Mastering FRENCH Vocabulary

Wolfgang Fischer and
Anne-Marie Le Plouhinec

Translated from German by Eric A. Bye, M.A., C.T.

All inquiries should be addressed to:
Barron's Educational Series, Inc.
250 Wireless Boulevard
Hauppauge, NY 11788
www.barronseduc.com

ISBN: 978-1-4380-7153-4
Library of Congress Control Number: 2011924977

Printed in the United States of America

9 8 7 6 5 4 3

Table of Contents

At a Glance

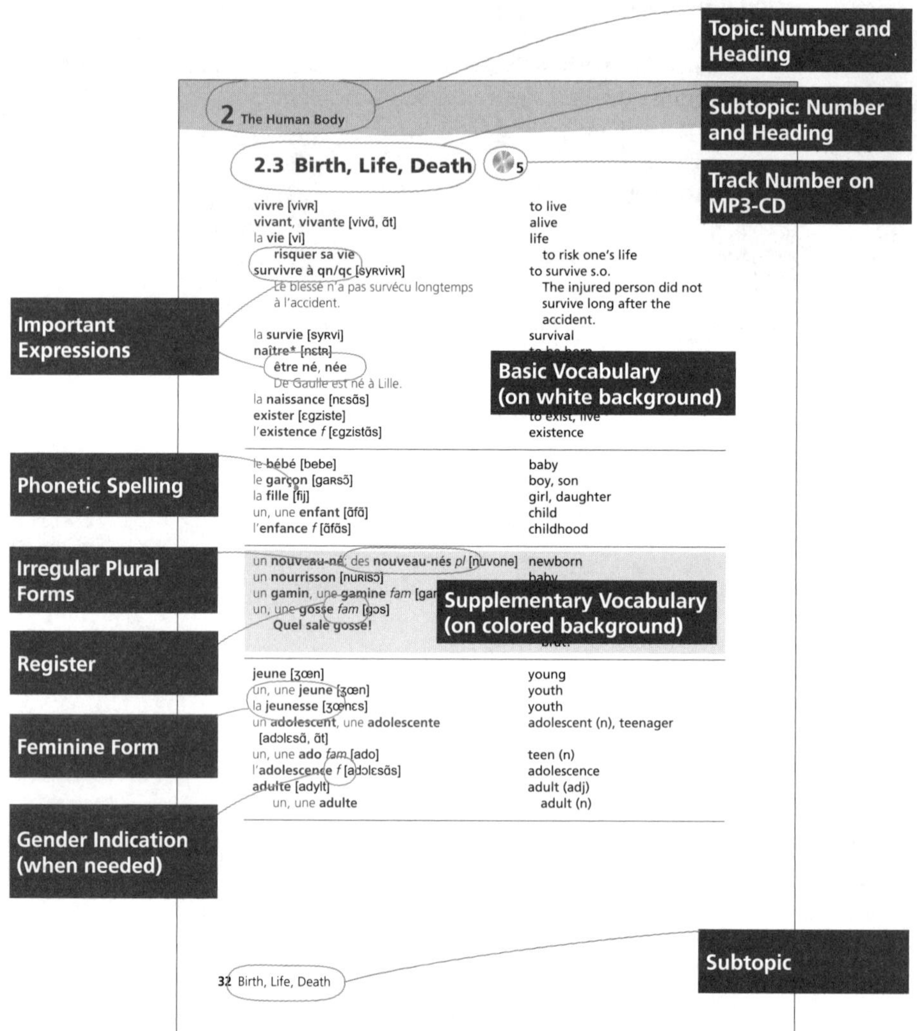

Topic: Number and Heading
Subtopic: Number and Heading
Track Number on MP3-CD
Important Expressions
Basic Vocabulary (on white background)
Phonetic Spelling
Irregular Plural Forms
Supplementary Vocabulary (on colored background)
Register
Feminine Form
Gender Indication (when needed)
Subtopic
2 The Human Body
2.3 Birth, Life, Death
5
vivre [vivʀ]
to live
vivant, vivante [vivɑ̃, ɑ̃t]
alive
la vie [vi]
life
risquer sa vie
to risk one's life
survivre à qn/qc [syʀvivʀ]
to survive s.o.
Le blessé n'a pas survécu longtemps à l'accident.
The injured person did not survive long after the accident.
la survie [syʀvi]
survival
naître* [nɛtʀ]
être né, née
De Gaulle est né à Lille.
la naissance [nɛsɑ̃s]
exister [ɛgziste]
l'existence f [ɛgzistɑ̃s]
existence
le bébé [bebe]
baby
le garçon [gaʀsɔ̃]
boy, son
la fille [fij]
girl, daughter
un, une enfant [ɑ̃fɑ̃]
child
l'enfance f [ɑ̃fɑ̃s]
childhood
un nouveau-né; des nouveau-nés pl [nuvone]
newborn
un nourrisson [nuʀisɔ̃]
un gamin, une gamine fam
un, une gosse fam [gɔs]
Quel sale gosse!
jeune [ʒœn]
young
un, une jeune [ʒœn]
youth
la jeunesse [ʒœnɛs]
youth
un adolescent, une adolescente [adɔlɛsɑ̃, ɑ̃t]
adolescent (n), teenager
un, une ado fam [ado]
teen (n)
l'adolescence f [adɔlɛsɑ̃s]
adolescence
adulte [adylt]
adult (adj)
un, une adulte
adult (n)
32 Birth, Life, Death

Introduction

Target Audience and Purpose

Mastering French Vocabulary, a book with an integral MP3-CD, is intended for students completing secondary school studies who want to review the basic vocabulary they have learned in a purposeful and subject-oriented manner. In more advanced French studies, students often struggle with the enormous and largely unorganized word glut encountered in directed or independent contact with authentic documents—whether in text, audio, or video format. The arrangement of this book into basic and supplementary vocabulary makes it possible to solidify or expand on known language, to systematize and put new lexical items into context, as well as to differentiate important things from less important ones. This book is also a reliable aid in producing verbal and written texts. It can help students create text analyses and commentaries, complete presentations and projects, and prepare purposefully for tests, examinations, or degrees in language.

This instructional book makes continued, broadened, and deeper vocabulary work more accessible for French students. It is particularly useful for translations and readings, the analysis and interpretation of demanding cultural or literary texts, and for competent, differentiated foreign language communication.

This book is appropriate for adults who wish to expand their cultural horizon, who desire to learn French for professional reasons, who are planning a stay in France, or who enjoy spending free time with French-language readings, television programs, and films in the original version.

Basis for This Vocabulary

In creating this comprehensive, practical basic and supplementary vocabulary, the following sources, among others, were examined and evaluated:

- vocabulary lists from the most recent instructional books;
- readings used in schools and in adult education;
- the electronic EU vocabulary book (which can be found on the Internet under the search word *EURODICAUTOM*);
- subthematic and culturally relevant articles and documents;
- lists of neologisms from current dictionaries.

The starting point for each term is contemporary language known as *langue courante*; however, with particularly common or current terms, the informal, down-to-earth slang was also included: *français familier* or *populaire*.

Vocabulary Structure and Presentation

There are many possible ways to structure a subject-oriented vocabulary; this book is based on a system of people and the circumstances around them. There are 24 major topics that are divided into 121 widely diversified subtopics. A thematic grouping of individual word entries within these subunits provides clarity and promotes learning in small, manageable segments.

A user-friendly layout based on the psychology of learning is intended to facilitate quick orientation and memory retention:

- Supplementary vocabulary is distinguished from basic vocabulary by a shaded background.
- Important idiomatic expressions in French are matched (if possible) by their counterparts in English.
- Rules separate the individual learning segments.
- A phonetic transcription is provided for every main entry.
- Verbs that form the *passé composé* with *être* are accompanied an asterisk (with the exception of reflexive verbs).
- Deviations from *français courant* are indicated with *fam (familier)* or *pop (populaire)*.
- A total of 85 Information Boxes are interspersed throughout the subjects and contain tips for clearing up common difficulties. (See list on p. 567.)
- At the end of the chapter a list of possible "false friends" selected from the subject in question helps to avoid particularly bothersome mistakes.
- Since learning and repeating vocabulary effectively enters the memory not only through reading and writing, but especially through hearing and speaking, all the words, sample sentences, and expressions included in the book are recorded on the accompanying CD as MP3 data. They are spoken by native speakers and can be listened to as tracks from subtopic to subtopic. A brief pause for thinking or pronunciation follows every main entry. By using the start/stop switch on their machine, students can of course also immediately repeat individual words, sentences, or expressions. (See track list on p. 571.)

The Main Concern

The primary goal of this book is effective vocabulary learning. For this reason there is no purely alphabetical arrangement of the vocabulary within the subchapter.

Memory stores vocabulary and word meanings in "networks." Therefore, anything that can help establish a relationship between a foreign-language term and its English equivalent will encourage understanding and strengthen retention. This knowledge of learning psychology is incorporated into the organization of this book: specifically, vocabulary is classified into manageable semantic units similar in content, which are grouped around a specific core subject. Within these semantic blocks other helpful associations are highlighted: synonyms (*terrible; horrible; épouvantable*); antonyms (*chaud – froid*); subordination (*meuble – siege – chaise*), semantic fields (*une rue; une route;*

une chaussée; une avenue); and word families (*dessiner; un dessin; un dessinateur, une dessinatrice*). These groupings produce lasting impressions and support memorization.

This type of organization of vocabulary, based on content and oral coherence, means that word entries are no longer designated as "basic" or "supplementary" based exclusively on their statistical frequency. This also means that terms with multiple meanings may appear in the basic vocabulary with their primary meaning, and also in the supplementary vocabulary with a secondary meaning. (For example, *une action* is entered in the basic vocabulary as *action*, but as *share* in the supplementary vocabulary.)

The Dangers of Bilingual Word Similarities

Word similarities are extremely significant in language receptive processes, and they harbor many dangers especially in the realm of second-language production. They encourage continual translation, and thus often lead to the transferal of native-language habits to the foreign language.

In order to mitigate these risks, this program places particular value on a syntagmatic embedding of the most frequently presented words:

- Relevant verb complements (e.g., *demander* ***qc à qn***) facilitate the syntactical connection.
- Sample sentences provide situational references and facilitate contextual understanding and retention. They show how the target word connects with other parts of the sentences, and they identify possible differences between the French and the English systems.
- Words are not always freely connectable in speech production. In many cases they involve predetermined combinations with nouns, adjectives, or verbs (e.g., *prendre du poids – to gain weight; faire attention à – to pay attention to*). In these combinations, English and French are clearly different from one another. These common word combinations pose the greatest difficulties for the active language learner and thus require targeted practice. The authors of this book are very focused on taking this fact into consideration.
- Idiomatic expressions (*locutions*) and proverbs (*proverbes*) show how imagination and playful wit can characterize a language. In many cases these expressions deviate from the basic meanings of the respective target words, but mastering them is part of linguistic and cross-cultural competence.

Overview of Symbols and Abbreviations

adj	*adjectif*	adjective
adv	*adverbe*	adverb
f	*féminin*	feminine
fam	*familier*	familiar, colloquial
loc	*locution*	idiom
m	*masculin*	masculine
n	*nom*	noun
péj	*péjoratif*	pejorative
pop	*populaire*	very informal, colloquial
prov	*proverbe*	proverb
qc	*quelque chose*	something
qn	*quelqu'un*	someone
s.o.		someone
s.o.'s		someone's
subj	*subjonctif*	subjunctive
v	*verbe*	verb, action word
*		verbs that form the *passé compose* with *être* (aside from the reflexive verbs)

Overview of Phonetic Symbols

The phonetic symbols used in this book follow the current *Petit Robert* and simplifications in the common instructional texts.

Vowels

[a]	m**a**d**a**me; **â**ge
[e]	caf**é**; mang**er**
[ɛ]	il f**ai**t; il m**e**t; adr**e**sse
[i]	**i**l; am**ie**
[ɔ]	d**o**micile; passep**o**rt
[o]	numér**o**; boul**ot**
[ø]	monsi**eur**; **Eu**rope
[œ]	**heu**re; c**œu**r; j**eu**ne
[ə]	l**e**; r**e**pas
[u]	r**ou**te; ép**ou**x
[v]	t**u**; r**ue**

Nasal Vowels

[ɑ̃]	d**an**s; contin**ent**
[ɛ̃]	itali**en**
[œ̃]	**un**
[ɔ̃]	**on**; n**om**

Consonants

[f]	**f**rère; **ph**oto
[v]	boule**v**ard; **v**isage
[s]	**s**œur; sta**t**ion; adole**sc**ent
[z]	phra**s**e; **z**éro
[ʒ]	**j**eune; reli**g**ion
[ʃ]	**ch**ose; **sh**ampooing
[ɲ]	ma**gn**ifique; si**gn**e
[ŋ]	park**ing**; camp**ing**
[ʀ]	p**r**énom; **R**ussie

Semiconsonants

[j]	bien; famille
[w]	**oui**; **toi**
[ɥ]	huit; bruit

An apostrophe (') is placed before an *h aspire*. This means that no liaison occurs, e.g., *le héros* [lə'hero], but *l'héroïne* [leʀɔin].

1

Personal Information

1.1 Personal Data  1

le **nom** [nɔ̃]	name
le **nom de famille**	last name, family name
le **prénom** [pʀenɔ̃]	first name
s'appeler [saple]	to be named
Comment t'appelles-tu?/ Comment tu t'appelles?	What is your name?

Monsieur; **messieurs** *pl* [məsjø, mesjø]	Mr.
madame; **mesdames** *pl* [madam, medam]	Mrs.
Madame Martin, née Dupont	Mrs. Martin, née Dupont
mademoiselle; **mesdemoiselles** *pl* [madmwazɛl, medmwazɛl]	Miss

INFO

Monsieur

The following abbreviations are commonly used:
M. (Monsieur), Mme (Madame), Mlle (Mademoiselle)
MM. (Messieurs), Mmes (Mesdames), Mlles (Mesdemoiselles)

In *polite forms of address* the name is not mentioned:

Bonjour, monsieur/madame/mademoiselle.	*Hello, good morning.*
Oui/Non/Merci, messieurs/mesdames/ mesdemoiselles.	*Yes/No/Thank you.*

In *greeting acquaintances* the name is often used:

Bonjour, Monsieur/Madame/ Mademoiselle Rigot	*Hello, Mr./Mrs./Miss Rigot.*

---

habiter qc/à [abite]	to live in
J'habite une maison neuve.	I live in a new house.
J'habite à Paris.	I live in Paris.
l'**adresse** *f* [adʀɛs]	address
un **domicile** [dɔmisil]	residence
sans domicile fixe	no fixed address
les **coordonnées** *fpl; fam* [kɔɔʀdɔne]	address and phone number, contact information
Donne-moi les coordonnées de Paul.	Give me Paul's address and phone number.
une **rue** [ʀy]	street
26, rue du Labrador	26 Rue du Labrador
une **route** [ʀut]	road, route

une **avenue** [avny]	avenue
un **boulevard** [bulvaʀ]	boulevard
une **place** [plas]	square
le **numéro** [nymeʀo]	(house) number
C'est **au numéro** 6 de la rue Rambuteau.	It is at 6 Rue Rambuteau.

INFO

Une rue - une route

J'ai rencontré Martine *dans la rue.*	*I bumped into Martine in the street (in town).*
Attention, il y a du verglas *sur la route.*	*Be careful, the road is icy.*

la **situation de famille** [sitɥasjɔ̃d(ə)famij]	marital status
le **mari** [maʀi]	husband
la **femme** [fam]	wife
se marier [s(ə)maʀje]	to get married
marié, **mariée** [maʀje]	married
le **mariage** [maʀjaʒ]	marriage

INFO

Se marier (avec qn), marier qn à/avec qn, épouser qn

se marier (avec qn)	*to marry s.o.*
Elle s'est mariée à l'église.	*She got married in the church.*
Elle s'est mariée avec mon frère.	*She married my brother.*
marier qn avec/à qn	*to marry s.o. to*
Ils ont marié leur fille au fils/avec le fils d'un gros industriel.	*They married their daughter to the son of a big industrialist.*
épouser qn	*to marry s.o.*
Céline a épousé son chef.	*Céline married her boss.*

l'**état civil** *m* [etasivil]	family status; personal information; registrar's office
Il faut aller faire signer ce formulaire à l'état civil.	This form must be signed at the registrar's office.
célibataire [selibatɛʀ]	single
une **mère célibataire**	single mother
un, une **célibataire**	single person, bachelor
se fiancer avec [s(ə)fjɑ̃seavɛk]	to become engaged to
fiancé, **fiancée** [fjɑ̃se]	engaged
un **fiancé**, une **fiancée**	fiancé(e)
épouser qn [epuze]	to marry s.o.
l'**époux** *m*, l'**épouse** *f* [epu, uz]	husband, wife
un **ménage** [menaʒ]	married couple
une **scène de ménage**	domestic dispute
le **conjoint**, la **conjointe** [kɔ̃ʒwɛ̃, wɛ̃t]	spouse
conjugal, **conjugale** [kɔ̃ʒygal]	marital, conjugal
le **lit conjugal**	marriage bed
le **PACS** (**Pacte civil de solidarité**) [paks]	civil union
pacsé, **pacsée** [pakse]	entered into civil union
se séparer de qn [s(ə)sepaʀe]	to separate from s.o.
Michel et Alice **se sont séparés**.	Michel and Alice have separated.
séparé, **séparée** [sepaʀe]	separated
la **séparation** [sepaʀasjɔ̃]	separation
divorcer de qn/(**d'**) **avec qn** [divɔʀse]	to divorce s.o.
Il a divorcé de sa 3e femme.	He got divorced from his third wife.
divorcé, **divorcée** [divɔʀse]	divorced (adj)
un **divorcé**, une **divorcée**	divorcé, divorcee
le **divorce** [divɔʀs]	divorce (n)
veuf, **veuve** [vœf, vœv]	widowed
un **veuf**, une **veuve**	widower, widow
orphelin, **orpheline** [ɔʀfəlɛ̃, in]	orphan (adj)
un **orphelin**, une **orpheline**	orphan (n)
un **père de famille** [pɛʀdəfamij]	father, family man
une **mère de famille** [mɛʀdəfamij]	mother, housewife

le **sexe** [sɛks]	gender, sex
masculin, **masculine** [maskylɛ̃, in]	male, masculine
féminin, **féminine** [feminɛ̃, in]	female, feminine

l'**âge** *m* [aʒ]	age
J'ai dix-huit ans. Et toi, **quel âge as-tu?**	I am eighteen. And how old are you?
âgé, **âgée** [aʒe]	old
Elle est âgée de 24 ans.	She is 24 years old.
un **an** [ɑ̃]	year

adulte [adylt]	adult (adj)
un, une **adulte**	adult (n)
un, une **enfant** [ɑ̃fɑ̃]	child
majeur, **majeure** [maʒœʀ]	s.o. of legal age (n)
la **majorité** [maʒɔʀite]	majority
mineur, **mineure** [minœʀ]	minor (n)
un film **interdit aux mineurs**	restricted movie (not for minors)
la **date de naissance** [datdənɛsɑ̃s]	date of birth
le **lieu de naissance** [ljød(ə)nɛsɑ̃s]	place of birth

1.2 Nationality, Language, Country  2

un **passeport** [paspɔʀ]	passport
les **papiers d'identité** *mpl* [papjedidɑ̃tite]	identification papers
une **carte d'identité** [kaʀtdidɑ̃tite]	identification card
un **continent** [kɔ̃tinɑ̃]	continent
un **pays** [pei]	country
une **nation** [nasjɔ̃]	nation
la **nationalité** [nasjɔnalite]	citizenship, nationality
Fatima va demander la nationalité française.	Fatima is going to request French citizenship.
(être) **d'origine**... [dɔʀiʒin]	(to be) of ... origin
C'est un Français **d'origine italienne**.	He is a Frenchman of Italian origin.
étranger, **étrangère** [etʀɑ̃ʒe, ɛʀ]	foreign
un **étranger**, une **étrangère**	foreigner
immigrer [imigʀe]	to immigrate
un **immigré**, une **immigrée**	immigrant (n)
Les immigrés ont parfois du mal à s'intégrer.	It is sometimes difficult for immigrants to integrate.
l'**immigration** *f* [imigʀasjɔ̃]	immigration
émigrer [emigʀe]	to emigrate
une **langue** [lɑ̃g]	language
la **langue maternelle**	native language
une **langue étrangère**	foreign language
bilingue [bilɛ̃g]	bilingual
l'**Europe** *f* [øʀɔp]	Europe
l'**Afrique** *f* [afʀik]	Africa
l'**Amérique** *f* [ameʀik]	America
l'**Asie** *f* [azi]	Asia

INFO

Residents–language

When referring to *members of a nation* or *an ethnic group,* the term is capitalized:

un Espagnol, une Espagnole	*a Spaniard, a Spanish woman*
un Allemand, une Allemande	*a German man, a German woman*
un Breton, une Bretonne	*a Breton man, a Breton woman*

On the other hand, *languages* are written with a lowercase letter:

l'espagnol; l'allemand; le français; le breton	*Spanish; German; French; Breton*

INFO

Être – aller – venir + country names

être/aller	*en* France (*la* France)	*to be in France / to go to France*
	en Italie (*l'*Italie *f*)	*to be in Italy / to go to Italy*
	en Iran (*l'*Iran = *m with initial vowel sound*)	*to be in Iran / to go to Iran*
	au Portugal (*le* Portugal)	*to be in Portugal / to go to Portugal*
	aux États-Unis (*les* États-Unis)	*to be in the USA / to go to the USA*
venir	*de* Belgique (*la* Belgique)	*to come from Belgium*
	*d'*Allemagne (*l'*Allemagne *f*)	*to come from Germany*
	*d'*Irak (*l'*Irak = *m with initital vowel sound*)	*to come from Iraq*
	du Mexique (*le* Mexique)	*to come from Mexico*
	des États-Unis (*les* États-Unis)	*to come from the USA*

l'**Australie** *f* [ɔstʀali]	Australia
la **France** [fʀɑ̃s]	France
français, **française** [fʀɑ̃nsɛ, ɛz]	French
l'**Allemagne** *f* [almaɲ]	Germany
allemand, **allemande** [almɑ̃, ɑ̃d]	German
la **Grande-Bretagne** [gʀɑ̃dbʀətaɲ]	Great Britain
britannique [bʀitanik]	British

l'**Angleterre** *f* [ɑ̃glətɛʀ]	England
anglais, **anglaise** [ɑ̃glɛ, ɛz]	English
l'**Italie** *f* [itali]	Italy
italien, **italienne** [italjɛ̃, jɛn]	Italian
l'**Espagne** *f* [ɛspaɲ]	Spain
espagnol, **espagnole** [ɛspaɲɔl]	Spanish
le **Portugal** [pɔʀtygal]	Portugal
portugais, **portugaise** [pɔʀtygɛ, ɛz]	Portuguese
la **Belgique** [bɛlʒik]	Belgium
belge [bɛlʒ]	Belgian
les **Pays-Bas** *mpl* [peiba]	Netherlands
néerlandais, **néerlandaise** [neɛʀlɑ̃dɛ, ɛz]	Dutch
la **Hollande** ['ɔlɑ̃d]	Holland
hollandais, **hollandaise** ['ɔlɑ̃dɛ, ɛz]	Dutch
le **Luxembourg** [lyksɑ̃buʀ]	Luxembourg
luxembourgeois, **luxembourgeoise** [lyksɑ̃buʀʒwa, waz]	Luxembourgian
l'**Autriche** *f* [otʀiʃ]	Austria
autrichien, **autrichienne** [otʀiʃjɛ̃, jɛn]	Austrian
la **Grèce** [gʀɛs]	Greece
grec, **grecque** [gʀɛk]	Greek
l'**Irlande** *f* [iʀlɑ̃d]	Ireland
irlandais, **irlandaise** [iʀlɑ̃dɛ, ɛz]	Irish
la **Finlande** [fɛ̃lɑ̃d]	Finland
finlandais, **finlandaise** [fɛ̃lɑ̃dɛ, ɛz]	Finnish
la **Suède** [sɥɛd]	Sweden
suédois, **suédoise** [sɥɛdwa, waz]	Swedish
la **Norvège** [nɔʀvɛʒ]	Norway
norvégien, **norvégienne** [nɔʀveʒjɛ̃, jɛn]	Norwegian
le **Danemark** [danmaʀk]	Denmark
danois, **danoise** [danwa, waz]	Danish
scandinave [skɑ̃dinav]	Scandinavian
la **Suisse** [sɥis]	Switzerland
suisse [sɥis]	Swiss *adj*
un, une **Suisse**, une **Suissesse** [sɥis, ɛs]	Swiss *n*
la **Russie** [ʀysi]	Russia
russe [ʀys]	Russian
la **Pologne** [pɔlɔɲ]	Poland
polonais, **polonaise** [pɔlɔnɛ, ɛz]	Polish
la **République tchèque** [ʀepybliktʃɛk]	Czech Republic
tchèque [tʃɛk]	Czech
la **Slovaquie** [slɔvaki]	Slovakia
slovaque [slɔvak]	Slovakian
la **Turquie** [tyʀki]	Turkey
turc, **turque** [tyʀk]	Turkish

l'**Albanie** *f* [albani]	Albania
albanais, **albanaise** [albanɛ, ɛz]	Albanian
la **Bulgarie** [bylgaʀi]	Bulgaria
bulgare [bylgaʀ]	Bulgarian
la **Roumanie** [ʀumani]	Romania
roumain, **roumaine** [ʀumɛ̃, ɛn]	Romanian
la **Hongrie** ['ɔ̃gʀi]	Hungary
hongrois, **hongroise** ['ɔ̃gʀwa, waz]	Hungarian
l'**Estonie** *f* [ɛstɔni]	Estonia
estonien, **estonienne** [ɛstɔjɛ̃, jɛn]	Estonian
la **Lettonie** [lɛtɔni]	Latvia
letton, **lettone** [lɛtɔ̃, ɔn]	Latvian
la **Lituanie** [litɥani]	Lithuania
lituanien, **lituanienne** [litɥanjɛ̃, jɛn]	Lithuanian
la **Biélorussie** [bjelɔʀysi]	Belarus
biélorusse [bjelɔʀys]	Belarusian
l'**Ukraine** *f* [ykʀɛn]	Ukraine
ukrainien, **ukrainienne** [ykʀɛnjɛ̃, jɛn]	Ukrainian
la **Croatie** [kʀoasi]	Croatia
croate [kʀɔat]	Croatian
la **Serbie** [sɛʀbi]	Serbia
serbe [sɛʀb]	Serbian
la **Slovénie** [slɔveni]	Slovenia
slovène [slɔvɛn]	Slovenian
la **Bosnie-Herzégovine** [bɔsniɛʀzegɔvin]	Bosnia-Herzegovina
bosniaque [bɔsnjak]	Bosnian

les **États-Unis** *mpl* [etazyni]	the United States
les **USA** *mpl* [yɛsa]	USA
américain, **américaine** [ameʀikɛ̃, ɛn]	American
le **Canada** [kanada]	Canada
canadien, **canadienne** [kanadjɛ̃, jɛn]	Canadian
le **Mexique** [mɛksik]	Mexico
mexicain, **mexicaine** [mɛksikɛ̃, ɛn]	Mexican
le **Brésil** [bʀezil]	Brazil
brésilien, **brésilienne** [bʀeziljɛ̃, jɛn]	Brazilian

la **Chine** [ʃin]	China
chinois, **chinoise** [ʃinwa, waz]	Chinese
le **Japon** [ʒapɔ̃]	Japan
japonais, **japonaise** [ʒapɔnɛ, ɛz]	Japanese
l'**Inde** *f* [ɛ̃d]	India
indien, **indienne** [ɛ̃djɛ̃, jɛn]	Indian

l'**Algérie** *f* [alʒeʀi]	Algeria
algérien, algérienne [alʒeʀjɛ̃, jɛn]	Algerian
le **Maroc** [maʀɔk]	Morocco
marocain, marocaine [maʀɔkɛ̃, ɛn]	Moroccan
la **Tunisie** [tynizi]	Tunisia
tunisien, tunisienne [tynizjɛ̃, jɛn]	Tunisian
le **Maghreb** [magʀɛb]	Maghreb
maghrébin, maghrébine [magʀebɛ̃, in]	Mahgrebi
l'**Égypte** *f* [eʒipt]	Egypt
égyptien, égyptienne [eʒipsjɛ̃, jɛn]	Egyptian

My Vocabulary

2

The Human Body

2.1 Body Parts, Organs 3

le **corps** [kɔʀ]	body
le corps humain	the human body
la **peau**; les **peaux** *pl* [po]	skin
le **sang** [sɑ̃]	blood
l'**os** *m*; les **os** *pl* [lɔs, lezo]	bone
Il n'**a que la peau sur les os.** *loc*	He is nothing but skin and bones.

le **crâne** [kʀɑn]	skull
avoir mal au crâne	to have a headache
le **cerveau**; les **cerveaux** *pl* [sɛʀvo]	brain
C'est le **cerveau de la bande**.	That is the brains of the group.
le **nerf** [nɛʀ]	nerve
le **système nerveux** [sistɛmnɛʀvø]	nervous system
l'**artère** *f* [aʀtɛʀ]	artery
la **veine** [vɛn]	vein
le **muscle** [myskl]	muscle
le **tendon** [tɑ̃dɔ̃]	tendon

la **tête** [tɛt]	head
des pieds à la tête	from head to toe
les **cheveux** *mpl* [ʃ(ə)vø]	hair
le **poil** [pwal]	(body) hair, fur
être à poil	to be naked

INFO

Cheveu - poil

le(s) cheveu(x)	*hair*
Mon père n'a presque plus de ***cheveux.***	*My father hardly has any hair left.*
le poil	*body hair; fur*
Elle se rase les ***poils*** des jambes.	*She shaves her legs.*

la **figure** [figyʀ]	face
le **visage** [vizaʒ]	face
le **front** [fʀɔ̃]	forehead
l'**oreille** *f* [ɔʀɛj]	ear
la **joue** [ʒu]	cheek
le **nez** [ne]	nose
Je me suis trouvé **nez à nez** avec mon chef.	I found myself nose to nose with my boss.

l'**œil** *m*; les **yeux** *pl* [lœj, lezjø]	eye
Je n'ai pas **fermé l'œil de la nuit**.	I didn't close my eyes all night.

INFO

Avoir + physical features

The *definite* as well as the *indefinite article* can be used with physical features:

Il a ***les/des*** cheveux roux.	*He has red hair.*
Elles ont ***les/des*** yeux noirs/clairs.	*They have black/light eyes.*

la **paupière** [popjɛʀ]	eyelid
le **cil** [sil]	eyelash
le **sourcil** [suʀsi]	eyebrow
froncer les sourcils	to knit one's brows

la **bouche** [buʃ]	mouth
la **lèvre** [lɛvʀ]	lip
la **langue** [lɑ̃g]	tongue
tirer la langue à qn	to stick your tongue out at s.o.
la **dent** [dɑ̃]	tooth
le **menton** [mɑ̃tɔ̃]	chin

le **cou** [ku]	neck
sauter au cou de qn	to throw your arms around s.o.'s neck
la **gorge** [gɔʀʒ]	throat
avoir un chat dans la gorge *loc*	to have a frog in your throat

l'**épaule** *f* [epol]	shoulder
le **dos** [do]	back
la **taille** [taj]	waist; size

le **squelette** [skəlɛt]	skeleton
la **nuque** [nyk]	neck
la **colonne vertébrale** [kɔlɔnvɛʀtebʀal]	spinal column
le **sein** [sɛ̃]	breast
les **seins**	the breasts
la **hanche** ['ɑ̃ʃ]	hip
les **fesses** *fpl* [fɛs]	buttocks
le **derrière** [dɛʀjɛʀ]	bottom

un **organe** [ɔʀgan]	organ
la **poitrine** [pwatʀin]	chest, bust
le **cœur** [kœʀ]	heart
Son cœur bat trop vite.	His/her heart is beating too fast.
le **ventre** [vɑ̃tʀ]	belly, abdomen
l'**estomac** *m* [ɛstɔma]	stomach
le **poumon** [pumɔ̃]	lung
le **foie** [fwa]	liver
le **rein** [ʀɛ̃]	kidney
l'**intestin** *m* [ɛ̃tɛstɛ̃]	intestine
le **bras** [bʀa]	arm
le **coude** [kud]	elbow
la **main** [mɛ̃]	hand
le **doigt** [dwa]	finger
montrer qn/qc du doigt	to point at s.o., s.th.
le **poignet** [pwaɲɛ]	wrist
le **poing** [pwɛ̃]	fist
serrer les poings	to clench the fists
le **pouce** [pus]	thumb
la **jambe** [ʒɑ̃b]	leg
le **genou**; les **genoux** *pl* [ʒ(ə)nu]	knee
le **pied** [pje]	foot
casser les pieds à qn *fam*	to annoy s.o.
la **cuisse** [kɥis]	thigh
la **cheville** [ʃ(ə)vij]	ankle
Il s'est foulé la cheville.	He sprained his ankle.
le **talon** [talɔ̃]	heel
l'**orteil** *m* [ɔʀtɛj]	toe
le **doigt de pied** [dwad(ə)pie]	toe

2.2 Sexuality and Reproduction 4

un **sentiment** [sɑ̃timɑ̃]	feeling
aimer [ɛme]	to love
Je ne l'aime pas d'amour, mais je l'aime bien.	I'm not in love with him, but I like him a lot.
amoureux, **amoureuse** [amuʀø, øz]	in love
être amoureux de qn	to be in love with s.o.
tomber* amoureux de qn	to fall in love with s.o.
l'**amour** *m* [amuʀ]	love
l'**affection** *f* [afɛksjɔ̃]	affection

faire la cour à qn [fɛʀlakuʀ]	to court s.o.
Il lui fait la cour depuis des mois.	He has been courting her for months.
flirter avec [flœʀte]	to flirt with
draguer qn *fam* [dʀage]	to come on to s.o.
Il l'a draguée toute la soirée.	He came on to her all evening.

un **ami**, une **amie** [ami]	friend
C'est son **petit ami**.	That is her boyfriend.
un **copain**, une **copine** *fam* [kɔpɛ̃, in]	friend
un **compagnon**, une **compagne** [kɔ̃paɲɔ̃, kɔ̃paɲ]	partner, live-in lover
un **amant** [amɑ̃]	lover
une **maîtresse** [mɛtʀɛs]	mistress, lover

une **liaison** [ljɛzɔ̃]	relationship
avoir une liaison orageuse avec qn	to have a stormy relationship with s.o.
fidèle [fidɛl]	faithful
être fidèle à qn	to be faithful to s.o.
infidèle [ɛ̃fidɛl]	unfaithful
être infidèle à qn	to be unfaithful to s.o.
tromper qn [tʀɔ̃pe]	to deceive

embrasser [ɑ̃bʀase]	to kiss
un **baiser** [beze]	kiss
caresser [kaʀɛse]	to caress
tendre [tɑ̃dʀ]	tender
la **tendresse** [tɑ̃dʀɛs]	tenderness
faire l'amour avec qn [fɛʀlamuʀ]	to make love to s.o.
coucher avec qn *fam* [kuʃe]	to make love with s.o., sleep with s.o.
Tout ce qu'il veut, c'est coucher avec elle.	All he wants is to go to bed with her.

vierge [vjɛʀʒ]	virgin
la **virginité** [viʀʒinite]	virginity
les **rapports sexuels** *mpl* [ʀapɔʀsɛksɥɛl]	sexual intercourse, intimate relations
la **puberté** [pybɛʀte]	puberty
Mon fils est **en pleine puberté**.	My son is right in the middle of puberty.
les **règles** *fpl* [ʀɛgl]	period, menstruation
sexuel, **sexuelle** [sɛksɥel]	sexual
le **sexe** [sɛks]	sex
la **sexualité** [sɛksɥalite]	sexuality
sexy *fam* [sɛksi]	sexy
désirer [deziʀe]	to desire
le **plaisir** [plɛziʀ]	pleasure
exciter [ɛksite]	to excite, arouse
érotique [eʀɔtik]	erotic
l'**érotisme** *m* [eʀɔtism]	eroticism
jouir [ʒwiʀ]	to have an orgasm
frigide [fʀiʒid]	frigid
les **organes génitaux** *mpl* [ɔʀganʒenito]	sexual organs, genitals
le **pénis** [penis]	penis
le **vagin** [vaʒɛ̃]	vagina
l'**orgasme** *m* [ɔʀgasm]	orgasm
l'**éjaculation** *f* [eʒakylasjɔ̃]	ejaculation
le **sperme** [spɛʀm]	sperm
Le virus du sida **se transmet par le sperme**.	The AIDS virus is transmitted with the sperm.
impuissant, **impuissante** [ɛ̃pɥisɑ̃, ɑ̃t]	impotent
l'**impuissance** *f* [ɛ̃pɥisɑ̃s]	impotence
hétérosexuel, **hétérosexuelle** [eteʀosɛksɥɛl]	heterosexual
hétéro *fam* [eteʀo]	heterosexual
homosexuel, **homosexuelle** [ɔmɔsɛksɥɛl]	homosexual
homo *fam* [ɔmɔ]	homosexual
pédé *péJ* [pede]	faggoty
un **pédé** *péJ*	faggot
lesbienne [lɛsbjɛn]	lesbian (adj)
une **lesbienne**	lesbian (n)

(être) **enceinte** [ɑ̃sɛ̃t]	(to be) pregnant
attendre un enfant [atɑ̃dʀɛ̃nɑ̃fɑ̃]	to be expecting a child
accoucher de [akuʃe]	to give birth to
Elle a accouché d'un beau garçon.	She gave birth to a beautiful boy.
l'**accouchement** *m* [akuʃmɑ̃]	birthing, labor
mettre au monde [mɛtʀomɔ̃d]	to give birth, bring into the world
Elle veut mettre son bébé au monde chez elle.	She would like to give birth at home.

la **reproduction** [ʀ(ə)pʀɔdyksjɔ̃]	reproduction
la **conception** [kɔ̃sɛpsjɔ̃]	conception
la **grossesse** [gʀosɛs]	pregnancy
une **fausse couche** [foskuʃ]	miscarriage
stérile [steʀil]	sterile
la **stérilité** [steʀilite]	sterility
fécond, féconde [fekɔ̃, ɔ̃d]	fertile
la **fécondité** [fekɔ̃dite]	fertility
féconder [fekɔ̃de]	to fertilize
la **fécondation** [fekɔ̃dasjɔ̃]	fertilization
la fécondation artificielle/in vitro	artificial insemination/ in vitro fertilization
un **moyen de contraception** [mwajɛ̃d(ə)kɔ̃tʀasɛpsjɔ̃]	a method of contraception
la **pilule** [pilyl]	the (birth control) pill
un **préservatif** [pʀezɛʀvatif]	condom
un **distributeur de préservatifs**	condom machine
avorter [avɔʀte]	to abort
se faire avorter	to get/have an abortion
un **avortement** [avɔʀtəment]	an abortion
une **I.V.G.** (**interruption volontaire de grossesse**) [iveʒe]	abortion, termination of pregnancy
le **contrôle des naissances** [kɔ̃tʀoldenɛsɑ̃s]	birth control

2.3 Birth, Life, Death  5

vivre [vivʀ]	to live
vivant, **vivante** [vivɑ̃, ɑ̃t]	alive
la **vie** [vi]	life
risquer sa vie	to risk one's life
survivre à qn/qc [syʀvivʀ]	to survive s.o.
Le blessé n'a pas survécu longtemps à l'accident.	The injured person did not survive long after the accident.
la **survie** [syʀvi]	survival
naître* [nɛtʀ]	to be born
être né, **née**	to be born
De Gaulle est né à Lille.	De Gaulle was born in Lille.
la **naissance** [nɛsɑ̃s]	birth
exister [ɛgziste]	to exist, live
l'**existence** *f* [ɛgzistɑ̃s]	existence

le **bébé** [bebe]	baby
le **garçon** [gaʀsɔ̃]	boy, son
la **fille** [fij]	girl, daughter
un, une **enfant** [ɑ̃fɑ̃]	child
l'**enfance** *f* [ɑ̃fɑ̃s]	childhood

un **nouveau-né**; des **nouveau-nés** *pl* [nuvone]	newborn
un **nourrisson** [nuʀisɔ̃]	baby
un **gamin**, une **gamine** *fam* [gamɛ̃, in]	little child
un, une **gosse** *fam* [gɔs]	kid, child
Quel sale gosse!	What a rotten kid/spoiled brat!

jeune [ʒœn]	young
un, une **jeune** [ʒœn]	youth
la **jeunesse** [ʒœnɛs]	youth
un **adolescent**, une **adolescente** [adɔlɛsɑ̃, ɑ̃t]	adolescent (n), teenager
un, une **ado** *fam* [ado]	teen (n)
l'**adolescence** *f* [adɔlɛsɑ̃s]	adolescence
adulte [adylt]	adult (adj)
un, une **adulte**	adult (n)

l'**âge** *m* [ɑʒ]	age
être d'un certain âge	to be of a certain age
le **3e âge** [tʀwazjɛmɑʒ]	retirement age, senior years
Il vit dans une **résidence pour le 3e âge**.	He lives in a retirement home.
âgé, **âgée** [ɑʒe]	old
Je suis **âgé de** 30 ans.	I am 30 (years old).
vieux, **vieil**, **vieille** [vjø, vjɛj]	old, elderly
Il est très vieux. Un vieil homme.	He is very old. An elderly man.
Une vieille dame.	An old lady.

vieillir [vjejiʀ]	to grow old
la **vieillesse** [vjɛjɛs]	(old) age
un **vieillard** [vjɛjaʀ]	old man, senior citizen
sénile [senil]	senile
centenaire [sɑ̃t(ə)nɛʀ]	centenarian (adj)
un, une **centenaire**	centenarian (n)
la **longévité** [lɔ̃ʒevite]	longevity
l'**espérance de vie** *f* [ɛspeʀɑ̃sdəvi]	life expectancy
L'espérance de vie des femmes est plus élevée que celle des hommes.	The life expectancy of women is greater than that of men.

se suicider [s(ə)sɥiside]	to commit suicide
le **suicide** [sɥisid]	suicide
mourir* [muʀiʀ]	to die
mourir d'un cancer du poumon	to die of lung cancer
mort, **morte** [mɔʀ, mɔʀt]	dead
Elle est morte d'un infarctus.	She died from a heart attack.
un **mort**, une **morte**	dead person
L'accident a fait deux morts.	The accident left two people dead.
mortel, **mortelle** [mɔʀtɛl]	mortal, fatal
une maladie mortelle	fatal disease
la **mort** [mɔʀ]	death
Attention, danger de mort!	Warning: Mortal Danger

INFO

La mort, etc.

Note the *article* and the *pronunciation*:

la mort [mɔʀ]	*death*
le mort [mɔʀ], *la* morte [mɔʀt]	*the dead person*

décéder* [desede]	to die
Il est décédé lundi dernier.	He died last Monday.
le **décès** [dese]	death
défunt, **défunte** [defœ̃, œ̃t]	dead, deceased
son défunt mari	her deceased husband
un **cadavre** [kadɑvʀ]	corpse, cadaver
le **deuil** [dœj]	mourning
être en deuil	to be in mourning
porter le deuil de qn	to be in mourning for s.o.
un **cimetière** [simtjɛʀ]	cemetery
la **tombe** [tɔ̃b]	grave, tomb
le **cercueil** [sɛʀkœj]	casket, coffin
enterrer [ɑ̃teʀe]	to bury
l'**enterrement** *m* [ɑ̃tɛʀmɑ̃]	burial
les **obsèques** *fpl* [ɔbsɛk]	funeral service
les **condoléances** *fpl* [kɔ̃dɔleɑ̃s]	condolences
présenter ses condoléances	to express one's condolences

2.4 Senses and Physical Reactions  6

voir [vwaʀ]	to see
visible [vizibl]	visible
C'est **visible à l'œil nu**.	It's visible to the naked eye.
visuel, **visuelle** [vizɥɛl]	visual
la **vue** [vy]	sight, vision
avoir la vue basse	to be nearsighted, have poor vision
regarder [ʀ(ə)gaʀde]	to look at, watch
un **regard** [ʀ(ə)gaʀ]	look, glance (n)
remarquer [ʀ(ə)maʀke]	to notice
observer [ɔpsɛʀve]	to observe
une **observation** [ɔpsɛʀvasjɔ̃]	observation
avoir le **sens de l'observation**	to have good observation skills
aveugle [avœgl]	blind
les **lunettes** *fpl* [lynɛt]	glasses *(See Information Box p. 46)*

reconnaître [R(ə)kɔnɛtR]	to recognize
apercevoir [apɛRsəvwaR]	to perceive, notice
s'apercevoir de qc [sapɛRsəvwaR]	to notice s.th.
Je ne me suis pas aperçu de son absence.	I did not notice his absence.
perceptible [pɛRsɛptibl]	perceptible, noticeable
un **coup d'œil** [kudœj]	glance (n)
jeter un coup d'œil sur qn/qc	to cast a glance on s.o./s.th.
cligner (**des yeux**) [kliɲe]	to blink
loucher [luʃe]	to squint
être myope [mjɔp]	to be nearsighted/myopic
être presbyte [pRɛsbit]	to be farsighted
la **cécité** [sesite]	blindness

entendre [ɑ̃tɑ̃dR]	to hear
écouter [ekute]	to listen (to)
le **son** [sɔ̃]	sound
le **bruit** [bRɥi]	noise
silencieux, **silencieuse** [silɑ̃sjø, jøz]	silent, quiet
le **silence** [silɑ̃s]	silence
La parole est d'argent et le silence est d'or. *prov*	Talk is silver, silence is golden.

INFO

Entendre – écouter

entendre	*to hear*
Qu'est-ce que c'est? J'entends des bruits.	*What's that? I hear noises.*
écouter	*to listen (to)*
Tais-toi, s'il te plaît. J'écoute les infos.	*Please be quiet. I am listening to the news.*

l'**ouïe** *f* [wi]	hearing
avoir l'ouïe très fine	to have good hearing
auditif, **auditive** [oditif, iv]	auditory
malentendant, **malentendante** [malɑ̃tɑ̃dɑ̃, ɑ̃t]	hard of hearing
un **malentendant**, une **malentendante**	hearing-impaired person
sourd, **sourde** [suR, suRd]	deaf
un **sourd**, une **sourde**	deaf person
Il **est sourd comme un pot**. *loc*	He is stone deaf.
être **sourd-muet, sourd-muette**	to be deaf-mute
un **sourd-muet**, une **sourd-muette**	deaf-mute (n)
la **surdité** [syRdite]	deafness

sentir [sɑ̃tiʀ]	to smell
Ça sent bon/mauvais.	That smells good/bad.
une **odeur** [ɔdœʀ]	odor, smell (n)
L'argent n'a pas d'odeur. *loc*	Money is not to be sniffed at.
goûter [gute]	to taste
le **goût** [gu]	taste, sense of taste, flavor
Ça **a un goût de** pomme.	It has an apple taste.
toucher [tuʃe]	to touch
N'y touche pas!	Don't touch!
le **toucher** [tuʃe]	sense of touch, touch (n)

INFO

Sentir

Note the ***nuances of meaning*** of ***sentir*** depending on context:

Je ne sens rien, j'ai un rhume.	*I don't smell anything; I have a cold.*
Beurk! Ce poisson sent.	*Yuck! This fish smells/stinks.*
Tu sens le tabac.	*You smell like tobacco.*
Viens sentir ces fleurs, elles sentent très bon/mauvais.	*Come smell these flowers; they smell very good/bad.*

The words ***bon/mauvais***, when used adverbially, do not change form.

dormir [dɔʀmiʀ]	to sleep
s'endormir [sɑ̃dɔʀmiʀ]	to go to sleep, fall asleep
le **sommeil** [sɔmɛj]	sleep, sleepiness
Je n'**ai** pas **sommeil**.	I am not sleepy.
se réveiller [s(ə)ʀevɛje]	to wake up
le **réveil** [ʀevɛj]	awakening (n)

réagir [ʀeaʒiʀ]	to react
une **réaction** [ʀeaksjɔ̃]	reaction
un **réflexe** [ʀeflɛks]	reflex
un **geste** [ʒɛst]	gesture
Il n'a pas **fait un geste** pour m'aider.	He didn't lift a finger to help me.

grandir [gʀɑ̃diʀ]	to grow up *(See Information Box p. 37)*
Ma fille a beaucoup grandi depuis Noël.	My daughter has grown a lot since Christmas.

grossir [gRosiR] — to put on weight, to become fat
  Il a **grossi de** cinq kilos. — He has gained eleven pounds.
maigrir [mɛgRiR] — to lose weight, to become thin

---

rougir [Ruʒir] — to blush
  Elle est timide, elle rougit dès qu'on la regarde. — She is timid; she blushes as soon as you look at her.
pâlir [paliR] — to turn pale
  Il a pâli quand il a entendu cette nouvelle. — He turned pale when he heard this news.

INFO

Verbs ending in -ir

Some *verbs ending in* -ir, the stem of which comes from an adjective, express a change of condition. Examples:
rougir *to turn red*; pâlir, blêmir *to turn pale*; grandir *to grow (up)*; grossir *to become fat, gain weight*; maigrir *to become thin, lose weight. In the compound tenses they are conjugated with* avoir.

2.5 Movements and Activities  7

agir [aʒiR] — to act
actif, **active** [aktif, iv] — active
inactif, **inactive** [inaktif, iv] — inactive
une **action** [aksjõ] — action
  une **femme d'action** — woman of action
une **activité** [aktivite] — activity
un **mouvement** [muvmɑ̃] — movement
bouger [buʒe] — to move
  Hier, je n'ai pas **bougé de chez moi**. — Yesterday I didn't leave the house.
s'arrêter [saRɛte] — to stop
rester* [Rɛste] — to remain, stay

---

un **acte** [akt] — act, action
  Il faut le **juger sur ses actes**. — He must be judged by his actions.
  un **acte de bonté** — act of kindness
remuer [Rəmye] — to move
se déplacer [s(ə)deplase] — to move, change location

---

marcher [maʀʃe]	to walk, go
la **marche**	walking (n)
La **marche à pied** est excellente pour la santé.	Walking is great for your health.
le **pas** [pa]	step (n)
Les soldats **marchent au pas**.	The soldiers march in step.
faire qc **pas à pas**	to do s.th. step by step

INFO

Going

In French *marcher* or *aller* (+ e.g., *à pied*) is used to express *to go* as a method of movement:

Pas si vite. Marche plus lentement.	*Not so fast. Walk more slowly.*
On y va à pied ou en voiture?	*Shall we walk or drive?*

Aller expresses pure movement and direction.

Je vais à Nantes.	*I am going/driving/flying/traveling to Nantes.*

aller* [ale]	to go
venir* [v(ə)niʀ]	to come
revenir* [ʀəv(ə)niʀ, ʀ(ə)vəniʀ]	to come back
revenir sur ses pas	to turn around
suivre qn/qc [sɥivʀ]	to follow s.o./s.th.
se diriger vers [s(ə)diʀiʒe]	to go toward

se rendre à [s(ə)ʀɑ̃dʀ]	to go to
s'approcher de qn/qc [sapʀɔʃe]	to approach s.o./s.th.
se rapprocher de qn/qc [s(ə)ʀapʀɔʃe]	to approach s.o./s.th.
accourir* [akuʀiʀ]	to come running
Je suis accouru dès que tu m'as appelé.	I came running as soon as you called me.
s'éloigner de [selwaɲe]	to go away from
se précipiter [s(ə)pʀesipite]	to rush
s'élancer [selɑ̃se]	to hasten
s'élancer au secours de qn	to rush to the aid of s.o.

avancer [avɑ̃se]	to advance
reculer [ʀ(ə)kyle]	to go back
reculer de trois pas	to go back three steps
retourner* [ʀ(ə)tuʀne]	to return, go back
se retourner [s(ə)ʀ(ə)tuʀne]	to turn around
Tout le monde **se retourne sur son passage**.	Everyone turns around when s/he goes by.
le **retour** [ʀ(ə)tuʀ]	return (n), return trip
sortir* [sɔʀtiʀ]	to go out
une **sortie** [sɔʀti]	exit (n)
Sortie de secours	emergency exit
entrer* [ɑ̃tʀe]	to enter, come in
une **entrée** [ɑ̃tʀe]	entrance
rentrer* [ʀɑ̃tʀe]	to return, come back
Ils sont rentrés de vacances.	They have returned from vacation.

---

courir [kuʀiʀ]	to run
une **course** [kuʀs]	race (n)
se dépêcher de faire qc [s(ə)depɛʃe]	to hurry to do s.th.
rapide *adj* [ʀapid]	fast, quick
Il est plus rapide que toi.	He is quicker than you.
vite *adv* [vit]	fast
Il court plus vite que toi.	He runs faster than you.
lent, **lente** [lɑ̃, lɑ̃t]	slowly

---

s'enfuir [sɑ̃fɥiʀ]	to flee
la **fuite** [fɥit]	flight
s'échapper [seʃape]	to escape, get away
se sauver *fam* [s(ə)sove]	to run away, save one's self
Sauvez-vous avant qu'il soit trop tard!	Get away before it's too late!
glisser [glise]	to slide, slip
traîner [tʀɛne]	to loiter

---

sauter [sote]	to jump
un **saut** [so]	jump (n)
un **saut périlleux**	flip (n), somersault
tomber* [tɔ̃be]	to fall
une **chute** [ʃyt]	fall (n)

---

monter* [mɔ̃te]	to go up (stairs), ascend
une **montée** [mɔ̃te]	ascent
descendre* [desɑ̃dʀ]	to go down (stairs), descend
descendre de voiture	to get out of a car
une **descente** [desɑ̃t]	descent

INFO

Monter, descendre, sortir, rentrer, retourner

The verbs *monter, descendre, sortir, rentrer*, and *retourner* change meaning depending on whether or not they are followed by a *direct object* (transitive usage) or not (intransitive usage). With *intransitive usage* the compound tenses are formed with *être*; with the *transitive* function they use *avoir*.

Elle ***est*** montée/descendue.	*She went upstairs/downstairs.*
Elle ***a*** monté/descendu la valise.	*She brought the suitcase upstairs/downstairs.*
Ils ***sont*** sortis/rentrés.	*They went out/came back in.*
Il ***a*** sorti/rentré la poubelle.	*He took the wastebasket out/brought the wastebasket back in.*
Elle ***est*** retournée à Paris.	*She returned to Paris.*
Il ***a*** retourné les cartes.	*He turned the cards over.*

voler [vɔle]	to fly
le **vol** [vɔl]	flight
nager [naʒe]	to swim
nager le crawl	to do the front crawl
la **natation** [natasjɔ̃]	swimming (n)
danser [dɑ̃se]	to dance
danser le rock	to dance rock
la **danse** [dɑ̃s]	dance (n)
s'exercer [sɛgzɛʀse]	to exercise, train, work out
un **exercice** [ɛgzɛʀsis]	exercise (n)

INFO

Voler, le vol

Voler and *le vol* are what's known as homonyms: depending on the *context*, *voler* can mean *to fly* or *to steal*, and *le vol* can mean *flight* or *theft*.

Les hirondelles volent bas aujourd'hui.	*Today the swallows are flying low.*
On m'a volé le porte-monnaie dans le métro.	*My wallet was stolen on the subway.*
un vol régulier/charter	*a scheduled/charter flight*
un vol à l'étalage	*shoplifting*

debout *adj; adv* [d(ə)bu]	standing
se mettre debout	to stand up
être debout	to stand, to be standing
se lever [s(ə)ləve]	to get up
se baisser [s(ə)bɛse]	to bend down, duck
assis, **assise** [asi, iz]	sitting, seated
être/rester assis, **assise**	to be/remain seated
s'asseoir [saswaʀ]	to sit down
Asseyez-vous.	Sit down.
se coucher [kuʃe]	to lie down
couché, **couchée** [kuʃe]	lying down (adj)
se reposer [s(ə)ʀ(ə)poze]	to rest
le **repos** [ʀ(ə)po]	rest (n)

à genoux [aʒ(ə)nu]	kneeling
être/se mettre à genoux	to kneel (down)
s'appuyer (**sur**) [sapɥje]	to lean (on)
s'allonger (**sur**) [salɔ̃ʒe]	to lie down (on), recline (on)
Allonge-toi sur le canapé.	Lie down on the sofa.
se détendre [s(ə)detɑ̃dʀ]	to relax
la **détente** [detɑ̃t]	relaxation
se redresser [s(ə)ʀ(ə)dʀɛse]	to sit up straight

montrer [mɔ̃tʀe]	to show
présenter [pʀezɑ̃te]	to present
présenter ses vœux	to offer one's best wishes
donner [dɔne]	to give
distribuer [distʀibɥe]	to distribute
Le facteur distribue le courrier.	The letter carrier distributes the mail.
rendre [ʀɑ̃dʀ]	to return, give back, deliver
tendre [tɑ̃dʀ]	to extend
tendre la main à qn	to hold out one's hand to s.o.
tenir [t(ə)niʀ]	to hold
attraper [atʀape]	to catch
prendre [pʀɑ̃dʀ]	to take
voler [vɔle]	to steal (*See Information Box p. 40*)
Qui vole un œuf vole un bœuf. *prov*	Steal a penny, steal a pound.

2.6 Appearance  8

beau, **bel**, **belle**; **beaux, belles** *pl* [bo, bɛl]	beautiful
un beau bébé ; un bel enfant ; une belle jeune fille	a beautiful baby; a beautiful child; a beautiful girl
la **beauté** [bote]	beauty
joli, **jolie** [ʒɔli]	pretty
laid, **laide** [lɛ, lɛd]	ugly
la **laideur** [lɛdœʀ]	ugliness

l'**aspect physique** [aspɛfizik]	physical appearance
le **physique** [fizik]	appearance, looks
avoir un physique avantageux	to look good
l'**apparence** *f* [apaʀɑ̃s]	appearance
avoir l'air (**de**) *m* [avwaʀlɛʀ]	to look (like)
Il a l'air d'un clochard.	He looks like a bum.
mignon, **mignonne** [miɲɔ̃, ɔn]	cute
affreux, **affreuse** [afʀø, øz]	frightful, ugly
moche *fam* [mɔʃ]	hideous, awful
ridé, **ridée** [ʀide]	wrinkled
une **ride** [ʀid]	wrinkle (n)

INFO

Avoir l'air + adjectif

After *avoir l'air*, the adjective generally agrees with the *subject*. With *female persons* the masculine form can also be used, however. In this case the word *air* (m) is the reference word.

Elle a l'air heureuse/heureux.	*She looks happy.*
Ces devoirs ont l'air difficiles.	*These assignments look difficult.*

la **taille** [taj]	size
un homme de petite taille	a man of small stature
grand, **grande** [gʀɑ̃, gʀɑ̃d]	large
petit, **petite** [p(ə)ti, it]	small
le **poids** [pwa]	weight
prendre/perdre du poids	to gain/lose weight
gros, **grosse** [gʀo, gʀos]	fat, big
gras, **grasse** [gʀɑ, gʀɑs]	fat
mince [mɛ̃s]	slender, slim
maigre [mɛgʀ]	thin, skinny
fort, **forte** [fɔʀ, fɔʀt]	strong, powerful

la **constitution** [kɔ̃stitysjɔ̃]	constitution
avoir une robuste constitution	to have a strong constitution
fragile [fʀaʒil]	fragile, delicate
musclé, **musclée** [myskle]	muscular
baraqué *fam*, **baraquée** [baʀake]	well-built, big and powerful
souple [supl]	supple, flexible, limber
la **souplesse** [suplɛs]	suppleness, flexibility
élance, **élancée** [elɑ̃se]	slender; gangly
svelte [svɛlt]	slender, svelte
corpulent, **corpulente** [kɔʀpylɑ̃, ɑ̃t]	corpulent, stout
la **corpulence** [kɔʀpylɑ̃s]	corpulence
une dame **de forte corpulence**	a full-figured/stout woman
trapu, **trapue** [tʀapy]	stocky

les **cheveux** *mpl* [ʃ(ə)vø]	hair
long, **longue** [lɔ̃, lɔ̃g]	long
avoir les cheveux longs	to have long hair
court, **courte** [kuʀ, kuʀt]	short
blond, **blonde** [blɔ̃, blɔ̃d]	blond
un **blond**, une **blonde**	blond, blonde (n)
roux, **rousse** [ʀu, ʀus]	red-headed
brun, **brune** [bʀœ̃, bʀyn]	brunette

chauve [ʃov]	bald
châtain [ʃatɛ̃]	light brown
Elle **a les cheveux châtains.**	She has brown hair.
Elle **est châtain.**	She is a brunette.
foncé, **foncée** [fɔ̃se]	dark (adj)
clair, **claire** [klɛʀ]	light (adj)

le **teint** [tɛ̃]	complexion
avoir le teint frais	to have a fresh complexion
bronzé, **bronzée** [bʀɔ̃ze]	tanned
pâle [pɑl]	pale
avoir des boutons *mpl* [avwaʀdebutɔ̃]	to have pimples
l'**acné** *f* [akne]	acne

2.7 Cosmetics and Grooming  9

la **toilette** [twalɛt]	grooming
faire sa toilette	to wash up
un **gant de toilette**	washcloth
un **bain** [bɛ̃]	bath
une **douche** [duʃ]	shower (n)
prendre une douche	to take a shower
chaud, **chaude** [ʃo, ʃod]	warm, hot
tiède [tjɛd]	lukewarm
froid, **froide** [fʀwa, fʀwad]	cold

---

propre [pʀɔpʀ]	clean
la **propreté** [pʀopʀəte]	cleanliness
sale [sal]	dirty
être sale comme un peigne *loc*	to be filthy
la **saleté** [salte]	dirt, filth
se laver [s(ə)lave]	to wash (oneself)
se nettoyer [s(ə)netwaje]	to clean (oneself)
le **savon** [savɔ̃]	soap

INFO

Propre

Some adjectives change their *meaning* depending on whether they are placed before or after the noun, e.g.:

un hôtel propre	*a clean hotel*
Il l'a écrit de sa propre main.	*He wrote it with his own hand.*
C'est une histoire vraie.	*That is a true story.*
C'est un vrai probléme.	*That is a real problem.*
une histoire drôle	*a funny story*
une drôle d'histoire	*a peculiar story*
un homme brave	*a brave man*
un brave type	*a good guy*
un ancien ministre	*a former minister*
un monument ancien	*an ancient monument*

l'**hygiène** [iʒjɛn]	hygiene
rincer [ʀɛ̃se]	to rinse
se rincer les cheveux	to rinse one's hair
frotter [fʀɔte]	to rub
une **trousse de toilette** [tʀusdətwalɛt]	toiletry kit
un **produit de beauté** [pʀɔdɥidbote]	cosmetic, beauty product
une **lotion** [lɔsjɔ̃]	lotion
un **pot de crème** (**hydratante**) [podkʀɛm(idʀatɑ̃t)]	container of (moisturizing) cream
un **déodorant** [deɔdɔʀɑ̃]	deodorant

sécher [seʃe]	to dry
Mes cheveux sèchent vite.	My hair dries quickly.
sec, **sèche** [sɛk, sɛʃ]	dry (adj)
une **serviette** (**de toilette**/**de bain**) [sɛʀvjɛt]	hand/bath towel
s'essuyer [sesɥije]	to dry (oneself) off
Essuie-toi les mains.	Dry your hands.

se brosser les dents [s(ə)bʀɔseledɑ̃]	to brush one's teeth
une **brosse à dents** [bʀɔsadɑ̃]	toothbrush
le **dentifrice** [dɑ̃tifʀis]	toothpaste
un **tube de dentifrice**	tube of toothpaste

une **brosse à cheveux** [bʀɔsaʃ(ə)vø]	hair brush
se peigner [s(ə)pɛɲe]	to comb one's hair
un **peigne** [pɛɲ]	comb
se coiffer [s(ə)kwafe]	to do one's hair
une **coiffure** [kwafyʀ]	hairstyle
Tu as changé de coiffure?	Do you have a new hairstyle?
un **coiffeur**, une **coiffeuse** [kwafœʀ, øz]	hairstylist, barber, hairdresser
aller chez le coiffeur	to go to the hairstylist
une **coupe de cheveux** [kupdəʃ(ə)vø]	haircut

INFO

Hairdresser

un coiffeur, une coiffeuse	*hairdresser (m. and f.)*
(se) coiffer	*to do one's hair*

Though English has the nouns *coiffure* and *coif* and the verb *coiffure*, all borrowed from French, they are not common in modern usage.

les **ciseaux** *mpl* [sizo]	scissors
un **shamp(o)oing** [ʃɑ̃pwɛ̃]	shampoo (n)
faire son shamp(o)oing	to wash one's hair
une **crème** [kʀɛm]	(facial)cream
une crème de jour/de nuit	day/night cream
un pot de crème (hydratante)	container of (moisturizing) cream

INFO

Plural terms

des ciseaux *mpl*, une paire de ciseaux	*(a pair of) scissors*
deux paires de ciseaux	*two pairs of scissors*

Similarly,

des lunettes *fpl*, une paire de lunettes	*a pair of glasses*
trios paires de lunettes	*three pairs of glasses*
des tenailles, *fpl*, une paire de tanailles	*(a pair of) tweezers*
deux paires de tenailles	*two pairs of tweezers*

Une tenaille is used as well as *des tenailles.*

un **brushing** [bʀœʃiŋ]	blow-dry (hairstyle) (n)
un **sèche-cheveu(x)** [sɛʃʃəvø]	hair-dryer (*See Information Box p.104*)
la **laque** [lak]	hairspray
la **barbe** [baʀb]	beard
porter la barbe	to have/wear a beard
la **moustache** [mustaʃ]	mustache
se raser [s(ə)ʀaze]	to shave
la **crème à raser**	shaving cream
un **rasoir (électrique)** [ʀazwaʀ]	(electric) razor
un **après-rasage** [apʀɛʀazaʒ]	aftershave
un **ongle** [ɔ̃gl]	(finger) nail
une **lime à ongles**	nail file
un **vernis à ongles**	nail polish
le **dissolvant** [disɔlvɑ̃]	nail polish remover
un **coton** [kɔtɔ̃]	cotton ball

se **maquiller** [s(ə)makije]	to put on makeup
le **maquillage** [makijaʒ]	makeup (n)
la **poudre** [pudʀ]	powder
le **mascara** [maskaʀa]	mascara
le **rouge à lèvres** [ʀuʒalɛvʀ]	lipstick
se démaquiller [s(ə)demakije]	to remove makeup
s'épiler [sepile]	to depilate, tweeze
une **pince à épiler**	depilatory tweezers
se parfumer [s(ə)paʀfyme]	to put on perfume
le **parfum** [paʀfɛ̃]	perfume
une **eau de toilette**; des **eaux de toilette** *pl* [odtwalɛt]	cologne, eau de toilette
un **flacon d'eau de toilette**	bottle of cologne

la **ligne** [liɲ]	figure (n)
surveiller sa ligne	to watch one's figure
se peser [s(ə)pəse]	to weigh oneself
une **balance** [balɑ̃s]	scale (n)
soigné, **soignée** [swaɲe]	well-groomed
un **institut de beauté** [ɛ̃stitydbote]	beauty salon
la **manucure** [manykyʀ]	manicure
la **pédicure** [pedikyʀ]	pedicure

False Friends

French Word	Actual Meaning	False Friend	Correct French Word
la figure	**face**	figure	*la taille, la ligne, la silhouette*
le front	**forehead**	front	*le devant, la façade*
impotent(e)	**immobile, disabled**	impotent	*impuissant(e)*
propre	**clean**	proper	*correct, correcte*
sale	**dirty**	sale	*une vente*
le talon	**heel**	talon	*la serre*
la toilette *les toilettes*	**grooming, washing** **restroom, bathroom**	toilet toilet (toilet bowl)	*la toilette, le WC* *la toilette, le WC* *(la cuvette)*

My Vocabulary

3

Health and Medicine

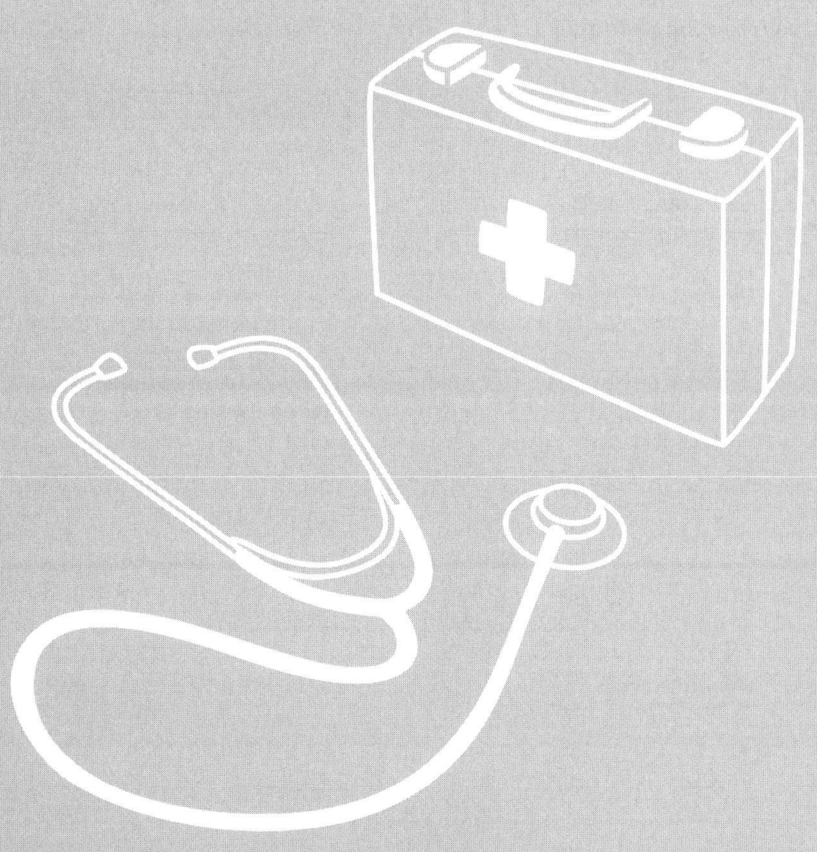

3.1 Health and Illness  10

sain, **saine** [sɛ̃, sɛn]	healthy
sain et sauf	safe and sound
la **santé** [sɑ̃te]	health
être en **bonne santé**	to be healthy
l'**état** (**de santé**) [eta(d(ə)sɑ̃te)]	state, condition (of health)
Elle est dans un **état grave**.	She is in serious condition.
être en forme [ɛtʀɑ̃fɔʀm]	to be in shape
avoir bonne/mauvaise mine [avwaʀbɔn/movɛzmin]	to look good/bad
se sentir bien/mal [s(ə)sɑ̃tiʀbjɛ̃/mal]	to feel good/bad
aller bien/mal [allebjɛ̃/mal]	to be well/unwell
Comment allez-vous? Bien, j'espère.	How are you? Good, I hope.

se porter bien/mal [s(ə)pɔʀtebjɛ̃/mal]	to be well/ill
être bien/mal portant, **portante** [ɛt(ʀə)bjɛ̃/malpɔʀtɑ̃, ɑ̃t]	to be well/ill
être bien/mal en point [ɛt(ʀə)bjɛ̃/malɑ̃pwɛ̃]	to be in good/bad shape
être épuisé, **épuisée** [epɥize]	to be exhausted
une **précaution** [pʀekosjɔ̃]	precaution
récupérer [ʀekypeʀe]	to recover
Je trouve qu'il met du temps à récupérer.	I find that he is slow to recover.
se remettre de qc [s(ə)ʀ(ə)mɛtʀ]	to get over s.th.
reprendre des forces [ʀ(ə)pʀɑ̃dʀdefɔʀs]	to get one's strength back
s'améliorer [sameljɔʀe]	to get better, improve
une **amélioration** [ameljɔʀasjɔ̃]	improvement
la **convalescence** [kɔ̃valɛsɑ̃s]	convalescence
guérir qn de qc [geʀiʀ]	to cure s.o. of s.th.
L'homéopathe m'a guéri de mon allergie.	The homeopath cured me of my allergy.
On ne guérit pas du sida.	AIDS is not curable.
guéri, **guérie** [geʀi]	cured, healed
la **guérison** [geʀizɔ̃]	cure (n)

fatiguer [fatige]	to tire, strain, get on the nerves
fatigué, **fatiguée** [fatige]	tired
la **fatigue** [fatig]	fatigue (n)
être mort de fatigue	to be dead tired
avoir sommeil [avwaʀsɔmɛj]	to be sleepy/tired
Je vais me coucher, j'ai sommeil.	I am going to bed, I am tired.
tomber de sommeil	to (nearly) drop from fatigue
se reposer [s(ə)ʀ(ə)pose]	to rest
le **repos** [ʀ(ə)po]	rest (n)
faible [fɛbl]	weak
la **faiblesse** [fɛblɛs]	weakness
fragile [fʀaʒil]	fragile, weak
Elle a une **santé fragile**.	Her health is fragile.

malade [malad]	ill, sick
tomber* gravement malade	to become seriously ill
un, une **malade** [malad]	sick person
une **maladie** [maladi]	illness
attraper une maladie grave	to acquire a serious illness

malin, **maligne** [malɛ̃, maliɲ]	malignant
bénin, **bénigne** [benɛ̃, beniɲ]	benign
une **tumeur bénigne**	benign tumor
héréditaire [eʀeditɛʀ]	hereditary
une **maladie héréditaire**	hereditary disease
génétique [ʒenetik]	genetic
la **manipulation génétique**	genetic engineering
contaminer [kɔ̃tamine]	to contaminate, infect
contagieux, **contagieuse** [kɔ̃taʒjø, jøz]	contagious
s'aggraver [sagʀɑve]	to get worse, deteriorate
Son état s'est aggravé rapidement.	His condition quickly deteriorated.
une **aggravation** [agʀavasjɔ̃]	worsening (n)
une **rechute** [ʀəʃyt]	relapse (n)
Elle a fait une rechute.	She suffered a relapse.

avoir mal (**à**) [avwaʀmal]	to feel pain
J'ai mal aux dents.	My teeth hurt.
(**se**) **faire mal** [(s(ə))fɛʀmal]	to hurt (oneself)
Ça me fait mal quand je bouge.	It hurts when I move.
Elle s'est fait mal en tombant.	She hurt herself when she fell.
le **mal**; les **maux** *pl* [mal, mo]	pain(s)
Ses maux de tête sont terribles.	His/Her headaches are terrible.
la **douleur** [dulœʀ]	pain (n)

les **symptômes** *mpl* [sɛ̃ptom]	symptoms
Il **présente tous les symptômes** de la grippe.	He exhibits all the symptoms of the flu.
les **troubles** *mpl* [tʀubl]	disorders
souffrir de qc [sufʀiʀ]	to suffer from s.th.
Il souffre d'une bronchite aiguë.	He is suffering from acute bronchitis.
la **tension** [tɑ̃sjɔ̃]	blood pressure
L'infirmière **a pris ma tension**.	The nurse checked my blood pressure.
prendre froid [pʀɑ̃dʀ(ə)fʀwa]	to catch a cold/chill
le **rhume** [ʀym]	cold, congestion
avoir/attraper un rhume	to have/catch a cold
le **rhume des foins**	hay fever
éternuer [etɛʀnɥe]	to sneeze
À tes souhaits! Ça fait trois fois que tu éternues.	God bless you! That's the third time you've sneezed.
avoir mal à la gorge [avwaʀmalalagɔʀʒ]	to have a sore throat
le **mal de gorge** [maldəgɔʀʒ]	sore throat
tousser [tuse]	to cough
la **toux** [tu]	cough (n)
un **refroidissement** [ʀ(ə)fʀwadismɑ̃]	cold (n)
une **infection** [ɛ̃fɛksjɔ̃]	infection
un **microbe** [mikʀɔb]	bacterium, microbe, pathogen
un **virus** [viʀys]	virus
une **angine** [ɑ̃ʒin]	angina
une **inflammation** [ɛ̃flamasjɔ̃]	inflammation, infection
une **bronchite** [bʀɔ̃ʃit]	bronchitis
une **pneumonie** [pnømɔni]	pneumonia
une **otite** [ɔtit]	inner ear infection
la **fièvre** [fjɛvʀ]	fever
un **accès de fièvre**	fever attack
la **grippe** [gʀip]	flu
être brûlant, **brûlante** [bʀylɑ̃, ɑ̃t]	to be burning (from fever)
transpirer [tʀɑ̃spiʀe]	to sweat
trembler [tʀɑ̃ble]	to tremble
garder le lit [gaʀdel(ə)li]	to stay in bed
un **thermomètre** [tɛʀmɔmɛtʀ]	thermometer
prendre sa température [pʀɑ̃dʀsatɑ̃peʀatyʀ]	to take one's temperature

les **courbatures** *fpl* [kuRbatyR]	sore/stiff muscles
la **sueur** [sɥœR]	sweat
être trempé de sueur	to be soaked with sweat
avoir des vertiges *mpl* [avwaRdevɛRtiʒ]	to feel dizzy
une **attaque** [atak]	stroke (n)
Il a eu une **attaque** (**d'apoplexie**).	He suffered a stroke.
une **crise** [kRiz]	attack (n)
une **crise cardiaque**	heart attack
une **crise de foie**	liver upset
un **infarctus** [ɛ̃faRktys]	infarction
le **cholestérol** [kɔlɛsteRɔl]	cholesterol
le **diabète** [djabɛt]	diabetes
les **rhumatismes** *mpl* [Rymatism]	rheumatism
le **cancer** [kɑ̃seR]	cancer
le **SIDA** [sida]	AIDS
être séropositif, **séropositive** [seRopozitif, iv]	to be HIV-positive
un **choc** [ʃok]	shock (n)
être en état de choc	to be in a state of shock
être allergique à [alɛRʒik]	to be allergic to
Je suis allergique aux fraises.	I am allergic to strawberries.
une **allergie** [alɛRʒi]	allergy
urgent, **urgente** [yRʒɑ̃, ɑ̃t]	urgent
un **accident** [aksidɑ̃]	accident
une **chute** [ʃyt]	fall
Il a **fait une chute mortelle.**	He took a fatal fall.
(**se**) **blesser** [s(ə)blɛse]	to hurt (oneself)
blessé, **blessée** [blɛse]	injured, hurt
Les victimes de l'accident sont **grièvement blessées**.	The accident victims are seriously injured. *(See Information Box p. 54)*
un **blessé**, une **blessée**	injured person
Cette collision a fait **trois blessés graves**.	This collision left three people seriously injured.
une **blessure** [blɛsyR]	injury, wound
(**se**) **couper** [s(ə)kupe]	to cut (oneself)
la **coupure** [kupyR]	cut (n)
saigner [seɲe]	to bleed
le **sang** [sɑ̃]	blood
Il a perdu beaucoup de sang.	He has lost a lot of blood.
se brûler [s(ə)bRyle]	to burn oneself
une **brûlure** [bRylyR]	burn (n)

INFO

Gravement/grièvement

grièvement (seriously) is used in connection with injuries (*blessé*/injured, wounded, *brûlé*/burned).

Ils se sont grièvement brûlés.	*They were seriously burned.*

Otherwise *gravement* is used as the adverb corresponding to *grave*.

Il est gravement malade.	*He is seriously ill.*

---

une **commotion cérébrale** [komosjɔ̃seʀebʀal]	concussion
une **plaie** [plɛ]	wound
une **plaie ouverte**	open wound
un **bleu** [blø]	bruise (n)
un **hématome** [ematom]	hematoma
une **bosse** [bɔs]	boil, lump
enflé, **enflée** [ɑ̃fle]	swollen
Après sa chute, il avait le genou enflé.	His knee was swollen after his fall.
une **ampoule** [ɑ̃pul]	blister (n) (*See Information Box p. 55*)
se démettre qc [s(ə)demɛtʀ]	to dislocate s.th.
Elle s'est démis l'épaule.	She dislocated her shoulder.
une **déchirure** [deʃiʀyʀ]	tear (n)
une **déchirure musculaire**	muscle tear
un **claquage** [klakaʒ]	strain (n)
se tordre qc [s(ə)tɔʀdʀ]	to twist s.th.
Je me suis tordu la cheville.	I twisted my ankle.
une **entorse** [ɑ̃tɔʀs]	sprain
se fouler qc [s(ə)fule]	to slightly sprain s.th.
une **foulure** [fulyʀ]	slight sprain
se fracturer qc [s(ə)fʀaktyʀe]	to break/fracture s.th.
une **fracture** [fʀaktyʀ]	fracture, break (n)
se casser le bras [s(ə)kasel(ə)bʀa]	to break one's arm
un **plâtre** [platʀ]	cast (n)
un **lumbago** [lɛ̃bago]	lumbago

---

le **régime** [ʀeʒim]	diet (n)
Nous sommes **au régime** sans sel.	We are on a salt-free diet.
suivre un régime	to be on a diet
l'**exercice** *m* [ɛgzɛʀsis]	exercise (n)
maigrir [mɛgʀiʀ]	to lose weight (*See Information Box p. 37*)
maigre [mɛgʀ]	thin
grossir [gʀosiʀ]	to put on weight
gros, **grosse** [gʀo, gʀos]	fat

INFO

Inflatables

The notion of a receptacle that swells, such as a blister, bladder, bubble, vesicle, or balloon, is expressed in various ways in French:

une ampoule Je me suis fait des ampoules aux pieds.	*(water, burn) blister* *I got blisters on my feet.*
une bulle Dans les bandes dessinées, les personnages s'expriement par bulles.	*a speech bubble (in comics)* *In the comics people talk with speech bubbles.*
une bulle de savon	*a soap bubble*

---

la **rougeole** [ʀuʒɔl]	measles
la **rubéole** [ʀybeɔl]	rubella
la **varicelle** [vaʀisɛl]	varicella, chicken pox
les **oreillons** *mpl* [ɔʀɛjɔ̃]	mumps
la **démangeaison** [demɑ̃ʒɛzɔ̃]	itch
un **abcès** [absɛ]	abscess

une **indigestion** [ɛ̃diʒɛsjɔ̃]	indigestion
la **diarrhée** [djaʀe]	diarrhea
s'empoisonner [sɑ̃pwazɔ̃ne]	to poison oneself
le **poison** [pwazɔ̃]	poison (n)
un **poison violent**	fact-acting poison
une **intoxication** [ɛ̃tɔksikasjɔ̃]	poisoning
une **intoxication alimentaire**	food poisoning
vomir [vɔmiʀ]	to vomit
une **appendicite** [apɛ̃disit]	appendicitis
se faire opérer de l'appendicite	to have one's appendix out

(**faire**) **une dépression nerveuse** [depʀesjɔ̃nɛʀvøz]	(to experience) a nervous breakdown
dépressif, **dépressive** [depʀɛsif, iv]	depressive, depressed
névrosé, **névrosée** [nevʀoze]	neurotic
une **maladie mentale** [maladimɑ̃tal]	mental illness

étouffer [etufe]	to smother, suffocate
s'asphyxier [sasfiksje]	to asphyxiate
s'évanouir [sevanwiʀ]	to faint, pass out
perdre connaissance [pɛʀdʀ(ə)kɔnɛsɑ̃s]	to lose consciousness
tomber* dans les pommes *fam* [tɔ̃bedɑ̃lepom]	to keel over
Dès qu'il voit du sang, il tombe dans les pommes.	He keels over as soon as he sees blood.

un **handicap** [ɑ̃dikap]	handicap (n)
handicapé, **handicapée** [ɑ̃dikape]	handicapped, disabled
un **handicapé**, une **handicapée**	handicapped person
un **handicapé physique/mental**	physically/mentally handicapped person
infirme [ɛ̃fiʀm]	disabled, handicapped (adj)
un, une **invalide** [ɛ̃valid]	disabled person, invalid (n)
un **invalide de guerre**	disabled veteran, war invalid

3.2 Medical Care  11

médical, **médicale** [medikal]	medical
une **visite médicale**	medical examination
la **médecine** [med(ə)sin]	medicine
un **médecin** [med(ə)sɛ̃]	doctor
le **médecin de famille**	family doctor
un **docteur** [dɔktœʀ]	doctor
un, une **généraliste** [ʒeneʀalist]	general practitioner
un, une **spécialiste** [spesjalist]	specialist
C'est un **spécialiste en pédiatrie**.	He is a specialist in pediatrics.
un **chirurgien**, une **chirurgienne** [ʃiʀyʀʒjɛ̃, jɛn]	surgeon
un **infirmier**, une **infirmière** [ɛ̃fiʀmje, jɛʀ]	nurse

un, une **toubib** *fam* [tubib]	doctor, doc
un, une **ophtalmologue** [ɔftalmɔlɔg]	ophthalmologist
un, une **ophtalmo** *fam* [ɔftalmo]	eye doctor, ophthalmologist
un, une **oto-rhino(-laryngologiste)**; des **oto-rhino-laryngologistes** *pl* [ɔtɔʀinolaʀɛ̃gɔlɔʒist]	otolaryngologist (ENT doctor)
un, une **oto-rhino**; des **oto-rhinos** *pl* [ɔtɔʀino]	
un, une **ORL** [oɛʀɛl]	ENT doctor
un, une **gynécologue** [ʒinekɔlɔg]	gynecologist
un, une **gynéco** *fam* [ʒineko]	OB-GYN
un, une **orthopédiste** [ɔʀtopedist]	orthopedic surgeon
un, une **pédiatre** [pedjɑtʀ]	pediatrician
un, une **dermatologue** [dɜʀmatɔlɔg]	dermatologist
un, une **dermato** *fam* [dɜʀmato]	dermatologist
un, une **psychiatre** [psikjɑtʀ]	psychiatrist
un, une **psy** *fam* [psi]	shrink
un, une **homéopathe** [ɔmeɔpat]	homeopath
l'**homéopathie** *f* [ɔmeɔpati]	homeopathy
les **médecines douces** *fpl* [med(ə)sindus]	alternative medicine(s)
l'**acupuncture** *f* [akypɔ̃ktyʀ]	acupuncture

un **patient**, une **patiente** [pasjɑ̃, ɑ̃t]	patient (n)
hospitalier, **hospitalière** [ɔspitalje, jɛʀ]	hospital (adj)
le **personnel hospitalier**	hospital personnel
un **hôpital** [ɔpital]	hospital
une **clinique** [klinik]	clinic
une **pharmacie** [faʀmasi]	pharmacy
un **pharmacien**, une **pharmacienne** [faʀmasjɛ̃, jɛn]	pharmacist

la **Sécurité sociale** [sekyRitesɔsjal]	social security (French social and health care system)
la **Sécu** *fam* [seky]	social security
une **feuille de maladie/de soins** [fœjdəmaladi/dəswɛ̃]	claim form
les **honoraires** *mpl* [ɔnɔRɛR]	doctor's fee
rembourser [Rɑ̃buRse]	to reimburse, cover
Ce médicament n'est pas remboursé par la Sécu.	This medication is not covered by social security.
un **certificat** (**médical**) [sɛRtifika(medikal)]	(medical) certificate

un **rendez-vous** [Rɑ̃devu]	appointment
Le docteur **reçoit sur rendez-vous**.	The doctor sees patients by appointment.
consulter [kɔ̃sylte]	to consult
Tu devrais consulter un spécialiste.	You should consult a specialist.
la **consultation** [kɔ̃syltasjɔ̃]	consultation
les **heures de consultation**	consultation hours
un **cabinet médical** [kabinɛmedikal]	medical practice
une **salle d'attente** [saldatɑ̃t]	waiting room
une **visite à domicile** [visitadɔmisil]	house call
examiner [ɛgzamine]	to examine
se faire examiner par qn	to be examined by s.o.
un **examen** [ɛgzamɛ̃]	examination

ausculter qn [ɔskylte]	to auscultate s.o., listen to one's heartbeat
un **diagnostic** [djagnɔstik]	diagnosis
faire un diagnostic	to make a diagnosis
prendre le pouls [pRɑ̃dR(ə)ləpu]	to check the pulse
une **ordonnance** [ɔRdɔnɑ̃s]	prescription
Le médecin a rédigé/délivré une ordonnance.	The doctor has written a prescription.

soigner [swaɲe]	to treat
Son docteur le soigne très bien.	He is getting very good treatment from his doctor.
le **soin** [swɛ̃]	care (n)
les **premiers soins**	first aid
traiter [tRɛte]	to treat
traiter une maladie	to treat a disease
le **traitement** [tRɛtmɑ̃]	treatment

une **piqûre** [pikyʀ]	shot
faire une piqûre à qn	to give s.o. a shot

INFO

Shots

Note the difference:

une piqûre	*a shot, a hypodermic injection*
une seringue	*a syringe, a hypodermic needle*

une **prise de sang** [pʀizdəsɑ̃]	blood sample
vacciner qn contre qc	to immunize/vaccinate s.o. for s.th.
J'ai été vacciné contre le tétanos.	I have been vaccinated for tetanus.
un **vaccin** [vaksɛ̃]	vaccine
une **transfusion sanguine** [tʀɑ̃sfyzjɔ̃sɑ̃gin]	blood transfusion
une **perfusion** [pɛʀfyzjɔ̃]	IV, drip (n)
Il doit **rester sous perfusion**.	He has to stay on a drip/IV.
une **greffe** [gʀɛf]	transplant
une **greffe d'organe**	organ transplant

un **médicament** [medikamɑ̃]	medication
prendre un médicament	to take a medication
un **comprimé** [kɔ̃pʀime]	pill, tablet
prescrire qc à qn [pʀɛskʀiʀ]	to prescribe s.th. for s.o.

le **mercurochrome** [mɛʀkyʀokʀom]	mercurochrome
le **coton** [kɔtɔ̃]	gauze
le **sparadrap** [spaʀadʀa]	adhesive bandage
un **pansement** [pɑ̃smɑ̃]	dressing
un **pansement adhésif**	adhesive dressing
une **pommade** [pɔmad]	salve
un **remède** [ʀ(ə)mɛd]	remedy (n)
C'est un **remède miracle** contre la toux.	It's a miracle cure for cough.
un **cachet** [kaʃɛ]	tablet
une **pilule** [pilyl]	pill
la **pilule**	contraceptive pill
des **gouttes** *fpl* [gut]	drops (n)
des **gouttes pour le nez**	nose drops
un **antibiotique** [ɑ̃tibjɔtik]	antibiotic (n)
un **calmant** [kalmɑ̃]	sedative, tranquilizer, painkiller

opérer [ɔpeʀe]	to operate
une **opération** [ɔpeʀasjɔ̃]	operation
subir une opération	to have an operation
sauver qn [sove]	to save s.o.

une **ambulance** [ɑ̃bylɑ̃s]	ambulance
le **SAMU** (**Service d'aide médicale d'urgence**) [samy]	emergency rescue, EMT
Il faut appeler le SAMU!	Call an ambulance!
un **C.H.U.** (**centre hospitalier universitaire**) [seaʃy]	university hospital
la **Croix-Rouge** [kʀwaʀuʒ]	Red Cross

un, une **dentiste** [dɑ̃tist]	dentist
la **dent** [dɑ̃]	tooth
avoir mal aux dents	to have a toothache
les **soins dentaires** *mpl* [swɛ̃dɑ̃tɛʀ]	dental care/treatment
un **cabinet dentaire** [kabinɛdɑ̃tɛʀ]	dental office

une **carie** [kaʀi]	cavity
plomber une dent [plɔ̃beyndɑ̃]	to fill a tooth
un **plombage** [plɔ̃bɑʒ]	filling (n)
une **couronne** [kuʀɔn]	(tooth) crown
un **dentier** [dɑ̃tje]	dentures, false teeth
un **appareil dentaire** [apaʀɛjdɑ̃tɛʀ]	braces, retainer, dental appliance
arracher [aʀaʃe]	to pull (out)
On lui a arraché une dent de sagesse.	She had a wisdom tooth pulled.

radiographier [ʀadjoɡʀafje]	to x-ray
une **radio(graphie)** [ʀadjo(ɡʀɑfi)]	X-ray (n)
Il vaudrait mieux faire une radio de votre jambe.	It would be better to x-ray your leg.
les **rayons** *mpl* [ʀɛjɔ̃]	rays
Les rayons X ont été découverts par Röntgen.	X-rays were discovered by Röntgen.
une **anesthésie** [anɛstesi]	anesthesia
une anesthésie locale/générale	local/general anesthesia
une **échographie** [ekoɡʀafi]	sonogram, ultrasound
un **électrocardiogramme** (**ECG**) [elɛktʀokaʀdjɔɡʀam]	electrocardiogram (ECG)
l'**IRM** (**Imagerie par Résonance Magnétique**) *f* [iɛʀɛm]	MRI (magnetic resonance imagery)
l'**RMN** (**Résonance Magnétique Nucléaire**) *f* [ɛʀɛmɛn]	NMR (nuclear magnetic resonance)
un **stimulateur cardiaque** [stimylatœʀkaʀdjak]	pacemaker
un **pacemaker** [pɛsmɛkœʀ]	pacemaker

3.3 Drugs, Tobacco, Alcohol  12

se droguer [s(ə)dʀɔɡe]	to take drugs
une **drogue** [dʀɔɡ]	drug (n)
une **drogue douce/dure**	soft/hard drugs
consommer de la drogue	to take/use drugs
fournir de la drogue	to deal drugs
drogué, **droguée** [dʀɔɡe]	addicted to drugs
un **drogué**, une **droguée**	drug addict
être dépendant, **dépendante** [depɑ̃dɑ̃, ɑ̃t]	to be addicted
être accro *fam* [akʀo]	to be hooked

la **toxicomanie** [tɔksikɔmani]	drug abuse
un, une **toxicomane** [tɔksikɔman]	drug addict
un, une **toxico** *fam* [tɔksiko]	junkie
un **trafiquant**, une **trafiquante** [tʀafikɑ̃, ɑ̃t]	(drug) dealer
un **dealer**/un **dealeur** [dilœʀ]	drug dealer
le **trafic de drogue** [tʀafikdədʀɔɡ]	drug trafficking

le **haschisch** [aʃiʃ]	hashish
le **hasch** *fam* [aʃ]	hash
la **marijuana** [maʀiʀwana/maʀiʒɥana]	marijuana
un **joint**; un **pétard** *fam* [ʒwɛ̃, petaʀ]	joint
l'**ecstasy** *f* [ekstazi]	ecstasy
un **stupéfiant** [stypefjɑ̃]	dope, drug
absorber des stupéfiants	to use drugs
se camer *fam* [s(ə)kame]	to be on drugs, to get stoned
la **came** *fam* [kam]	drugs, stuff
la **cocaïne** [kɔkain]	cocaine
la **coke** *fam* [kɔk]	coke
la **neige** *fam* [nɛʒ]	coke, snow
l'**héroïne** *f* [eʀɔin]	heroin
se piquer *fam* [s(ə)pike]	to shoot up
se shooter *fam* [səʃute]	to shoot up
le **crack** [kʀak]	crack (cocaine)
la **méthadone** [metadɔn]	methadone
La méthadone est un produit de substitution.	Methadone is a replacement product.
le **LSD** [ɛlɛsde]	LSD
une **dose** [doz]	dose (n)
s'injecter une dose d'héroïne	to inject a dose of heroin
une **overdose**/une **surdose**	overdose (n)
le **manque** [mɑ̃k]	withdrawal symptoms
être en manque	to experience withdrawal symptoms
flipper *fam* [flipe]	to trip (out)
une **thérapie** [teʀapi]	therapy
se soumettre à une thérapie	to undergo therapy
se désintoxiquer [dezɛ̃tɔksike]	to go through rehab
la **désintoxication** [dezɛ̃tɔksikasjɔ̃]	withdrawal
suivre une **cure de désintoxication**	to go through rehab
être clean *fam* [klin]	to be clean
fumer [fyme]	to smoke
Défense de fumer.	No smoking.
la **fumée** [fyme]	smoke (n)
un **fumeur**, une **fumeuse** [fymœʀ, øz]	smoker
C'est un **gros fumeur**.	He's a heavy smoker.
une **zone non-fumeurs**	non-smoking area
le **tabac** [taba]	tobacco
un **bureau de tabac**	tobacco shop

le **tabagisme** [tabaʒism]	nicotine addiction
une campagne de lutte contre le tabagisme	anti-smoking campaign
la **nicotine** [nikɔtin]	nicotine
le **goudron** [gudʀɔ̃]	tar
une **cigarette** [sigaʀɛt]	cigarette
une **cigarette bout filtre/sans filtre**	filter/non-filter cigarette
un **paquet de cigarettes**	pack of cigarettes
rouler une cigarette	to roll a cigarette
un **cigare** [sigaʀ]	cigar
une **pipe** [pip]	pipe
un **briquet** [bʀikɛ]	cigarette lighter
une **allumette** [alymɛt]	match
une **boîte d'allumettes**	box of matches
une **clope** *fam* [klɔp]	cigarette, smoke (n)
Tu peux me **passer une clope**?	Pass me a smoke, will you?
une **cartouche de cigarettes** [kaʀtuʃdəsigaʀɛt]	carton of cigarettes
un **mégot** [mego]	a (cigarette) butt
la **cendre** [sɑ̃dʀ]	ash
un **cendrier** [sɑ̃dʀije]	ashtray
boire [bwaʀ]	to drink
boire un coup (**de trop**)	to take one drink (too many)
boire dans un verre	to drink from a glass
boire à la bouteille	to drink from the bottle
un **buveur**, une **buveuse** [byvœʀ, øz]	drinker
prendre un verre [pʀɑ̃dʀɛ̃vɛʀ]	to have a drink
Viens prendre un verre à la maison!	Come have a drink at the house!
l'**alcool** *m* [alkɔl]	alcohol
l'**alcoolisme** *m* [alkɔlism]	alcoholism
alcoolique [alkɔlik]	alcoholic (adj)
un, une **alcoolique**	alcoholic (n)
l'**abus** *m* [aby]	abuse (n)
L'abus d'alcool est dangereux pour la santé.	Alcohol abuse is dangerous to your health.

ivre [ivʀ]	drunk (adj)
l'**ivresse** *f* [ivʀɛs]	drunkenness
un, une **ivrogne** [ivʀɔɲ]	drunk (person) (n)
soûl, soûle [su, sul]	drunk (adj)
noir *fam*, **noire** [nwaʀ]	soused, plastered
beurré *fam*, **beurrée** [bœʀe]	soused, plastered
prendre une cuite *fam* [pʀɑ̃dʀynkɥit]	to get smashed
avoir la gueule de bois [avwaʀlagœldəbwa]	to have a hangover
un **alcootest** [alkɔtɛst]	sobriety test
le **taux d'alcoolémie** [todalkɔlemi]	blood alcohol level

False Friends

French Word	Actual Meaning	False Friend	Correct French Word
blesser	**to hurt/injure**	to bless	*bênir*
la gorge	**throat**	to gorge (on)	*se gaver (de)*
le médecin	**doctor**	medicine	*le médicament*

My Vocabulary

4

Psyche, Mind, Behavior

4.1 Feelings  13

se sentir [s(ə)sɑ̃tiʀ]	to feel
sentimental, **sentimentale** [sɑ̃timɑ̃tal]	sentimental
le **sentiment** [sɑ̃timɑ̃]	sentiment, feeling
éprouver un sentiment de joie	to experience a feeling of joy
ému, **émue** [emy]	moved (adj)
Elle est **émue aux larmes**.	She is moved to tears.
émotif, **émotive** [emɔtif, iv]	sensitive, emotional
émouvant, **émouvante** [emuvɑ̃, ɑ̃t]	moving (adj)
l'**émotion** *f* [emosjɔ̃]	emotion
réagir **sous l'effet de l'émotion**	to react emotionally

ressentir qc [ʀ(ə)sɑ̃tiʀ]	to feel s.th.
ressentir de la pitié pour qn	to feel pity for s.o.
manifester [manifɛste]	to express
manifester sa joie	to express one's joy
refouler [ʀ(ə)fule]	to suppress
refouler un sentiment de haine	to suppress a feeling of hatred
surmonter [syʀmɔ̃te]	to overcome, surmount
surmonter son chagrin	to overcome one's sorrow
la **passion** [pasjɔ̃]	passion
toucher [tuʃe]	to touch
Sa gentillesse me touche beaucoup.	His/her kindness is very touching to me.

aimer [ɛme]	to like, love
amoureux, **amoureuse** [amuʀø, øz]	in love
être amoureux de qn	to be in love with s.o.
Il est **tombé amoureux**.	He has fallen in love.
admirer [admiʀe]	to admire
l'**admiration** *f* [admiʀasjɔ̃]	admiration
éprouver de l'admiration pour qn	to feel admiration for s.o.
un **admirateur**, une **admiratrice** [admiʀatœʀ, tʀis]	admirer
adorer [adɔʀe]	to adore, love
adorable [adɔʀabl]	adorable, sweet, nice
détester [detɛste]	to detest, hate

haïr ['aiʀ]	to hate
la **haine** ['ɛn]	hatred
éprouver de la haine pour qn/qc	to hate s.o./s.th.
le **dégoût** [degu]	disgust, revulsion
Son égoïsme **m'inspire du dégoût**.	His/her egotism disgusts me.
être dégoûté, **dégoûtée** [degute]	to be disgusted

la **joie** [ʒwa]	joy
sauter de joie	to jump for joy
s'amuser (**à**) [samyze]	to have fun, amuse oneself (by)
Les enfants s'amusent à embêter le voisin.	The children have fun annoying the neighbor.
rire (**de**) [ʀiʀ]	to laugh (about)
rigoler *fam* [ʀigɔle]	to laugh, have fun
sourire [suʀiʀ]	to smile
heureux, **heureuse** (**de**) [øʀø, øz]	happy (about)
Je suis heureuse d'avoir pris cette décision.	I am happy I made this decision.
le **bonheur** [bɔnœʀ]	happiness, good fortune (*See Information Box p. 144*)
Le malheur des uns fait le bonheur des autres. *prov*	One man's joy is another man's sorrow.
content, **contente** (**de**) [kɔ̃tɑ̃, ɑ̃t]	happy (about), content (with)
Je suis content de te voir en bonne santé.	I am happy to see you in good health.
plaire [plɛʀ]	to please
Carine plaît beaucoup à Pierre.	Carine is very pleasing to Pierre.
le **plaisir** [pleziʀ]	pleasure
prendre plaisir à qc	to take pleasure in s.th.

joyeux, **joyeuse** [ʒwajø, øz]	cheerful, happy, joyous
être d'humeur joyeuse	to be cheerful
l'**enthousiasme** *m* [ɑ̃tuzjasm]	enthusiasm
se réjouir de qc [s(ə)ʀeʒwiʀ]	to be happy/glad about s.th.
Je me réjouis de la savoir heureuse.	I am glad to know that she is happy.
l'**excitation** *f* [ɛksitasjɔ̃]	excitement

malheureux, **malheureuse** (**de**) [maløʀø, øz]	unhappy, unfortunate
le **malheur** [malœʀ]	bad luck, misfortune
pleurer [plœʀe]	to cry
pleurer de joie	to cry for joy
une **larme** [laʀm]	a tear

mélancolique [melɑ̃kɔlik]	melancholy (adj)
la **mélancolie** [melɑ̃kɔli]	melancholy (n)
nostalgique [nɔstalʒik]	nostalgic
la **nostalgie** [nɔstalʒi]	nostalgia, longing
avoir la nostalgie du temps passé	to feel nostalgic for the past
pleurnicher [plœʀniʃe]	to whine, whimper
Cet enfant pleurniche sans arrêt.	This child whines constantly.
sangloter [sɑ̃glɔte]	to sob
le **chagrin** [ʃagʀɛ̃]	grief
le **chagrin d'amour**	lovesickness
souffrir de qc [sufʀiʀ]	to suffer from s.th.
Elle souffre de l'absence de son ami.	She is suffering from the absence of her friend.
la **souffrance** [sufʀɑ̃s]	suffering, pain
être déprimé, **déprimée** [depʀime]	to be depressed
la **dépression** [depʀɛsjɔ̃]	depression
le **deuil** [dœj]	mourning
être en deuil de qn	to be in mourning for s.o.
subir qc [sybiʀ]	to experience s.th.
Il a subi une lourde perte.	He has experienced/suffered a heavy loss.
supporter [sypɔʀte]	to bear
troubler [tʀuble]	to trouble
s'effondrer [sefɔ̃dʀe]	to go to pieces, crumble
Quand elle a appris la nouvelle, elle s'est effondrée.	She went to pieces when she heard the news.

espérer (**faire**) **qc** [ɛspeʀe]	to hope (to do s.th.)
J'espère te revoir bientôt!	I hope to see you again soon!
l'**espoir** *m* [ɛspwaʀ]	hope (n)
perdre l'espoir	to lose hope
l'**espérance** *f* [ɛspeʀɑ̃s]	hope (n)
désespérer de qn/qc [dezɛspeʀe]	to give up hope on s.o./s.th.
Je désespère de lui faire comprendre ça.	I give up hope of making him understand it.
être désespéré, **désespérée** [dezɛspeʀe]	to be desperate, distressed
le **désespoir** [desɛspwaʀ]	despair (n)
être au désespoir	to be in despair

la **confiance** [kɔ̃fjɑ̃s]	confidence
Je lui **accorde toute ma confiance**.	I put my entire confidence in him.
faire confiance à qn	to trust s.o.
avoir confiance en qn	to have confidence in s.o.
se méfier de qn/qc [s(ə)mefje]	to mistrust s.o./s.th.
Je me méfie de ses sourires hypocrites.	I mistrust his hypocritical smiles.
la **méfiance** [mefjɑ̃s]	mistrust (n)

la **peur** [pœʀ]	fear (n)
avoir peur (**de**)	to be afraid (of)
J'ai peur des chiens.	I am afraid of dogs.
J'ai peur que Martin soit malade.	I'm afraid that Martin is sick.
craindre [kʀɛ̃dʀ]	to fear
Les marins craignent la tempête.	Seamen fear the storm.
craindre que + *subj*	to fear that
Je crains que nous ayons des ennuis.	I fear that we will experience some problems.
la **crainte** [kʀɛ̃t]	fear (n)

INFO

Fear

The word *fear* has various counterparts in French, depending on the context:

la peur	*fear (general)*
une peur bleue	*mortal fear*
N'ayez pas peur!	*Don't be afraid!*
la crainte	*fear, apprehension*
Soyez sans crainte!	*Don't worry!*
l'angoisse *f*	*anguish*
un cri d'angoisse	*a cry of anguish*
l'anxiété *f*	*anxiety, anxiousness, inner turmoil*
envisager l'avenir avec anxiété	*to look to the future with anxiety*

s'inquiéter de qc [sɛ̃kjete]	to worry about s.th.
Je m'inquiète du retard de mon fils.	I am worried about my son's lateness.
inquiet, **inquiète** [ɛ̃kjɛ, ɛt]	troubled, uneasy
Nous sommes inquiets de ne pas avoir de ses nouvelles.	We are troubled because we have not heard from him/her.
l'**inquiétude** *f* [ɛ̃kjetyd]	worry (n), unease
se faire du souci [s(ə)fɛʀdysusi]	to worry
On **s'**est **fait du souci pour** toi.	We were worried about you.
l'**angoisse** *f* [ɑ̃gwas]	anguish (n)
horrible [ɔʀibl]	horrible
terrifier qn [teʀifje]	to terrify s.o.
L'explosion nous a terrifiés.	The explosion terrified us.
la **terreur** [teʀœʀ]	terror
anxieux, **anxieuse** [ɑ̃ksjø, jøz]	anxious

la **honte** ['ɔ̃t]	shame (n)
Tu me **fais honte**.	You shame me.
avoir honte de qn/qc	to be ashamed of s.o./s.th.
se moquer de qn/qc [s(ə)mɔke]	to make fun of s.o./s.th.
la **pitié** [pitje]	pity (n)
avoir pitié de qn	to have pity on s.o.

mépriser qn [mepʀize]	to scorn s.o.
le **mépris** [mepʀi]	scorn (n)
être jaloux, jalouse de qn [ʒalu, uz]	to be jealous of s.o.
Il est jaloux de tous ses amis.	He is jealous of all his friends.
la **jalousie** [ʒaluzi]	jealousy
être déçu, déçue [desy]	to be disappointed
la **déception** [desɛpsjɔ̃]	disappointment
envieux, envieuse [ɑ̃vjø, jøz]	envious
l'**envie** *f* [ɑ̃vi]	envy (n)
en vouloir à qn [ɑ̃vulwaʀ]	to be angry with s.o.
Je lui en veux de m'avoir trompé.	I am angry with him/her because he/she deceived me.

être embarrassé, embarrassée [ɑ̃baʀase]	to be embarrassed
Je ne sais pas quoi faire, je suis très embarrassé.	I don't know what to do; I am very embarrassed.
l'**embarras** *m* [ɑ̃baʀa]	embarrassment
se résigner à [s(ə)ʀeziɲe]	to resign oneself to
Il s'est résigné à ne plus la voir.	He has resigned himself to not seeing her again.
la **résignation** [ʀeziɲasjɔ̃]	resignation
être vexé, vexée [vɛkse]	to be irritated, upset, offended
ne pas s'en faire [nəpasɑ̃fɛʀ]	not to worry
Ne t'en fais pas, demain ça ira mieux.	Don't worry, tomorrow things will be better.
s'ennuyer de qn [sɑ̃nɥije]	to miss s.o.
Elle s'ennuie de ses parents.	She misses her parents.
l'**ennui** *m* [ɑ̃nɥi]	boredom, tedium

4.2 Thoughts, Imagination, Desires  14

penser à [pɑ̃se]	to think about
Elle pense souvent à lui.	She often thinks of him.
la **pensée** [pɑ̃se]	thought (n)
une **idée** [ide]	idea
changer d'idée	to change one's mind
réfléchir à/sur qc [ʀefleʃiʀ]	to think/reflect about s.th.
J'ai réfléchi à/sur votre argument.	I have thought about your point.
une **réflexion** [ʀeflɛksjɔ̃]	reflection
la **raison** [ʀɛzɔ̃]	reason (n)
perdre la raison	to lose one's senses/mind

intelligent, **intelligente** [ɛ̃teliʒɑ̃, ɑ̃t]	intelligent
l'**intelligence** *f* [ɛ̃teliʒɑ̃s]	intelligence
intellectuel, **intellectuelle** [ɛ̃telɛktɥɛl]	intellectual (adj)
comprendre [kɔ̃pʀɑ̃dʀ]	to understand
Je n'y comprends rien.	I don't understand anything about it.
la **compréhension** [kɔ̃pʀeɑ̃sjɔ̃]	understanding, comprehension

le **sens** [sɑ̃s]	sense (n)
le **bon sens**	common sense
le **non-sens**	nonsense
logique [lɔʒik]	logical
la **logique**	logic

une **opinion** [ɔpiɲɔ̃]	opinion
se faire une opinion sur qc	to form an opinion about s.th.
vrai, **vraie** [vʀɛ]	true, correct (*See Information Box p. 44*)
la **vérité** [veʀite]	truth
une **erreur** [eʀœʀ]	error, mistake (n)
Vous avez commis une erreur.	You have made a mistake.
L'erreur est humaine. *prov*	To err is human.
se tromper [s(ə)tʀɔ̃pe]	to be mistaken

savoir [savwaʀ]	to know, be able to
le **savoir**	knowledge, ability
connaître [kɔnɛtʀ]	to know, meet
connaître un poème **par cœur**	to know a poem by heart
la **connaissance** [kɔnɛsɑ̃s]	knowledge, familiarity
les **connaissances en français**	knowledge of French
théorique [teɔʀik]	theoretical
une **théorie** [teɔʀi]	theory

deviner [d(ə)vine]	to guess
une **devinette** [dəvinɛt]	riddle
poser une devinette à qn	to pose a riddle to s.o.
prévoir [pʀevwaʀ]	to foresee, predict
C'était à prévoir.	That was foreseeable./You could see that coming.
une **prévision** [pʀevizjɔ̃]	prediction, prognosis
les **prévisions météorologiques**	weather forecast
constater qc [kɔ̃state]	to determine, ascertain s.th.
une **constatation** [kɔ̃statasjɔ̃]	findings, determination

retenir qc [ʀ(ə)təniʀ]	to retain s.th.
Je n'arrive jamais à retenir votre nom.	I can never remember your name.
se rappeler qn/qc [s(ə)ʀap(ə)le]	to remember s.o./s.th.
se souvenir de [s(ə)suv(ə)niʀ]	to remember
Je ne me souviens plus de ton adresse.	I no longer remember your address.
oublier qc/de faire qc [ublije]	to forget s.th./to do s.th.

INFO

Rappeler

se rappeler qn/qc	*to remember s.o./s.th.*
Tu te rappelles notre prof de maths?	*Do you remember our math teacher?*
rappeler qc à qn	*to remind s.o. of s.th.*
Cela me rappelle mon enfance.	*That reminds me of my childhood.*
rappeler à qn de faire qc	*to remind s.o. to do s.th.*
Rappelle-moi de mettre le réveil.	*Remind me to set the alarm clock.*

la **mémoire** [memwaʀ]	memory
avoir la mémoire courte	to have a short memory
douter de qc/que + *subj* [dute]	to doubt s.th.
Je doute de sa sincérité.	I doubt his sincerity.
On doute qu'il dise la vérité.	We doubt that he is telling the truth.
un **doute** [dut]	doubt (n)
confondre avec [kɔ̃fɔ̃dʀ]	to confuse with, mistake for
Je l'ai confondue avec sa sœur.	I mistook her for her sister.
confus, **confuse** [kɔ̃fy, yz]	confused
la **confusion** [kɔ̃fyzjɔ̃]	confusion

analyser [analize]	to analyze
comparer qn/qc à qn/qc [kɔ̃paʀe]	to compare s.o./s.th. to s.o./s.th.
distinguer de [distɛ̃ge]	to distinguish between
distinguer le bien du mal	to distinguish the good from the bad
reconnaître [ʀ(ə)kɔnɛtʀ]	to recognize
se rendre compte de qc [s(ə)ʀɑ̃dʀ(ə)kɔ̃t]	to realize s.th.
Elle ne s'est pas rendu compte de son erreur.	She did not realize her error.
conclure [kɔ̃klyʀ]	to conclude
une conclusion [kɔ̃klyzjɔ̃]	conclusion
J'en tire les conclusions qui s'imposent.	I draw the necessary conclusions from that.
juger qn/qc [ʒyʒe]	to judge s.o./s.th.
juger qn sur ses actes	to judge s.o. by his/her actions
le **jugement** [ʒyʒmɑ̃]	judgment
un **préjugé** [pʀeʒyʒe]	prejudice (n)
Les préjugés ont la vie dure.	Prejudices live a long life.
croire qn/qc [kʀwaʀ]	to believe s.o./s.th.
un **avis** [avi]	opinion, view (n)
À mon avis, tu devrais t'excuser.	In my view, you should apologize.
être d'avis que	to be of the opinion that
un **point de vue** [pwɛ̃dvy]	viewpoint
partager le point de vue de qn	to share s.o.'s point of view
une **impression** [ɛ̃pʀesjɔ̃]	impression
J'ai l'impression que tu te moques de moi.	I have the impression that you are making fun of me.
proposer qc à qn/à qn de faire qc [pʀɔpoze]	to suggest s.th. to s.o./that s.o. do s.th.
la **proposition** [pʀɔpozisjɔ̃]	proposition, suggestion
s'imaginer (**faire**) **qc** [simaʒine]	to imagine (doing) s.th.
Les jeunes s'imaginent avoir toujours raison.	Young people imagine that they are always right.
l'**imagination** *f* [imaʒinasjɔ̃]	imagination
supposer [sypoze]	to suppose
Je suppose que tu es en colère contre lui.	I suppose you are angry with him.
rêver (**de**) [ʀeve]	to dream (about/of)
un **rêve** [ʀɛv]	dream (n)
vouloir [vulwaʀ]	to wish, want
Tu veux bien qu'on aille au cinéma?	Do you want to go to the movies?
la **volonté** [vɔlɔ̃te]	will, intention (n)

demander [d(ə)mɑ̃de] — to request, ask for, demand
souhaiter faire qc [swete] — to want/wish to do s.th.
désirer faire qc [dezire] — to want to do s.th.
le **désir** [dezir] — desire (n)
préférer (**faire**) **qc** [prefere] — to prefer (to do) s.th.
  Je préfère ne pas la rencontrer. — I prefer not to meet her.
avoir envie de qc [avwarɑ̃vi] — to feel like having s.th.
  J'ai envie d'une glace. — I feel like having an ice cream cone.

il vaut mieux [ilvomjø] — it is better
  Il vaut mieux ne pas le déranger. — It is better not to disturb him.
  Il vaut mieux qu'on s'en aille. — It is better that we leave.

INFO

Demander

demander qc je demande une explication.	*to demand, request s.th.* *I demand an explanation.*
demander qn On demande Mme Caradec au téléphone.	*to request s.o.* *Mrs. Caradec is wanted on the phone.*
demander qc à qn Tu pourrais demander le chemin à cet agent.	*to ask s.th. of s.o.* *You could ask this policeman for directions.*
demander à qn de faire qc Demandez-lui de nous attendre.	*to ask s.o. to do s.th.* *Ask him to wait for us.*

volontaire [vɔlɔ̃tɛr] — voluntary
involontaire [ɛ̃vɔlɔ̃tɛr] — involuntary
  un **homicide involontaire** — involuntary manslaughter
imposer qc à qn [ɛ̃poze] — to require s.th. of s.o.
exiger qc [ɛgziʒe] — to require, to demand s.th.
  J'exige tes excuses. — I demand an apology from you.

être exigeant, **exigeante** [ɛgziʒɑ̃, ɑ̃t] — to be demanding
  Il **est** très **exigeant envers** lui-même. — He is very demanding of himself.

une **exigence** [ɛgziʒɑ̃s] — requirement, demand (n)
arbitraire [arbitrɛr] — arbitrary
  une décision arbitraire — arbitrary decision
résolu, **résolue** [rezɔly] — resolute, determined
  Je suis bien résolu à lui dire ses quatre vérités. — I am determined to give him/her a piece of my mind.
la **résolution** [rezɔlysjɔ̃] — resolution

un **objectif** [ɔbʒɛktif]	goal
un **but** [byt]	goal, purpose
poursuivre un but/un objectif précis	to pursue a goal/specific purpose
un **projet** [pʀɔʒɛ]	plan, project (n)
faire des projets pour les vacances	to make plans for a vacation
un **plan** [plɑ̃]	plan (n)
tirer des plans	to make plans
une **intention** [ɛ̃tɑ̃sjɔ̃]	intention
Ma mère est **pleine de bonnes intentions**.	My mother is full of good intentions.
avoir l'intention de faire qc	to have the intention to do s.th.
envisager (**de faire**) **qc** [ɑ̃vizaʒe]	to intend (to do) s.th.
songer à [sɔ̃ʒe]	to think/dream of
Elle songe à émigrer.	She is thinking of emigrating.
tenir à ce que + *subj* [t(ə)niʀ]	to insist that/on
Je tiens à ce que tu fasses tes devoirs.	I insist that you do your homework.
accepter [aksɛpte]	to accept
refuser (**de faire**) **qc** [ʀ(ə)fyze]	to refuse (to do) s.th.
Elle refuse de nous aider.	She refuses to help us.
Elle refuse qu'on lui vienne en aide.	She refuses to let anyone help her.
renoncer à (**faire**) **qc** [ʀ(ə)nɔ̃se]	to give up (doing) s.th.
Nous renonçons à lui faire comprendre notre point de vue.	We give up trying to make her understand our point of view.
s'opposer à [sɔpoze]	to oppose
éviter de faire qc [evite]	to avoid doing s.th.
empêcher qn de faire qc [ɑ̃pɛʃe]	to prevent s.o. from doing s.th.
Son père veut l'empêcher de se marier.	His father wants to prevent him from marrying.

4.3 Character, Behavior  15

caractériser [kaʀakteʀize]	to characterize
caractéristique de [kaʀakteʀistik]	characteristic of
Cette affirmation est caractéristique de sa pensée.	This assertion is characteristic of his/her thinking.
le **caractère** [kaʀaktɛʀ]	character
avoir bon/mauvais caractère	to have a good/bad character
le **trait de caractère**	character trait
le **tempérament** [tɑ̃peʀamɑ̃]	temperament
l'**état d'esprit** *m* [etadɛspʀi]	state of mind, attitude, mindset
naturel, **naturelle** [natyʀɛl]	natural
le **naturel**	disposition, nature
Il est d'un naturel agréable.	He has a pleasant disposition.
une **qualité** [kalite]	quality
un **défaut** [defo]	defect, fault (n)

---

la **mentalité** [mɑ̃talite]	mentality
la **personnalité** [pɛʀsɔnalite]	personality
se comporter [s(ə)kɔ̃pɔʀte]	to behave, carry oneself
Il s'est mal comporté envers toi.	He behaved badly toward you.
le **comportement** [kɔ̃pɔʀtəmɑ̃]	behavior, conduct (n)
la **vertu** [vɛʀty]	virtue
le **vice** [vis]	vice
L'oisiveté est mère de tous les vices. *prov*	Idleness is the origin of all vices.

---

l'**humeur** *f* [ymœʀ]	mood, humor
agréable [agʀeabl]	pleasant, agreeable
aimable [ɛmabl]	friendly, nice
l'**amabilité** *f* [amabilite]	kindness
charmant, **charmante** [ʃaʀmɑ̃, ɑ̃t]	charming
Il est d'une humeur charmante.	He is in a delightful/charming mood.
le **charme** [ʃaʀm]	charm (n)
gentil, **gentille** [ʒɑ̃ti, ij]	nice, kind
Sois gentil, apporte-moi mes lunettes.	Be so kind as to bring me my glasses.
la **gentillesse** [ʒɑ̃tijɛs]	kindness
sympa(**thique**) [sɛ̃pa(tik)]	nice
la **sympathie** [sɛ̃pati]	sympathy

INFO

Humeur – humour

Humeur (mood) and *humour* (humor) are not the same. *Difference:*

l'humeur *f*	*mood*
être de bonene/mauvais humeur	*to be in a good/bad mood*
Elle est d'humeur changeante	*She is moody.*
l'humour *m*	*humor*
Il manque totalement d'humour.	*He has absolutely no sense of humor.*

ouvert, **ouverte** [uvɛʀ, ɛʀt]	open (adj)
avoir l'esprit ouvert	to have an open mind; to be a free spirit
équilibré, **équilibrée** [ekilibʀe]	balanced
l'**humour** *m* [ymuʀ]	humor
avoir de l'humour	to have a sense of humor
manquer d'humour	to have no sense of humor
déterminé, **déterminée** [detɛʀmine]	determined
un, une **risque-tout** [ʀiskətu]	daredevil, risk-taker
optimiste [ɔptimist]	optimistic
un, une **optimiste**	optimist
l'**optimisme** *m* [ɔptimism]	optimism
satisfait, **satisfaite** [satisfɛ, ɛt]	satisfied, pleased
la **satisfaction** [satisfaksjɔ̃]	satisfaction
afficher sa satisfaction	to show one's appreciation
obtenir satisfaction	to obtain satisfaction
tolérant, **tolérante** [tɔleʀɑ̃, ɑ̃t]	tolerant, patient
bienveillant, **bienveillante** [bjɛ̃vɛjɑ̃, jɑ̃t]	benevolent

désagréable [dezagʀeabl]	disagreeable, unfriendly
méchant, **méchante** [meʃɑ̃, ɑ̃t]	naughty, wicked, unkind
la **méchanceté** [meʃɑ̃ste]	naughtiness, nastiness
sévère [sevɛʀ]	strict, severe
la **sévérité** [seveʀite]	strictness, severity
la **colère** [kɔlɛʀ]	anger
se mettre en colère	to become angry
être en colère	to be angry
la **rage** [ʀaʒ]	anger, rage
Ça m'a mis dans une rage folle.	That made me wild with anger.

INFO

-age

Polysyllabic nouns that end in ***-age*** generally are *masculine*.

un garage	*garage*
un étage	*floor, story (in a building)*
un passage	*passage*
le massage	*massage*
le dopage	*doping*

Monosyllabic words ending in *-age*, on the other hand, are usually *feminine*:

une cage	*cage*
la rage	*rage*
une page	*page*

agité, **agitée** [aʒite]	agitated, restless
insolent, **insolente** [ɛ̃sɔlɑ̃, ɑ̃t]	insolent
arrogant, **arrogante** [aʀɔgɑ̃, ɑ̃t]	arrogant
gâté, **gâtée** [gate]	spoiled
un enfant gâté	spoiled child
râleur *fam*, **râleuse** [ʀɑlœʀ, øz]	grouchy, nagging
grossier, **grossière** [gʀosje, jɛʀ]	gross, coarse
Quel grossier personnage!	What a coarse individual!
brutal, **brutale** [bʀytal]	brutal
une **brute** [bʀyt]	brute (n)
une **sale brute**	vulgar person/beast/so-and-so
la **brutalité** [bʀytalite]	brutality

bon, **bonne** [bɔ̃, bɔn]	good
la **bonté** [bɔ̃te]	goodness
tendre [tɑ̃dʀ]	tender
adresser un regard tendre à qn	to direct a tender glance at s.o.
la **tendresse** [tɑ̃dʀɛs]	tenderness
sensible [sɑ̃sibl]	sensitive
la **sensibilité** [sɑ̃sibilite]	sensitivity
une **sensibilité à fleur de peau**	squeamishness, over-sensitivity
généreux, **généreuse** [ʒeneʀø, øz]	generous
la **générosité** [ʒeneʀozite]	generosity

avoir le cœur sur la main [avwaʀləkœʀsyʀlamɛ̃]	to be very generous
avoir un faible pour [avwaʀɛ̃fɛbl]	to have a weakness for
Luc a un faible pour les blondes.	Luc has a weakness for blondes.
idéaliste [idealist]	idealistic
un, une **idéaliste**	idealist
réaliste [ʀealist]	realistic
un, une **réaliste**	realist
inhumain, **inhumaine** [inymɛ̃, ɛn]	inhuman
Je trouve son attitude inhumaine.	I find his/her attitude inhuman.
insensible (à) [ɛ̃sɑ̃sibl]	insensitive (to)
un, une **égoïste** [egɔist]	egotist
égoïste [egɔist]	egotistical
Les hommes sont tous des égoïstes.	All men are egotists.
l'**égoïsme** *m* [egɔism]	egotism
avare [avaʀ]	miserly, stingy
juste [ʒyst]	fair, just
Elle est sévère mais juste.	She is strict, but fair.
la **justice** [ʒystis]	justice, fairness
honnête [ɔnɛt]	honest
l'**honnêteté** *f* [ɔnɛtte]	honesty
Ayez l'honnêteté de reconnaître votre erreur.	Have the honesty to acknowledge your error.
franc, **franche** [fʀɑ̃, fʀɑ̃ʃ]	sincere, genuine, frank
digne de foi [diɲdəfwa]	credible, trustworthy
Ne crois pas tout ce qu'il dit, il n'est pas digne de foi.	Don't believe everything he says; he is not trustworthy.
sincère [sɛ̃sɛʀ]	sincere
mes vœux les plus sincères	my most sincere best wishes
la **sincérité** [sɛ̃seʀite]	sincerity
modeste [mɔdɛst]	modest
la **modestie** [mɔdɛsti]	modesty
serviable [sɛʀvjabl]	helpful, obliging
injuste [ɛ̃ʒyst]	unjust, unfair
l'**injustice** *f* [ɛ̃ʒystis]	injustice
malhonnête [malɔnɛt]	dishonest
la **malhonnêteté** [malɔnɛtte]	dishonesty

menteur, **menteuse** [mɑ̃tœʀ, øz]	lying, untruthful
un **menteur**, une **menteuse**	liar
traiter qn de menteur	to call s.o. a liar
hypocrite [ipokʀit]	hypocritical
un, une **hypocrite**	hypocrite
l'**hypocrisie** *f* [ipokʀizi]	hypocrisy
malin, **maligne** [malɛ̃, maliɲ]	crafty, sly
À malin, malin et demi. *loc*	There is always someone who will outwit you.
une **joie maligne**	spiteful gloating
rusé, **rusée** [ʀyze]	cunning, sly, crafty
rusé comme un renard *loc*	sly as a fox
la **ruse** [ʀyz]	cunning (adj)
arriver* à qc par la ruse	to achieve s.th. through cunning
corrompu, **corrompue** [kɔʀɔ̃py]	corrupt (adj)
la corruption [kɔʀypsjɔ̃]	corruption
orgueilleux, **orgueilleuse** [ɔʀgøjø, jøz]	proud, haughty
l'**orgueil** *m* [ɔʀgœj]	haughtiness, pride
L'orgueil précède la chute. *loc*	Pride goes before a fall.
vaniteux, **vaniteuse** [vanitø, øz]	vain
la **vanité** [vanite]	vanity
rancunier, **rancunière** [ʀɑ̃kynje, jɛʀ]	resentful
se venger de [səvɑ̃ʒe]	to get even with, avenge
Je vais me venger de vos moqueries.	I will get even with you for your teasing.
faire du tort à qn [fɛʀdytɔʀ]	to cause harm to s.o., do s.o. an injustice
Cet article dans le journal lui a fait du tort.	This newspaper article has done him harm.
un **scrupule** [skʀypyl]	scruple

gai, **gaie** [ge/gɛ]	happy
Tu n'as pas l'air très gai.	You don't look too happy.
la **gaieté/gaîté** [gete]	happiness, merriness, mirth
drôle [dʀol]	merry, fun (*See Information Box p. 44*)
Arrête, tu n'es vraiment pas drôle!	Stop, you really are not being funny!
amusant, **amusante** [amyzɑ̃, ɑ̃t]	amusing, funny
comique [kɔmik]	comical, funny
original, **originale** [ɔʀiʒinal]	original, witty
intéressant, **intéressante** [ɛ̃teʀesɑ̃, ɑ̃t]	interesting

triste [tʀist]	sad
la **tristesse** [tʀistɛs]	sadness
ennuyeux, **ennuyeuse** [ɑ̃nɥijø, jøz]	boring, unpleasant
être mécontent, **mécontente** [mekɔ̃tɑ̃, ɑ̃t]	to be unhappy
Elle **est mécontente de** son nouveau chef.	She is unhappy with her new boss.

renfermé, **renfermée** [ʀɑ̃fɛʀme]	withdrawn
Elle est **renfermée sur elle-même**.	She is withdrawn into herself.
déséquilibré, **déséquilibrée** [dezekilibʀe]	unbalanced
borné, **bornée** [bɔʀne]	bigoted, closed-minded
têtu, **têtue** [tety]	stubborn
Tu es **têtu comme une mule**. *loc*	You are as stubborn as a mule.
pessimiste [pesimist]	pessimistic
un, une **pessimiste**	pessimist
le **pessimisme** [pesimism]	pessimism
intolérant, **intolérante** [ɛ̃tɔleʀɑ̃, ɑ̃t]	intolerant
malveillant, **malveillante** [malvɛjɑ̃, ɑ̃t]	malicious, spiteful, hateful

calme [kalm]	calm (adj)
Ne t'énerve pas, reste calme.	Don't get excited, keep calm.
tranquille [tʀɑ̃kil]	calm (adj)
Laisse-moi tranquille.	Leave me alone.
décontracté, **décontractée** [dekɔ̃tʀakte]	relaxed

nerveux, **nerveuse** [nɛʀvø, øz]	nervous, agitated
énervant, **énervante** [enɛʀvɑ̃, ɑ̃t]	annoying
fatigant, **fatigante** [fatigɑ̃, ɑ̃t]	tiring
bizarre [bizaʀ]	strange, odd, bizarre
fou, **fol**, **folle** [fu, fɔl]	crazy
un fol espoir	a foolish hope
un amour fou	a passionate love
compliqué, **compliquée** [kɔ̃plike]	complicated
difficile [difisil]	difficult (*See Information Box p. 437*)

timide [timid]	timid
la **timidité** [timidite]	timidity
complexé, **complexée** [kɔ̃plɛkse]	inhibited, uptight
peureux, **peureuse** [pøʀø, øz]	fearful
hésitant, **hésitante** [ezitɑ̃, ɑ̃t]	hesitant, indecisive
lâche [lɑʃ]	cowardly
un, une **lâche**	coward
Il s'est comporté **en lâche**.	He behaved like a coward.
craintif, **craintive** [kʀɛ̃tif, iv]	fearful
trouillard, **trouillarde** *fam* [tʀujaʀ, jaʀd]	timid, anxious
la trouille *fam* [tʀuj]	the jitters
Vas-y toi; moi, j'ai la trouille.	You go; I have the jitters.

rapide [ʀapid]	fast, quick, rapid
dynamique [dinamik]	dynamic
un jeune cadre dynamique	dynamic young manager
avoir de la volonté [avwaʀd(ə)lavolɔ̃te]	to be strong-willed
énergique [enɛʀʒik]	energetic
l'**énergie** *f* [enɛʀʒi]	energy, power
déborder d'énergie	to be overflowing with energy
autoritaire [ɔtɔʀitɛʀ]	authoritarian

efficace [efikas]	efficient, capable
Pour cet emploi, il faut quelqu'un d'efficace.	We need someone capable for this job.
ambitieux, **ambitieuse** [ɑ̃bisjø, jøz]	ambitious
l'**ambition** *f* [ɑ̃bisjɔ̃]	ambition
consciencieux, **consciencieuse** [kɔ̃sjɑ̃sjø, jøz]	conscientious

lent, **lente** [lɑ̃, lɑ̃t]	slow
Il a **l'esprit** plutôt **lent.**	He is rather slow-witted.
mou, **mol**, **molle** [mu, mɔl]	soft
faible [fɛbl]	weak
Elle est trop faible avec ses enfants.	She is too indulgent with her children.
paresseux, **paresseuse** [paʀesø, øz]	lazy
un **paresseux**, une **paresseuse**	lazy person
la **paresse** [paʀɛs]	laziness

désordonné, **désordonnée** [dezɔʀdɔne]	disorderly, messy
flemmard, **flemmarde** *fam* [flɛmaʀ, aʀd]	lazy, sluggish
indifférent, **indifférente** [ɛ̃difeʀɑ̃, ɑ̃t]	indifferent, passive
Il est **indifférent à** ce qui se passe autour de lui.	He is indifferent to what goes on around him.
l'**indifférence** *f* [ɛ̃difeʀɑ̃s]	indifference

bête [bɛt]	dumb
Il **est bête comme ses pieds**. *loc*	He is brainless.
la **bêtise** [betiz]	stupidity
faire des bêtises	to do stupid things
stupide [stypid]	stupid, dumb
la **stupidité** [stypidite]	stupidity
idiot, **idiote** [idjo, idjɔt]	idiotic, stupid, dumb
un **idiot**, une **idiote**	idiot

courageux, **courageuse** [kuʀaʒø, øz]	brave, courageous
le **courage** [kuʀaʒ]	courage
fier, **fière de** [fjɛʀ]	proud of
Ils sont fiers de leurs enfants.	They are proud of their children.
la **fierté** [fjɛʀte]	pride

sage [saʒ]	good, well-behaved
être sage comme une image *loc*	to be extremely well-behaved
prudent, **prudente** [pʀydɑ̃, ɑ̃t]	careful
la **prudence** [pʀydɑ̃s]	care (n)
agir avec prudence	to act with care
diplomate [diplɔmat]	diplomatic
raisonnable [ʀɛzɔnabl]	reasonable
poli, **polie** [pɔli]	polite
la **politesse** [pɔlitɛs]	politeness
discret, **discrète** [diskʀɛ, ɛt]	discrete, inconspicuous
la **discrétion** [diskʀesjɔ̃]	discretion, tact
faire preuve de discrétion	to be thoughtful, considerate
sérieux, **sérieuse** [seʀjø, jøz]	serious
Cet homme **est** très **sérieux dans** son travail.	This man is very serious about his work.
être sérieux comme un pape *loc*	to be dead serious

compréhensif, **compréhensive** [kɔ̃pʀeɑ̃sif, iv]	understanding (adj)
attentif, **attentive** [atɑ̃tif, iv]	attentive
prêter une oreille attentive à qn	to listen attentively to s.o.
conciliant, **conciliante** [kɔ̃siljɑ̃, ɑ̃t]	accommodating, obliging
réfléchi, **réfléchie** [ʀefleʃi]	deliberate, thoughtful
Il n'agit pas à la légère, il est réfléchi.	He doesn't do things lightly; he is deliberate.
brave [bʀav]	brave, decent (*See Information Box p. 44*)
C'est un **brave type**. *fam*	He's a decent fellow.
faire le brave	to play the hero

imprudent, **imprudente** [ɛ̃pʀydɑ̃, ɑ̃t]	careless
l'**imprudence** *f* [ɛ̃pʀydɑ̃s]	carelessness
impoli, **impolie** [ɛ̃poli]	impolite
indiscret, **indiscrète** [ɛ̃diskʀɛ, ɛt]	indiscreet, tactless
une **indiscrétion** [ɛ̃diskʀesjɔ̃]	indiscretion
commettre une indiscrétion	to commit an indiscretion
curieux, **curieuse** [kyʀjø, jøz]	curious
Il **est curieux comme un singe**. *loc*	He is extremely curious.
la **curiosité** [kyʀjozite]	curiosity
bavard, **bavarde** [bavaʀ, aʀd]	talkative, chatty

distingué, **distinguée** [distɛ̃ge]	distinguished
avoir de la classe [avwaʀd(ə)laklas]	to have class
Elle a une classe folle!	She is really classy!
snob [snɔb]	snobbish
un, une **snob**	snob
vulgaire [vylgɛʀ]	vulgar, ordinary

4.4 Activities and Skills  16

actif, **active** [aktif, iv]	active, energetic
inactif, **inactive** [inaktif, iv]	inactive, idle
l'**activité** *f* [aktivite]	activity
Il est **débordant d'activité**.	He is bursting with activity.
agir [aʒiʀ]	to act
une **action** [aksjɔ̃]	action
passer à l'action	to go into action
réagir [ʀeaʒiʀ]	to react
une **réaction** [ʀeaksjɔ̃]	reaction
déclencher une réaction	to trigger a reaction

adroit, **adroite** [adʀwa, wat]	skillful, adroit
l'**adresse** *f* [adʀɛs]	skill
Ce sport demande beaucoup d'adresse.	This sport requires lots of skill.
maladroit, **maladroite** [maladʀwa, wat]	awkward, clumsy
la **maladresse** [maladʀɛs]	awkwardness, clumsiness
capable (**de**) [kapabl]	capable (of)
incapable (**de**) [ɛ̃kapabl]	incapable (of)
Elle est incapable de voyager seule.	She is not capable of traveling alone.

la **capacité** [kapasite]	ability, capacity
l'**incapacité** *f* [ɛ̃kapasite]	inability
être dans l'incapacité de faire qc	to be incapable of doing s.th.
la **faculté** [fakylte]	ability
Dans son domaine, il **fait preuve de facultés** étonnantes.	He has amazing abilities in his field.
le **savoir-faire** [savwaʀfɛʀ]	know-how, ability *(See Information Box p. 450)*
habile [abil]	clever, skilled
Il est très **habile de** ses mains.	He is very skilled with his hands.
malhabile [malabil]	clumsy, unskilled
l'**habileté** *f* [abil(ə)te]	skill
compétent, **compétente** [kɔ̃petɑ̃, ɑ̃t]	competent
la **compétence** [kɔ̃petɑ̃s]	competence, expertise
Il est connu pour ses **compétences en informatique**.	He is known for his expertise with computers.
incompétent, **incompétente** [ɛ̃kɔ̃petɑ̃, ɑ̃t]	incompetent
l'**incompétence** *f* [ɛ̃kɔ̃petɑ̃s]	incompetence, deficiency

décider (**de faire**) **qc** [deside]	to decide (to do) s.th.
J'ai décidé de faire du sport régulièrement.	I have decided to play sports regularly.
se décider à faire qc [s(ə)deside]	to decide, make up one's mind about s.th.
Je me suis enfin décidé à lui dire la vérité.	I have finally decided to tell him the truth.
être décidé, **décidée à** [deside]	to be determined to
Je suis bien décidé à arrêter de fumer.	I have determined to quit smoking.
une **décision** [desizjɔ̃]	decision
prendre une décision importante	to make an important decision
préparer qc [pʀepaʀe]	to prepare s.th.
se préparer à faire qc [s(ə)pʀepaʀe]	to prepare to do s.th.
une **préparation** [pʀepaʀasjɔ̃]	preparation
hésiter à faire qc [ezite]	to hesitate to do s.th.
J'hésite à lui prêter ma voiture.	I hesitate to loan him my car.
l'**hésitation** *f* [ezitasjɔ̃]	hesitation

projeter [pʀɔj(ə)te]	to intend, plan
s'engager dans qc/à faire qc [sɑ̃gaʒe]	to commit to s.th./to doing s.th.
Elle s'est engagée dans une aventure dangereuse.	She got involved in a dangerous adventure.
Il s'est engagé à me rendre l'argent avant Noël.	He comitted to returning the money to me before Christmas.
se forcer à faire qc [s(ə)fɔʀse]	to force oneself to do s.th.
Je me suis forcé à manger les légumes.	I forced myself to eat the vegetables.
s'efforcer de faire qc [sefɔʀse]	to force oneself to do s.th.
Il s'efforçait de rester calme.	He forced himself to remain calm.
se garder de faire qc [s(ə)gaʀde]	to keep oneself from doing s.th.
céder [sede]	to yield, succumb, give in
céder à une envie	to give in to a craving

essayer de faire qc [eseje]	to try to do s.th.
un **essai** [esɛ]	attempt (n)
faire un essai	to make an attempt
risquer de faire qc [ʀiske]	to risk doing s.th.
On risque de tout perdre à vouloir trop gagner. *prov*	If you try to win too much, you risk losing everything.
réussir à faire qc [ʀeysiʀ]	to succeed in doing s.th.
Blériot a réussi à traverser la Manche en avion.	Blériot succeeded in crossing the Channel by plane.
une **réussite** [ʀeysit]	success
arriver* à faire qc [aʀive]	to manage to do s.th., succeed in doing s.th.
Je ne suis pas arrivé à réparer la voiture.	I have not succeeded in repairing the car.
oser faire qc [oze]	to dare to do s.th.
Il n'ose pas l'inviter à dîner.	He doesn't dare to invite him/her to dinner.
résoudre [ʀezudʀ]	to resolve
résoudre un problème	to solve a problem
échouer à/dans [eʃwe]	to fail at/in
Elle a échoué dans ses projets.	She failed in her plans.
un **échec** [eʃɛk]	failure, flop (n)

une **tentative** [tɑ̃tativ]	attempt (n)
oublier (**de faire qc**) [ublie]	to forget (to do s.th.)
l'**oubli** *m* [ubli]	oblivion, neglect, forgetfulness
tomber* dans l'oubli	to fade into obscurity
négliger [negliʒe]	to neglect
la **négligence** [negliʒɑ̃s]	negligence

un **effort** [efɔʀ]	effort
faire des efforts	to exert effort
avoir du mal à faire qc [avwaʀdymal]	to have trouble doing s.th.
J'ai du mal à croire tes explications.	It is hard for me to believe your explanations.
avoir de la peine à faire qc [avwaʀd(ə)lapɛn]	to have trouble doing s.th.
J'ai eu de la peine à porter ma valise.	It was difficult for me to carry my suitcase.
se débrouiller [s(ə)debʀuje]	to manage, make out
Débrouille-toi tout seul.	Figure it out by yourself.

une **tâche** [taʃ]	task
entreprendre une tâche	to take on a task
élaborer qc [elabɔʀe]	to develop s.th., work s.th. out
se charger de qc [s(ə)ʃaʀʒe]	to take care of s.th.
Tu apportes le vin, et je me charge du dessert.	You bring the wine and I will take care of the dessert.
accomplir qc [akɔ̃pliʀ]	to accomplish s.th.
exécuter [ɛgzekyte]	to carry out
se donner la peine [s(ə)dɔnelapɛn]	to take the trouble
Il ne s'est même pas donné la peine de me répondre.	He didn't even take the trouble to answer me.
faire de son mieux [fɛʀdəsɔ̃mjø]	to do one's best
J'ai fait de mon mieux, mais ce n'est pas très réussi.	I did my best, but it didn't work out.
(se) **perfectionner** [(s(ə))pɛʀfɛksjɔne]	to perfect, improve (oneself)
se tirer d'affaire [s(ə)tiʀedafɛʀ]	to get out of difficulty

INFO

Tache – tâche

They are pronounced the same, but have totally different meanings. *Watch out for the accent!*

une t**a**che	*spot, stain*
Ton pantalon est plein de taches.	*Your pants are full of stains.*
une t**â**che	*task*
Tu n'auras pas la tâche facile.	*That will not be an easy task for you.*

créer [kʀee]	to create
un parfum créé par Chanel	a perfume created by Chanel
la **création** [kʀeasjɔ̃]	creation
inventer [ɛ̃vɑ̃te]	to invent
une **invention** [ɛ̃vɑ̃sjɔ̃]	invention
faire breveter une invention	to have an invention patented
réaliser [ʀealize]	to realize, fulfill
réaliser ses projets	to bring one's plans to fruition
la **réalisation** [ʀealizasjɔ̃]	realization, attainment
imiter [imite]	to imitate
une **imitation** [imitasjɔ̃]	imitation

faire attention à [fɛʀatɑ̃sjɔ̃]	to pay attention to, be attentive to
Fais attention à la marche.	Watch out for the step.

faire exprès de faire qc [fɛʀɛkspʀɛ]	to do s.th. intentionally
faire semblant (**de faire qc**) [fɛʀsɑ̃blɑ̃]	to pretend (to do s.th.)
Il fait semblant de dormir.	He is pretending to be asleep.

faire qc en vain [fɛʀɑ̃vɛ̃]	to do s.th. in vain/for nothing/ without success
Je l'ai cherché en vain.	I looked for him without success.
faire qc en personne [fɛʀɑ̃pɛʀsɔn]	to do s.th. oneself
faire qc en cachette [fɛʀɑ̃kaʃɛt]	to do s.th. in secret
Les enfants ont fumé en cachette.	The children smoked in secret.
faire qc avec/sans peine [fɛʀavɛk/sɑ̃pɛn]	to do s.th. with/without trouble/effort
Est-ce qu'on peut apprendre le français sans peine?	Is it possible to learn French without effort?
faire qc avec/sans succès [fɛʀavɛk/sɑ̃syksɛ]	to do s.th. with/without success
faire qc volontiers [fɛʀvɔlɔ̃tje]	to do s.th. willingly

perdre [pɛʀdʀ]	to lose
la **perte** [pɛʀt]	loss
une **grosse perte**	major loss
chercher [ʃɛʀʃe]	to look for, search, seek
Qui cherche trouve. *prov*	Seek and you shall find.
trouver [tʀuve]	to find
retrouver [ʀ(ə)tʀuve]	to rediscover, find again
partager [paʀtaʒe]	to share

diriger [diʀiʒe]	to direct, lead
Mon père dirige une entreprise importante.	My father is in charge of an important company.
organiser [ɔʀganize]	to organize
l'**organisation** *f* [ɔʀganizasjɔ̃]	organization
avoir le sens de l'organisation	to be a good organizer
choisir [ʃwaziʀ]	to choose
le **choix** [ʃwa]	choice
faire son choix	to make a choice
Je n'ai pas le choix.	I have no choice.

parler [paʀle]	to speak
chanter [ʃɑ̃te]	to sing
chanter juste/faux	to sing on/off key
écouter [ekute]	to listen
Tu ne m'écoutes jamais.	You never listen to me.
entendre [ɑ̃tɑ̃dʀ]	to hear
Tu as entendu ce bruit?	Did you hear that noise?
lire [liʀ]	to read
la **lecture** [lɛktyʀ]	reading (n)
écrire [ekʀiʀ]	to write

regarder [R(ə)gaRde]	to look at
un **regard** [R(ə)gaR]	a look, glance
jeter un regard sur	to cast a glance at
observer [ɔpsɛRve]	to observe
une **observation** [ɔpsɛRvasjɔ̃]	observation
avoir le sens de l'observation	to have good powers of observation
remarquer [R(ə)maRke]	to notice
une **remarque** [R(ə)maRk]	remark (n)
s'intéresser à [sɛ̃teRese]	to be interested in
Je m'intéresse beaucoup à la politique.	I am very interested in politics.
un **intérêt** [ɛ̃teRɛ]	interest
C'est sans intérêt.	That is uninteresting.

se désintéresser de [s(ə)dezɛ̃teRese]	to lose interest in
Je me désintéresse complètement de ce sujet.	I have totally lost interest in this subject.
le **désintérêt** [dezɛ̃teRɛ]	disinterest
abandonner [abɑ̃dɔne]	to abandon, give up
apercevoir [apɛRsəvwaR]	to notice
s'apercevoir de qc [sapɛRsəvwaR]	to notice s.th.
Je me suis aperçu qu'il me manquait 100 euros.	I noticed that I was missing 100 euros.
concevoir [kɔ̃s(ə)vwaR]	to conceive
Je **conçois mal** que tu aies fait ça.	I find it hard to believe/ conceive you did that.
se faire une idée de qc [s(ə)fɛRynide]	to have/form an idea about s.th.
tenir compte de qc [t(ə)niRkɔ̃t]	to consider s.th.
Tu ne tiens jamais compte de mon avis.	You never consider my opinion.

réclamer [Reklame]	to claim
réclamer des dommages-intérêts	to claim damages/ compensation
acquérir qc [akeRiR]	to acquire s.th.
Bien mal acquis ne profite jamais. *prov*	Ill got, ill spent.
une **acquisition** [akizisjɔ̃]	acquisition

attribuer [atʀibye]	to attribute, award
On a attribué le prix Nobel de Littérature à Günter Grass en 1999.	The 1999 Nobel Prize for literature was awarded to Günter Grass.
(se) **répartir** [(s(ə))ʀepaʀtiʀ]	to divide up
On se répartit les tâches domestiques.	We divide up the household chores.
la **répartition** [ʀepaʀtisjɔ̃]	division, sharing
accorder qc à qn [akɔʀde]	to grant s.th. to s.o.
Je lui ai accordé 8 jours de réflexion.	I granted him a week to think about it.
destiner qc à qn [destine]	to intend s.th. for s.o.
Cette lettre lui est destinée.	This letter is intended for him.

False Friends

French Word	Actual Meaning	False Friend	Correct French Word
brave	**nice**	brave	*courageux*
le regard	**glance, look**	regard	*égard*
sensible	**sensitive**	sensible	*sensé(e)*

My Vocabulary

5

Food, Clothing, Shopping

5.1 Eating and Drinking  17

manger [mɑ̃ʒe]	to eat
l'**appétit** *m* [apeti]	appetite
manger de bon appétit	to eat heartily
«L'appétit vient en mangeant.»	*Appetite comes with eating.*
la **faim** [fɛ̃]	hunger
avoir faim	to be hungry
avoir une faim de loup *loc*	to be famished/hungry as a bear
mourir* de faim	to die of starvation
avoir envie de qc [avwaʀɑ̃vi]	to desire/feel like having s.th.

affamé, **affamée** [afame]	hungry
à jeun [aʒœ̃]	fasting
Il faut prendre ce médicament à jeun.	This medication must be taken on an empty stomach.
dévorer [devoʀe]	to devour
bouffer *fam* [bufe]	to chow down, gorge
digérer [diʒeʀe]	to digest
souper [supe]	to have a late dinner
le **souper**	late dinner
savourer [savuʀe]	to savor
la **saveur** [savœʀ]	taste (n), tastiness

boire [bwaʀ]	to drink
boire à la bouteille	to drink from the bottle
boire dans un verre	to drink from a glass
une **boisson** [bwasɔ̃]	a drink, beverage
la **soif** [swaf]	thirst (n)
avoir soif	to be thirsty

un **aliment** [alimɑ̃]	food
l'**alimentation** *f* [alimɑ̃tasjɔ̃]	food, nutrition, diet
se nourrir (**de**) [s(ə)nuʀiʀ]	to eat
la **nourriture** [nuʀityʀ]	food
avaler [avale]	to swallow
avaler de travers	to swallow the wrong way/ choke on food

gourmand, **gourmande** [guʀmɑ̃, ɑ̃d]	gluttonous
un **gourmand**, une **gourmande**	glutton
la **gourmandise** [guʀmɑ̃diz]	gluttony
un **gourmet** [guʀmɛ]	gourmet (n)
grignoter [gʀiɲɔte]	to nibble, snack
Elle n'a pas d'appétit. Elle a juste grignoté une biscotte.	She has no appetite. She just nibbles a biscuit.
mâcher [mɑʃe]	to chew

un **repas** [R(ə)pɑ]	meal
se mettre à table [s(ə)mɛtRatabl]	to sit down at the table (to eat)
servir qc (**à qn**) [sɛRviR]	to serve s.th. (to s.o.)
Je vous sers encore un peu de viande?	May I serve you a little more meat?
se servir [s(ə)sɛRviR]	to serve oneself
Sers-toi, je t'en prie.	Please help yourself.
déjeuner [deʒœne]	to have lunch
le **déjeuner**	lunch
le **petit déjeuner** [p(ə)tideʒœne]	breakfast
prendre le petit déjeuner	to have breakfast
goûter [gute]	to taste, try
Il faut absolument **goûter à** ce fromage.	You absolutely must try this cheese.
le **goûter** [gute]	snack (n)
dîner [dine]	to have dinner
le **dîner**	dinner

le **goût** [gu]	taste (n)
avoir du goût	to be tasty
Bizarre, ce poulet **a un goût de** poisson.	Strange, the chicken tastes like fish.
bon, **bonne** [bɔ̃, bɔn]	good
sucré, **sucrée** [sykRe]	sweet
salé, **salée** [sale]	salty
amer, **amère** [amɛR]	bitter
acide [asid]	sour, acidic

cru, **crue** [kRy]	raw
un camembert **au lait cru**	raw-milk camembert
cuit, **cuite** [kɥi, kɥit]	cooked
dur, **dure** [dyR]	hard
mou, **mol**, **molle** [mu, mɔl]	soft
tendre [tɑ̃dR]	tender
Ce bifteck est vraiment tendre.	This steak is really tender.

épais, **épaisse** [epɛ, ɛs]	thick
gras, **grasse** [gRɑ, gRɑs]	fatty
maigre [mɛgR]	lean
une tranche de jambon maigre	a slice of lean ham
lourd, **lourde** [luR, luRd]	heavy (to digest) *(See Information Box p. 437)*
On ne va plus dans ce restaurant, la cuisine y est trop lourde.	We won't go back to this restaurant; the food there is too heavy.
léger, **légère** [leʒe, ʒɛR]	light
allégé, **allégée** [aleʒe]	reduced-fat, light
un fromage allégé	low-fat cheese

le **régime** [ʀeʒim]	diet (n)
être au régime	to be on a diet
se mettre au régime	to go on a diet
les **produits diététiques** *mpl* [prɔdɥidjetetik]	low-calorie/diet foods
sec, **sèche** [sɛk, sɛʃ]	dry
du **saucisson sec**	dry/hard-cured sausage
frais, **fraîche** [fʀɛ, fʀɛʃ]	fresh
pur, **pure** [pyʀ]	pure
100 % pur jus de fruits	100% pure fruit juice

appétissant, **appétissante** [apetisɑ̃, ɑ̃t]	appetizing
rafraîchissant, **rafraîchissante** [ʀafʀɛʃisɑ̃, ɑ̃t]	refreshing
Cette boisson est très rafraîchissante.	This drink is very refreshing.
indigeste [ɛ̃diʒɛst]	hard to digest
Ma mère trouve la cuisine à l'huile indigeste.	My mother finds foods cooked in oil hard to digest.

le **café** [kafe]	coffee
un **express** [ɛkspʀɛs]	espresso
le **thé** [te]	tea
boire un **thé au citron**	to drink a cup of tea with lemon
le **lait** [lɛ]	milk
le lait entier	whole milk
le lait écrémé	skim milk
un **chocolat** [ʃɔkɔla]	chocolate milk, cocoa
le **sucre** [sykʀ]	sugar
le **sucre en morceaux**	sugar cubes
une **sucrette** [sykʀɛt]	sweetener

une **cafetière** [kaftjɛʀ]	coffee pot
une **théière** [tejɛʀ]	teapot

une **baguette** [bagɛt]	baguette
une **tartine** [taʀtin]	slice of bread and butter
un **croissant** [kʀwasɑ̃]	croissant
le **pain** [pɛ̃]	bread
une **tranche de pain**	slice of bread
le **pain complet**	whole-grain bread
un **petit pain**	roll
le **pain de mie**	sandwich bread
du **pain grillé**	toast
un **grille-pain**	toaster
une **brioche** [bʀiɔʃ]	brioche
une **biscotte** [biskɔt]	zwieback, melba

le **beurre** [bœʀ]	butter
la **confiture** [kɔ̃fityʀ]	jam, jelly
le **miel** [mjɛl]	honey
un **œuf**; des **œufs** *pl* [œf, ø]	egg(s)
un **œuf à la coque**	soft-boiled egg
un **œuf sur le plat**	fried egg
le **muesli** [mysli]	muesli

le **hors-d'œuvre** ['ɔʀdœvʀ]	appetizer
une **entrée** [ɑ̃tʀe]	first course
une **soupe** [sup]	soup
la **charcuterie** [ʃaʀkytʀi]	cold cuts
un **pâté** [pɑte]	pâté
le **jambon** [ʒɑ̃bɔ̃]	ham
le **jambon cru**	cured ham
le **jambon blanc**	cooked ham
le **saucisson** [sosisɔ̃]	salami
une **omelette** [ɔmlɛt]	omelet
les **crudités** *fpl* [kʀydite]	raw vegetables, crudité

varié, **variée** [vaʀje]	varied
Il y a des hors-d'œuvre variés au menu.	There is an assortment of appetizers on the menu.
un **casse-croûte** [kaskʀut]	snack (n)
le **potage** [pɔtaʒ]	soup
la **soupe à l'oignon** [supalɔɲɔ̃]	onion soup

le **poisson** [pwasɔ̃]	fish
la **truite** [tʀɥit]	trout
la **sole** [sɔl]	sole
le **saumon** [somɔ̃]	salmon
le **saumon fumé**	smoked salmon
le **thon** [tɔ̃]	tuna
le **thon à l'huile**	tuna in oil
le **hareng** ['aʀɑ̃]	herring
la **sardine** [saʀdin]	sardine
les **fruits de mer** *mpl* [fʀɥidmɛʀ]	seafood
les **moules** *fpl* [mul]	mussels

la **viande** [vjɑ̃d]	meat
le **bœuf** [bøf]	beef
le **veau** [vo]	veal
le **porc** [pɔʀ]	pork
le **mouton** [mutɔ̃]	mutton
l'**agneau** *m* [aɲo]	lamb
la **volaille** [vɔlɑj]	poultry
le **poulet** [pulɛ]	chicken
le **canard** [kanaʀ]	duck

la **dinde** [dɛ̃d]	turkey
le **lapin** [lapɛ̃]	rabbit
le **gibier** [ʒibje]	wild game

---

le **bifteck** [biftɛk]	beef steak
le **steak** [stɛk]	steak
le **rôti** [ʀoti/ʀɔti]	roast
la **sauce** [sos]	gravy, sauce
le **foie** [fwa]	liver
une **côtelette** [kotlɛt/kɔtlɛt]	chop
une **escalope** [ɛskalɔp]	cutlet
un **filet** [filɛ]	filet
une **entrecôte** [ɑ̃tʀəkot]	rib steak
une **saucisse** [sosis]	sausage

INFO

Le foie – la foi – la fois

Same pronounciation, different spellings. *Note the homophones.*

le foie [fwa]	*liver*
du foie gras	*foie gras*
la foi [fwa]	*faith*
Il n'y a que la foi qui sauve. *loc*	*A likely story.*
la fois [fwa]	*time*
Une fois n'est pas coutume. *loc*	*One swallow does not make a spring.*

---

saignant, **saignante** [sɛɲɑ̃, ɑ̃t]	rare
à point [apwɛ̃]	medium
bien cuit, **bien cuite** [bjɛ̃kɥi, it]	well done
Deux steaks saignants, et un bien cuit, s'il vous plaît.	Two rare steaks, and one well done, please.

---

le **légume** [legym]	vegetable *(See Information Box p. 99)*
la **pomme de terre** [pɔmdətɛʀ]	potato
les **pommes de terre à l'eau**	boiled potatoes
les **pommes de terre sautées**	roasted potatoes
la **purée de pommes de terre**	mashed potatoes
les (**pommes**) **frites** *fpl* [(pɔm)fʀit]	French fries
la **purée** [pyʀe]	puree, mash (n)
la **carotte** [kaʀɔt]	carrot
Les carottes sont cuites. *fam*	The carrots are cooked./ There is nothing more one can do.
une **tomate** [tɔmat]	tomato
les **haricots verts** *mpl* ['aʀikovɛʀ]	green beans

les **petits pois** *mpl* [p(ə)tipwa]	peas
les **asperges** *fpl* [aspɛʀʒ]	asparagus
le **champignon** [ʃɑ̃piɲɔ̃]	mushroom
l'**oignon** *m* [ɔɲɔ̃]	onion
le **chou**; les **choux** *pl* [ʃu]	cabbage
la **choucroute** [ʃukʀut]	sauerkraut

INFO

Le(s) légume(s)

The translation for vegetables, *in the plural form, is* les légumes. *In referring to a single vegetable, the singular term* un legume *is used.*

l'**aubergine** *f* [obɛʀʒin]	eggplant
le **brocoli** [bʀɔkɔli]	broccoli
le **chou-fleur**; les **choux-fleurs** *pl* [ʃuflœʀ]	cauliflower
les **épinards** *mpl* [epinaʀ]	spinach
l'**artichaut** *m* [aʀtiʃo]	artichoke
le **concombre** [kɔ̃kɔ̃bʀ]	cucumber
le **cornichon** [kɔʀniʃɔ̃]	pickle
le **poivron** [pwavʀɔ̃]	bell pepper
l'**ail** *m*; les **ails** *mpl* [aj]	garlic

le **riz** [ʀi]	rice
les **nouilles** *fpl* [nuj]	noodles
les **pâtes** *fpl* [pɑt]	pasta

la **salade** [salad]	salad
une **salade composée**	mixed salad
une **salade de fruits**	fruit salad
la **vinaigrette** [vinɛgʀɛt]	vinaigrette dressing
la **mayonnaise** [majɔnɛz]	mayonnaise

une **endive** [ɑ̃div]	endive
une (**chicorée**) **frisée** [(ʃikɔʀe)fʀize]	frisée (lettuce)
une **laitue** [lɛty]	lettuce
assaisonner [asɛzɔne]	to dress (a salad)
l'**assaisonnement** *m* [asɛzɔnmɑ̃]	seasoning, dressing (n)

les **produits laitiers** *mpl* [pʀɔdɥilɛtje]	dairy products
le **fromage** [fʀɔmaʒ]	cheese
le **fromage blanc**	cream cheese
le **camembert** [kamɑ̃bɛʀ]	camembert
le **gruyère** [gʀɥjɛʀ]	Gruyère
le **yaourt** [jauʀt]	yogurt
le **yog(h)ourt** [jɔguʀt]	yogurt
la **crème fraîche** [kʀɛmfʀɛʃ]	crème fraîche

les **fruits** *mpl* [fʀɥi]	fruit(s)
les **fruits secs**	dried fruit(s)
une **pomme** [pɔm]	apple
une **poire** [pwaʀ]	pear
une **pêche** [pɛʃ]	peach
une **banane** [banan]	banana
une **orange** [ɔʀɑ̃ʒ]	orange
un **ananas** [anana(s)]	pineapple
un **melon** [m(ə)lɔ̃]	melon
du **raisin** [ʀɛzɛ̃]	grapes
un **grain de raisin**	grape
une **cerise** [s(ə)ʀiz]	cherry
une **prune** [pʀyn]	plum
travailler pour des prunes *loc*	to work for peanuts
une **fraise** [fʀɛz]	strawberry
une **framboise** [fʀɑ̃bwaz]	raspberry

le **dessert** [desɛʀ]	dessert
un **gâteau**; des **gâteaux** *pl* [gɑto]	cake
un **gâteau à la crème**	cream cake
une **tarte** [taʀt]	tart
des **pâtisseries** *fpl* [pɑtisʀi]	pastries
une **glace** [glas]	ice cream
une **glace à la vanille**	vanilla ice cream
le **parfum** [paʀfœ̃]	flavor
Quel parfum? Fraise ou chocolat?	What flavor? Strawberry or chocolate?
une **mousse au chocolat** [musoʃɔkɔla]	chocolate mousse
la **crème** [kʀɛm]	cream
un **bonbon** [bɔ̃bɔ̃]	candy

INFO

Dessert – désert

Note the difference between:

le dessert [desɛʀ]	*dessert*
le désert [dezɛʀ]	*desert, wasteland*

une **coupe** [kup]	cup
Comme dessert, je vous recommande une **coupe de glace**.	For dessert, I recommend a dish of ice cream.
un **flan** [flɑ̃]	flan
la **crème Chantilly** [kʀɛmʃɑ̃tiji]	whipped cream
la **compote** [kɔ̃pɔt]	compote
une **crêpe** [kʀɛp]	crepe, pancake
une **gaufre** [gofʀ]	waffle
un **gâteau sec**; des **gâteaux secs** *pl* [gatosɛk]	scone

l'**eau** (**minérale**) *f*; les **eaux** (**minérales**) *pl* [o(mineʀal)]	(mineral) water
l'**eau gazeuse**	carbonated/sparkling water
un **jus** (**de fruits**) [ʒy(d(ə)fʀɥi)]	(fruit) juice
verser [vɛʀse]	to pour
une **limonade** [limɔnad]	lemonade, soft drink
un **sirop** [siʀo]	syrup
un **coca** [kɔka]	cola
vider [vide]	to empty
Il a **vidé son verre d'une traite**.	He emptied his glass in one gulp.

l'**alcool** *m* [alkɔl]	alcohol
une **boisson sans alcool**	non-alcoholic drink
la **bière** [bjɛʀ]	beer
une **bière blonde**	light beer
une **bière brune**	dark beer
le **vin** [vɛ̃]	wine
un **vin de table**	table wine
le (**vin**) **blanc**	white wine
le (**vin**) **rouge**	red wine
le (**vin**) **rosé**	rosé wine
le **champagne** [ʃɑ̃paɲ]	champagne
le (**vin**) **mousseux** [(vɛ̃)musø]	sparkling wine
le **cidre** [sidʀ]	cider
un **tire-bouchon** [tiʀbuʃɔ̃]	corkscrew *(See Information Box p.104)*
un **ouvre-bouteille** [uvʀəbutɛj]	bottle opener *(See Information Box p.104)*
À votre santé! [avɔtʀəsɑ̃te]	To your health!
À la vôtre! *fam*	Cheers!

trinquer à [tʀɛ̃ke]	to drink a toast to
Trinquons à la santé des jeunes mariés!	Let's drink to the health of the newlyweds!
ivre [ivʀ]	drunk
soûl *fam*, **soûle** [su, sul]	drunk, smashed

les **épices** *fpl* [epis]	spices
épicer [epise]	to spice
épicé, épicée [epise]	spiced
le **thym** [tɛ̃]	thyme
le **laurier** [lɔʀje]	bay leaf
le **persil** [pɛʀsi]	parsley
la **ciboulette** [sibulɛt]	chives
les **fines herbes** *fpl* [finzɛʀb]	culinary herbs
les **herbes de Provence** *fpl* [ɛʀbdəpʀɔvɑ̃s]	herbes de Provence
la **vanille** [vanij]	vanilla
la **cannelle** [kanɛl]	cinnamon

5.2 Cooking, Baking, and Meals 

cuisiner [kɥizine]	to cook *(See Information Box p. 103)*
la **cuisine** [kɥizin]	kitchen
un **livre de cuisine**	cookbook
un **cuisinier**, une **cuisinière** [kɥizinje, jɛʀ]	cook, chef
un **plat** [pla]	dish, meal
un **plat cuisiné**	TV dinner
un **four** [fuʀ]	oven
mettre au four	to put into the oven, bake
un (**four à**) **micro-ondes**	microwave (oven)

une **cuisinière** [kɥizinjeʀ]	stove
une **plaque de cuisson** [plakdəkɥisɔ̃]	hot plate
une plaque à induction	induction cooker
à feu doux [afødu]	over low heat
faire cuire à feu doux	to cook over low heat, simmer

un **réfrigérateur** [ʀefʀiʒeʀatœʀ]	refrigerator
un **frigidaire** [fʀiʒidɛʀ]	refrigerator
un **frigo** *fam* [fʀigo]	fridge, refrigerator
congeler [kɔ̃ʒ(ə)le]	to freeze
un **congélateur** [kɔ̃ʒelatœʀ]	freezer

griller [gʀije]	to grill
rôtir [ʀotiʀ/ʀɔtiʀ]	to roast
faire chauffer [fɛʀʃofe]	to warm up, heat
réchauffer [ʀeʃofe]	to heat up
refroidir [ʀəfʀwadiʀ]	to cool
brûlant, **brûlante** [bʀylɑ̃, ɑ̃t]	boiling hot
chaud, **chaude** [ʃo, ʃod]	hot, warm
Mange pendant que c'est chaud.	Eat while it's hot.

INFO

Cooking

Depending on the context, *cook* can be translated in several ways:

cuisiner/faire la cuisine	*to cook the food*
Mon frère cuisine très bien.	*My brother cooks very well.*
Tu sais faire la cuisine?	*Can you cook?*
cuire	*to cook (through)*
cuire de four	*to bake*
Les lentilles doivent cuire 40 minutes.	*The lentils have to cook for 40 minutes.*
faire cuire	*to cook*
faire cuire un œuf	*to cook a hard-boiled egg*
Va te faire cuire un œuf. ***fam***	*Go cook an egg! (Go fly a kite!)*
faire	*to make, cook, prepare*
faire du thé/du café	*to make tea/coffee*
bouillir	*to boil*
L'eau bout à 100 degrés.	*Water boils at 100 degrees Centigrade.*
faire bouillir qc	*to boil s.th.*
faire bouillir du lait	*to boil some milk*

tiède [tjɛd] — lukewarm, tepid
froid, **froide** [fʀwa, fʀwad] — cold

---

un **récipient** [ʀesipjɑ̃] — container
une **casserole** [kasʀɔl] — saucepan
une **marmite** [maʀmit] — cooking pot
une **cocotte-minute**; les **cocottes-minute** *pl* [kɔkɔtminyt] — pressure cooker(s)
une **poêle** [pwal] — frying pan
une **friteuse** [fʀitøz] — deep fat fryer
la **graisse** [gʀɛs] — grease

INFO

Masculine/feminine

une poêle (à frire)	*(frying) pan*
un poêle	*heating stove/floor furnace*
un poêle à bois	*wood stove*

une **recette** [ʀəsɛt]	recipe
préparer [pʀepaʀe]	to prepare
éplucher [eplyʃe]	to peel
couper [kupe]	to cut
découper [dekupe]	to cut up
hacher ['aʃe]	to chop, mince
mélanger [melɑ̃ʒe]	to mix
ajouter qc (**à qc**) [aʒute]	to add s.th. (to s.th.)

---

remuer [ʀəmɥe]	to stir
fouetter [fwɛte]	to beat, whip
la **crème fouettée**	whipped cream
battre [batʀ]	to beat
battre les œufs **en neige**	to beat the egg whites until stiff
un **mixeur** [miksœʀ]	mixer
un **mixer** [miksœʀ]	mixer

---

une **boîte** [bwat]	can
un **ouvre-boîte**(**s**)	can opener
une **conserve** [kɔ̃sɛʀv]	canned food
une boîte de conserve	can

INFO

Plural

According to the new spelling (1990), composite words of the type *verb* + *noun* behave like a *simple noun*. That is, in the plural, the noun uses only one plural marker:

un porte-monnaie	des porte-monnaies	*wallets*
un ouvre-boîte	des ouvre-boîtes	*can openers*
un sèche-cheveu	des sèche-cheveux	*hair dryers*

This new spelling is accepted.

The traditional spelling varies:

un porte-monnaie	des porte-monnaie
un ouvre-boîte(s)	des ouvre-boîte(s)
un sèche-cheveux	des sèche-cheveux

---

l'**huile** *f* [ɥil]	oil
le **vinaigre** [vinɛɡʀ]	vinegar
une **cuillerée** (**de qc**) [kɥij(e)ʀe]	a spoonful (of s.th.)

---

saler [sale]	to salt
le **sel** [sɛl]	salt
Ajoutez **une pincée de sel**.	Add a pinch of salt.

poivrer [pwavʀe]	to pepper
le **poivre** [pwavʀ]	pepper
le **piment** [pimɑ̃]	chili pepper, cayenne pepper
la **moutarde** [mutaʀd]	mustard

la **farine** [faʀin]	flour
la **levure** [l(ə)vyʀ]	yeast
la **pâte** [pɑt]	dough
la **pâte brisée**	short pastry
la **pâte feuilletée**	flaky pastry, puff pastry
la **pâte levée**	yeast dough

un **moule** [mul]	baking form, mould

la **table** [tabl]	table
mettre la table	to set the table
débarrasser la table	to clear the table
une **nappe** [nap]	tablecloth
une **serviette** (**de table**) [sɛʀvjɛt (d(ə)tabl)]	napkin
une **corbeille à pain** [kɔʀbɛjapɛ̃]	bread basket

INFO

With and without a handle

une corbeille	*basket (without a handle)*
une corbeille à papier	*paper basket*
un panier	*basket (with a handle)*
un panier à provisions	*shopping basket*
un panier à salade *fam*	*salad basket (for drip drying washed salad); slang = paddy wagon*

une **carafe** [kaʀaf]	carafe
un **plateau**; des **plateaux** *pl* [plato]	tray
un **plateau de fromages**	cheese plate
un **saladier** [saladje]	salad bowl
une **soupière** [supjɛʀ]	soup bowl

la **vaisselle** [vɛsɛl]	dishes, dishware
faire la vaisselle	to do the dishes
une **assiette** [asjɛt]	plate
une **assiette plate**	dinner plate
une **assiette creuse**	soup bowl
un **verre** [vɛʀ]	glass
une **tasse** [tas]	cup *(See Information Box p. 225)*
une **coupe** [kup]	bowl, cup
une **soucoupe** [sukup]	saucer
un **bol** [bɔl]	bowl

le **couvert** [kuvɛʀ]	place setting
mettre le couvert	to set the table
un **couteau**; des **couteaux** *pl* [kuto]	knife
une **cuillère**/une **cuiller** [kɥijɛʀ]	spoon
une **cuillère à soupe**	soupspoon, tablespoon
une **petite cuillère**/une **cuillère à café**	teaspoon
une **fourchette** [fuʀʃɛt]	fork

5.3 Articles of Clothing  19

un **vêtement** [vɛtmɑ̃]	article of clothing
s'habiller [sabije]	to get dressed
Il a sauté dans l'eau **tout habillé**.	He jumped into the water fully dressed.
les **habits** *mpl* [abi]	clothing
se déshabiller [s(ə)dezabije]	to undress
nu, **nue** [ny]	naked
les **fringues** *fpl fam* [fʀɛ̃g]	gear
mettre [mɛtʀ]	to put on
Mets ton manteau.	Put your coat on.
à l'endroit [alɑ̃dʀwa]	right-side-out
à l'envers [alɑ̃vɛʀ]	backwards, inside-out
Il a mis son pull à l'envers.	He put his sweater on inside-out.
enlever [ɑ̃l(ə)ve]	to take off
enlever sa chemise	to take off one's shirt
porter [pɔʀte]	to wear
changer de qc [ʃɑ̃ʒe]	to change
changer de chaussettes	to change socks
se changer [s(ə)ʃɑ̃ʒe]	to change clothes
Elle s'est changée.	She changed clothes.
se couvrir [s(ə)kuvʀiʀ]	to dress warm
Couvre-toi, il fait froid!	Dress warm, it's cold out!

doublé, **doublée** [duble]	lined
la **doublure** [dublyʀ]	lining
essayer [eseje]	to try on
Je voudrais essayer la **taille au-dessus**.	I would like to try the next larger size.
aller à qn [alea]	to fit s.o., suit s.o.
Cet ensemble lui va **à ravir**.	This outfit fits her beautifully.
aller avec qc [aleavɛk]	to go with s.th.
Cette cravate ne va pas avec ta chemise.	This tie does not go with your shirt.
assorti [asɔʀti], **assortie**	matching
une jupe et un chemisier assortis	a skirt and a matching blouse

un **pantalon** [pɑ̃talɔ̃]	pants
un **short** [ʃɔʀt]	shorts
un **jean** [dʒin]	jeans
une **robe** [ʀɔb]	dress
une **robe du soir**	evening dress
une **jupe** [ʒyp]	skirt
une **mini**(**jupe**)	miniskirt

une **ceinture** [sɛ̃tyʀ]	belt
Il va falloir **se serrer la ceinture**. *loc*	We will have to tighten our belts.
un **bouton** [butɔ̃]	button (n)
une **fermeture éclair** [fɛʀmətyʀeklɛʀ]	zipper (n)
Remonte ta fermeture éclair.	Zip up.
une **fermeture velcro** [fɛʀmətyʀvɛlkʀo]	Velcro fastener
le **velcro** [vɛlkʀo]	Velcro
coudre [kudʀ]	to sew
une **machine à coudre**	sewing machine
la **couture** [kutyʀ]	sewing
la haute couture	haute couture, high fashion
recoudre [ʀ(ə)kudʀ]	to sew, mend
une **aiguille** [egɥij]	needle
Autant chercher une aiguille dans une botte de foin. *loc*	It's like looking for a needle in a haystack.
une **épingle** [epɛ̃gl]	pin
des **ciseaux** *mpl* [sizo]	scissors *(See Information Box p. 46)*
un **fil** [fil]	thread
déchirer [deʃiʀe]	to tear
repriser [ʀ(ə)pʀize]	to stitch
un **trou** [tʀu]	hole

une **chemise** [ʃ(ə)miz]	shirt
Il **change d'avis comme de chemise**. *loc*	He changes his mind the way he changes his shirt.
un **chemisier** [ʃ(ə)mizje]	blouse
un **tee-shirt**; des **tee-shirts** *pl* [tiʃœʀt]	T-Shirt
un **T-shirt**; des **T-shirts** *pl* [tiʃœʀt]	T-Shirt
un **pull** [pyl]	sweater, pullover
un **sweat-shirt**; des **sweat-shirts** *pl* [switʃœʀt]	sweatshirt
un **sweat** [swit]	sweatshirt

un **survêtement** [syʀvɛtmɑ̃]	training suit, sweat suit
un **jogging** [dʒɔgiŋ]	jogging suit
un **col** [kɔl]	collar
un **col en V**	V-neck
un **col roulé**	turtleneck
une **manche** [mɑ̃ʃ]	sleeve
une **chemise à manches courtes**	a short-sleeved shirt
faire la manche *fam*	to beg, panhandle
une **poche** [pɔʃ]	pocket

un **manteau**; des **manteaux** *pl* [mɑ̃to]	coat
un **imperméable** [ɛ̃pɛʀmeabl]	raincoat
un **imper** *fam* [ɛ̃pɛʀ]	raincoat
un **anorak** [anɔʀak]	parka
un **blouson** [bluzɔ̃]	coat, jacket
un **costume** [kɔstym]	suit
un **costume trois pièces**	three-piece suit

un **tailleur** [tajœʀ]	lady's suit; tailor
un **ensemble** [ɑ̃sɑ̃bl]	combination (suit), ensemble
On ne peut pas acheter la veste sans la jupe, c'est un ensemble.	The jacket cannot be bought without the skirt; it's an ensemble.

INFO

Clothing nuances

une veste	*jacket, sport coat*
un veston Le veston de mon costume est trop large.	*sport coat, jacket (of a suit)* *The jacket for my suit is too big.*
un gilet un gilet de sauvetage	*vest (e.g., for a three-piece suit)* *life vest*

un **chapeau**; des **chapeaux** *pl* [ʃapo]	hat
une **casquette** [kaskɛt]	cap
une **casquette de base-ball**	baseball cap
un **bonnet** [bɔnɛ]	knitted hat
un **béret** (**basque**) [beʀɛ(bask)]	beret
des **sous-vêtements** *mpl* [suvɛtmɑ̃]	underwear
un **soutien-gorge**; des **soutiens-gorge(s)** *pl* [sutjɛ̃gɔʀʒ]	bra
un **slip** [slip]	panties, brief
un **collant** [kɔlɑ̃]	tights, panty hose
un **bas** [bɑ]	stocking
des **chaussettes** *fpl* [ʃosɛt]	socks
la **lingerie** [lɛ̃ʒʀi]	lingerie
une **culotte** [kylɔt]	underpants
Chez les Dupont, c'est la femme qui **porte la culotte**.	At the Dupont's, it's the woman who wears the pants.
une **petite culotte** (en dentelle)	(lace) panties
un **caleçon** [kalsɔ̃]	drawers, long-johns
un **tricot de corps** [tʀikod(ə)kɔʀ]	undershirt
un **maillot de corps** [majod(ə)kɔʀ]	undershirt
un **body** [bɔdi]	body shirt
les **socquettes** *fpl* [sɔkɛt]	ankle socks
un **peignoir** [pɛɲwaʀ]	(bath)robe
la **layette** [lɛjɛt]	baby clothes, layette
un **maillot de bain** [majodbɛ̃]	bathing suit
un (**maillot**) **deux-pièces** [(mɑjo) døpjɛs]	bikini, two-piece suit
un **bikini** [bikini]	bikini
un **slip de bain** [slipdəbɛ̃]	bathing trunks
un **pyjama** [piʒama]	pajamas
une **chemise de nuit** [ʃ(ə)mizdənɥi]	night shirt
une **robe de chambre** [ʀɔbdəʃɑ̃bʀ]	housecoat, robe
un **tablier** [tablije]	apron
un **tablier de cuisine**	kitchen apron
une **blouse** [bluz]	smock, work coat
La femme de ménage porte une blouse pour protéger ses vêtements.	The cleaning lady wears a smock to protect her clothing.
une **salopette** [salɔpɛt]	overalls
un **bleu de travail**; des **bleus de travail** *pl* [blødətʀavaj]	work clothes

des **chaussures** *fpl* [ʃosyʀ]	shoes
une **paire de chaussures**	pair of shoes
des **bottes** *fpl* [bɔt]	boots
en avoir plein les bottes *fam*	to be fed up
des **baskets** *fpl* [baskɛt]	gym shoes
des **tennis** *fpl* [tenis]	tennis shoes
des **sandales** *fpl* [sɑ̃dal]	sandals
des **escarpins** *mpl* [ɛskaʀpɛ̃]	pumps
à talons hauts/plats [atalɔ̃o/pla]	high-heeled, flat
à talons aiguilles [atalɔ̃egɥij]	with spike heels
des **pantoufles** *fpl* [pɑ̃tufl]	slippers
des **chaussons** *mpl* [ʃosɔ̃]	slippers; booties
la **pointure** [pwɛ̃tyʀ]	size (for shoes)
Quelle pointure fais-tu?	What size shoe do you wear?
chausser [ʃose]	to put on shoes; to wear a size ... shoe
Je **chausse du 46**.	My shoe size is 46.
laver [lave]	to wash
une **machine à laver**	washing machine
la **lessive** [lɛsiv]	laundry; wash; laundry detergent
faire la lessive	to do the laundry
le **linge** [lɛ̃ʒ]	linen, underwear
mouillé, **mouillée** [muje]	wet
humide [ymid]	damp, moist
sec, **sèche** [sɛk, sɛʃ]	dry
sécher [seʃe]	to dry
une **corde** (**à linge**) [kɔʀd(alɛ̃ʒ)]	(clothes)line
une **pince** (**à linge**) [pɛ̃s(alɛ̃ʒ)]	clothespin
étendre le linge [etɑ̃dʀləlɛ̃ʒ]	to hang out the wash
essorer le linge [esɔʀel(ə)lɛ̃ʒ]	to spin dry the wash
un **sèche-linge** [sɛʃlɛ̃ʒ]	clothes dryer *(See Information Box p.104)*
nettoyer [nɛtwaje]	to clean
faire nettoyer une veste	to have a jacket cleaned
une **tache** [taʃ]	spot, stain *(See Information Box p. 88)*
enlever une tache	to remove a spot
une **teinturerie** [tɛ̃tyʀʀi]	dry cleaner
un **pressing** [pʀɛsiŋ]	dry cleaner
une **laverie** (**automatique**) [lavʀi (otomatik)]	laundromat
rétrécir [ʀetʀesiʀ]	to shrink
Ce pull a rétréci au lavage.	This sweater shrank in the wash.

repasser [ʀ(ə)pase]	to iron
une **table/planche à repasser**	ironing board
le **fer à repasser**	iron (n)
un fer à vapeur	steam iron
le **repassage** [ʀ(ə)pasaʒ]	ironing (n)
froissé, **froissée** [fʀwase]	wrinkled

chic [ʃik]	chic, stylish
élégant, **élégante** [elegɑ̃, ɑ̃t]	elegant
la **mode** [mɔd]	fashion
à la mode	fashionable
moderne [mɔdɛʀn]	modern
la **qualité** [kalite]	quality
un tissu de bonne qualité	a good-quality fabric
nouveau, **nouvel**, **nouvelle**; **nouveaux**, **nouvelles** *pl* [nuvo, nuvɛl]	new
neuf, **neuve** [nœf, nœv]	new
usé, **usée** [yze]	used, worn
un vieux jean **usé aux genoux**	an old pair of jeans worn in the knees
propre [pʀɔpʀ]	clean *(See Information Box p. 44)*
sale [sal]	dirty

INFO

Mode

Mode may be spelled the same way and pronounced the same way, but watch the article. It makes all the difference.

la mode	*fashion*
Elle est habillée à la dernière mode.	*She is dressed in the latest style.*
un défilé de mode	*fashion show*
le mode	*means, manner*
le mode d'emploi	*instructions for use*

INFO

New

neuf, neuve	une voiture neuve	*a new car (i.e., fresh from the factory)*
nouveau, nouvel, nouvelle	une nouvelle voiture (= une autre voiture)	*a new car (i.e., different from the old/former car)*

démodé, **démodée** [demɔde]	outdated, old-fashioned
avoir du goût [avwaʀdygu]	to have good taste
s'habiller **avec goût**	to dress tastefully
le **look** *fam* [luk]	appearance, look (n)
avoir un **look d'enfer**	to have a cool look
un **modèle** [mɔdɛl]	model (n)
C'est le même modèle mais en bleu.	This is the same model, but in blue.

la **taille** [taj]	size
C'est **à ma taille**.	That is my size.
Comme taille, je fais du 38.	I take a size 38.
court, **courte** [kuʀ, kuʀt]	short *(See Information Box p. 164)*
long, **longue** [lɔ̃, lɔ̃g]	long
large [laʀʒ]	wide, loose, large
étroit, **étroite** [etʀwa, etʀwat]	tight
serré, **serrée** [seʀe]	tight
une veste **serrée à la taille**	a jacket cinched/tapered at the waist

retoucher [ʀ(ə)tuʃe]	to alter
une **retouche** [ʀ(ə)tuʃ]	alteration
raccourcir [ʀakuʀsiʀ]	to shorten
J'ai raccourci mon pantalon.	I shortened my pants.
rallonger [ʀalɔ̃ʒe]	to lengthen

chaud, **chaude** [ʃo, ʃod]	warm
un vêtement chaud pour l'hiver	warm winter clothing
confortable [kɔ̃fɔʀtabl]	comfortable
épais, **épaisse** [epɛ, ɛs]	thick
léger, **légère** [leʒe, ʒɛʀ],	light *(See Information Box p. 437)*
un tissu épais/léger	thick/thin fabric
fin, **fine** [fɛ̃, fin]	thin

un **tissu** [tisy]	cloth/fabric
une **étoffe** [etɔf]	cloth/fabric
une étoffe souple	soft fabric
le **cuir** [kɥiʀ]	leather
un blouson **en cuir véritable**	real leather jacket
le **coton** [kɔtɔ̃]	cotton
une chemise **100% coton**	100% cotton shirt
la **laine** [lɛn]	wool
un pull **en pure laine**	pure wool sweater
les **fibres synthétiques** *fpl* [fibʀ(ə)sɛ̃tetik]	synthetic fibers
une **microfibre** [mikʀofibʀ]	microfiber
la **soie** [swa]	silk
la **dentelle** [dɑ̃tɛl]	lace
le **velours** [v(ə)luʀ]	velvet
la **fourrure** [fuʀyʀ]	fur
un **manteau de fourrure**	a fur coat
uni, **unie** [yni]	plain, solid, one-color
imprimé, **imprimée** [ɛ̃pʀime]	printed
un tissu imprimé à petites fleurs	floral-print fabric
rayé, **rayée** [ʀeje]	striped
à rayures [aʀejyʀ]	striped
à carreaux [akaʀo]	checked
une **veste à carreaux écossais**	plaid jacket
à pois [apwa]	polka-dotted

broder [bʀɔde]	to embroider
la **broderie** [bʀɔdʀi]	embroidery
un **crochet** [kʀɔʃɛ]	crochet hook
faire du crochet	to crochet
tricoter [tʀikɔte]	to knit
les **aiguilles à tricoter**	knitting needles
le **tricot** [tʀiko]	knitting

5.4 Jewelry and Accessories  20

un **bijou**; des **bijoux** *pl* [biʒu]	jewel
une **chaîne** [ʃɛn]	chain
une **montre** [mɔ̃tʀ]	watch
regarder l'heure à sa montre	to check one's watch

une **bague** [bag]	ring
Il lui a mis la bague au doigt.	He put a ring on her finger. (He married her.)
une **alliance** [aljɑ̃s]	wedding ring
un **bracelet** [bʀaslɛ]	bracelet
un **collier** [kɔlje]	necklace
une **boucle d'oreille** [bukl(ə)dɔʀɛj]	earring
une **broche** [bʀɔʃ]	brooch

précieux, **précieuse** [pʀesjø, jøz]	precious, valuable
en or [ɑ̃nɔʀ]	(made of) gold
une **montre en or**	a gold watch
doré, **dorée** [dɔʀe]	gold-plated, gilded
en argent [ɑ̃naʀʒɑ̃]	(made of) silver
argenté, **argentée** [aʀʒɑ̃te]	silver-plated

un **joyau**; des **joyaux** *pl* [ʒwajo]	jewel, gem
les **joyaux de la couronne**	the crown jewels
un **diamant** [djamɑ̃]	diamond
une **perle** [pɛʀl]	pearl
une **pierre précieuse** [pjɛʀpʀesjøz]	precious stone
un **bijou fantaisie** [biʒufɑ̃tɛzi]	costume jewelry
du **toc** [tɔk]	fake, junk
C'est du toc, ça se voit tout de suite!	That's a fake, it's obvious right away!

un **accessoire** [akseswaʀ]	accessory
un **sac** [sak]	bag
un **sac à main**	handbag
les **lunettes** *fpl* [lynɛt]	glasses (*See Information Box p. 46)*
porter des **lunettes de soleil**	to wear sunglasses
un **foulard** [fulaʀ]	scarf
une **écharpe** [eʃaʀp]	shawl
un **gant** [gɑ̃]	glove
une **paire de gants**	pair of gloves
Cela lui **va comme un gant**. *loc*	That fits him/her like a glove.
une **cravate** [kʀavat]	necktie

un **nœud** [nø]	knot
faire un nœud (de cravate)	to tie a knot (in a necktie)
un **nœud papillon**	bow tie
un **mouchoir** [muʃwaʀ]	handkerchief
un **parapluie** [paʀaplɥi]	umbrella

5.5 Shopping  21

un **magasin** [magazɛ̃]	store, shop
un **magasin de jouets**	toy shop
un **grand magasin**	department store
un **marché** [maʀʃe]	market
faire son marché	to go shopping
un **supermarché** [sypɛʀmaʀʃe]	supermarket
un **hypermarché** [ipɛʀmaʀʃe]	superstore
une **grande surface** [gʀɑ̃dsyʀfas]	supermarket, superstore
un **centre commercial** [sɑ̃tʀəkɔmɛʀsjal]	shopping center, mall
une **boutique** [butik]	shop, boutique
le **petit commerce** [p(ə)tikɔmɛʀs]	retail
un **traiteur** [tʀɛtœʀ]	caterer
un **étalage** [etalaʒ]	display
un **rayon** [ʀejɔ̃]	department
le **rayon parfumerie**	cosmetics/perfume department
un **distributeur automatique** [distʀibytœʀɔtɔmatik]	automat
une **boucherie** [buʃʀi]	butcher shop
aller* à la boucherie	to go to the butcher shop
un **boucher**, une **bouchère** [buʃe, ɛʀ]	butcher
aller* chez le boucher	to go to the butcher's
une **charcuterie** [ʃaʀkytʀi]	deli, sausage shop
un **charcutier**, une **charcutière** [ʃaʀkytje, ɛʀ]	delicatessen worker

INFO

Butcher or delicatessen?

une charcuterie	*is a store that sells sausage products and cold cuts.*
une boucherie	*is a butcher shop where mostly fresh meat is sold.*
une boucherie-characuterie	*This shop is a combination of the two.*

une **boulangerie** [bulɑ̃ʒʀi]	bakery
un **boulanger**, une **boulangère** [bulɑ̃ʒe, ɛʀ]	baker
une **pâtisserie** [pɑtisʀi]	pastry shop
un **pâtissier**, une **pâtissière** [pɑtisje, jɛʀ]	confectioner, pastry chef
une **épicerie** [episʀi]	grocery store
On trouve tout, à l'**épicerie du coin**.	The grocery store on the corner has everything.
un **épicier**, une **épicière** [episje, jɛʀ]	grocer
une **librairie** [libʀɛʀi]	book shop
un, une **libraire** [libʀɛʀ]	book seller
une **papeterie** [papɛtʀi/pap(ə)tʀi]	stationery store
un **bureau de tabac**; des **bureaux de tabac** *pl* [byʀodtaba]	tobacco shop
une **parfumerie** [paʀfymʀi]	perfumery
une **vitrine** [vitʀin]	display window
faire du lèche-vitrine(s)	to go window shopping
acheter [aʃte]	to buy
un **achat** [aʃa]	purchase (n)
faire ses achats	to go shopping
faire les courses *fpl* [fɛʀlekuʀs]	to go shopping/run errands
un **client**, une **cliente** [klijɑ̃, ɑ̃t]	client/customer
être bon client	to be a good customer
la **clientèle** [klijɑ̃tɛl]	clientele
Les prix bas attirent la clientèle.	Low prices attract customers.
vendre [vɑ̃dʀ]	to sell
un **vendeur**, une **vendeuse** [vɑ̃dœʀ, øz]	sales person
marchander [maʀʃɑ̃de]	to haggle
la **marchandise** [maʀʃɑ̃diz]	merchandise (n)
un **marchand**, une **marchande** [maʀʃɑ̃, ɑ̃d]	merchant
le **marchand de journaux**	newspaper seller
un **article** [aʀtikl]	article, item
Nous n'**avons** pas **cet article en magasin**.	We don't carry that item.

emballer [ɑ̃bale]	to wrap
un **emballage** [ɑ̃balaʒ]	wrapping, packaging (n)
déballer [debale]	to unwrap
un **paquet-cadeau**; des **paquets-cadeaux** *pl* [pakɛkado]	gift box
la **vente par correspondance** [vɑ̃tpaʀkɔʀɛspɔ̃dɑ̃s]	mail-order business
un **catalogue** [katalɔg]	catalog
commander [kɔmɑ̃de]	to order
commander qc **sur catalogue**	to order s.th. from the catalog

une **tranche** [tʀɑ̃ʃ]	slice (n)
trois tranches de jambon	three slices of ham
un **morceau**; des **morceaux** *pl* [mɔʀso]	piece
Un morceau de bœuf pour quatre personnes, s'il vous plaît.	A piece of beef for four people, please.
un **litre** [litʀ]	liter
un **kilo**(**gramme**) [kilo(gʀam)]	kilo(gram)
une **livre** [livʀ]	pound
une livre de beurre	a pound of butter

désirer [deziʀe]	to want, desire
Et à part ça, vous désirez?	Would you like something else?
avoir besoin de qc [avwaʀbəzwɛ̃]	to need s.th.
J'ai besoin d'un nouveau jean.	I need some new jeans.
avoir envie de qc [avwaʀɑ̃vi]	to feel like having s.th.
choisir [ʃwaziʀ]	to choose

faire la queue [fɛʀlakø]	to wait in line
Eh, vous! Faites la queue comme tout le monde!	Hey, you! Get in line like everybody else!
un **chariot** [ʃaʀjo]	shopping cart
la **caisse** [kɛs]	register, checkout
un **caissier**, une **caissière** [kɛsje, jɛʀ]	cashier
Combien? [kɔ̃bjɛ̃]	How much?
coûter [kute]	to cost
Ça fait/coûte combien?	How much is it?
Ça coûte une fortune.	It costs a fortune.
cher, **chère** [ʃɛʀ]	expensive
Ça **coûte** trop **cher**.	It is too expensive.
augmenter [ɔgmɑ̃te]	to increase, go up
Les prix augmentent sans arrêt.	Prices keep going up.
baisser [bese]	to go down
bon marché [bɔ̃maʀʃe]	cheap
meilleur marché [mɛjœʀ maʀʃe]	cheaper

gratuit [gʀatɥi, ɥit], **gratuite**	free
une **réduction** [ʀedyksjɔ̃]	price reduction, discount
les **soldes** *mpl* [sɔld]	special offers, sale, closeouts
acheter un vêtement **en solde**	to buy an article of clothing on sale

INFO

Les erreurs se paient cher

In some *fixed locutions* an *adjective* is used instead of an *adverb*, e.g.:

coûter/acheter/payer cher	*to cost/pay/purchase for a lot of money*
travailler dur	*to work hard*
peser lourd	*to be heavy*
sentir bon/mauvais	*to smell good/bad*

coûteux, **coûteuse** [kutø, øz]	costly, expensive
les **coûts** *mpl* [ku]	costs (n)
faire un prix à qn [fɛʀɛ̃pʀi]	to give s.o. a discount/good price
une **offre spéciale** [ɔfʀ(ə)spesjal]	special offer
en promotion [ɑ̃pʀɔmosjɔ̃]	on special offer
acheter un article en promotion	to buy an item on discount/ markdown

l'**argent** *m* [aʀʒɑ̃]	money
dépenser [depɑ̃se]	to spend
Il dépense plus qu'il ne gagne.	He spends more than he earns.
la **monnaie** [mɔnɛ]	change
rendre la monnaie	to give the change
une **pièce de monnaie**	coin
le **porte-monnaie**	wallet, purse *(See Information Box p. 104)*
l'**euro** *m* [øʀo]	euro
18 euros, ça fait combien, en dollars?	How much is 18 euros in dollars?
un **billet** (**de banque**) [bijɛ(d(ə)bɑ̃k)]	banknote, bill
un **portefeuille** [pɔʀtəfœj]	wallet
Je ne mets jamais ma carte de crédit dans mon portefeuille.	I never put my credit card in my wallet.

payer [peje]	to pay
payer cher	to pay a lot
le **prix** [pʀi]	price (n)
C'est **hors de prix**!	That is exorbitant/ unaffordable!

payer comptant [pejekɔ̃tɑ̃]	to pay in cash
C'est moins cher, si on paie comptant?	Is it cheaper if you pay in cash?
payer cash [pejekaʃ]	to pay in cash

False Friends

French Word	Actual Meaning	False Friend	Correct French Word
une blouse	**work coat, smock**	blouse	*une chemisier*
un costume	**man's suit**	costume	*un déguisement*
la librairie	**bookstore**	library	*une bibliothèque*
la monnaie	**change**	money	*l'argent*
une robe	**dress**	robe	*un peignoir, une robe de chambre*
une veste	**suit jacket**	vest	*un gilet*

My Vocabulary

6

Living

6.1 Construction, Houses, Buildings, and Occupants

 22

bâtir [batiʀ]	to build
un **terrain à bâtir**	building site
un **bâtiment** [batimɑ̃]	building (n)
construire [kɔ̃stʀɥiʀ]	to construct
faire construire une maison	to have a house built
la **construction** [kɔ̃stʀyksjɔ̃]	construction
transformer [tʀɑ̃sfɔʀme]	to remodel
l'**architecture** *f* [aʀʃitɛktyʀ]	architecture
un, une **architecte** [aʀʃitɛkt]	architect
un **plan** [plɑ̃]	plan, blueprint

un **matériau** [mateʀjo]	material
des **matériaux de construction**	construction materials
une **pierre** [pjɛʀ]	stone
une **brique** [bʀik]	brick
une **tuile** [tɥil]	roofing tile
un **toit de tuiles**	tile roof
le **béton** [betɔ̃]	concrete
une construction **en béton armé**	reinforced concrete construction

un **immeuble** [imœbl]	building (n)
une **tour** [tuʀ]	tower, high-rise *(See Information Box p. 201)*
les **tours de la Défense**	the high-rise office buildings of la Défense (office district on the edge of Paris)
un/une **HLM** (**habitation à loyer modéré**) [aʃɛlɛm]	a residential area with subsidized housing
un **appartement** [apaʀtəmɑ̃]	apartment
un **appartement de luxe**	deluxe apartment
l'**espace** *m* [ɛspas]	space, room
manquer d'espace	to have too little space

un **édifice** [edifis]	building (n)
un **building** [b(y)ildiŋ]	high-rise (n)
la **façade** [fasad]	facade
l'**extérieur** *m* [ɛksteʀjœʀ]	exterior
L'extérieur du château ne paie pas de mine.	The outside of the castle isn't much to look at.
l'**intérieur** *m* [ɛ̃teʀjœʀ]	interior
un **appartement en copropriété** [apaʀtəmɑ̃ɑ̃kɔ̃pʀɔpʀijete]	condominium
un **studio** [stydjo]	studio apartment
un **deux-pièces** [døpjɛs]	two-room apartment
un **duplex** [dyplɛks]	duplex

un **F3** [ɛftʀwa]	three-room apartment
meublé, **meublée** [mœble]	furnished
Il a trouvé un **studio meublé**.	He found a furnished apartment.
luxueux, **luxueuse** [lyksɥø, øz]	luxurious
spacieux, **spacieuse** [spasjø, jøz]	roomy, spacious
un grand appartement aux pièces spacieuses	a large apartment with spacious rooms
à l'étroit [aletʀwa]	cramped for space
de grand standing [dəgʀɑ̃stɑ̃diŋ]	luxury
un **appartement de grand standing**	a luxury apartment
les **charges** *fpl* [ʃaʀʒ]	additional expenses
Le loyer s'élève à 800 euros **sans les charges**.	The rent is 800 euros not counting extras.

une **maison** [mɛzɔ̃]	house
une **maison individuelle**	single-family house
une **maison préfabriquée**	pre-fabricated house
un **pavillon** [pavijɔ̃]	single-family house
un **pavillon de banlieue**	single-family suburban house
une **villa** [vila]	villa
la **résidence** [ʀezidɑ̃s]	residence, housing area
le **lieu de résidence**	place of residence
une **résidence secondaire**	second residence, vacation home

loger [lɔʒe]	to live, reside
loger dans un appartement modeste	to live in a modest apartment
un **logement** [lɔʒmɑ̃]	apartment
habiter [abite]	to live, reside
habiter qc	to live in s.th.
une **habitation** [abitasjɔ̃]	dwelling, housing

déménager [demenaʒe]	to move (houses)
J'ai déménagé de Reims à Lyon.	I have moved from Reims to Lyon.
le **déménagement** [demenaʒmɑ̃]	move (n)
emménager (**dans**) [ɑ̃menaʒe]	to move in
Elle a emménagé dans l'appartement du troisième.	She has moved into the apartment on the fourth floor.
s'installer [sɛ̃stale]	to settle in, take up residence

un **robinet** [ʀɔbinɛ]	faucet
ouvrir/fermer le robinet	to turn on/off the faucet
un **évier** [evje]	sink
le **carrelage** [kaʀlaʒ]	tiles

un, une **propriétaire** [pRɔpRijetɛR]	owner
une **propriété** [pRɔpRijete]	property
posséder [pɔsede]	to own
louer [lue]	to rent
Chambre à louer.	Room for rent.
le **loyer** [lwaje]	rent (n)
un, une **locataire** [lɔkatɛR]	renter, tenant
un, une **sous-locataire**	subleaser, sublessee
la **location** [lɔkasjɔ̃]	rental, lease
mettre en location	to put up for rent
un **habitant**, une **habitante** [abitɑ̃, ɑ̃t]	inhabitant
un **voisin**, une **voisine** [vwazɛ̃, in]	neighbor
un, une **concierge** [kɔ̃sjɛRʒ]	concierge, superintendent
un **gardien**, une **gardienne** [gaRdjɛ̃, jɛn]	janitor, groundskeeper
la **porte** [pɔRt]	door
Qui a frappé à la porte?	Who knocked on the door?
sonner [sɔne]	to ring (a doorbell)
On a sonné!	Somebody rang the door bell!
une **sonnette** [sɔnɛt]	bell
donner un coup de sonnette	to ring the bell
une **serrure** [seRyR]	lock (n)
une **clé**/une **clef** [kle]	key
fermer à clé	to lock
une **entrée** [ɑ̃tRe]	entrance
la **porte d'entrée**	front door
un **couloir** [kulwaR]	corridor
le **rez-de-chaussée** [Redʃose]	first floor, ground floor
un **étage** [etaʒ]	floor
J'habite au 3e (étage).	I live on the fourth floor.
un **escalier** [eskalje]	stair, staircase
monter/descendre l'escalier	to go up/down the stairs
Il a monté péniblement l'escalier.	He walked up the staircase with difficulty.
l'**ascenseur** *m* [asɑ̃sœR]	elevator
appeler l'ascenseur	to call for the elevator

le **hall d'entrée** ['oldɑ̃tʀe]	lobby, entrance hall
un **digicode** [diʒikɔd]	digital access code
La porte d'entrée est **équipée d'un digicode**.	The front door has an electronic lock.
un **interphone** [ɛ̃tɛʀfɔn]	intercom
le **palier** [palje]	landing
un **voisin de palier**	landing/corridor neighbor
le **grenier** [gʀənje]	attic

une **pièce** [pjɛs]	room
un (**appartement de**) **trois pièces**	three-room apartment
une **salle à manger** [salamɑ̃ʒe]	dining room
une **salle de séjour** [saldəseʒuʀ]	living room
un **salon** [salɔ̃]	living room
une **chambre** [ʃɑ̃bʀ]	bedroom
la **chambre** (**à coucher**)	bedroom
la **chambre d'amis**	guest room
une **cuisine** [kɥizin]	kitchen
une **kitchenette** [kitʃənɛt]	kitchenette

une **salle de bains** [saldəbɛ̃]	bathroom (one which includes a shower or tub)
les **W.-C.** *mpl* [vese]	bathroom, restroom, powder room
Les W.-C. sont occupés.	The bathroom is occupied.
les **toilettes** *fpl* [twalɛt]	restroom, bathroom
le(s) **cabinet(s)** *mpl* [kabinɛ]	restroom, bathroom
les **toilettes**	toilet (n)
la **cuvette**	toilet bowl

un **toit** [twa]	roof
une **cheminée** [ʃəmine]	chimney
le **sol** [sɔl]	floor
le **sous-sol**	cellar, basement
la **cave** [kav]	cellar

une **terrasse** [teʀas]	terrace
un **balcon** [balkɔ̃]	balcony
un **jardin** [ʒaʀdɛ̃]	garden
un **garage** [gaʀaʒ]	garage *(See Information Box p. 78)*
Tu as sorti la voiture du garage?	Did you back the car out of the garage?

6.2 Home and Furnishings  23

un **mur** [myʀ]	wall
le **plafond** [plafɔ̃]	ceiling
le **plancher** [plɑ̃ʃe]	floor
un **coin** [kwɛ̃]	corner
une **marche** [maʀʃ]	step, stair
rater une marche	to miss/trip on a step

un **tapis** [tapi]	rug
un **tapis persan**	a Persian rug
la **moquette** [mɔkɛt]	carpet
le **parquet** [paʀkɛ]	parquet floor

une **porte** [pɔʀt]	door
une **fenêtre** [f(ə)nɛtʀ]	window
regarder par la fenêtre	to look out the window
une **vitre** [vitʀ]	pane of glass
faire les vitres	to clean the windows

un **volet** [vɔlɛ]	shutter (n)
ouvrir les volets	to open the shutters
un **store** [stɔʀ]	blind, shade
descendre le store	to lower the shade
un **rideau**; des **rideaux** *pl* [ʀido]	curtain
un **rideau de douche**	shower curtain
le **papier peint** [papjepɛ̃]	wallpaper
Il serait temps de **changer les papiers peints**.	It's about time to replace the wallpaper.

une **baignoire** [bɛɲwaʀ]	bathtub
un **lavabo** [lavabo]	(bathroom) sink
une **douche** [duʃ]	shower
installer [ɛ̃stale]	to install
installer une cabine de douche	to put in a shower stall

équiper [ekipe]	to equip, outfit
une cuisine **équipée d'une hotte aspirante**	a kitchen equipped with an exhaust fan
un **four** [fuʀ]	oven
un **réfrigérateur** [ʀefʀiʒeʀatœʀ]	refrigerator
un **frigo** *fam* [fʀigo]	fridge
Mets le coca au frigo.	Put the cola in the fridge.

le **chauffage** [ʃofaʒ]	heat (n)
faire installer le **chauffage central**	to have central heating installed
un **radiateur** [ʀadjatœʀ]	radiator

un **poêle** [pwal]	heating stove *(See Information Box p. 103)*
un **poêle à mazout**	oil furnace

l'**électricité** *f* [elɛktʀisite]	electricity, current
le **gaz** [gaz]	gas
une **cuisinière à gaz**	gas stove
la **lumière** [lymjɛʀ]	light

un **interrupteur** [ɛ̃teʀyptœʀ]	(light) switch
le **courant** (**électrique**) [kuʀɑ̃(elɛktʀik)]	(electrical) current
Il y a une **coupure de courant**.	The power is out.
une **prise** (**de courant**)	wall socket, plug
un **bouton** [butɔ̃]	button, switch
éclairer [ekleʀe]	to illuminate
Cette lampe **éclaire mal**.	This lamp doesn't throw much light.
l'**éclairage** *m* [eklɛʀaʒ]	illumination, lighting
un éclairage indirect	indirect lighting
un **lampadaire** [lɑ̃padɛʀ]	floor lamp

confortable [kɔ̃fɔʀtabl]	comfortable
inconfortable [ɛ̃kɔ̃fɔʀtabl]	uncomfortable
le **confort** [kɔ̃fɔʀ]	comfort (n)
un **appartement tout confort**	an apartment with all the modern conveniences

un **meuble** [mœbl]	piece of furniture
des meubles Louis XV	Louis XV-style furniture
une **table** [tabl]	table
un **bureau**; des **bureaux** *pl* [byʀo]	desk; office
une **chaise** [ʃɛz]	chair
un **fauteuil** [fotœj]	armchair
un **coussin** [kusɛ̃]	cushion

INFO

Bedding

un coussin	*cushion, pad*
Il me faut un coussin, mon siège est trop bas.	*I need a cushion, my seat is too low.*
un oreiller	*(bed) pillow*
Il dort avec deux oreillers.	*He sleeps with two pillows.*

l'**ameublement** *m* [amœbləmɑ̃]	furnishings
un **canapé** [kanape]	sofa, couch
un **canapé en cuir**	leather sofa
un **sofa** [sɔfa]	sofa
un **lit** [li]	bed
un **grand lit**	double bed
une **table de nuit/de chevet** [tabldənɥi/dəʃ(ə)vɛ]	night table
une **armoire** [ARmwaR]	wardrobe, armoire
une **armoire à glace**	mirrored wardrobe
un **placard** [plakaR]	closet, built-in cabinet
un **tiroir** [tiRwaR]	drawer
une **commode** [kɔmɔd]	dresser, bureau
une **étagère** [etaʒɛR]	shelf
ranger des livres sur les étagères	to arrange books on the shelves
un **cadre** [kɑdR]	frame
un **tableau**; des **tableaux** *pl* [tablo]	picture
accrocher un tableau	to hang a picture
une **lampe** [lɑ̃p]	lamp
allumer/éteindre une lampe	to turn on/off a lamp
un **vase** [vaz]	vase
une **glace** [glas]	mirror
un **miroir** [miRwaR]	mirror

INFO

Vase

le vase	*the* **vase**
un vase en cristal	*crystal vase*
la vase	*the* **mud, slush**
Cette carpe a un goût de vase.	*This carp tastes like mud.*

6.3 Household and Housework  24

le **ménage** [menaʒ]	household
faire le ménage	to do the housework
une **femme de ménage**	cleaning lady
l'**ordre** *m* [ɔʀdʀ]	order (n)
le **désordre** [dezɔʀdʀ]	disorder
ranger [ʀɑ̃ʒe]	to tidy up
Range ta chambre.	Tidy up your room.

les **travaux ménagers** *mpl* [tʀavomenaʒe]	housework
la **ménagère** [menaʒɛʀ]	housewife
le **maître**, la **maîtresse de maison** [mɛtʀə, mɛtʀɛsdəmɛzɔ̃]	the man, lady of the house
donner un coup de main à qn [dɔneɛ̃kud(ə)mɛ̃]	to give s.o. a hand

salir [saliʀ]	to dirty
sale [sal]	dirty
la **saleté** [salte]	filth
propre [pʀɔpʀ]	clean (adj) *(See Information Box p. 44)*
la **propreté** [pʀɔpʀəte]	cleanliness
laver [lave]	to wash
laver qc à la main	to wash s.th. by hand
le **lavage** [lavaʒ]	the wash
nettoyer [netwaje]	to clean
le **nettoyage** [netwajaʒ]	(dry) cleaning
essuyer [esɥije]	to dry, wipe off
essuyer la vaisselle	to dry the dishes
frotter [fʀɔte]	to rub

un **aspirateur** [aspiʀatœʀ]	vacuum cleaner
passer l'aspirateur	to run the vacuum cleaner
épousseter [epuste]	to dust
aérer [aeʀe]	to air out
Il faudrait aérer, ça sent le renfermé.	This needs airing out; it smells musty.
un **produit d'entretien** [pʀɔdɥidɑ̃tʀətjɛ̃]	cleaning product

brosser [bRɔse]	to brush
une **brosse** [bRɔs]	brush (n)
un **chiffon** [ʃifɔ̃]	rag
balayer [baleje]	to sweep
un **balai** [balɛ]	broom
donner un coup de balai	to sweep (up)
la **poussière** [pusjɛR]	dust
un **chiffon à poussière**	dust rag

un **appareil** [apaRɛj]	device, appliance
les **appareils électro-ménagers**	electric appliances
une **machine** [maʃin]	machine
électrique [elɛktRik]	electric
une **pile** [pil]	battery
fonctionner [fɔ̃ksjɔne]	to function
la **garantie** [gaRɑ̃ti]	guarantee (n)
être sous garantie	to be under guarantee

un **équipement** [ekipmɑ̃]	equipment
l'**équipement ménager**	household equipment, appliances
une **machine à laver** [maʃinalave]	washing machine
un **sèche-linge** [sɛʃlɛ̃ʒ]	dryer *(See Information Box p. 104)*
un **lave-vaisselle** [lavvɛsɛl]	dishwasher *(See Information Box p. 104)*

la **vaisselle** [vɛsɛl]	dishes
faire la vaisselle	to do/wash the dishes
faire la cuisine [fɛRlakɥizin]	to cook

la **lessive** [lɛsiv]	the wash, laundry; laundry detergent
le **linge** [lɛ̃ʒ]	linens; the wash
repasser [R(ə)pase]	to iron

allumer [alyme]	to turn on
éteindre [etɛ̃dR]	to turn off
faire du feu [fɛRdyfø]	to light a fire
chauffer [ʃofe]	to heat, warm (up)
Il fait chauffer le lait.	He is warming up the milk.

un **chauffe-eau** [ʃofo]	hot-water heater *(See Information Box p. 104)*
un **court-circuit**; des **courts-circuits** *pl* [kuRsiRkɥi]	short-circuit (n)
les **plombs** *mpl* [plɔ̃]	fuses
Les plombs ont sauté.	The fuses have blown.

faire le lit [fɛʀləli]	to make the bed
un **drap** [dʀa]	sheet
changer les draps	to change the sheets
une **couverture** [kuvɛʀtyʀ]	blanket
un **oreiller** [ɔʀɛje]	(bed) pillow
une **couette** [kwɛt]	down comforter/duvet
se glisser sous la couette	to slide under the covers
un **édredon** [edʀədɔ̃]	comforter
un **traversin** [tʀavɛʀsɛ̃]	bolster
mettre la table [mɛtʀ(ə)latabl]	to set the table
débarrasser [debaʀase]	to clean up
enlever [ɑ̃l(ə)ve]	to take away
N'enlève pas mon verre, s'il te plaît.	Don't take my glass, please.
la **poubelle** [pubɛl]	waste basket
les **ordures** *fpl* [ɔʀdyʀ]	trash
les ordures ménagères	household trash
un **vide-ordures** [vidɔʀdyʀ]	garbage disposal *(See Information Box p. 104)*
les **déchets** *mpl* [deʃɛ]	garbage
les **épluchures** *fpl* [eplyʃyʀ]	peelings

False Friends

French Word	Actual Meaning	False Friend	Correct French Word
un appareil	**device**	apparel	*les vêtements*
un coin	**corner**	coin	*la monnaie*
une pile	**battery**	pile	*un tas/une pile*
un store	**blinds**	store	*un magasin*

My Vocabulary

7
Private Life, Social Relationships

7.1 People, Family  25

la **famille** [famij]	family
une **famille nombreuse**	large family
une **fête de famille**	family celebration

INFO

All in the family

familier, familière	*familiar*	un visage familier	*familiar face*
	casual, relaxed	un comportement familier	*(excessively) familiar behavior*
	conversational	le langage familier	*conversational language*
familial, familiale	*family-related*	une entreprise familale	*family business*
		Il a des ennuis familiaux.	*He has family problems.*

fonder une famille [fɔ̃deynfamij]	to start a family
la **vie de famille** [vidfamij]	family life
avoir de la famille à [avwaʀd(ə)lafamij]	to have relatives in
un **membre de la famille** [mɑ̃bʀd(ə)lɑfɑmij]	family member
le **planning familial** [planiŋfamiljal]	family planning
une **famille monoparentale** [fɑmijmɔnopaʀɑ̃tal]	single-parent family
une **famille recomposée** [fɑmijʀ(ə)kɔ̃poze]	blended family
l'**union libre** *f* [ynjɔ̃libʀ]	common-law marriage
le **concubinage** [kɔ̃kybinaʒ]	common-law marriage
vivre en concubinage/en union libre	to live in a common-law marriage

les **parents** *mpl* [paʀɑ̃]	parents
le **père** [pɛʀ]	father
le **papa** [papa]	dad
la **mère** [mɛʀ]	mother
la **maman** [mamɑ̃]	mom

parent, **parente** [paʀɑ̃, ɑ̃t]	related
un **parent**, une **parente**	parent, relative
un parent proche/éloigné	close/distant relative
la **parenté** [paʀɑ̃te]	relationship
par alliance [paʀaljɑ̃s]	by marriage
C'est mon oncle par alliance.	That is my uncle by marriage.
les **liens de parenté** *mpl* [ljɛ̃ d(ə) paʀɑ̃te]	family ties
paternel, **paternelle** [patɛʀnɛl]	paternal
maternel, **maternelle** [matɛʀnɛl]	maternal
ma **grand-mère maternelle**	my maternal grandmother

marié, **mariée** [maʀje]	married
un **marié**, une **mariée**	groom, bride
le **mari** [maʀi]	husband
la **femme** [fam]	wife
une femme enceinte	pregnant woman
un **couple** [kupl]	couple
vivre en couple	to live together

l'**époux** *m*, l'**épouse** *f* [epu, uz]	spouse
le **droit de garde** [dʀwad(ə)gaʀd]	custody
Leur père a obtenu le droit de garde.	Their father won custody.
la **pension alimentaire** [pɑ̃sjɔ̃alimɑ̃tɛʀ]	alimony

l'**enfant** *m* [ɑ̃fɑ̃]	child
un **enfant unique**	only child
élever un enfant	to raise a child
le **bébé** [bebe]	baby
le **fils** [fis]	son
le **garçon** [gaʀsɔ̃]	boy
la **fille** [fij]	girl; daughter
le **frère** [fʀɛʀ]	brother
le **demi-frère**	half brother
la **sœur** [sœʀ]	sister
la **demi-sœur**	half sister

fraternel, **fraternelle** [fRatɛRnɛl]	fraternal
un **jumeau**, une **jumelle**; des **jumeaux, des jumelles** *pl* [ʒymo, ʒymɛl]	twin (n)
des **vrais jumeaux**	identical twins
des **sœurs jumelles**	twin sisters
majeur, **majeure** [maʒœR]	of legal age
un **majeur**, une **majeure**	person of legal age
la **majorité** [maʒɔRite]	majority; legal age
mineur, **mineure** [minœR]	minor (adj)
un **mineur**, une **mineure**	minor (n)
Ce film est **interdit aux mineurs**.	This film is not for minors..
aîné, **aînée** [ene]	elder *(with siblings)*
l'**aîné**/l'**aînée**	eldest (n)
C'est l'aînée de trois filles.	That is the eldest of three daughters.
cadet, **cadette** [kadɛ, ɛt]	younger *(with siblings)*
Elle a un frère cadet.	She has a younger brother.
le **cadet**, la **cadette**	younger brother/sister
adoptif, **adoptive** [adɔptif, iv]	adopted
le **fils adoptif** de mon ami	my friend's adopted son

les **grands-parents** *mpl* [gRɑ̃paRɑ̃]	grandparents
la **grand-mère** [gRɑ̃mɛR]	grandmother
la **mamie** *fam* [mami]	grandma
la **mémé** *fam* [meme]	grandma
le **grand-père** [gRɑ̃pɛR]	grandfather
le **pap** /le **papi** *fam* [papi]	grandpa
le **pépé** *fam* [pepe]	grandpa

un, une **ancêtre** [ɑ̃sɛtR]	ancestor
les **arrière-grands-parents** *mpl* [aRjɛRgRɑ̃paRɑ̃]	great-grandparents
un **arrière-grand-père** [aRjɛRgRɑ̃pɛR]	great-grandfather
une **arrière-grand-mère** [aRjɛRgRɑ̃mɛR]	great-grandmother
descendre de [desɑ̃dR]	to be descended from
descendre d'une famille noble	to come from a noble family
les **descendants** *mpl* [desɑ̃dɑ̃]	descendants
la **descendance** [desɑ̃dɑ̃s]	progeny
avoir une descendance nombreuse	to have lots of descendants

les **petits-enfants** *mpl* [p(ə)tizɑ̃fɑ̃]	grandchildren
la **petite-fille** [p(ə)titfij]	granddaughter
le **petit-fils** [p(ə)tifis]	grandson

les **arrière-petits-enfants** *mpl* [aʀjɛʀp(ə)tizɑ̃fɑ̃]	great-grandchildren
un **arrière-petit-fils** [aʀjɛʀp(ə)tifis]	great-grandson
une **arrière-petite-fille** [aʀjɛʀp(ə)titfij]	great-granddaughter

INFO

Plurals: Be Careful!

As a component of *composite nouns,* the adverb *arrière* is invariable.

ses arrière-petits-enfants	*his great-grandchildren*

When composite nouns consist of an *adjective* + *noun*, both elements take -s in the plural.

mes grands-pères	*my grandfathers*
des cartes postales	*postcards*

l'**oncle** *m* [ɔ̃kl]	uncle
la **tante** [tɑ̃t]	aunt
le **neveu** [n(ə)vø]	nephew
la **nièce** [njɛs]	niece
le **cousin**, la **cousine** [kuzɛ̃, in]	cousin
un **cousin germain**	first cousin
une cousine au 2e degré	second cousin

le **parrain** [paʀɛ̃]	godfather
la **marraine** [maʀɛn]	godmother
le **filleul**, la **filleule** [fijœl]	godchild
les **beaux-parents** *mpl* [bopaʀɑ̃]	parents-in-law, inlaws
le **beau-père**; les **beaux-pères** *pl* [bopɛʀ]	father-in-law; step-father
la **belle-mère** [bɛlmɛʀ]	mother-in-law; step-mother
le **gendre** [ʒɑ̃dʀ]	son-in-law
la **belle-fille** [bɛlfij]	daughter-in-law

7.2 Greetings and Goodbyes 

arriver [aʀive]	to arrive
rencontrer qn [ʀɑ̃kɔ̃tʀe]	to meet s.o.
saluer [salɥe]	to greet
Saluez-le de ma part!	Say hello for me!
Bonjour! [bɔ̃ʒuʀ]	Hello!
Bonjour, M./Mme Pennec!	Hello, Mr./Mrs. Pennec!
Salut! [saly]	Hi!
Allô? [alo]	Hello. *(on telephone)*
Allô, qui est à l'appareil?	Hello, who is this?
Bonsoir! [bɔ̃swaʀ]	Good evening!
partir* [paʀtiʀ]	to leave
se séparer [s(ə)sepaʀe]	to separate
Bonne nuit! [bɔnnɥi]	Goodnight!
Au revoir. [ɔʀvwaʀ]	Good-bye.
Madame; **Mesdames** *pl* [madam, medam]	Madam
une **dame**	lady
Mademoiselle; **Mesdemoiselles** *pl* [madmwazɛl, medmwazɛl]	Miss
une **demoiselle**	young lady
Monsieur; **Messieurs** *pl* [məsjø, mesjø]	Mister
un **monsieur**	man, gentleman
À bientôt. [abjɛ̃to]	See you soon.
À plus tard. [aplytaʀ]	See you later.
À tout à l'heure. [atutalœʀ]	See you soon.
À ce soir. [asəswaʀ]	See you tonight.
À demain. [ad(ə)mɛ̃]	See you tomorrow.
présenter qn à qn [pʀezɑ̃te]	to introduce s.o. to s.o.
Permettez-moi de vous présenter M./Mme Moreau.	May I introduce Mr./Mrs. Moreau (to you)?
Je la leur présente.	I will introduce her to them.
Je te présente à elle.	I will introduce you to her.
se présenter	to introduce oneself
Enchanté, Enchantée. [ɑ̃ʃɑ̃te]	How do you do? Nice to meet you.
Enchanté/Heureux de faire votre connaissance.	Very pleased to meet you.
Bienvenu, Bienvenue. [bjɛ̃v(ə)ny]	Welcome.

chéri, **chérie** [ʃeʀi]	dear
mon amour [mɔ̃namuʀ]	my love, my dear
mon petit, **ma petite** [mɔ̃p(ə)ti, map(ə)tit]	my little one

mon cher, **ma chère** [mɔ̃ʃɛʀ, maʃɛʀ]	my darling
mon vieux, **ma vieille** *fam* [mɔ̃vjø, mavjɛj]	old boy, old girl
mon chou *fam* [mɔ̃ʃu]	my dear
mon trésor *fam* [mɔ̃tʀezɔʀ]	my sweetheart
mon lapin *fam* [mɔ̃lapɛ̃]	my sweetie

7.3 Young People 27

un, une **jeune** [ʒœn]	youth (n), young person
la **jeunesse** [ʒœnɛs]	youth
un **jeune homme** [ʒœnɔm]	young man
un **garçon** [gaʀsɔ̃]	boy
une (**jeune**) **fille** [(ʒœn)fij]	girl
les **jeunes gens** *mpl* [ʒœnʒɑ̃]	young people
un **adolescent**, une **adolescente** [adɔlesɑ̃, ɑ̃t]	adolescent, teenager
un, une **ado** *fam* [ado]	teen(ager)

un **mec** *fam* [mɛk]	guy
une **nana** *fam* [nana]	chick
l'**âge ingrat** *m* [aʒɛ̃gʀa]	awkward age
Mon fils est **en plein dans l'âge ingrat**.	My son is right in the middle of the awkward age.
pubertaire [pybɛʀtɛʀ]	pubescent
la **puberté** [pybɛʀte]	puberty

un **ami**, une **amie** [ami]	friend
un **petit ami**, une **petite amie**	boy/girl friend
un **copain**, une **copine** [kɔpɛ̃, in]	buddy
un, une **pote** *fam* [pɔt]	pal
une soirée sympa entre potes	fun evening with friends
se rencontrer [s(ə)ʀɑ̃kɔ̃tʀe]	to meet (up)
sortir* avec qn [sɔ̃ʀtiʀ]	to go out with s.o.
Il sort avec Sylvie depuis 3 semaines.	He has been going out with Sylvie for three weeks.
sortir* ensemble	to go out together
un **groupe** [gʀup]	group
une **bande** [bɑ̃d]	group, crowd, gang

une **association** (**sportive**) [asɔsjasjɔ̃(spɔʀtiv)]	(sports) club
devenir membre d'une association	to join a club
faire du sport [fɜʀdyspɔʀ]	to play sports
une **MJC** (**maison des jeunes et de la culture**) [ɛmʒise]	youth center
une **discothèque** [diskɔtɛk]	disco(theque)
danser [dɑ̃se]	to dance
aller*/sortir* en boîte *fam* [ale/sɔʀtiʀɑ̃bwat]	to go to a (dance) club

INFO

Faisons du sport!

Generally, faire de + *definite article* + *type of sport* is used to express the act of *playing a sport.*

Elle fait de la voile.	*She sails.*
Nous faisons de la natation.	*We swim.*
Il fait du tennis (= Il joue au tennis).	*He plays tennis.*
Tu fais du ski?	*Do you ski?*

un **concert** [kɔ̃sɛʀ]	concert
un **concert** (**de**) **rock**	rock concert
le **rap** [ʀap]	rap
un **rappeur**, une **rappeuse** [ʀapœʀ, øz]	rapper
un **fan** [fan]	fan
un **tube** *fam* [tyb]	hit
le **top 50** [tɔ̃psɛ̃kɑ̃t]	hit parade
Ce tube est en tête du Top 50.	This hit is at the top of the charts.

un **conflit** [kɔ̃fli]	conflict
un **conflit de générations**	generation gap
un **problème** [pʀɔblɛm]	problem
le **dialogue** [djalɔg]	dialogue
l'**autorité** *f* [ɔtɔʀite]	authority
l'autorité parentale	parental authority
la **révolte** [ʀevɔlt]	revolt (n), rebellion
critique [kʀitik]	critical
être critique à l'égard de qn	to be critical of s.o.
la **critique** [kʀitik]	criticism
contredire qn [kɔ̃tʀədiʀ]	to contradict s.o.
Sa fille le contredit sans arrêt.	His daughter continually contradicts him.
s'entendre bien/mal avec qn [sɑ̃tɑ̃dʀbjɛ̃/mal]	to get along well/badly with s.o.

se confier à qn [s(ə)kɔ̃fje]	to confide in s.o.
la **confiance** [kɔ̃fjɑ̃s]	trust (n)
avoir confiance en qn/faire confiance à qn	to trust, have confidence in s.o.
compréhensif, compréhensive [kɔ̃pʀeɑ̃sif, iv]	understanding (adj).
la **compréhension** [kɔ̃pʀeɑ̃sjɔ̃]	understanding (n)
Elle se plaint **du manque de compréhension** de ses parents.	She complains of her parents' lack of understanding.
l'**incompréhension** *f* [ɛ̃kɔ̃ʀeɑ̃sjɔ̃]	lack of understanding
remettre qn/qc en question [ʀ(ə)mɛtʀɑ̃kɛstjɔ̃]	to question s.th./s.o.
se brouiller [s(ə)bʀuje]	to quarrel
Elle s'est brouillée avec son copain.	She quarreled with her friend.
en vouloir à qn (**de qc/de faire qc**) [ɑ̃vulwaʀ]	to be angry with s.o. (because of s.th./for having done s.th.)
Je lui en veux de son égoïsme.	I resent his egotism.
fuguer [fyge]	to run away
une **fugue** [fyg]	flight, running away (n)

l'**agression** *f* [agʀesjɔ̃]	aggression
être victime d'une agression	to fall victim to an attack
une **bagarre** [bagaʀ]	brawl, fight
la **violence** [vjɔlɑ̃s]	violence
violent, **violente** [vjɔlɑ̃, ɑ̃t]	violent
détruire [detʀɥiʀ]	to destroy

un **zonard**, une **zonarde** *fam* [zonaʀ, aʀd]	thug (from deprived area), hooligan
un **loubard**, une **loubarde** *fam* [lubaʀ, aʀd]	lout
mal tourner [maltuʀne]	to turn out bad
J'ai peur qu'il **finisse par mal tourner**.	I'm afraid he is going to turn out bad.
s'en sortir [sɑ̃sɔʀtiʀ]	to end up all right
Elle a des problèmes, mais je crois qu'elle va s'en sortir.	She has some problems, but I think she will end up okay.
la **délinquance juvénile** [delɛ̃kɑ̃sʒyvenil]	juvenile delinquency
un **casseur**, une **casseuse** *fam* [kasœʀ, øz]	(street) ruffian
un **graffiti** [gʀafiti]	graffiti (n)
un **tag** [tag]	sprayed graffiti
un **tagueur**, une **tagueuse** [tagœʀ, øz]	graffiti sprayer
le **verlan** [vɛʀlɑ̃]	(street) slang

INFO

Verlan

Verlan is a language spoken mainly by young people, which is based roughly on transposing syllables: (à) l'envers *backwards* → verlan. Examples: metro → tromé; bizarre → zarbi; femme → meuf; blouson → zomblou.

7.4 Social Groups, Living Conditions, Behavior

28

les **gens** *mpl* [ʒɑ̃]	people
la **population** [pɔpylasjɔ̃]	population
la **population active**	work/labor force
les **jeunes** *mpl* [ʒœn]	young people
la **jeunesse** [ʒœnɛs]	youth
la **vieillesse** [vjɛjɛs]	old age
le **3e âge** [tʀwazjɛmaʒ]	old age, senior years
Il y a des tarifs réduits **pour le 3e âge**.	Prices are reduced for senior citizens.

les **vieux** *mpl* [vjø]	old people
les **personnes âgées** *fpl* [pɛʀsɔn(z)aʒe]	the elderly
une **génération** [ʒeneʀasjɔ̃]	generation
la **génération 68**	the generation of '68
le fossé entre les générations	generation gap

social, **sociale** [sɔsjal]	social
une **couche sociale**	social stratum
la **société** [sɔsjete]	society
le **milieu** [miljø]	milieu, backgroud
venir d'un **milieu social défavorisé**	to come from a disadvantaged background
une **communauté** [kɔmynote]	community
un **groupe** [gʀup]	group
un **groupe ethnique minoritaire**	ethnic minority group
une **classe sociale** [klassɔsjal]	social class

aisé, **aisée** [eze]	well off, moneyed
un **milieu aisé**	a comfortable background
moyen, **moyenne** [mwajɛ̃, jɛn]	middle, average
les **classes moyennes**	the middle class
bourgeois, **bourgeoise** [buʀʒwa, waz]	bourgeois, middle-class (adj)
un **bourgeois**, une **bourgeoise**	middle-class person
la **bourgeoisie** [buʀʒwazi]	bourgeoisie, middle class (n)
populaire [pɔpylɛʀ]	common, popular
Il est **issu des couches populaires**.	He comes from a modest background.
ouvrier, **ouvrière** [uvʀije, ijɛʀ]	working (adj)
la **classe ouvrière**	the working class
un **ouvrier**, une **ouvrière**	a (blue-collar) worker, laborer

les **conditions de vie** *fpl* [kɔ̃disjɔ̃d(ə)vi]	living conditions
le **niveau de vie**; les **niveaux de vie** *pl* [nivod(ə)vi]	standard of living
le **train de vie** [tʀɛ̃dəvi]	lifestyle
s'accroître [sakʀwatʀ]	to increase
Le taux de chômage s'est encore accru.	The unemployment index has gone up again.
une **augmentation** [ɔgmɑ̃tasjɔ̃]	increase (n)
une **augmentation de salaire**	a raise, salary increase
une **réduction** [ʀedyksjɔ̃]	reduction
la **réduction du temps de travail** (**RTT**)	cutback in working hours

riche [Riʃ]	rich
la **richesse** [Riʃɛs]	wealth
le **capital** [kapital]	capital, wealth
amasser un **capital important**	to amass significant wealth
la **fortune** [fɔRtyn]	fortune
pauvre [povR]	poor
la **pauvreté** [povRəte]	poverty
la **misère** [mizɛR]	poverty
tomber* dans la misère	to fall into poverty
démuni, **démunie** [demyni]	destitute

INFO

Fortune – chance – bonheur

la fortune	*fortune (fate); property; fortune*
faire fortune	*to become rich*
la roue de la fortune	*wheel of fortune*
la chance	*luck*
avoir de la chance	*to be lucky*
Bonne chance!	*Good luck!*
le bonheur	*happiness; good fortune*
un bonheur sans nuages	*pure happiness*

privilégié, **privilégiée** [pRivileʒje]	privileged
un **privilège** [pRivilɛʒ]	privilege
fortuné, **fortunée** [fɔRtyne]	prosperous, rich
les **revenus** *mpl* [Rəv(ə)ny/R(ə)vəny]	income (n)
l'**impôt sur le revenu**	income tax
la **prospérité** [pRɔspeRite]	prosperity
les **ressources** *fpl* [RəsuRs]	resources
disposer de ressources illimitées	to have unlimited resources

un **chômeur**, une **chômeuse** [ʃomœR, øz]	jobless/unemployed person
le **chômage** [ʃomaʒ]	unemployment
Elle **est au chômage** depuis 6 mois.	She has been out of work for six months.
le **RMI** (**revenu minimum d'insertion**) [ɛRɛmi]	minimum state unemployement insurance for workers over 25
un, une **RMIste** [ɛRɛmist]	*recipient of above*
le **minimum vital** [minimɔmvital]	subsistence level income
l'**aide sociale** *f* [ɛdsɔsjal]	welfare, social services
un, une **SDF** (un, une **sans domicile fixe**) [ɛsdeɛf]	homeless person
un, une **sans-abri** [sɑ̃zabRi]	homeless person

un **clochard**, une **clocharde** [klɔʃaʀ, aʀd]	bum (n)
mendier [mɑ̃dje]	to beg
un **mendiant**, une **mendiante** [mɑ̃djɑ̃, ɑ̃t]	beggar

appauvri, **appauvrie** [apovʀi]	impoverished
économiquement faible [ekɔnɔmikmɑ̃fɛbl]	low-income
un, une **économiquement faible**	a low-income person
une allocation réservée aux économiquement faibles	subsidy for low-income people
le **prolétariat** [pʀɔletaʀja]	proletariat

immigrer [imigʀe]	to immigrate
Sa famille a immigré en 1960.	His/Her family immigrated in 1960.
un **immigré**, une **immigrée** [imigʀe]	immigrant (n)
l'**immigration** *f* [imigʀasjɔ̃]	immigration
l'immigration clandestine	illegal immigration
s'intégrer [sɛ̃tegʀe]	to integrate
s'intégrer dans la société	to blend into society
l'**intégration** *f* [ɛ̃tegʀasjɔ̃]	integration

précaire [pʀekɛʀ]	precarious
se trouver dans une situation précaire	to find oneself in a precarious situation
les **déshérités** *mpl* [dezeʀite]	the needy, disadvantaged
un, une **sans-papiers** [sɑ̃papje]	illegal immigrant
lutter pour la légalisation des sans-papiers	to struggle for the legalization of illegal aliens
marginal, **marginale** [maʀʒinal]	marginal
un **marginal**, une **marginale**	dropout, alternative person
exclu, **exclue** [ɛkskly]	excluded
un **exclu**, une **exclue**	(social) outcast (n)
l'**exclusion** *f* [ɛksklyzjɔ̃]	exclusion
la **fracture sociale** [fʀaktyʀsɔsjal]	social gap
le **quart-monde** [kaʀmɔ̃d]	fourth world

accepter [aksɛpte]	to accept
rejeter [ʀ(ə)ʒəte/ʀəʒ(ə)te]	to reject
Les étrangers se sentent souvent rejetés.	Foreigners often feel rejected.
s'adapter [sadapte]	to adapt
l'**adaptation** *f* [adaptasjɔ̃]	adaptation
être en conflit avec qn [ɛtʀɑ̃kɔ̃fli]	to be in conflict with s.o.
respecter [ʀɛspɛkte]	to respect
tolérer [tɔleʀe]	to tolerate
la **tolérance** [tɔleʀɑ̃s]	tolerance

l'**intolérance** *f* [ɛ̃tɔleʀɑ̃s]	intolerance
avoir pitié de qn [avwaʀpitje]	to take pity on s.o.
Ayez pitié de moi.	Have pity on me.
faire pitié à qn [fɜʀpitje]	to inspire pity in s.o.
Le voir dans cet état me fait pitié.	I pity him when I see him in this condition.
aider [ede]	to help
aider qn à faire qc	to help s.o. do s.th.
encourager [ɑ̃kuʀaʒe]	to encourage
décourager [dekuʀaʒe]	to discourage
Ne te décourage pas si vite!	Don't get discouraged so quickly!
soutenir [sut(ə)niʀ]	to support
Leurs amis les ont beaucoup soutenus.	Their friends gave them lots of support.
avoir des problèmes *mpl* [avwaʀdepʀɔblɛm]	to have problems/difficulties
une **épreuve** [epʀœv]	trial, test (n)
subir une dure épreuve	to undergo a severe test
le **souci** [susi]	worry, care (n)
se faire du souci	to worry
la **difficulté** [difikylte]	difficulty
inquiéter [ɛ̃kjete]	to worry, upset
L'augmentation de la criminalité inquiète les pouvoirs publics.	The increase in crime worries the authorities.
l'**inquiétude** *f* [ɛ̃kjetyd]	worry (n)
maltraiter [maltʀɛte]	to mistreat
bousculer [buskyle]	to jostle
dépendre de [depɑ̃dʀ]	to depend on
dépendant, **dépendante** (**de**) [depɑ̃dɑ̃, ɑ̃t]	dependent (on)
indépendant, **indépendante** (**de**) [ɛ̃depɑ̃dɑ̃, ɑ̃t]	independent (of, from)
délivrer de [delivʀe]	to deliver, free from
Nous voilà **délivrés de nos soucis**.	Now we are free of worry.
se libérer de [s(ə)libeʀe]	to free oneself from
Elle s'est libérée de l'influence de ses parents.	She freed herself from the influence of her parents.
libre [libʀ]	free

responsable [rɛspɔ̃sabl]	responsible
être responsable de	to be responsible for
Je me sens responsable de ma sœur.	I feel responsible for my sister.
la **responsabilité** [rɛspɔ̃sabilite]	responsibility
protéger [pʀɔteʒe]	to protect
la **protection** [pʀɔtɛksjɔ̃]	protection
sauver [sove]	to save

solidaire [sɔlidɛʀ]	showing solidarity
se sentir solidaire des marginaux	to feel solidarity with the fringe groups
la **solidarité** [sɔlidaʀite]	solidarity
porter secours à qn [pɔʀtes(ə)kuʀ]	to help, come to the aid of s.o.

7.5 Relationships and Connections  29

amical, **amicale** [amikal]	friendly
un **ami**, une **amie** [ami]	friend
un ami intime	close friend
l'**amitié** *f* [amitje]	friendship
faire qc **par amitié pour qn**	to do s.th. for s.o. out of friendship
aimable [ɛmabl]	kind, friendly
Merci, vous êtes très aimable.	Thank you; you are very kind.
l'**amabilité** *f* [amabilite]	kindness
un **copain**, une **copine** [kɔpɛ̃, in]	buddy, pal
un, une **camarade** [kamaʀad]	comrade, friend
C'est un ancien **camarade de classe**.	He is an old classmate.
un **voisin**, une **voisine** [vwazɛ̃, in]	neighbor
un, une **collègue** [kɔlɛg]	colleague

connaître [kɔnɛtʀ]	to know
faire la connaissance de qn [fɛʀlakɔnɛsɑ̃s]	to meet/get to know s.o.
J'ai fait sa connaissance hier.	I met her/him yesterday.
être en contact avec [ɛtʀɑ̃kɔ̃takt]	to be in touch with
une **relation** [ʀ(ə)lasjɔ̃]	relationship (n)
entretenir des relations amicales avec qn	to have friendly relations with s.o.
des **rapports** *mpl* [ʀapɔʀ]	relations
avoir des rapports tendus avec qn	to have a tense relationship with s.o.

fréquenter qn [fʀekɑ̃te]	to visit s.o. frequently, socialize with s.o.
une **liaison** [ljɛzɔ̃]	connection, relationship
être attiré, **attirée par qn** [atiʀe]	to be attracted to s.o.
J'ai toujours été attiré par elle.	I have always been attracted to her.
charmer qn [ʃaʀme]	to charm s.o.
apprécier [apʀesje]	to appreciate

vouvoyer [vuvwaje]	to address in formal terms (i.e., using *vous*)
tutoyer [tytwaje]	to address in familiar terms (i.e., using *tu*)
On se vouvoie ou on se tutoie?	Shall we speak in formal or informal terms?
faire la bise à qn [fɛʀlabiz]	to give s.o. a kiss
serrer la main à qn [seʀelamɛ̃]	to shake hands with s.o.
être poli, **polie** [pɔli]	to be polite
être gentil, **gentille** [ʒɑ̃ti, ij]	to be nice
Sois gentil avec ta sœur.	Be nice to your sister.
l'**ambiance** *f* [ɑ̃bjɑ̃s]	mood, atmosphere
froid, **froide** [fʀwa, fʀwad]	cold
Pendant toute la réunion, l'ambiance a été froide.	There was a cold atmosphere during the whole meeting.
agréable [agʀeabl]	pleasant
tendu, tendue [tɑ̃dy]	tense
détendu, **détendue** [detɑ̃dy]	relaxed

sympa(**thique**) [sɛ̃pa(tik)]	nice, friendly
la **sympathie** [sɛ̃pati]	sympathy, affection
antipathique [ɑ̃tipatik]	disagreeable
Jean m'est très antipathique.	Jean is very disagreeable with me.
l'**antipathie** *f* [ɑ̃tipati]	dislike
Elle m'inspire une profonde antipathie.	She inspires deep dislike in me.

affectueux, **affectueuse** [afektyø, øz]	affectionate
l'**affection** *f* [afɛksjɔ̃]	affection
chaleureux, **chaleureuse** [ʃaløʀø, øz]	warm
un accueil chaleureux	warm welcome
cordial, **cordiale** [kɔʀdjal]	cordial
une atmosphère cordiale	cordial atmosphere
mépriser qn [mepʀize]	to scorn s.o.
le **mépris** [mepʀi]	scorn (n)
s'attirer le mépris de qn	to attract the scorn of s.o.
être hostile à qn [ɔstil]	to be hostile to s.o.
Tout le monde lui était hostile.	Everyone was hostile to him.
l'**hostilité** *f* [ɔstilite]	hostility

embrasser [ɑ̃bʀase]	to kiss
caresser [kaʀɛse]	to caress
courir après qn [kuʀiʀ]	to pursue, chase after s.o.
Pourquoi est-ce que tu cours encore après cette fille?	Why are you still chasing that girl?
draguer *fam* [dʀage]	to hit on, chat up
repousser [ʀ(ə)puse]	to reject

fidèle [fidɛl]	faithful
être fidèle à qn	to be faithful to s.o.
Elle est fidèle à ses amis.	She is faithful to her friends.
la **fidélité** [fidelite]	fidelity
l'**infidélité** *f* [ɛ̃fidelite]	infidelity
tromper qn [tʀɔ̃pe]	to deceive s.o.
décevoir qn [des(ə)vwaʀ]	to let s.o. down
la **déception** [desɛpsjɔ̃]	disappointment
jaloux, **jalouse** [ʒalu, uz]	jealous
être jaloux de qn/qc	to be jealous of s.o./s.th.
la **jalousie** [ʒaluzi]	jealousy
soupçonner qn [supsɔne]	to suspect s.o.
Je le soupçonne de me tromper.	I suspect that he is betraying me.
le **soupçon** [supsɔ̃]	suspicion
éveiller les soupçons de qn	to arouse s.o.'s suspicions

féliciter [felisite]	to congratulate
féliciter qn pour/de son travail	to congratulate s.o. on his/her work
un **compliment** [kɔ̃plimɑ̃]	compliment (n)
imiter [imite]	to imitate
l'**imitation** *f* [imitasjɔ̃]	imitation
se moquer de [s(ə)mɔke]	to make fun of, mock
faire marcher qn *fam* [fɛʀmaʀʃe]	to pull s.o.'s leg
Tu veux me faire marcher, ou quoi?	Are you pulling my leg or what?

aller* voir qn [alevwaʀ]	to visit s.o.
inviter à [ɛ̃vite]	to invite to
J'ai invité les Dupont à dîner.	I have invited the Duponts to dinner.
une **invitation** [ɛ̃vitasjɔ̃]	invitation
une **visite** [vizit]	visit (n)
rendre visite à qn	to visit s.o.
recevoir [ʀ(ə)səvwaʀ/ʀəs(ə)vwaʀ]	to receive
Dans cette grande maison, on peut recevoir beaucoup de monde.	We can host many people in this large house.

INFO

Visiting

aller/venis voir qn Cet(te) après-midi, on va voir notre tante. Venez me voir demain.	*to visit s.o.* *This afternoon we will visit our aunt.* *Come visit/see me tomorrow.*
rendre visite à qn Si vous le permettez, nous vous rendrons visite après-demain.	*to visit s.o., to pay s.o. a visit (more formally)* *With your permission, we will visit you the day after tomorrow.*
visiter qc Tu as déjà visité le Louvre?	*to visit s.th.* *Have you already visited the Louvre?*

la **compagnie** [kɔ̃paɲi]	company
accueillir qn [akœjiʀ]	to welcome s.o.
un **accueil** [akœj]	welcome (n), reception, hospitality
adopter qn [adɔpte]	to adopt s.o.
s'intéresser à [sɛ̃teʀese]	to be interested in
Il s'intéresse beaucoup à toi.	He is very interested in you.
concerné, **concernée** [kɔ̃sɛʀne]	concerned
se sentir concerné par un problème	to be concerned by a problem
s'ennuyer [sɑ̃nɥije]	to be bored
Qu'est-ce qu'on s'ennuie ici!	It is so boring here!
seul, **seule** [søl]	alone, lonely
Je me sens seul.	I feel lonely.
la **solitude** [sɔlityd]	solitude
retrouver qn [ʀ(ə)tʀuve]	to meet s.o. (again)
revoir qn [ʀ(ə)vwaʀ]	to see s.o. again
Ils ne se sont jamais revus.	They never saw each other again.
quitter qn [kite]	to leave s.o.
Ne me quitte pas!	Don't leave me!
perdre de vue [pɛʀdʀ(ə)dəvy]	to lose sight/track of
Après la fac, on s'est perdu de vue.	After college, we lost track of each other.

faire ses adieux *mpl* [fɛʀsezadjø]	to say good-bye
rompre avec qn [ʀɔ̃pʀ]	to break up with s.o.
Elle a rompu avec son fiancé.	She split up with her fiancé.
une **rupture** [ʀyptyʀ]	separation
les **retrouvailles** *fpl* [ʀ(ə)tʀuvaj]	reunion
On va fêter nos retrouvailles.	We are going to celebrate our getting back together.

attendre [atɑ̃dʀ]	to wait for
aller* chercher qn [aleʃɛʀʃe]	to pick s.o. up
On ira te chercher à la gare.	We will pick you up at the train station.
accompagner qn [akɔ̃paɲe]	to accompany s.o.
amener qn [am(ə)ne]	to bring s.o.
emmener qn [ɑ̃m(ə)ne]	to take s.o.
ramener qn [ʀam(ə)ne]	to bring s.o. back
Je l'ai ramené en voiture.	I brought him back home by car.

INFO

When you want to bring or take s.o./s.th.

Mener (*to lead*) and its composites (amener = *to bring/take along*, ramener = *to bring back, return*, emmener = *to take along*) are used especially with *persons*; porter (*to carry*) and its composites (apporter = *to bring*, rapporter = *to bring back*, emporter = *to take with/away*) are used mainly with *things* or when something *is being carried*.

Si tu veux, tu peux ***amener*** ton cousin.	*If you want you can bring your cousin along.*
Apporte-moi mes lunettes, s'il te plaît.	*Bring me my glasses, please.*
Vous pourriez m'***emmener*** à l'aéroport?	*Could you take me to the airport?*
une pizza à ***emporter***	*one pizza to take out*

fort, **forte** [fɔʀ, fɔʀt]	strong
la **force** [fɔʀs]	strength
faible [fɛbl]	weak
la **faiblesse** [fɛblɛs]	weakness
patient, **patiente** [pasjɑ̃, jɑ̃t]	patient (adj)
Elle ne s'énerve jamais, elle est très patiente.	She never gets irritated; she is very patient.
la **patience** [pasjɑ̃s]	patience
impatient, **impatiente** [ɛ̃pasjɑ̃, jɑ̃t]	impatient
l'**impatience** *f* [ɛ̃pasjɑ̃s]	impatience

regretter [ʀ(ə)gʀete]	to regret
Nous regrettons de l'avoir laissé partir.	We are sorry we let him leave.
le **regret** [ʀ(ə)gʀɛ]	regret (n)
gaffer *fam* [gafe]	to blunder
faire une gaffe *fam* [fɛʀyngaf]	to make a blunder
faire de la peine à qn [fɛʀd(ə)lapɛn]	to cause s.o. grief
Tu me fais de la peine.	You give me grief.
humilier qn [ymilje]	to humiliate s.o.
une **humiliation** [ymiljasjɔ̃]	humiliation
subir une humiliation	to suffer humiliation
vexer qn [vɛkse]	to offend, bother s.o.
Elle est **vexée pour un oui ou pour un non.**	She is bothered by every trifle.
gêner qn [ʒene]	to embarrass/perplex s.o.
calmer qn [kalme]	to calm s.o.
J'ai eu du mal à la calmer.	I had difficulty calming her.
consoler qn [kɔ̃sɔle]	to comfort, console s.o.
la **consolation** [kɔ̃sɔlasjɔ̃]	consolation
s'énerver [senɛʀve]	to get worked up
Ne t'énerve pas pour ça!	Don't get worked up over that!
se fâcher [s(ə)fɑʃe]	to get angry
se fâcher tout rouge	to become furious
furieux, **furieuse** [fyʀjø, øz]	furious
récompenser [ʀekɔ̃pɑ̃se]	to reward
une **récompense** [ʀekɔ̃pɑ̃s]	reward (n)
punir [pyniʀ]	to punish
se faire punir	to be punished
la **punition** [pynisjɔ̃]	punishment
contraindre qn à [kɔ̃tʀɛ̃dʀ]	to force s.o. to
Tu ne pourras pas l'y contraindre.	You can't force him to do it.
la **contrainte** [kɔ̃tʀɛ̃t]	coercion
dominer qn [dɔmine]	to dominate s.o.
la **domination** [dɔminasjɔ̃]	domination
priver qn de qc [pʀive]	to deprive s.o. of s.th.; to withhold s.th. from s.o.
Si tu continues, tu seras **privé de dessert**.	If you keep that up, you won't get any dessert.
poursuivre qn [puʀsɥivʀ]	to pursue, hound s.o.
poursuivre qn en justice	to institute proceedings against s.o./to sue s.o.

reprocher qc à qn [ʀ(ə)pʀɔʃe]	to reproach s.o. for s.th.
Je lui reproche beaucoup son attitude.	I certainly reproach him for his attitude.
Je te reproche de ne penser qu'à toi.	I reproach you for thinking only of yourself.
un **reproche** [ʀ(ə)pʀɔʃ]	reproach (n)
se disputer avec qn [s(ə)dispyte]	to argue with s.o.
une **dispute** [dispyt]	argument
une **querelle** [kəʀɛl]	quarrel (n)
traiter qn de qc/comme qc [tʀɛte]	to treat s.o. like s.th.
Ils l'ont traité d'imbécile.	They treated him like an imbecile.
faire une scène à qn [fɛʀynsɛn]	to make a scene in front of s.o.
se réconcilier avec [s(ə)ʀekɔ̃silje]	to reconcile with
la **réconciliation** [ʀekɔ̃siljasjɔ̃]	reconciliation
la **réconciliation franco-allemande**	the German-French reconciliation
s'arranger avec [saʀɑ̃ʒe]	to agree, compromise with
la **chance** [ʃɑ̃s]	luck *(See Information Box p. 144)*
Tu as de la chance d'avoir du travail.	You are lucky to have work.
avoir la chance de faire qc	to have the luck to do s.th.
Bonne chance!	Good luck!
avoir du succès [avwaʀdysyksɛ]	to experience success
la **malchance** [malʃɑ̃s]	bad luck
être poursuivi par la malchance	to be hounded by bad luck
être bien/mal avec qn [ɛtʀbjɛ̃/mal]	to get along well/badly with s.o.
Il vaut mieux être bien avec son chef.	It's better to be on good terms with your boss.
frapper [fʀape]	to strike
battre [batʀ]	to beat
un **coup** [ku]	a blow
un **coup de pied**	a kick
un **coup de poing**	a punch
gifler qn [ʒifle]	to slap s.o.
une **gifle** [ʒifl]	slap (n)
provoquer qn [pʀɔvɔke]	to provoke s.o.
une **provocation** [pʀɔvɔkasjɔ̃]	provocation

le **bien-être** *sans pl* [bjɛ̃nɛtʀ]	well-being
être à l'aise [ɛtʀalɛz]	to feel comfortable, be at ease
s'épanouir [sepanwiʀ]	to blossom, achieve one's potential
Elle s'épanouit de jour en jour.	She blossoms more from day to day.
le **prestige** [pʀɛstiʒ]	prestige
jouir d'un grand prestige auprès de qn	to enjoy high prestige with s.o.

7.6 Possession and Ownership  30

avoir [avwaʀ]	to have
Nous avons une maison en Bretagne.	We have a house in Brittany.
appartenir à qn [apaʀtəniʀ]	to belong to s.o.
Ce sac ne m'appartient pas.	This bag is not mine.
À qui est …? [akiɛ]	Whose is…?
À qui sont ces gants?	Whose gloves are these?
être à qn [ɛtʀ]	to belong to s.o.
être à (moi; toi; lui, elle; nous; vous; eux, elles)	to be (mine; yours; his; hers; ours; yours; theirs)
N'y touche pas. **C'est à moi.**	Don't touch. That's mine.
posséder [pɔsede]	to possess
la **possession** [pɔsesjɔ̃]	possession
prendre possession de qc	to take possession of s.th.
propre [pʀɔpʀ]	own (adj) *(See Information Box p. 44)*
C'est son propre appartement.	That is his own apartment.
un, une **propriétaire** [pʀɔpʀijetɛʀ]	owner
la **propriété** [pʀɔpʀijete]	property
Propriété privée.	Private property.
être le/la/les … **de qn** [ɛtʀlə/la/le]	to be s.o.'s...
C'est la voiture de Marcel.	That is Marcel's car.

disposer de qc [dispɔze]	to have s.th.
Il dispose d'une petite fortune.	He has a small fortune.
détenir [det(ə)niʀ]	to own
le(s) **bien(s)** *m(pl)* [bjɛ̃]	belongings, estate
Elle a donné tous ses biens à l'Église.	She gave her entire estate to the church.
prospère [pʀɔspɛʀ]	prosperous
une entreprise prospère	a prosperous business
la **prospérité** [pʀɔspeʀite]	prosperity

acquérir qc [akeʀiʀ]	to acquire s.th.
une **acquisition** [akizisjɔ̃]	acquisition
Ce Picasso, c'est sa **dernière acquisition**.	This Picasso is his most recent acquisition.
un **placement** [plasmɑ̃]	investment
faire un bon placement	to make a good investment
une **action** [aksjɔ̃]	share (n)

le **testament** [tɛstamɑ̃]	(final) will (n)
coucher qn sur son testament	to name s.o. in one's will
hériter [eʀite]	to inherit
hériter de qn	to inherit from s.o.
hériter (**de**) **qc**	to inherit s.th.
l'**héritage** *m* [eʀitaʒ]	inheritance
faire un bel héritage	to get a good inheritance
un **héritier**, une **héritière** [eʀitje, jɛʀ]	heir, heiress
le **patrimoine** [patʀimwan]	estate, wealth
sauvegarder le patrimoine	to conserve the estate

My Vocabulary

8

Education and Training

8.1 Education  31

élever [el(ə)ve]	to raise
éduquer [edyke]	to bring up, raise
l'**éducation** *f* [edykasjɔ̃]	education
un **éducateur**, une **éducatrice** [edykatœʀ, tʀis]	educator

cultivé, **cultivée** [kyltive]	cultured
la **culture** [kyltyʀ]	culture
la **culture générale**	general education
former qn [fɔʀme]	to train s.o.
la **formation** [fɔʀmasjɔ̃]	training (n)
la **formation continue**	continuing education
la **formation permanente**	continuing education

instruit, **instruite** [ɛ̃stʀɥi, it]	educated, literate
l'**instruction** *f* [ɛ̃stʀyksjɔ̃]	instruction, knowledge
Elle **a de l'instruction.**	She has sound knowledge.

enseigner qc à qn [ɑ̃seɲe]	to teach s.th. to s.o.
J'enseigne le japonais à des adultes.	I teach Japanese to adults.
l'**enseignement** *m* [ɑ̃sɛɲ(ə)mɑ̃]	instruction
l'**enseignement primaire**	primary education
l'**enseignement secondaire**	secondary education
l'**enseignement supérieur**	higher education
un **enseignant**, une **enseignante** [ɑ̃sɛɲɑ̃, ɑ̃t]	teacher

savoir [savwaʀ]	to know (how), be able *(See Information Box p. 450)*
Cet enfant sait beaucoup de choses.	This child knows many things.
le **savoir** [savwaʀ]	knowledge
connaître [kɔnɛtʀ]	to know, be familiar
Je n'y connais rien.	I don't know anything about it.
les **connaissances** *fpl* [kɔnɛsɑ̃s]	knowledge
ignorer [iɲɔʀe]	to not know, to be unaware

le **talent** [talɑ̃]	talent
être doué, douée (**pour**) [due]	to be gifted (in)
Elles sont douées pour le dessin.	They are gifted in drawing.
le **don** [dɔ̃]	gift
avoir un don pour les langues	to have a gift for languages
être fort, forte/faible en [fɔʀ, fɔʀt/fɛbl],	to be strong/weak in
la **mémoire** [memwaʀ]	memory

un **but** [byt]	goal
poursuivre un but	to pursue a goal
motiver [mɔtive]	to motivate
la **motivation** [mɔtivasjɔ̃]	motivation
se concentrer [s(ə)kɔ̃sɑ̃tʀe]	to concentrate
la **concentration** [kɔ̃sɑ̃tʀasjɔ̃]	concentration
l'**attention** *f* [atɑ̃sjɔ̃]	attention, attentiveness
faire attention à qc	to pay attention to s.th.
être attentif, **attentive** [atɑ̃tif, iv]	to be attentive
Elle n'est pas attentive en classe.	She is not attentive in class.
faire des progrès *mpl* [fɛʀdepʀɔgʀɛ]	to make progress
Ma fille a fait des progrès en maths.	My daughter has made some progress in math.

apprendre qc à qn [apʀɑ̃dʀ]	to teach s.th. to s.o.
Elle a appris le violon à tous ses enfants.	She taught violin to all her children.
paresseux, **paresseuse** [paʀesø, øz]	lazy
la **paresse** [paʀɛs]	laziness
travailleur, **travailleuse** [tʀavajœʀ, jøz]	industrious, diligent, hardworking
appliqué, **appliquée** [aplike]	diligent
comprendre [kɔ̃pʀɑ̃dʀ]	to understand
la **compréhension** [kɔ̃pʀeɑ̃sjɔ̃]	understanding (n)

autoritaire [ɔtɔʀitɛʀ]	authoritarian
l'**autorité** *f* [ɔtɔʀite]	authority
exercer son autorité sur qn	to wield one's authority over s.o.
sévère [sevɛʀ]	harsh
la **discipline** [disiplin]	discipline
refuser de **se plier à la discipline**	to refuse to submit to discipline

servir de modèle à [sɛRviRdəmɔdɛl]	to serve as a model for
récompenser qn de qc [Rekɔ̃pɑ̃se]	to compensate s.o. for s.th.
une **récompense** [Rekɔ̃pɑ̃s]	compensation
indulgent, **indulgente** [ɛ̃dylʒɑ̃, ɑ̃t]	indulgent
l'**indulgence** *f* [ɛ̃dylʒɑ̃s]	indulgence
faire preuve d'indulgence	to exercise leniency
exiger qc de qn [egziʒe]	to demand/require s.th. of s.o.
J'exige de toi que tu fasses un effort.	I insist that you make an effort.
être exigeant, **exigeante** [egziʒɑ̃, ɑ̃t]	to be demanding
obéir à [ɔbeiR]	to obey
obéir à un ordre	to obey an order
punir [pyniR]	to punish
une **punition** [pynisjɔ̃]	punishment

8.2 Teaching, School  32

une **école** [ekɔl]	school
une **école publique**	public school
une **école privée**	private school
une **école primaire/élémentaire**	primary/elementary school
une **école mixte**	co-ed school
un **écolier**, une **écolière** [ekɔlje, jɛR]	pupil

le **système éducatif** [sistɛmedykatif]	education system
le **système scolaire** [sistɛmskɔlɛR]	school system
la **scolarité** [skɔlaRite]	schooling
la **scolarité obligatoire**	compulsory education
une **année scolaire** [aneskɔlɛR]	school year
la **rentrée** (**des classes**) [Rɑ̃tRe(deklas)]	beginning of the academic year
les **fournitures scolaires** *fpl* [fuRnityRskɔlɛR]	school supplies

le **jardin d'enfants** [ʒaRdɛ̃dɑ̃fɑ̃]	kindergarten, preschool
l'**école maternelle** / la **maternelle** [(ekɔl)matɛRnɛl]	kindergarten
le **CP** (**cours préparatoire**) [sepe]	1st grade
le **CE1** (**cours élémentaire première année**) [seeœ̃]	2nd grade
le **CE2** (**cours élémentaire deuxième année**) [seedø]	3rd grade
le **CM1** (**cours moyen première année**) [seɛmœ̃]	4th grade
le **CM2** (**cours moyen deuxième année**) [seɛmdø]	5th grade

le **collège** [kɔlɛʒ]	middle school, junior high school
le **lycée** [lise]	high school
le **lycée professionnel** (**LP**)	vocational high school
un **lycéen**, une **lycéenne** [liseɛ̃, ɛn]	secondary-school student
une **école de commerce** [ekɔldəkɔmɛʀs]	business school
un **établissement d'éducation spécialisée** [etablismɑ̃dedykasjɔ̃spesjalize]	special education institution
un **centre de formation professionnelle** [sɑ̃tʀdəfɔʀmasjɔ̃pʀɔfɛsjɔnɛl]	vocational training center
un **internat** [ɛ̃tɛʀna]	boarding school
être en pension [ɛtʀɑ̃pɑ̃sjɔ̃]	to be in boarding school
un, une **professeur** [pʀɔfesœʀ]	teacher, professor
un, une **professeur des écoles**	elementary school teacher
un, une **prof** *fam* [pʀɔf]	teacher, prof(essor)
un **instituteur**, une **institutrice** *vx* [ɛ̃stitytœʀ, tʀis]	elementary school teacher
un, une **instit** *vx, fam* [ɛ̃stit]	elementary school teacher
un **proviseur** [pʀɔvizœʀ]	principal *(high school)*
un **principal**, une **principale** [pʀɛ̃sipal]	principal *(middle school)*
surveiller [syʀvɛje]	to oversee
un **surveillant**, une **surveillante** [syʀvɛjɑ̃, jɑ̃t]	supervisor, chaperone
un **pion**, une **pionne** *fam* [pjɔ̃, pjɔn]	supervisor
un, une **élève** [elɛv]	student
une **classe** [klɑs]	class
une salle (de classe)	classroom
Les Français **ont classe** l'après-midi aussi.	The French have classes in the afternoons too.
passer dans la classe supérieure	to move up to the next grade
redoubler (**une classe**)	to repeat (a grade)
un **échange** (**scolaire**) [eʃɑ̃ʒ(skɔlɛʀ)]	student exchange
Les enfants sont partis à Nîmes **en échange scolaire**.	The children have gone to Nîmes on a student exchange.
un **correspondant**, une **correspondante** [kɔʀɛspɔ̃dɑ̃, ɑ̃t]	pen pal

un, une **analphabète** [analfabɛt]	illiterate person
un **cancre** *fam* [kɑ̃kʀ]	slacker, dunce
tricher [tʀiʃe]	to cheat
faire l'école buissonnière [fɜʀlekɔlbɥisɔnjɛʀ]	to play hooky
sécher un cours *fam* [seʃeɛ̃kuʀ]	to skip a class
la **retenue** [ʀət(ə)ny/ʀ(ə)təny]	detention
une (**heure de**) **colle** *fam* [(œʀdə)kɔl]	(an hour of) detention
Le prof m'a donné une heure de colle.	The teacher gave me an hour of detention.

présent, **présente** [pʀezɑ̃, ɑ̃t]	present (adj)
la **présence** [pʀezɑ̃s]	presence
absent, **absente** [absɑ̃, ɑ̃t]	absent
l'**absence** *f* [absɑ̃s]	absence
En cas d'absence, il faut apporter un mot d'excuse.	In case of absence, a sick note is required.

réussir (**à faire**) **qc** [ʀeysiʀ]	to succeed (in doing s.th.)
réussir un contrôle	to do well on a test
Il **réussit dans tout** ce qu'il entreprend.	He succeeds at everything he undertakes.
Tu ne réussiras pas à me convaincre.	You will not succeed in convincing me.
la **réussite** [ʀeɥsit]	success
échouer à qc [eʃue]	to fail at s.th.
échouer à un examen	to fail an exam
un **échec** [eʃɛk]	failure
rater qc [ʀate]	to fail s.th., miss s.th.
le **baccalauréat** [bakalɔʀea]	baccalaureate (secondary-school leaving exam)
le **bac** *fam* [bak]	French baccalaureate
passer le bac	to take the baccalaureate exam

le **brevet** (**des collèges**) [bʀəvɛ]	diploma
Elle a été **reçue au brevet**.	She got her diploma.
le **BEP** (**brevet d'études professionnelles**) [beəpe]	diploma in a vocational secondary school
le **CAP** (**certificat d'aptitude professionnelle**) [seape]	*roughly equivalent to an apprenticeship diploma*

les **devoirs** *mpl* [dəvwaʀ]	homework
Fais tes devoirs.	Do your homework.
un **exercice** [egzɛʀsis]	exercise (n)
une **difficulté** [difikylte]	difficulty
un texte **bourré de difficultés**	a text crammed with difficulties
une **question** [kɛstjɔ̃]	question (n)
poser une question à qn	to ask s.o. a question
répondre à une question	to answer a question
interroger [inteʀɔʒe]	to ask
une **interrogation** (**écrite**) [inteʀɔgasjɔ̃(ekʀit)]	(written) test
une **interro** *fam* [ɛ̃teʀo]	test (n)
J'ai raté l'interro d'anglais.	I flunked the English test.
une **composition** [kɔ̃pozisjɔ̃]	essay
un **contrôle** [kɔ̃tʀol]	test (n)
noter [nɔte]	to grade
Ce prof note sévèrement.	This teacher is a hard grader.
une **note** [nɔt]	grade (n)
le **bulletin scolaire** [byltɛ̃skɔlɛʀ]	report card
un **résultat** [ʀezylta]	result
le **niveau**; les **niveaux** *pl* [nivo]	level (n)
Le niveau de la classe est lamentable.	The level of the class is pathetic.
la **moyenne** [mwajɛn]	average (n)
Il n'**aura** pas **la moyenne en** anglais.	He will not pass in English.
une **dictée** [dikte]	dictation
l'**orthographe** *f* [ɔʀtɔgʀaf]	spelling
faux, **fausse** [fo, fos]	false
une **faute** [fot]	error, mistake (n)
Ta dictée est pleine de **fautes d'orthographe**.	Your dictation is filled with spelling errors.
correct, **correcte** [kɔʀɛkt]	correct, right
le **corrigé** [kɔʀiʒe]	answer key, correction
le **vocabulaire** [vɔkabylɛʀ]	vocabulary; dictionary
avoir un vocabulaire riche/pauvre	to have a rich/weak vocabulary
un **mot** [mo]	word
employer le mot juste	to use the right word
l'**usage** *m* [yzaʒ]	usage
la **grammaire** [gʀamɛʀ]	grammar

parler [parle]	to speak
une **expression** [ɛkspresjɔ̃]	expression
l'expression orale/écrite	oral/written expression
le **langage** [lɑ̃gaʒ]	language
La grammaire définit les règles du langage.	Grammar defines the rules of a language.
la **langue** [lɑ̃g]	language
la **langue des jeunes**	language of youth
le **niveau de langue**	language level
familier, **familière** [familje, ljɛr]	familiar
populaire [pɔpylɛr]	popular, common
une **expression familière/populaire**	familiar/popular expression
littéraire [literɛr]	literary
utiliser la langue littéraire	to use literary language

écrire [ekrir]	to write
Ça s'écrit comment?	How do you write/spell that?
donner sa réponse **par écrit**	to answer in writing
l'**écriture** *f* [ekrityr]	writing (n)
prendre des notes *fpl* [prɑ̃drdenɔt]	to take notes

le **cours** [kur]	course, class
suivre un **cours de géographie**	to take a geography course
copier qc (**sur qn**) [kɔpje]	to copy s.th. (from s.o.)
Elle a copié sur sa voisine.	She copied from her neighbor.
recopier [r(ə)kɔpje]	to copy
la **copie** [kɔpi]	paper, exercise, class work

INFO

Cour(s/t, e/se/ses)

la cour **[kur]**	*courtyard*
le cours **[kur]**	*course, class, course of a river*
le court (de tennis) **[kur]**	*(tennis) court*
la course **[kurs]**	*race, running*
les courses **[kurs]**	*shopping, errands*
court, courte **[kur, kurt]**	*short*

lire [liʀ]	to read
la **lecture** [lɛktyʀ]	reading (n)
un **livre** [livʀ]	book
un **bouquin** *fam* [bukɛ̃]	light novel
un **manuel** (**scolaire**) [manɥɛl(skɔlɛʀ)]	text(book)
un **dictionnaire** [diksjɔnɛʀ]	dictionary
un **dictionnaire unilingue**	monolingual dictionary
un **dictionnaire bilingue**	bilingual dictionary
une **lettre** [lɛtʀ]	letter
une **page** [paʒ]	page
un **chapitre** [ʃapitʀ]	chapter
la **table des matières** [tabl(ə)dematjɛʀ]	table of contents
une **bibliothèque** [biblijɔtɛk]	library

expliquer [ɛksplike]	to explain
une **explication** [ɛksplikasjɔ̃]	explanation
un **texte** [tɛkst]	text
compréhensible [kɔ̃pʀeɑ̃sibl]	understandable
incompréhensible [ɛ̃kɔ̃pʀeɑ̃sibl]	unintelligible

décrire qc [dekʀiʀ]	to describe s.th.
une **description** [dɛskʀipsjɔ̃]	description
faire une description réaliste de qc	to describe s.th. realistically
définir [definiʀ]	to define
une **définition** [definisjɔ̃]	definition

résumer [ʀezyme]	to summarize
un **résumé** [ʀezyme]	summary
faire un **bref résumé** de l'action	to briefly summarize the plot
commenter [kɔmɑ̃te]	to comment
un **commentaire** [kɔmɑ̃tɛʀ]	commentary

un **exposé** [ɛkspoze]	paper, report (n)
une **dissertation** [disɛʀtasjɔ̃]	dissertation
rédiger une dissertation	to write a dissertation
une **rédaction** [ʀedaksjɔ̃]	essay, composition
un **brouillon** [bʀujɔ̃]	rough draft, outline

discuter de qc [diskyte]	to discuss s.th.
une **discussion** [diskysjɔ̃]	discussion
engager la discussion	to open the discussion
un **débat** [deba]	debate (n)
mener un débat	to conduct a debate

une **leçon** [l(ə)sɔ̃]	lesson
réciter [ʀesite]	to recite
réciter un poème à son père	to recite a poem to one's father
par cœur [paʀkœʀ]	by heart
apprendre une poésie par cœur	to learn a poem by heart
retenir qc [ʀ(ə)təniʀ/ʀət(ə)niʀ]	to remember, memorize s.th.
oublier [ublije]	to forget

traduire [tʀadɥiʀ]	to translate
traduire en français	to translate into French
une **traduction** [tʀadyksjɔ̃]	translation
un **traducteur**, une **traductrice** [tʀadyktœʀ, tʀis]	translator
signifier [siɲifje]	to mean
Que signifie «die Sonne» en français?	How do you say *the sun* in French?
la **signification** [siɲifikasjɔ̃]	meaning (n)

un **chiffre** [ʃifʀ]	number, numeral
un **nombre** [nɔ̃bʀ]	number
compter [kɔ̃te]	to count
compter jusqu'à 100	to count up to 100
calculer [kalkyle]	to calculate
calculer mentalement	to calculate mentally

un **problème** [pʀɔblɛm]	problem
un **problème de maths**	a math problem
résoudre [ʀezudʀ]	to solve
une **solution** [sɔlysjɔ̃]	solution
prouver [pʀuve]	to prove
une **preuve** [pʀœv]	proof
apporter la preuve que la terre tourne autour du soleil	to provide evidence that the earth rotates around the sun

une **image** [imaʒ]	picture, image
dessiner [desine]	to draw
dessiner qc **au crayon**	to draw s.th. in pencil
un **dessin** [desɛ̃]	drawing (n)
les **ciseaux** *mpl* [sizo]	scissors *(See Information Box p. 46)*
le **scotch®** [skɔtʃ]	cellophane tape

un **cahier** [kaje]	notebook
un **classeur** [klasœʀ]	(loose-leaf) binder
une **feuille** [fœj]	paper
une **feuille de papier**	sheet of paper
un **cartable** [kaʀtabl]	school bag
une **serviette** [sɛʀvjɛt]	briefcase

une **trousse** [tʀus]	pencil case
un **stylo** [stilo]	pen
écrire **au stylo**	to write in pen
un **stylo** (**à**) **bille**	ballpoint pen
un **stylo** (**à**) **plume**	fountain pen
l'**encre** *f* [ɑ̃kʀ]	ink
une **cartouche** [kaʀtuʃ]	cartridge
un **crayon** [kʀɛjɔ̃]	pencil
des **crayons de couleur**	colored pencils
un **taille-crayon** [tajkʀɛjɔ̃]	pencil sharpener *(See Information Box p. 104)*
une **gomme** [gɔm]	eraser
une **règle** [ʀɛgl]	ruler
une **équerre** [ekɛʀ]	square (i.e., the tool)
un **rapporteur** [ʀapɔʀtœʀ]	protractor
un **compas** [kɔ̃pa]	compass
tracer un cercle au compas	to draw a circle with a compass
un **tableau** (**noir**); des **tableaux** (**noirs**) *pl* [tablo(nwaʀ)]	(black)board
effacer le tableau	to erase the blackboard
la **craie** [kʀɛ]	chalk
une **éponge** [epɔ̃ʒ]	sponge
un **tableau blanc interactif**; des **tableaux blancs interactifs** *pl* [tabloblɑ̃ɛ̃tɛʀaktif]	whiteboard
le **programme** [pʀɔgʀam]	syllabus
Le **programme d'histoire** est très dense.	The history syllabus is very full.
une **matière** [matjɛʀ]	subject
une **matière principale**	major subject
une **matière obligatoire**	required course
une **matière facultative**	elective course
choisir une matière en option	to choose an elective
l'**emploi du temps** *m* [ɑ̃plwadytɑ̃]	course schedule
un emploi du temps chargé	full course schedule
la **récréation** [ʀekʀeasjɔ̃]	break, recess
la **récré** *fam* [ʀekʀe]	break, recess
la **cour de récré**	playground, schoolyard
la **cantine** [kɑ̃tin]	cafeteria
aller* en étude/permanence/perm *fam* [aleɑ̃netyd/pɛʀm(anɑ̃s)]	to be on detention

les **mathématiques** *fpl* [matematik]	mathematics
les **maths** *fpl fam* [mat]	math
l'**algèbre** *f* [alʒɛbʀ]	algebra
la **géométrie** [ʒeɔmetʀi]	geometry
une **calculette** [kalkylɛt]	calculator
l'**informatique** *f* [ɛ̃fɔʀmatik]	computer science
une **opération** [ɔpeʀasjɔ̃]	operation; mathematical procedure
les quatre **opérations fondamentales**	the four basic operations
additionner [adisjɔne]	to add
une **addition** [adisjɔ̃]	sum, addition
soustraire [sustʀɛʀ]	to subtract
une **soustraction** [sustʀaksjɔ̃]	subtraction
multiplier [myltiplije]	to multiply
multiplier par 3	to multiply by 3
une **multiplication** [myltiplikasjɔ̃]	multiplication
la **table de multiplication**	multiplication table
diviser [divize]	to divide
On ne peut pas **diviser par** 0.	Division by 0 is not possible.
une **division** [divizjɔ̃]	division
la **physique** [fizik]	physics
la **chimie** [ʃimi]	chemistry
les **SVT** *fpl* (**Sciences de la Vie et de la Terre**) [ɛsvete]	natural sciences (biology, geology, astronomy)
la **biologie** [bjɔlɔʒi]	biology
la **technologie** [tɛknɔlɔʒi]	technology
une **langue** [lɑ̃g]	language
la **langue maternelle**	native language
une **langue étrangère**	foreign language
le **français** [fʀɑ̃sɛ]	French *(See Information Box p. 20)*
l'**anglais** *m* [ɑ̃glɛ]	English
l'**allemand** *m* [almɑ̃]	German
l'**espagnol** *m* [ɛspaɲɔl]	Spanish
l'**italien** *m* [italjɛ̃]	Italian
le **latin** [latɛ̃]	Latin
le **grec** [gʀɛk]	Greek
l'**histoire** *f* [istwaʀ]	history
l'**Histoire de France**	history of France
la **géographie** [ʒeɔgʀafi]	geography
l'**histoire-géo** *f fam* [istwaʀʒeo]	social studies
l'**instruction civique** *f* [ɛ̃stʀyksjɔ̃sivik]	civics
la **philosophie** [filɔzɔfi]	philosophy

la **musique** [myzik]	music
l'**éducation musicale** *f* [edykasjɔ̃myzikal]	music education
l'**éducation artistique** *f* [edykasjɔ̃aʀtistik]	(graphic) art
les **arts plastiques** *mpl* [aʀplastik]	fine arts
les **travaux manuels** *mpl* [tʀavomanɥɛl]	tech(nical) studies

l'**EPS** *f* (**éducation physique et sportive**) [əpeɛs]	physical education
la **gymnastique** [ʒimnastik]	gymnastics
la **gym** *fam* [ʒim]	gymnastics

8.3 University, Science, and Research  33

l'**université** *f* [yniveʀsite]	university
la **faculté** [fakylte]	school, university
la **fac** *fam* [fak]	university
la **fac**(**ulté**) **des lettres**	faculty of arts
la **fac**(**ulté**) **des sciences**	faculty of sciences
la **fac**(**ulté**) **de droit**	faculty of law
une **grande école** [gʀɑ̃dekɔl]	(elite) college
une **classe préparatoire** [klaspʀepaʀatwaʀ]	preparatory studies (for an elite school)
une **prépa** *fam* [pʀepa]	prep school

s'inscrire [sɛ̃skʀiʀ]	to register, matriculate, enroll
Julien s'est inscrit en fac(ulté) de médecine.	Julien enrolled in medical school.
l'**inscription** *f* [ɛ̃skʀipsjɔ̃]	matriculation, registration
l'**École des Beaux-Arts** *f* [ekɔldebozaʀ]	fine arts academy
les **Beaux-Arts** *mpl* [bozaʀ]	fine arts academy
un **IUT** (**Institut universitaire de Technologie**) [iyte]	technical college
l'**université populaire** *f* [univeʀsitepɔpylɛʀ]	community college

scientifique [sjɑ̃tifik]	scientific
un, une **scientifique**	scientist
la **science** [sjɑ̃s]	science
les **sciences humaines**	humanities
les **sciences naturelles**	natural sciences
les **sciences économiques**	economics
les **sciences politiques**	political science
le **progrès** [pʀɔgʀɛ]	progress
la **recherche** [ʀəʃɛʀʃ]	research
faire de la recherche	to conduct research
un **centre de recherche**	research center
un **chercheur**, une **chercheuse** [ʃɛʀʃœʀ, øz]	researcher
un **savant**, une **savante** [savɑ̃, ɑ̃t]	scientist, researcher, academic

la **recherche fondamentale** [ʀəʃɛʀʃfɔ̃damɑ̃tal]	basic research
le **CNRS** (**Centre national de la recherche scientifique**) [seɛnɛʀɛs]	national research center
la **biochimie** [bjɔʃimi]	biochemistry
une **réaction chimique** [ʀeaksjɔ̃ʃimik]	chemical reaction
une **réaction en chaîne** [ʀeaksjɔ̃ɑ̃ʃɛn]	chain reaction
la **classification** [klasifikasjɔ̃]	classification
la classification périodique des éléments	periodic table of elements
cellulaire [selylɛʀ]	cellular
la **biologie cellulaire**	cellular biology
la **cellule** [selyl]	cell
le **gène** [ʒɛn]	gene
la **génétique** [ʒenetik]	genetic
le **génie génétique** [ʒeniʒenetik]	genetic engineering
les **manipulations génétiques** *fpl* [manipylasjɔ̃]	gene modification

une **théorie** [teɔʀi]	theory
expérimental, **expérimentale** [ɛkspeʀimɑ̃tal]	experimental
une **expérience** [ɛkspeʀjɑ̃s]	experiment (n)
un **laboratoire** [labɔʀatwaʀ]	laboratory
un **labo** *fam* [labo]	lab
vérifier [veʀifje]	to verify, validate, prove
démontrer [demɔ̃tʀe]	to demonstrate
Je vais **te démontrer par a + b** que j'ai raison.	I am going to show you in black and white that I am right.
une **démonstration** [demɔ̃stʀasjɔ̃]	demonstration, proof

INFO

No experiments!

The French word *expérience* translates into several meanings in English:

une expérience	*1. experiment, trial; 2. experience*
faire/se livrer à des expériences	*to experiment, conduct experiments*
avoir de l'expérience	*to have experience*
par expérience	*through experience*
expérimenter	*to experiment*
expérimenter un nouveau procédé	*to test a new procedure*

---

inventer [ɛ̃vɑ̃te]	to invent
une **invention** [ɛ̃vɑ̃sjɔ̃]	invention
un **inventeur**, une **inventrice** [ɛ̃vɑ̃tœʀ, tʀis]	inventor
découvrir [dekuvʀiʀ]	to discover
une **découverte** [dekuvɛʀt]	discovery
la **médecine** [med(ə)sin]	medicine
la **médecine générale**	general practice
la **médecine dentaire**	dental medicine
la **médecine vétérinaire**	veterinary medicine
la **biologie** [bjɔlɔʒi]	biology
un, une **biologiste** [bjɔlɔʒist]	biologist
un, une **chimiste** [ʃimist]	chemist
la **psychologie** [psikɔlɔʒi]	psychology
un **mathématicien**, une **mathématicienne** [matematisjɛ̃, jɛn]	mathematician
un **physicien**, une **physicienne** [fizisjɛ̃, jɛn]	physician
étudier [etydje]	to study
étudier le droit	to study law
les **études** *fpl* [etyd]	studies
faire des études de médecine	to study medicine
un **étudiant**, une **étudiante** [etydjɑ̃, jɑ̃t]	student
un étudiant **en lettres**	student of language and literature, liberal arts student

une **chaire** [ʃɛʀ]	chair, professorship
un **assistant**, une **assistante** [asistɑ̃, ɑ̃t]	assistant
un **cours magistral** [kuʀmaʒistʀal]	lecture, course
les **travaux pratiques** (**TP**) *mpl* [tʀavopʀatik (tepe)]	practical work
les **travaux dirigés** (**TD**) *mpl* [tʀavodiʀiʒe (tede)]	tutorials, workshops
un **cours par correspondance** [kuʀpaʀkɔʀɛspɔ̃dɑ̃s]	correspondence course
un **cours du soir** [kuʀdyswaʀ]	evening course
suivre un cours du soir	to take a night class

un **candidat**, une **candidate** [kɑ̃dida, at]	candidate
être candidat à un examen	to be a candidate for an exam
un **examen** [ɛgzamɛ̃]	exam
passer/réussir un examen	to take/pass an exam
un **concours** [kɔ̃kuʀ]	competition
se préparer à un concours/à un examen	to prepare for a competition/exam
être reçu à un concours/un examen	to pass in a competition/entrance exam
un **certificat** [sɛʀtifika]	certificate, diploma
un **diplôme** [diplom]	degree, diploma

une **UV** (**unité de valeur**) [yve]	credit (n)
un **DEUG** (**diplôme d'études universitaires générales**) [dœg]	(general 2-year university diploma)
Il me manque encore trois UV pour avoir le DEUG.	I need just three more credits to get my diploma.
la **licence** [lisɑ̃s]	degree
faire une **licence d'anglais**	to take a degree in English
la **maîtrise** [mɛtʀiz]	master's degree
passer sa maîtrise	to do a master's

une **cité universitaire** [siteynivɛʀsitɛʀ]	university campus
une **cité U** *fam* [sitey]	campus
le **restaurant universitaire** [ʀɛstɔʀɑ̃ynivɛʀsitɛʀ]	commons, dining hall
le **resto U** *fam* [ʀɛstoy]	commons, dining hall
une **bourse** [buʀs]	scholarship
une **colocation** [kolɔkasjɔ̃]	shared housing

False Friends

French Word	Actual Meaning	False Friend	Correct French Word
la course	**race, running**	(academic) course	*un cours*
un crayon	**pencil**	crayon	*une craie grasse/à la cire*
la démonstration	**proof; exhibition**	demonstration (protest)	*la manifestation*

My Vocabulary

9
Professional and Work World

9.1 Tools and Production  34

un **outil** [uti]	tool
une **boîte à outils**	toolbox
fixer qc [fikse]	to fasten, attach s.th.
accrocher qc [akʀɔʃe]	to hang up s.th.
monter qc [mɔ̃te]	to mount/assemble s.th.
le **montage** [mɔ̃taʒ]	mounting, assembly
faire marcher qc [fɛʀmaʀʃe]	to operate s.th.
Je n'arrive pas à faire marcher le lecteur DVD.	I can't get the DVD player to work.
réparer [ʀepaʀe]	to repair
une **réparation** [ʀepaʀasjɔ̃]	repair (n)

l'**outillage** *m* [utijaʒ]	tool, hand tool
un **établi** [etabli]	workbench
un **étau**; des **étaux** *pl* [eto]	vice

un **marteau**; des **marteaux** *pl* [maʀto]	hammer(n)
se servir de [s(ə)sɛʀviʀ]	to use
un **clou** [klu]	nail (n)
enfoncer un clou	to drive in a nail
arracher un clou	to pull a nail
une **échelle** [eʃɛl]	ladder
utiliser [ytilize]	to use
employer [ɑ̃plwaje]	to use
le **mode d'emploi** [mɔddɑ̃plwa]	operating instructions, manual
suivre le mode d'emploi	to follow the manual

une **pince** [pɛ̃s]	pliers
une **pince coupante**	cutting pliers
une **pince universelle**	slip joint pliers
des **tenailles** *fpl*, une **tenaille** [t(ə)nɑj]	pincers *(See Information Box p. 46)*
une **vis** [vis]	screw (n)
un **tournevis** [tuʀnəvis]	screwdriver
une **clé** [kle]	wrench (n)
une **clé anglaise/à molette**	monkey wrench
un **niveau à bulle**; des **niveaux à bulle** *pl* [nivoabyl]	level (n)
un **mètre** (**pliant**) [mɛtʀə(plijɑ̃)]	(folding) rule
une **hache** ['aʃ]	hatchet (n)
scier [sje]	to saw
une **scie** [si]	saw (n)
une **scie à métaux**	hack saw
une **scie circulaire/sauteuse**	circular saw/jigsaw
une **perceuse** (**électrique**) [pɛʀsøz (elɛktʀik)]	(electric) drill
percer [pɛʀse]	to drill (through)
une **cheville** [ʃ(ə)vij]	dowel, peg
enfoncer une cheville	to insert a peg
un **écrou** [ekʀu]	nut
un **boulon** [bulɔ̃]	bolt (n)
serrer un boulon	to tighten a bolt
un **rabot** [ʀabo]	plane (n)
raboter [ʀabɔte]	to plane
raboter une planche	to plane a board
un **burin** [byʀɛ̃]	chisel (n)
une **lime** [lim]	file (n)
limer [lime]	to file
une **truelle** [tʀyɛl]	trowel

une **lampe de poche** [lɑ̃pdəpɔʃ]	flashlight
une **pile** [pil]	battery
une **pile rechargeable**	rechargeable battery
un **canif** [kanif]	pocket knife
des **ciseaux** *mpl* [sizo]	scissors *(See Information Box p. 46)*
couper [kupe]	to cut
découper [dekupe]	to cut off, out, up
découper une feuille de papier	to cut up a piece of paper

9.2 Office, Office Items  35

un **bureau**; des **bureaux** *pl* [byʀo]	office; desk
un **article de bureau**	office item
l'**équipement de bureau**	office equipment
une **salle de réunion** [saldəʀeynjɔ̃]	meeting room
une **table** [tabl]	table
un **tiroir** [tiʀwaʀ]	drawer
une **chaise** [ʃɛz]	chair
une **étagère** [etaʒɛʀ]	shelf
classer [klɑse]	to file, sort
classer les dossiers **par ordre alphabétique**	to arrange files in alphabetical order
un **classeur** [klɑsœʀ]	file cabinet
une **fiche** [fiʃ]	file card
un **fichier** [fiʃje]	index card file
remettre un fichier à jour	to update a card index
les **fournitures** *fpl* [fuʀnityʀ]	supplies
les **fournitures de bureau**	office supplies
une **chemise** [ʃ(ə)miz]	folder
un **agenda** [aʒɛ̃da]	appointment book, planner
un **calendrier** [kɑlɑ̃dʀije]	calendar
un **bloc-notes** [blɔknɔt]	notepad
le **papier** [papje]	paper
le **papier à lettres**	stationery
l'**en-tête** *m* [ɑ̃tɛt]	letterhead
le **papier à en-tête**	letterhead paper
une **enveloppe** [ɑ̃v(ə)lɔp]	envelope
un **timbre** [tɛ̃bʀ]	stamp (n)
un **stylo** (à) **plume** [stilo(a)plym]	fountain pen
l'**encre** *f* [ɑ̃kʀ]	ink
une **cartouche** [kaʀtuʃ]	(ink) cartridge
un **stylo** (à) **bille** [stilo(a)bij]	ballpoint pen
un **crayon** [kʀɛjɔ̃]	pencil
un **taille-crayon**	pencil sharpener *(See Information Box p.104)*
un **marqueur** [maʀkœʀ]	highlighter
souligner au marqueur	to highlight (with a marker)
un **feutre** [føtʀ]	felt-tip pen, marker
la **colle** [kɔl]	glue
un tube de colle	tube of glue

un **trombone** [tʀɔ̃bɔn]	paper clip
une **agrafe** [agʀaf]	staple (n)
une **agrafeuse** [agʀaføz]	stapler
une **perforatrice** [pɛʀfɔʀatʀis]	hole punch
une **perforeuse** [pɛʀfɔʀøz]	hole punch
le **ruban adhésif** [ʀybɑ̃adezif]	adhesive/cellophane tape
surligner [syʀliɲe]	to highlight
un **surligneur** [syʀliɲœʀ]	highlighter

téléphoner à qn [telefɔne]	to phone s.o.
J'ai essayé de lui téléphoner, mais c'était occupé.	I tried to telephone him, but the line was busy.
un **téléphone** [telefɔn]	telephone (n)
donner/recevoir un coup de téléphone	to make/receive a telephone call
appeler qn [ap(ə)le]	to call s.o.
rappeler qn [ʀap(ə)le]	to call s.o. back
un **appel** (**téléphonique**) [apɛl(telefɔnik)]	(telephone) call
un **répondeur** [ʀepɔ̃dœʀ]	answering machine
Il y a trois messages sur le répondeur.	There are three messages on the answering machine.
faxer qc à qn [fakse]	to fax s.th. to s.o.
un **fax** [faks]	a fax (message)
envoyer qc **par fax**	to send s.th. by fax

dicter [dikte]	to dictate
un **dictaphone** [diktafɔn]	dictaphone
un **télécopieur** [telekɔpjœʀ]	fax machine
une **télécopie** [telekɔpi]	fax (n)

photocopier [fɔtɔkɔpje]	to photocopy
une **photocopie** [fɔtɔkɔpi]	photocopy (n)
des **photocopies couleur**	color photocopies
une **photocopieuse** [fɔtɔkɔpjøz]	photocopier
un **photocopieur** [fɔtɔkɔpjœʀ]	photocopier

un **ordinateur** [ɔʀdinatœʀ]	computer
un **ordinateur personnel** (**PC**)	PC
un (**ordinateur**) **portable** [(ɔʀdinatœʀ)pɔʀtabl]	laptop
un **cédérom** (**CD-ROM**) [sedeʀɔm]	CD-ROM
une **imprimante** [ɛ̃pʀimɑ̃t]	printer
une **imprimante** (à) **laser/à jet d'encre**	laser/inkjet printer
un **scanneur** [skanœʀ]	scanner
un **scanner** [skanɛʀ]	scanner
un **vidéoprojecteur** [videopʀɔʒɛktœʀ]	video projector

9.3 Professional Training and Professions

 36

apprendre qc à qn [apʀɑ̃dʀ]	to teach s.th. to s.o.
C'est moi qui lui ai appris le français.	I'm the one who taught him French.
apprendre (**à faire**) **qc** [apʀɑ̃dʀ]	to learn (to do) s.th.
un **apprenti**, une **apprentie** [apʀɑ̃ti]	apprentice, trainee
un **apprentissage** [apʀɑ̃tisaʒ]	apprenticeship
faire son apprentissage (chez)	to serve an apprenticeship (with)
devenir* [dev(ə)niʀ]	to become
Il a décidé de devenir pilote.	He has decided to become a pilot.
la **formation professionnelle** [fɔʀmasjɔ̃pʀɔfɛsjɔnɛl]	professional training
un **atelier** [atəlje]	workshop

la **population active** [pɔpylasjɔ̃aktiv]	workforce
les **catégories socioprofessionnelles** *fpl* [kategɔʀisɔsjopʀɔfesjɔnɛl]	socio-professional categories; professional classes
la **vie professionnelle** [vipʀɔfɛsjɔnɛl]	professional life
l'**activité professionnelle** *f* [aktivitepʀɔfɛsjɔnɛl]	professional activity
Il est… **de profession**. [pʀɔfɛsjɔ̃]	He is a … by profession.
Il est danseur de profession.	He is a dancer by profession.
le **secteur primaire** [sɛktœʀpʀimɛʀ]	primary sector (agriculture, fishing, mining)
le **secteur secondaire** [sɛktœʀsəgɔ̃dɛʀ]	secondary sector (industry)
le **secteur tertiaire** [sɛktœʀtɛʀsjɛʀ]	services sector
(**travailler**) **à son compte** [asɔ̃kɔ̃t]	to be self-employed
Il fait des économies pour **s'installer à son compte**.	He is saving in order to go out on his own.
les **professions libérales** *fpl* [pʀɔfɛsjɔ̃libeʀal]	liberal professions

un **stage** [staʒ]	internship, practicum
faire un stage en entreprise	to do an internship
un, une **stagiaire** [staʒjɛʀ]	trainee, intern
la **période d'essai** [peʀjɔddesɛ]	trial period
se perfectionner [s(ə)pɛʀfɛksjɔne]	to improve oneself, continue studies
le **perfectionnement** [pɛʀfɛksjɔnmɑ̃]	skills training, professional development
faire un stage de perfectionnement	to take a continuing education course
se spécialiser [s(ə)spesjalize]	to specialize
un, une **spécialiste** [spesjalist]	specialist
se qualifier [s(ə)kalifje]	to qualify
qualifié, **qualifiée** [kalifje]	qualified (adj)
expérimenté, **expérimentée** [ɛkspeʀimɑ̃te]	experienced (adj)
la **qualification** [kalifikasjɔ̃]	qualification
se recycler [s(ə)ʀ(ə)sikle]	to get retrained
C'est un métier où on doit se recycler régulièrement.	That's a profession in which regular training is required.
le **recyclage** [ʀ(ə)siklaʒ]	retraining
l'**industrie** *f* [ɛ̃dystʀi]	industry
un **industriel**, une **industrielle** [ɛ̃dystʀijɛl]	industrial
un **PDG** (**président-directeur général**) [pedeʒe]	CEO
un **directeur**, une **directrice** [diʀɛktœʀ, tʀis]	manager
un, une **chef** [ʃɛf]	boss, employer, manager
un **chef d'entreprise**	business owner
une **entreprise** [ɑ̃tʀəpʀiz]	company
une **entreprise de travaux publics**	public works company
un **entrepreneur**, une **entrepreneuse** [ɑ̃tʀəpʀənœʀ, øz]	entrepreneur
une **société** [sɔsjete]	company
une **affaire** [afɛʀ]	company, business
monter une affaire d'import-export	to build an import-export business
le **siège social** [sjɛʒsɔsjal]	corporate headquarters
un **cadre** [kadʀ]	executive, manager
un **cadre supérieur**	upper-level manager
un **cadre moyen**	mid-level manager
un **employé**, une **employée** [ɑ̃plwaje]	employee
un, une **comptable** [kɔ̃tabl]	accountant
un, une **secrétaire** [səkʀetɛʀ]	secretary
une **secrétaire de direction**	executive secretary

occuper un poste/une fonction [ɔkypeɛ̃pɔst/ynfɔ̃ksjɔ̃]	to occupy a position, perform a function
occuper un poste à responsabilité	to have a position of responsibility
faire carrière [fɛʀkaʀjɛʀ]	to make a career
Il a fait carrière dans l'automobile.	He made his career in the automotive industry.
une **promotion** [pʀɔmosjɔ̃]	promotion

un **ouvrier**, une **ouvrière** [uvʀije, ijɛʀ]	worker
un **manœuvre** [manœvʀ]	laborer
Il **travaille comme manœuvre** sur un chantier.	He works as a laborer on a construction site.
un **contremaître**, une **contremaîtresse** [kɔ̃tʀəmɛtʀ, tʀɛs]	foreman

INFO

Ouvrier

un ouvrier qualifié	*skilled worker*
un ouvrier spécialisé (OS)	*semiskilled laborer*

l'**administration** *f* [administʀasjɔ̃]	administration
le **service public** [sɛʀvispyblik]	public service
un, une **fonctionnaire** [fɔ̃ksjɔnɛʀ]	civil servant
un **facteur**, une **factrice** [faktœʀ, tʀis]	mail carrier
un **postier**, une **postière** [pɔstje, jɛʀ]	postal employee
un **agent** (**de police**) [aʒɑ̃(d(ə)pɔlis)]	(police) officer
un **policier**, une **policière** [pɔlisje, jɛʀ]	police officer
un **pompier** [pɔ̃pje]	firefighter

l'**enseignement** *m* [ɑ̃sɛɲ(ə)mɑ̃]	school system, education
l'**enseignement public**	public education
l'**enseignement privé/libre**	private education
un **enseignant**, une **enseignante** [ɑ̃sɛɲɑ̃, ɑ̃t]	teacher
un, une **professeur** [pʀɔfɛsœʀ]	teacher, professor
un, une **professeur des écoles**	elementary school teacher
un, une **prof** *fam* [pʀɔf]	teacher, professor
un **instituteur**, une **institutrice** *vx* [ɛ̃stitytœʀ, tʀis]	elementary school teacher
un, une **instit** *vx, fam* [ɛ̃stit]	elementary school

un **éducateur**, une **éducatrice** [edykatœʀ, tʀis]	pre-school teacher, educator
un **travailleur social**, une **travailleuse sociale** [tʀavajœʀ, øz sɔsjal]	social worker

INFO

Homme ou femme?

In French. for *most professional designations,* there are both a *masculine* and a *feminine* form:

un vendeur	une vendeuse
un acteur	une actrice
un infirmier **(nurse)**	une infirmière
un secrétaire	une secrétaire

In addition, for many professions, there is just one (usually masculine) form: un écrivain, un ingénieur, un maire, un médecin.

Many professions originally exercised by men are now open to women as well, so with time (and by legislation) they have taken on a feminine form, but this practice has not yet gained universal acceptance. (E.g., une avocate, une juge, une metteuse en scène, une ministre, une deputée.)

le **commerce** [kɔmɛʀs]	commerce, business
le **petit commerce**	retail sector
un **représentant**, une **représentante** [ʀəpʀesɑ̃tɑ̃, ɑ̃t]	representative, agent
un **commerçant**, une **commerçante** [kɔmɛʀsɑ̃, ɑ̃t]	business person
un **marchand**, une **marchande** [maʀʃɑ̃, ɑ̃d]	merchant
un **vendeur**, une **vendeuse** [vɑ̃dœʀ, øz]	sales person
Elle a trouvé une **place de vendeuse**.	She got a job as a sales lady.
un **boulanger**, une **boulangère** [bulɑ̃ʒe, ɛʀ]	baker
un **pâtissier**, une **pâtissière** [pɑtisje, jɛʀ]	pastry chef
un **boucher**, une **bouchère** [buʃe, ɛʀ]	butcher
un **charcutier**, une **charcutière** [ʃaʀkytje, jɛʀ]	butcher
un **bijoutier**, une **bijoutière** [biʒutje, jɛʀ]	jeweler
un, une **libraire** [libʀɛʀ]	book seller
un **pharmacien,** une **pharmacienne** [faʀmasjɛ̃, jɛn],	pharmacist
un **opticien**, une **opticienne** [ɔptisjɛ̃, jɛn]	optician

un **cuisinier**, une **cuisinière** [kɥizinje, jɛʀ]	cook, chef
un **serveur**, une **serveuse** [sɛʀvœʀ, øz]	waiter, waitress
un **garçon** [gaʀsɔ̃]	waiter
Garçon, l'addition, s'il vous plaît!	Waiter, the check please!
l'**hôtellerie** *f* [ɔ/otɛlʀi]	hotel, hospitality industry
un **hôtelier**, une **hôtelière** [ɔ/otəlje, jɛʀ]	hotel operator
la **restauration** [ʀɛstɔʀasjɔ̃]	food service industry, restaurant business
La **restauration rapide** est en plein boom.	The fast-food industry is booming.
un **restaurateur**, une **restauratrice** [ʀɛstɔʀatœʀ, tʀis]	restaurateur
un **gérant**, une **gérante** [ʒeʀɑ̃, ɑ̃t]	manager
la **médecine** [med(ə)sin]	medicine
la **médecine du travail**	industrial/occupational medicine
les **professions médicales** *fpl* [pʀɔfɛsjɔ̃medikal]	medical professions
un **médecin** [med(ə)sɛ̃]	doctor
un, une **généraliste** [ʒeneʀalist]	general practitioner
un **chirurgien,** une **chirurgienne** [ʃiʀyʀʒjɛ̃, jɛn]	surgeon
un **infirmier**, une **infirmière** [ɛ̃fiʀmje, jɛʀ]	nurse
un, une **dentiste** [dɑ̃tist]	dentist
un, une **vétérinaire** [veteʀinɛʀ]	veterinarian
un, une **kinésithérapeute** [kineziteʀapøt]	physical therapist
un, une **kiné** *fam* [kine]	physical therapist
un **esthéticien**, une **esthéticienne** [ɛstetisjɛ̃, ɛn]	esthetician, beautician
le **bâtiment** [bɑtimɑ̃]	construction (industry)
Le **secteur du bâtiment** est en crise.	The construction industry is in serious trouble.
un, une **architecte** [aʀʃitɛkt]	architect
un **ingénieur** [ɛʒenjœʀ]	engineer
un **artisan**, une **artisane** [aʀtizɑ̃, an]	artisan
un, une **peintre** [pɛ̃tʀ]	painter
un **peintre en bâtiment**(**s**)	(house) painter
un **électricien**, une **électricienne** [elɛktʀisjɛ̃, jɛn]	electrician

un **maçon** [masɔ̃]	mason
un **plombier** [plɔ̃bje]	plumber
un **menuisier**, une **menuisière** [mənɥizje, jɛʀ]	finish carpenter
un **couvreur**, une **couvreuse** [kuvʀœʀ, øz]	roofer

l'**informatique** *f* [ɛ̃fɔʀmatik]	computer science
un **informaticien**, une **informaticienne** [ɛ̃fɔʀtisjɛ̃, jɛn]	computer specialist
un **programmeur**, une **programmeuse** [pʀɔgʀamœʀ, øz]	programmer
un **électronicien**, une **électronicienne** [elɛktʀɔnisjɛ̃, jɛn]	electronics engineer/technician
un **technicien**, une **technicienne** [tɛknisjɛ̃, jɛn]	technician
une **technicienne en électronique**	electronics technician

les **transports en commun** *mpl* [tʀɑ̃spɔʀɑ̃kɔmɛ̃]	public transportation
Il y a une grève des transports en commun.	There is a public transportation strike.
un **chauffeur** [ʃofœʀ]	driver
un **chauffeur de taxi**	taxi driver
un **conducteur**, une **conductrice** [kɔ̃dyktœʀ, tʀis]	driver, conductor
un **conducteur de bus**	bus driver
un, une **pilote** [pilɔt]	pilot
un **pilote de ligne**	airline pilot
une **hôtesse de l'air** [otɛsdəlɛʀ]	flight attendant, stewardess
un **steward** [stiwaʀt]	flight attendant, steward

l'**agriculture** *f* [agʀikyltyʀ]	agriculture
un **agriculteur**, une **agricultrice** [agʀikyltœʀ, tʀis]	agriculturist, farmer
un **cultivateur**, une **cultivatrice** [kyltivatœʀ, tʀis]	agriculturist, farmer
un **paysan**, une **paysanne** [peizɑ̃, an]	peasant
un **ouvrier agricole**, une **ouvrière agricole** [uvʀije, ijɛʀagʀikɔl]	farm worker
un **jardinier**, une **jardinière** [ʒaʀdinje, jɛʀ]	gardener

les **services** *mpl* [sɛʀvis]	services
un, une **garagiste** [gaʀaʒist]	(auto) mechanic, repair shop owner
un **mécanicien**, une **mécanicienne** [mekanisjɛ̃, jɛn]	mechanic

un **gardien**, une **gardienne** [gaʀdjɛ̃, jɛn]	caretaker, guard, caregiver, warden
une **gardienne de musée**	museum attendant
une **femme de ménage** [famdəmenaʒ]	cleaning lady
la **justice** [ʒystis]	justice
porter une affaire devant la justice	to bring a matter before the courts
un, une **juge** [ʒyʒ]	judge (n)
un **juge d'instruction**	investigating judge
un **procureur** [pʀɔkyʀœʀ]	prosecuting attorney
un **avocat**, une **avocate** [avɔka, at]	attorney, lawyer
les **finances** *fpl* [finɑ̃s]	finances
Mes finances sont au plus bas.	My financial situation is on the skids.
un **banquier**, une **banquière** [bɑ̃kje, jɛʀ]	banker
un **caissier**, une **caissière** [kɛsje, jɛʀ]	cashier, teller
la **politique** [pɔlitik]	politics
Elle s'est lancée dans la politique.	She has gone into politics.
un **homme**, une **femme politique** [ɔm/fampɔlitik]	politician
un **politicien**, une **politicienne** *péj* [pɔlitisjɛ̃, jɛn]	politician
un, une **ministre** [ministʀ]	minister
un **député**, une **députée** [depyte]	elected member
un député socialiste	socialist deputy
un **maire** [mɛʀ]	mayor
passer devant M./Mme le maire	to get married
l'**armée** *f* [aʀme]	army
s'engager dans l'armée	to enlist in the army
un **militaire** [militɛʀ]	soldier
un **soldat**, une **soldate** [sɔlda, at]	soldier
un **général** [ʒeneʀal]	general
la **marine** [maʀin]	navy
la **marine marchande**	merchant marine
un **marin** [maʀɛ̃]	sailor, seaman
un **marin-pêcheur**	commercial fisherman
un **capitaine** [kapitɛn]	captain

le **journalisme** [ʒuʀnalism]	journalism
un, une **journaliste** [ʒuʀnalist]	journalist
un **journaliste à la radio/télévision**	radio/television journalist
un, une **reporter** [ʀ(ə)pɔʀtɛʀ/øʀ]	reporter
un **rédacteur**, une **rédactrice** [ʀedaktœʀ, tʀis]	editor
un **rédacteur**, une **rédactrice en chef**	editor-in-chief
un, une **photographe** [fɔtɔgʀaf]	photographer
un **photographe de presse**	press photographer

le **tourisme** [tuʀism]	tourism
un, une **guide** [gid]	(travel) guide
Suivez le guide.	Follow the guide.
un, une **interprète** [ɛ̃tɛʀpʀɛt]	interpreter

le **spectacle** [spɛktakl]	performance, show
donner un spectacle	to put on a show
un **acteur**, une **actrice** [aktœʀ, tʀis]	actor, actress
un **musicien**, une **musicienne** [myzisjɛ̃, jɛn]	musician
un, une **artiste** [aʀtist]	artist
un **auteur**, une **autrice/une auteure** [otœʀ, tʀis]	author
un **écrivain**, une (**femme**) **écrivain** [ekʀivɛ̃]	writer

l'**ANPE** *f* (**Agence nationale pour l'emploi**) [aɛnpeə]	employment agency
être inscrit à l'ANPE	to be registered with the employment agency
l'**orientation professionnelle** *f* [ɔ̃ʀjɑ̃tasjɔ̃pʀɔfɛsjɔnɛl]	vocational guidance
un **employeur**, une **employeuse** [ɑ̃plwajœʀ, jøz]	employer
un **candidat**, une **candidate** [kɑ̃dida, at]	candidate, applicant
postuler à/pour [pɔstyle]	to apply for
Elle a postulé pour un emploi de puéricultrice.	She has applied for a job as a child care nurse.
poser sa candidature [pozesakɑ̃didatyʀ]	to apply
un **curriculum vitae** (**CV**) [kyʀikulɔmvite (seve)]	résumé, CV
Prière de joindre à votre candidature un **CV détaillé**.	Please attach a detailed résumé to your application.
les **débouchés** *mpl* [debuʃe]	career opportunities

9.4 Work and Working Conditions  37

travailler [tʀavaje]	to work
travailler à plein temps/à temps complet	to work full time
travailler à mi-temps	to work half-time
travailler à temps partiel	to work part-time
travailler à la chaîne	to do production line work
travailler à domicile	to work at home
le **travail** [tʀavaj]	work (n)
le **travail au noir**	moonlighting
le **temps de travail**	work hours
un **contrat de travail**	work contract
le **marché du travail**	labor/job market
un **travailleur**, une **travailleuse** [tʀavajœʀ, jøz]	worker
un **travailleur immigré**	foreign worker
le **personnel** [pɛʀsɔnel]	personnel

le **partage du travail** [paʀtaʒdytʀavaj]	job sharing
la **réduction du temps de travail** (**RTT**) [ʀedyksjɔ̃dytɑ̃d(ə)tʀavaj (ɛʀtete)]	cutback in work hours
l'**horaire à la carte** *m* [ɔʀɛʀalakaʀt]	flextime
l'**intérim** *m* [ɛ̃teʀim]	temporary work
une **agence d'intérim**	temp agency
faire les trois huit [fɛʀletʀwa'ɥit]	to work round the clock
embaucher [ɑ̃boʃe]	to hire
embaucher du personnel supplémentaire	to hire additional personnel
l'**embauche** *f* [ɑ̃boʃ]	hiring
un **CDD** (**contrat à durée déterminée**) [sedede]	fixed-term contract
un **CDI** (**contrat à durée indéterminée**) [sedei]	open-ended contract

employer [ɑ̃plwaje]	to employ
un **employé**, une **employée** [ɑ̃plwaje]	employee
l'**emploi** *m* [ɑ̃plwa]	employment
être sans emploi	to be unemployed
engager [ɑ̃gaʒe]	to hire
Il a été **engagé comme chauffeur**.	He was hired as a driver.
un **poste** (**de travail**) [pɔst (d(ə)tʀavaj]	job
un **boulot** *fam* [bulo]	job, work, gig
vivre de **petits boulots**	to do odd jobs
actif, **active** [aktif, iv]	(gainfully) employed

une **activité** [aktivite]	activity
un **métier** [metje]	profession, trade
Elle exerce le **métier de journaliste**.	She works as a professional journalist.
un **job** *fam* [dʒɔb]	job
un **retraité**, une **retraitée** [ʀ(ə)tʀete]	retired person
la **retraite** [ʀ(ə)tʀɛt]	retirement
partir à la retraite	to retire

gagner [gaɲe]	to earn
gagner de l'argent	to earn money
gagner sa vie	to earn one's living
un **salaire** [salɛʀ]	salary
une **augmentation de salaire**	a raise in salary
un **salarié**, une **salariée** [salaʀje]	salaried person
une **heure supplémentaire** [œʀsyplemɑ̃tɛʀ]	overtime
une **heure sup** *fam* [œʀsyp]	hour of overtime

le **traitement** [tʀɛtmɑ̃]	salary, remuneration
les **revenus** *mpl* [ʀ(ə)vəny/ʀəv(ə)ny]	income
une **indemnité** [ɛ̃dɛmnite]	benefit, compensation
toucher une **indemnité de licenciement**	to get severance pay
une **prime** [pʀim]	bonus
avoir droit à une **prime de fin d'année**	to be entitled to a year-end bonus
les **ressources** *fpl* [ʀ(ə)suʀs]	(financial) resources
le **niveau de vie**; les **niveaux de vie** *pl* [nivod(ə)vi]	standard of living
le **pouvoir d'achat** [puvwaʀdaʃa]	purchasing power
la baisse du pouvoir d'achat	decrease in purchasing power
les **charges annexes** (**au salaire**) *fpl* [ʃaʀʒanɛks (osalɛʀ)]	payroll deductions
les **prestations sociales** *fpl* [pʀɛstasjɔ̃sɔsjal]	social security benefits

produire [pʀɔdɥiʀ]	to produce
la **production** [pʀɔdyksjɔ̃]	production
un **produit** [pʀɔdɥi]	product
importer [ɛ̃pɔʀte]	to import
l'**importation** *f* [ɛ̃pɔʀtasjɔ̃]	importation
exporter [ɛkspɔʀte]	to export
l'**exportation** *f* [ɛkspɔʀtasjɔ̃]	exportation
l'**import-export** *m* [ɛ̃pɔʀɛkspɔʀ]	import-export
la **vente** [vɑ̃t]	sale

un **jour ouvrable** [ʒuʀuvʀabl]	work day
un **jour férié** [ʒuʀfeʀje]	day off, holiday
le **congé** [kɔ̃ʒe]	vacation, time off
donner congé à qn	to lay off, dismiss s.o.
les **congés payés**	paid vacation
faire le pont [fɛʀl(ə)pɔ̃]	to take a long weekend

une **offre d'emploi** [ɔfʀdɑ̃plwa]	job offer
une **demande d'emploi** [dəmɑ̃ddɑ̃plwa]	job application
un **demandeur**, une **demandeuse d'emploi** [dəmɑ̃dœʀ, øzdɑ̃plwa]	(job) applicant
créer (**des emplois**) [kʀee (dezɑ̃plwa)]	to create (jobs)
supprimer (**des emplois**) [sypʀime (dezɑ̃plwa)]	to eliminate (jobs)
La robotisation supprime des emplois.	Full automation leads to job losses.

la **main-d'œuvre**; les **mains-d'œuvre** *pl* [mɛ̃dœvʀ]	(manual) labor
employer de la main-d'œuvre bon marché	to use cheap labor
un **travail manuel** [tʀavajmanɥɛl]	manual labor
l'**automation**/l'**automatisation** *f* [ɔtɔmasjɔ̃/ɔtɔmatizasjɔ̃]	automation
rationaliser [ʀasjɔnalize]	to streamline
la **rationalisation** [ʀasjɔnalizasjɔ̃]	streamlining
délocaliser [delɔkalize]	to outsource
De nombreuses firmes délocalisent leurs usines.	Many companies are outsourcing their factories.
la **délocalisation** [delɔkalizasjɔ̃]	outsourcing
la **mondialisation** [mɔ̃djalizasjɔ̃]	globalization

le **chômage** [ʃomaʒ]	unemployment
l'**accroissement du taux de chômage**	increase in the unemployment rate
un **chômeur**, une **chômeuse** [ʃomœʀ, øz]	unemployed person
un **chômeur de longue durée**	long-term unemployed person
un **chômeur en fin de droits**	unemployment benefits recipient
le **chômage partiel** [ʃomaʒpaʀsjɛl]	temporary work
l'**allocation** (**de**) **chômage** *f* [alɔkasjɔ̃(d(ə))ʃomaʒ]	unemployment compensation
toucher une allocation chômage	to receive unemployment compensation
licencier [lisɑ̃sje]	to fire, let go
Il a peur de **se faire licencier**.	He is afraid of being terminated.
le **licenciement** [lisɑ̃simɑ̃]	firing (n)
renvoyer [ʀɑ̃vwaje]	to fire, boot out

économiser [ekɔnɔmize]	to save
économique [ekɔnɔmik]	economic
la **crise économique**	economic crisis
l'**économie** *f* [ekɔnɔmi]	economy
une **difficulté** [difikylte]	difficulty
faire face aux difficultés	to confront the difficulties
responsable de [ʀɛspɔ̃sabl]	responsible for
Il est responsable de la production.	He is responsible for production.
une **organisation** [ɔʀganizasjɔ̃]	organization
une **expansion** [ɛkspɑ̃sjɔ̃]	expansion
l'**expansion économique**	economic expansion
la **faillite** [fajit]	bankruptcy, insolvency
faire faillite	to go bankrupt
déposer son bilan [depozesɔ̃bilɑ̃]	to file for bankruptcy, go bankrupt
un **dépôt de bilan** [depodbilɑ̃]	bankruptcy claim
revendiquer [ʀ(ə)vɑ̃dike]	to claim
revendiquer une augmentation de salaire	to demand, claim a salary increase
une **revendication** [ʀ(ə)vɑ̃dikasjɔ̃]	demand, claim (n)
des **revendications salariales**	wage demand
une **manifestation** [manifɛstasjɔ̃]	demonstration
une **manifestation silencieuse**	silent protest
une **manif** *fam* [manif]	demonstration
une **grève** [gʀɛv]	strike (n)
faire grève	to go on strike
un, une **gréviste** [gʀevist]	striker
mener une action [m(ə)neynaksjɔ̃]	to carry out militant actions
les **partenaires sociaux** *mpl* [paʀtənɛʀsɔsjo]	partners in labor negotiations
Le dialogue a repris entre les partenaires sociaux.	Dialogue has resumed between the partners in labor negotiations.
un **conflit social** [kɔ̃flisɔsjal]	social conflict
contester [kɔ̃tɛste]	to protest
une **contestation** [kɔ̃tɛstasjɔ̃]	protest (n)
lutter [lyte]	to struggle
la **lutte** [lyt]	struggle (n)
une **consultation de la base** [kɔ̃syltasjɔ̃d(ə)labaz]	strike vote
un **préavis de grève** [pʀeavid(ə)gʀɛv]	strike declaration
un **lock-out** [lɔkaut]	lockout
le **SMIC** [smik]	minimum wage
gagner le SMIC	to earn minimum wage
être payé au SMIC	to be paid minimum wage

se réunir [s(ə)ReyniR]	to meet
une **réunion** [Reyɲɔ̃]	meeting (n)
négocier [negɔsje]	to negotiate
Les syndicats ont négocié avec le patronat une augmentation de salaire.	The unions negotiated a salary increase with management.
une **négociation** [negɔsjasjɔ̃]	negotiation
syndical, **syndicale** [sɛ̃dikal]	union (adj)
un **délégué syndical**, une **déléguée syndicale**	union delegate
un **syndicat** [sɛ̃dika]	union
patronal, **patronale** [patRɔnal]	employer, management (adj)
un **patron**, une **patronne** [patRɔ̃, ɔn]	employer (n)
un **accord** [akɔR]	agreement
signer un accord	to sign an agreement
un **accord sur les salaires** [akɔRsyRlesalɛR]	salary agreement
un **délégué**, une **déléguée du personnel** [delegedypɛRsɔnɛl]	labor representative
une **convention collective** [kɔ̃vɑ̃sjɔ̃kɔlɛktiv]	collective agreement

False Friends

French Word	Actual Meaning	False Friend	Correct French Word
l'affaire	business (dealings)	affair	*un liaison (amoureux)*
fixer	*to fasten*	to fix	*réparer*
un patron	boss	patron (customer) patron (arts)	*un client* *un protecteur*
un trombone	paperclip	trombone	*un trombone*

My Vocabulary

10

Leisure Activities

10.1 Pastimes, Hobbies, and Games  38

les **loisirs** *mpl* [lwaziʀ]	leisure activities, pastimes
un **hobby** ['ɔbi]	hobby
se distraire [s(ə)distʀɛʀ]	to have fun, amuse oneself
une **distraction** [distʀaksjɔ̃]	distraction, entertainment
passer son temps à faire qc [pasesɔ̃tɑ̃afɛʀ]	to spend one's time doing s.th.
Il passe son temps à bouquiner.	He spends his time browsing.
un **passe-temps** [pastɑ̃]	pastime
avoir envie de [avwʀɑ̃vi]	to feel like
Tu as envie d'aller au cinéma?	Do you feel like going to the movies?

se détendre [s(ə)detɑ̃dʀ]	to relax
la **détente** [detɑ̃t]	relaxation
se relaxer [s(ə)ʀ(ə)lakse]	to relax
un **divertissement** [divɛʀtismɑ̃]	entertainment, diversion

actif, **active** [aktif, iv]	active
une **activité** [aktivite]	activity
participer à qc [paʀtisipe]	to participate in s.th.
participer à un stage de judo	to take part in a judo class

collectionner [kɔlɛksjɔne]	to collect
une **collection** [kɔlɛksjɔ̃]	collection
une **collection de timbres**	stamp collection
un **collectionneur**, une **collectionneuse** [kɔlɛksjɔnœʀ, øz]	collector
un **album** [albɔm]	album

lire [liʀ]	to read
la **lecture** [lɛktyʀ]	reading
Elle est **plongée dans sa lecture**.	She is immersed in her reading.
les **mots croisés** *mpl* [mokʀwaze]	crossword puzzle

jouer à (**un jeu**) [ʒwe]	to play (a game)
un **jeu** [ʒø]	game
la règle du jeu	rules of the game
les **cartes** *fpl* [kaʀt]	cards
les **dés** *mpl* [de]	dice
les **échecs** *mpl* [eʃɛk]	chess
un **jeu de société** [ʒød(ə)sɔsjete]	board game
un **puzzle** [pœzl/pœzœl]	puzzle
un puzzle de 5 000 pièces	5000-piece puzzle

INFO

Jouer à/de

jouer à (un jeu) Ils jouent au foot/aux cartes/ aux échecs/aux Indiens	*They are playing soccer/cards/ chess/Indians.*
jouer de/d'(un instrument) Elles jouent du piano/de la flûte/ de l'harmonica.	*They play piano/flute/harmonica.*

In addition to *jouer, faire* can also be used with *musical instruments*; for example:

Tu joues se l'accordéon? Non, je fais de la clarinette.	*Do you play the accordion?* *No, I play the clarinet.*

le **jeu de boules** *fpl* [ʒød(ə)bul]	bowling
la **pétanque** [petɑ̃k]	pétanque
faire une partie de pétanque	to play a game of pétanque

bricoler [bʀikɔle]	to putter, tinker
le **bricolage** [bʀikɔlaʒ]	tinkering, puttering around
un **magasin de bricolage**	home improvement store
un **bricoleur**, une **bricoleuse** [bʀikɔlœʀ, øz]	handyman, do-it-yourselfer
coller [kɔle]	to glue
la **colle** [kɔl]	glue (n)
la **colle à bois**	wood glue
fabriquer [fabʀike]	to make
la **poterie** [pɔtʀi]	pottery

INFO

Things people do with their hands

Performing manual tasks is often expressed by the expression *faire de* + *handicraft*.

Nous faisons de la peinture sur soie.	*We do silk painting.*
Il fait du tricot/crochet.	*He knits/crochets.*

une **photo** [fɔto]	photo
faire/prendre une photo	to take a photo
prendre qn/qc en photo	to take a photo of s.o./s.th.
un **appareil photo** [apaʀɛjfɔto]	camera
un **appareil** (**photo**) **numérique**	digital camera

une **caméra** [kameʀa]	(television/video) camera
un **caméscope** (**numérique**) [kameskɔp(nymeʀik)]	(digital) video camera
la **vidéo** [video]	video
une **cassette vidéo**	video cassette
un **DVD** [devede]	DVD
graver un DVD	to burn a DVD
une **carte mémoire** [kaʀtmemwaʀ]	memory card
filmer [filme]	to film
un **film** [film]	film (n)
la **musique** [myzik]	music
Tu fais de la musique?	Do you play music?
le **rythme** [ʀitm]	rhythm
jouer de qc [ʒwe]	to play s.th. *(See Information Box p. 195)*
danser [dɑ̃se]	to dance
aller danser en boîte	to go dancing in a nightclub
la **danse** [dɑ̃s]	dance (n)
peindre [pɛ̃dʀ]	to paint
la **peinture** [pɛ̃tyʀ]	picture, painting
faire de la peinture	to paint
un **peintre** [pɛ̃tʀ]	painter
un **peintre du dimanche**	Sunday painter
dessiner [desine]	to draw
jardiner [ʒaʀdine]	to garden
un **jardin** [ʒaʀdɛ̃]	garden, yard
un **jardin potager**	vegetable garden
le **jardinage** [ʒaʀdinaʒ]	gardening
planter [plɑ̃te]	to plant
une **plante** [plɑ̃t]	plant (n)
cultiver [kyltive]	to grow
Il cultive des légumes dans son jardin.	He grows vegetables in his garden.
une **fleur** [flœʀ]	flower (n)
l'**herbe** *f* [ɛʀb]	grass
les **mauvaises herbes**	weeds
se promener [s(ə)pʀɔm(ə)ne]	to go for a walk
Viens, on va **se promener au grand air**.	Come, we are going for a walk in the fresh air.
une **promenade** [pʀɔm(ə)nad]	walk (n)
une **promenade à/en vélo**	bike ride

se balader *fam* [s(ə)balade]	to take a walk, stroll
On va se balader?	Shall we take a stroll?
une **balade** *fam* [balad]	walk, stroll (n)
une **randonnée** [ʀɑ̃dɔne]	hike, tour (n)
un **randonneur**, une **randonneuse** [ʀɑ̃dɔnœʀ, øz]	hiker
une **excursion** [ɛkskyʀsjɔ̃]	excursion
le **cyclotourisme** [siklotuʀism]	bicycle touring

chasser [ʃase]	to hunt
la **chasse** [ʃas]	hunting (n)
aller* à la chasse	to go hunting
un **fusil de chasse**	a hunting gun
un **chasseur**, une **chasseuse** [ʃasœʀ, øz]	hunter
pêcher [pɛʃe]	to fish
la **pêche** (**à la ligne**) [pɛʃ(alaliɲ)]	fishing, angling
manger le **produit de sa pêche**	to eat the fish caught
un **pêcheur**, une **pêcheuse** [pɛʃœʀ, øz]	fisher(man)
un **pêcheur à la ligne**	angler

10.2 Sports  39

sportif, **sportive** [spɔʀtif, iv]	athletic
un **sportif**, une **sportive**	athlete
une **association sportive**	sports club
une **manifestation sportive**	sporting event
une **rencontre sportive**	sports competition, meet
le **sport** [spɔʀ]	sport (n)
faire du sport	to play sports

pratiquer (**une discipline sportive**) [pʀatike (yndisiplinspɔʀtiv)]	to practice (a sport)
Simon pratique la natation.	Simon is a swimmer.
athlétique [atletik]	athletic
un, une **athlète** [atlɛt]	athlete
un **sportif**, une **sportive de haut niveau** [spɔʀtif, spɔʀtivdəonivo]	elite athlete

s'entraîner [sɑ̃tʀɛne]	to train
l'**entraînement** *m* [ɑ̃tʀɛnmɑ̃]	training
un **entraîneur**, une **entraîneuse** [ɑ̃tʀɛnœʀ, øz]	trainer, coach
un **moniteur**, une **monitrice** [mɔnitœʀ, tʀis]	coach, instructor

être en forme [ɛtʀɑ̃fɔʀm]	to be in shape/fit
être fort, **forte** [fɔʀ, fɔʀt]	to be strong
la **force** [fɔʀs]	strength
transpirer [tʀɑ̃spiʀe]	to sweat

un, une **adversaire** [advɛʀsɛʀ]	opponent
siffler [sifle]	to whistle
un, une **arbitre** [aʀbitʀ]	referee
la **mi-temps** [mitɑ̃]	halftime
une **prolongation** [pʀɔlɔ̃gasjɔ̃]	overtime
un **supporter**, une **supportrice** [sypɔʀtɛʀ/œʀ, tʀis]	fan

un **club** [klœb]	club, association
faire partie d'un **club de foot**	to belong to a soccer club
une **équipe** [ekip]	team
un **match** [matʃ]	match, game
un **match aller/retour**	first match/return match (i.e., in soccer)
un **tournoi** [tuʀnwa]	tournament
disputer un tournoi	to compete in a tournament

un **stade** [stad]	stadium
un **gymnase** [ʒymnaz]	gymnasium
un **terrain de sport** [teʀɛ̃d(ə)spɔʀ]	athletic field

une **course** [kuʀs]	race (n) *(See Information Box p. 164)*
le **départ** [depaʀ]	start (n)
donner le départ d'une course	to start a race
l'**arrivée** *f* [aʀive]	finish
franchir la ligne d'arrivée	to cross the finish line

un **résultat** [ʀezylta]	results
battre [batʀ]	to beat
Bordeaux a battu Monaco 2 à 1.	Bordeaux beat Monaco 2 to 1.
gagner (**qc/contre qn**) [gaɲe]	to win (s.th./over s.o.)
gagnant, **gagnante** [gaɲɑ̃, ɑ̃t]	winning (adj)
un **gagnant**, une **gagnante**	winner
Les deux équipes gagnantes se retrouveront en finale.	The two winning teams will meet in the finals.
perdre (**qc/contre qn**) [pɛʀdʀ]	to lose (s.th./s.o.)
J'ai perdu mon dernier match de tennis.	I lost my last tennis match.
perdant, **perdante** [pɛʀdɑ̃, ɑ̃t]	losing (adj)
un **perdant**, une **perdante**	loser

vaincre [vɛ̃kʀ]	to win, beat
Il a vaincu son adversaire.	He beat his opponent.
un **vainqueur** [vɛ̃kœʀ]	winner
sortir* vainqueur d'une épreuve	to emerge victorious in a competition
victorieux, **victorieuse** [viktɔʀjø, jøz]	victorious
une **victoire** [viktwaʀ]	victory
remporter une victoire	to gain a victory
(**faire**) **match nul** [(fɛʀ)matʃnyl]	(to end in) a tie
une **défaite** [defɛt]	defeat (n)
la **revanche** [ʀ(ə)vɑ̃ʃ]	rematch, grudge match
prendre sa revanche	to get revenge
tirer au sort [tiʀeosɔʀ]	to draw lots
le **tirage au sort** [tiʀaʒosɔʀ]	draw (n)

un **champion**, une **championne** [ʃɑ̃pjɔ̃, jɔn]	champion (n)
un **championnat** [ʃɑ̃pjɔna]	championship
le **championnat du monde**	world championship
le **classement** [klɑsmɑ̃]	ranking (n)
une **compétition** [kɔ̃petisjɔ̃]	competition
une **compétition par équipes**	team competition
une **compétition individuelle**	individual competition
un **exploit** [ɛksplwa]	feat
un **record** [ʀ(ə)kɔʀ]	record (n)
détenir un record	to hold a record
battre un record	to break a record
améliorer un record	to set a new record

une **coupe** [kup]	cup, trophy
la **coupe du Monde**	World Cup
une **médaille** [medaj]	medal (n)
une médaille d'or/d'argent/de bronze	gold/silver/bronze medal
les **Jeux Olympiques** *mpl* [ʒøzɔlɛ̃pik]	Olympic Games
un **titre** [titʀ]	title
C'est son deuxième titre olympique.	That is his second Olympic victory.
un **participant**, une **participante** [paʀtisipɑ̃, ɑ̃t]	participant
un **favori**, une **favorite** [favɔʀi, it]	favorite
La favorite a gagné haut la main.	The favorite won easily.
un **défi** [defi]	challenge
lancer un défi à qn	to challenge s.o.

un **amateur**, une **amatrice** [amatœʀ, tʀis]	amateur
Ils font du cyclisme **en amateurs**.	They are amateur cyclists.
un **professionnel**, une **professionnelle** [pʀɔfɛsjɔnɛl]	professional (n)
un, une **pro** *fam* [pʀo]	pro (n)
un **joueur**, une **joueuse** [ʒwœʀ, øz]	player
un joueur de tennis professionnel	professional tennis player

un **ballon** [balɔ̃]	(large) ball
un **ballon de foot**(**ball**)	soccer ball
le **foot**(**ball**) [fut(bol)]	soccer
un **terrain de foot** [teʀɛ̃dəfut]	soccer field
un **but** [by(t)]	goal
le **gardien de but**	goalie, goal tender
marquer un but	to score a goal
le **rugby** [ʀygbi]	rugby
le **volley-ball** [vɔlɛbol]	volleyball
le **volley** *fam* [vɔlɛ]	volleyball
le **basket-ball** [baskɛtbol]	basketball
le **basket** *fam* [baskɛt]	basketball
le **hand-ball** ['ɑ̃dbal]	handball
le **hand** *fam* ['ɑ̃d]	handball

une **balle** [bal]	ball
une **balle de tennis**	tennis ball
jouer au tennis [ʒweotenis]	to play tennis
une **raquette** [ʀakɛt]	(tennis) racket
le **ping-pong** [piŋpɔ̃g]	ping-pong
le **filet** [filɛ]	net
La balle a atterri dans le filet.	The ball hit the net.
le **golf** [gɔlf]	golf

le **service** [sɛʀvis]	serve (n)
perdre son service	to lose the serve
une **manche** [mɑ̃ʃ]	set (n)
un **jeu** [ʒø]	game
la **balle de match** [baldəmatʃ]	match point
mener [m(ə)ne]	to lead
mener (**par**) **4 jeux à 2**	to lead with four games to two
le **jeu décisif** [ʒødesizif]	tie-breaker
remporter le jeu décisif	to win the tie-breaker

un **vélo** [velo]	bicycle, bike
faire du vélo	to cycle, ride a bicycle
une **bicyclette** [bisiklɛt]	bicycle
un **VTT** (**vélo tout terrain**) [vetete]	mountain bike
le **cyclisme** [siklism]	cycling

un, une **cycliste** [siklist]	cyclist
pédaler [pedale]	to pedal
un **tour** [tuʀ]	tour (n)
une **étape** [etap]	stage (n)
un **maillot** [majo]	(cycling) jersey
le maillot jaune	yellow jersey

INFO

Le/la tour

le tour	*tour, round trip, trip*
le Tour de France	*Tour de France*
un tour en voiture	*a (small) car trip, quick spin*
faire le tour du monde	*to travel around the world*
la tour	*tower*
la tour Eiffel	*Eiffel Tower*
la tour de contrôle	*control tower*

se doper [s(ə)dɔpe]	to dope, use performance-enhancing drugs
Le contrôle a confirmé que le coureur s'était dopé.	The test confirmed that the racer had used drugs.
le **dopage** [dɔpaʒ]	doping *(See Information Box p. 78)*
le **doping** [dɔpiŋ]	doping, drug use
la **lutte anti-dopage** [lytɑ̃tidɔpaʒ]	anti-doping campaign

les **patins à roulettes** *mpl* [patɛ̃aʀulɛt]	roller skates
les **rollers** *mpl* [ʀɔlœʀ]	inline skates
faire du roller	to do inline skating
un **skateboard** [skɛtbɔʀd]	skateboard

l'**athlétisme** *m* [atletism]	track and field
courir [kuʀiʀ]	to run
Il n'a pas couru assez vite.	He didn't run fast enough.
la **course** (**à pied**) [kuʀs(apje)]	(foot) race
sauter [sote]	to jump
le **saut** [so]	jump (n)
le **saut en longueur**	long jump
le **saut en hauteur**	high jump
le **saut à la perche**	pole vault
lancer [lɑ̃se]	to throw
lancer une balle	to throw a ball

un **sauteur**, une **sauteuse** [sotœʀ, øz]	jumper
un sauteur en longueur/en hauteur	long/high jumper
le **lancer** [lɑ̃se]	throwing (n)
le lancer du poids/du disque	shot put, discus throw
un **lanceur**, une **lanceuse** [lɑ̃sœʀ, øz]	thrower
une lanceuse de poids	shot-putter
le **poids** [pwa]	shot put
le **disque** [disk]	discus
le **javelot** [ʒavlo]	javelin
le **marteau** [marto]	hammer
le **jogging** [dʒɔgiŋ]	jogging, distance running
le **footing** [futiŋ]	jogging, running

la **gymnastique** [ʒimnastik]	gymnastics
faire de la gymnastique	to do gymnastics
la **gym** *fam* [ʒim]	gymnastics
un, une **gymnaste** [ʒimnast]	gymnast

les **sports d'hiver** *mpl* [spɔʀdivɛʀ]	winter sports
la **neige** [nɛʒ]	snow (n)
skier [skje]	to ski
le **ski** [ski]	ski, skiing (n)
un **skieur**, une **skieuse** [skjœʀ, jøz]	skier
un **snowboard** [snobɔʀd]	snowboard (n)
une **luge** [lyʒ]	luge (n)
une **piste** [pist]	trail
skier **hors-piste**	to ski off-trail

le **ski alpin** [skialpɛ̃]	alpine skiing
la **descente** [desɑ̃t]	downhill (n)
un **remonte-pente** [ʀ(ə)montpɑ̃t]	ski lift *(See Information Box p. 104)*
un **téléski** [teleski]	ski lift, tow
le **tire-fesses** *fam* [tiʀfɛs]	t-bar *(See Information Box p. 104)*
un **télésiège** [telesjɛʒ]	chair lift
le **ski de fond** [skidfɔ̃]	cross-country skiing
le **saut à ski** [soaski]	ski jumping
patiner [patine]	to skate
le **patinage** [patinaʒ]	skating (n)
le **patinage artistique**	figure skating
le **patinage de vitesse**	speed skating
les **patins à glace** *mpl* [patɛ̃aglas]	ice skates
le **hockey sur glace** ['ɔkɛsyʀglas]	ice hockey
une **patinoire** [patinwaʀ]	skating rink
un **patineur**, une **patineuse** [patinœʀ, øz]	skater
grimper [gʀɛ̃pe]	to climb

un, une **alpiniste** [alpinist]	mountain climber, alpinist
faire de l'alpinisme *m* [fɛʀd(ə)lalpinism]	to do mountain climbing, mountaineering
escalader [ɛskalade]	to climb
escalader la face nord du Mont-Blanc	to climb the north face of Mont-Blanc
une **escalade** [ɛskalad]	ascent, climb (n)
les **sports nautiques** *mpl* [spɔʀnotik]	water sports
nager [naʒe]	to swim
nager en piscine/**dans** la mer	to swim in a pool/in the ocean
la **natation** [natasjɔ̃]	swimming (n)
un **nageur**, une **nageuse** [naʒœʀ, øz]	swimmer
plonger [plɔ̃ʒe]	to dive
Elle a **plongé du tremplin** de 3 mètres.	She dove from the three-meter board.
un **plongeur**, une **plongeuse** [plɔ̃ʒœʀ, øz]	diver
la **plongée** (**sous-marine**) [plɔ̃ʒe (sumaʀin)]	(underwater) diving
la **brasse** [bʀas]	breaststroke
nager la brasse	to do the breaststroke
le **crawl** [kʀol]	crawl (n)
la **voile** [vwal]	sail, sailing (n)
faire de la voile	to go sailing
un **bateau**; des **bateaux** *pl* [bato]	boat, ship
un **bateau à voiles**	sailboat, sailing ship
la **planche à voile** [plɑ̃ʃavwal]	windsurfing
le **surf** [sœʀf]	surfing
l'**aviron** *m* [aviʀɔ̃]	rowing; oar
ramer [ʀame]	to row
un **canoë** [kanɔe]	canoe (n)
descendre la Dordogne **en canoë**	to go down the Dordogne in a canoe
une **régate** [ʀegat]	regatta

les **sports de combat** *mpl* [spɔʀdəkɔ̃ba]	combat sports
l'**escrime** *f* [ɛskʀim]	fencing
la **boxe** [bɔks]	boxing
un **combat de boxe**	boxing match
la **lutte** [lyt]	wrestling
le **judo** [ʒydɔ]	judo
le **culturisme** [kyltyʀism]	body building
une **salle de culturisme**	body building gym
faire du cheval [fɛʀdyʃ(ə)val]	to ride (horses)
l'**équitation** *f* [ekitasjɔ̃]	equitation; horseback riding
un **concours hippique** [kɔ̃kuʀipik]	riding competition

10.3 Theater, Movies, and Film 

le **théâtre** [teɑtʀ]	theater (n)
faire du théâtre	to perform (drama) on stage
une **pièce de théâtre**	play (n)
monter une pièce (**de théâtre**)	to produce a play
une **scène** [sɛn]	stage (n)
entrer* en scène	to come on stage
mettre en scène	to stage, direct, produce
la **mise en scène**	production
un **metteur en scène**	director
le **décor** [dekɔʀ]	scenery, set
les **costumes** *mpl* [kɔstym]	costumes
le **rideau**; les **rideaux** *pl* [ʀido]	curtain
Le rideau se lève/tombe.	The curtain rises/falls.
les **coulisses** *fpl* [kulis]	wings
représenter [ʀ(ə)pʀezɑ̃te]	to perform, put on stage
une **représentation** [ʀ(ə)pʀezɑ̃tasjɔ̃]	performance
la **première** [pʀəmiɛʀ]	premiere
un **spectacle** [spɛktakl]	show, performance
un **spectateur**, une **spectatrice** [spɛktatœʀ, tʀis]	spectator
le **public** [pyblik]	audience, public
Cette pièce a du succès **auprès du grand public**.	This play is successful with the general public.

assister à [asiste]	to attend
Nous avons assisté à une représentation de *l'Avare.*	We attended a performance of *l'Avare.*
l'**auditoire** *m* [oditwaʀ]	audience
un auditoire attentif	attentive audience
un **acte** [akt]	act (n)
une **pièce en trois actes**	a play in three acts
un **entracte** [ɑ̃tʀakt]	intermission
l'**action** *f* [aksjɔ̃]	action, plot
L'action se déroule à Paris.	The action takes place in Paris.
une **scène** [sɛn]	scene
la 1ère scène de l'acte II	scene 1, act II
une **troupe** [tʀup]	troupe, acting company
un **comédien**, une **comédienne** [kɔmedjɛ̃, jɛn]	actor, comedian
une **vedette** [vədɛt]	star
une **star** [staʀ]	star
un **rôle** [ʀol]	role
le **rôle principal**	lead role
un **rôle secondaire**	supporting role
un **petit rôle**	small, minor role
un **figurant**, une **figurante** [figyʀɑ̃, ɑ̃t]	extra (n)
la **distribution** [distʀibysjɔ̃]	cast (n)
un **personnage** [pɛʀsɔnaʒ]	character
Quel est le **personnage principal** de la pièce?	Who is the main character in the play?
jouer [ʒwe]	to play
Il joue ce rôle pour la 200e fois.	He is playing this role for the two-hundredth time.
le **jeu** [ʒø]	playing (n)
interpréter [ɛ̃tɛʀpʀete]	to interpret
répéter qc [ʀepete]	to rehearse
une **répétition** [ʀepetisjɔ̃]	rehearsal
la (**répétition**) **générale**	dress rehearsal
diriger [diʀiʒe]	to direct
débuter [debyte]	to debut
avoir le trac [avwaʀlətʀak]	to have stage fright

comique [kɔmik]	comic, funny, comical
une **comédie** [kɔmedi]	comedy
une **comédie musicale**	musical comedy
dramatique [dʀamatik]	dramatic
un **drame** [dʀam]	drama, play
tragique [tʀaʒik]	tragic
une **tragédie** [tʀaʒedi]	tragedy

la **caisse** [kɛs]	ticket office
un **billet** [bijɛ]	ticket
faire la queue [fɛʀlakø]	to wait in line
complet, **complète** [kɔ̃plɛ, ɛt]	full, sold out
Ce théâtre **affiche complet** jusqu'à la fin de la saison.	This theater is sold out up to the end of the season.
le **vestiaire** [vɛstjɛʀ]	cloakroom
le **programme** [pʀɔgʀam]	program
être au programme	to be on the program

un **succès** [syksɛ]	success
obtenir un succès fou	to be a smashing success
applaudir qn/qc [aplodiʀ]	to applaud s.o./s.th.
les **applaudissements** *mpl* [aplodismɑ̃]	applause
un **échec**	failure, flop
Cette mise en scène a été un **échec total**.	This production was a total failure.
siffler [sifle]	to whistle

un **triomphe** [tʀiɔ̃f]	triumph (n)
triomphal, **triomphale** [tʀiɔ̃fal]	triumphant
huer ['ɥe]	to boo
un **bide** *fam* [bid]	flop (n)

la **salle** [sal]	hall
le **rang** [ʀɑ̃]	row
la **place** [plas]	seat, place
Les places ne sont pas numérotées.	The seats are not numbered.

le **cinéma** [sinema]	movie(s)
une salle de cinéma	movie theater
un **film** [film]	film
tourner un film	to shoot a film
un **film muet/parlant**	a silent movie
filmer [filme]	to film
une **caméra** [kameʀa]	(movie) camera
un **studio** [stydjo]	studio
passer à [pase]	to be in the theaters, to run
Ce film ne passe plus à Paris.	This film is no longer running in Paris.
une **séance** [seɑ̃s]	performance
la séance de 17 heures	the 5:00 P.M. performance

cinématographique [sinematɔgʀafik]	film
l'**industrie cinématographique**	film/movie industry
un, une **cinéphile** [sinefil]	movie goer, film lover
un **ciné-club**; des **ciné-clubs** *pl* [sineklœb]	film club
un **film de science-fiction** [filmdəsjɑ̃sfiksjɔ̃]	science fiction film
le **suspense** [syspɛns]	suspense
un **film policier** [filmpɔlisje]	crime movie
un **film d'aventures** [filmdavɑ̃tyʀ]	adventure, action movie
un **western** [wɛstɛʀn]	western (n)
un **documentaire** [dɔkymɑ̃tɛʀ]	documentary
un **dessin animé** [desɛ̃anime]	animated film
un **long-métrage** [lɔ̃metʀaʒ]	feature film
un **court-métrage** [kuʀmetʀaʒ]	short film
en noir et blanc [ɑ̃nwaʀeblɑ̃]	in black-and-white
(**en**) **couleurs** [ɑ̃kulœʀ]	in color
la **télévision en couleurs**	color television

un **acteur**, une **actrice** [aktœʀ, tʀis]	actor, actress
réaliser [ʀealize]	to film, produce
Ce film a été réalisé avec un petit budget.	This film was made on a low budget.
un **réalisateur**, une **réalisatrice** [ʀealizatœʀ, tʀis]	director
un **cascadeur**, une **cascadeuse** [kaskadœʀ, øz]	stuntperson

le **scénario** [senaʀjo]	screenplay
un, une **scénariste** [senaʀist]	(screen) writer
la **prise de son** [pʀizdəsɔ̃]	audio recording
le **montage** [mɔ̃taʒ]	film editing
le **mixage** [miksaʒ]	mixing
les **effets spéciaux** *mpl* [efɛspesjo]	special effects
le **trucage** [tʀykaʒ]	special effects
un **gros plan** [gʀoplɑ̃]	close-up (n)
On voit le héros **en gros plan**.	The hero is seen in close-up.
un **ralenti** [ʀalɑ̃ti]	slow motion (scene)
Et maintenant, la même scène **au ralenti**.	And now, the same scene in slow motion.
un **retour en arrière** [ʀ(ə)tuʀɑ̃naʀjɛʀ]	flashback (n)
un **flash-back** [flaʃbak]	flashback (n)
le **générique** [ʒeneʀik]	credits
tenir l'affiche [t(ə)niʀlafiʃ]	to have a run
Ce film tient l'affiche depuis deux ans.	This movie has been running for two years.

une **version** [vɛʀsjɔ̃]	version
en version originale (**VO**)	in original version
en version originale sous-titrée	in original version with subtitles
en version française (**VF**)	in French version
doubler [duble]	to dub
le **doublage** [dublaʒ]	dubbing

10.4 Celebrations  41

fêter [fɛte]	to celebrate
une **fête** [fɛt]	celebration, party, name day
Aujourd'hui, c'est la fête de Michel.	Today is Michel's name day.
un **jour de fête**	holiday, feast day

le **réveillon** [ʀevɛjɔ̃]	réveillon *(Christmas or New Year's Eve celebration)*
le **jour de l'An** [ʒuʀdəlɑ̃]	New Year's Day
(le) **carnaval** [kaʀnaval]	Carnival
la **Fête du Travail** [fɛtdytʀavaj]	Labor Day
la **Fête Nationale** (**14 juillet**) [fɛtnasjɔnal(katɔʀz(ə)ʒɥijɛ)]	French national holiday (July 14)
une **fête foraine** [fɛtfɔʀɛn]	carnival, fair

une **fête de famille** [fɛtdəfamij]	family party, celebration
un **anniversaire** [anivɛʀsɛʀ]	birthday
baptiser [batize]	to baptize
le **baptême** [batɛm]	baptism
le **mariage** [maʀjaʒ]	marriage, wedding
les **noces** *fpl* [nɔs]	marriage, wedding
le **voyage de noces**	honeymoon
la **noce** [nɔs]	wedding celebration
la **fête des mères/pères** [fɛtdemɛʀ/pɛʀ]	Mother's Day, Father's Day
célébrer [selebʀe]	to celebrate
une **cérémonie** [seʀemɔni]	ceremony
une cérémonie officielle	official ceremony
les **noces d'or** *fpl* [nɔsdɔʀ]	golden wedding anniversary
féliciter qn de/pour qc [felisite]	to congratulate s.o. for s.th.
On l'a félicité de/pour son succès.	He was congratulated for his success.
les **félicitations** *fpl* [felisitasjɔ̃]	congratulations (n)
Toutes nos félicitations!	Hearty congratulations!
présenter ses vœux à qn [pʀezɑ̃tesevø]	to give s.o. your best wishes
Je vous présente mes meilleurs vœux.	I give you my best wishes.
souhaiter qc à qn [swete]	to wish s.th. to/for s.o.
Je te souhaite un joyeux Noël.	I wish you a merry Christmas.
Bonne année! [bɔnane]	Happy New Year!
Joyeuses fêtes! [ʒwajøzfɛt]	Happy holidays!
Bonne fête! [bɔnfɛt]	Happy birthday/name day!
Joyeux anniversaire! [anivɛʀsɛʀ]	Happy birthday!
inviter qn à [ɛ̃vite]	to invite s.o. to
un **invité**, une **invitée** [ɛ̃vite]	guest
une **invitation** [ɛ̃vitasjɔ̃]	invitation
lancer une invitation	to make an invitation
recevoir [ʀəs(ə)vwaʀ, ʀ(ə)səvwaʀ]	to receive
une **réception** [ʀesɛpsjɔ̃]	reception
retrouver qn [ʀ(ə)tʀuve]	to meet s.o. (again)
se réunir [s(ə)ʀeyniʀ]	to get together, meet

un **dîner** [dine]	dinner
faire un bon dîner	to have a good dinner
un **repas** (**de fête**) [R(ə)pa (d(ə)fɛt)]	feast, banquet
un **festin** [fɛstɛ̃]	banquet, lavish feast
un **gâteau**; des **gâteaux** *pl* [gɑto]	cake
souffler les bougies du gâteau d'anniversaire	to blow out the candles on a birthday cake
le **champagne** [ʃɑ̃paɲ]	champagne
sabler le champagne	to drink champagne, to celebrate

un **banquet** [bɑ̃kɛ]	banquet
trinquer à [tRɛ̃ke]	to toast, drink to
Trinquons à la santé des jeunes mariés.	Let's drink to the health of the newlyweds.
porter un toast à qn/qc [pɔRteɛ̃tost]	to make a toast to s.o./s.th.

s'amuser (à) [samyze]	to have fun, amuse oneself (with, at, by)
le **plaisir** [pleziR]	pleasure
Ses yeux brillent de plaisir.	His/her eyes gleam with pleasure.
joyeux, **joyeuse** [ʒwajø, øz]	merry, happy
la **joie** [ʒwa]	joy
sauter de joie	to jump for joy
rire [RiR]	to laugh
le **rire** [RiR]	laughter
rigoler *fam* [Rigɔle]	to laugh
l'**ambiance** *f* [ɑ̃bjɑ̃s]	mood, atmosphere
une ambiance animée	lively atmosphere
ému, **émue** [emy]	moved (adj)
être ému aux larmes	to be moved to tears
l'**émotion** *f* [emosjɔ̃]	emotion

s'habiller [sabije]	to get dressed
un **habit** [abi]	a garment
L'habit ne fait pas le moine. *prov*	Clothes don't make the man.
se faire beau, **belle**; **beaux, belles** *pl* [s(ə)fɛRbo, bɛl]	to deck out, spruce up

un **bal** [bal]	ball
un bal populaire	public dance
un bal masqué	masked ball
se déguiser [s(ə)degize]	to masquerade
Il **s'est déguisé en pirate**.	He is dressed up as a pirate.
le **déguisement** [degizmɑ̃]	costume, masquerade

False Friends

French Word	Actual Meaning	False Friend	Correct French Word
un anniversaire	**birthday**	anniversary	*un anniversaire de mariage*
le footing	**jogging**	footing	*la base, l'équilibre*
un habit	**article of clothing**	habit	*une habitude*
réaliser	**to produce, film**	to realize	*se rendre compte*
les vacances	**vacation**	vacancy	*un poste vacant*

My Vocabulary

11

Travel and Tourism

11.1 Travel and Travel Preparations  42

les **vacances** *fpl* [vakɑ̃s]	vacation
Bonnes vacances!	Have a good vacation!
passer ses vacances en Espagne	to spend vacation in Spain
un **vacancier**, une **vacancière** [vakɑ̃sje, jɛʀ]	vacationer
le **congé** [kɔ̃ʒe]	vacation
prendre un **jour de congé**	to take a vacation day, day off work
un, une **touriste** [tuʀist]	tourist
le **tourisme** [tuʀism]	tourism
l'**industrie du tourisme**	tourism industry
la **pleine saison** [plɛnsɛzɔ̃]	busy, high season
hors saison [ɔʀsɛzɔ̃]	off-season
Si vous le pouvez, allez-y plutôt hors saison.	If you can, go in the off-season.
voyager [vwajaʒe]	to travel
un **voyage** [vwajaʒ]	trip (n)
partir* en voyage	to leave on a trip
un **voyage organisé**	group tour
un **voyageur**, une **voyageuse** [vwajaʒœʀ, øz]	traveler
un **tour** [tuʀ]	trip *(See Information Box p. 201)*
un **circuit** [siʀkɥi]	trip, tour
faire un circuit à travers le Massif central	to take a tour through the Massif Central
séjourner [seʒuʀne]	to stay, visit somewhere
un **séjour** [seʒuʀ]	stay (n)
un **estivant**, une **estivante** [ɛstivɑ̃, ɑ̃t]	summer guest, vacationer
un **voyage à prix forfaitaire** [vwajazapʀifɔʀfɛtɛʀ]	package tour
un **voyage d'études** [vwajaʒdetyd]	educational trip
un **voyage d'affaires** [vwajaʒdafɛʀ]	business trip
un **voyage d'agrément** [vwajaʒdagʀemɑ̃]	pleasure trip
un **voyage de noces** [vwajaʒdənɔs]	honeymoon
une **agence de voyage** [aʒɑ̃sdəvwajaʒ]	travel agency
un **syndicat d'initiative** [sɛ̃dikadinisjativ]	tourist information office

un **office de/du tourisme** [ɔfisdə/dyturism]	tourist office
un **projet** (**de voyage**) [pʀɔʒɛ (d(ə)vwajaz)]	(travel) plan
se renseigner sur qc [s(ə)ʀɑ̃sɛɲe]	to get information about s.th.
Nous nous sommes renseignés sur les prix des circuits en car.	We got information about the prices of bus tours.
un **renseignement** [ʀɑ̃sɛɲmɑ̃]	information
s'informer sur [sɛ̃fɔʀme]	to find out about
une **information** [ɛ̃fɔʀmasjɔ̃]	information
un **catalogue** [katalɔg]	catalog
un **prospectus** [pʀɔspɛktys]	brochure
recommander qc à qn [ʀ(ə)kɔmɑ̃de]	to recommend s.th. to s.o.
Nous vous recommandons l'hôtel Bellevue.	We recommend the Bellevue Hotel.
les **documents de voyage** *mpl* [dɔkymɑ̃d(ə)vwajaʒ]	travel documents

accompagner qn [akɔ̃paɲe]	to accompany s.o.
un **accompagnateur**, une **accompagnatrice** [akɔ̃paɲatœʀ, tʀis]	(travel) companion
un **voyagiste** [vwajaʒist]	tour operator
un **tour opérateur** [tuʀɔpeʀatœʀ]	tour operator

réserver [ʀezɛʀve]	to reserve
(faire) réserver une chambre	to reserve a room
une **réservation** [ʀezɛʀvasjɔ̃]	reservation
confirmer une réservation	to confirm a reservation
annuler [anyle]	to cancel

les **bagages** *mpl* [bagaʒ]	baggage
les **bagages à main**	hand baggage
une **valise** [valiz]	suitcase
(**dé**)**faire sa valise**	to (un)pack one's suitcase
un **sac** [sak]	bag
un **sac à dos**	backpack (n)
préparer [pʀepaʀe]	to prepare
préparer ses affaires	to get one's affairs in order
les **préparatifs** *mpl* [pʀepaʀatif]	preparations
une **liste** [list]	list (n)

un **guide** [gid]	guide (n)
une **carte routière** [kaʀtʀutjɛʀ]	road map
un **itinéraire** [itineʀɛʀ]	itinerary, route
un **itinéraire bis**	alternate route

partir* (**pour**) [paRtiR]	to leave (for)
Elle est partie pour l'Espagne.	She left for Spain.
partir seul	to leave alone (unaccompanied)
le **départ** [depaR]	departure
la **destination** [destinasjɔ̃]	destination
arriver* [aRive]	to arrive
arriver à destination	to reach one's destination
l'**arrivée** *f* [aRive]	arrival

un **passager**, une **passagère** [pasaʒe, ɛR]	passenger
un **contrôleur**, une **contrôleuse** [kɔ̃tRolœR, øz]	ticket inspector
un **contrôle** [kɔ̃tRol]	inspection
un **guichet** [giʃɛ]	(ticket) window
un **billet** [bijɛ]	ticket
un **billet de train/d'avion**	train/plane ticket
composter son billet	to cancel/void/validate one's ticket
un **aller simple** [alesɛ̃pl]	one-way ticket
un **aller** (**et**) **retour** [ale(e)R(ə)tuR]	round-trip ticket
un **supplément** [syplemɑ̃]	surcharge

un **train** [tRɛ̃]	train
un **train rapide**	express train
un **train direct**	direct train
voyager en train	to travel by train
manquer/rater *fam* le train	to miss the train
le **TGV** (**train à grande vitesse**) [teʒeve]	TGV, high-speed train
monter* dans le TGV	to board the TGV
descendre* du TGV	to get off the TGV
la **correspondance** [kɔRɛspɔ̃dɑ̃s]	connection, transfer
attendre la correspondance (pour)	to wait for the connection (for)
une **gare** [gaR]	(railroad) station
la **consigne** [kɔ̃siɲ]	baggage room
la **consigne automatique**	baggage lockers
un **quai** [kɛ]	platform
une **voie** [vwa]	track (n)
Le train pour Bordeaux partira de la voie 12.	The train for Bordeaux will leave from track 12.
la **classe** [klas]	class (n)
voyager en première/seconde (classe)	to travel first/second class
l'**horaire** *m* [ɔRɛR]	timetable, (flight) schedule
le **retard** [R(ə)taR]	delay (n)
On est parti avec **une heure de retard**.	We left an hour late.

une **voiture** [vwatyʀ]	car, coach
un **compartiment** [kɔ̃paʀtimɑ̃]	compartment
un **wagon-lit** [vagɔ̃li]	sleeping car
une **couchette** [kuʃɛt]	couchette
une **voiture-couchettes** [vwatyʀkuʃɛt]	sleeping car
un **wagon-restaurant** [vagɔ̃ʀɛstɔʀɑ̃]	dining car

un **avion** [avjɔ̃]	airplane
prendre l'avion	to take the plane, travel by plane
un **aéroport** [aeʀɔpɔʀ]	airport
voler [vɔle]	to fly *(See Information Box p. 40)*
un **vol** [vɔl]	flight *(See Information Box p. 40)*

décoller [dekɔle]	to take off
le **décollage** [dekɔlaʒ]	takeoff (n)
atterrir [ateʀiʀ]	to land
L'avion a atterri à 8 heures 24.	The plane landed at 8:24 A.M.
l'**atterrissage** *m* [ateʀisaʒ]	landing (n)

un **bateau**; des **bateaux** *pl* [bato]	ship
un **ferry**(-**boat**); des **ferrys, ferries, ferry-boats** *pl* [feʀi(bot)]	ferry
un **port** [pɔʀ]	port
un **port de plaisance**	marina
à bord [abɔʀ]	on board
naviguer à bord d'un voilier	to travel on board a sailboat
avoir le mal de mer [avwaʀl(ə)maldəmɛʀ]	to be seasick

un **bac** [bak]	ferry (n)
une **croisière** [kʀwazjɛʀ]	cruise (n)
s'embarquer [sɑ̃baʀke]	to board, embark
s'embarquer pour la Crète	to embark for Crete
débarquer [debaʀke]	to disembark
faire escale [fɛʀɛskal]	to make a stopover

un **car** [kaʀ]	(tour) bus
prendre le car pour Nîmes	to take the bus to Nîmes
une **autoroute** [otoʀut]	highway
une **autoroute à péage**	toll road
une **aire** [ɛʀ]	area
une **aire de repos/de pique-nique**	rest/picnic area
une **aire de service**	service area
une **aire de stationnement**	parking area

une **carte d'identité** [kaʀtdidɑ̃tite]	ID card
une **pièce d'identité** [pjɛsdidɑ̃tite]	identification, pass
présenter une pièce d'identité	to present identification
un **passeport** [paspɔʀ]	passport
un passeport biométrique/électronique	biometric/electronic passport
en règle [ɑ̃ʀɛgl]	in order
Votre passeport n'est pas en règle.	Your passport is not in order.
valable [valabl]	valid
périmé, **périmée** [peʀime]	expired, outdated
un **visa** [viza]	visa
une **frontière** [fʀɔ̃tjɛʀ]	border (n)
la **douane** [dwan]	customs
passer la douane	to go through customs
un **douanier** [dwanje]	customs agent
déclarer qc [deklaʀe]	to declare s.th.
Vous avez quelque chose à déclarer?	Do you have anything to declare?
fouiller [fuje]	to search
un **souvenir** [suv(ə)niʀ]	souvenir
un **pays** [pei]	country
partir* pour un **pays lointain**	to leave for a distant land
une **région** [ʀeʒjɔ̃]	region
une **région touristique**	tourist region
étranger, **étrangère** [etʀɑ̃ʒe, ɛʀ]	foreign
un **étranger**, une **étrangère**	foreigner
l'**étranger** *m* [etʀɑ̃ʒe]	foreign countries
à l'étranger	overseas
international, **internationale** [ɛ̃tɛʀnasjɔnal]	international (adj)
exotique [ɛgzɔtik]	exotic
l'**exotisme** *m* [ɛgzɔtism]	exoticism
le **folklore** [fɔlklɔʀ]	folklore
visiter qc [vizite]	to visit s.th. *(See Information Box p. 150)*
une **visite** [vizit]	visit (n)
un **visiteur**, une **visiteuse** [vizitœʀ, øz]	visitor
découvrir [dekuvʀiʀ]	to discover
une **découverte** [dekuvɛʀt]	discovery
une **aventure** [avɑ̃tyʀ]	adventure
partir à l'aventure	to go on an adventure

une **excursion** [ɛkskyʀsjɔ̃]	excursion
faire une **excursion en montagne**	to take a hike in the mountains
une **randonnée** [ʀɑ̃dɔne]	hike (n)
faire une **randonnée à pied**	to hike
faire une **randonnée à bicyclette**	to take a bike tour
un **chemin de grande randonnée** (**GR**)	long hiking trail
un **sentier** [sɑ̃tje]	path
la **mer** [mɛʀ]	sea *(See Information Box p. 370)*
une maison avec **vue sur la mer**	house with an ocean view
la **plage** [plaʒ]	beach
le **sable** [sabl]	sand
se baigner [s(ə)beɲe]	to swim, bathe
la **baignade** [bɛɲad]	swimming area; swimming
Baignade interdite.	No swimming.
se reposer [səʀ(ə)poze]	to rest, recover
le **repos** [ʀ(ə)po]	rest (n)
prendre un repos bien mérité	to take a well deserved rest
un **bain de soleil** [bɛ̃dsɔlɛj]	sunbathing (n)
un **coup de soleil** [kudsɔlɛj]	sunburn
en plein soleil [ɑ̃plɛ̃sɔlɛj]	in full sun
les **lunettes de soleil** *fpl* [lynɛtdəsɔlɛj]	sunglasses
l'**ambre solaire** *m* [ɑ̃bʀ(ə)sɔlɛʀ]	sunscreen
bronzer [bʀɔ̃ze]	to tan
bronzé, **bronzée** [bʀɔ̃ze]	tanned
le **bronzage** [bʀɔ̃zaʒ]	tanning *(See Information Box p. 78)*
la (**mer**) **Méditerranée** [(mɛʀ) mediteʀane]	Mediterranean (Sea)
l'(**océan**) **Atlantique** *m* [(ɔsean) atlɑ̃tik]	Atlantic (Ocean)
la **Manche** [mɑ̃ʃ]	English Channel
la **mer du Nord** [mɛʀdynɔʀ]	North Sea
la **mer Baltique** [mɛʀbaltik]	Baltic Sea
la **campagne** [kɑ̃paɲ]	country(side)
la **montagne** [mɔ̃taɲ]	mountains
la **neige** [nɛʒ]	snow

un **parc naturel** [paʀknatyʀɛl]	nature reserve, conservation area
en plein air [ɑ̃plɛnɛʀ]	outdoors
un **restaurant en plein air**	outdoor restaurant
au grand air [ogʀɑ̃tɛʀ]	in the fresh air
passer ses journées dehors/au grand air	to spend the days outdoors/ in the fresh air
se détendre [s(ə)detɑ̃dʀ]	to relax
se relaxer [s(ə)ʀ(ə)lakse]	to relax

11.2 Lodging  43

un **hôtel** [ɔ/otɛl]	hotel
une **pension** (**de famille**) [pɑ̃sjɔ̃ (d(ə)famij)]	guest house
une **auberge de jeunesse** [obɛʀʒd(ə)ʒœnɛs]	youth hostel
un **club** (**de vacances**) [klœb (d(ə)vakɑ̃s)]	(vacation) club
un **village de vacances** [vilaʒdəvakɑ̃s]	resort town
un **appartement**/une **maison de vacances** [apaʀtəmɑ̃/mɛzɔ̃d(ə)vakɑ̃s]	vacation apartment/house
louer [lwe]	to rent
chambre à louer	room for rent
une **location** [lɔkasjɔ̃]	rental (house)
libre [libʀ]	available, vacancy
complet, **complète** [kɔ̃plɛ, ɛt]	full, no vacancy
L'hôtel affiche complet.	The hotel is full.

l'**hôtellerie** *f* [ɔ/otɛlʀi]	hotel trade
un **hôtelier**, une **hôtelière** [ɔ/otəlje, jɛʀ]	hotel owner/operator
loger [lɔʒe]	to stay
loger chez l'habitant	to stay with a local
le **logement** [lɔʒmɑ̃]	accommodations, lodging
une **chambre d'hôte** [ʃɑ̃bʀ(ə)dot]	guest room, bed and breakfast
un **chalet** [ʃalɛ]	chalet
un **gîte rural** [ʒitʀyʀal]	country vacation accommodations

une **chambre** [ʃɑ̃bʀ]	room
une **chambre simple**	single room
une **chambre double**	double room
la **clé/clef** [kle]	key
le **lit** [li]	bed
un **grand lit**	double bed
un lit supplémentaire	additional bed

la **catégorie** [kategɔʀi]	category, class
confortable [kɔ̃fɔʀtabl]	comfortable
le **confort** [kɔ̃fɔʀ]	comfort
une **chambre tout confort**	a room with every modern convenience
le **luxe** [lyks]	luxury
un **hôtel de luxe**	luxury hotel
une **étoile** [etwal]	star
un **hôtel/restaurant 3 étoiles**	a three-star hotel/restaurant

un **prix forfaitaire** [pʀifɔʀfɛtɛʀ]	flat fee, all-inclusive price
la **nuit**(**ée**) [nɥi(te)]	night
Combien coûte la nuit(ée), en single/pour une personne?	How much per night for one person?
la **note** [nɔt]	bill (n)
présenter la note	to submit the bill
hors de prix ['ɔʀdəpʀi]	unaffordable
modéré, **modérée** [mɔdeʀe]	moderate, inexpensive

une **salle de bains** [saldəbɛ̃]	bathroom
se doucher [s(ə)duʃe]	to take a shower
une **douche** [duʃ]	shower (n)
prendre une douche	to take a shower
un **lavabo** [lavabo]	sink
les **W.-C.** *mpl* [vese]	toilet

une **terrasse** [teʀas]	terrace
un **balcon** [balkɔ̃]	balcony
donner sur [dɔne]	to look out over
Ma chambre donne sur la rue.	My room looks out over the street.
calme [kalm]	quiet
bruyant, **bruyante** [bʀɥijɑ̃, jɑ̃t]	noisy
central, **centrale** [sɑ̃tʀal]	central
une **piscine** [pisin]	swimming pool

la **réception** [ʀesɛpsjɔ̃]	reception (desk)
déposer ses clés à la réception	to leave the keys at the reception
le **hall** ['ol]	lobby, reception hall
l'**ascenseur** *m* [asɑ̃sœʀ]	elevator

en **demi-pension** [ɑ̃d(ə)mipɑ̃sjɔ̃]	with half-board
une chambre en demi-pension	room with half-board
en pension complète [ɑ̃pɑ̃sjɔ̃kɔ̃plɛt]	room and board
le **petit déjeuner** [p(ə)tideʒœne]	breakfast
Le petit déjeuner est compris dans le prix de la chambre.	Breakfast is included in the price of the room.
le **personnel** [pɛʀsɔnɛl]	staff, service
une **femme de chambre** [famdəʃɑ̃bʀ]	chambermaid

camper [kɑ̃pe]	to camp
le **camping** [kɑ̃piŋ]	camping
un **terrain de camping**	campground
faire du camping	to camp
Le **camping sauvage** est interdit ici.	Camping is not permitted here.
une **tente** [tɑ̃t]	tent (n)
monter la tente	to set up/pitch the tent
une **caravane** [kaʀavan]	(camping) trailer
un **campingcar** [kɑ̃piŋkaʀ]	camper (vehicle), RV

une **station** [stasjɔ̃]	vacation resort
une **station thermale**	thermal spa
une **station balnéaire**	spa, beach resort
une **station de sports d'hiver**	winter sports resort
une **colonie de vacances** [kɔlɔnid(ə)vakɑ̃s]	summer camp
une **colo** *fam* [kolo]	camp
partir en colo	to go to a summer camp

11.3 Gastronomy 

un **restaurant** [ʀɛstɔʀɑ̃]	restaurant
aller manger au restaurant	to eat in a restaurant
un **hôtel-restaurant** [ɔ/otɛlʀɛstɔʀɑ̃]	hotel and restaurant
un **bar** [baʀ]	bar
un **bistro**(**t**) [bistʀo]	pub, bar
un **café** [kafe]	café, coffee shop

un **salon de thé** [salɔ̃d(ə)te]	café, teahouse
un **libre-service** [libʀəsɛʀvis]	self-serve restaurant, cafeteria
un **self** *fam* [sɛlf]	self-serve restaurant
un **fast-food**; des **fast-foods** *pl* [fastfud]	fast-food restaurant
une **brasserie** [bʀasʀi]	restaurant, tavern
un **restauroute/restoroute** [ʀɛstoʀut]	roadside restaurant

un **patron**, une **patronne** [patʀɔ̃, ɔn]	chef, owner
un, une **chef** [ʃɛf]	chef
un restaurant tenu par un grand chef	restaurant run by a famous chef
un **cuisinier**, une **cuisinière** [kɥizinje, jɛʀ]	cook (n)
un **maître d'hôtel** [mɛtʀdotɛl]	headwaiter, maître d'
un **garçon** [gaʀsɔ̃]	waiter
Garçon, 2 cafés, s'il vous plaît.	Waiter, two coffees, please.
servir qn/qc [sɛʀviʀ]	to serve s.o./s.th.
On vous sert, Madame?	Is someone waiting on you?
le **service** [sɛʀvis]	service
un **serveur**, une **serveuse** [sɛʀvœʀ, øz]	waiter, waitress, server

un **client**, une **cliente** [klijɑ̃, ɑ̃t]	customer
la **clientèle** [klijɑ̃tɛl]	clientele
un **consommateur**, une **consommatrice** [kɔ̃sɔmatœʀ, tʀis],	customer (in a bar)
une **consommation** [kɔ̃sɔmasjɔ̃]	drink (n)
Ils mettent longtemps à apporter les consommations.	It's taking a long time for them to bring us the drinks.

gastronomique [gastʀɔnɔmik]	gastronomical, gourmet
un **menu gastronomique**	gourmet menu
la **gastronomie** [gastʀɔnɔmi]	gastronomy, culinary art
une **spécialité** [spesjalite]	specialty
la **spécialité du chef**	specialty of the house
typique de [tipik]	typical of/for
C'est un plat typique de la région.	This dish is typical for the area.
local, **locale** [lɔkal]	local
une **coutume locale**	local custom
goûter [gute]	to taste
déguster [degyste]	to taste, sample
déguster une douzaine d'huîtres	to eat a dozen oysters
une **dégustation** [degystasjɔ̃]	tasting, sampling
une **dégustation de vins**	wine tasting

le **menu** [məny]	menu
la **carte** [kaʀt]	menu
choisir un plat **à la carte**	to select a dish à la carte
la **carte des vins**	wine list
un **plat** [pla]	dish (n)
un **plat cuisiné**	ready-to-serve meal
le **plat du jour**	daily special

commander [kɔmɑ̃de]	to order
une **commande** [kɔmɑ̃d]	order (n)
Pourriez-vous **prendre les commandes**, s'il vous plaît?	Could you please take the orders?
proposer [pʀɔpoze]	to suggest

recommandé, recommandée [ʀ(ə)kɔ̃mɑ̃de]	recommended
renommé, renommée [ʀ(ə)nɔme]	well-known, famous
La Bourgogne est renommée pour ses vins.	Burgundy is famous for its wines.
conseiller [kɔ̃seje]	to advise, recommend
Quel vin pourriez-vous me conseiller?	Which wine could you recommend?
déconseiller [dekɔ̃seje]	to advise against

un **apéritif** [apeʀitif]	aperitif, pre-dinner drink
un **hors-d'œuvre** ['ɔʀdœvʀ]	appetizer, hors-d'oeuvre
des hors-d'œuvre variés	assorted hors-d'oeuvres
une **entrée** [ɑ̃tʀe]	first course, appetizer
le **plat de résistance** [plad(ə)ʀezistɑ̃s]	main course
le **plat principal** [plapʀɛ̃sipal]	main course
le **plateau de fromages** [platod(ə)fʀɔmaʒ]	cheese plate
un **dessert** [desɛʀ]	dessert *(See Information Box p. 100)*
au choix [oʃwa]	choice of
Vous pouvez prendre au choix du fromage ou un dessert.	You have a choice of cheese or a dessert.
un **digestif** [diʒestif]	digestif, after-dinner drink, cordial

la **cave** [kav]	(wine) cellar
un **vin de pays** [vɛ̃d(ə)pei]	local wine
une **bouteille** [butɛj]	bottle (n)
un **bouchon** [buʃɔ̃]	cork (n)
un **tire-bouchon**	corkscrew *(See Information Box p. 104)*
un **verre** [vɛʀ]	glass

INFO

What we use to drink

un verre d'eau	*a glass of water*
un verre à eau	*a water glass*
un verre de vin	*a glass of wine*
un verre à vin	*a wine glass*
une tasse de café	*a cup of coffee*
une tasse à café	*a coffee cup*

un **grand cru** [gʀɑ̃kʀy]	fine wine
un **pichet** [piʃɛ]	pitcher, tankard
une **carafe** [kaʀaf]	carafe
une **carafe d'eau**	pitcher of water
un **seau à glace**; des **seaux à glace** *pl* [soaglas]	ice bucket
un **glaçon** [glasɔ̃]	ice cube

un **guide** (**gastronomique**) [gid(gastʀɔnɔmik)]	(restaurant) guide
une **étoile** [etwal]	star
Ce restaurant a deux étoiles dans le guide Michelin.	This restaurant has two stars in the Michelin Guide.

le **prix** [pʀi]	price
le **tarif** [taʀif]	price
le **tarif des consommations**	drink prices
l'**addition** *f* [adisjɔ̃]	bill (n)
service compris [sɛʀviskɔ̃pʀi]	tip included
le **pourboire** [puʀbwaʀ]	tip (n)
laisser un pourboire généreux	to leave a generous tip
une **réclamation** [ʀeklamasjɔ̃]	complaint
faire une réclamation	to complain

11.4 Sightseeing  45

visiter qc [vizite]	to visit s.th. *(See Information Box p. 150)*
une **visite** (**guidée**) [vizit(gide)]	(guided) visit, tour
un **visiteur**, une **visiteuse** [vizitœʀ, øz]	visitor
touristique [tuʀistik]	touristy
une ville touristique	a touristy city
une **curiosité** (**touristique**) [kyʀjozite(tuʀistik)]	point of interest
un **site** [sit]	site, place
une **attraction** [atʀaksjɔ̃]	attraction
La tour Eiffel est une attraction pour les touristes.	The Eiffel Tower is a tourist attraction.
pittoresque [pitɔʀɛsk]	picturesque
un **monument** (**historique**) [mɔnymɑ̃ (istɔʀik)]	(historic) monument
un **château**; des **châteaux** *pl* [ʃɑto]	castle
un **château fort**	fortress
Ce château a été classé monument historique.	This castle has been declared a historic monument.
des **ruines** *fpl* [ʀɥin]	ruins
une **église en ruine**	church ruins
des **murs** *mpl* [myʀ]	walls
un **palais** [palɛ]	palace
un palais ancien	ancient palace
une **forteresse** [fɔʀtəʀɛs]	fortress
des **remparts** *mpl* [ʀɑ̃paʀ]	ramparts
un (**spectacle**) **son et lumière** [(spɛktakl)sɔ̃elymjɛʀ]	sound and light presentation
assister à un son et lumière	to attend a sound and light show
une **église** [egliz]	church
une **cathédrale** [katedʀal]	cathedral
une **cathédrale romane/gothique**	Romanesque/Gothic cathedral
un **musée** [myze]	museum
un **musée d'art moderne**	modern art museum
un **écomusée**	open-air museum

une **chapelle** [ʃapɛl]	chapel
une **basilique** [bazilik]	basilica
un **arc** [aʀk]	arch
l'**Arc de Triomphe**	Arch of Triumph
une **colonne** [kɔlɔn]	column

un **quartier** [kaʀtje]	precinct, neighborhood
une **place** [plas]	square
un **marché** (**aux puces**) [maʀʃe(opys)]	(flea) market
une **tour** [tuʀ]	tower *(See Information Box p. 201)*
On a une vue splendide du haut de la tour.	There is a wonderful view from the top of the tower.
un **pont** [pɔ̃]	bridge

un **parc** [paʀk]	park
une **fontaine** [fɔ̃tɛn]	fountain
un **jet d'eau**; des **jets d'eau** *pl* [ʒɛdo]	fountain

un **plan** [plɑ̃]	map
un **dépliant** [deplijɑ̃]	leaflet
un **tour** (**de la ville**) [tuʀ(d(ə)lavil)]	(city) tour *(See Information Box p. 201)*
un **circuit touristique** [siʀkɥituʀistik]	tour
l'**entrée** *f* [ɑ̃tʀe]	entry, admission
L'entrée au musée est gratuite pour les enfants.	Entry into the museum is free for children.

les **heures d'ouverture** *fpl* [œʀduvɛʀtyʀ]	hours of operation
la **fermeture hebdomadaire** [fɛʀmətyʀɛbdɔmadɛʀ]	closing day; closed on...

False Friends

French Word	Actual Meaning	False Friend	Correct French Word
un car	**(tour) bus**	car	*une voiture*
une cave	**cellar**	cave	*une grotte*
l'entrée	**appetizer course**	entrée	*le plat principal*

My Vocabulary

12

Art, Music, Literature

12.1 Graphic Arts  46

artistique [aʀtistik]	artistic
l'**art** *m* [aʀ]	art
les **beaux-arts**	fine arts
les **arts plastiques**	plastic arts (*painting, sculpture*)
les **arts graphiques**	graphic arts
une **œuvre d'art**	work of art
un, une **artiste** [aʀtist]	artist
un **artiste peintre**	painter

peindre [pɛ̃dʀ]	to paint
la **peinture** [pɛ̃tyʀ]	paint; painting
un **peintre** [pɛ̃tʀ]	painter
un **atelier** [atəlje]	studio; workshop
un **modèle** [mɔdɛl]	model
poser [poze]	to pose
Elle pose pour des peintres célèbres.	She is a model for famous painters.

l'**École des Beaux-Arts** *f* [ekɔldebozaʀ]	fine arts school, academy
les **Beaux-Arts** *mpl* [bozaʀ]	fine arts school, academy
faire ses études aux Beaux-Arts	to study at the art academy
la **peinture à l'huile** [pɛ̃tyʀalɥil]	oil painting
une **aquarelle** [akwaʀɛl]	watercolor (n)
un **nu** [ny]	nude (n)
une **nature morte** [natyʀmɔʀt]	still life (n)
un **pinceau**; des **pinceaux** *pl* [pɛ̃so]	artist's brush
une **palette** [palɛt]	palette

un **tableau**; des **tableaux** *pl* [tablo]	picture
une **toile** [twal]	canvas
encadrer [ɑ̃kadʀe]	to frame
un **cadre** [kadʀ]	frame (n)
un **portrait** [pɔʀtʀɛ]	portrait
un **autoportrait**	self-portrait
un **paysage** [peizaʒ]	landscape

dessiner [desine]	to draw
un **dessin** [desɛ̃]	drawing (n)
un **dessinateur**, une **dessinatrice** [desinatœʀ, tʀis]	designer; draftsman
un **crayon** [kʀɛjɔ̃]	pencil
un **portrait au crayon**	pencil portrait

un **pastel** [pastɛl]	pastel (n)
un **fusain** [fyzɛ̃]	charcoal, charcoal drawing
une esquisse au fusain	a charcoal sketch
graver [gʀave]	to engrave
une **gravure** [gʀavyʀ]	engraving, etching (n)
un **graveur** [gʀavœʀ]	etcher, engraver, print maker

un **original** [ɔʀiʒinal]	original (n)
L'original se trouve au musée du Louvre.	The original is in the Louvre.
une **reproduction** [ʀ(ə)pʀɔdyksjɔ̃]	reproduction
une **copie** [kɔpi]	copy

collectionner [kɔlɛksjɔne]	to collect
une **collection** [kɔlɛksjɔ̃]	collection
un **collectionneur**, une **collectionneuse** [kɔlɛksjɔnœʀ, øz]	collector
un **faux** [fo]	fake
L'expertise a révélé que c'était un faux.	Expert examination showed that it was a fake.
un, une **faussaire** [fosɛʀ]	faker, forger

un **musée** [myze]	museum
exposer [ɛkspoze]	to exhibit
une **exposition** [ɛkspozisjɔ̃]	exposition, exhibit
une **exposition permanente/temporaire**	permanent/temporary, special exhibit
une **galerie** [galʀi]	(art) gallery
visiter qc [vizite]	to visit s.th., look around *(See Information Box p. 150)*
une **visite** [vizit]	visit (n)
une visite guidée	guided visit

impressionniste [ɛ̃pʀesjɔnist]	impressionist (adj)
un, une **impressionniste**	impressionist (n)
l'**impressionnisme** *m* [ɛ̃pʀesjɔnism]	impressionism
expressionniste [ɛkspʀesjɔnist]	expressionist (adj)
un, une **expressionniste**	expressionist (n)
l'**expressionnisme** *m* [ɛkspʀesjɔnism]	expressionism
le **cubisme** [kybism]	cubism
le **surréalisme** [syʀealism]	surrealism
l'**art nouveau** *m* [aʀnuvo]	art nouveau
réaliste [ʀealist]	realistic
figuratif, **figurative** [figyʀatif, iv]	representational, figurative, objective
abstrait, **abstraite** [abstʀɛ, ɛt]	abstract
Après une période figurative, il s'est tourné vers l'art abstrait.	After a representational period he turned to abstract art.

l'**architecture** *f* [aʀʃitɛktyʀ]	architecture
Notre-Dame de Paris est un exemple célèbre de l'architecture gothique.	Notre-Dame in Paris is a famous example of Gothic architecture.
un, une **architecte** [aʀʃitɛkt]	architect
un **projet** [pʀɔʒɛ]	project, plan
un **plan** [plɑ̃]	plan, design, schedule, map
monumental, monumentale [mɔnymɑ̃tal]	monumental, immense
un **monument** [mɔnymɑ̃]	monument

le **style** [stil]	style
le **style roman**	Romanesque style
le **style gothique**	Gothic style
le **style médiéval**	medieval style
le **style baroque**	baroque style
le **style classique**	classical style

créer [kʀee]	to create
la **créativité** [kʀeativite]	creativity
réaliser [ʀealize]	to realize, carry out
la **réalisation** [ʀealizasjɔ̃]	realization, attainment, completion
La réalisation de ce projet a duré 5 ans.	Completion of this project took five years.

sculpter [skylte]	to sculpt, model, shape, carve
la **sculpture** [skyltyʀ]	sculpture (n)
une **statue** [staty]	statue
une **statue de/en bronze**	bronze statue
un **buste** [byst]	bust
un **bas-relief** [baʀəliɛf]	bas-relief, low relief
le **marbre** [maʀbʀ]	marble
une colonne en marbre de Carrare	column of Carrara marble
modeler [mɔd(ə)le]	to model, shape
l'**argile** *f* [aʀʒil]	clay
la **poterie** [pɔtʀi]	pottery
faire de la poterie	to make pottery
la **céramique** [seʀamik]	ceramics

beau, **bel**, **belle; beaux, belles** *pl* [bo, bɛl]	beautiful
la **beauté** [bote]	beauty
laid, **laide** [lɛ, lɛd]	ugly
la **laideur** [lɛdœʀ]	ugliness
célèbre [selɛbʀ]	famous
inconnu, **inconnue** [ɛ̃kɔny]	unknown
anonyme [anɔnim]	anonymous
une œuvre anonyme	anonymous work

12.2 Music and Musical Performances  47

musical, **musicale** [myzikal]	musical
une **comédie musicale**	musical comedy
la **musique** [myzik]	music
faire de la musique	to play music
la **musique moderne**	modern music
la **musique folklorique**	folk music
la **musique classique**	classical music
une **école de musique**	music school
un **musicien**, une **musicienne** [myzisjɛ̃, jɛn]	musician
un **son** [sɔ̃]	sound
une **note** [nɔt]	note
écouter [ekute]	to listen *(See Information Box p. 35)*

---

la **musique instrumentale** [myzikɛ̃stʀymɑ̃tal]	instrumental music
la **musique orchestrale** [myzikɔʀkɛstʀal]	orchestral music
la **musique vocale** [myzikvɔkal]	vocal music, singing
le **conservatoire** [kɔ̃sɛʀvatwaʀ]	conservatory, music school
la **gamme** [gam]	scale (n)
faire ses gammes	to practice scales
la **gamme majeure**	major scale
la **gamme mineure**	minor scale
harmonieux, **harmonieuse** [aʀmɔnjø, jøz]	harmonious
l'**harmonie** *f* [aʀmɔni]	harmony
la **mesure** [m(ə)zyʀ]	measure (n)
jouer en mesure	to play in time, keep time

---

un **instrument** [ɛ̃stʀymɑ̃]	instrument *(See Information Box p. 195)*
une **flûte** [flyt]	flute
prendre des cours de **flûte à bec**	to take recorder lessons
une **guitare** [gitaʀ]	guitar
un **violon** [vjɔlɔ̃]	violin
une **trompette** [tʀɔ̃pɛt]	trumpet
une **clarinette** [klaʀinɛt]	clarinet
un **piano** [pjano]	piano
apprendre le piano	to learn to play the piano
un **orgue**; des **orgues** *fpl* [ɔʀg]	organ
un **orgue électronique**	electronic organ, keyboard
une **batterie** [batʀi]	drum set

un **instrument à cordes** [ɛ̃stʀymɑ̃akɔʀd]	stringed instrument
un **instrument à vent** [ɛ̃stʀymɑ̃avɑ̃]	wind instrument
un **instrument à percussion** [ɛ̃stʀymɑ̃apɛʀkysjɔ̃]	percussion instrument
un **alto** [alto]	viola
un **violoncelle** [vjɔlɔ̃sɛl]	cello
une **contrebasse** [kɔ̃tʀəbas]	(stringed) bass
une **harpe** ['aʀp]	harp
un **hautbois** ['obwa]	oboe
un **piano à queue** [pjanoakœ]	grand piano, concert piano
une **mélodie** [melɔdi]	melody
un **air** [ɛʀ]	melody, air, tune
un air gai et entraînant	a lively, high-spirited tune
un **rythme** [ʀitm]	rhythm
un **mouvement** [muvmɑ̃]	movement
le **premier mouvement** de la sonate «Au clair de lune»	the first movement of the sonata "Au clair de lune"
une **symphonie** [sɛ̃fɔni]	symphony
une **sonate** [sɔnat]	sonata
une **sonate pour piano**	piano sonata
un **concerto** [kɔ̃sɛʀto]	concerto
un concerto pour violon et orchestre	concerto for violin and orchestra
un **quatuor** [kwatɥɔʀ]	quartet
un **quatuor à cordes**	string quartet
la **musique de chambre** [myzikdəʃɑ̃bʀ]	chamber music
un **morceau**; des **morceaux** *pl* [mɔʀso]	(musical) piece
jouer un morceau de musique	to play a musical piece
chanter [ʃɑ̃te]	to sing
chanter en direct	to sing live
chanter en play-back	to mime, lip-synch
un **chanteur**, une **chanteuse** [ʃɑ̃tœʀ, øz]	singer
un **chant** [ʃɑ̃]	song
une **chanson** [ʃɑ̃sɔ̃]	song
un **chœur** [kœʀ]	chorus
Chantons tous **en chœur**.	Let's all sing in chorus.
une **chorale** [kɔʀal]	chorale, choir
chanter dans une chorale	to sing in a chorus
un **lied** [lid]	song, lied
un **opéra** [ɔpeʀa]	opera

un **ballet** [balɛ]	ballet
danser [dɑ̃se]	to dance
un **danseur**, une **danseuse** [dɑ̃sœʀ, øz]	dancer
le **jazz** [dʒɑz]	jazz (n)
le **rock** [ʀɔk]	rock (n)
un **groupe** [gʀup]	group, band
jouer de la batterie dans un groupe de rock	to play drums in a rock band
la **musique pop** [myzikpɔp]	pop music
le **reggae** [ʀege]	reggae (n)
le **rap** [ʀap]	rap (n)
la **techno** [tɛkno]	techno (n)
un **concert** [kɔ̃sɛʀ]	concert
un **orchestre** [ɔʀkɛstʀ]	orchestra
un **chef d'orchestre**	orchestra conductor
diriger [diʀiʒe]	to conduct
un, une **soliste** [sɔlist]	soloist
un **gala** [gala]	gala
un **récital** [ʀesital]	recital, solo performance
donner un **récital de chant**	to present a singing recital
un **festival** [fɛstival]	festival
une **tournée** [tuʀne]	tour
s'abonner à qc [sabɔne]	to subscribe to s.th.
s'abonner à l'opéra	to subscribe/get a season's ticket to the opera
un **abonnement** [abɔnmɑ̃]	subscription
un **abonnement pour la saison**	season's subscription
un **abonné**, une **abonnée** [abɔne]	subscriber
un **billet** [bijɛ]	ticket
une **salle de concert** [saldəkɔ̃sɛʀ]	concert hall
un **music-hall**; des **music-halls** *pl* [myzikol]	music hall
le **parterre** [paʀtɛʀ]	orchestra (seating area)
le **balcon** [balkɔ̃]	balcony
une **loge** [lɔʒ]	box
être aux 1ères loges *loc*	to be up close/in premier seating
une **représentation** [ʀəpʀezɑ̃tasjɔ̃]	presentation, performance
interpréter [ɛ̃tɛʀpʀete]	to interpret
Elle interprète Mozart à merveille.	She is a marvelous interpreter of Mozart.
un, une **interprète** [ɛ̃tɛʀpʀɛt]	interpreter

un, une **virtuose** [viʀtɥoz]	virtuoso
Il joue du violon **en virtuose**.	He is a virtuoso violinist.
le **talent** [talɑ̃]	talent
doué, **douée** [due]	gifted
un **enfant prodige** [ɑ̃fɑ̃pʀɔdiʒ]	child prodigy
une **cantatrice** [kɑ̃tatʀis]	female (opera) singer
une **diva** [diva]	diva, celebrated female singer

applaudir [aplodiʀ]	to applaud
les **applaudissements** *mpl* [aplodismɑ̃]	applause
siffler [sifle]	to whistle
critiquer [kʀitike]	to criticize
un, une **critique** [kʀitik]	critic
Les critiques ont été très sévères.	The critics were very harsh.
la **critique** [kʀitik]	criticism

un **microphone** [mikʀɔfɔn]	microphone
un **micro** *fam* [mikʀo]	mic
un **amplificateur** [ɑ̃plifikatœʀ]	amplifier
un **ampli** *fam* [ɑ̃pli]	amp
la **sonorisation** [sɔnɔʀizasjɔ̃]	public address system
la **sono** *fam* [sɔno]	PA system
La sono est trop forte.	The PA/sound is too loud.
un **décibel** [desibɛl]	decibel

enregistrer [ɑ̃ʀ(ə)ʒistʀe]	to record
un **enregistrement** [ɑ̃ʀ(ə)ʒistʀəmɑ̃]	recording
un (**disque**) **compact** [(disk)kɔ̃pakt]	compact disc
un **CD** [sede]	CD
Son dernier CD est sorti il y a deux semaines.	His latest CD was released two weeks ago.

12.3 Literature  48

littéraire [liteʀɛʀ]	literary
un **texte littéraire**	literary text
un **texte non-littéraire**	non-fiction text
le **genre littéraire**	(literary) genre
un **prix littéraire**	literary prize
la **littérature** [liteʀatyʀ]	literature
la **littérature de** (**quai de**) **gare**	mass-market literature
la **littérature engagée**	engaged literature (with social and political commitments)
les **lettres** *fpl* [lɛtʀ]	language and literature, humanities
un **homme**/une **femme de lettres**	writer, author
les **époques littéraires** *fpl* [epɔkliteʀɛʀ]	literary eras
les **courants littéraires** *mpl* [kuʀɑ̃liteʀɛʀ]	literary currents, movements
le **classicisme** [klasisism]	classicism
le **romantisme** [ʀɔmɑ̃tism]	romanticism
le **réalisme** [ʀealism]	realism
le **naturalisme** [natyʀalism]	naturalism
le **symbolisme** [sɛ̃bɔlism]	symbolism
l'**existentialisme** *m* [egzistɑ̃sjalism]	existentialism
Sartre est le chef de file de l'existentialisme français.	Sartre is the leading proponent of French existentialism.
écrire [ekʀiʀ]	to write
un **écrivain** [ekʀivɛ̃]	writer, author
un **auteur**, une **autrice**/une **auteure** [otœʀ, tʀis]	author
un **romancier**, une **romancière** [ʀɔmɑ̃sje, jɛʀ]	novelist
un **poète** [pɔɛt]	poet
un **éditeur**, une **éditrice** [editœʀ, tʀis]	editor, publisher
une **édition** [edisjɔ̃]	edition
acheter un livre dans une **édition de poche**	to buy a book in a pocket edition
une **maison d'édition**	publishing house
paraître [paʀɛtʀ]	to appear, come out
vient de paraître	has just come out

une **œuvre** [œvʀ]	work (n)
les **œuvres complètes** de Balzac	Balzac's collected works
un **ouvrage** [uvʀaʒ]	work (n)
publier un ouvrage	to publish a book/work
un **passage** [pasaʒ]	passage *(See Information Box p. 78)*
un **extrait** [ɛkstʀɛ]	excerpt

un **livre** [livʀ]	book
un **bouquin** *fam* [bukɛ̃]	light novel
le **titre** [titʀ]	title
une **page** [paʒ]	page *(See Information Box p. 78)*
un **chapitre** [ʃapitʀ]	chapter
un **volume** [vɔlym]	volume
une encyclopédie en 24 volumes	encyclopedia in 24 volumes
un **tome** [tɔm]	volume
la **table des matières** [tabl(ə)dematjɛʀ]	table of contents
la **couverture** [kuvɛʀtyʀ]	cover
le **dos du livre** [dodylivʀ]	spine (of book)

une **bande dessinée** (**BD**) [bɑ̃ddesine (bede)]	comic strip
un **album** [albɔm]	issue, book
J'ai tous les albums d'Astérix.	I have all the issues of Astérix.
un **dessinateur**, une **dessinatrice** [desinatœʀ, tʀis]	illustrator
illustrer qc [ilystʀe]	to illustrate s.th.
l'**illustration** *f* [ilystʀasjɔ̃]	illustration
un **illustrateur**, une **illustratrice** [ilystʀatœʀ, tʀis]	illustrator

une **bulle** [byl]	speech balloon
Les personnages des BD s'expriment par bulles.	Characters in comic strips speak in balloons.
un **scénario** [senaʀjo]	script; story
un, une **scénariste** [senaʀist]	script writer; screenwriter
humoristique [ymɔʀistik]	humorous
un **dessin humoristique**	caricature, cartoon
l'**humour** *m* [ymuʀ]	humor
une **planche** [plɑ̃ʃ]	plate

12.4 Prose, Nonfiction  49

la **prose** [pRoz]	prose
un **roman** [Rɔmɑ̃]	novel
un **roman d'aventures**	adventure novel
un **roman policier**/un **polar** *fam*	crime novel, whodunit
un **roman de science-fiction**	science fiction novel
un **roman à l'eau de rose**	novelette, romance novel

une **nouvelle** [nuvɛl]	novella, short story
un **conte** [kɔ̃t]	story, tale, fairy tale
un **conte satirique**	satirical tale
un **conte de fées**	fairy tale
une **biographie** [bjɔgRafi]	biography
une **autobiographie** [otobjɔgRafi]	autobiography
les **mémoires** *mpl* [memwaR]	memoir
une **légende** [leʒɑ̃d]	legend
un **traité** [tRɛte]	treatise, discourse
un **traité de philosophie**	philosophical treatise
un **essai** [esɛ]	essay
un **discours** [diskuR]	speech, talk (n)
faire/prononcer un discours	to give a speech
une **lettre** [lɛtR]	letter
Les *Lettres persanes* de Montesquieu sont pleines d'ironie.	Montesquieu's *Lettres persanes* are filled with irony.
un **proverbe** [pRɔvɛRb]	proverb

la **tension** [tɑ̃sjɔ̃]	tension
le **suspense** [syspɛns]	suspense
le **fil de l'action** [fild(ə)laksjɔ̃]	plot (line), action
interrompre le fil de l'action par un commentaire	to interrupt the action with commentary
le **fil conducteur** [filkɔ̃dyktœR]	thread
le **déroulement** [deRulmɑ̃]	unfolding, unwinding
un **retour en arrière** [R(ə)tuRɑ̃naRjɛR]	flashback
une **allusion** [a(l)lyzjɔ̃]	allusion
faire allusion à qn/qc	to allude to s.o./s.th.
un **lieu commun** [ljøkɔmɛ̃]	platitude, cliché
Ce livre accumule les lieux communs.	This book teems with platitudes.

un **article** [aʀtikl]	article
consacrer un long article à un événement	to devote a long article to an event
un **document** [dɔkymɑ̃]	document (n)
adapter [adapte]	adapt
Il a adapté son roman pour la télévision.	He adapted his novel for television.
intégral, **intégrale** [ɛ̃tegʀal]	entire, unabridged
l'**œuvre intégrale** d'un écrivain	a writer's unabridged works
abrégé, **abrégée** [abʀeʒe]	abridged, shortened
une **version abrégée**	abridged version

une **publication** [pyblikasjɔ̃]	publication
une **anecdote** [anɛkdɔt]	anecdote
Il paraît que cette anecdote est véridique.	It seems that this anecdote is based on fact.
un **témoignage** [temwaɲaʒ]	statement, testimony
un témoignage (im)partial	(im)partial testimony
journalistique [ʒuʀnalistik]	journalistic
un **texte journalistique**	newspaper text
captivant, **captivante** [kaptivɑ̃, ɑ̃t]	captivating, exciting
passionnant, **passionnante** [pasjɔnɑ̃, ɑ̃t]	exciting

un **récit** [ʀesi]	account, report (n)
une **histoire** [istwaʀ]	story
fictif, **fictive** [fiktif, iv]	fictitious
la **fiction** [fiksjɔ̃]	fiction
C'est de la pure fiction.	That is pure fiction.
un **portrait** [pɔʀtʀɛ]	portrait
dresser un portrait de qn	to do a portrait of s.o.

narratif, **narrative** [naʀatif, iv]	narrative
Le poème comporte quelques éléments narratifs.	The poem includes some narrative elements.
un **narrateur**, une **narratrice** [naʀatœʀ, tʀis]	narrator
un **narrateur omniscient**	omniscient narrator
la **perspective** [pɛʀspɛktiv]	perspective
l'**optique** *f* [ɔptik]	point of view
se placer dans l'**optique du lecteur**	to see things from the reader's viewpoint

un, une **journaliste** [ʒuʀnalist]	journalist
un **reportage** [ʀ(ə)pɔʀtaʒ]	reporting
un **compte rendu** [kɔ̃tʀɑ̃dy]	report
une **interview** [ɛ̃tɛʀvju]	interview (n)
accorder une interview à la télévision	to do an interview on television

observer [ɔpsɛʀve]	to observe
une **observation** [ɔpsɛʀvasjɔ̃]	observation
affirmer [afiʀme]	to affirm, claim
Il affirme que cette histoire est vraie.	He claims that this story is true.
une **affirmation** [afiʀmasjɔ̃]	affirmation, claim
réfléchir à/sur qc [ʀefleʃiʀ]	to reflect on s.th.
une **réflexion** [ʀeflɛksjɔ̃]	reflection
s'accorder un **temps de réflexion**	to take some time for reflection
mettre en relief [mɛtʀɑ̃ʀəljɛf]	to emphasize, show clearly
mettre en évidence [mɛtʀɑ̃nevidɑ̃s]	to present clearly, emphasize
souligner [suliɲe]	to underline, emphasize
Ce critique met en relief/met en évidence/souligne la gravité du problème.	This critic shows/stresses/underlines the seriousness of the situation.
exagérer [ɛgzaʒeʀe]	to exaggerate
une **exagération** [ɛgzaʒeʀasjɔ̃]	exaggeration
un **point de vue** [pwɛ̃dvy]	point of view
une (**prise de**) **position** [(pʀizdə)pɔzisjɔ̃]	position, statement
prendre clairement position sur qc	to take a clear position on s.th.
une **opinion** [ɔpiɲɔ̃]	opinion
donner son opinion sur qc	to give one's opinion on s.th.
un **avis** [avi]	opinion, view
à mon avis	in my view
un **argument** [aʀgymɑ̃]	argument, contention
prouver [pʀuve]	to prove
Rien ne prouve que ce soit vrai.	There is nothing to prove that is true.
contredire qn [kɔ̃tʀədiʀ]	to contradict s.o.
une **thèse** [tɛz]	assertion, claim, theory
formuler une thèse	to formulate a theory
une **hypothèse** [ipɔtɛz]	hypothesis
avancer une hypothèse	to put forth a hypothesis, hypothesize
une **antithèse** [ɑ̃titɛz]	antithesis
une **synthèse** [sɛ̃tɛz]	synthesis
faire la synthèse de qc	to synthesize s.th.

s'engager pour qc [sɑ̃gaʒe]	to commit to, undertake s.th.
s'adresser à qn [sadʀɛse]	to address s.o.
L'auteur s'adresse avant tout à la jeunesse.	The author addresses youth above all.
une **question** [kɛstjɔ̃]	question (n)
un **problème** [pʀɔblɛm]	problem

être convaincu, convaincue que [kɔ̃vɛ̃ky]	to be convinced that
une **conviction** [kɔ̃viksjɔ̃]	conviction
ma conviction profonde	my deep conviction
une **intention** [ɛ̃tɑ̃sjɔ̃]	intention
avoir l'intention de faire qc	to have the intention of doing s.th.
approuver [apʀuve]	to approve
lu et approuvé	read and approved

12.5 Poetry

50

poétique [pɔetik]	poetic
l'œuvre poétique de Prévert	the poetic work of Prévert
un **poète** [pɔɛt]	poet
la **poésie** [pɔezi]	poetry
un **poème** [pɔɛm]	poem
lyrique [liʀik]	lyrical
le **lyrisme** [liʀism]	lyricism; lyric poetry

un **recueil** [ʀəkœj]	collection
un **recueil de poèmes**	collection of poems
une **anthologie** [ɑ̃tɔlɔʒi]	anthology
une anthologie de la **poésie française**	anthology of French poetry
un **cycle** [sikl]	cycle
un **sonnet** [sɔnɛ]	sonnet
une **ode** [od]	ode
une **ballade** [balad]	ballad
une **fable** [fabl]	fable
les fables de La Fontaine	the fables of La Fontaine

sentimental, **sentimentale** [sɑ̃timɑ̃tal]	sentimental
le **sentiment** [sɑ̃timɑ̃]	feeling, sentiment
l'**humeur** *f* [ymœʀ]	mood *(See Information Box p. 77)*
être d'humeur joyeuse	to be in a joyful mood
l'**état d'âme** *m* [etadɑm]	mood, state of mind
l'**atmosphère** *f* [atmɔsfɛʀ]	atmosphere

imagé, **imagée** [imaʒe]	colorful, figurative
une expression imagée	a colorful expression
une **image** [imaʒ]	image
un style **riche en images**	a style rich in imagery
une **métaphore** [metafɔʀ]	metaphor
symbolique [sɛ̃bɔlik]	symbolic
un **symbole** [sɛ̃bɔl]	symbol
le **rythme** [ʀitm]	meter
un **enjambement** [ɑ̃ʒɑ̃bmɑ̃]	enjambement, run-on line
une **syllabe** [silab]	syllable
un **octosyllabe** [ɔktɔsilab]	octosyllable
un **alexandrin** [alɛksɑ̃dʀɛ̃]	alexandrine verse
un **dodécasyllabe** [dodekasilab]	dodecasyllable
une **allitération** [aliteʀasjɔ̃]	alliteration
une **césure** [sezyʀ]	caesura
la **forme** [fɔʀm]	form
un **poème à forme fixe**	fixed-verse poem
une **strophe** [stʀɔf]	stanza
une **strophe de quatre vers**	four-verse stanza, quatrain
un **refrain** [ʀəfʀɛ̃]	refrain
un **vers** [vɛʀ]	verse, line
la **versification** [vɛʀsifikasjɔ̃]	study of verse, art of poetry, versification
un **tercet** [tɛʀsɛ]	tercet
un **quatrain** [katʀɛ̃]	quatrain
Le sonnet se compose de deux quatrains et de deux tercets.	A sonnet is made up of two quatrains and two tercets.
rimer avec qc [ʀime]	to rhyme with s.th.
Amour rime avec *toujours*.	*Amour* rhymes with *toujours*.
la **rime** [ʀim]	rhyme (n)
une **rime pauvre/riche**	poor/rich rhyme
une **rime plate** (**aa bb**)	rhyming couplet
une **rime croisée** (**ab ab**)	alternating rhyme
sonore [sɔnɔʀ]	sonorous
la **sonorité** [sɔnɔʀite]	sonority

12.6 Drama  51

le **théâtre** [teɑtʀ]	theater
tragique [tʀaʒik]	tragic
la **tragédie** [tʀaʒedi]	tragedy
comique [kɔmik]	comical
la **comédie** [kɔmedi]	comedy
dramatique [dʀamatik]	dramatic
un auteur dramatique	playwright
le **drame** [dʀam]	drama, play

le **comique** [kɔmik]	humor, comedy
le **comique de situation**	situational comedy
le **comique de caractère**	character comedy
le **comique de langage**	wordplay comedy

une **pièce** (**de théâtre**) [pjɛs (d(ə)teɑtʀ)]	play, theatrical piece
une **pièce en prose**	prose piece
une **pièce en vers**	play in verse
un **acte** [akt]	act (n)
une pièce en cinq actes	a play in five acts
un **tableau**; des **tableaux** *pl* [tablo]	scene
un drame en trois tableaux	a play in three scenes
une **scène** [sɛn]	scene
la scène précédente	preceding scene
la scène suivante	following scene
l'**action** *f* [aksjɔ̃]	action
L'action se déroule dans l'Antiquité.	The action takes place in Antiquity.
l'**action principale**	main plot
l'**action secondaire**	sub-plot

le **point de départ** [pwɛ̃d(ə)depaʀ]	point of departure
L'action a pour point de départ l'assassinat du roi.	The point of departure is the assassination of the king.
l'**exposition** *f* [ɛkspozisjɔ̃]	introduction, preface
l'**intrigue** *f* [ɛ̃tʀig]	plot (n)
le **mobile** [mɔbil]	motive
le **nœud** [nø]	crux, key point
Le nœud du drame se forme à l'acte III, scène 4.	The crux of the play comes in act III, scene 4.
le **point culminant** [pwɛ̃kylminɑ̃]	highpoint, climax
le **coup de théâtre** [kudteɑtʀ]	theatrical twist
un **quiproquo** [kipʀɔko]	misunderstanding, mix-up
le **malentendu** [malɑ̃tɑ̃dy]	misunderstanding
Toute l'histoire repose sur un malentendu.	The entire story is based on a misunderstanding.

le **dénouement** [denumɑ̃]	unraveling, denouement
un dénouement heureux	happy ending
fatal, **fatale** [fatal]	fatal
une issue fatale	fatal outcome
un **héros**, une **héroïne** ['eʀo, eʀɔin]	hero, heroine
un, une **protagoniste** [pʀɔtagɔnist]	protagonist, main character, central figure
un **dialogue** [djalɔg]	dialogue
un **monologue** [mɔnɔlɔg]	monologue
L'action est interrompue par un long monologue.	The action is interrupted by a long monologue.
représenter [ʀəpʀezɑ̃te]	to present, put on
une **représentation** [ʀəpʀezɑ̃tasjɔ̃]	presentation
la **première** [pʀəmjɛʀ]	premiere, first performance
assister à une **première mondiale**	to attend a world premiere
mettre en scène [mɛtʀɑ̃sɛn]	to direct
la **mise en scène** [mizɑ̃sɛn]	direction
le **metteur en scène** [mɛtœʀɑ̃sɛn]	director
monter une pièce [mɔ̃teynpjɛs]	to direct
la **répétition** [ʀepetisjɔ̃]	rehearsal
la (**répétition**) **générale**	dress rehearsal
le **public** [pyblik]	audience
un **rôle** [ʀol]	role
le **premier rôle**	leading role
jouer [ʒwe]	to play
Elle joue ce rôle à merveille.	She plays this role marvelously.
le **jeu** [ʒœ]	acting, playing (n)
un **comédien**, une **comédienne** [kɔmedjɛ̃, jɛn]	actor, actress
un **acteur**, une **actrice** [aktœʀ, tʀis]	(film) actor, actress
un **figurant**, une **figurante** [figyʀɑ̃, ɑ̃t]	extra (n)
débuter [debyte]	to make one's debut
avoir le trac [avwaʀl(ə)tʀak]	to have stage fright

12.7 Working with Texts  52

une **idée** [ide]	idea
exposer ses idées	to state one's ideas
une **pensée** [pɑ̃se]	thought (n)
prendre parti pour/contre [pʀɑ̃dʀpaʀti]	to side with/against
se révolter (**contre**) [s(ə)ʀevɔlte]	to revolt, rebel (against)
critiquer [kʀitike]	to criticize
la **critique** [kʀitik]	criticism
s'élever contre [sel(ə)ve]	to protest against
Cet écrivain s'élève contre la violence.	This writer is protesting against violence.
distraire [distʀɛʀ]	to distract, amuse
Le but de l'auteur est de distraire son public.	The author's goal is to amuse his audience.
amuser [amyze]	to amuse
le **genre** [ʒɑ̃ʀ]	genre, type
le **genre dramatique**	drama, dramatic genre
une **œuvre** [œvʀ]	work (n)
un **chef d'œuvre**	masterpiece
être tiré, **tirée de** [tiʀe]	to be taken from
Ce passage est tiré d'une nouvelle de Le Clézio.	This passage is taken from a novella by Le Clézio.
le **titre** [titʀ]	title
le **sous-titre**	subtitle
un **cycle** [sikl]	cycle
Ce poème fait partie d'un cycle.	This poem is part of a cycle.
une **trilogie** [tʀilɔʒi]	trilogy
C'est le **premier volet d'une trilogie**.	This is the first part of a trilogy.
s'intituler [sɛ̃tityle]	to be titled
Le roman s'intitule *Germinal*.	The novel is titled *Germinal*.
un **sujet** [syʒɛ]	subject, topic
un sujet d'actualité	current topic
le **thème** [tɛm]	topic, subject
il s'agit de [ilsaʒidə]	it is about, deals with, involves
Il s'agit d'un discours sur l'éducation.	It involves a discourse on education.
il est question de [ilɛkɛstjɔ̃də]	it is a question of, deals with
Au premier acte, il est question de la guerre.	It deals with war in the first act.

traiter (**de**) **qc** [tʀɛte]	to deal with s.th.
L'auteur traite un sujet délicat.	The author deals with a delicate subject.
parler de qc [paʀle]	to speak of s.th.

la **structure** [stʀyktyʀ]	structure
se diviser en [s(ə)divize]	to be divided into
Cet ouvrage se divise en trois récits.	This work is divided into three stories.
se composer de [s(ə)kɔ̃pɔze]	to consist of
comporter [kɔ̃pɔʀte]	to include, contain, consist of
Sa tragédie comporte deux parties principales.	His tragedy consists of two main parts.
une **phase** [faz]	phase, stage
un **chapitre** [ʃapitʀ]	chapter
chapitre 2, ligne 14	chapter 2, line 14

une **narration** [naʀasjɔ̃]	narrative
l'**introduction** *f* [ɛ̃tʀɔdyksjɔ̃]	introduction
le **début** [deby]	beginning, start
le **développement** [dev(ə)lɔpmɑ̃]	development
Le développement de l'intrigue est interrompu par des retours en arrière.	The plot development is interrupted by flashbacks.
la **partie principale** [paʀtipʀɛ̃sipal]	main part
le **tournant** [tuʀnɑ̃]	turning point
Le tournant de l'action se situe au chapitre suivant.	The turning point in the action is in the following chapter.
la **conclusion** [kɔ̃klyzjɔ̃]	conclusion
un essai dont la conclusion manque de logique	an essay whose conclusion lacks logic
la **fin** [fɛ̃]	end (n)
à la fin	at the end

analyser [analize]	to analyze
une **analyse** (**de texte**) [analiz (d(ə)tɛkst)]	analysis (of text)
expliquer [ɛksplike]	to explain
une **explication de texte** [ɛksplikasjɔ̃d(ə)tɛkst]	interpretation of text
commenter [kɔmɑ̃te]	to comment
un **commentaire** [kɔmɑ̃tɛʀ]	commentary
rédiger un commentaire de texte	to compose a commentary on a text
peser le pour et le contre [pəzel(ə)puʀel(ə)kɔ̃tʀ]	to weigh the pluses and minuses
un **avantage** [avɑ̃taʒ]	advantage
un **inconvénient** [ɛ̃kɔ̃venjɑ̃]	disadvantage
résumer [ʀezyme]	to summarize

un **résumé** [Rezyme]	summary
faire un bref résumé du passage	to do a brief summary of the passage
un **paragraphe** [paRagRaf]	paragraph
un **extrait** [ɛkstRɛ]	excerpt

d'abord [dabɔR]	at first, firstly
Tout d'abord, l'auteur présente ses personnages.	First of all, the author introduces his characters.
pour commencer [puRkɔmɑ̃se]	at the start, to begin with, first
ensuite [ɑ̃sɥit]	then, next
Ensuite, il parle de ses intentions.	Then he speaks of his intentions.
de plus [dəplys]	in addition
en effet [ɑ̃nefɛ]	in fact
En effet, il explique ses idées d'une manière remarquable.	In fact, he explains his ideas in a remarkable way.
donc [dɔ̃k]	thus, therefore
enfin [ɑ̃fɛ̃]	finally
Enfin, il résume les différents aspects du problème.	Finally, he sums up the different aspects of the problem.
finalement [finalmɑ̃]	finally
pour finir [puRfiniR]	finally, in the end
en conclusion [ɑ̃kɔ̃klyzjɔ̃]	in conclusion
En conclusion, on peut dire que son argumentation est convaincante.	In conclusion, it can be said that his line of reasoning is convincing.
bref [bRɛf]	in short
Bref, je trouve que l'auteur a tort.	In short, I find that the author is wrong.
dans l'ensemble [dɑ̃lɑ̃sɑ̃bl]	overall, all in all
pourtant [puRtɑ̃]	however, (and) yet
Le héros est sincère, et pourtant il n'est pas sympathique.	The hero is sincere, and yet he is not sympathetic.

en premier lieu [ɑ̃pRəmjeljø]	in the first place
En premier lieu, il faut signaler la clarté de la langue.	First of all, we must mention the clarity of the language.
par conséquent [paRkɔ̃sekɑ̃]	as a result, consequently
pour conclure [puRkɔ̃klyR]	finally, in conclusion, to conclude

interpréter [ɛ̃tɛʀpʀete]	to interpret
une **interprétation** [ɛ̃tɛʀpʀetasjɔ̃]	interpretation
le **contexte** [kɔ̃tɛkst]	context
replacer un extrait dans son contexte	to put an excerpt back into context
le **plan** [plɑ̃]	plan, structure, organization
un **détail**; des **détails** *pl* [detaj]	detail (n)
un **message** [mɛsaʒ]	message
dégager le message d'un texte	to figure out the message in a text
la **signification** [siɲifikasjɔ̃]	meaning
symboliser [sɛ̃bɔlize]	to symbolize
un **symbole** [sɛ̃bɔl]	symbol
une **méthode** [metɔd]	method
les **moyens** (**d'expression**) *mpl* [mwajɛ̃ (dɛkspʀesjɔ̃)]	means (of expression)
décrire qc [dekʀiʀ]	to describe s.th.
une **description** [dɛskʀipsjɔ̃]	description
énumérer [enymeʀe]	to enumerate, list
une **énumération** [enymeʀasjɔ̃]	enumeration
Ce passage comporte de nombreuses énumérations.	This passage contains many enumerations.
comparer qn/qc à qn/qc [kɔ̃paʀe]	to compare s.o./s.th. to s.o./s.th.
une **comparaison** [kɔ̃paʀɛzɔ̃]	comparison
une **répétition** [ʀepetisjɔ̃]	repetition
se dérouler [s(ə)deʀule]	to unfold
le **déroulement de l'action** [deʀulmɑ̃d(ə)laksjɔ̃]	the unfolding of the plot
se situer [s(ə)sitɥe]	to be placed, located
La scène se situe à la fin de l'acte II.	The scene is found at the end of act II.
se passer [s(ə)pase]	to happen, take place
L'histoire se passe à Marseille.	The story takes place in Marseille.
le **lieu** [ljø]	place (n), setting
le **temps** [tɑ̃]	time
Molière ne respecte pas toujours les **unités de lieu**, **de temps** et **d'action**.	Molière does not always respect the unity of place, time, and action.
contenir [kɔ̃t(ə)niʀ]	to contain
le **contenu** [kɔ̃t(ə)ny]	contents
le **fond** [fɔ̃]	substance
analyser le fond et la forme	to analyze the substance and form

un **héros**, une **héroïne** ['eRo, eRoin]	hero, heroine
le **personnage principal/central** [pɛRsɔnaʒpRɛ̃sipal/sɑ̃tRal]	main/central character
un **personnage secondaire** [pɛRsɔnaʒs(ə)gɔ̃dɛR]	minor character
présenter [pRezɑ̃te]	to present
Dans le premier chapitre, l'auteur présente les personnages centraux.	In the first chapter the author presents the main characters.
le **caractère** [kaRaktɛR]	character, essence
Le caractère de chaque protagoniste est décrit avec précision.	The character of each protagonist is described precisely.
un **type** [tip]	epitome, embodiment
C'est le **type même** du héros romantique.	He is the embodiment of the romantic hero.

le **style** [stil]	style
une poésie écrite dans un **style élaboré**	poetry written in an elaborate style
un **style limpide**	clear style
un **style concis**	succinct style
un **style dépouillé**	austere style
un **style recherché**	elegant, literary style
un **style ampoulé**	inflated, exaggerated style
un **moyen stylistique** [mwajɛ̃stilistik]	stylistic means
La variété des moyens stylistiques contribue au lyrisme de l'œuvre.	The variety of stylistic means contributes to the work's lyricism.
l'**ironie** *f* [iRɔni]	irony
une **figure de style** [figyRdəstil]	stylistic device
une **mise en relief** [mizɑ̃Rəljɛf]	highlighting (n)
au sens propre/figuré [osɑ̃spRɔpR/figyRe]	in the true/figurative sense
Il utilise cette expression au sens figuré.	He uses this expression in the figurative sense.

False Friends

French Word	Actual Meaning	False Friend	Correct French Word
un éditeur	**publisher**	editor	*un rédacteur, une rédactrice*
le génie	**genius**	genie	*un djinn*

My Vocabulary

13
History, Religion, Philosophy

13.1 History  53

historique [istɔʀik]	historic, historical
un **événement historique**	historical event
l'**histoire** *f* [istwaʀ]	history
l'**histoire ancienne**	ancient history
l'**histoire moderne**	modern history
l'**histoire contemporaine**	contemporary history
un **historien**, une **historienne** [istɔʀjɛ̃, jɛn]	historian
avoir lieu [avwaʀljø]	to take place, occur
La guerre de Trente Ans a eu lieu au XVIIe siècle.	The Thirty Years' War took place in the seventeenth century.
se passer [s(ə)pase]	to happen, occur, take place
durer (**de**… **à**) [dyʀe]	to last (from...to)
La Première Guerre mondiale a duré de 1914 à 1918.	The First World War lasted from 1914 to 1918.
au début de [odebydə]	at the beginning of
L'avion a été inventé au début du XXe siècle.	The airplane was invented at the beginning of the twentieth century.
à la fin de [alafɛ̃də]	at the end of
remonter à [ʀ(ə)mɔ̃te]	to go back to
Cette coopération remonte aux années 80.	This collaboration goes back to the eighties.
le **siècle** [sjɛkl]	century
av./ap. J.-C. (**avant/après Jésus-Christ**) [avɑ̃/apʀɛʒesykʀi(st)]	B.C./A.D. (before/after Christ)
en 1200 ap. J.-C.	in 1200 A.D.
au Ve siècle av. J.-C.	in the fifth century B.C.

---

la **Gaule** [gol]	Gaul (n)
gaulois, **gauloise** [golwa, waz]	gallic
un **Gaulois**, une **Gauloise**	Gaul (person)
romain, **romaine** [ʀɔmɛ̃, ɛn]	Roman (adj)
un **Romain**, une **Romaine**	Roman (n)
gallo-romain, **gallo-romaine** [galoʀɔmɛ̃, ɛn]	Gallo-Roman
l'**époque gallo-romaine**	the Gallo-Roman epoch

---

une **ère** [ɛʀ]	era, age, period
une **époque** [epɔk]	epoch, period
à l'époque des Croisades	at the time of the Crusades
préhistorique [pʀeistɔʀik]	prehistoric

la **préhistoire** [pʀeistwaʀ]	prehistory
l'**âge de la pierre/du bronze** [aʒd(ə)lapjɛʀ/dybʀɔ̃z]	Stone/Bronze Age
antique [ɑ̃tik]	antique
l'**Antiquité** *f* [ɑ̃tikite]	antiquity
les **Anciens** *mpl* [ɑ̃sjɛ̃]	ancients
médiéval, **médiévale** [medjeval]	medieval
Carcassonne est une ville médiévale.	Carcassonne is a medieval city.
le **Moyen(-)Âge** [mwajɛnɑʒ]	Middle Ages
les **Croisades** *fpl* [kʀwazad]	Crusades
la **Renaissance** [ʀənɛsɑ̃s]	Renaissance
la **Réforme** [ʀefɔʀm]	Reform
l'**Absolutisme** *m* [absɔlytism]	Absolutism
l'**Ancien Régime** *m* [ɑ̃sjɛ̃ʀeʒim]	Ancien Régime *(age of absolutism in France before 1789)*

découvrir [dekuvʀiʀ]	to discover
Christophe Colomb a découvert l'Amérique.	Christopher Columbus discovered America.
une **découverte** [dekuvɛʀt]	discovery
conquérir [kɔ̃keʀiʀ]	to conquer
une **conquête** [kɔ̃kɛt]	conquest
fonder [fɔ̃de]	to found, establish
colonial, **coloniale** [kɔlɔnjal]	colonial
un empire colonial	colonial empire
une **colonie** [kɔlɔni]	colony
un, une **esclave** [ɛsklav]	slave (n)

la **monarchie** [mɔnaʀʃi]	monarchy
royal, **royale** [ʀwajal]	royal (adj)
un **roi** [ʀwa]	king
une **reine** [ʀɛn]	queen
le **royaume** [ʀwajom]	kingdom
régner [ʀeɲe]	to reign
Louis XIV **a régné en souverain absolu**.	Louis XIV reigned as an absolute monarch.
le **règne** [ʀɛɲ]	reign (n)
un **empire** [ɑ̃piʀ]	empire
le **Premier Empire** (1804–1814)	the First Empire
le **Second Empire** (1852–1870)	the Second Empire
un **empereur**, une **impératrice** [ɑ̃pʀœʀ, ɛ̃peʀatʀis]	emperor, empress
Charlemagne a été **sacré empereur** en 800.	Charlemagne was crowned emperor in 800.

un **monarque** [mɔnaʀk]	monarch
succéder à [syksede]	to succeed
Louis XV a succédé à Louis XIV.	Louis XV succeeded Louis XIV.
une **dynastie** [dinasti]	dynasty
la dynastie des Carolingiens	Carolingian dynasty

la **population** [pɔpylasjɔ̃]	population
le **peuple** [pœpl]	people
une **révolution** [ʀevɔlysjɔ̃]	revolution
la **Révolution**	French Revolution
la **Marseillaise** [maʀsɛjɛz]	Marseillaise *(French National Anthem)*
Liberté, **Égalité**, **Fraternité** [libɛʀte, egalite, fʀatɛʀnite]	Liberty, Equality, Fraternity
«Liberté, Égalité, Fraternité» est la devise de la France.	"Liberty, Equality, Fraternity" is the motto of France.

le **clergé** [klɛʀʒe]	clergy
noble [nɔbl]	noble
un, une **noble**	nobleman/noblewoman
la **noblesse** [nɔblɛs]	nobility
un **privilège** [pʀivilɛʒ]	privilege
bourgeois, **bourgeoise** [buʀʒwa, waz]	bourgeois (adj)
un **bourgeois**, une **bourgeoise**	bourgeois (n)
la **bourgeoisie** [buʀʒwazi]	bourgeoisie
le **tiers état** [tjɛʀzeta]	Third Estate
98 % de la population appartenaient au tiers état.	The Third Estate makes up 98% of the population.
les **états généraux** *mpl* [etaʒeneʀo]	Estates-General
la **prise de la Bastille** [pʀizdəlabastij]	storming of the Bastille
guillotiner [gijɔtine]	to execute by guillotine
la **guillotine** [gijɔtin]	guillotine
exécuter [ɛgzekyte]	to execute
une **exécution** [ɛgzekysjɔ̃]	execution
les **droits de l'homme** *mpl* [dʀwad(ə)lɔm]	human rights
la **séparation des pouvoirs** [sepaʀasjɔ̃depuvwaʀ]	separation of powers
le **pouvoir législatif**	legislative power
le **pouvoir exécutif**	executive power
le **pouvoir judiciaire**	judicial power

la **guerre** [gɛʀ]	war
une **guerre civile**	civil war
déclarer la guerre	to declare war
faire la guerre	to wage war
battre [batʀ]	to beat
Napoléon Ier a été battu à Waterloo.	Napoleon I was beaten at Waterloo.
occuper [ɔkype]	to occupy
l'**occupation** *f* [ɔkypasjɔ̃]	occupation
sous l'occupation	under the occupation
libérer [libeʀe]	to liberate
la **libération** [libeʀasjɔ̃]	liberation
la **paix** [pɛ]	peace
conclure un traité de paix	to sign a peace treaty
faire la paix	to make peace
un **armistice** [aʀmistis]	armistice
signer l'armistice	to sign the armistice

combattre [kɔ̃batʀ]	to combat, fight
combattre pour la liberté	to fight for liberty
le **combat** [kɔ̃ba]	combat (n)
lutter [lyte]	to struggle
la **lutte** [lyt]	struggle (n)
envahir (**qc**) [ɑ̃vaiʀ]	to invade s.th.
Le pays a été envahi par les troupes ennemies.	The country was invaded by enemy troops.
une **invasion** [ɛ̃vazjɔ̃]	invasion
un **envahisseur** [ɑ̃vaisœʀ]	invader
dévaster [devaste]	to devastate
La guerre a dévasté le pays.	War devastated the country.
dominer [dɔmine]	to dominate
torturer [tɔʀtyʀe]	to torture
la **torture** [tɔʀtyʀ]	torture (n)
Le prisonnier a été **soumis à la torture**.	The prisoner was subjected to torture.
vaincre [vɛ̃kʀ]	to conquer

le **vainqueur** [vɛ̃kœʀ]	victor
victorieux, **victorieuse** [viktɔʀjø, jøz]	victorious
sortir* victorieux d'un combat	to emerge victorious from combat
une **victoire** [viktwaʀ]	victory
la **gloire** [glwaʀ]	glory
une **défaite** [defɛt]	defeat (n)
une **débâcle** [debɑkl]	debacle, catastrophe
perdre [pɛʀdʀ]	to lose
«La France a perdu une bataille! Mais la France n'a pas perdu la guerre!» *(de Gaulle)*	"France has lost a battle! But France has not lost the war!"
le **vaincu**, la **vaincue** [vɛ̃ky]	the vanquished, conquered
les **négociations** *fpl* [negɔsjasjɔ̃]	negotiations
les **négociations de paix**	peace negotiations

la **Première Guerre mondiale** [pʀəmjɛʀgɛʀmɔ̃djal]	World War I
la **Seconde Guerre mondiale** [s(ə)gɔ̃dgɛʀmɔ̃djal]	World War II
la **Collaboration** [kɔ(l)labɔʀasjɔ̃]	Collaboration *(cooperation with the Axis powers in WWII)*
la **Résistance** [ʀezistɑ̃s]	Resistance *(French resistance movement 1940–1944)*
entrer dans la Résistance	to go into the Resistance
le **Débarquement** [debaʀkəmɑ̃]	D-day

la **Guerre franco-allemande** (**1870–1871**) [gɛʀfʀɑ̃koalmɑ̃d]	Franco-Prussian War (1870–1871)
la (**I**ère**-V**e) **République** [ʀepyblik]	(First–Fifth) Republic
les **relations franco-allemandes** *fpl* [ʀ(ə)lasjɔ̃fʀɑ̃koalmɑ̃d]	French-German relations
l'**OFAJ** *m* (**Office franco-allemand pour la jeunesse**) [ɔfaʒ]	French-German Youth Office
la **réunification** [ʀeynifikasjɔ̃]	reunification
la réunification de l'Allemagne	reunification of Germany
la **CECA** (**Communauté européenne du charbon et de l'acier**) [seka]	European Coal and Steel Community
le **Marché commun** [maʀʃekɔmɛ̃]	Common Market
l'**Union européenne** *f* (**UE**) [ynjɔ̃øʀɔpeɛn]	European Union (EU)
la **BCE** (**Banque centrale européenne**) [beseø]	ECB (European Central Bank)

13.2 Religion  54

religieux, **religieuse** [R(ə)liʒjø, jøz]	religious
un **religieux**, une **religieuse**	brother, sister of an order
la **religion** [R(ə)liʒjɔ̃]	religion
la **théologie** [teɔlɔʒi]	theology

la **Bible** [bibl]	Bible
l'**Ancien**/le **Nouveau Testament** [ɑ̃sjɛ̃/nuvotɛstamɑ̃]	Old/New Testament
le **Coran** [kɔRɑ̃]	Koran

la **foi** [fwa]	faith *(See Information Box p. 98)*
avoir la foi	to be a believer
croire (à/en) [kRwaR]	to believe in
croyant, **croyante** [kRwajɑ̃, jɑ̃t]	devout, faithful, religious
un **croyant**, une **croyante**	person of faith
prier [pRije]	to pray
la **prière** [pRijɛR]	prayer
faire ses prières	to say one's prayers

INFO

What people believe in

croire qn/qc	*to believe s.o./s.th.*
Il ne croit même pas ses amis.	*He doesn't even believe his friends.*
Tu crois tout ce qu'on te raconte?	*Do you believe everything you are told?*
croire à qn/qc	*to believe in s.o./s.th.*
Tu crois à l'avenir de l'Europe?	*Do you believe in the future of Europe?*
croire en Dieu	*to believe in God*
Je crois en Dieu, mais pas au diable.	*I believe in God, but not in the devil.*

chrétien, **chrétienne** [kʀetjɛ̃, jɛn]	Christian (adj)
un **chrétien**, une **chrétienne**	Christian (n)
la **foi chrétienne**	Christian faith
le **christianisme** [kʀistjanism]	Christianity
catholique [katɔlik]	Catholic (adj)
un, une **catholique**	Catholic (n)
un **catholique pratiquant**	practicing Catholic
le **catholicisme** [katɔlisism]	Catholicism
protestant, **protestante** [pʀɔtɛstɑ̃, ɑ̃t]	Protestant (adj)
un **protestant**, une **protestante**	Protestant (n)
le **protestantisme** [pʀɔtɛstɑ̃tism]	Protestantism

islamique [islamik]	Islamic
l'**Islam** *m* [islam]	Islam
musulman, **musulmane** [myzylmɑ̃, an]	Muslim (adj)
un **musulman**, une **musulmane**	Muslim (n)
le **ramadan** [ʀamadɑ̃]	Ramadan
se convertir à [s(ə)kɔ̃vɛʀtiʀ]	to convert to
Il s'est converti à l'Islam.	He converted to Islam.
juif, **juive** [ʒɥif, ʒɥiv]	Jewish
un **juif**, une **juive**	Jew (n)
le **Judaïsme** [ʒydaism]	Judaism
israélite [isʀaelit]	Israeli (adj)
un, une **israélite**	Israeli, Israelite
l'**hindouisme** *m* [ɛ̃duism]	Hinduism
le **bouddhisme** [budism]	Buddhism
une **secte** [sɛkt]	sect
l'**athéisme** *m* [ateism]	atheism
laïque [laik]	lay, secular
aller à l'école laïque	to go to a non-religious school
la **laïcité** [laisite]	secularism, separation of church and state
la **liberté du culte** [libɛʀtedykylt]	religious freedom

l'**Église** *f* [egliz]	Church *(institution)*
la séparation de l'Église et de l'État	separation of church and state
une **église** [egliz]	church (building)
une **cathédrale** [katedʀal]	cathedral
le **pape** [pap]	pope
un **prêtre** [pʀɛtʀ]	priest
un **curé** [kyʀe]	priest, father (Catholic clergyman)
M. le curé	Father
un **pasteur** [pastœʀ]	pastor, minister

un **temple** [tɑ̃pl]	temple; evangelical church
une **mosquée** [mɔske]	mosque
une **synagogue** [sinagɔg]	synagogue
une **paroisse** [paʀwas]	parish
le curé de notre paroisse	our parish priest
le **clergé** [klɛʀʒe]	clergy
un membre du clergé	member of the clergy
un **évêque** [evɛk]	bishop
un **archevêque** [aʀʃəvɛk]	archbishop
un **moine** [mwan]	monk
une (**bonne**) **sœur** *fam* [(bɔn) sœʀ]	nun, sister
un **ordre** (**religieux**) [ɔʀdʀ (ʀ(ə)liʒjø)]	(religious) order
un **couvent** [kuvɑ̃]	convent
entrer au couvent	to enter a convent
un **monastère** [mɔnastɛʀ]	monastery

Dieu [djø]	God
Jésus-Christ [ʒesykʀi(st)]	Jesus Christ
le **ciel**; les **cieux** *mpl poétique, biblique* [sjɛl, sjø]	heaven
«Notre Père qui êtes aux cieux.»	"Our Father who art in Heaven."
un **ange** [ɑ̃ʒ]	angel
le **paradis** [paʀadi]	paradise, heaven
le **diable** [djɑbl]	devil
l'**enfer** *m* [ɑ̃fɛʀ]	hell

saint, **sainte** [sɛ̃, sɛ̃t]	holy
un **Saint**, une **Sainte**	saint
la **Sainte Vierge**	Holy Virgin
le **Saint Esprit**	Holy Spirit
sacré, **sacrée** [sakʀe]	holy, sacred
solennel, **solennelle** [sɔlanɛl]	solemn
la **communion solennelle**	holy communion
un **miracle** [miʀakl]	miracle
la **résurrection** [ʀezyʀɛksjɔ̃]	resurrection
la **croix** [kʀwa]	cross
faire le signe de croix	to make the sign of the cross, cross oneself
pieux, **pieuse** [pjø, pjøz]	pious
un **dogme** [dɔgm]	dogma

l'**instruction religieuse** *f* [ɛ̃stʀyksjɔ̃ʀ(ə)liʒjøz]	religious education
baptiser [batize]	to baptize
le **baptême** [batɛm]	baptism
la (**première**) **communion** [(pʀəmjɛʀ)kɔmyɲɔ̃]	(first) communion
la **confirmation** [kɔ̃fiʀmasjɔ̃]	confirmation
le **mariage** [maʀjaʒ]	marriage
le **mariage civil**	civil ceremony
le **mariage religieux**	church ceremony

la **messe** [mɛs]	Mass
dire la messe	to say Mass
le **péché** [peʃe]	sin
se confesser [s(ə)kɔ̃fɛse]	to confess
la **confession** [kɔ̃fɛsjɔ̃]	confession
entendre qn en confession	to hear s.o.'s confession
être de confession protestante	to be of Protestant denomination
prêcher [pʀɛʃe]	to preach
prêcher la tolérance	to preach tolerance
un **prêche** [pʀɛʃ]	preacher
bénir [beniʀ]	to bless
Le prêtre bénit les fidèles.	The priest blesses the faithful.

Noël [nɔɛl]	Christmas
Joyeux Noël!	Merry Christmas!
le **père Noël**	Santa Claus
Vendredi saint [vɑ̃dʀədisɛ̃]	Good Friday
Pâques *fpl* [pak]	Easter
Joyeuses Pâques!	Happy Easter!
l'**Ascension** *f* [asɑ̃sjɔ̃]	Ascension
la **Pentecôte** [pɑ̃tkot]	Pentecost
la **Fête-Dieu**; les **Fêtes-Dieu** *pl* [fɛtdjø]	Corpus Christi
l'**Assomption** *f* [asɔ̃psjɔ̃]	Assumption (of Mary)
la **Toussaint** [tusɛ̃]	All Saints' Day

13.3 Philosophy  55

philosophique [filɔzɔfik]	philosophical
un conte philosophique	philosophical tale
la **philosophie** [filɔzɔfi]	philosophy
un, une **philosophe** [filɔzɔf]	philosopher
la **métaphysique** [metafizik]	metaphysics
l'**éthique** *f* [etik]	ethics
l'**esthéthique** *f* [ɛstetik]	esthetics
la **logique** [lɔʒik]	logic
le **siècle des lumières** [sjɛkldelymjɛʀ]	Age of Enlightenment
l'**idéalisme** *m* [idealism]	idealism
l'**empirisme** *m* [ɑ̃piʀism]	empiricism
le **matérialisme** [mateʀjalism]	materialism
l'**existentialisme** *m* [ɛgzistɑ̃sjalism]	existentialism
«L'existentialisme est un humanisme.» *(Sartre)*	"Existentialism is a humanism."
penser [pɑ̃se]	to think
«Je pense donc je suis.» *(Descartes)*	"I think, therefore I am."
la **pensée** [pɑ̃se]	thought, thinking (n)
un **penseur**, une **penseuse** [pɑ̃sœʀ, øz]	thinker
une **idée** [ide]	idea
échanger des idées	to exchange ideas, thoughts
théorique [teɔʀik]	theoretical
une **théorie** [teɔʀi]	theory
émettre une théorie	to postulate a theory
spirituel, **spirituelle** [spiʀitɥɛl]	spiritual
l'**esprit** *m* [ɛspʀi]	spirit
la **matière** [matjɛʀ]	matter
une **notion** [nosjɔ̃]	notion

la **méthode** [metɔd]	method
la **doctrine** [dɔktʀin]	doctrine
le **modèle** [mɔdɛl]	model
le **principe** [pʀɛ̃sip]	principle
Il est contre **par principe**.	He is against it on principle.
concevoir [kɔ̃s(ə)vwaʀ]	to conceive
la **conception** [kɔ̃sɛpsjɔ̃]	conception
le **terme** [tɛʀm]	term, word, expression
un **acte** [akt]	action
juger qn **sur ses actes**	to judge s.o. by his actions
douter [dute]	to doubt
douter de l'existence de Dieu	to doubt the existence of God
le **doute** [dut]	doubt (n)
mettre qc en doute	to put s.th. in doubt, to doubt s.th.
l'**apparence** *f* [apaʀɑ̃s]	appearance
ne pas se fier aux apparences	not to be deceived by appearances
l'**utopie** *f* [ytɔpi]	Utopia
l'**ignorance** *f* [iɲɔʀɑ̃s]	ignorance
le **hasard** ['azaʀ]	chance

les **mœurs** *fpl* [mœʀ(s)]	morality, morals
le **bien** [bjɛ̃]	good
le **mal** [mal]	evil
moral, **morale** [mɔʀal]	moral, ethical
la **morale** [mɔʀal]	morality

INFO

A tricky switch

In English, the words "moral" and "morale" have different meanings, although they are spelled similarly. The same observation can be made of the French words *"le moral"* and *"la morale."* Be careful though! Their meanings may be the opposite of what you expect. See below:

le moral	*morale (emotional condition), mood, state of mind*
remonter le moral à qn	*to cheer s.o. up*
la morale	*morality, ethics, moral doctrine*
donner une leçon de morale à qn	*to give s.o. a sermon (on morality)*

raisonner [ʀɛzɔne]	to reason
raisonnable [ʀɛzɔnabl]	reasonable
la **raison** [ʀɛzɔ̃]	reason, understanding (n)
le **raisonnement** [ʀɛzɔnmɑ̃]	reasoning
suivre un raisonnement logique	to follow logical reasoning
un **argument** [aʀgymɑ̃]	argument
un argument pour/contre	argument for/against
le **sens** [sɑ̃s]	sense
donner un sens à sa vie	to give sense to one's life
le **bon sens** [bɔ̃sɑ̃s]	common sense
agir **en dépit du bon sens**	to act against good sense
la **contradiction** [kɔ̃tʀadiksjɔ̃]	contradiction
le **symbole** [sɛ̃bɔl]	symbol

l'**origine** *f* [ɔʀiʒin]	origin
causer [koze]	to cause
la **cause** [koz]	cause (n)
un **effet** [efɛ]	effect
À petite cause grands effets. *loc*	Small cause, large effects.
la **volonté** [vɔlɔ̃te]	will (n)

l'**individu** *m* [ɛ̃dividy]	individual (n)
l'**être** *m* [ɛtʀ]	being; existence (n)
l'**essence** *f* [esɑ̃s]	essence
exister [ɛgziste]	to exist
l'**existence** *f* [ɛgzistɑ̃s]	existence
«L'existence précède l'essence.» *(Sartre)*	"Existence precedes essence."
la **mort** [mɔʀ]	death *(See Information Box p. 33)*
mourir de sa belle mort	to die a natural death
le **néant** [neɑ̃]	nothingness, void

concret, **concrète** [kɔ̃kʀɛ, ɛt]	concrete
abstrait, **abstraite** [abstʀɛ, ɛt]	abstract
réel, **réelle** [ʀeɛl]	real
réaliste [ʀealist]	realistic
la **réalité** [ʀealite]	reality
l'**expérience** *f* [ɛkspeʀjɑ̃s]	experience; experiment *(See Information Box p. 171)*
une **expérience vécue**	personal experience
tenter l'expérience	to risk an attempt

élémentaire [elemɑ̃tɛʀ]	elementary
définitif, **définitive** [definitif, iv]	definitive, final
empirique [ɑ̃piʀik]	empirical, based on experience

vrai, **vraie** [vʀɛ]	true
véritable [veʀitabl]	true, veritable
la **vérité** [veʀite]	truth
certain, **certaine** [sɛʀtɛ̃, ɛn]	certain, sure
Je suis **sûr et certain**.	I am absolutely positive.
la **certitude** [sɛʀtityd]	certainty
incertain, **incertaine** [ɛ̃sɛʀtɛ̃, ɛn]	uncertain
l'**incertitude** *f* [ɛ̃sɛʀtityd]	uncertainty
être dans l'incertitude au sujet de qc	to be unsure about s.th.
l'**erreur** *f* [eʀœʀ]	error
faire erreur	to err
L'erreur est humaine. *loc*	To err is human.
faux, **fausse** [fo, fos]	false
faire fausse route	to be on the wrong track

une **œuvre** [œvʀ]	work (n)
les **œuvres complètes** de Voltaire	the complete works of Voltaire
un **ouvrage** [uvʀaʒ]	work, book
un ouvrage philosophique	a philosophical work
un **essai** [esɛ]	essay
un **traité** [tʀɛte]	treatise

False Friends

French Word	Actual Meaning	False Friend	Correct French Word
antique	**ancient**	antique	*l'antiquité*
le hasard	**chance**	hazard	*un risque*
miserable	**destitute, shabby**	miserable	*malheureux, très mal*

14

State, Law, Politics

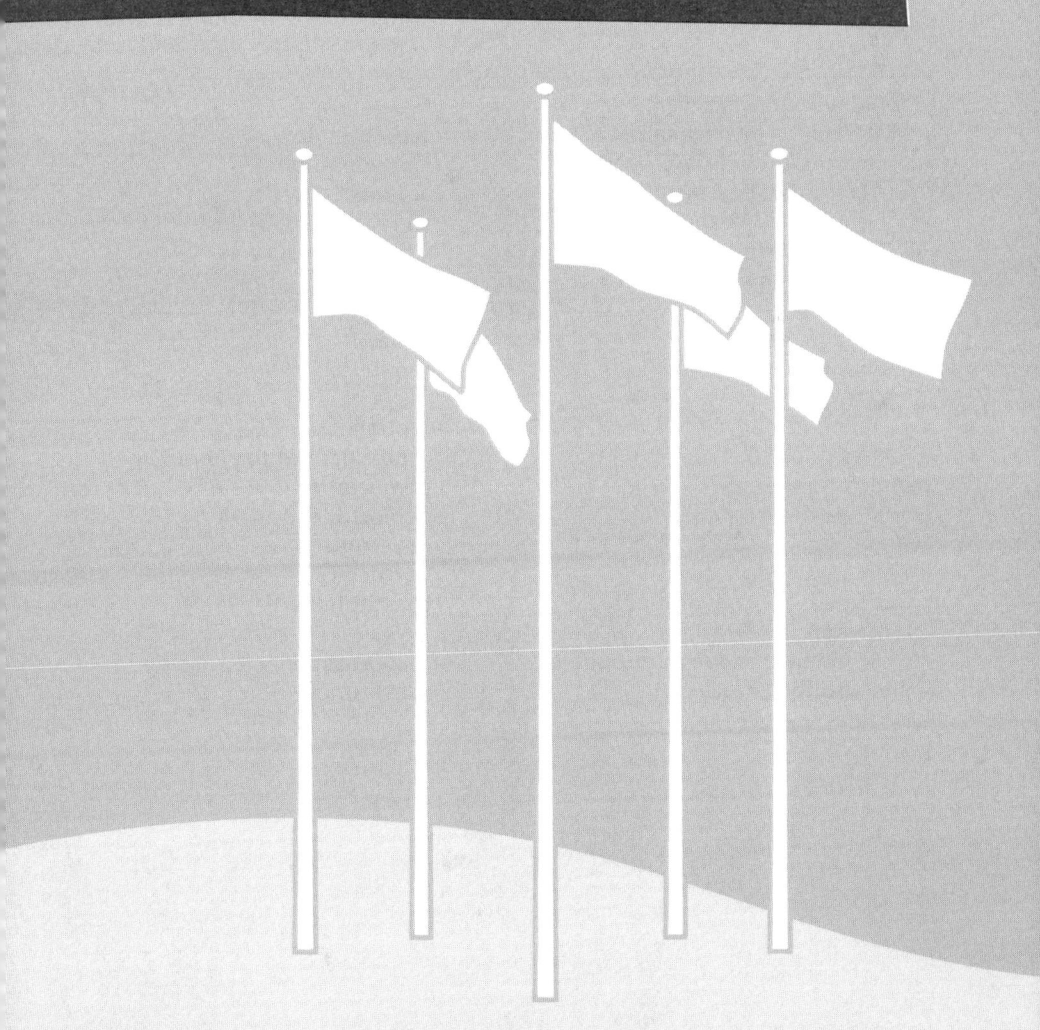

14.1 Constitution, National Institutions  56

le **pays** [pei]	country
l'**État** *m* [eta]	state
«L'État, c'est moi.» *(Louis XIV)*	"I am the State."
national, **nationale** [nasjɔnal]	national
l'**hymne national**	national anthem
la **nation** [nasjɔ̃]	nation
la **nationalité** [nasjɔnalite]	nationality, citizenship
demander la nationalité française	to request French citizenship
être de nationalité espagnole	to be of Spanish nationality
la **patrie** [patʀi]	homeland, fatherland
le **drapeau**; les **drapeaux** *pl* [dʀapo]	flag
hisser le drapeau tricolore	to raise the tricolor (French) flag
le **fédéralisme** [fedeʀalism]	federalism
un **État fédéral** [etafedeʀal]	federal state
une **confédération** [kɔ̃fedeʀasjɔ̃]	confederation
la **Confédération helvétique**	Swiss Confederation
le **Chancelier** (**allemand**), la **Chancelière** (**allemande**) [ʃɑ̃səlje, jɛʀ (almɑ̃(d))]	(German) Chancellor
la **société** [sɔsjete]	society
républicain, **républicaine** [ʀepyblikɛ̃, ɛn]	republican
la **république** [ʀepyblik]	republic
le **président de la République**	president of the Republic
démocratique [demɔkʀatik]	democratic
un **régime démocratique**	democratic form of government
la **démocratie** [demɔkʀasi]	democracy
constitutionnel, **constitutionnelle** [kɔ̃stitysjɔnɛl]	constitutional
une **monarchie constitutionnelle**	constitutional monarchy
la **constitution** [kɔ̃stitysjɔ̃]	constitution

le **pouvoir** [puvwaʀ]	power
le **pouvoir législatif**	legislative power
le **pouvoir exécutif**	executive power
le **pouvoir judiciaire**	judicial power
la **séparation des pouvoirs**	separation of powers
la **prise du pouvoir**	seizure of power
être au pouvoir	to be in power
la **liberté de conscience** [libɛʀtedkɔ̃sjɑ̃s]	freedom of conscience
la **liberté d'opinion** [libɛʀtedɔpinjɔ̃]	freedom of opinion
la **liberté du culte** [libɛʀtedykylt]	religious freedom
les **droits fondamentaux** *mpl* [dʀwafɔ̃damɑ̃to]	civil rights
les **droits de l'homme** *mpl* [dʀwadlɔm]	human rights
la **Déclaration des droits de l'homme**	Declaration of Human Rights
garantir [gaʀɑ̃tiʀ]	to guarantee, assure
proclamer [pʀɔklame]	to proclaim, announce
Les résultats du vote seront proclamés demain.	The results of the vote will be announced tomorrow.
la **proclamation** [pʀɔklamasjɔ̃]	proclamation
la proclamation de la République	proclamation of the Republic
l'**autodétermination** *f* [otodetɛʀminasjɔ̃]	self-determination
le **droit à l'autodétermination**	right of self-determination

individuel, **individuelle** [ɛ̃dividyɛl]	individual, personal
les libertés individuelles	personal liberties
un **individu** [ɛ̃dividy]	individual (n)
Tous les individus sont égaux devant la loi.	All individuals are equal before the law.
un **citoyen**, une **citoyenne** [sitwajɛ̃, jɛn]	citizen
la **liberté** [libɛʀte]	liberty
l'**égalité** *f* [egalite]	equality
la **fraternité** [fʀatɛʀnite]	fraternity

un **ressortissant**, une **ressortissante** [R(ə)sɔRtisɑ̃, ɑ̃t]	national (n)
les ressortissants français à l'étranger	French nationals overseas
un, une **compatriote** [kɔ̃patRiɔt]	compatriot
un, une **patriote** [patRiɔt]	patriot
le **patriotisme** [patRijɔtism]	patriotism
le **nationalisme** [nasjɔnalism]	nationalism
nationaliste [nasjɔnalist]	nationalistic
un, une **nationaliste**	nationalist
le **chauvinisme** [ʃovinism]	chauvinism, exaggerated patriotism
chauvin, **chauvine** [ʃovɛ̃, in]	chauvinistic
un **chauvin**, une **chauvine**	chauvinist (n)

électoral, **électorale** [elɛktɔRal]	electoral
se faire inscrire sur une **liste électorale**	to get registered on a voting list
un **électeur**, une **électrice** [elɛktœR, tRis]	voter
un **candidat**, une **candidate** [kɑ̃dida, at]	candidate
désigner un candidat	to nominate a candidate
la **voix** [vwa]	voice, vote (n)

la **participation** [paRtisipasjɔ̃]	participation
La **participation au vote** a été très faible.	Voter turnout was very low.
s'abstenir [sapstəniR]	to abstain
Les électeurs ont été **nombreux à s'abstenir**.	Many voters abstained.
une **abstention** [apstɑ̃sjɔ̃]	abstention
une **circonscription** (**électorale**) [siRkɔ̃skRipsjɔ̃(elɛktɔRal)]	constituency, electoral district
un **bureau de vote**; des **bureaux de vote** *pl* [byRod(ə)vɔt]	polling site
une **urne** [yRn]	ballot box
déposer son bulletin dans l'urne	to put one's vote into the ballot box
un **bulletin** (**de vote**) [byltɛ̃(d(ə)vɔt)]	ballot
un **bulletin blanc**	blank ballot
un **bulletin nul**	void ballot

INFO

Elections and choices

une élection	*election*
l'élection présidentielle	*presidential election*
être candidat à l'élection présidentielle	*to be a candidate in the presidential election*
les (élections) législatives	*legislative elections*
se présenter aux élections législatives	*to be a candidate for legislative elections*
les (élections) régionales	*regional elections*
les (élections) cantonales	*cantonal elections*
les (élections) municipales	*municipal elections*
les (élections) européennes	*European elections*
les élections anticipées	*early elections*
envisager des élections anticipées	*to consider early elections*
élire qn	*to elect s.o.*
Les citoyens ont élu un nouveau Président.	*The citizens elected a new President.*
voter qc	*to vote on s.th.*
voter une loi	*to vote on a law*
voter pour qn	*to vote for s.o.*
un vote	*vote (n)*
exercer son droit de vote	*to exercise one's voting rights*
le suffrage	*suffrage*
le suffrage universel	*universal suffrage*
le suffrage indirect	*indirect vote*
le scrutin	*voting*
le scrutin secret	*secret ballot*
le scrutin/suffrage majoritaire	*majority vote*
le scrutin/suffrage proportionnel	*proportional representation*
un tour de scrutin	*round of voting*
au 1er/2e tour	*in the first/second round of voting*
Il a été élu au deuxième/2e tour.	*He was elected in the second round of voting.*
dépouiller le scrutin	*to count the votes*

la **majorité** [maʒɔRite]	majority
la **majorité absolue**	absolute majority
la **majorité relative**	plurality
Au 2e tour, la majorité relative suffit.	In the second round of voting a plurality is sufficient.
être en ballottage [ɛtRɑ̃balɔtaʒ]	to be in the runoff
un **référendum** [RefeRɛ̃dɔm/RefeRɑ̃dɔm]	referendum
un **plébiscite** [plebisit]	plebiscite
présidentiel, **présidentielle** [pRezidɑ̃sjɛl]	presidential
les **élections présidentielles**	presidential elections
le **Président**, la **Présidente** [pRezidɑ̃, ɑ̃t]	president
gouverner [guvɛRne]	to govern
gouvernemental, **gouvernementale** [guvɛRnəmɑ̃tal]	governmental
le **gouvernement** [guvɛRnəmɑ̃]	government
renverser le gouvernement	to overthrow the government
un, une **ministre** [ministR]	minister
le **Premier ministre**	prime minister
un **Ministre-président**	minister-president *(in German states)*
un **chef d'État** [ʃɛfdeta]	head of state
Les chefs d'État de l'UE se sont réunis à Londres.	The EU heads of state met in London.
le **chef de l'État** [ʃɛfdəleta]	chief/head of state
Le chef de l'État s'est adressé aux Français.	The chief of state addressed the French people.
le **chef du gouvernement** [ʃɛfdyguvɛRnəmɑ̃]	head of state
la **cohabitation** [kɔabitasjɔ̃]	*situation where the French President is in political opposition to the majority in the National Assembly*
un gouvernement de cohabitation	cohabitation government
le **Conseil des ministres** [kɔ̃sɛjdeministR]	council of ministers
le, la **ministre des Affaires étrangères**	minister of foreign affairs
le, la **ministre de l'Intérieur**	minister of the interior
le, la **ministre des Finances**	minister of finance
le, la **ministre de l'Éducation nationale**	minister of education
le, la **garde des Sceaux** [gaRd(ə)deso]	attorney general
un, une **secrétaire d'État** [s(ə)kRetɛRdeta]	secretary of state
la **secrétaire d'État à la condition féminine**	secretary of state for women's issues

un **remaniement ministériel** [ʀ(ə)manimɑ̃ministeʀjɛl]	government shakeup
procéder à un remaniement ministériel	to carry out a government shakeup
démissionner [demisjɔne]	to resign
la **démission** [demisjɔ̃]	resignation
donner sa démission	to submit one's resignation
succéder à [syksede]	to follow/succeed
la **succession** [syksesjɔ̃]	succession
assurer/prendre la succession de qn	to succeed s.o.

parlementaire [paʀləmɑ̃tɛʀ]	parliamentary
un, une **parlementaire**	parliamentarian (n)
une **session parlementaire**	parliamentary session
le **parlement** [paʀləmɑ̃]	parliament
une **séance** [seɑ̃s]	session
une **loi** [lwa]	law
un **projet de loi**	draft bill
adopter une loi	to adopt a law
promulguer une loi	to pass a law
rejeter une loi	to vote down a law

l'**Assemblée nationale** *f* [asɑ̃blenasjɔnal]	French National Assembly
un **député**, une **députée** [depyte]	delegate, representative
les députés de l'opposition	opposition representatives
le **Sénat** [sena]	senate
un **sénateur**, une **sénatrice** [senatœʀ, tʀis]	senator
la **question de confiance** [kɛstjɔ̃dkɔ̃fjɑ̃s]	vote of confidence
poser la question de confiance	to request a vote of confidence
une **motion de censure** [mosjɔ̃dsɑ̃syʀ]	a vote of non-confidence
voter une motion de censure	to vote on a non-confidence motion
dissoudre [disudʀ]	to dissolve
dissoudre l'Assemblée	to dissolve the Assembly
la **dissolution** [disɔlysjɔ̃]	dissolution
prononcer la dissolution de l'Assemblée	to announce the dissolution of the Assembly
la **législature** [leʒislatyʀ]	legislature
les **indemnités parlementaires** *fpl* [ɛ̃dɛmniteparləmɑ̃tɛʀ]	parliamentary allowance, pay and perks

14.2 Public Administration  57

une **institution** [ɛ̃stitysjɔ̃]	institution
les institutions de la République	institutions of the Republic
officiel, **officielle** [ɔfisjɛl]	official (adj)
une déclaration officielle	official declaration
un, une **fonctionnaire** [fɔ̃ksjɔnɛʀ]	government official, civil servant
une **fonction** [fɔ̃ksjɔ̃]	function
exercer [ɛgzɛʀse]	to exercise
exercer le pouvoir	to exercise power
occuper [ɔkype]	to occupy
occuper un poste important	to occupy an important position
être responsable de [ʀɛspɔ̃sabl]	to be responsible for

les **autorités** *fpl* [ɔtɔʀite]	authorities
se plaindre **auprès des autorités**	to complain to the authorities
administratif, **administrative** [administʀatif, iv]	administrative
le **service administratif**	administration, management
l'**administration** *f* [administʀasjɔ̃]	administration
bureaucratique [byʀokʀatik]	bureaucratic
la **bureaucratie** [byʀokʀasi]	bureaucracy
une **demande** [d(ə)mɑ̃d]	request (n)
faire une demande auprès de qn	to make a request to s.o.
un **formulaire** [fɔʀmylɛʀ]	form
remplir un formulaire	to fill out a form
un **questionnaire** [kɛstjɔnɛʀ]	questionnaire
un **certificat** [sɛʀtifika]	certificate
faire établir un **certificat de mariage**	to have a marriage certificate issued
un **extrait** (**de naissance**) [ɛkstʀɛ(d(ə)nɛsɑ̃s)]	(short-form) birth certificate
un **permis** [pɛʀmi]	permit
un **permis de séjour**	residence permit
délivrer un **permis de conduire**	to issue a driver's license
prolonger (**le passeport/la carte d'identité**) [pʀɔlɔ̃ʒe]	to renew (a passport/ID card)

une **capitale** [kapital]	capital city
communal, **communale** [kɔmynal]	communal
une **commune** [kɔmyn]	township, municipality
La France a plus de 36 000 communes.	France has more than 36,000 townships.
un **maire** [mɛʀ]	mayor
M./Mme le maire	Mr./Mrs. Mayor
une **mairie** [mɛʀi]	town hall
l'**hôtel de ville** *m* [ɔ/otɛldəvil]	city hall *(in larger cities)*
un **habitant**, une **habitante** [abitɑ̃, ɑ̃t]	resident, inhabitant

municipal, **municipale** [mynisipal]	municipal
le **Conseil municipal**	municipal council
la **municipalité** [mynisipalite]	municipality
un **conseiller**, une **conseillère** [kɔ̃seje, jɛʀ]	counselor
une conseillère municipale	municipal councilwoman

régional, **régionale** [ʀeʒjɔnal]	regional
le **Conseil régional**	regional council
une **région** [ʀeʒjɔ̃]	region
départemental, **départementale** [depaʀtəmɑ̃tal]	departmental
une route départementale	departmental road *(rural road)*
un **département** [depaʀtəmɑ̃]	department
un **arrondissement** [aʀɔ̃dismɑ̃]	precinct, arrondissement *(subdivision of a département in France)*
un **canton** [kɑ̃tɔ̃]	canton *(subdivision of an arrondissement)*

un **préfet** [pʀefɛ]	prefect *(national representative in a département)*
une **préfecture** [pʀefɛktyʀ]	prefecture *(main town of a département)*
la **sous-préfecture**	subprefecture *(main town of an arrondissement)*
la **régionalisation** [ʀeʒjɔnalizasjɔ̃]	regionalization
central, **centrale** [sɑ̃tʀal]	central
centralisé, **centralisée** [sɑ̃tʀalize]	centralized
La France est un pays centralisé.	France is a centralized country.
la **centralisation** [sɑ̃tʀalizasjɔ̃]	centralization
décentralisé, **décentralisée** [desɑ̃tʀalize]	decentralized
la **décentralisation** [desɑ̃tʀalizasjɔ̃]	decentralization

la **Métropole** [metʀɔpɔl]	motherland
Ils vont quitter la Guadeloupe pour aller en Métropole.	They are going to leave Guadeloupe and move to the motherland.
une **métropole** [metʀɔpɔl]	metropolis
la **France métropolitaine** [fʀɑ̃smetʀɔpɔlitɛn]	metropolitan France
les **D.O.M.-R.O.M.** (**départements et régions d'outre-mer**) *mpl* [dɔmʀɔm]	overseas départements and regions
un **territoire** [teʀitwaʀ]	territory
l'**aménagement du territoire**	regional development planning

fiscal, **fiscale** [fiskal]	tax (adj)
la **fraude fiscale**	tax fraud
le **fisc** [fisk]	Internal Revenue Service
un **percepteur**, une **perceptrice** [pɛʀsɛptœʀ, tʀis]	revenue officer
imposer qn [ɛ̃poze]	to assess s.o. (for taxes)
On **impose les contribuables en fonction de** leurs revenus.	The taxpayers are assessed based on their income.
imposable [ɛ̃pozabl]	subject to taxation
les **impôts** *mpl* [ɛ̃po]	taxes
payer des impôts	to pay taxes
les **impôts sur le revenu**	income taxes
déclarer [deklaʀe]	to declare
Il ne déclare pas tout ce qu'il gagne.	He does not declare everything that he earns.
une **déclaration d'impôts** [deklaʀasjɔ̃dɛ̃po]	tax declaration
le, la **contribuable** [kɔ̃tʀibyabl]	taxpayer

14.3 Parties, Political Systems  58

politique [pɔlitik]	political
la **politique**	politics
faire de la politique	to be involved in politics
un **régime** [ʀeʒim]	form of government; regime
un **régime totalitaire**	totalitarian regime
un **système** [sistɛm]	system, form, regime
instaurer un système démocratique	to set up a democratic system

un **homme d'État** [ɔmdeta]	statesman
un **homme**, une **femme politique** [ɔm/fampɔlitik]	politician
un **politicien**, une **politicienne** *péj* [pɔlitisjɛ̃, jɛn]	politician
diriger [diʀiʒe]	to lead
gouverner [guvɛʀne]	to govern
le **gouvernement** [guvɛʀnəmɑ̃]	government, cabinet
Le Premier ministre forme son gouvernement.	The Prime Minister is putting together his cabinet.

un **dirigeant**, une **dirigeante** [diʀiʒɑ̃, ɑ̃t]	director, leader *(in parties, trade unions)*
un **leader** [lidœʀ]	leader
le leader de l'opposition	opposition leader
assumer une responsabilité [asymeynʀɛspɔ̃sabilite]	to take on a responsibility
Elle assume une responsabilité au sein du gouvernement.	She is taking on a governmental responsibility.
un **message** [mesaʒ]	message
Le président a adressé un message clair aux syndicats.	The president sent a clear message to the trade unions.
consulter qn [kɔ̃sylte]	to consult s.o.
consulter les électeurs (par référendum)	to consult the voters (by referendum)
une **consultation** [kɔ̃syltasjɔ̃]	referendum, public opinion poll

un **parti** [paʀti]	party
un **parti conservateur**	conservative party
le **parti gaulliste**	Gaullist Party
un **parti libéral**	Liberal Party
un **parti chrétien-démocrate**	Christian-Democratic Party
un **parti socialiste**	Socialist Party
un **parti communiste**	Communist Party
être majoritaire (au parlement/ gouvernement) [maʒɔʀitɛʀ]	to have a majority
être minoritaire [minɔʀitɛʀ]	to be in the minority
indépendant, **indépendante** [ɛ̃depɑ̃dɑ̃, ɑ̃t]	independent (adj)
l'**opposition** *f* [ɔpozisjɔ̃]	opposition

adhérer [adeʀe]	to belong
un **adhérent**, une **adhérente** [adeʀɑ̃, ɑ̃t]	member
un **membre** [mɑ̃bʀ]	member
un **militant**, une **militante** [militɑ̃, ɑ̃t]	active party member
les **militants de base**	member of the party base
un **sympathisant**, une **sympathisante** [sɛ̃patizɑ̃, ɑ̃t]	sympathizer

la **gauche** [goʃ]	left (n)
l'**extrême gauche**	extreme left
la **droite** [dʀwat]	right (n)
l'**extrême droite**	extreme right
être de droite/de gauche	to be (politically) on the right/left
les **partis de droite/de gauche**	parties of the right/left

un **courant politique** [kuʀɑ̃pɔlitik]	political current
un courant modéré	moderate (political) current
une **union** [ynjɔ̃]	union
un **groupe parlementaire** [gʀuppaʀləmɑ̃tɛʀ]	parliamentary group, faction
se rallier à [s(ə)ʀalje]	to agree with, get behind
Le député s'est rallié au groupe communiste.	The representative got behind the communist faction.
une **coalition** [kɔalisjɔ̃]	coalition
une **alliance** [aljɑ̃s]	alliance
un, une **adversaire** [advɛʀsɛʀ]	opponent
une **intrigue** [ɛ̃tʀig]	scheme
un **scandale** [skɑ̃dal]	scandal
être impliqué dans un scandale politique	to be implicated in a political scandal

un, une **capitaliste** [kapitalist]	capitalist (n)
le **capitalisme** [kapitalism]	capitalism
un, une **socialiste** [sɔsjalist]	socialist (n)
le **socialisme** [sɔsjalism]	socialism
un, une **communiste** [kɔmynist]	communist (n)
le **communisme** [kɔmynism]	communism
un, une **fasciste** [faʃist]	fascist (n)
le **fascisme** [faʃism]	fascism
un, une **écologiste** [ekɔlɔʒist]	ecologist (n)
l'**écologie** *f* [ekɔlɔʒi]	ecology, environmental protection

le **PS** (**Parti socialiste**) [peɛs]	Socialist Party
le **PC** (**Parti communiste**) [pese]	Communist Party
l'**UMP** *m* (**Union pour un mouvement populaire**) [uɛmpe]	Union for a Popular Movement (conservative party)
le **MoDem** (**Mouvement démocrate**) [mɔdɛm]	Democratic Movement (Party)
les **Verts** *mpl* [vɛʀ]	The Green Party
le **FN** (**Front National**) [ɛfɛn]	National Front (radical right party)

un **programme** [pʀɔgʀam]	program (n)
un **changement** [ʃɑ̃ʒmɑ̃]	change (n)
une **initiative** [inisjativ]	initiative
prendre une initiative	to take an initiative
une **mesure** [m(ə)zyʀ]	measure (n)
prendre des mesures efficaces contre le chômage	to take effective measures against unemployment

14.4 Laws, Justice, Crime  59

légal, **légale** [legal]	legal
une **loi** [lwa]	law
respecter une loi	to obey a law
violer une loi	to break a law
la **légalité** [legalite]	legality
illégal, **illégale** [ilegal]	illegal
l'**illégalité** *f* [ilegalite]	illegality
le **droit** [dʀwa]	law; right
un **étudiant en droit**	law student

le **droit pénal** [dʀwapenal]	criminal law
le **droit civil** [dʀwasivil]	civil law
le **code pénal** [kɔdpenal]	penal code
le **code civil** [kɔdsivil]	civil code
un **dossier** [dosje]	case, file
rouvrir un dossier	to re-open a case
un **article** [aʀtikl]	paragraph, article

juste [ʒyst]	just, fair
la **justice** [ʒystis]	justice
poursuivre qn en justice	to sue s.o.
injuste [ɛ̃ʒyst]	unjust, unfair
une **injustice** [ɛ̃ʒystis]	injustice
être victime d'une injustice	to be victim of an injustice

un **tribunal** [tʀibynal]	court, tribunal
passer devant le tribunal	to appear before the court
une **cour** (**de justice**) [kuʀ(dəʒystis)]	court (of justice)
le **procès** [pʀɔsɛ]	trial
le **Tribunal correctionnel** [tʀibynalkɔʀɛksjɔnɛl]	criminal court
la **Cour d'assises** [kuʀdasiz]	Assize Court
en première instance [ɑ̃pʀəmjɛʀɛ̃stɑ̃s]	in trial court
être condamné en première instance	to be convicted in trial court
faire appel [fɛʀapɛl]	to appeal
L'accusé a l'intention de faire appel.	The defendant intends to appeal.
casser un jugement [kaseɛ̃ʒyʒmɑ̃]	to overturn, reverse a judgment
la **Cour de cassation** [kuʀdəkasasjɔ̃]	court of cassation (supreme court)

une **affaire** [afɛʀ]	matter, case
une **affaire de corruption**	corruption case
juger qn [ʒyʒe]	to judge s.o.
être jugé pour qc	to be convicted of s.th.
un **jugement** [ʒyʒmɑ̃]	verdict, judgment, sentence
prononcer un jugement	to deliver a verdict
un, une **juge** [ʒyʒ]	judge (n)
un, une **juge d'instruction**	investigative judge
un **avocat**, une **avocate** (**de la défense**) [avɔka, at (d(ə)ladefɑ̃s)]	(defense) attorney, lawyer
un **jury** [ʒyʀi]	jury
un **juré**, une **jurée** [ʒyʀe]	juror

le **procureur** (**général**) [pʀɔkyʀœʀ(ʒeneʀal)]	prosecuting attorney, prosecutor
la **défense** [defɑ̃s]	defense (n)
prendre la défense de qn	to defend s.o.
plaider [plɛde]	to plead
plaider non-coupable	to plead not guilty
le **verdict** [vɛʀdikt]	verdict
La cour a prononcé son verdict.	The court has delivered its verdict.
des **circonstances atténuantes** *fpl* [siʀkɔ̃stɑ̃satenyɑ̃t]	extenuating circumstances
accorder des circonstances atténuantes à l'accusé	to grant the defendant extenuating circumstances
la **prescription** [pʀɛskʀipsjɔ̃]	statute of limitations
avec préméditation [avɛkpʀemeditasjɔ̃]	with premeditation

la **légitime défense** [leʒitimdefɑ̃s]	self-defense
plaider la légitime défense	to plead self-defense
se repentir de qc [səʀ(ə)pɑ̃tiʀ]	to repent of s.th.
Il se repent de son crime.	He is sorry for his crime.

interroger [ɛ̃teʀɔʒe]	to interrogate, question
interroger l'accusé	to interrogate the defendant
un **interrogatoire** [ɛ̃teʀɔgatwaʀ]	interrogation, hearing
procéder à un interrogatoire	to conduct an interrogation
une **question** [kɛstjɔ̃]	question (n)

témoigner pour/en faveur de/contre qn [temwaɲe]	to testify for/against s.o.
un, une **témoin** [temwɛ̃]	witness (n)
appeler un témoin à la barre	to call a witness to the stand
l'audition des témoins	evidentiary hearing, examination of witnesses
un **témoignage** [temwaɲaʒ]	testimony
un **faux témoignage**	false testimony
à charge [aʃaʀʒ]	for the prosecution
à décharge [adeʃaʀʒ]	for the defense
un témoin à charge/à décharge	witness for the prosecution/ defense
déposer en faveur de/contre qn [depoze]	to depose in favor of /against s.o.
une **déposition** [depozisjɔ̃]	deposition
le **serment** [sɛʀmɑ̃]	oath
prêter serment	to take an oath
affirmer qc sous serment	to state under oath

accuser qn de qc [akyze]	to accuse s.o. of s.th.
Il a été accusé de vol.	He was accused of theft.
une **accusation** [akyzasjɔ̃]	accusation
porter une accusation grave contre qn	to bring a serious accusation against s.o.
un **accusé**, une **accusée** [akyze]	accused (n)
la **vérité** [veʀite]	truth
mentir [mɑ̃tiʀ]	to lie
un **mensonge** [mɑ̃sɔ̃ʒ]	lie (n)
être coupable (**de qc**) [kupabl]	to be guilty (of s.th.)
la **culpabilité** [kylpabilite]	guilt
avoir **un doute sur la culpabilité** de l'accusé	to have a doubt about the guilt of the accused
innocent, **innocente** [inɔsɑ̃, ɑ̃t]	innocent
être reconnu innocent	to be declared innocent
l'**innocence** *f* [inɔsɑ̃s]	innocence

un **cas** [ka]	case
prouver [pʀuve]	to prove
une **preuve** [pʀœv]	proof
apporter la preuve de la culpabilité de qn	to produce proof of s.o.'s guilt
avouer [avwe]	to confess, admit
un **aveu** [avœ]	confession
passer aux aveux	to confess
nier [nje]	to deny
L'accusé nie tout en bloc.	The accused denies everything.

condamner qn à qc [kɔ̃dane]	to condemn, convict, sentence s.o. to s.th.
L'accusée a été condamnée à 6 mois de prison.	The accused was sentenced to six months in prison.
la **condamnation** [kɔ̃danasjɔ̃]	sentencing, punishment
infliger une condamnation à qn	to sentence s.o.
un **condamné**, une **condamnée** [kɔ̃dane]	convict (n)
un **condamné à mort**	death row inmate
punir qn de/pour qc [pyniʀ]	to punish s.o. for s.th.
une **prison** [pʀizɔ̃]	prison
faire de la prison	to serve time (in prison)
un **prisonnier**, une **prisonnière** [pʀizɔnje, jɛʀ]	prisoner
Un prisonnier s'est évadé.	A prisoner has escaped.
libérer qn [libeʀe]	to free/release s.o.
être **libéré pour** bonne conduite	to be released for good conduct
la **liberté** [libɛʀte]	freedom
remettre qn en liberté	to release s.o., grant s.o. freedom

une **plainte** [plɛ̃t]	charge (n), lawsuit, complaint
porter plainte	to file a complaint, press charges
déposer une plainte	to file a demand for prosecution
inculper qn (**de qc**) [ɛ̃kylpe]	to charge, accuse s.o. of s.th.
Il a été inculpé de meurtre.	He was charged with murder.
une **inculpation** [ɛ̃kylpasjɔ̃]	accusation, charge, indictment
comparaître (**en justice**) [kɔ̃paʀɛtʀ]	to appear (in court)
comparaître (**en justice**) **pour** vol à main armée	to appear in court for armed robbery
la **détention provisoire** [detɑ̃sjɔ̃pʀɔvizwaʀ]	custody
Elle a **fait trois mois de détention provisoire.**	She spent three months in custody.

un **délinquant**, une **délinquante** [delɛ̃kɑ̃, ɑ̃t]	delinquent (n)
la **délinquance** [delɛ̃kɑ̃s]	delinquency
La **délinquance juvénile** est en augmentation.	Juvenile delinquency is on the rise.
un **prévenu**, une **prévenue** [pʀev(ə)ny]	suspect (n)
un, une **récidiviste** [ʀesidivist]	recidivist, habitual criminal
le **non-lieu** [nɔ̃ljø]	non-suit/dismissal
obtenir un non-lieu	to obtain a dismissal
acquitter qn [akite]	to acquit s.o.
Le prévenu a été acquitté.	The suspect was acquitted.
un **acquittement** [akitmɑ̃]	acquittal
une **amende** [amɑ̃d]	fine (n)
une **sanction** [sɑ̃ksjɔ̃]	sanction, punishment
une **peine** [pɛn]	penalty
la **peine de mort**	death penalty
avec sursis [avɛksyʀsi]	probation
6 mois de prison avec sursis	six months in prison with probation
la **réclusion à perpétuité** [ʀeklyzjɔ̃apɛʀpetɥite]	life sentence
une **erreur judiciaire** [eʀœʀʒydisjɛʀ]	judicial error, miscarriage of justice

les **forces de l'ordre** *fpl* [fɔʀsdəlɔʀdʀ]	law enforcement forces
la **police** [pɔlis]	police (n)
un **agent de police**	police officer
un **poste** (**de police**)	(police) station
policier, **policière** [pɔlisje, jɛʀ]	police (adj)
une **enquête policière**	police investigation
un **policier**, une **policier**/une **policière**	police officer
un, une **gendarme** [ʒɑ̃daʀm]	police officer
un, une **commissaire** [kɔmisɛʀ]	commissioner
un **commissariat** [kɔmisaʀja]	superintendent's office, police station
enquêter [ɑ̃kɛte]	to investigate
enquêter sur qn/qc	to investigate s.o./s.th.
une **enquête** [ɑ̃kɛt]	investigation, inquiry
mener l'enquête	to conduct an investigation
un **flic** *fam* [flik]	cop

un **contractuel**, une **contractuelle** [kɔ̃tʀaktyɛl]	auxiliary police officer
la **police judiciaire** (**PJ**) [pɔlisʒydisjɛʀ (peʒi)]	police detective, criminal investigator
la **Gendarmerie nationale** [ʒɑ̃daʀməʀinasjɔnal]	(national) police
un, une **CRS** (**Compagnie Républicaine de Sécurité**) [seɛʀɛs]	CRS force (special mobile police force in France)
rechercher [ʀ(ə)ʃɛʀʃe]	to hunt, search for
une **piste** [pist]	trail; clue (n)
suivre une piste	to follow a trail
une **trace** [tʀas]	clue
des **empreintes digitales** *fpl* [ɑ̃pʀɛ̃tdiʒital]	fingerprints
prendre les empreintes digitales de qn	to take s.o.'s fingerprints
suspect, **suspecte** [syspɛ(kt), ɛkt]	suspicious (adj)
un **suspect**, une **suspecte**	suspect (n)
soupçonner qn [supsɔne]	to suspect s.o.
un **soupçon** [supsɔ̃]	suspicion
Les soupçons se portent sur son mari.	Suspicion is directed to her husband.
une **rafle** [ʀafl]	raid, crackdown
les **poursuites** *fpl* [puʀsɥit]	criminal prosecution
abandonner les poursuites contre qn	to discontinue prosecution against s.o.
un **mandat** [mɑ̃da]	mandate, order, warrant, summons
délivrer un **mandat d'amener**	to deliver a summons
un **mandat d'arrêt**	arrest warrant
mettre qn en examen [mɛtʀɑ̃nɛgzamɛ̃]	to launch a preliminary investigation against s.o.
la **garde à vue** [gaʀdavy]	police custody
une **perquisition** [pɛʀkizisjɔ̃]	search (n)
un **indice** [ɛ̃dis]	clue, evidence
une **pièce à conviction** [pjɛsakɔ̃viksjɔ̃]	exhibit, evidence

criminel, **criminelle** [kʀiminɛl]	criminal (adj)
un **acte criminel**	criminal act
un **crime** [kʀim]	crime
commettre un crime	to commit a crime
tuer [tye]	to kill
blesser [blese]	to wound
une **arme** [aʀm]	weapon
une **victime** [viktim]	victim
arrêter [aʀɛte]	to arrest
une **arrestation** [aʀɛstasjɔ̃]	arrest (n)
procéder à une arrestation	to perform an arrest

un **délit** [deli]	offense, crime
prendre qn en flagrant délit	to catch s.o. red-handed
un **meurtre** [mœʀtʀ]	murder (n)
assassiner [asasine]	to murder
un **assassinat** [asasina]	murder (n)
un **assassin** [asasɛ̃]	murderer
violer [vjɔle]	to rape
un **viol** [vjɔl]	rape (n)
un **mobile** [mɔbil]	motive
un **alibi** [alibi]	alibi
vérifier un alibi	to check, verify an alibi

une **bagarre** [bagaʀ]	fight (n)
violent, **violente** [vjɔlɑ̃, ɑ̃t]	violent
la **violence** [vjɔlɑ̃s]	violence
céder face à la violence	to yield to force

une **attaque** [atak]	attack (n)
voler [vɔle]	to steal *(See Information Box p. 40)*
un **vol** [vɔl]	theft *(See Information Box p. 40)*
un **vol à main armée**	armed robbery
un **voleur**, une **voleuse** [vɔlœʀ, øz]	thief, robber
Au voleur!	Stop thief!
piquer *fam* [pike]	to swipe, filch

kidnapper [kidnape]	to kidnap
un **kidnappeur**, une **kidnappeuse** [kidnapœʀ, øz]	kidnapper
enlever qn [ɑ̃l(ə)ve]	to abduct s.o.
un **enlèvement** [ɑ̃lɛvmɑ̃]	abduction
une **prise d'otage** [pʀizdɔtaʒ]	hostage-taking
une **rançon** [ʀɑ̃sɔ̃]	ransom
faire chanter qn [fɛʀʃɑ̃te]	to blackmail s.o.
un **chantage** [ʃɑ̃taʒ]	blackmail/extortion
un **maître-chanteur** [mɛtʀ(ə)ʃɑ̃tœʀ]	blackmailer/extortionist
un **malfaiteur** [malfɛtœʀ]	felon, delinquent
un **escroc** [ɛskʀo]	cheat, con man, crook
une **escroquerie** [ɛskʀɔkʀi]	fraud, scam
un **gangster** [gɑ̃gstɛʀ]	gangster
cambrioler [kɑ̃bʀijɔle]	to break in, burglarize
un **cambriolage** [kɑ̃bʀijɔlaʒ]	burglary, break-in
un **cambrioleur**, une **cambrioleuse** [kɑ̃bʀijɔlœʀ, øz]	burglar
une **bande** [bɑ̃d]	gang
un **hold-up** ['ɔldœp]	holdup, robbery

un **réseau**; des **réseaux** *pl* [ʀezo]	network, ring
démanteler un réseau de trafiquants de drogue	to break up a drug trafficking ring
un, une **complice** [kɔ̃plis]	accomplice (n)

14.5 Organizations, Unions  60

une **association** [asɔsjasjɔ̃]	association
syndical, **syndicale** [sɛ̃dikal]	union
un **délégué syndical**, une **déléguée syndicale**	union delegate
un **syndicat** [sɛ̃dika]	union
un, une **syndicaliste** [sɛ̃dikalist]	unionist, union representative
le **syndicalisme** [sɛ̃dikalism]	organized labor

se syndiquer [s(ə)sɛ̃dike]	to unionize
adhérer [adeʀe]	to belong
un **adhérent**, une **adhérente** [adeʀɑ̃, ɑ̃t]	member
s'organiser [sɔʀganize]	to organize

un **salarié**, une **salariée** [salaʀje]	employee
un **travailleur**, une **travailleuse** [tʀavajœʀ, jøz]	worker
un **patron**, une **patronne** [patʀɔ̃, ɔn]	boss
le **patronat** [patʀɔna]	employers, management

les **partenaires sociaux** *mpl* [paʀtənɛʀsɔsjo]	management and labor
un **employeur**, une **employeuse** [ɑ̃plwajœʀ, øz]	employer
le **comité d'entreprise** [kɔmitedɑ̃tʀəpʀiz]	employee organization
une **convention collective** [kɔ̃vɑ̃sjɔ̃kɔlɛktiv]	collective agreement
un **conflit social** [kɔ̃flisɔsjal]	labor dispute

protester [pʀɔtɛste]	to protest
une **protestation** [pʀɔtɛstasjɔ̃]	protest (n)
revendiquer [ʀ(ə)vɑ̃dike]	to demand
une **revendication** [ʀ(ə)vɑ̃dikasjɔ̃]	demand (n)

une **grève** [gʀɛv]	strike (n)
Une **grève générale** a paralysé le pays.	A general strike has paralyzed the country.
une **grève sauvage**	wildcat strike
faire (**la**) **grève**	to strike
se mettre en grève	to go out on strike
être en grève	to be on strike
un, une **gréviste** [gʀevist]	striker

contester [kɔ̃tɛste]	to protest
une **contestation** [kɔ̃tɛstasjɔ̃]	challenge (n), protest (movement)
se rassembler [s(ə)ʀasɑ̃ble]	to assemble
un **rassemblement** [ʀasɑ̃bləmɑ̃]	assembly
lancer un ordre de grève [lɑ̃seɛ̃nɔʀdʀ(ə)dəgʀɛv]	to issue a strike order
débrayer [debʀeje]	to walk out, stop work
un **débrayage** [debʀɛjaʒ]	walkout, warning strike
un **piquet de grève** [pikɛdgʀɛv]	picket (n)
un **briseur**, une **briseuse de grève** [bʀizœʀ, øzdəgʀɛv]	strike breaker, scab
un **lock-out** [lɔkaut]	lockout

se réunir [s(ə)ʀeyniʀ]	to meet
une **réunion** [ʀeynjɔ̃]	meeting (n)
discuter de qc [diskyte]	to discuss s.th.
une **discussion** [diskysjɔ̃]	discussion
une **solution** [sɔlysjɔ̃]	solution
un **compromis** [kɔ̃pʀɔmi]	compromise (n)
parvenir à un compromis	to reach a compromise
un **résultat** [ʀezylta]	result (n)
reprendre le travail [ʀ(ə)pʀɑ̃dʀlətʀavaj]	to go back to work

négocier [negɔsje]	to negotiate
une **négociation** [negɔsjasjɔ̃]	negotiation
engager des négociations	to enter into negotiations
un **négociateur**, une **négociatrice** [negɔsjatœʀ, tʀis]	negotiator
un **accord** [akɔʀ]	agreement
un **médiateur**, une **médiatrice** [medjatœʀ, tʀis]	mediator
une **consultation de la base** [kɔ̃syltasjɔ̃d(ə)labaz]	strike vote

14.6 Domestic Politics  61

l'**identité** *f* [idɑ̃tite]	identity
l'identité culturelle	cultural identity
une **minorité** [minɔʀite]	minority
être en minorité	to be in the minority
l'**autonomie** *f* [otonomi]	autonomy
autonomiste [otonomist]	autonomist
un **mouvement autonomiste**	autonomy movement

les **us et coutumes** *mpl* [ysekutym]	customs and traditions
se plier aux us et coutumes d'un pays	to adapt to the customs and traditions of a country
les **particularités** *fpl* [paʀtikylaʀite]	distinctive features
préserver [pʀezɛʀve]	to preserve
préserver les traditions	to keep the traditions alive
un, une **séparatiste** [sepaʀatist]	separatist (n)
le **séparatisme** [sepaʀatism]	separatism

l'**origine** *f* [ɔʀiʒin]	origin
le **pays d'origine**	country of origin
la (**double**) **nationalité** [(dublə)nasjɔnalite]	(dual) citizenship, (double) nationality

le **Code de la nationalité** [kɔddəlanasjɔnalite]	citizenship law
un **Français**, une **Française de souche** [fʀɑ̃sɛ/sɛzdəsuʃ]	native French person
clandestin, **clandestine** [klɑ̃dɛstɛ̃, tin]	illegal
un **clandestin**, une **clandestine**	illegal alien
l'**afflux** *m* [afly]	influx
L'afflux de clandestins sur le marché du travail pose des problèmes.	The influx of illegal aliens into the labor market poses problems.
un **Maghrébin**, une **Maghrébine** [magʀebɛ̃, bin]	Maghrebi (n)
un, une **beur**/une **beurette** *fam* [bœʀ, ʀɛt]	beur (n) *(a child born in France to Maghrebi immigrants)*

immigrer [imigʀe]	to immigrate
immigré, **immigrée** [imigʀe]	immigrant (adj)
un **immigré**, une **immigrée**	immigrant (n)
un **travailleur immigré**	migrant worker
une **immigrée clandestine**	illegal alien
l'**immigration** *f* [imigʀasjɔ̃]	immigration
l'**immigration sauvage**	illegal immigration

émigrer [emigʀe]	to emigrate
un **émigré**, une **émigrée** [emigʀe]	emigrant (n)
l'**émigration** *f* [emigʀasjɔ̃]	emigration
se réfugier [s(ə)ʀefyʒje]	to flee
un **réfugié**, une **réfugiée** [ʀefyʒje]	refugee
accueillir des réfugiés politiques	to admit political refugees

---

raciste [ʀasist]	racist (adj)
un, une **raciste**	racist (n)
le **racisme** [ʀasism]	racism
On constate une montée inquiétante du racisme.	A disturbing increase in racism is evident.
la **discrimination** [diskʀiminasjɔ̃]	discrimination
la discrimination raciale	racial discrimination

---

persécuter [pɛʀsekyte]	to persecute
Elle a été **persécutée en raison de** ses convictions politiques.	She was persecuted for her political beliefs.
la **persécution** [pɛʀsekysjɔ̃]	persecution
l'**exil** *m* [ɛgzil]	exile (n)
s'exiler [sɛgzile]	to go into exile
un **opposant**, une **opposante** [ɔpozɑ̃, ɑ̃t]	opponent
un **opposant au régime**	opponent of the regime
s'expatrier [sɛkspatʀije]	to leave one's homeland, emigrate
s'expatrier pour échapper aux persécutions	to leave one's country to escape persecution
xénophobe [gzenɔfɔb]	xenophobic
la **xénophobie** [gzenɔfɔbi]	xenophobia
le **préjugé** [pʀeʒyʒe]	prejudice
Les préjugés ont la vie dure.	Prejudices die hard.
rejeter [ʀ(ə)ʒəte/ʀəj(ə)te]	to reject
le **rejet** [ʀ(ə)ʒɛ]	rejection
la **haine** ['ɛn]	hatred
éprouver de la haine pour qn	to feel hatred for s.o.
exclure qn (**de**) [ɛksklyʀ]	to exclude s.o. (from)
l'**exclusion** *f* [ɛksklyzjɔ̃]	exclusion
donner la priorité à la lutte contre l'exclusion	to give priority to the struggle against exclusion
expulser qn [ɛkspylse]	to expel s.o.
On a expulsé les clandestins du territoire français.	The illegal aliens were expelled from French territory.
l'**expulsion** *f* [ɛkspylsjɔ̃]	expulsion
renvoyer [ʀɑ̃vwaje]	to send back
Ils ont été renvoyés dans leur pays d'origine.	They were sent back to their country of origin.

la **tolérance** [tɔleʀɑ̃s]	tolerance
l'**intolérance** *f* [ɛ̃tɔleʀɑ̃s]	intolerance
s'intégrer [sɛ̃tegʀe]	to integrate
intégré, **intégrée** [ɛ̃tegʀe]	integrated
l'**intégration** *f* [ɛ̃tegʀasjɔ̃]	integration
un **permis de séjour** [pɛʀmidseʒuʀ]	residency permit
accorder un permis de séjour à qn	to grand s.o. a residency permit
un **permis de travail** [pɛʀmidtʀavaj]	work permit
l'**asile** (**politique**) *m* [azil(pɔlitik)]	(political) asylum
un **demandeur d'asile**	asylum seeker
le **droit d'asile**	right of asylum
demander l'asile politique	to request political asylum
accorder l'asile politique à qn	to grant political asylum to s.o.
un pays d'asile	country of asylum
un foyer pour demandeurs d'asile	shelter for asylum seekers

multiculturel, **multiculturelle** [myltikyltyʀɛl]	multicultural
se faire naturaliser [s(ə)fɛʀnatyʀalize]	to become naturalized
la **naturalisation** [natyʀalizasjɔ̃]	naturalization
Elle a demandé sa naturalisation, mais elle ne l'a pas obtenue.	She requested naturalization, but she didn't get it.
le **droit du sol** [dʀwadysɔl]	jus soli *(citizenship according to birthright)*
La France applique le droit du sol.	France applies jus soli.
le **droit du sang** [dʀwadysɑ̃]	jus sanguinis *(citizenship based on parentage)*

s'opposer à [sɔpoze]	to oppose
l'**opposition** *f* [ɔpozisjɔ̃]	opposition
manifester (**en faveur de/contre**) [manifɛste]	to demonstrate (in favor of/against)
un **manifestant**, une **manifestante** [manifɛstɑ̃, ɑ̃t]	demonstrator
une **manifestation** [manifɛstasjɔ̃]	demonstration
une **manif** *fam* [manif]	demonstration
une manif pacifique/non-violente	a peaceful/non-violent demonstration
l'**ordre** *m* [ɔʀdʀ]	order (n)
troubler l'ordre public	to disturb public order
rétablir l'ordre	to reestablish order
la **violence** [vjɔlɑ̃s]	violence
la **non-violence**	non-violence

la **désobéissance civile** [dezɔbeisɑ̃ssivil]	civil disobedience
appeler à la désobéissance civile	to invoke civil disobedience
boycotter [bɔjkɔte]	to boycott
une **banderole** [bɑ̃dʀɔl]	banner
Les manifestants ont déployé leurs banderoles.	The demonstrators unrolled their banners.
un **tract** [tʀakt]	flyer, leaflet
distribuer des tracts	to distribute leaflets
militer (**en faveur de/contre**) [milite]	to campaign for/against s.th.
la **lutte** [lyt]	combat, struggle (n)
engager la lutte contre	fight, campaign against
lutter pour/contre qn/qc [lyte]	campaign for/against s.o./s.th.
le **combat** [kɔ̃ba]	fight (n)
se révolter contre [s(ə)ʀevɔlte]	to revolt against
une **révolte** [ʀevɔlt]	revolt, rebellion
une révolte armée	armed revolt, rebellion
révolutionnaire [ʀevɔlysjɔnɛʀ]	revolutionary
un, une **révolutionnaire**	revolutionary (n)
une **révolution** [ʀevɔlysjɔ̃]	revolution
libérer [libeʀe]	to free, liberate, release
la **libération** [libeʀasjɔ̃]	liberation
des **troubles** *mpl* [tʀubl]	unrest, disturbances
une **émeute** [emøt]	riot (n)
déclencher une émeute	to trigger, prompt a riot
se soulever contre [s(ə)sul(ə)ve]	to rise up against
une **insurrection** [ɛ̃syʀɛksjɔ̃]	insurrection
un **coup d'État** [kudeta]	coup d'état
prendre le pouvoir à la suite d'un coup d'État	to take power following a coup d'état
la **répression** [ʀepʀesjɔ̃]	repression
La répression de la révolte a été sanglante.	The repression of the rebellion was bloody.
la **torture** [tɔʀtyʀ]	torture (n)
un, une **terroriste** [teʀɔʀist]	terrorist (n)
appartenir à un **réseau terroriste**	to belong to a terrorist network
le **terrorisme** [teʀɔʀism]	terrorism
un **attentat** [atɑ̃ta]	assassination attempt
commettre un **attentat à la bombe**	to commit a bomb attack
un **acte de sabotage** [aktdəsabɔtaʒ]	act of sabotage

14.7 International Relations, Globalization, Europe

 62

étranger, **étrangère** [etʀɑ̃ʒe, ʒɛʀ]	foreign
la **politique étrangère**	foreign policy
le **ministre/ministère des Affaires étrangères**	minister of foreign affairs
l'**étranger** *m* [etʀɑ̃ʒe]	abroad
puissant, puissante [pɥisɑ̃, ɑ̃t]	powerful
la **puissance** [pɥisɑ̃s]	power
une **puissance nucléaire**	nuclear power/atomic weapons state
une **grande puissance**	major (military) power
l'**ONU** *f* (**Organisation des Nations Unies**) [ony]	UN (United Nations)
l'**OTAN** *f* (**Organisation du traité de l'Atlantique Nord**) [otɑ̃]	NATO (North Atlantic Treaty Organization)
la **diplomatie** [diplɔmasi]	diplomacy
un, une **diplomate** [diplɔmat]	diplomat (n)
une **ambassade** [ɑ̃basad]	embassy
un **ambassadeur**, une **ambassadrice** [ɑ̃basadœʀ, dʀis]	ambassador
consulaire [kɔ̃sylɛʀ]	consular
un **consul** [kɔ̃syl]	consul
un **consulat** [kɔ̃syla]	consulate
le consulat (général) de France à Francfort	the French consulate (general) in Frankfurt
sous-développé, **sous-développée** [sudev(ə)lɔpe]	underdeveloped
un **pays sous-développé**	underdeveloped country
le **sous-développement** [sudev(ə)lɔpmɑ̃]	underdevelopment
le **tiers-monde** [tjɛʀmɔ̃d]	Third World
les pays du tiers-monde	third-world countries
un **pays en voie de développement** [peiɑ̃vwad(ə)dev(ə)lɔpmɑ̃]	developing nation
l'**aide au développement** *f* [ɛdodev(ə)lɔpmɑ̃]	development aid
un **pays émergent** [peiemɛʀʒɑ̃]	emerging nation

la **relation** [ʀ(ə)lasjɔ̃]	relation
les **relations internationales**	international relations
entretenir/rompre des relations diplomatiques	maintain/break diplomatic relations
les **rapports** *mpl* [ʀapɔʀ]	relations
Les rapports entre les deux pays sont tendus.	The relations between the two countries are strained.
la **tension** [tɑ̃sjɔ̃]	tension
une **crise** [kʀiz]	crisis
l'**hégémonie** *f* [eʒemɔni]	hegemony, supremacy
une **rivalité** [ʀivalite]	rivalry
un **désaccord** [dezakɔʀ]	disagreement
être en désaccord avec qn	to be in disagreement with s.o.
la **détérioration** [deteʀjɔʀasjɔ̃]	deterioration
une **querelle** [kəʀɛl]	quarrel
un **conflit** [kɔ̃fli]	conflict
un **conflit armé**	armed conflict
la **pression** [pʀesjɔ̃]	pressure
exercer une pression sur qn	to exert pressure on s.o.
s'affronter [safʀɔ̃te]	to confront
une **confrontation** [kɔ̃fʀɔ̃tasjɔ̃]	confrontation
La confrontation semble inévitable.	A confrontation seems inevitable.
une **intervention** [ɛ̃tɛʀvɑ̃sjɔ̃]	intervention
une **réunion** [ʀeynjɔ̃]	meeting
un **sommet** [sɔmɛ]	summit
un sommet des pays industrialisés	a summit of the industrialized countries
une **réunion au sommet**	summit meeting
une **rencontre** [ʀɑ̃kɔ̃tʀ]	meeting
des **rencontres bilatérales**	bilateral meetings
une **conférence** [kɔ̃feʀɑ̃s]	conference
Une **conférence internationale sur l'environnement** a lieu à Rome.	An international conference on the environment is taking place in Rome.

la **neutralité** [nøtʀalite]	neutrality
une **consultation** [kɔ̃syltasjɔ̃]	consultation
des **consultations bilatérales**	bilateral consultations
la **détente** [detɑ̃t]	détente
poursuivre une **politique de détente**	to pursue a policy of détente
une **amélioration** [ameljɔʀasjɔ̃]	improvement
un **entretien** [ɑ̃tʀətjɛ̃]	conversation, talk
un **entretien secret**	secret talks
un **accord** [akɔʀ]	agreement
conclure un accord	to enter into an agreement
un **pacte** [pakt]	pact
une **entente** [ɑ̃tɑ̃t]	agreement, understanding
un **traité** [tʀete]	treaty
signer un traité	to sign a treaty
ratifier un traité	to ratify a treaty
violer un traité	to violate a treaty

coopérer [kɔɔpeʀe]	to cooperate, work together
la **coopération** [kɔɔpeʀasjɔ̃]	cooperation
un **échange** [eʃɑ̃ʒ]	exchange (n)
un **échange scolaire**	student exchange
être jumelé, **jumelée** [ʒymle]	to be paired, partnered with
Strasbourg est jumelé avec Stuttgart.	Strasbourg is a sister city with Stuttgart.
un **jumelage** [ʒymlaʒ]	twinning (of cities)

un **ennemi héréditaire** [en(ə)mieʀeditɛʀ]	historical/hereditary/sworn enemy
se rapprocher de qn/qc [s(ə)ʀapʀɔʃe]	to approach s.o./s.th.
un **rapprochement** [ʀapʀɔʃmɑ̃]	rapprochement
se réconcilier [s(ə)ʀekɔ̃silje]	to reconcile
se réconcilier avec son ennemi	to reconcile with one's enemy
une **réconciliation** [ʀekɔ̃siljasjɔ̃]	reconciliation
la **réconciliation franco-allemande**	Franco-German reconciliation
un **allié**, une **alliée** [alje]	ally
une **alliance** [aljɑ̃s]	alliance
le **Traité sur la coopération franco-allemande** [tʀetesyʀlakɔɔpeʀasjɔ̃fʀɑ̃koalmɑ̃d]	Franco-German Cooperation Treaty
francophone [fʀɑ̃kɔfɔn]	francophone
Le Sénégal est un pays francophone.	Senegal is a francophone country.
la **francophonie** [fʀɑ̃kɔfɔni]	francophonie/French-speaking countries and regions

mondial, **mondiale** [mɔ̃djal]	worldwide, global
l'**économie mondiale**	world, global economy
le **marché mondial**	global market
le **commerce mondial**	global commerce
la **mondialisation** [mɔ̃djalizasjɔ̃]	globalization
la **globalisation** [glɔbalizasjɔ̃]	globalization
le **sommet économique mondial** [sɔmɛekɔnɔmik]	world economic summit
le **G8** (**groupe des Huit**) [ʒe'ɥit]	G8 (Group of Eight)
Le G8 soutient la mondialisation du commerce.	The G8 supports the globalization of commerce.
un, une **altermondialiste** [altɛʀmɔ̃djalist]	globalization opponent
boycotter [bɔjkɔte]	to boycott
un **boycott**(**age**) [bɔjkɔt(aʒ)]	boycott (n)
une **sanction** [sɑ̃ksjɔ̃]	sanction (n)
décréter des sanctions envers un état	to impose sanctions on a country
un **embargo** [ɑ̃baʀgo]	embargo
lever l'embargo contre un pays	to lift, repeal the embargo against a country
une **multinationale** [myltinasjɔnal]	multinational corporation
rationaliser [ʀasjɔnalize]	to rationalize
la **rationalisation** [ʀasjɔnalizasjɔ̃]	rationalization
délocaliser [delɔkalize]	to delocalize
la **délocalisation** [delɔkalizasjɔ̃]	delocalization
une **fusion** [fyzjɔ̃]	fusion
la **libéralisation** [libeʀalizasjɔ̃]	liberalization
le **libre-échange** [libʀeʃɑ̃ʒ]	free exchange
le **commerce extérieur** [kɔmɛʀsɛksteʀjœʀ]	foreign trade
importer [ɛ̃pɔʀte]	to import
l'**importation** *f* [ɛ̃pɔʀtasjɔ̃]	import, importation
exporter [ɛkspɔʀte]	to export
l'**exportation** *f* [ɛkspɔʀtasjɔ̃]	export, exportation
investir [ɛ̃vɛstiʀ]	to invest
investir à l'étranger	to invest abroad
un **investissement** [ɛ̃vɛstismɑ̃]	investment
l'**interdépendance économique** *f* [ɛ̃tɛʀdepɑ̃dɑ̃sekɔnɔmik]	economic interdependence

européen, **européenne** [øʀɔpeɛ̃, ɛn]	European
l'**Europe** *f* [øʀɔp]	Europe
l'**Union européenne** (**UE**) *f* [ynjɔ̃øʀɔpeɛn]	European Union (EU)
un **pays membre** [peimɑ̃bʀ]	member country
un **membre fondateur** [mɑ̃bʀfɔ̃datœʀ]	founding member
l'**élargissement** *m* [elaʀʒismɑ̃]	expansion
Tout le monde n'est pas favorable à l'élargissement de l'Union européenne.	Not everyone is in favor of expanding the European Union.
le **Marché intérieur européen** [maʀʃeɛ̃teʀjœʀøʀɔpeɛ̃]	European domestic market
l'**union économique** *f* [ynjɔ̃ekɔnɔmik]	economic union
l'**union monétaire** *f* [ynjɔ̃mɔnetɛʀ]	monetary union
la **monnaie unique** [mɔnɛynik]	common currency
l'**euro** *m* [øro]	euro
la **zone euro** [zonøro]	euro zone

le **Parlement européen** [paʀləmɑ̃øʀɔpeɛ̃]	European Parliament
siéger [sjeʒe]	to be headquartered
Le Parlement européen siège à Strasbourg.	The European Parliament is headquartered in Strasbourg.
un **siège** [sjɛʒ]	seat (in Parliament)
le **Conseil de l'Europe** [kɔ̃sɛjdəløʀɔp]	Council of Europe
le **Conseil des ministres** [kɔ̃sɛjdeministʀ]	Council of Ministers
la **Commission européenne** [kɔmisjɔ̃øʀɔpeɛn]	European Commission
la **Banque centrale européenne** (**BCE**) [bɑ̃ksɑ̃tʀaløʀɔpeɛn(beseə)]	European Central Bank (ECB)
le **Système monétaire européen** (**SME**) [sistemɔnetɛʀøʀopeɛn(ɛsɛmø)]	European Monetary System (EMS)
le **pacte de stabilité et de croissance** [paktdəstabiliteekʀwasɑ̃s]	stability and growth agreement

14.8 Peace, War, Military  63

la **paix** [pɛ]	peace
faire la paix avec qn	to make peace with s.o.
signer un **traité de paix**	to sign a peace treaty
la **guerre** [gɛʀ]	war (n)
la **guerre civile**	civil war
une **déclaration de guerre**	declaration of war
faire la guerre à qn/à un pays	to make war on s.o./a country
déclarer la guerre	to declare war

un **plan** [plɑ̃]	plan (n)
attaquer [atake]	to attack
une **attaque** [atak]	attack (n)
mener une action [məneynaksjɔ̃]	to conduct a campaign
une **bataille** [bataj]	battle (n)
la **défense** [defɑ̃s]	defense
le **ministre de la Défense**	the Minister of Defense
ennemi, **ennemie** [en(ə)mi]	enemy (adj)
une **nation ennemie**	an enemy nation
l'**ennemi héréditaire**	historical, sworn enemy

hostile [ɔstil]	hostile
les **hostilités** *fpl* [ɔstilite]	hostilities
Tout le monde souhaite la fin des hostilités.	Everyone wants an end to the hostilities.
combattre [kɔ̃batʀ]	to fight
un **combattant**, une **combattante** [kɔ̃batɑ̃, ɑ̃t]	combatant; soldier
une **provocation** [pʀɔvɔkasjɔ̃]	provocation
un **avertissement** [avɛʀtismɑ̃]	warning
lancer un dernier avertissement à qn	to send a final warning to s.o.
un **ultimatum** [yltimatɔm]	ultimatum
L'ultimatum expirera demain.	The ultimatum expires tomorrow.
bombarder [bɔ̃baʀde]	to bombard
un **bombardement** [bɔ̃baʀdəmɑ̃]	bombardment
la **dissuasion** [disɥazjɔ̃]	deterrence
la **force de dissuasion**	power of deterrence

militaire [militɛʀ]	military (adj)
un, une **militaire**	soldier
un **militaire de carrière**	career soldier
un **soldat**, une **soldate** [sɔlda, at]	soldier
un **uniforme** [ynifɔʀm]	uniform
une **caserne** [kazɛʀn]	barracks

le **service militaire** (**obligatoire**) [sɛʀvismilitɛʀ(ɔbligatwaʀ)]	(compulsory) military service
le **service civil** [sɛʀvissivil]	civil service
faire son service militaire/civil	to do one's military/civil service
un **conscrit** [kɔ̃skʀi]	draftee
un **appelé** [ap(ə)le]	draftee, conscript (n)
une **recrue** [ʀəkʀy]	recruit (n)
un, une **volontaire** [vɔlɔ̃tɛʀ]	volunteer
demander des volontaires pour une mission	to ask for volunteers for a mission
s'engager [sɑ̃gaʒe]	to enlist (willingly)
un **objecteur de conscience** [ɔbjɛktœʀdəkɔ̃sjɑ̃s]	conscientious objector
obtenir le statut d'objecteur de conscience	to be granted conscientious objector status
pacifiste [pasifist]	pacifist (adj)
un, une **pacifiste**	pacifist (n)
le **pacifisme** [pasifism]	pacifism
déserter [dezɛʀte]	to desert
un **déserteur** [dezɛʀtœʀ]	deserter

armer qn de qc [aʀme]	to arm s.o. with s.th.
une **arme** [aʀm]	weapon
une arme conventionnelle	conventional weapon
une arme chimique	chemical weapon
une arme nucléaire	nuclear weapon
une **armée** [aʀme]	army
un **coup de feu** [kudfø]	shot (n)
un **fusil** [fyzi]	gun
une **bombe** [bɔ̃b]	bomb
une **bombe atomique**	atomic bomb
une **mine** [min]	mine
exploser [ɛksploze]	to explode
détruire [detʀɥiʀ]	to destroy

l'**armement** *m* [aʀməmɑ̃]	armament; arming
la **course aux armements**	arms race
le **contrôle des armements**	arms control
réduire l'armement nucléaire	to reduce nuclear weaponry
le **désarmement** [dezaʀməmɑ̃]	disarmament
une **troupe** [tʀup]	troop
une **division** [divizjɔ̃]	division
un **bataillon** [batajɔ̃]	battalion
un **officier** [ofisje]	officer
un **général** [ʒeneʀal]	general
recevoir un ordre [ʀəsəvwaʀɛ̃nɔʀdʀ]	to receive an order
l'**armée de métier** *f* [aʀmed(ə)metje]	professional army
l'**armée de terre** *f* [aʀmedtɛʀ]	army
un **char** [ʃaʀ]	tank
tirer sur [tiʀe]	to fire on
L'armée a tiré sur des civils.	The army fired on civilians.
l'**armée de l'air** *f* [aʀmedlɛʀ]	air force
un **avion de chasse** [avjɔ̃d(ə)ʃas]	fighter plane
une **fusée** [fyze]	rocket
la **marine** [maʀin]	navy
un **sous-marin** [sumaʀɛ̃]	submarine
un **sous-marin nucléaire**	nuclear submarine
un **porte-avions** [pɔʀtavjɔ̃]	aircraft carrier *(See Information Box p. 104)*
les **forces armées** *fpl* [fɔʀs(əz)aʀme]	armed forces
la **force de frappe** [fɔʀsdəfʀap]	strike/assault force
intervenir* [ɛ̃tɛʀvəniʀ]	to intervene
une **intervention** [ɛ̃tɛʀvɑ̃sjɔ̃]	intervention
les **pertes** *fpl* [pɛʀt]	losses
On déplore de lourdes pertes.	People deplore heavy losses.
une **victoire** [viktwaʀ]	victory
remporter la victoire	to win a victory
vaincre [vɛ̃kʀ]	to conquer
le **vainqueur** [vɛ̃kœʀ]	conqueror
sortir* vainqueur de	to emerge victorious from
un **vaincu**, une **vaincue** [vɛ̃ky]	loser, vanquished (n)
une **défaite** [defɛt]	defeat (n)
subir une défaite	to suffer defeat
se rendre [s(ə)ʀɑ̃dʀ]	to surrender
Les vaincus se sont rendus à l'ennemi.	The vanquished surrendered to the enemy.

une **frontière** [fʀɔ̃tjɛʀ]	border
franchir la frontière	to cross the border
un **incident** [ɛ̃sidɑ̃]	incident
Un incident grave s'est produit.	A serious incident resulted.
occuper [ɔkype]	to occupy
l'**occupation** *f* [ɔkypasjɔ̃]	occupation

une **agression** [agʀesjɔ̃]	attack, aggression
un **agresseur** [agʀesœʀ]	aggressor
un **attaquant**, une **attaquante** [atakɑ̃, ɑ̃t]	attacker
repousser l'attaquant	to fight off the attacker
le **couvre-feu** [kuvʀəfø]	curfew
l'**état d'urgence** *m* [etadyʀʒɑ̃s]	state of emergency, martial law
déclarer l'état d'urgence	to declare a state of emergency
envahir [ɑ̃vaiʀ]	to invade
envahir un pays	to invade a country
un **envahisseur** [ɑ̃vaisœʀ]	invader
résister à l'envahisseur	to resist, stand up against the invader
une **invasion** [ɛ̃vazjɔ̃]	invasion
dévaster [devaste]	to lay waste, devastate
un **crime de guerre** [kʀimdəgɛʀ]	war crime
poursuivre qn pour crimes de guerre	to persecute s.o. for war crimes
un **criminel**, une **criminelle de guerre** [kʀiminɛldəgɛʀ]	war criminal

un **prisonnier**, une **prisonnière** [pʀizɔnje, jɛʀ]	prisoner
un **prisonnier de guerre**	prisoner of war
un **camp** (**de prisonniers**) [kɑ̃(d(ə)pʀizɔnje)]	(prison) camp
un **camp de concentration**	concentration camp
une **victime** [viktim]	victim
blessé, **blessée** [blese]	wounded, injured
un **blessé**, une **blessée**	wounded, injured (person)
un blessé, une blessée grave	seriously wounded person
tuer [tɥe]	to kill
mort, **morte** [mɔʀ, mɔ̃ʀt]	dead *(See Information Box p. 33)*
un **mort**, une **morte**	dead person, fatality

fuir [fɥiʀ]	to flee
La population civile a fui devant l'ennemi.	The civilian population fled from the enemy.
s'enfuir [sɑ̃fɥiʀ]	to flee
Ils ont profité de l'obscurité pour s'enfuir.	They took advantage of darkness to flee.
la **fuite** [fɥit]	flight
prendre la fuite	to take flight
capituler [kapityle]	to capitulate, surrender
L'armée a **capitulé sans conditions**.	The army surrendered unconditionally.
la **capitulation** [kapitylasjɔ̃]	surrender, capitulation
un **armistice** [aʀmistis]	armistice
violer l'armistice	to violate, break the armistice

résister à [ʀeziste]	to resist
la **résistance** [ʀezistɑ̃s]	resistance
un **résistant**, une **résistante** [ʀezistɑ̃, ɑ̃t]	resistance fighter
trahir [tʀaiʀ]	to betray
Il a trahi sa patrie.	He betrayed his country.
une **trahison** [tʀaizɔ̃]	treason, betrayal
un **traître**, une **traîtresse** [tʀɛtʀ, tʀɛs]	traitor
exécuter [ɛgzekyte]	to execute
une **exécution** [ɛgzekysjɔ̃]	execution

False Friends

French Word	Actual Meaning	False Friend	Correct French Word
demander	**to request**	to demand	*exiger*
la Marine	**Navy**	Marine	*le fusilier marin*
une prescription	**a regulation**	(medical) prescription	*une ordonnance*
violer	**to rape**	to violate	*transgresser*

My Vocabulary

15
Economy and Business

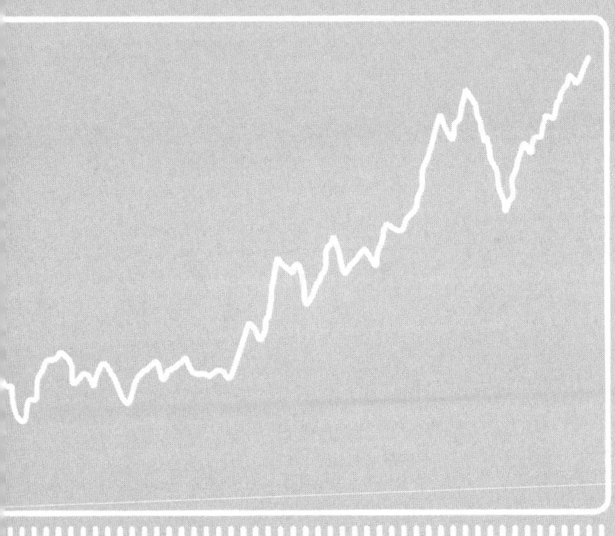

15.1 Agriculture, Fishing, and Mining  64

agricole [agʀikɔl]	agricultural
un **ouvrier**, une **ouvrière agricole**	agricultural worker
l'**agriculture** *f* [agʀikyltyʀ]	agriculture
un **agriculteur**, une **agricultrice** [agʀikyltœʀ, tʀis]	farmer
un **cultivateur**, une **cultivatrice** [kyltivatœʀ, tʀis]	farmer
un **paysan**, une **paysanne** [peizɑ̃, an]	peasant
une **ferme** [fɛʀm]	farm
un **fermier**, une **fermière** [fɛʀmje, jɛʀ]	farmer, tenant farmer

le **secteur primaire** [sɛktœʀpʀimɛʀ]	primary sector
les **ressources naturelles** *fpl* [ʀ(ə)suʀsnatyʀɛl]	natural resources
rural [ʀyʀal], **rurale**	rural
la **population rurale**	rural population
l'**exode rural**	urbanization, rural flight
exploiter [ɛksplwate]	to cultivate, till
un **exploitant**, une **exploitante agricole** [ɛksplwatɑ̃(t)agʀikɔl]	farmer
une **exploitation agricole** [ɛksplwatasjɔ̃agʀikɔl]	farm
une **coopérative** [k(ɔ)ɔpeʀativ]	cooperative
une **coopérative viticole**	vintners' cooperative
l'**équipement** *m* [ekipmɑ̃]	equipment
un **tracteur** [tʀaktœʀ]	tractor

campagnard, **campargnarde** [kɑ̃paɲaʀ, aʀd]	country (adj)
La **vie campagnarde** lui plaît beaucoup.	He likes country life very much.
la **campagne** [kɑ̃paɲ]	the country
habiter **à la campagne**	to live in the country
un **champ** [ʃɑ̃]	field
un **champ de blé**	wheat field
un **pré** [pʀe]	meadow, pasture
une **forêt** [fɔʀɛ]	forest

cultiver [kyltive]	to cultivate
la surface cultivée	crop acreage
la **culture** [kyltyʀ]	cultivation
pratiquer la **culture des fruits et légumes**	to grow fruits and vegetables
un **produit** [pʀɔdɥi]	product
un **produit agricole**	agricultural product

le **rendement** [Rɑ̃dmɑ̃]	yield, harvest
la **chute des prix** [ʃytdepRi]	fall in prices

labourer [labuRe]	to plow, cultivate
une **charrue** [ʃaRy]	plow (n)
moissonner [mwasɔne]	to harvest (grain)
la **moisson** [mwasɔ̃]	(grain) harvest
une **moissonneuse-batteuse** [mwasɔnøzbatøz]	combine (n)
les **primeurs** *mpl* [pRimœR]	early crops
la **culture maraîchère** [kyltyRmaRεʃεR]	truck farming, market gardening
un **maraîcher**, une **maraîchère** [maReʃe, εR]	vegetable farmer, truck farmer
l'**engrais** *m* [ɑ̃gRε]	fertilizer
un **pesticide** [pεstisid]	pesticide
Les arbres fruitiers sont **traités aux pesticides**.	Fruit trees are treated with pesticides.
un **insecticide** [ε̃sεktisid]	insecticide

élever [el(ə)ve]	to raise
Il élève des chèvres dans le Cantal.	He raises goats in Cantal.
l'**élevage** *m* [el(ə)vaʒ]	livestock breeding
un **éleveur**, une **éleveuse** [el(ə)vœR, øz]	breeder

le **bétail** [betaj]	livestock
le **pâturage** [patyRaʒ]	pasture
En automne, le bétail quitte les pâturages et rentre à l'étable.	In the fall, the livestock leaves the pasture and goes back to the barn.
la **surproduction** [syRpRɔdyksjɔ̃]	overproduction
les **quotas** *mpl* [kɔta]	quotas
les **quotas laitiers**	dairy quotas

la **vigne** [viɲ]	grapevine; vineyard
le **vignoble** [viɲɔbl]	vineyard; wine producing area
Le vignoble français fournit de très grands crus.	The French vineyards produce some great vintages.
un **vigneron**, une **vignerone** [viɲ(ə)Rɔ̃, ɔn]	vintner
un **viticulteur**, une **viticultrice** [vitikyltœR, tRis]	vintner, wine grower
le **vin** [vε̃]	wine

viticole [vitikɔl]	wine growing, viticulture
une **région viticole**	wine-producing region
vendanger [vɑ̃dɑ̃ʒe]	to pick grapes
les **vendanges** *fpl* [vɑ̃dɑ̃ʒ]	grape harvest (n)
pêcher [pɛʃe]	to fish
la **pêche** [pɛʃ]	fishing (n)
la **pêche au large**	deep-sea fishing
la **pêche à la ligne**	angling *(with a fishing rod)*
une **canne à pêche**	fishing rod
un **pêcheur**, une **pêcheuse** [pɛʃœʀ, øz]	fisher(man)
un **marin-pêcheur**	commercial fisher(man)
un **filet** [filɛ]	net (n)
la **pisciculture** [pisikyltyʀ]	fish farming
les **coquillages** *mpl* [kɔkijaʒ]	shellfish
les **crustacés** *mpl* [kʀystase]	crustaceans, shellfish
les **richesses du sous-sol** *fpl* [ʀiʃɛsdysusɔl]	natural resources, treasures of the soil
les **matières premières** *fpl* [matjɛʀpʀəmjɛʀ]	raw materials
un pays **riche/pauvre en matières premières**	a country rich/poor in raw materials
le **charbon** [ʃaʀbɔ̃]	carbon
une **mine** [min]	mine (n)
une **mine à ciel ouvert**	strip mine, surface mine
un **mineur** [minœʀ]	miner
la **houille** ['uj]	(bituminous) coal, hard coal
le **lignite** [liɲit]	lignite, (brown/soft) coal
une **région minière** [ʀeʒjɔ̃minjɛʀ]	mining region
une **galerie** [galʀi]	tunnel, gallery
un **gisement** [ʒizmɑ̃]	deposit (n)
un **gisement abondant**	rich deposit
Le gisement est épuisé.	The deposit is exhausted.
extraire [ɛkstʀɛʀ]	to extract
traiter [tʀɛte]	to treat, process
Traiter les minerais est coûteux.	It is costly to process minerals.

15.2 Industry and Trades  65

industriel, **industrielle** [ɛ̃dystʀijɛl]	industrial
un **industriel**, une **industrielle**	industrialist
une **région industrielle**	industrial region
une **zone industrielle** (**ZI**)	industrial area
un **secteur industriel**	industrial sector
l'**industrie** *f* [ɛ̃dystʀi]	industry
l'**industrie lourde**	heavy industry
l'**industrie automobile**	automobile industry
l'**industrie aéronautique**	aeronautics industry
l'**industrie électronique**	electronics industry

s'industrialiser [sɛ̃dystʀijalize]	to become industrialized
Cette région s'est fortement industrialisée dans les années 80.	This region became very industrialized during the '80s.
l'**industrialisation** *f* [ɛ̃dystʀijalizasjɔ̃]	industrialization
une **industrie(-)clé** [ɛ̃dystʀikle]	(key) industry
l'**industrie sidérurgique** *f* [ɛ̃dystʀisideʀyʀʒik]	steel industry
l'**industrie métallurgique** *f* [ɛ̃dystʀimetalyʀʒik]	metals industry
l'**industrie textile** *f* [ɛ̃dystʀitekstil]	textile industry
l'**industrie agro-alimentaire** *f* [ɛ̃dystʀiagʀoalimɑ̃tɛʀ]	food processing industry
une **industrie de pointe** [ɛ̃dystʀid(ə)pwɛ̃t]	leading-edge industry
l'**industrie chimique et pharmaceutique** *f* [ɛ̃dystʀiʃimikefaʀmasøtik]	chemical and pharmaceutical industry
une **branche** [bʀɑ̃ʃ]	branch
une **branche** industrielle **en plein essor**	booming industrial branch

une **usine** [yzin]	factory
s'installer [sɛ̃stale]	to locate
De nombreuses entreprises se sont installées en province.	Many companies have located in the countryside.
l'**installation** *f* [ɛ̃stalasjɔ̃]	facility, plant
une **machine** [maʃin]	machine
un **robot** [ʀɔbo]	robot

implanter [ɛ̃plɑ̃te]	to locate
l'**implantation** *f* [ɛ̃plɑ̃tasjɔ̃]	installation, establishment
protester contre l'implantation d'une centrale nucléaire	to protest against the establishment of a nuclear power plant
l'**essor** *m* [esɔʀ]	boom
la **récession** [ʀesesjɔ̃]	recession
délocaliser [delɔkalize]	to outsource
Cette firme a délocalisé une partie de sa production.	This company has outsourced a part of its production.
la **délocalisation** [delɔkalizasjɔ̃]	outsourcing (n)
restructurer [ʀəstʀyktyʀe]	to restructure
la **restructuration** [ʀəstʀyktyʀasjɔ̃]	restructuring (n)
se reconvertir [s(ə)ʀ(ə)kɔ̃vɛʀtiʀ]	to reorganize
la **reconversion** [ʀ(ə)kɔ̃vɛʀsjɔ̃]	reorganization, refitting
la **robotisation** [ʀɔbɔtizasjɔ̃]	robotization
l'**automation/automatisation** *f* [ɔtɔmasjɔ̃, ɔtɔmatizasjɔ̃]	automation

un **travailleur**, une **travailleuse** [tʀavajœʀ, øz]	worker
un **ouvrier**, une **ouvrière** [uvʀije, ijɛʀ]	worker, laborer
un **ouvrier qualifié**	technician, skilled worker
un **ouvrier spécialisé** (**OS**)	semiskilled worker

la **main-d'œuvre**; les **mains-d'œuvre** *pl* [mɛ̃dœvʀ]	manpower, labor force
avoir besoin de main d'œuvre qualifiée	to need qualified manpower
travailler à la chaîne [tʀavajealaʃɛn]	to work on an assembly line

se concentrer [s(ə)kɔ̃sɑ̃tʀe]	to be concentrated
la **concentration** [kɔ̃sɑ̃tʀasjɔ̃]	concentration
une **crise** [kʀiz]	crisis
L'industrie automobile **est en crise**.	The auto industry is in crisis.
un secteur **touché par la crise**	a sector affected by the crisis

fabriquer [fabʀike]	to produce, manufacture
la **fabrication** [fabʀikasjɔ̃]	manufacturing
la **fabrication en** (**grande**) **série**	series production
un **fabricant**, une **fabricante** [fabʀikɑ̃, ɑ̃t]	manufacturer, producer
produire [pʀɔdɥiʀ]	to produce
un **produit** [pʀɔdɥi]	product
lancer un produit sur le marché	to bring a product to market

producteur, **productrice** [pRɔdyktœR, tRis]	producing (adj)
un **producteur**, une **productrice**	manufacturer, producer
un **pays producteur de pétrole**	petroleum-producing country
la **production** [pRɔdyksjɔ̃]	production
les **biens de consommation** *mpl* [bjɛ̃d(ə)kɔ̃sɔmasjɔ̃]	consumer goods, expendable goods
les **biens d'équipement** *mpl* [bjɛ̃dekipmɑ̃]	capital goods
les **produits** (**semi-**)**finis** *mpl* [pRɔdɥi(semi)fini]	finished/semi-manufactured product
la **finition** [finisjɔ̃]	finishing (n)
artisanal, **artisanale** [aRtizanal]	handcrafted, artisanal (adj)
une **entreprise artisanale**	craft enterprise
l'**artisanat** *m* [aRtizana]	handicraft
un **artisan**, une **artisane** [aRtizɑ̃, an]	artisan, crafts person
un **atelier** [atəlje]	workshop

15.3 Business  66

une **entreprise** [ɑ̃tRəpRiz]	enterprise, business
une **entreprise de travaux publics**	public works enterprise
une **compagnie** (**Cie**) [kɔ̃paɲi]	company
une **firme** [fiRm]	firm
un **groupe** [gRup]	group
le **siège social** [sjɛʒsɔsjal]	headquarters, home office
une **maison** [mɛzɔ̃]	firm, business
la **maison mère**	main office
une **maison de gros**	wholesale firm
une **multinationale** [myltinasjɔnal]	multinational corporation
une **SA** (**Société anonyme**) [ɛsa]	corporation
une **SARL** (**Société à responsabilité limitée**) [ɛsaɛRɛl]	limited liability company
une **PME** (**Petites et moyennes entreprises**) [peɛmə]	small or medium-size business
une **succursale** [sykyRsal]	branch (n)
ouvrir une succursale à l'étranger	to open a foreign branch
un, une **chef** [ʃɛf]	boss
le **chef d'entreprise**	principal of the firm
diriger [diRiʒe]	to direct, manage
la **direction** [diRɛksjɔ̃]	top management

un **directeur**, une **directrice** [diʀɛktœʀ, tʀis]	director
le **PDG** (**président-directeur général**) [pedeʒe]	CEO
un **patron**, une **patronne** [patʀɔ̃, ɔn]	boss

le **personnel** [pɛʀsɔnɛl]	personnel, staff, workforce
un **cadre** [kadʀ]	executive, manager
un **cadre supérieur**	upper-level manager
un **cadre moyen**	mid-level manager
un **supérieur**, une **supérieure** [syperjœʀ]	superior (n)
un **employé**, une **employée** [ɑ̃plwaje]	employee
un, une **collègue** [kɔlɛg]	colleague
un **poste** [pɔst]	job, position
occuper un poste important	to have an important job
une **fonction** [fɔ̃ksjɔ̃]	function (n)
exercer une fonction de cadre	to have a leadership position
responsable de [ʀɛspɔ̃sabl]	responsible for

les **effectifs** *mpl* [efɛktif]	workforce, personnel
réduire les effectifs de moitié	to cut the workforce in half
un **collaborateur**, une **collaboratrice** [kɔ(l)labɔʀatœʀ, tʀis]	coworker
un **manager** [manadʒœʀ/ɛʀ]	manager
embaucher [ɑ̃boʃe]	to hire
L'entreprise embauche des ouvriers qualifiés.	The company is hiring skilled workers.
l'**embauche** *f* [ɑ̃boʃ]	hiring (n)
le **comité directeur** [kɔmitediʀɛktœʀ]	executive board
le **conseil de surveillance** [kɔ̃sɛjdəsyʀvɛjɑ̃s]	board of directors, supervisory board

la **concurrence** [kɔ̃kyʀɑ̃s]	competition
faire face à la concurrence étrangère	to face foreign competition
un **concurrent**, une **concurrente** [kɔ̃kyʀɑ̃, ɑ̃t]	competitor
la **perte** [pɛʀt]	loss
produire à perte	to produce at a loss

les **affaires** *fpl* [afɛʀ]	business
un **homme**, une **femme d'affaires**	businessman, businesswoman
Il est en Italie **pour affaires**.	He is in Italy on business.
le **chiffre d'affaires** [ʃifʀ(ə)dafɛʀ]	volume of sales
investir dans [ɛ̃vɛstiʀ]	to invest in
un **investissement** [ɛ̃vɛstismɑ̃]	investment
amortir ses investissements	to amortize, redeem one's investments
fusionner [fyzjɔne]	to merge, consolidate
fusionner pour rester compétitif	to merge in order to remain competitive
une **fusion** [fyzjɔ̃]	merger
la **comptabilité** [kɔ̃tabilite]	accounting
les **frais** *mpl* [fʀɛ]	expenses
les **charges** *fpl* [ʃaʀʒ]	additional, incidental expenses
le **bénéfice** [benefis]	profit (n)
réinvestir ses bénéfices	to reinvest one's profits
un **déficit** [defisit]	deficit
déposer son bilan [depozesɔ̃bilɑ̃]	to file for bankruptcy
faire faillite [fɛʀfajit]	to go bankrupt
une faillite frauduleuse	fraudulent bankruptcy

15.4 Technology  67

technique [tɛknik]	technical/technological
la **technique** [tɛknik]	technology
la **technique de pointe**	leading-edge technology
un **technicien**, une **technicienne** [tɛknisjɛ̃, jɛn]	technician, engineer
le **progrès** [pʀɔgʀɛ]	progress (n)
un **équipement** [ekipmɑ̃]	equipment, hardware
un **dispositif** [dispozitif]	device
le (**service**) **technico-commercial** [(sɛʀvis)tɛknikokɔmɛʀsjal]	commercial-technical department
technologique [tɛknɔlɔʒik]	technological
avoir une avance technologique sur qn	to have a technological advantage over s.o.
la **technologie** [tɛknɔlɔʒi]	technology
les technologies nouvelles	new technologies

le **savoir-faire** [savwaRfɛR]	know-how *(See Information Box p. 450)*
un **brevet** (**d'invention**) [bRəvɛ(dɛ̃vɑ̃sjɔ̃)]	patent
déposer un brevet	to register, take out a patent
la **haute technologie** ['ottɛknɔlɔʒi]	high technology (n)
le **transfert de technologie** [tRɑ̃sfɛRdətɛknɔlɔʒi]	technology transfer
le **génie génétique** [ʒeniʒenetik]	genetic engineering
un **parc technologique** [paRktɛknɔlɔʒik]	technology park
une **technopole** [tɛknɔpɔl]	technology center, park
La recherche et l'industrie sont réunies dans les technopoles.	Research and industry are brought together in technology parks.

inventer [ɛ̃vɑ̃te]	to invent
une **invention** [ɛ̃vɑ̃sjɔ̃]	invention
un **inventeur**, une **inventrice** [ɛ̃vɑ̃tœR, tRis]	inventor
un **ingénieur** [ɛ̃ʒenjœR]	engineer
scientifique [sjɑ̃tifik]	scientific (adj)
un, une **scientifique**	scientist
une **méthode** [metɔd]	method
agir **avec méthode**	to proceed methodically

un **moteur** [mɔtœR]	motor (n)
automatique [ɔtɔmatik]	automatic
électrique [elɛktRik]	electric
l'**électricité** *f* [elɛktRisite]	electricity
une **panne d'électricité**	power outage
électronique [elɛktRɔnik]	electronic
l'**électronique** *f*	electronics

nucléaire [nykleɛR]	nuclear, atomic
un **réacteur nucléaire**	nuclear reactor
le **nucléaire**	nuclear power
une manifestation contre le nucléaire	demonstration against nuclear power
une **centrale nucléaire**	nuclear power plant
un **incident** [ɛ̃sidɑ̃]	incident
Un incident technique a provoqué l'arrêt de la centrale électrique.	A technical incident caused the shutdown of the power plant.

spatial, **spatiale** [spasjal]	space (adj)
un **vaisseau spatial**	space ship
une **navette/station spatiale**	space shuttle, station
la **navigation spatiale**	space travel, flight
un, une **astronaute** [astʀonot]	astronaut
une **fusée** [fyze]	rocket
un **satellite** [satelit]	satellite
sur orbite [syʀɔʀbit]	in orbit
mettre un satellite **sur orbite**	to put a satellite into orbit

15.5 Commerce and Service Industries  68

commercial, **commerciale** [kɔmɛʀsjal]	commercial
le **commerce** [kɔmɛʀs]	commerce
un (**petit**) **commerçant** [kɔmɛʀsɑ̃]	retailer, small-business owner
Les petits commerçants sont contre l'ouverture du centre commercial.	The independent retailers are opposed to the opening of the shopping mall.

le **secteur tertiaire** [sɛktœʀtɛʀsjɛʀ]	service sector
le **commerce intérieur/extérieur** [kɔmɛʀsɛ̃teʀjœʀ/ɛksteʀjœʀ]	domestic/foreign commerce
le **commerce de gros/de détail** [kɔmɛʀsdəgʀo/dədetaj]	wholesale/retail
la **balance commerciale** [balɑ̃skɔmɛʀsjal]	balance of trade; commercial balance sheet
un, une **grossiste** [gʀosist]	wholesaler
un **détaillant**, une **détaillante** [detajɑ̃, ɑ̃t]	retailer
un, une **VRP** (**Voyageur de commerce, représentant et placier**) [veɛʀpe]	agent, sales representative, rep
une **commission** [kɔmisjɔ̃]	commission
travailler à la commission	to work on commission

le **marché** [maʀʃe]	market
aller* faire son marché	to buy on the market
marchander [maʀʃɑ̃de]	to haggle, bargain
un **marchand**, une **marchande** [maʀʃɑ̃, ɑ̃d]	dealer
une **marchandise** [maʀʃɑ̃diz]	merchandise
proposer sa marchandise à bas prix	to offer one's merchandise at a low price
un **magasin** [magazɛ̃]	store

un **client**, une **cliente** [klijɑ̃, jɑ̃t]	customer, client
un **client**, une **cliente fidèle**	loyal client
la **clientèle** [klijɑ̃tɛl]	clientele
un **consommateur**, une **consommatrice** [kɔ̃sɔmatœʀ, tʀis]	consumer
acheter [aʃ(ə)te]	to buy, purchase
un **acheteur**, une **acheteuse** [aʃ(ə)tœʀ, øz]	buyer
un **achat** [aʃa]	purchase (n)
commander [kɔmɑ̃de]	to order
une **commande** [kɔmɑ̃d]	order (n)
vendre [vɑ̃dʀ]	to sell
un **vendeur**, une **vendeuse** [vɑ̃dœʀ, øz]	salesperson
la **vente** [vɑ̃t]	sale
la **vente par correspondance**	mail-order business
la **vente en gros/au détail**	wholesale/retail
la **vente aux enchères**	auction
les **soldes** *mpl* [sɔld]	sale, clearance, closeout
un **contrat** [kɔ̃tʀa]	contract (n)
signer un contrat	to sign a contract

la **distribution** [distʀibysjɔ̃]	distribution
fournir [fuʀniʀ]	to supply
un **fournisseur**, une **fournisseuse** [fuʀnisœʀ, øz]	supplier

le **prix** [pʀi]	price (n)
la **facture** [faktyʀ]	bill (n)
envoyer [ɑ̃vwaje]	to send
Envoyez-nous votre bon de commande.	Send us your order form.
livrer [livʀe]	to deliver
la **livraison** [livʀɛzɔ̃]	delivery

la **taxe** [taks]	tax
exempt de taxes	tax-exempt
le **prix HT** (**hors taxes**) [pʀiɔʀtaks]	price without taxes and duties
le **prix TTC** (**toutes taxes comprises**) [pʀitetese]	price including all taxes
la **TVA** (**Taxe à la valeur ajoutée**) [tevea]	value added tax
une **remise** [ʀ(ə)miz]	reduction, discount
un **rabais** [ʀabɛ]	discount, rebate

un **article** [aʀtikl]	article, item
Cet article est épuisé.	This item is out of stock.
la **marque** [maʀk]	brand (n)
une **étiquette** [etikɛt]	label; price tag
la **garantie** [gaʀɑ̃ti]	guarantee (n)
un appareil **sous garantie**	an appliance under guarantee
faire de la publicité [fɛʀd(ə)lapyblisite]	to advertise

l'**offre** *f* [ɔfʀ]	offer (n)
la **demande** [d(ə)mɑ̃d]	demand (n)
Les prix varient **en fonction de l'offre et de la demande**.	Prices vary based on supply and demand.
importer [ɛ̃pɔʀte]	to import
l'**importation** *f* [ɛ̃pɔʀtasjɔ̃]	import, importation
exporter [ɛkspɔʀte]	to export
l'**exportation** *f* [ɛkspɔʀtasjɔ̃]	export, exportation

expédier [ɛkspedje]	to send
expédier qc contre remboursement	to send s.th. C.O.D.
un **colis** [kɔli]	package (n)
un **échantillon** [eʃɑ̃tijɔ̃]	sample (n)
un **entrepôt** [ɑ̃tʀəpo]	warehouse
le **stock** [stɔk]	stock (n)
être en rupture de stock	to be out of stock
écouler le stock	to sell off the inventory

15.6 Money, Banking  69

l'**argent** *m* [aʀʒɑ̃]	money
l'**argent de poche**	pocket money
avoir de l'argent sur soi	to have some money on oneself
compter [kɔ̃te]	to count
la **monnaie** [mɔnɛ]	change, coins
avoir de la monnaie	to have some change
rendre la monnaie	to give the change

financer [finɑ̃se]	to finance
financer l'achat d'une maison	to finance the purchase of a house
les **finances** *fpl* [finɑ̃s]	finances, funds
le **financement** [finɑ̃smɑ̃]	financing (n)
un **financier** [finɑ̃sje]	financier
les **sous** *mpl fam* [su]	cents
ne pas avoir un sou en poche	to have not a penny in one's pocket
le **fric** *fam* [fʀik]	dough
une **unité monétaire** [ynitemɔnetɛʀ]	currency, monetary unit
un **euro** [øʀo]	euro
un **cent** (**d'euro**) [sɛnt(døʀo)]	eurocent
un **centime** (**d'euro**) [sɑ̃tim(døʀo)]	eurocent
un **porte-monnaie** [pɔʀt(ə)mɔnɛ]	wallet *(See Information Box p. 104)*
un **portefeuille** [pɔʀt(ə)fœj]	wallet, portfolio
avoir un portefeuille bien rempli	to have a fat wallet
gérer son portefeuille	to manage one's portfolio
les **devises** *fpl* [dəviz]	currencies
une **devise forte/faible**	strong/weak currency
le **taux de change** [todʃɑ̃ʒ]	exchange rate
les **recettes** *fpl* [ʀ(ə)sɛt]	revenue, income
dévaluer [devalɥe]	to devalue
la **dévaluation** [devalɥasjɔ̃]	devaluation
l'**inflation** *f* [ɛ̃flasjɔ̃]	inflation
gratuit, **gratuite** [gʀatɥi, ɥit]	free (adj)
coûter [kute]	to cost
Ça coûte trop cher.	That is too expensive.
payer [peje]	to pay
payer comptant/cash	to pay cash
dépenser [depɑ̃se]	to spend
Il dépense son argent sans compter.	He spends money by the fistful.
les **dépenses** *fpl* [depɑ̃s]	expenses
la **valeur** [valœʀ]	value (n)
coûteux, **coûteuse** [kutø, øz]	costly, expensive
le **coût** [ku]	cost (n)
régler [ʀegle]	to pay, settle up
régler une facture **en espèces**	to pay a bill in cash
du **liquide** [likid]	cash
payer qc **en liquide**	to pay cash for s.th.

économiser [ekɔnɔmize]	to save
économe [ekɔnɔm]	thrifty, economical
Il n'est pas avare, il est seulement économe.	He is not miserly; he is merely thrifty.
les **économies** *fpl* [ekɔnɔmi]	savings (n)
faire des économies	to save money
la **fortune** [fɔʀtyn]	fortune
faire fortune	to become rich
épargner [epaʀɲe]	to save
l'**épargne** *f* [epaʀɲ]	saving (n)
un **épargnant**, une **épargnante** [epaʀɲɑ̃, ɑ̃t]	individual investor, saver
un **livret d'épargne** [livʀɛdepaʀɲ]	savings book
la **caisse d'épargne** [kɛsdepaʀɲ]	savings bank
une **tirelire** [tiʀliʀ]	piggy bank
prêter [pʀete]	to lend, borrow
Elle lui a prêté 2 000 euros.	She loaned him 2000 euros.
un **prêt** [pʀɛ]	loan (n)
accorder un prêt à des conditions intéressantes	to grant a loan on favorable terms
un **crédit** [kʀedi]	credit; balance
faire crédit	to advance, give credit
emprunter qc à qn [ɑ̃pʀɛ̃te]	to loan s.th. to s.o.
Je ne sais plus à qui j'ai emprunté ce DVD.	I can't remember who I loaned that DVD to.
un **emprunt** [ɑ̃pʀɛ̃]	loan (n)
rembourser [ʀɑ̃buʀse]	to pay back
un **remboursement** [ʀɑ̃buʀsəmɑ̃]	payback, reimbursement
devoir qc à qn [devwaʀ]	to owe s.th. to s.o.
Vous me devez une grosse somme.	You owe me a lot of money.
la **dette** [dɛt]	debt
faire des dettes	to incur debt
s'endetter [sɑ̃dɛte]	to go into debt
les **intérêts** *mpl* [ɛ̃teʀɛ]	interest
le **taux d'intérêt**	interest rate
une **hypothèque** [ipɔtɛk]	mortgage
prendre une hypothèque sur qc	to take out a mortgage on s.th.

une **banque** [bɑ̃k]	bank (n)
un **banquier**, une **banquière** [bɑ̃kje]	banker
un **guichet** [giʃɛ]	(bank) window
la **caisse** [kɛs]	cash register
passer à la caisse	to go to the register, check out
un **caissier**, une **caissière** [kɛsje, jɛʀ]	cashier
changer [ʃɑ̃ʒe]	to change
changer de l'argent	to change money
changer ses euros en dollars	to change one's euros into dollars
le **change** [ʃɑ̃ʒ]	(currency) exchange (n)

INFO

Banks and benches

une banque [bɑ̃k]	*bank (financial institution)*
la BNP (Banque Nationale de Paris)	*BNP (one of France's largest banks)*
un banc [bɑ̃]	*bench (for sitting)*
un banc public	*park bench*

une **agence** [aʒɑ̃s]	agency
une **succursale** [sykyʀsal]	branch
un **coffre**(**-fort**) [kɔfʀə(fɔʀ)]	safe
un **distributeur automatique** (**de billets**) [distʀibytœʀɔtɔmatik(d(ə)bijɛ)]	ATM/automated teller machine

un **compte** (**en banque**) [kɔ̃t(ɑ̃bɑ̃k)]	(bank) account
un **compte courant**	checking account
ouvrir un compte	to open an account
un numéro de compte	account number
déposer de l'argent sur son compte	to deposit money into one's account
retirer de l'argent [ʀ(ə)tiʀed(ə)laʀʒɑ̃]	to withdraw money
une (**grosse**) **somme** [(gʀos)sɔm]	(large) sum of money
un montant de... [mɔ̃tɑ̃də]	an amount of...
On a reçu une facture d'un montant de 2 500 euros.	We have received a bill in the amount of 2500 euros.

un **relevé de compte** [ʀəl(ə)ve/ʀ(ə)ləved(ə)kɔ̃t]	bank statement
le **solde** [sɔld]	account balance

le **découvert** [dekuvɛʀ]	overdraft, line of credit
La banque m'a accordé un découvert de 10 000 euros.	The bank granted me a line of credit of 10,000 euros.
être à découvert	to be overdrawn
débiter [debite]	to debit
le **débit** [debi]	debit (n)
créditer [kʀedite]	to credit
Mon compte a été crédité de 1 000 euros.	My account was credited 1000 euros.
virer [viʀe]	to transfer, remit
un **virement** [viʀmɑ̃]	transfer (n)
un **prélèvement automatique** [pʀelɛvmɑ̃ɔtɔmatik]	direct debit (n)
verser [vɛʀse]	to pay, remit
un **versement** [vɛʀsəmɑ̃]	payment

un **chèque** [ʃɛk]	check (n)
encaisser un chèque	to cash a check
une **carte bancaire** [kaʀt(ə)bɑ̃kɛʀ]	bank card
une **carte de crédit** [kaʀtdəkʀedi]	credit card
payer par carte (de crédit)	to pay with a credit card
le **code secret** [kɔdsəkʀɛ]	PIN number

un **chéquier** [ʃekje]	checkbook
un **carnet de chèques** [kaʀnɛdʃɛk]	checkbook
faire/rédiger un chèque (**à l'ordre de qn**) [fɛʀ/ʀediʒeɛ̃ʃɛk]	to make a check out (to s.o.)
signer [siɲe]	to sign
signer un chèque	to sign a check
la **signature** [siɲatyʀ]	signature
falsifier une signature	to forge a signature

la **Bourse** [buʀs]	stock market
spéculer [spekyle]	to speculate
la **spéculation** [spekylasjɔ̃]	speculation
un **spéculateur**, une **spéculatrice** [spekylatœʀ, tʀis]	speculator
une **action** [aksjɔ̃]	share (n)
la **hausse** ['os]	increase, rise (n)
Mes actions **sont en hausse**.	My shares are up.
la **baisse** [bɛs]	fall (n)
un **dividende** [dividɑ̃d]	dividend
un **titre** [titʀ]	security
placer [plase]	to invest
un **placement** [plasmɑ̃]	investment
les **fonds d'investissement** *mpl* [fɔ̃dɛ̃vɛstismɑ̃]	investment funds

15.7 Insurance  70

assurer [asyʀe]	to insure
s'assurer contre qc [sasyʀe]	to insure against s.th.
s'assurer contre les inondations	to insure for flooding
une **assurance** [asyʀɑ̃s]	insurance
une **assurance obligatoire**	compulsory insurance
un **assuré**, une **asssurée** [asyʀe]	insured (n)

une **assurance vie** [asyʀɑ̃svi]	life insurance
une **assurance maladie** [asyʀɑ̃smaladi]	health insurance
une **assurance auto**(**mobile**) [asyʀɑ̃sɔtɔ/oto(mɔbil)]	auto insurance
une **assurance accidents** [asyʀɑ̃saksidɑ̃]	accident insurance
On va **résilier notre assurance accidents**.	Our accident insurance is going to be cancelled.
une **assurance vieillesse** [asyʀɑ̃svjɛjɛs]	old age insurance
contracter une assurance vieillesse	to take out old age insurance
une **assurance dépendance** [asyʀɑ̃sdepɑ̃dɑ̃s]	long-term/nursing care insurance
une **assurance responsabilité civile** [asyʀɑ̃sʀɛspɔ̃sabilitesivil]	liability insurance
une **assurance tous risques** [asyʀɑ̃stuʀisk]	comprehensive insurance
cotiser [kɔtize]	to pay in
une **cotisation** [kɔtizasjɔ̃]	payment, contribution
les **prestations** *fpl* [pʀɛstasjɔ̃]	benefits

une **compagnie d'assurances** [kɔ̃paɲidasyʀɑ̃s]	insurance company
un **assureur** [asyʀœʀ]	insurer
une **police d'assurance** [pɔlisdasyʀɑ̃s]	insurance policy
un **contrat** [kɔ̃tʀa]	contract (n)

couvrir qc [kuvʀiʀ]	to cover s.th.
Cette assurance couvre à peu près tous les risques.	This insurance covers nearly all risks.
une **prime** [pʀim]	premium (n)
un **bonus** [bɔnys]	premium, bonus
un **malus** [malys]	supplementary premium

un **accident** [aksidɑ̃]	accident
déclarer un accident	to report an accident
une **déclaration** [deklaʀasjɔ̃]	(accident) report

un **constat** (**à l'**)**amiable** [kõsta(al)amjabl]	amicable report *(without police)*
un **formulaire** [fɔʀmylɛʀ]	form (n)
remplir un formulaire	to fill out a form
un **sinistre** [sinistʀ]	claim, loss
les **dégâts** *mpl* [dega]	damage(s)
s'assurer contre les dégâts des eaux	to insure oneself against water damage
les **dommages** *mpl* [dɔmaʒ]	damages
les **dommages** (**et**) **intérêts** *mpl* [dɔmaʒ(e)ɛ̃teʀɛ]	damages and interest
dédommager qn [dedɔmaʒe]	to indemnify, compensate s.o.
L'assurance ne m'a toujours pas dédommagé.	I still not have been compensated by the insurance.
indemniser qn de qc/pour qc [ɛ̃dɛmnize]	to indemnify s.o. for s.th.
Il a été indemnisé pour ses frais d'hôpital.	He was reimbursed for his hospital expenses.
une **indemnisation** [ɛ̃dɛmnizasjõ]	compensation, reimbursement

la **Sécurité sociale** [sekyʀitesɔsjal]	social security
la **Sécu** *fam* [seky]	social security
une **caisse d'assurance maladie** [kɛsdasyʀɑ̃smaladi]	health insurance
une **caisse de retraite** [kɛsdəʀ(ə)tʀɛt]	pension fund
une **allocation** [alɔkasjõ]	stipend, award, payment
toucher une allocation	to receive aid, a subsidy
les **allocations familiales**	family allowances
l'**allocation de maternité**	maternity benefit
l'**allocation de chômage**	unemployment benefit
les **Assedic** *fpl* (**Associations pour l'emploi dans l'industrie et le commerce**) [asedik]	unemployment insurance
les **charges sociales** *fpl* [ʃaʀʒ(ə)sɔsjal]	social security compensations
une **mutuelle** [mytɥɛl]	mutual insurance company

False Friends

French Word	Actual Meaning	False Friend	Correct French Word
un concours	**competition**	concourse (hall)	*un hall*
labourer	**to plow**	laborer	*un ouvrier*

My Vocabulary

16

Communication and Mass Media

16.1 Telecommunications 

téléphoner à qn [telefɔne]	to phone s.o.
Depuis une heure, il téléphone à Marie.	He has been on the phone with Marie for an hour.
le **téléphone** [telefɔn]	telephone (n)
Marc est là? On le demande au téléphone.	Is Marc here? The phone is for him.
un **coup de téléphone**	(telephone) call
donner un coup de téléphone à qn	to call s.o.
répondre au téléphone	to answer the phone
joindre qn au téléphone	to reach s.o. by phone
un **coup de fil** *fam* [kudfil]	telephone call
passer un coup de fil à qn	to call s.o., to give s.o. a ring
recevoir un coup de fil	to get a call
le **combiné** [kɔ̃bine]	receiver/handset
décrocher/raccrocher (le combiné)	to pick up/hang up (the phone)
sonner [sɔne]	to ring
Le téléphone sonne.	The phone is ringing.
une **sonnerie** [sɔnʀi]	ringing, ring tone

la **télécommunication** [telekɔmynikasjɔ̃]	telecommunications
les **Télécom** [telekɔm]	telecom
un **abonné**, une **abonnée** [abɔne]	subscriber, customer
Il n'y a pas d'abonné au numéro que vous avez demandé.	There is no one listed with the number you requested.
un **numéro vert** [nymeʀovɛʀ]	toll-free number
un **appel en PCV** [apɛlɑ̃peseve]	collect call
l'**indicatif** *m* [ɛ̃dikatif]	area code
la **tonalité** [tɔnalite]	dial tone

une **communication** (**téléphonique**) [kɔmynikasjɔ̃(telefɔnik)]	(telephone) connection, phone conversation
La communication est très mauvaise.	The connection is very poor.
appeler qn [ap(ə)le]	to call s.o.
un **appel** [apɛl]	call (n)
rappeler qn [ʀap(ə)le]	to call s.o. back
Pourriez-vous rappeler dans un quart d'heure?	Could you call back in fifteen minutes?
un **correspondant**, une **correspondante** [kɔʀɛspɔ̃dɑ̃, ɑ̃t]	interlocutor/party called

un **numéro** [nymeʀo]	number
composer/faire un numéro	to dial a number
se tromper de numéro	to dial the wrong number
les **coordonnées** *fpl* [kɔɔʀdɔne]	contact information
les **renseignements** (**téléphoniques**) *mpl* [ʀɑ̃sɛɲmɑ̃(telefɔnik)]	directory assistance
le **standard** [stɑ̃daʀ]	switchboard

la **ligne** (**téléphonique**) [liɲ (telefɔnik)]	(phone) line
Les lignes sont encombrées.	The lines are overloaded.
être en dérangement [ɛtʀɑ̃deʀɑ̃ʒmɑ̃]	to be out of order
La ligne est en dérangement.	The line is out of order.
occupé, **occupée** [ɔkype]	busy
Impossible de téléphoner à Luc, c'est toujours occupé.	It's impossible to call Luc; the line is always busy.

un **portable** [pɔʀtabl]	cell phone
un **texto** [tɛksto]	text (message)
envoyer un texto	to send a text (message)
un **SMS** [ɛsɛmɛs]	text message
un **message multimedia** (**MMS**) [mesaʒmyltimedja, ɛmɛmɛs]	multimedia message
une **cabine** (**téléphonique**) [kabin(telefɔnik)]	phone booth
une **télécarte** [telekaʀt]	telephone card
un **répondeur** (**automatique**) [ʀepɔ̃dœʀ(otɔmatik)]	answering machine
le **bip sonore** [bipsɔnɔʀ]	beep (n)
Vous pouvez laisser votre message après le bip sonore.	You can leave your message after the beep.

la **téléphonie mobile** [telefɔnimɔbil]	mobile communications
un **forfait** [fɔʀfɛ]	flat rate
le **téléphone de voiture** [telefɔndəvwatyʀ]	car phone
un **kit mains libres** [kitmɛ̃libʀ]	hands-free device
un **publiphone** [pyblifɔn]	public telephone

faxer qc à qn [fakse]	to fax s.th. to s.o.
un **fax** [faks]	fax (n)
envoyer un fax	to send a fax

une **télécopie** [telekɔpi]	fax (message)
un **télécopieur** [telekɔpjœʀ]	fax machine

un **annuaire** [anɥɛʀ]	phone book
les **pages jaunes** *fpl* [paʒʒon]	yellow pages
être sur la liste rouge [ɛtʀsyʀlalistəʀuʒ]	to have an unlisted number

INFO

Telephoning in France

Allô! J'écoute.	*Hello! (said by the person receiving the call)*
Qui est à l'appareil?	*Who is calling?*
Pouvez-vous me passer...?	*May I speak with...?*
Je vous passe...	*I'll connect you to...*
Restez en ligne!	*One moment please.*
Ne coupez pas!	*Don't hang up!*
Ne quittez pas!	*Please stay on the line.*
Il y a erreur!	*You have the wrong number.*

16.2 Mail  72

la **Poste** [pɔst]	post office
poster une lettre [pɔsteynlɛtʀ]	to mail a letter
postal, **postale** [pɔstal]	postal (adj)
un **bureau de poste**; des **bureaux de poste** *pl* [byʀod(ə)pɔst]	post office
un **guichet** [giʃɛ]	window
une **boîte aux lettres** [bwatolɛtʀ]	mailbox

poste restante [pɔst(ə)ʀɛstɑ̃t]	general delivery, poste restante
envoyer une lettre poste restante	to send a letter by poste restante
la **boîte postale** (**BP**) [bwatpɔstal (bepe)]	post office box (P.O. Box)
CEDEX (**courrier d'entreprise à distribution exceptionnelle**) [sedɛks]	*pickup service for company and official mail*

un **facteur**, une **factrice** [faktœʀ, tʀis]	letter carrier
distribuer [distʀibɥe]	to deliver
la **distribution** [distʀibysjɔ̃]	delivery

une **tournée** [tuʀne]	(letter carrier's) route
Le facteur commence sa tournée à 8 heures.	The mailman starts his route at 8:00 A.M.
trier [tʀije]	to sort (mail)
le **tri** [tʀi]	sorting (n)
un **centre de tri** (**postal**)	(mail) sorting center
le **courrier** [kuʀje]	mail
le **courrier prioritaire**	priority mail
écrire [ekʀiʀ]	to write
envoyer [ɑ̃vwaje]	to send
recevoir [ʀəs(ə)vwaʀ/ʀ(ə)səvwaʀ]	to receive
une **lettre** [lɛtʀ]	letter
une **lettre recommandée**	registered letter
une **lettre exprès**	express mail
en recommandé [ɑ̃ʀ(ə)kɔmɑ̃de]	by registered mail
envoyer qc en recommandé	to send s.th. by registered mail
par avion [paʀavjɔ̃]	airmail
expédier une lettre par avion	to send a letter airmail
une **carte postale** [kaʀt(ə)pɔstal]	postcard
un **imprimé** [ɛ̃pʀime]	printed matter
un **paquet** [pakɛ]	package (n)
un **colis** [kɔli]	package (n)
un **colis contre remboursement**	collect package
à l'attention de [alatɑ̃sjɔ̃də]	to the attention of
à l'attention de Mme Fournier	to the attention of Mrs. Fournier
faire suivre [fɛʀsɥivʀ]	to forward
Prière de faire suivre.	Please forward.
par retour du courrier [paʀʀətuʀdykuʀje]	by return mail
répondre à une lettre par retour du courrier	to answer a letter by return mail
ci-joint, **ci-jointe** [sijwɛ̃, jwɛ̃t]	included, enclosed, attached
Veuillez trouver ci-joint(s) les documents demandés.	Please find enclosed the requested documents.
expédier [ɛkspedje]	to mail, dispatch
réexpédier [ʀeɛkspedje]	to forward, send back
l'**expéditeur** *m*, l'**expéditrice** *f* [ɛkspeditœʀ, tʀis]	sender
le, la **destinataire** [dɛstinatɛʀ]	addressee
le **mailing** [meliŋ]	direct mail
le **publipostage** [pyblipɔstaʒ]	direct mail, junk mail
un **mandat** [mɑ̃da]	money order
un **compte chèque postal** (**CCP**) [kɔ̃tʃɛkpɔstal (sesepe)]	postal check account

une **enveloppe** [ɑ̃v(ə)lɔp]	envelope
une **enveloppe timbrée**	stamped envelope
un **timbre**(**-poste**); des **timbres**(**-poste**) *pl* [tɛ̃bʀə(pɔst)]	(postage) stamp
l'**adresse** *f* [adʀɛs]	address
le **code postal** [kɔdpɔstal]	postal code
le **cachet** (**de la poste**) [kaʃɛ(d(ə)lapɔst)]	postmark

affranchir [afʀɑ̃ʃiʀ]	to stamp
affranchir une lettre **au tarif en vigueur**	to stamp a letter with the current postage
le **port** [pɔʀ]	postage
franco de port	postpaid
les **tarifs postaux** *mpl* [taʀifpɔsto]	postal rates
la **surtaxe** [syʀtaks]	surtax
le **distributeur** (**de timbres**) [distʀibytœʀ(d(ə)tɛ̃bʀ)]	stamp machine
un **carnet** (**de timbres**) [kaʀnɛ(d(ə)tɛ̃bʀ)]	book of stamps

16.3 Television, Radio 73

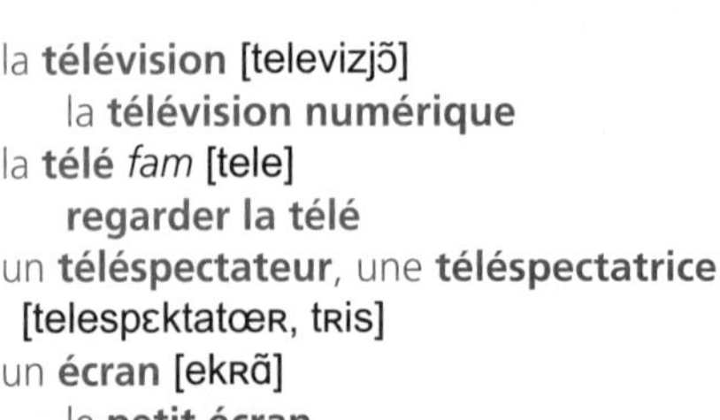

la **télévision** [televizjɔ̃]	television
la **télévision numérique**	digital television
la **télé** *fam* [tele]	TV
regarder la télé	to watch TV
un **téléspectateur**, une **téléspectatrice** [telespɛktatœʀ, tʀis]	television viewer
un **écran** [ekʀɑ̃]	screen
le **petit écran**	television, small screen

un **téléviseur** [televizœʀ]	television set
un **poste de télé**(**vision**) [pɔstdətele(vizjɔ̃)]	television set
s'acheter un **poste de télévision portatif**	to buy a portable TV
la **télévision par câble** [televizjɔ̃paʀkabl]	cable TV
la **télévision par satellite** [televizjɔ̃paʀsatelit]	satellite TV
une **antenne** [ɑ̃tɛn]	antenna
une **antenne parabolique**	satellite dish
Je **rends l'antenne** à nos studios à Paris.	Back to our studios in Paris.
une **chaîne codée** [ʃɛnkɔde]	coded television program
un **décodeur** [dekɔdœʀ]	decoder
la **réception** [ʀesɛpsjɔ̃]	reception
La réception est très mauvaise.	The reception is very poor.

un **récepteur** [ʀesɛptœʀ]	receiver
capter [kapte]	to receive
On n'arrive pas à capter la 5.	We can't get channel 5.

le **programme** [pʀɔgʀam]	(television) program
une **chaîne** [ʃɛn]	television broadcaster network
une **chaîne publique**	public broadcaster
une **chaîne privée**	private broadcaster
une **chaîne payante**	pay-TV
la **télécommande** [telekɔmɑ̃d]	remote control
zapper [zape]	to channel surf

audiovisuel, **audiovisuelle** [odjovizɥɛl]	audiovisual
la **télévision commerciale** [televizjɔ̃kɔmɛʀsjal]	commercial television
émettre [emɛtʀ]	to broadcast
émettre 24 heures sur 24	to broadcast around the clock
un **émetteur** [emɛtœʀ]	broadcaster
diffuser [difyze]	to broadcast, transmit
diffuser de la musique	to broadcast music
rediffuser [ʀ(ə)difyze]	to rebroadcast, rerun
Ce débat sera rediffusé demain matin.	This debate will be rebroadcast tomorrow morning.
une **rediffusion** [ʀ(ə)difyzjɔ̃]	rerun (n)
l'**audimat** *m* [odimat]	audience rating
Cette émission fait monter l'audimat.	This program increases the ratings.
la **redevance** [ʀ(ə)dəvɑ̃s]	license fee

la **radio** [ʀadjo]	radio
une **station** (**de radio**)	radio station
écouter la radio	to listen to the radio *(See Information Box p. 35)*
un **poste** (**de radio**) [pɔst(d(ə)ʀadjo)]	radio
écouter les nouvelles au poste/à la radio	to listen to the news on the radio
un **transistor** [tʀɑ̃zistɔʀ]	transistor radio
un **microphone** [mikʀɔfɔn]	microphone
un **micro** *fam* [mikʀo]	mic
l'**écoute** *f* [ekut]	listening (n)
Vous êtes **à l'écoute d'**Europe 1.	You are listening to Europe 1.

un **radioréveil** [ʀadjoʀevɛj]	clock radio
un **auditeur**, une **auditrice** [oditœʀ, tʀis]	listener
l'**audience** *f* [odjɑ̃s]	audience, listeners
radiophonique [ʀadjɔfɔnik]	radio (adj)
une **pièce radiophonique**	radio play
les **grandes ondes** (**GO**) *fpl* [gʀɑ̃dzɔ̃d (ʒeo)]	long wave
recevoir une émission sur grandes ondes	to receive a broadcast on long wave
les **ondes moyennes** (**OM**) *fpl* [ɔ̃dmwajɛn(oɛm)]	medium wave
les **petites ondes** *fpl* [p(ə)titzɔ̃d]	medium frequency
les **ondes courtes** *fpl* [ɔ̃dkuʀt]	short wave
la **modulation de fréquence** (**FM**) [mɔdylasjɔ̃d(ə)fʀekɑ̃s (ɛfɛm)]	FM, frequency modulation

les **actualités** *fpl* [aktɥalite]	news
regarder les actualités (télévisées)	to watch the (TV) news
informer qn sur qc [ɛ̃fɔʀme]	to inform s.o. of s.th.
les **informations** *fpl* [ɛ̃fɔʀmasjɔ̃]	news, newscast
les **infos** *fpl fam* [ɛ̃fo]	news
le **journal** (**télévisé**) [ʒuʀnal(televize)]	TV news
un **événement/évènement** [evɛnmɑ̃]	event
suivre le cours des événements	to follow the course of the events
être au courant (**de qc**) [ɛtʀokuʀɑ̃]	to be informed (of s.th.)
un **envoyé spécial**, une **envoyée spéciale** [ɑ̃vwajespesjal]	special correspondent
un **reportage** [ʀ(ə)pɔʀtaʒ]	report (n)
un, une **reporter** [ʀ(ə)pɔʀtɛʀ/ʀ(ə)pɔʀtœʀ]	reporter
interviewer [ɛ̃tɛʀvjuve]	to interview
une **interview** [ɛ̃tɛʀvju]	interview (n)
donner/accorder une interview	to grant an interview

retransmettre [ʀ(ə)tʀɑ̃smɛtʀ]	to relay
une **retransmission** [ʀ(ə)tʀɑ̃smisjɔ̃]	relay (n)
en duplex [ɑ̃dyplɛks]	conference call
en différé [ɑ̃difeʀe]	time-delay, pre-recorded
retransmettre un match en différé	to relay a game in time-delay
un **flash** (**d'information**) [flaʃ(dɛ̃fɔʀmasjɔ̃)]	(news) flash

un **téléfilm** [telefilm]	TV film
une **série télévisée** [seʀitelevize]	TV series
un **jeu télévisé** [ʒøtelevize]	game show, quiz show
un **présentateur**, une **présentatrice** [pʀezɑ̃tatœʀ, tʀis]	moderator, host
un **animateur**, une **animatrice** [animatœʀ, tʀis]	moderator, host
un **feuilleton** [fœjtɔ̃]	serial drama, soap opera
un **épisode** [epizɔd]	episode
les **variétés** *fpl* [vaʀjete]	entertainment/variety show
un **soap-opéra**; des **soap-opéras** *pl* [sopɔpeʀa]	soap opera
la **télé-réalité** [teleʀealite]	reality TV
la **météorologie** [meteɔʀɔlɔʒi]	weather forecast
la **météo** *fam* [meteo]	weather (forecast)
publicitaire [pyblisitɛʀ]	advertising (adj)
un **spot publicitaire**	commercial (n)
la **publicité** [pyblisite]	advertising (n)
la **pub** *fam* [pyb]	ads
un **studio** [stydjo]	studio
un **enregistrement** [ɑ̃ʀ(ə)ʒistʀəmɑ̃]	recording (n)
une **émission** [emisjɔ̃]	broadcast (n)
une **émission en direct**	direct broadcast
une **émission sportive**	sports broadcast
le **public** [pyblik]	audience, listeners
un **invité**, une **invitée** [ɛ̃vite]	guest

16.4 Image and Sound Recordings  74

photographier [fɔtɔgʀafje]	to photograph
la **photographie** [fɔtɔgʀafi]	photograph (n)
une **photo** [fɔto]	photo
prendre une photo	to take a photo
prendre qn/qc en photo	to take a picture of s.o./s.th.
un, une **photographe** [fɔtɔgʀaf]	photographer
un **appareil photo** [apaʀɛjfɔto]	camera
un **appareil** (**photo**) **numérique**	digital camera
une **carte mémoire** [kaʀtmemwaʀ]	memory card
un **motif** [mɔtif]	subject
un **portrait** [pɔʀtʀɛ]	portrait
un **polaroïd** [pɔlaʀɔid]	instant camera, Polaroid
un **flash** [flaʃ]	flash
un **réglage** [ʀeglaʒ]	setting, adjustment

un (**appareil**) **reflex** [(apaʀej)ʀeflɛks]	reflex camera
le **viseur** [vizœʀ]	viewfinder
l'**objectif** *m* [ɔbʒɛktif]	lens
un **mégapixel** [megapiksɛl]	megapixel
une **pellicule** [pelikyl]	film (n)
développer un film/une pellicule	to develop a film
le **développement** [dev(ə)lɔpmɑ̃]	developing (n)
un **négatif** [negatif]	negative (n)
le **format** [fɔʀma]	format (n)
une **diapo**(**sitive**) [djapo(zitiv)]	slide (n)
projeter des diapositives	to show slides
(**en**) **couleurs** [(ɑ̃)kulœʀ]	(in) color
(**en**) **noir et blanc** [(ɑ̃)nwaʀeblɑ̃]	(in) black and white
une photo en couleurs/en noir et blanc	color/black-and-white photo
net, **nette** [nɛt]	clear
flou, **floue** [flu]	fuzzy, blurred
mat, **mate** [mat]	matte
brillant, **brillante** [bʀijɑ̃, ɑ̃t]	glossy
une **épreuve** [epʀœv]	print (n)
Vous voulez vos **épreuves en mat** ou **en brillant**?	Do you want matte or glossy prints?
agrandir [agʀɑ̃diʀ]	to enlarge
un **agrandissement** [agʀɑ̃dismɑ̃]	enlargement
un **tirage** [tiʀaʒ]	printing (n)
filmer [filme]	to film
un **film** [film]	film (n)
tourner un film	to shoot a film
une **caméra** [kameʀa]	(movie) camera
zoomer [zume]	to zoom
le **zoom** [zum]	zoom (n)
un **caméscope numérique** [kameskɔp(nymeʀik)]	digital video recorder
un **magnétoscope** [maɲetɔskɔp]	video recorder
une **vidéocassette** [videokasɛt]	videocassette
un **lecteur de DVD** [lɛktœʀd(ə)devede]	DVD player
un **lecteur laser vidéo** [lɛktœʀlazɛʀvideo]	DVD player

écouter [ekute]	to listen
le **son** [sɔ̃]	sound, volume
le **volume** [vɔlym]	volume
baisser le volume	to turn down the volume
enregistrer [ɑ̃ʀ(ə)ʒistʀe]	to record
un **enregistrement** [ɑ̃ʀ(ə)ʒistʀəmɑ̃]	recording (n)
un **disque** [disk]	record (n)
un **tourne-disque**	record player, turntable
un **CD**/un **compact** [sede, kɔ̃pakt]	CD
un **lecteur de compacts/CD**	CD player
une **platine laser** [platinlazɛʀ]	CD player
une **chaîne hi-fi** [ʃɛnifi]	hi-fi
une (**chaîne**) **stéréo** [(ʃɛn)steʀeo]	stereo
une **cassette** (**K 7**) [kasɛt]	cassette
un **magnétophone** [maɲetɔfɔn]	cassette recorder, tape recorder
un **lecteur de cassettes** [lɛktœʀdəkasɛt]	cassette recorder
une **radiocassette** [ʀadjokasɛt]	radio-cassette recorder
un (**lecteur**) **MP3** [(lɛktœʀ)ɛmpetʀwɑ]	MP3 player
une **enceinte** [ɑ̃sɛ̃t]	speaker
un **casque** [kask]	headset, earphones
les **écouteurs** *mpl* [ekutœʀ]	headphones

16.5 Print and Books  75

les (**mass**)**médias** *mpl* [(mas)medja]	(mass) media
la **presse** [pʀɛs]	press
un **journal**; des **journaux** *pl* [ʒuʀnal, o]	newspaper
un **journal régional/national**	regional/national newspaper
lire [liʀ]	to read
la **lecture** [lɛktyʀ]	reading (n)
un **lecteur**, une **lectrice** [lɛktœʀ, tʀis]	reader
paraître [paʀɛtʀ]	to be published, to appear
une **revue** [ʀ(ə)vy]	magazine
une **revue spécialisée**	specialty magazine
un **magazine** [magazin]	magazine
un **magazine de mode**	fashion magazine
un **périodique** [peʀjɔdik]	periodical
un **illustré** [ilystʀe]	periodical, magazine

la **presse du cœur** [pʀɛ̃sdykœʀ]	pulp magazines
la **presse à sensation/à scandale** [pʀɛsasɑ̃sasjɔ̃/askɑ̃dal]	tabloid press
un **canard** *fam* [kanaʀ]	local rag
publier [pyblije]	to publish
une **publication** [pyblikasjɔ̃]	publication
imprimer [ɛ̃pʀime]	to print
une **imprimerie** [ɛ̃pʀimʀi]	print shop
la **mise en page** [mizɑ̃paʒ]	layout
tirer à [tiʀe]	to have a circulation of…
Le journal tire à 400 000 exemplaires.	The paper has a circulation of 400,000.
un **tirage** [tiʀaʒ]	printing (n)
à grand tirage	large run, printing
un tirage de 200 000 exemplaires	a run of 200,000 copies
la **diffusion** [difyzjɔ̃]	distribution
éditer [edite]	to publish
une **édition** [edisjɔ̃]	edition
Édition spéciale! Demandez France-Soir!	Special Edition! Buy *France-Soir!*
une **édition du soir**	evening edition
une **maison d'édition**	publisher, publishing house
un **éditeur**, une **éditrice** [editœʀ, tʀis]	publisher; editor
un **quotidien** [kɔtidjɛ̃]	daily (newspaper)
un **hebdomadaire** [ɛbdɔmadɛʀ]	weekly newspaper
un **hebdo** *fam* [ɛbdo]	weekly (n)
un **mensuel** [mɑ̃sɥɛl]	monthly (publication)
un **supplément** [syplemɑ̃]	supplement (n)
un **supplément week-end/du dimanche**	weekend/Sunday supplement

un, une **journaliste** [ʒuʀnalist]	journalist
un, une **reporter** [ʀ(ə)pɔʀtɛʀ/tœʀ]	reporter
un **grand reporter**	special correspondent
un **reportage** [ʀ(ə)pɔʀtaʒ]	report (n)
la **rédaction** [ʀedaksjɔ̃]	editing, editorial staff/work
un **rédacteur**, une **rédactrice** [ʀedaktœʀ, tʀis]	editor
une **rédactrice en chef**	editor-in-chief

une **agence de presse** [aʒɑ̃sdəpʀɛs]	news agency/wire service
un **correspondant**, une **correspondante** [kɔʀɛspɔ̃dɑ̃, ɑ̃t]	correspondent
un **éditorial** [editɔʀjal]	editorial/feature story
un, une **éditorialiste** [editɔʀjalist]	editorial writer
la **couverture** [kuvɛʀtyʀ]	front page
le **titre** [titʀ]	title
un **gros titre**	headline
la **une** [layn]	front page
Cette catastrophe a fait la une de tous les journaux.	This disaster made it to the front page of all the papers.
la **manchette** [mɑ̃ʃɛt]	lead story
le **sommaire** [sɔmɛʀ]	table of contents
une **page** [paʒ]	page *(See Information Box p. 78)*
une **colonne** [kɔlɔn]	column
une **rubrique** [ʀybʀik]	heading, caption
une **enquête** [ɑ̃kɛt]	inquiry, investigation
Nos reporters ont mené l'enquête.	Our reporters did the investigation.
un **sondage** [sɔ̃daʒ]	survey, poll
les **faits divers** *mpl* [fɛdivɛʀ]	miscellany
un **compte rendu** [kɔ̃tʀɑ̃dy]	report (n)
une **chronique** (**théâtrale**) [kʀɔnik (teɑtʀal)]	culture section
un **scoop** [skup]	scoop, exclusive report
le **courrier des lecteurs** [kuʀjedelɛktœʀ]	letters to the editor
le **courrier du cœur** [kuʀjedykœʀ]	advice column
un **texte** [tɛkst]	text
un **article** [aʀtikl]	article
rédiger un article	to write an article
un **sujet** [syʒɛ]	topic, subject
traiter un sujet sérieux	to treat a serious topic

exclusif, **exclusive** [ɛksklyzif, iv]	exclusive (adj)
l'**exclusivité** *f* [ɛksklyzivite]	exclusivity
Ce reportage **paraît en exclusivité** dans notre magazine.	This report appears exclusively in our magazine.
objectif, **objective** [ɔbʒɛktif, iv]	objective (adj)
l'**objectivité** *f* [ɔbʒɛktivite]	objectivity
subjectif, **subjective** [sybʒɛktif, iv]	subjective
la **subjectivité** [sybʒɛktivite]	subjectivity
divertissant, **divertissante** [divɛʀtisɑ̃, ɑ̃t]	amusing, entertaining
instructif, **instructive** [ɛ̃stʀyktif, iv]	informative, educational

informer [ɛ̃fɔʀme]	to inform
l'**information** *f* [ɛ̃fɔʀmasjɔ̃]	information
les **informations internationales**	international news
une **nouvelle** [nuvɛl]	news item
les **nouvelles locales**	local news
Tu as lu les **dernières nouvelles**?	Have you read the most recent news?
de source sûre/de bonne source [dəsuʀsəsyʀ/dəbɔnsuʀs]	from a reliable/good source
Selon une information de source sûre, les impôts vont augmenter.	According to a reliable source, taxes are going to increase.
un **détail**; des **détails** *pl* [detaj]	detail (n)
résumer [ʀezyme]	to summarize
un **résumé** [ʀezyme]	summary, résumé
en résumé	in summary

la **publicité** [pyblisite]	advertising
la **pub** *fam* [pyb]	advertising
une **annonce** [anɔ̃s]	ad (n)
les **petites annonces**	classified ad
passer une annonce	to advertise, take out an ad

un **roman feuilleton** [ʀɔmɑ̃fœjtɔ̃]	serialized novel
la **suite** [sɥit]	sequel, continuation
à suivre [asɥivʀ]	to be continued

l'**opinion** *f* [ɔpiɲɔ̃]	opinion
la **position** [pɔzisjɔ̃]	position
prendre position pour ou contre	to take a stance for or against
le **point de vue** [pwɛ̃d(ə)vy]	viewpoint
un **commentaire** [kɔmɑ̃tɛʀ]	commentary
influencer [ɛ̃flyɑ̃se]	to influence
l'**influence** *f* [ɛ̃flyɑ̃s]	influence (n)
critiquer [kʀitike]	to criticize
la **critique** [kʀitik]	criticism
Le dernier film de Depardieu a eu de bonnes critiques.	Depardieu's latest film had good reviews.
un, une **critique** [kʀitik]	critic

la **tendance** (**politique**) [tɑ̃dɑ̃s(pɔlitik)]	(political) leaning
orienté, **orientée** [ɔʀjɑ̃te]	biased
(être) orienté à droite/à gauche	(to be) biased to the right/left
la **liberté de la presse** [libɛʀted(ə)laprɛs]	freedom of the press
la **censure** [sɑ̃syʀ]	censorship
manipuler [manipyle]	to manipulate
une **campagne de presse** [kɑ̃paɲdəpʀɛs]	press campaign

un **kiosque** [kjɔsk]	kiosk
un **numéro** [numeʀo]	issue
Le dernier numéro de Paris-Match est épuisé.	The latest issue of *Paris-Match* is sold out.
s'abonner à qc [sabɔne]	to subscribe to s.th.
un **abonnement** [abɔnmɑ̃]	subscription

un **livre** [livʀ]	book
un **bouquin** *fam* [bukɛ̃]	light novel
un **chapitre** [ʃapitʀ]	chapter
la **table des matières** [tabl(ə)dematjɛʀ]	table of contents
la **préface** [pʀefas]	preface
l'**avant-propos** *m* [avɑ̃pʀɔpo]	foreword
une **librairie** [libʀɛʀi]	bookshop
Mon nouveau livre sort en librairie la semaine prochaine.	My new book will be in the bookshops next week.
une **librairie-papeterie**	book and stationery store
un, une **libraire** [libʀɛ̃ʀ]	bookseller
une **bibliothèque** [bibliɔtɛk]	library
un, une **bibliothécaire** [bibliɔtekɛʀ]	librarian

un **best-seller**; **best-sellers** *pl* [bɛstsɛlɛʀ]	best seller
un **exemplaire** [ɛgzɑ̃plɛʀ]	copy
un **exemplaire broché/relié**	softcover/hardcover copy
la **reliure** [ʀəljyʀ]	binding (n)
une **brochure** [bʀɔʃyʀ]	brochure
les **droits d'auteur** *mpl* [dʀwadotœʀ]	copyright, intellectual property rights
une **collection** [kɔlɛksjɔ̃]	book series
une **collection de poche**	pocket book series
une **collection classique**	classical series
Ce roman vient de paraître dans la collection Folio.	This novel has just come out in the Folio series.
les **œuvres complètes** *fpl* [œvʀəkɔ̃plɛt]	complete works
la **version** [vɛʀsjɔ̃]	version
lire un roman **en version originale**	to read a novel in the original version
la **version intégrale**	unabridged version
la **version abrégée et adaptée**	abridged, adapted version
une **faute d'impression** [fotdɛ̃pʀɛsjɔ̃]	misprint (n)

16.6 Multimedia, Computers, Internet

multimédia [myltimedja]	multimedia (adj)
le **multimédia**	multimedia (n)
la **technologie de l'information** [tɛknɔlɔʒid(ə)lɛ̃fɔʀmasjɔ̃]	information technology
l'**informatique** *f* [ɛ̃fɔʀmatik]	computer science
le **langage informatique** [lɑ̃gaʒɛ̃fɔʀmatik]	computer language
un **informaticien**, une **informaticienne** [ɛ̃fɔʀmatisjɛ̃, jɛn]	computer specialist, IT specialist

un **ordinateur** [ɔʀdinatœʀ]	computer
un **PC** [pese]	PC
allumer/éteindre son PC	to turn on/off one's computer
un **micro-ordinateur**; **micro-ordinateurs** *pl* [mikʀoɔʀdinatœʀ]	microcomputer, personal computer
un **portable** [pɔʀtabl]	laptop
une **puce** [pys]	chip (n)
démarrer (**le PC**) [demaʀe(ləpese)]	to power/boot up (the PC)
arrêter (**le portable**) [aʀete(ləpɔʀtabl)]	to stop/shut down (the laptop)

un **processeur** [pRɔsesœR]	processor
un **système d'exploitation** [sistɛmdɛksplwatasjɔ̃]	operating system
une **mémoire** [memwaR]	memory
une **mémoire morte** (**ROM**)	ROM
une **mémoire vive** (**RAM**)	RAM
la **capacité de mémoire**	memory, storage capacity
le **disque dur** [diskədyR]	hard drive
un **cédérom** (**CD-ROM**) [sedeRɔm]	CD-ROM
un **lecteur de cédérom**	CD-ROM reader
introduire un CD-ROM dans le lecteur	to put a CD-ROM into the drive
une **clé USB** [kleyɛsbe]	USB flash drive
un **router** [Rutœr]	router
le **réseau sans fil**; les **réseaux sans fil** *pl* [Rezosɑ̃fil]	wireless network
le **matériel** [mateRjɛl]	hardware
le **logiciel** [lɔʒisjɛl]	software
le **progiciel** [pRɔʒisjɛl]	software packet
programmer [pRɔgRame]	to program
un **programme** [pRɔgRam]	program (n)
charger un programme	to install a program
un **programmeur**, une **programmeuse** [pRɔgRamœR, øz]	programmer
le **langage de programmation** [lɑ̃gaʒdəpRɔgRamasjɔ̃]	programming language
installer [ɛ̃stale]	to install
Je n'arrive pas à installer ce programme.	I can't install this program.
l'**installation** *f* [ɛ̃stalasjɔ̃]	installation
traiter [tRɛte]	to process
traiter des données	to process data
le **traitement de texte** [tRɛtmɑ̃d(ə)tɛkst]	word processing (program)
une **carte mémoire** [kaRtmemwaR]	memory card
une **carte graphique** [kaRtgRafik]	graphics card
une **carte son** [kaRtsɔ̃]	sound card
un **tableur** [tablœR]	spreadsheet program
un **grapheur** [gRafœR]	graphics program

un **moniteur** [mɔnitœʀ]	monitor (n)
un **écran** [ekʀɑ̃]	screen/monitor
un écran de 19 pouces	19-inch monitor
un **économiseur d'écran** [ekɔnɔmizœʀdekʀɑ̃]	screen saver
un **clavier** [klavje]	keyboard
taper [tape]	to type
une **touche** [tuʃ]	key
une **souris** [suʀi]	mouse
la touche droite de la souris	right click on the mouse
un **tapis** (**de**) **souris**	mouse pad
un **curseur** [kyʀsœʀ]	cursor
faire glisser le curseur	to move the cursor
la **flèche** [flɛʃ]	arrow
cliquer [klike]	to click (with the mouse)
double-cliquer sur l'icône	double-click on the icon
une **commande** [kɔmɑ̃d]	command (n)
imprimer [ɛ̃pʀime]	to print
une **imprimante** [ɛ̃pʀimɑ̃t]	printer
une **imprimante** (**à**) **laser**	laser printer
une **imprimante à jet d'encre**	inkjet printer
scanner [skane]	to scan
un **scanneur** [skanœʀ]	scanner
un **scanner** [skanɛʀ]	scanner

le **répertoire** [ʀepɛʀtwaʀ]	index, directory
un **fichier** [fiʃje]	file
ouvrir/fermer un fichier	to open/close a file
Pour revenir au menu principal, il faut fermer ce fichier.	To return to the main menu, this file must be closed.
l'**accès** *m* [aksɛ]	access (n)
le **mot de passe** [modpas]	password
valider [valide]	to validate/press the enter key
les **données** *fpl* [dɔne]	data
un **support de données**	data storage device
une **banque de données**	databank
entrer des données dans l'ordinateur	to input data into the computer
consulter des données	to retrieve data

saisir des données [seziʀdedɔne]	to capture, collect data
la **saisie** (**de données**) [sezi(dədɔne)]	data collection
transférer des données [tʀɑ̃sfeɑ̃dedɔne]	to transfer data
le **transfert** (**de données**) [tʀɑ̃sfɛʀ(dədɔne)]	(data) transfer (n)
stocker [stɔke]	to store
éditer [edite]	to edit
se bloquer [s(ə)blɔke]	to crash
se planter [s(ə)plɑ̃te]	to crash
le **plantage** [plɑ̃taʒ]	crash (n)
un **bogue**/un **bug** [bɔg, bœg]	bug/program error

formater [fɔʀmate]	to format
mémoriser [memɔʀize]	to store
mettre en mémoire [mɛtʀɑ̃memwaʀ]	to store
sauvegarder [sovgaʀde]	to back up, save
Il faut sauvegarder le texte avant de fermer le fichier.	The text must be saved before the file is closed.
mettre à jour [mɛtʀaʒuʀ]	to update
Cela fait longtemps que ce fichier n'a pas été mis à jour.	This file has not been updated for a long time.
la **mise à jour** [mizaʒuʀ]	update (n)
copier [kɔpje]	to copy
couper [kupe]	to cut
coller [kɔle]	to paste
effacer [efase]	to erase
la **corbeille** [kɔʀbɛj]	trash/recycle bin

le **menu** [məny]	menu
le **contrôle du menu**	menu control/prompting/mode
la **barre de menu** [baʀdəməny]	menu bar
la **barre d'outils**	toolbar
la **barre de tâches**	taskbar
une **interface** [ɛ̃tɛʀfas]	interface (n)

un **jeu électronique** [ʒøelɛktʀɔnik]	computer game
un **jeu vidéo** [ʒøvideo]	video game
une **console de jeux vidéo**	play station
une **manette de jeu** [manɛtdəʒø]	joystick
une **image virtuelle** [imaʒviʀtɥɛl]	virtual image

Internet/le **Net** *m* [(ɛ̃tɛʀ)nɛt]	Internet
le **web/WEB** [wɛb]	web
le **modem** [mɔdɛm]	modem
l'**ADSL** *f* [adeɛsɛl]	DSL
un **forfait** [fɔʀfɛ]	flat rate

un **utilisateur**, une **utilisatrice** [ytilizatœʀ, tʀis]	user
le **nom d'utilisateur**	user name
un, une **internaute** [ɛ̃tɛʀnot]	Internet surfer
un, une **cybernaute** [sibɛʀnot]	Internet surfer
naviguer (**sur Internet**) [navige(syʀɛ̃tɛʀnɛt)]	to surf (on the Internet)
surfer [sœʀfe]	to surf
On a passé 3 heures à surfer/naviguer sur le Net.	We spent three hours surfing on the Internet.
un **moteur de recherche**	search engine
un **mot-clé** [mokle]	key word

un **navigateur** [navigatœʀ]	browser
un **serveur** [sɛʀvœʀ]	server
télécharger qc du serveur	to download s.th. from the server
un **fournisseur d'accès** [fuʀnisœʀdaksɛ]	access provider

le **branchement Internet** [bʀɑ̃ʃmɑ̃ɛ̃tɛʀnɛt]	Internet connection
ouvrir la session [uvʀiʀlasesjɔ̃]	to sign on
clore la session [klɔʀlasesjɔ̃]	to sign off
se connecter [s(ə)kɔnɛkte]	to log on
se déconnecter [s(ə)dekɔnɛkte]	to log off
être connecté, **connectée** [kɔnɛkte]	to be online
être déconnecté, **déconnectée** [dekɔnɛkte]	to be offline
la **connexion** [kɔnɛksjɔ̃]	connection
en ligne [ɑ̃liɲ]	online
travailler en ligne	to work online
hors ligne ['ɔʀliɲ]	offline
accéder à Internet/à l'internet [aksedeaɛ̃tɛʀnɛt, alɛ̃tɛʀnɛt]	to access, log onto the Internet
un **cybercafé** [sibɛʀkafe]	cyber/internet café

une **page d'accueil** [paʒdakœj]	homepage
un **site** [sit]	website
s'installer un site sur Internet	to set up a web page
un **lien** [ljɛ̃]	link
un **hyperlien** [ipɛʀljɛ̃]	hyperlink
un **hypertexte** [ipɛʀtɛkst]	hypertext
télécharger [teleʃaʀʒe]	to download
un **logiciel gratuit** [lɔʒisjɛlgʀatɥi]	freeware

le **courrier électronique** [kuʀjeelɛtʀɔnik]	e-mail
un **courriel**/un **e-mail**; des **e-mails** *pl* [kuʀjɛl, imɛl]	e-mail (message)
envoyer un e-mail	to send an e-mail
une **adresse électronique** [adʀɛselɛktʀɔnik]	e-mail address
un **arobas** [aʀɔbas]	[*at* symbol], @
une **arobase** [aʀɔbaz]	[*at* symbol], @
un **message** [mesaʒ]	message (n)
une **annexe** [anɛks]	attachment
une **pièce jointe** [pjɛsʒwɛ̃t]	attachment
le **spam** [spam]	spam
chatter [tʃate]	to chat
le **chat** [tʃat]	chat (n)
le **bavardage** [bavaʀdaʒ]	chat (n)

le **service en ligne** [sɛʀvisɑ̃liɲ]	e-service, online service
les **opérations bancaires à domicile** *fpl* [ɔpeʀasjɔ̃bɑ̃kɛʀadɔmisil]	home banking, e-banking
commercer sur Internet [kɔmɛʀsesyʀɛ̃tɛʀnɛt]	to do business over the Internet
le **commerce sur Internet** [kɔmɛʀssyʀɛ̃tɛʀnɛt]	e-commerce
la **vente par Internet** [vɑ̃tpaʀɛ̃tɛʀnɛt]	e-commerce
l'**E.A.O.** (**enseignement assisté par ordinateur**) *m* [əao]	computer-supported instruction
appendre sur Internet [apʀɑ̃dʀsyrɛ̃tɛʀnɛt]	to study, take classes online
le **télétravail** [teletʀavaj]	telecommuting
la **boîte aux lettres** (**électronique**) [bwatolɛtʀ(elɛktrɔnik)]	(electronic) mailbox
relever la boîte aux lettres (électronique)	to check e-mail
un **forum de discussion** [fɔʀɔmdədiskysjɔ̃]	internet forum
un **pare-feu**; des **pare-feu(x)** *pl* [paʀfø]	firewall
un **virus** [viʀys]	virus
un (logiciel) **anti-virus**	anti-virus program

pirater un programme [piʀateœ̃pʀɔgʀam]	to pirate a program
un **pirate** [piʀat]	hacker
le **piratage** [piʀataʒ]	software piracy, hacking
un **ver informatique** [vɛʀɛ̃fɔʀmatik]	worm
un **cheval de Troie** [ʃ(ə)valdətʀwɑ]	Trojan

False Friends

French Word	Actual Meaning	False Friend	Correct French Word
un couvert	**place setting**	cover	*une couverture*
un libraire	**bookseller**	library	*la bibliothèque*
un numero	**issue**	number	*un chiffre, un nombre*

My Vocabulary

17

Transportation, Vehicles

17.1 Private Transportation  77

un **moyen de transport** [mwajɛ̃d(ə)tʀɑ̃spɔʀ]	means of transportation
une **voiture** [vwatyʀ]	automobile, car
aller* quelque part **en voiture**	to go somewhere by car
une **voiture de location**	rental car
une **voiture d'occasion**	used car
un **camion** [kamjɔ̃]	truck
une **moto** [moto]	motorcycle
une **mobylette**/une **mob** *fam* [mɔb(ilɛt)]	motorbike, moped
un **scooter** [skutœʀ/skutɛʀ]	motor scooter
un **vélo** [velo]	bicycle, bike
aller* à/en vélo	to go by bike
faire du vélo	to ride a bike
une **bicyclette** [bisiklɛt]	bicycle

INFO

Getting around

En/à + a noun with no article generally indicates a means of getting around.

Nous sommes arrivés en voiture.	*We came by car.*
Elle est partie à/en vélo.	*She left by bicycle.*
Ils ont fait une promenade à pied/à cheval.	*They took a walk/horseback ride.*

Par + a noun with an article generally indicates *public transportation*.

Ils est venu par le train/par le car de 8 heures.	*He arrived on the 8 o'clock train/bus.*

un **véhicule** [veikyl]	vehicle
un **véhicule utilitaire**	light truck/van, utility vehicle
une **auto**(**mobile**) [oto(mɔbil)]	automobile
un, une **automobiliste** [oto/ɔtɔmɔbilist]	driver
un **motard** [mɔtaʀ]	motorcyclist, biker
un **break** [bʀɛk]	station wagon
un **monospace** [mɔnɔspas]	van
une **décapotable** [dekapɔtabl]	convertible
un, une **4x4 (quatre quatre)** [kat(ʀə)kat(ʀə)]	four-by-four/all-wheel drive/SUV
une **camionnette** [kamjɔnɛt]	pickup truck
un **vélomoteur** [velomɔtœʀ]	moped
un **deux-roues** [døʀu]	two-wheeler (bicycle/ motorcycle)
une **auto-école**; des **auto-écoles** *pl* [otoekɔl]	driving school
un **moniteur d'auto-école**	driving instructor

un **piéton**, une **piétonne** [pjetɔ̃, ɔn]	pedestrian
un **passage** [pasaʒ]	passage *(See Information Box p. 78)*
un **passage** (**pour**) **piétons/clouté**	(pedestrian) crosswalk
un **trottoir** [tʀɔtwaʀ]	sidewalk

conduire [kɔ̃dɥiʀ]	to drive
Mon père n'aime pas conduire la nuit.	My father does not like to drive at night.
la **conduite** [kɔ̃dɥit]	driving, manner of driving
la **conduite accompagnée**	driving for 16-year-olds in the presence of an adult licensed driver
un **conducteur**, une **conductrice** [kɔ̃dyktœʀ, tʀis]	driver
circuler [siʀkyle]	to drive, get around
On circule mal dans Paris.	Driving in Paris is difficult.
la **circulation** [siʀkylasjɔ̃]	traffic
une circulation dense/fluide	heavy/flowing traffic
le **trafic** [tʀafik]	traffic

démarrer [demaʀe]	to start
mettre en marche [mɛtʀɑ̃maʀʃ]	to start
la **clé** (**de contact**) [kle(d(ə)kɔ̃takt)]	(ignition) key
couper le contact	to turn off the ignition
arrêter/couper le moteur [aʀɛte/kupel(ə)mɔtœʀ]	to shut off the motor

la **boîte de vitesses** [bwatdəvitɛs]	transmission
une boîte de vitesses automatique	automatic transmission
embrayer [ɑ̃bʀeje]	to engage the clutch
l'**embrayage** *m* [ɑ̃bʀɛjaʒ]	clutch (n)
débrayer [debʀeje]	to disengage the clutch
une **vitesse** [vitɛs]	speed (n)
passer une vitesse	to engage a gear
passer en 4e (**vitesse**)	to shift into fourth (gear)
changer de vitesse	to change gear
la **marche avant/arrière** [maʀʃavɑ̃/aʀjɛʀ]	drive/reverse
passer la marche arrière	to go into reverse

rouler [ʀule]	to drive
rouler à 90 à l'heure	to drive 90 km per hour
rouler prudemment	to drive carefully
la **vitesse** (**maximale**) [vitɛs(maksimal)]	speed limit
à toute vitesse	at top speed
La vitesse est limitée à 50 km/h.	The speed limit is 50 km/h.
avancer [avɑ̃se]	to drive ahead
reculer [ʀ(ə)kyle]	to back up
ralentir [ʀalɑ̃tiʀ]	to slow down
Tu devrais ralentir, on roule trop vite.	You should drive more slowly; we are going too fast.
s'arrêter [saʀɛte]	to stop
Tu aurais dû t'arrêter au feu rouge.	You should have stopped at the red light.
klaxonner [klaksɔne]	to blow the horn

accélérer [akseleʀe]	to accelerate
l'**accélérateur** *m* [akseleʀatœʀ]	accelerator
appuyer à fond sur l'accélérateur	to floor it
une **pédale** [pedal]	pedal (n)
freiner [fʀene]	to brake
le **frein** [fʀɛ̃]	brake (n)
le **frein à main**	hand brake
donner un coup de frein	to tap the brake
l'**ABS (système antiblocage)** *m* [abeɛs]	ABS/anti-lock braking system
l'**ESP (correcteur électronique de trajectoire)** *m* [øɛspe]	electronic stability control/ESC
rouler en pleins phares [ʀuleɑ̃plɛ̃faʀ]	to drive with high beams on
rouler en codes [ʀuleɑ̃kɔd]	to drive with low beams on
rouler en feux de croisement [ʀuleɑ̃fød(ə)kʀwazmɑ̃]	to drive with low beams on

le **volant** [vɔlɑ̃]	steering wheel
prendre le volant	to take the wheel
être au volant	to be at the wheel, drive
tourner [tuʀne]	to turn
un **virage** [viʀaʒ]	curve (n)
à gauche [agoʃ]	to/on the left
En Grande-Bretagne, on roule à gauche.	In Great Britain people drive on the left.
à droite [adʀwat]	to/on the right
tourner à droite	to turn right
tout droit [tudʀwa]	straight ahead
faire un détour [fɛʀɛ̃detuʀ]	to make a detour
passer [pase]	to pass/get through
Tu as le temps de passer.	You have enough time to pass.
dépasser [depase]	to pass
Interdiction de dépasser.	No passing.
doubler [duble]	to pass

faire demi-tour [fɛʀd(ə)mituʀ]	to turn around/back
une **déviation** [devjasjɔ̃]	detour (n)
À cause des travaux (routiers), il y a des déviations partout.	Because of the (road) construction there are detours everywhere.
tenir sa droite [t(ə)niʀsadʀwat]	to drive, stay on the right
Tu es incapable de tenir ta droite.	You are incapable of staying to the right.
serrer à droite [seʀeadʀwat]	to stay to the right
rater un virage *fam* [ʀateœ̃viʀaʒ]	to miss, get pulled out of the curve
zigzaguer [zigzage]	to zigzag
déraper [deʀape]	to skid, spin
La voiture a dérapé sur la route verglacée.	The car skidded on the icy road.
un **chantier** [ʃɑ̃tje]	construction site
Chaussée déformée. [ʃosedefɔʀme]	Rough road surface.
les **gravillons** *mpl* [gʀavijɔ̃]	loose gravel
Attention, gravillons!	Watch for loose gravel!

stationner [stasjɔne]	to park
stationner en double file	to double park
le **stationnement** [stasjɔnmɑ̃]	parking (n)
une zone à **stationnement payant**	paid parking area
Stationnement interdit.	No Parking.
se garer [s(ə)gaʀe]	to park
un **parking** [paʀkiŋ]	parking space/lot
un **parking souterrain**	underground parking

un **parcmètre** [paʀkmɛtʀ]	parking meter
un **horodateur** [ɔʀodatœʀ]	parking ticket vending machine
la **zone bleue** [zonblø]	short-term parking area
N'oublie pas que tu es en zone bleue.	Don't forget that you are in a short-term parking area.

une **route** [ʀut]	route *(See Information Box p. 17)*
une (**route**) **nationale** (**RN**)	national route (like a federal highway)
la route de Paris à Versailles	the route from Paris to Versailles
une **autoroute** [otoʀut]	superhighway
prendre l'autoroute	to take the highway
une **entrée** [ɑ̃tʀe]	on-ramp
une **sortie** [sɔʀti]	exit, off-ramp
On quittera l'autoroute à la prochaine sortie.	We will get off the highway at the next exit.

une **rue** [ʀy]	street *(See Information Box p. 17)*
un **chemin** [ʃ(ə)mɛ̃]	road
se tromper de chemin	to get lost, take the wrong road
un **carrefour** [kaʀfuʀ]	intersection, crossroad
des **feux de signalisation** *mpl* [fød(ə)siɲalizasjɔ̃]	traffic light
un **feu** (**tricolore**) [fø(tʀikɔlɔʀ)]	traffic light
passer au (**feu**) **rouge**	to go through a red light
griller un feu rouge	to run a red light
le **réseau routier**; les **réseaux routiers** *pl* [ʀezoʀutje]	road network, system
une **voie express** [vwaɛkspʀɛs]	express highway
emprunter la voie express	to take the highway
une **bretelle** [bʀətɛl]	ramp
un **échangeur** [eʃɑ̃ʒœʀ]	interchange (n)
le **péage** [peaʒ]	tollbooth
une **autoroute à péage**	toll road
un (**boulevard**) **périphérique** [(bulvaʀ)peʀifeʀik]	beltway *(around a city)*
le **périph** *fam* [peʀif]	beltway *(around a city)*
une **rocade** [ʀɔkad]	beltway, bypass
un **croisement** [kʀwazmɑ̃]	crossroad, intersection (rural roads)
un **rond-point** [ʀɔ̃pwɛ̃]	rotary, traffic circle
un **sens giratoire** [sɑ̃sʒiʀatwaʀ]	rotary, traffic circle
une **voie sans issue** [vwasɑ̃zisy]	dead-end street
une **impasse** [ɛ̃pas]	dead-end street
une **piste cyclable** [pist(ə)siklabl]	bicycle path
un **bouchon** [buʃɔ̃]	traffic jam, congestion
Bouchon dans 3 kilomètres!	Traffic jam in three kilometers!
un **embouteillage** [ɑ̃butɛjaʒ]	traffic jam
bloquer [blɔke]	to block
Un accident a bloqué la route.	An accident has blocked the road.
un **encombrement** [ɑ̃kɔ̃bʀəmɑ̃]	traffic jam, holdup
être coincé dans les encombrements	to be stuck in traffic
un **ralentissement** [ʀalɑ̃tismɑ̃]	slow traffic
l'**heure d'affluence** *f* [œʀdaflyɑ̃s]	rush hour
l'**heure de pointe** *f* [œʀdəpwɛ̃t]	rush hour
Impossible de circuler **aux heures de pointe**.	It's impossible to drive during rush hour.
une **station-service**; des **station-service(s)** *pl* [stasjɔ̃sɛʀvis]	gas/service station
l'**essence** *f* [esɑ̃s]	gasoline

faire le plein [fɛʀləplɛ̃]	to fill it up
le **super sans-plomb** [sypɛʀsɑ̃plɔ̃]	super-unleaded
le **gazole** [gazɔl]	diesel fuel
le **gasoil** [gazwal]	diesel fuel
le **GPL** (**gaz de pétrole liquéfié**) [ʒepeɛl]	liquid propane gas, propane
vérifier [veʀifje]	to check
l'**huile** *f* [ɥil]	oil
vérifier le niveau d'huile	to check the oil level

consommer [kɔ̃sɔme]	to use, consume
Ma voiture consomme 10 litres aux cent.	My car uses 10 liters per 100 kilometers.
la **consommation** [kɔ̃sɔmasjɔ̃]	use, consumption
un **pot d'échappement** [podeʃapmɑ̃]	exhaust pipe
un **pot catalytique** [pokatalitik]	catalytic converter

le **moteur** [mɔtœʀ]	motor
un (**moteur**) **diesel** [(mɔtœʀ)djezɛl]	diesel motor
une **panne** [pan]	breakdown (n)
tomber*/être en panne	to have a breakdown
On est tombé en panne d'essence.	We have run out of gas.
un **garage** [gaʀaʒ]	garage, mechanic shop *(See Information Box p. 78)*
emmener la voiture au garage	to take the car to the garage
un, une **garagiste** [gaʀaʒist]	mechanic
réparer [ʀepaʀe]	to repair
une **réparation** [ʀepaʀasjɔ̃]	repair (n)

un **moteur hybride** [mɔtœʀibʀid]	hybrid motor
dépanner [depane]	to troubleshoot; to tow
une **dépanneuse** [depanøz]	tow truck
le **service de dépannage** [sɛʀvisdədepanaʒ]	tow service
une **bougie** [buʒi]	sparkplug
changer les bougies	to change the (spark) plugs
une **vidange** [vidɑ̃ʒ]	oil change
remorquer [ʀ(ə)mɔʀke]	to tow
La dépanneuse nous a remorqués jusqu'au garage le plus proche.	The tow truck towed us to the nearest garage.
faire réviser (**sa voiture**) [fɛʀʀevize(savwatyʀ)]	to have one's car inspected
une **révision** [ʀevizjɔ̃]	inspection
un **centre de contrôle technique** [sɑ̃tʀ(ə)dəkɔ̃tʀoltɛknik]	technical inspection center

une **roue** [ʀu]	wheel
la **roue de secours**	spare tire
changer une roue	to change a tire
un **pneu** [pnø]	tire
monter les pneus d'hiver	to put on the snow tires
la **pression** [pʀesjɔ̃]	pressure
la pression des pneus	tire pressure
gonfler [gɔ̃fle]	to inflate, pump up

crever [kʀəve]	to have a flat
J'ai crevé.	I have a flat.
une **crevaison** [kʀəvɛzɔ̃]	puncture (n)
un **cric** (**d'automobile**) [kʀik(dotomɔbil)]	jack (n)

l'**éclairage** *m* [eklɛʀaʒ]	lighting
un **phare** [faʀ]	headlight
allumer les phares	to turn on the headlights
le **feu arrière** [føaʀjɛʀ]	taillight

un **clignotant** [kliɲɔtɑ̃]	blinker, turn signal
mettre le clignotant à gauche	to put on the left blinker
un **pare-chocs** [paʀʃɔk]	bumper *(See Information Box p. 104)*
un **pare-brise** [paʀbʀiz]	windshield *(See Information Box p. 104)*
un **essuie-glace** [esɥiglas]	windshield wiper *(See Information Box p. 104)*
un **lave-glace** [lavglas]	windshield washer *(See Information Box p. 104)*

le **code de la route** [kɔddəlaʀut]	traffic regulations
la **priorité** [pʀijɔʀite]	priority, right of way
Priorité à droite.	Right of way is on the right.
respecter la priorité	to yield the right of way
avoir la priorité sur	to have right of way over
un **panneau**; des **panneaux** *pl* [pano]	(road) sign
(un) **sens interdit** [sɑ̃sɛ̃tɛʀdi]	one-way street, no entrance
s'engager dans un sens interdit	to go the wrong way on a one-way street
(un) **sens unique** [sɑ̃synik]	one-way street

une **infraction** [ɛ̃fʀaksjɔ̃]	infraction, violation
Il a **commis une infraction au** code de la route.	He violated the rules of the road.
une **interdiction** (**de dépasser**) [ɛ̃tɛʀdiksjɔ̃(d(ə)depase)]	no passing
respecter une interdiction	to comply with a prohibition
un **excès de vitesse** [ɛksɛdvitɛs]	speeding (n)
une **amende pour excès de vitesse**	speeding fine
une **limitation de vitesse** [limitasjɔ̃dvitɛs]	speed limit
(un) **rappel** [ʀapɛl]	reminder of a previous road sign

un **contrôle** [kɔ̃tʀol]	inspection
les **papiers** *mpl* [papje]	(car) documents
présenter ses papiers à la police	to show one's papers to the police
le **permis** (**de conduire**) [pɛʀmi(d(ə)kɔ̃dɥiʀ)]	(driver's) license
passer son permis (de conduire)	to get one's driver's license
On lui a retiré le permis de conduire.	His driver's license was revoked.
être assuré, **assurée contre qc** [asyʀe]	to be insured against s.th.
une **assurance** [asyʀɑ̃s]	insurance
une **assurance tous risques**	comprehensive insurance

la **carte grise** [kaʀtəgʀiz]	vehicle registration
la **carte verte** [kaʀtəvɛʀt]	green insurance card
une **vignette** [viɲɛt]	tax sticker

dangereux, dangereuse [dɑ̃ʒʀø, øz]	dangerous
un virage dangereux	dangerous curve
un **danger** [dɑ̃ʒe]	danger
Tu es un vrai **danger public**!	You are a real public danger!
un **risque** [ʀisk]	risk (n)
courir un risque	to run a risk
prendre des risques	to take risks
un **accident** [aksidɑ̃]	accident
L'accident s'est produit à la sortie du village.	The accident happened on the way out of town.

un **chauffard** [ʃofaʀ]	road hog
un **alcootest** [alkɔtɛst]	sobriety test
Son alcootest a été positif.	His alcohol test was positive.
écraser [ekʀaze]	to run over
Elle s'est fait écraser par un chauffard ivre.	She was run over by a drunk driver.
une **collision** [kɔlizjɔ̃]	collision
une **victime** [viktim]	victim
porter secours à qn [pɔʀtes(ə)kuʀ]	to aid, help s.o.
les **premiers secours**	first aid
un **témoin** [temwɛ̃]	witness (n)

la **police** [pɔlis]	police
un **poste** (**de police**) [pɔst(d(ə)pɔlis)]	police station
Il a passé la nuit au poste.	He spent the night in the police station.
un **commissariat** [kɔmisaʀja]	police station
un **agent** (**de police**) [aʒɑ̃(d(ə)pɔlis)]	(police) officer
un **flic** *fam* [flik]	cop

un **contractuel**, une **contractuelle** [kɔ̃tʀaktɥɛl]	auxiliary police officer
une **contravention** [kɔ̃tʀavɑ̃sjɔ̃]	(violation) ticket
un **papillon** *fam* [papijɔ̃]	parking ticket
une **amende** [amɑ̃d]	fine (n)
un **procès-verbal** (**PV**); des **procès-verbaux** *pl* [pʀɔsɛvɛʀbal (peve)]	traffic/parking ticket
La contractuelle lui a mis un PV.	The (auxiliary) officer gave him a ticket.

la **ceinture de sécurité** [sɛ̃tyʀdəsekyʀite]	seatbelt
attacher sa ceinture de sécurité	to fasten one's seatbelt
un **airbag** [ɛʀbag]	airbag
un **coussin gonflable** [kusɛ̃gɔ̃flabl]	airbag
un **toit ouvrant** [twauvʀɑ̃]	sun roof
la **climatisation** [klimatizasjɔ̃]	air conditioning
la **clim** *fam* [klim]	AC
un **GPS** [ʒepeɛs]	GPS
un **système de navigation** [sistɛmdənavigasjɔ̃]	navigation system
un **limiteur de vitesse** [limitœʀdəvitɛs]	speed limiter/governor

17.2 Public Transportation 

transporter [tʀɑ̃spɔʀte]	to transport
le **transport** [tʀɑ̃spɔʀ]	transport
voyager [vwajaʒe]	to travel
voyager en/par le train	to travel by train
un **voyage** [vwajaʒ]	trip
Bon voyage!	Have a good trip!
un **voyageur**, une **voyageuse** [vwajaʒœʀ, øz]	traveler
un **passager**, une **passagère** [pasaʒe, ɛʀ]	passenger

le **transport routier** [tʀɑ̃spɔʀ]	road transport
le **transport ferroviaire/aérien/maritime/fluvial**	rail/air/ocean/river transport
le **réseau** (**ferroviaire**); les **réseaux** (**ferroviaires**) *pl* [ʀezo(fɛʀɔvjɛʀ)]	(railroad) system, railway
les **transports en commun** *mpl* [tʀɑ̃spɔʀɑ̃kɔmɛ̃]	public transportation
emprunter les transports en commun	to use public transportation

un **autobus** [oto/ɔtɔbys]	bus/motor coach
un **bus** [bys]	bus
un **arrêt de bus/d'autobus**	bus stop
un **conducteur**, une **conductrice de bus**	bus driver
un **autocar** [oto/ɔtɔkaʀ]	tour bus
un **car** [kaʀ]	bus
Le car pour Brive partira à 9 heures 15.	The bus for Brive leaves at 9:15.
une **gare routière** [gaʀʀutjɛʀ]	bus station
un **taxi** [taksi]	taxi
appeler un taxi	to call/hail a taxi
un **chauffeur de taxi**	taxi driver
un **trajet** [tʀaʒɛ]	trip
Je fais ce trajet tous les jours.	I make this trip every day.
le **RER** (**Réseau express régional**) [ɛʀəɛʀ]	regional rail rapid transit system
un **métro** [metʀo]	subway
une **ligne de métro**	subway line
une **station de métro**	subway station

faire la navette [fɛRlanavɛt]	to commute
J'aime mieux faire la navette tous les jours qu'habiter à Paris.	I prefer commuting every day to living in Paris.
desservir [desɛRviR]	to stop (at a train station)
Ce train ne dessert pas la gare de Corbeil.	This train does not stop at the Corbeil train station.
une **rame de métro** [Ramdəmetro]	subway
le **tram**(**way**) [tRam(wɛ)]	streetcar

la **SNCF** (**Société nationale des chemins de fer français**) [ɛsɛnseɛf]	French national railway
un **train** [tRɛ̃]	train
un **TGV** (**train à grande vitesse**) [teʒeve]	TGV *(French high-speed train)*
un **train de voyageurs** [tRɛ̃dvwajaʒœR]	passenger train
une **locomotive** [lɔkɔmɔtiv]	locomotive
un **wagon** [vagɔ̃]	car
un **wagon-lit**	sleeping car
un **wagon-restaurant**	dining car
un **compartiment** [kɔ̃paRtimɑ̃]	compartment
un **compartiment** (**non-**)**fumeurs**	non-smoking compartment
une **place** [plas]	seat
(faire) réserver une place	to reserve a seat
une **place assise/debout**	seat/standing place
une **banquette** [bɑ̃kɛt]	bench
une **couchette** [kuʃɛt]	couchette, berth
une **voiture-couchettes**	sleeping car
une **gare** [gaR]	train station
un **quai** [kɛ]	platform
une **voie** [vwa]	platform
Le train pour Brest part de la voie 2.	The train to Brest leaves from platform 2.
les **rails** *mpl* [Raj]	rails

un **train de banlieue** [tRɛ̃d(ə)bɑ̃ljø]	local, commuter train
les **grandes lignes** *fpl* [gRɑ̃dliɲ]	long-distance lines
le **terminus** [tɛRminys]	terminus, end station
à destination de... [adɛstinasjɔ̃də]	in the direction of...
Le TGV à destination de Stuttgart partira à 13 heures 30.	The TGV for Stuttgart leaves at 13:30.
en provenance de [ɑ̃pRɔv(ə)nɑ̃sdə]	arriving from...
Le train en provenance de Lille arrivera en retard.	The train from Lille will arrive late.

un **ticket** [tikɛ]	ticket
un **aller simple** [alesɛ̃pl]	one-way ticket
un **aller (et) retour** [ale(e)ʀ(ə)tuʀ]	round-trip ticket
un aller-retour pour Strasbourg	round-trip ticket for Strasburg
un **distributeur de tickets** [distʀibytœʀdətikɛ]	ticket vending machine
composter [kɔ̃pɔste]	to void, cancel, validate
composter son billet	to void, validate one's ticket
un **contrôleur**, une **contrôleuse** [kɔ̃tʀolœʀ, øz]	ticket inspector
valable [valabl]	valid
Votre billet n'est plus valable.	Your ticket is no longer valid.
(**en**) **1ère classe** [(ɑ̃)pʀəmjɛʀklas]	(in) first class
Elle voyage toujours en 1ère (classe).	She always travels first class.
(**en**) **2e classe** [(ɑ̃)døzjɛmklas]	(in) second class
un **carnet** [kaʀnɛ]	book of tickets
Un **carnet de tickets** (de métro), s'il vous plaît.	A book of (subway) tickets, please.
une **carte orange** [kaʀtɔʀɑ̃ʒ]	travel pass
une carte orange pour trois zones	travel pass for three zones
une **réduction** [ʀedyksjɔ̃]	reduction, discount
une **réduction famille nombreuse**	family discount

attendre (**le bus, le train**...) [atɑ̃dʀ]	to wait for (the bus, the train...)
une **salle d'attente** [saldatɑ̃t]	waiting room
prendre le métro [pʀɑ̃dʀ]	to take the subway
On y va en taxi ou on prend le métro?	Shall we take a taxi or the subway?
rater (**le bus**...) *fam* [ʀate]	to miss (the bus...)
Si tu ne te dépêches pas, tu vas rater ton bus.	If you don't hurry you are going to miss your bus.
manquer (**le bus**...) [mɑ̃ke]	to miss (the bus...)
monter* (**dans le bus**...) [mɔ̃te]	to get on (the bus...) *(See Information Box p. 40)*
En voiture, s.v.p.! [ɑ̃vwatyʀsilvuplɛ]	All aboard, please!
Les voyageurs pour Lyon en voiture, s'il vous plaît!	Passengers for Lyon please get on the bus!
descendre* (**du bus**...) [desɑ̃dʀ]	to get off (the bus...) *(See Information Box p. 40)*
changer (**de bus**...) [ʃɑ̃ʒe]	to change (bus...)
Pour aller à «Odéon», il faut changer à «Châtelet».	To get to "Odéon" you have to change at "Châtelet."
la **correspondance** [kɔʀɛspɔ̃dɑ̃s]	connection
attendre la correspondance	to wait for the connecting train

les **renseignements** *mpl* [ʀɑ̃sɛɲmɑ̃]	information
un **horaire** [ɔʀɛʀ]	timetable, schedule
Renseigne-toi sur les **horaires des trains pour** Nantes.	Find out the timetable for trains to Nantes.
le **départ** [depaʀ]	departure
l'**heure de départ**	departure time
l'**arrivée** *f* [aʀive]	arrival
l'**heure d'arrivée**	arrival time
en avance [ɑ̃navɑ̃s]	early
Nous sommes en avance.	We are early.
à l'heure [alœʀ]	on time
Le car est parti à l'heure.	The bus left on time.
ponctuel, **ponctuelle** [pɔ̃ktɥɛl]	punctual
en retard [ɑ̃ʀ(ə)taʀ]	late
Le train est en retard.	The train is late.
annulé, **annulée** [anyle]	canceled
Le vol de 9 heures est **annulé en raison des grèves**.	The 9:00 flight is canceled because of the strike.

un **avion** [avjɔ̃]	airplane
prendre l'avion pour…	to fly/take the plane to…
un **hélicoptère** [elikɔptɛʀ]	helicopter
une **compagnie aérienne** [kɔ̃paɲiaeʀjɛn]	airline
voler [vɔle]	to fly *(See Information Box p. 40)*
Au retour, nous volons de nuit.	On the return trip, we fly at night.
un **vol régulier** [vɔlʀegylje]	scheduled flight
un (**vol**) **charter** [(vɔl)ʃaʀtɛʀ]	charter (flight)
une **piste** [pist]	runway
L'avion **se pose sur la piste**.	The plane touches down on the runway.
un **aéroport** [aeʀɔpɔʀ]	airport
un **aérodrome** [aeʀodʀom]	airport, airfield
une **aérogare** [aeʀogaʀ]	terminal
un **terminal** [tɛʀminal]	terminal
Les vols internationaux partent du terminal B.	International flights leave from terminal B.

l'**enregistrement** (**des bagages**) *m* [ɑ̃ʀ(ə)ʒistʀəmɑ̃(debagaʒ)]	baggage check
embarquer [ɑ̃baʀke]	to go on board
l'**embarquement** *m* [ɑ̃baʀkəmɑ̃]	boarding
la **carte d'embarquement**	boarding pass
un **pilote** [pilɔt]	pilot
un **commandant de bord** [kɔmɑ̃dɑ̃d(ə)bɔʀ]	flight commander
un **steward** [stiwaʀt]	attendant, steward
une **hôtesse de l'air** [otɛsdəlɛʀ]	attendant, stewardess
les **ventes hors-taxes** *fpl* [vɑ̃tɔʀtaks]	duty-free sales
décoller [dekɔle]	to take off
L'avion a décollé de la piste 03.	The plane took off from runway 03.
le **décollage** [dekɔlaʒ]	takeoff (n)
atterrir [ateʀiʀ]	to land
l'**atterrissage** *m* [ateʀisaʒ]	landing (n)
une **escale** [ɛskal]	stopover (n)
faire escale	to make a stopover
le **décalage horaire** [dekalaʒɔʀɛʀ]	time difference
Il y a 9 heures de décalage (horaire) entre Paris et San Francisco.	There is a time difference of nine hours between Paris and San Francisco.

un **bateau**; des **bateaux** *pl* [bato]	ship
un **ferry**(**-boat**); des **ferrys, ferries, ferry-boats** *pl* [feʀi(bot)]	ferry
traverser [tʀavɛʀse]	to cross
une **traversée** [tʀavɛʀse]	crossing (n)
la traversée de la Manche	crossing the Channel
un **port** [pɔʀ]	port
arriver* à bon port	to arrive safely in port
un **capitaine** [kapitɛn]	captain
un **marin** [maʀɛ̃]	sailor, seaman
à bord [abɔʀ]	on board
Il était marin à bord du Titanic.	He was a sailor on board the *Titanic*.
monter* à bord	to go onboard

un **navire** [naviʀ]	(large) ship
Le navire met le cap sur Tahiti.	The ship is heading toward Tahiti.
naviguer [navige]	to navigate
la **navigation** [navigasjɔ̃]	navigation
un **paquebot** [pak(ə)bo]	passenger ship
une **croisière** [kʀwazjɛʀ]	cruise (n)
un **équipage** [ekipaʒ]	crew
les **membres d'équipage**	crew members
le **mal de mer** [maldəmɛʀ]	seasickness
un **cargo** [kaʀgo]	cargo ship, freighter
le **fret** [fʀɛt]	freight
charger le fret dans la cale	to stow the freight in the hold
un **pétrolier** [petʀɔlje]	oil tanker
une **péniche** [peniʃ]	barge
un **canal**; des **canaux** *pl* [kanal, o]	canal
Les péniches naviguent sur les canaux.	The barges sail on the canals.
une **écluse** [eklyz]	lock (n)

les **bagages** *mpl* [bagaʒ]	baggage
les **bagages à main**	hand baggage
la **consigne** [kɔ̃siɲ]	baggage room, locker
laisser ses bagages à la consigne (automatique)	to leave one's bags in the baggage room/locker
un **porteur** [pɔʀtœʀ]	porter
un **chariot** [ʃaʀjo]	baggage cart
mettre ses bagages sur le chariot	to put one's bags onto the cart

un **semi-remorque**; des **semi-remorques** *pl* [səmiʀ(ə)mɔʀk]	semi-trailer
un **routier** [ʀutje]	long-haul trucker
un **camionneur** [kamjɔnœʀ]	truck driver
la **marchandise** [maʀʃɑ̃diz]	merchandise, goods
un **train de marchandises**	freight train

False Friends

French Word	Actual Meaning	False Friend	Correct French Word
un break	**station wagon**	a break	*une pause*
valable	**valid**	valuable	*cher, de valeur*

My Vocabulary

18

Nature, Environment, Ecology

18.1 Universe, Earth  79

l'**espace** *m* [ɛspas]	space
le **ciel** [sjɛl]	sky
solaire [sɔlɛʀ]	solar
le **système solaire**	solar system
le **soleil** [sɔlɛj]	sun
une **étoile** [etwal]	star
une **étoile filante**	shooting star

universel, **universelle** [ynivɛʀsɛl]	universal
l'**univers** *m* [ynivɛʀ]	universe
une **galaxie** [galaksi]	galaxy
la **voie lactée** [vwalakte]	Milky Way
la **constellation** [kɔ̃stelasjɔ̃]	constellation
une **comète** [kɔmɛt]	comet
un **météore** [meteɔʀ]	meteor
un **astre** [astʀ]	star, heavenly body
une **année-lumière**; des **années-lumière** *pl* [anelymjɛʀ]	light year
une **éclipse** [eklips]	eclipse
une éclipse totale/partielle	total/partial eclipse
une **planète** [planɛt]	planet

lunaire [lynɛʀ]	lunar
la **lune** [lyn]	moon
être dans la lune *loc*	to be absent-minded
la **pleine lune**	full moon
la **lune de miel**	honeymoon
croître [kʀwatʀ]	to wax
décroître [dekʀwatʀ]	to wane
terrestre [teʀɛstʀ]	earthly
la **terre** [tɛʀ]	earth
tourner autour de la terre	to rotate around the earth
le **globe (terrestre)** [glɔb(teʀɛstʀ)]	globe

le **pôle** [pol]	pole
le **pôle Nord/Sud**	North/South Pole
le **cercle polaire** [sɛʀkl(ə)polɛʀ]	polar circle
l'**hémisphère** *m* [emisfɛʀ]	hemisphere
l'**hémisphère nord**	northern hemisphere
la **rotation** [ʀɔtasjɔ̃]	rotation, revolution
La rotation de la Terre sur elle-même dure 24 heures.	It takes 24 hours for the earth to make one revolution.
un **axe** [aks]	axis
l'**équateur** *m* [ekwatœʀ]	equator
les **tropiques** *mpl* [tʀɔpik]	tropics
le **tropique du Cancer/du Capricorne**	Tropic of Cancer/Capricorn
un **fuseau horaire**; des **fuseaux horaires** *pl* [fyzoɔʀɛʀ]	time zone

l'**air** *m* [ɛʀ]	air
être au grand air	to be out in the fresh air
un **gaz** [gaz]	gas
l'**ozone** *m* [ozon/ɔzɔn]	ozone
l'**oxygène** *m* [ɔksiʒɛn]	oxygen
l'**atmosphère** *f* [atmɔsfɛʀ]	atmosphere
respirer [ʀɛspiʀe]	to breathe
respirer **à pleins poumons**	to breathe deeply
la **respiration** [ʀɛspiʀasjɔ̃]	breathing (n)

graviter [gʀavite]	to orbit, circle
Le satellite gravite autour de la Terre.	The satellite orbits around the Earth.
la **gravitation** [gʀavitasjɔ̃]	gravitation
attirer [atiʀe]	to attract
L'aimant attire le fer.	The magnet attracts iron.
l'**attraction** *f* [atʀaksjɔ̃]	attraction
l'**attraction terrestre**	gravitational pull
un **satellite** [satelit]	satellite
La Lune est un satellite de la Terre.	The moon is a satellite of the Earth.
une **orbite** [ɔʀbit]	orbit
mettre un satellite **sur orbite**	to put a satellite into orbit
l'**apesanteur** *f* [apəzɑ̃tœʀ]	weightlessness
se trouver **en état d'apesanteur**	to be in a state of weightlessness, zero gravity

l'**astronautique** *f* [astʀonotik]	astronautics, space travel
un, une **astronaute** [astʀonot]	astronaut
un, une **cosmonaute** [kɔsmɔnot]	cosmonaut
spatial, **spatiale** [spasjal]	space (adj)
la **recherche spatiale**	space research
un **vaisseau spatial**	space ship
une **navette/station spatiale**	space shuttle/station
une **fusée** [fyze]	rocket
lancer une fusée dans l'espace	to launch a rocket into space
une **soucoupe volante** [sukupvɔlɑ̃t]	flying saucer
un **OVNI** (**objet volant non-identifié**) [ɔvni]	UFO (unidentified flying object)
Il croit fermement aux OVNI et aux extraterrestres.	He believes firmly in UFOs and extraterrestrials.

18.2 Geography  80

géographique [ʒeɔgʀafik]	geographic
la **géographie** [ʒeɔgʀafi]	geography
une **carte** (**de géographie**)	(geographic) map
le **nord** [nɔʀ]	north
le **sud** [syd]	south
l'**est** *m* [ɛst]	east
l'**ouest** [wɛst]	west
le **paysage** [peizaʒ]	landscape
la **nature** [natyʀ]	nature

un **atlas** [atlɑs]	atlas
un **parallèle** [paʀalɛl]	parallel (n), (degree of) latitude
à la hauteur du 20e parallèle	at the twentieth parallel
un **méridien** [meʀidjɛ̃]	longitude, meridian
être situé, **située à** [sitɥe]	to be located on
... **degrés de latitude** (**nord/sud**) [dəgʀed(ə)latityd(nɔʀ/syd)]	of ... degrees north/south latitude
Paris est situé à 48 degrés de latitude nord.	Paris is located at a latitude of 48 degrees north.
... **degrés de longitude** (**est/ouest**) [dəgʀed(ə)lɔ̃ʒityd(ɛst/wɛst)]	of ... degrees east/west longitude
les **quatre points cardinaux** *mpl* [katʀ(ə)pwɛ̃kaʀdino]	the four cardinal directions

septentrional, **septentrionale** [sɛptɑ̃tʀijɔnal]	northern
méridional, **méridionale** [meʀidjɔnal]	southern
oriental, **orientale** [ɔʀjɑ̃tal]	eastern
occidental, **occidentale** [ɔksidɑ̃tal]	western
le **monde** [mɔ̃d]	world
Il a voyagé dans le **monde entier**.	He has traveled all over the world.
terrestre [tɛʀɛstʀ]	land
les **animaux terrestres**	land animals
la **terre** [tɛʀ]	earth, soil
un **continent** [kɔ̃tinɑ̃]	continent
la **surface** [syʀfas]	surface, area
La France a une surface de 550 000 km².	France has an area of 550,000 km².
un **pays** [pei]	country
une **région** [ʀeʒjɔ̃]	region
une **région sauvage**	wilderness, uninhabited areas
une **province** [pʀɔvɛ̃s]	province
s'étendre sur [setɑ̃dʀ]	to extend over
Cette forêt s'étend sur 200 hectares.	This forest extends over 200 hectares.
une **frontière** [fʀɔ̃tjɛʀ]	border
une **frontière naturelle**	natural border
un **plateau**; des **plateaux** *pl* [plato]	plateau
une **plaine** [plɛn]	plain
La Beauce est une plaine fertile.	La Beauce is a fertile plain.
plat, **plate** [pla, plat]	flat
en terrain plat	on flat ground
la **superficie** [sypɛʀfisi]	surface
l'**étendue** *f* [etɑ̃dy]	size, extent
un **bassin** [basɛ̃]	basin
le Bassin parisien	Paris Basin

le **relief** [Rəljɛf]	relief, terrain
montagneux, **montagneuse** [mɔ̃taɲø, øz]	mountainous
une **région montagneuse**	mountainous region
une **montagne** [mɔ̃taɲ]	mountain
une **colline** [kɔlin]	hill
volcanique [vɔlkanik]	volcanic
une **éruption volcanique**	volcanic eruption
un **volcan** [vɔlkɑ̃]	volcano
un **volcan en activité**	active volcano

une **chaîne de montagnes** [ʃɛndəmɔ̃taɲ]	mountain chain
l'**altitude** *f* [altityd]	altitude, height
Le village **est situé à une altitude de** 1 200 mètres.	The village is located at an altitude of 1200 meters.
une **pente** [pɑ̃t]	slope
Le sol descend **en pente douce**.	The ground slopes gently downward.
un **glacier** [glasje]	glacier
fondre [fɔ̃dR]	to melt
une **grotte** [gRɔt]	cave

un **sommet** [sɔmɛt]	peak, summit
monter* au sommet	to climb to the summit
s'élever à [sel(ə)ve]	to reach
Le Mont Blanc s'élève à 4 807 m.	Mont Blanc reaches 4807 meters.
un **col** [kɔl]	mountain pass
une **vallée** [vale]	valley
une **gorge** [gɔRʒ]	ravine, gorge
la **hauteur** ['otœR]	height
La hauteur de la Tour Montparnasse est de 209 m.	The height of the Montparnasse Tower is 209 meters.
haut, **haute** ['o, 'ot]	high
une montagne **haute de** 3 000 m	a 3000-meter-high mountain
bas, **basse** [ba, bas]	low
L'avion vole très bas.	The plane is flying very low.

les Alpes *fpl* [lezalp]	Alps
les Pyrénées *fpl* [lepiRene]	Pyrenees
le Massif Central [ləmasifsɑ̃tRal]	Massif Central
les Vosges *fpl* [levoʒ]	Vosges

le Jura [ləʒyRa]	Jura
les Ardennes *fpl* [lezaRdɛn]	Ardennes
la Forêt-Noire [lafɔRɛnwaR]	Black Forest

une **forêt** [fɔʀɛ]	forest
la **forêt vierge**	virgin forest
un **bois** [bwa]	forest, woods
se promener **dans les bois**	to walk in the woods
la **campagne** [kɑ̃paɲ]	country(side)
désertique [dezɛʀtik]	desert (adj)
un **désert** [dezɛʀ]	desert *(See Information Box p. 100)*

le **sol** [sɔl]	soil
un sol fertile	fertile soil
le **terrain** [teʀɛ̃]	terrain
un terrain aride	arid terrain
boisé, **boisée** [bwaze]	wooded, forested
l'**érosion** *f* [eʀozjɔ̃]	erosion
la **désertification** [dezɛʀtifikasjɔ̃]	desertification
Le déboisement entraîne un phénomène de désertification.	Deforestation leads to desertification.

l'**eau** *f*; les **eaux** *fpl* [o]	water
Les **eaux de pluie** ont grossi la rivière.	The rainwater swelled the river.
un **lac** [lak]	lake
profond, **profonde** [pʀɔfɔ̃, ɔ̃d]	deep
une eau peu profonde	shallow water
la **profondeur** [pʀɔfɔ̃dœʀ]	depth
La gorge a une profondeur de 250 mètres.	The gorge is 250 meters deep.

le lac de Constance [ləlakdəkɔ̃stɑ̃s]	Lake Constance
le lac Léman [ləlaklemɑ̃]	Lake Geneva
un **étang** [etɑ̃]	pond

maritime [maʀitim]	maritime, coastal
le **climat maritime**	maritime climate
la **mer** [mɛʀ]	sea *(See Information Box p. 370)*
aller* au bord de la mer	to go to the seashore
un **océan** [ɔseɑ̃]	ocean
les **marées** *fpl* [maʀe]	tides
la **marée haute/basse**	high/low tide
à marée haute/basse	at high/low tide
une **vague** [vag]	wave (n)

INFO

Watch out for sound-alikes!

In French there are a number of words that are pronounced alike (*homophones*) but written differently, and they have different meanings:

la mer [mɛʀ]	*the sea*
la mère [mɛʀ]	*the mother*
le maire [mɛʀ]	*the mayor*

l'(océan) **Atlantique** *m* [l(ɔseɑ̃)atlɑ̃tik]	Atlantic Ocean
la (mer) **Méditerranée** [la(mɛʀ)mediteʀane]	Mediterranean (Sea)
la mer du Nord [lamɛʀdynɔʀ]	North Sea
la mer Baltique [lamɛʀbaltik]	Baltic Sea
une **mer intérieure** [mɛʀɛ̃teʀjœʀ]	inland sea
la Manche [lamɑ̃ʃ]	English Channel
le Pacifique/l'océan pacifique *m* [ləpasifik/lɔseɑ̃pasifik]	Pacific Ocean
l'océan Indien *m* [lɔseɑ̃ɛ̃djɛ̃]	Indian Ocean

un **fleuve** [flœv]	river (that empties into the sea)
La ville est située **au bord d'un fleuve**.	The city is located next to a river.
se jeter dans [s(ə)j(ə)tedɑ̃]	to empty into
La Seine se jette dans la Manche.	The Seine empties into the English Channel.
navigable [navigabl]	navigable
une **rivière** [ʀivjɛʀ]	river
couler [kule]	to flow
une **source** [suʀs]	spring (n)
prendre sa source	to originate

un **ruisseau**; des **ruisseaux** *pl* [ʀɥiso]	brook
un **courant** [kuʀɑ̃]	current
un **torrent** [tɔʀɑ̃]	mountain stream, torrent
L'orage a transformé le ruisseau en **torrent rapide**.	The storm turned the brook into a raging torrent.
une **chute d'eau**; des **chutes d'eau** *pl* [ʃytdo]	waterfall
une **cascade** [kaskad]	(small) waterfall
en amont [ɑ̃namɔ̃]	upstream
une ville située au bord de la Seine, **en amont de** Paris	a city located on the Seine, upstream from Paris
en aval [ɑ̃naval]	downstream

un **affluent** [aflyɑ̃]	tributary
le **confluent** [kɔ̃flyɑ̃]	junction, confluence
Lyon se trouve **au confluent du** Rhône et de la Saône.	Lyon is located at the confluence of the Rhône and the Saône.
l'**embouchure** *f* [ɑ̃buʃyʀ]	mouth
la Seine [lasɛn]	the Seine
la Loire [lalwaʀ]	the Loire
le Rhône [ləʀon]	the Rhône
la Garonne [lagaʀɔn]	the Garonne
le Rhin [ləʀɛ̃]	the Rhine
la Marne [lamaʀn]	the Marne
la Meuse [lamøz]	the Meuse
la Saône [lason]	the Saône
la Dordogne [ladɔʀdɔɲ]	the Dordogne
la Moselle [lamɔzɛl]	the Moselle
le Danube [lədanyb]	the Danube
une **côte** [kot]	coast
Cet été, nous allons **sur la Côte d'Azur**.	This summer we are going to the Côte d'Azur.
une **rive** [ʀiv]	shore, bank
sur la rive droite du fleuve	on the right bank of the river
un **rivage** [ʀivaʒ]	shore
une **plage** [plaʒ]	beach
le **sable** [sabl]	sand
rocheux, **rocheuse** [ʀɔʃø, øz]	rocky
La Bretagne a des côtes rocheuses.	Brittany has rocky coasts.
un **rocher** [ʀɔʃe]	rock
une **île** [il]	island
une **baie** [bɛ]	bay
un **golfe** [gɔlf]	gulf
une **presqu'île** [pʀɛskil]	peninsula
une **falaise** [falɛz]	cliff
une **dune** [dyn]	dune
le **littoral** [litɔʀal]	shoreline
Les complexes hôteliers défigurent le littoral.	The hotel complexes mar the shoreline.

18.3 Climate, Weather  81

climatique [klimatik]	climatic
le **climat** [klima]	climate
le **climat méditerranéen**	Mediterranean climate
le **climat océanique**	ocean climate
le climat continental/tropical	continental/tropical climate
le **climat polaire**	polar climate
un **climat rude/(mal)sain**	harsh/unhealthy climate
une **zone** [zon]	zone
une **zone tempérée**	temperate zone
une **saison** [sɛzɔ̃]	season
la **saison des pluies**	rainy season

---

le **temps** [tɑ̃]	weather
la **météorologie** [meteɔʀɔlɔʒi]	meteorology, weather report
la **météo** *fam* [meteo]	weather report, meteorology
un, une **météorologiste** [meteɔʀɔlɔʒist]	meteorologist
le **bulletin météo**(**rologique**) [byltɛ̃meteo(ɔʀɔlɔʒik)]	weather report, forecast
les **prévisions météo**(**rologiques**) *fpl* [pʀevizjɔ̃meteo(ɔʀɔlɔʒik)]	weather forecast
un **changement** [ʃɑ̃ʒmɑ̃]	change
variable [vaʀjabl]	variable
Le temps sera variable sur la moitié nord du pays.	The weather will be variable over the northern half of the country.
la **pression atmosphérique** [pʀesjɔ̃atmɔsfeʀik]	barometric pressure
La pression est en hausse/en baisse.	Pressure is rising/falling.
les **hautes/basses pressions**	high/low pressure
un **baromètre** [baʀɔmɛtʀ]	barometer
Le baromètre est descendu.	The barometer has fallen.

---

un **anticyclone** [ɑ̃tisiklon]	high (n)
une **dépression** [depʀɛsjɔ̃]	low (n)

la **température** [tɑ̃peʀatyʀ]	temperature
un **degré** [dəgʀe]	degree
20 degrés au-dessus/au-dessous de zéro	20 degrees above/below zero
plus [plys]	above
moins [mwɛ̃]	below
Il fait plus/moins 15.	It is 15 above/below.
à l'ombre [alɔ̃bʀ]	in the shade
Il fait 35 degrés à l'ombre.	It is 35 degrees in the shade.
un **thermomètre** [tɛʀmɔmɛtʀ]	thermometer
baisser [bese]	to go down, decrease
La température a **baissé de 15 degrés** depuis hier.	The temperature has gone down 15 degrees since yesterday.
monter* [mɔ̃te]	to rise, go up, increase
moyen, **moyenne** [mwajɛ̃, ɛn]	average (adj)
À Paris, au mois d'août, la température moyenne est de 18,7 degrés.	In Paris in August, the average temperature is 18.7 degrees.
la **moyenne annuelle** [mwajɛnanɥɛl]	the yearly average
Il fait beau. [ilfɛbo]	The weather is nice.
Il fait bon. [ilfɛbɔ̃]	The weather is pleasant.
Il fait chaud. [ilfɛʃo]	It is hot (out).
la **chaleur** [ʃalœʀ]	heat
une vague de chaleur	heat wave
froid, **froide** [fʀwa, də]	cold (adj)
le **froid**	cold
Il fait froid.	It is cold (out).
tiède [tjɛd]	mild, warm
doux, **douce** [du, dus]	mild
frais, **fraîche** [fʀɛ, fʀɛʃ]	fresh, cool
Les nuits sont fraîches.	The nights are cool.
la **fraîcheur** [fʀɛʃœʀ]	coolness, chill (n)

le **ciel** [sjɛl]	sky
le **soleil** [sɔlɛj]	sun
Il fait soleil.	It is sunny.
Le soleil brille.	The sun is shining.
Le soleil tape.	The sun is beating down.
Le soleil se lève/se couche.	The sun rises/sets.
le **lever/coucher de/du soleil**	sunrise/sunset
un **rayon de soleil**	sunbeam
sec, **sèche** [sɛk, sɛʃ]	dry
un été très sec	a very dry summer
agréable [agʀeabl]	pleasant

la **canicule** [kanikyl]	dog-days, sweltering heat
s'éclaircir [seklɛʀsiʀ]	to lighten, clear
Le ciel s'éclaircit.	The sky is clearing.
une **éclaircie** [eklɛʀsi]	clearing (n)
s'améliorer [sameljɔʀe]	to improve
une **amélioration** [ameljɔʀasjɔ̃]	improvement
Une amélioration arrive par l'ouest.	Improvement is coming from the west.

pleuvoir [pløvwaʀ]	to rain
Il pleut.	It is raining.
la **pluie** [plɥi]	rain (n)
La pluie tombe sans arrêt.	The rain falls without stop.
une **goutte** [gut]	drop (n)
nuageux, **nuageuse** [nɥaʒø, øz]	cloudy
Le ciel est très nuageux.	The sky is very cloudy.
un **nuage** [nɥaʒ]	cloud
Il fait mauvais. [ilfɛmovɛ]	The weather is bad.
Il fait lourd. [ilfɛluʀ]	The weather is sultry/muggy/oppressive.
orageux, **orageuse** [ɔʀaʒø, øz]	stormy
un **orage** [ɔʀaʒ]	storm
Il y a de l'orage dans l'air.	There is a storm in the air.
le **tonnerre** [tɔnɛʀ]	thunder
Le tonnerre gronde au loin.	Thunder rumbles in the distance.
un **éclair** [eklɛʀ]	flash of lightning
la **foudre** [fudʀ]	bolt of lightning
La foudre est tombée sur sa maison.	Lightning struck the house.
humide [ymid]	damp, humid
l'**humidité** *f* [ymidite]	humidity, dampness
le **brouillard** [bʀujaʀ]	fog
un brouillard à couper au couteau *loc*	fog as thick as pea soup

se couvrir [s(ə)kuvʀiʀ]	to cloud over
Le ciel se couvre rapidement.	The sky clouds over quickly.
couvert, **couverte** [kuvɛʀ, ɛʀt]	cloudy
maussade [mosad]	bleak, dismal
Il fait un temps maussade.	The weather is dismal.
pluvieux, **pluvieuse** [plyvjø, øz]	rainy
un automne pluvieux	a rainy fall
(**Il fait**) **un temps de chien** *fam* [(ilfɛ)ɛ̃tɑ̃d(ə)ʃjɛ̃]	The weather is rotten.
une **perturbation** [pɛʀtyʀbasjɔ̃]	disturbance
une **averse** [avɛʀs]	downpour
Le soleil arrive à percer entre deux averses.	The sun breaks through between two downpours.
pleuvoir à verse [pløvwaʀavɛʀs]	to rain buckets
Ne sors pas sans ton parapluie, il pleut à verse.	Don't go out without your umbrella; it is raining buckets.
des **précipitations** *fpl* [pʀesipitasjɔ̃]	precipitation
être trempé, **trempée** [tʀɑ̃pe]	to be soaked
Je **suis trempé jusqu'aux os**.	I am soaked to the bone.
la **brume** [bʀym]	mist
un **arc-en-ciel**; des **arcs-en-ciel** *pl* [aʀkɑ̃sjɛl]	rainbow

le **vent** [vɑ̃]	wind
un **vent glacial**	icy wind
Le vent souffle fort.	The wind is blowing hard.
Il fait du vent.	It is windy.
La direction du vent a changé.	The wind direction has changed.
une **tempête** [tɑ̃pɛt]	storm
La tempête s'est calmée.	The storm has abated.

une **brise** [bʀiz]	breeze
une brise légère	light breeze
un **courant d'air** [kuʀɑ̃dɛʀ]	draft
une **rafale** [ʀafal]	gust
une rafale violente	violent gust

neiger [neʒe]	to snow
la **neige** [nɛʒ]	snow (n)
un **flocon de neige**	snowflake
La neige tombe à gros flocons.	Snow is falling in big flakes.
la **glace** [glas]	ice
geler [ʒ(ə)le]	to freeze
Il gèlera au-dessus de 400 m.	It will freeze above 400 meters.
le **gel** [ʒɛl]	frost
le **verglas** [vɛʀgla]	black ice
déraper sur une plaque de verglas	to slide on a sheet of black ice

la **gelée** [ʒ(ə)le]	frost, freeze
Les **gelées tardives** ont abîmé les fleurs.	The late frosts ruined the flowers.
un **froid de canard** *fam* [fʀwadkanaʀ]	bitter cold
le **givre** [ʒivʀ]	frost
la **grêle** [gʀɛl]	hail (n)
le **dégel** [deʒɛl]	thaw (n)

18.4 Matter, Substances

 82

une **matière** [matjɛʀ]	substance
un **matériau**; des **matériaux** *pl* [mateʀjo]	material
solide [sɔlid]	solid (adj)
un **solide**	solid (n)
liquide [likid]	liquid (adj)
un **liquide**	fluid, liquid (n)
Au-dessous de 0 degré, l'eau passe de l'état liquide à l'état solide.	At zero degrees water changes from a liquid to a solid state.
gazeux, **gazeuse** [gazø, øz]	gaseous
de l'**eau gazeuse**	carbonated water
un **gaz** [gaz]	gas
des **gaz toxiques**	toxic gases
se composer de [s(ə)kɔ̃poze]	to be composed of
L'air se compose de plusieurs gaz.	Air is composed of several gases.
contenir [kɔ̃t(ə)niʀ]	to contain

INFO

Matière – matériel – matériau

la matière	*matter, substance*
un pays riche en matières premières	*a country rich in raw materials*
le matériau	*material*
les matériaux de construction	*construction materials*
le matériel	*equipment*
le matériel de camping	*camping gear/equipment*

un **élément** [elemɑ̃]	element
un **atome** [atom]	atom
une **molécule** [mɔlekyl]	molecule
une **substance** (**in**)**organique** [sypstɑ̃s(in)ɔʀganik]	(in)organic substance
l'**oxygène** *m* [ɔksiʒɛn]	oxygen
une **bouteille d'oxygène**	bottle of oxygen
l'**hydrogène** *m* [idʀɔʒɛn]	hydrogen
le **carbone** [kaʀbɔn]	carbon
l'**azote** *m* [azɔt]	nitrogen

fragile [fʀaʒil]	fragile
fin, **fine** [fɛ̃, fin]	fine, delicate
épais, **épaisse** [epɛ, epɛs]	thick

soluble [sɔlybl]	soluble
Le sel est soluble dans l'eau.	Salt is water soluble.
inflammable [ɛ̃flamabl]	flammable

la **pierre** [pjɛʀ]	stone (n)
une maison **en pierre**	stone house
une **pierre précieuse**	precious stone
minéral, **minérale** [mineʀal]	mineral
la **chimie minérale**	inorganic chemistry
le **sable** [sabl]	sand
le **ciment** [simɑ̃]	cement
le **béton** [betɔ̃]	concrete
une **construction en béton armé**	reinforced concrete construction
le **verre** [vɛʀ]	glass
du verre opaque/transparent	opaque/clear glass

l'**ardoise** *f* [aʀdwaz]	slate
un **toit en ardoise**	slate roof
le **grès** [gʀɛ]	sandstone
le **granit** [gʀanit]	granite
la **craie** [kʀɛ]	chalk
le **plâtre** [plɑtʀ]	plaster
l'**argile** *f* [aʀʒil]	clay
modeler un buste **en argile**	to sculpt a bust in clay
la **porcelaine** [pɔʀsəlɛn]	porcelain
un service **en porcelaine** de Sèvres	Sèvres porcelain service
la **céramique** [seʀamik]	ceramic
le **cristal** [kʀistal]	crystal

métallique [metalik]	metallic
le **métal** [metal]	metal
le **fer** [fɛʀ]	iron
l'**acier** *m* [asje]	steel
l'**or** *m* [ɔʀ]	gold
avoir une **chaîne en or**	to have a gold chain
l'**argent** *m* [aʀʒɑ̃]	silver
un **bijou en argent**	silver jewelry

un **minerai** [minʀɛ]	ore
l'exploitation du **minerai de fer**	iron ore extraction
le **cuivre** [kɥivʀ]	copper
l'**étain** *m* [etɛ̃]	tin
le **bronze** [bʀɔ̃z]	bronze
le **zinc** [zɛ̃g]	zinc
le **plomb** [plɔ̃]	lead
avoir un sommeil de plomb *loc*	to sleep like a log
le **laiton** [lɛtɔ̃]	brass
un **alliage** [aljaʒ]	alloy
la **tôle** [tol]	sheet metal
la **tôle ondulée**	corrugated sheet metal
fondre [fɔ̃dʀ]	to melt
La glace fond au-dessus de 0 degré.	Ice melts above zero degrees.
souder [sude]	to weld, solder, braze

le **coton** [kɔtɔ̃]	cotton
un t(ee)-shirt **100 % coton**	100% cotton T-shirt
la **soie** [swa]	silk
le **cuir** [kɥiʀ]	leather
la **laine** [lɛn]	wool

la **fibre** [fibʀ]	fiber
une **fibre naturelle/synthétique**	natural/synthetic fiber
une **microfibre** [mikʀofibʀ]	microfiber
filer [file]	to spin
le **lin** [lɛ̃]	linen

le **bois** [bwa]	wood
le **papier** [papje]	paper
le **carton** [kaʀtɔ̃]	cardboard
ranger qc dans une **boîte en carton**	to store s.th. in a cardboard box

chimique [ʃimik]	chemical
un **produit chimique**	chemical product
la **chimie** [ʃimi]	chemistry
le **pétrole** [petʀɔl]	petroleum
un **produit pétrolier** [pʀɔdɥipetʀɔlje]	petroleum product
l'**essence** *f* [esɑ̃s]	gasoline
le **plastique** [plastik]	plastic
une **bouteille en plastique**	plastic bottle
la **colle** [kɔl]	glue, paste

le **carburant** [kaʀbyʀɑ̃]	fuel
être en panne de carburant	to be out of fuel
la **pétrochimie** [petʀoʃimi]	petroleum chemistry
un **pipeline** [piplin/pajplajn]	pipeline
un **oléoduc** [ɔleɔdyk]	petroleum pipeline
le **mazout** [mazut]	heating oil
faire remplir la **cuve à mazout**	to have the oil tank filled
le **goudron** [gudʀɔ̃]	tar
le **polystyrène** [pɔlistiʀɛn]	polystyrene, styrofoam

18.5 Plants and Garden  83

végétal, **végétale** [veʒetal]	plant (adj)
une **graisse végétale**	vegetable fat
un **végétal**; des **végétaux** *pl* [veʒetal, o]	plant (n)
la **végétation** [veʒetasjɔ̃]	vegetation
une **végétation luxuriante**	lush vegetation
planter [plɑ̃te]	to plant
une **plante** [plɑ̃t]	plant (n)
une **plantation** [plɑ̃tasjɔ̃]	planting (n)
l'**herbe** *f* [ɛʀb]	grass
la **mauvaise herbe**	weed
pousser [puse]	to grow
jardiner [ʒaʀdine]	to (work in the) garden
un **jardin** [ʒaʀdɛ̃]	garden (n)
un (**jardin**) **potager**	vegetable garden
un **jardinier**, une **jardinière** [ʒaʀdinje, jɛʀ]	gardener
entretenir [ɑ̃tʀət(ə)niʀ]	to maintain, take care of
récolter [ʀekɔlte]	to harvest
la **récolte** [ʀekɔlt]	harvest (n)

la **flore** [flɔʀ]	flora, plant world
une **racine** [ʀasin]	root
prendre racine	to take root
une **tige** [tiʒ]	stalk, stem
un **bourgeon** [buʀʒɔ̃]	bud (n)
semer [səme]	to sow
une **graine** [gʀɛn]	seed (n)
irriguer [iʀige]	to water
l'**irrigation** *f* [iʀigasjɔ̃]	watering, irrigation
l'**arrosage** *m* [aʀozaʒ]	watering (n)
L'arrosage des jardins est interdit en période de grande sécheresse.	It is forbidden to water gardens during very dry spells.
un **arrosoir** [aʀozwaʀ]	watering can

un **arbre** [aʀbʀ]	tree
un **arbre fruitier**	fruit tree
une **branche** [bʀɑ̃ʃ]	branch
une **feuille** [fœj]	leaf
Le sol est couvert de **feuilles mortes**.	The ground is covered with dead leaves.
un **buisson** [bɥisɔ̃]	bush

un **tronc** [tʀɔ̃]	trunk
le **feuillage** [fœjaʒ]	foliage, leaves
un **arbre à feuillage persistant**	evergreen tree
une **haie** ['ɛ]	hedge
Le jardin est entouré d'une haie.	The yard is surrounded by a hedge.
un **arbuste** [aʀbyst]	bush
un **chêne** [ʃɛn]	oak
un meuble **en chêne massif**	furniture made of solid oak
un **bouleau**; des **bouleaux** *pl* [bulo]	birch
un **hêtre** ['ɛtʀ]	beech
un **orme** [ɔʀm]	elm
un **peuplier** [pøplije]	poplar, cottonwood
un **saule** [sol]	willow
un **pin** [pɛ̃]	pine
une **pomme de pin**	pinecone
un **sapin** [sapɛ̃]	fir
décorer le **sapin de Noël**	to decorate the Christmas tree
un **platane** [platan]	plane (tree)
une allée **bordée de platanes**	boulevard lined with plane trees
un **tilleul** [tijœl]	linden
un **palmier** [palmje]	palm tree

un **fruit** [fʀɥi]	fruit
un **fruit mûr/vert**	ripe/unripe fruit
les **fruits**	fruits
une **pomme** [pɔm]	apple
une **tarte aux pommes**	apple pie
une **poire** [pwaʀ]	pear
une **prune** [pʀyn]	plum
une **cerise** [s(ə)ʀiz]	cherry
une **pêche** [pɛʃ]	peach
avoir la pêche *fam*	to feel great
un **abricot** [abʀiko]	apricot
la **confiture d'abricots**	apricot jam
une **fraise** [fʀɛz]	strawberry
le **raisin** [ʀɛzɛ̃]	grape
une **grappe de raisins**	bunch of grapes
une **olive** [ɔliv]	olive

un **verger** [vɛʀʒe]	orchard
un **pommier** [pɔmje]	apple tree
un **poirier** [pwaʀje]	pear tree
faire le poirier	to do a headstand
un **noisetier** [nwaz(ə)tje]	hazelnut bush
un **noyer** [nwaje]	walnut tree
un **pêcher** [pɛʃe]	peach tree
un **cerisier** [s(ə)ʀizje]	cherry tree
un **prunier** [pʀynje]	plum tree
un **olivier** [ɔlivje]	olive tree
un **cassis** [kasis]	black currant bush
la **liqueur**/la **crème de cassis**	cassis, black currant liqueur
une **groseille** [gʀɔzɛj]	currant
la **gelée de groseilles**	currant jelly
une **mûre** [myʀ]	blackberry
une **ronce** [ʀɔ̃s]	bramble bush

fleurir [flœʀiʀ]	to flower, bloom
une **fleur** [flœʀ]	flower (n)
un **arbre en fleurs**	tree in blossom
offrir un **bouquet de fleurs** à qn	to give s.o. a bouquet of flowers
se faner [s(ə)fane]	to wilt
une **rose** [ʀoz]	rose
une **tulipe** [tylip]	tulip

une **pâquerette** [pɑkʀɛt]	daisy
une **jonquille** [ʒɔ̃kij]	daffodil
une **violette** [vjɔlɛt]	violet
le **lilas** [lila]	lilac
le **muguet** [mugɛ]	lily of the valley
le **coquelicot** [kɔkliko]	poppy
une **marguerite** [maʀgəʀit]	marguerite, daisy
effeuiller la marguerite	to pluck daisy petals (she loves me, she loves me not...)
un **tournesol** [tuʀnəsɔl]	sunflower
la **bruyère** [bʀyjɛʀ]	heather
le **genêt** [ʒənɛ]	gorse
un **œillet** [œjɛ]	carnation
un **glaïeul** [glajœl]	gladiolus
un **lys** [lis]	lily
un **bouton** [butɔ̃]	bud
un **bouton de rose**	rosebud

le **légume** [legym]	**vegetable** *(See Information Box p. 99)*
une bonne **soupe de légumes**	a good vegetable soup
la **carotte** [kaʀɔt]	carrot
la **pomme de terre** [pɔmdətɛʀ]	potato
la **patate** *fam* [patat]	potato, spud
le **chou**; les **choux** *pl* [ʃu]	cabbage
la **tomate** [tɔmat]	tomato
le **champignon** [ʃɑ̃piɲɔ̃]	mushroom
Je ne suis pas sûr que ce champignon soit comestible.	I am not sure that this mushroom is edible.

une **courgette** [kuʀʒɛt]	zucchini
une **aubergine** [obɛʀʒin]	eggplant
un **artichaut** [aʀtiʃo]	artichoke
un **poivron** [pwavʀɔ̃]	(bell) pepper
un **concombre** [kɔ̃kɔ̃bʀ]	cucumber
une **salade** [salad]	salad
des **épinards** *mpl* [epinaʀ]	spinach
mettre du beurre dans les épinards *fam*	to earn some extra income

les **céréales** *fpl* [seReal]	grains
le **blé** [ble]	wheat
un **champ de blé**	wheat field
le **maïs** [mais]	corn
du **maïs transgénique**	genetically engineered corn
le **froment** [fRɔmɑ̃]	wheat
la **farine de froment**	wheat flour
l'**orge** *f* [ɔRʒ]	barley
le **seigle** [sɛgl]	rye
du **pain de seigle**	rye bread
l'**avoine** *f* [avwan]	oats
le **colza** [kɔlza]	raps, canola
la **betterave** [bɛtRav]	beet
la **betterave à sucre**	sugar beet

18.6 Animals, Animal Husbandry 

la **faune** [fon]	fauna
la faune et la flore des régions tropicales	the flora and fauna of the tropical regions
un **animal**; des **animaux** *pl* [animal, o]	animal
un **animal domestique**	house pet
utile [ytil]	useful
nuisible [nɥisibl]	harmful
Les rats sont des animaux nuisibles.	Rats are vermin.
une **bête** [bɛt]	animal, beast
une **bête sauvage**	wild animal
une **race** [Ras]	breed
un **chien de race**	purebred dog

mâle [mɑl]	male (adj)
le **mâle**	male (n)
une **girafe mâle**	male giraffe
femelle [fəmɛl]	female (adj)
la **femelle**	female (n)
La jument est la femelle du cheval.	A mare is a female horse.
un **mammifère** [mamifɛʀ]	mammal
un **carnivore** [kaʀnivɔʀ]	carnivore
un **herbivore** [ɛʀbivɔʀ]	herbivore
une **espèce** [ɛspɛs]	species
une **espèce protégée**	protected species
une espèce **en voie de disparition**	endangered species
apprivoiser [apʀivwaze]	to tame
dresser [dʀɛse]	to train
dompter [dɔ̃(p)te]	to tame, subdue

un **cheval**; des **chevaux** *pl* [ʃ(ə)val, o]	horse
un **taureau**; des **taureaux** *pl* [tɔʀo]	bull
une **vache** [vaʃ]	cow
la **maladie de la vache folle** (**ESB**)	mad cow disease
un **bœuf**; des **bœufs** *pl* [bœf, bø]	steer
un **veau**; des **veaux** *pl* [vo]	calf
un **mouton** [mutɔ̃]	sheep
une **chèvre** [ʃɛvʀ]	goat
un **cochon** [kɔʃɔ̃]	pig
une **étable** [etabl]	barn
rentrer les vaches à l'étable	to put the cows back into the barn

INFO

Not for vegetarians!

un cochon	*pig*
C'est donner de la confiture aux cochons. *loc*	*That's casting pearls before swine.*
le porc	*pork*
une côtelette de porc	*pork chop*
Les musulmans ne mangent pas de porc.	*Muslims do not eat pork.*

un **étalon** [etalɔ̃]	stallion
une **jument** [ʒymɑ̃]	mare
un **poney** [pɔnɛ]	pony
un **âne**, une **ânesse** [an, anɛs]	donkey

une **écurie** [ekyʀi]	stable
un **troupeau**; des **troupeaux** *pl* [tʀupo]	herd, flock
Le chien de berger rassemble le troupeau de moutons.	The sheepdog herds the flock of sheep together.
une **brebis** [bʀəbi]	ewe
un **agneau**, une **agnelle**; **des agneaux** *pl* [aɲo, aɲɛl]	lamb

la **volaille** [vɔlaj]	poultry
un **coq** [kɔk]	rooster
Le coq chante *cocorico*.	The rooster sings *cock-a-doodle-doo!*
une **poule** [pul]	hen
avoir la chair de poule	to have goose bumps
un **poussin** [pusɛ̃]	chick
un **canard** [kanaʀ]	duck

la **basse-cour** [baskuʀ]	small animals, chicken yard
une **oie** [wa]	goose
une **dinde** [dɛ̃d]	turkey
un **cygne** [siɲ]	swan

un **chien**, une **chienne** [ʃjɛ̃, ʃjɛn]	dog
Attention, **chien méchant**.	Beware of Dog.
un **temps de chien**	miserable weather
aboyer [abwaje]	to bark
mordre [mɔʀdʀ]	to bite
une **niche** [niʃ]	doghouse
un **chat**, une **chatte** [ʃa, ʃat]	cat
avoir un chat dans la gorge *loc*	to have a frog in one's throat

la **queue** [kø]	tail
la **gueule** [gœl]	mouth, jaws
se jeter dans la gueule du loup *loc*	to venture into the lion's den
une **patte** [pat]	paw, leg

INFO

Jambe – patte

la jambe	*(human) leg*
la patte L'homme a deux jambes est le chein a quatre pattes.	*(animal) leg, paw* *Humans have two legs and dogs have four paws.*

une **souris** [suʀi]	mouse
un **rat** [ʀa]	rat
un **hamster** ['amstɛʀ]	hamster
un **cochon d'Inde** [kɔʃɔ̃dɛ̃d]	guinea pig
un **lapin** [lapɛ̃]	rabbit
un **oiseau**; des **oiseaux** *pl* [wazo]	bird
un **drôle d'oiseau** *fam*	an odd bird, peculiar fellow
l'**aile** *f* [ɛl]	wing
le **bec** [bɛk]	beak
un **nid** [ni]	nest
faire son nid	to nest
un **œuf**; des **œufs** *pl* [œf, ø]	egg
pondre un œuf	to lay an egg
une **cage** [kaʒ]	cage
un **perroquet** [peʀɔkɛ]	parrot
un **pigeon** [piʒɔ̃]	pigeon
une **cigogne** [sigɔɲ]	stork
La cigogne est un oiseau migrateur.	The stork is a migratory bird.
un **aigle** [ɛgl]	eagle
un **moineau**; des **moineaux** *pl* [mwano]	sparrow
une **mésange** [mezɑ̃ʒ]	chickadee
un **merle** [mɛʀl]	blackbird
une **hirondelle** [iʀɔ̃dɛl]	swallow
Une hirondelle ne fait pas le printemps. *prov*	One swallow does not make spring.
une **alouette** [alwɛt]	lark
un **rossignol** [ʀɔsiɲɔl]	nightingale
un **poisson** [pwasɔ̃]	fish
un **poisson de mer**	ocean fish
un **poisson d'eau douce**	freshwater fish
un **poisson rouge**	goldfish
un **aquarium** [akwaʀjɔm]	aquarium
une **truite** [tʀɥit]	trout
un **hareng** ['aʀɑ̃]	herring
un **requin** [ʀəkɛ̃]	shark
une **baleine** [balɛn]	whale
un **dauphin** [dofɛ̃]	dolphin
un **serpent** [sɛʀpɑ̃]	snake
un **serpent venimeux**	poisonous snake
un **crocodile** [kʀɔkɔdil]	crocodile
des **larmes de crocodile**	crocodile tears

un **reptile** [Rɛptil]	reptile
ramper [Rɑ̃pe]	to crawl
un **lézard** [lezaR]	lizard
une **vipère** [vipɛR]	viper
une **tortue** [tɔRty]	turtle/tortoise
une **grenouille** [gRənuj]	frog
un **lion**, une **lionne** [ljɔ̃, ljɔn]	lion, lioness
la **part du lion**	lion's share
un **tigre**, une **tigresse** [tigR, tigRɛs]	tiger, tigress
un **loup**, une **louve** [lu, luv]	wolf
avoir une faim de loup *loc*	to be hungry as a bear
un **singe** [sɛ̃ʒ]	ape, monkey
un **fauve** [fov]	wild animal
un **ours**; des **ours** *pl* [uRs]	bear
un **renard** [R(ə)naR]	fox
rusé comme un renard *loc*	sly as a fox
un **prédateur** [pRedatœR]	predator
une **proie** [pRwa]	prey
Le faucon s'est jeté sur sa proie.	The hawk pounced on its prey.
le **gibier** [ʒibje]	game
une **trace** [tRas]	trail (n)
chasser [ʃase]	to hunt
la **chasse** [ʃas]	hunting
aller* à la **chasse au gros gibier**	to go big-game hunting
un **insecte** [ɛ̃sɛkt]	insect
une **larve** [laRv]	larva
une **mouche** [muʃ]	fly
Quelle mouche t'a piqué? *fam*	What's eating you?
une **guêpe** [gɛp]	wasp
avoir une **taille de guêpe**	to have a wasp waist
un **moustique** [mustik]	mosquito
un **papillon** [papijɔ̃]	butterfly
une **coccinelle** [kɔksinɛl]	ladybug
une **fourmi** [fuRmi]	ant
avoir des fourmis dans les jambes	to have pins and needles in one's legs
une **abeille** [abɛj]	bee
l'**apiculture** *f* [apikyltyR]	apiculture
un **apiculteur**, une **apicultrice** [apikyltœR, tRis]	beekeeper

18.7 Ecology, Environmental Protection, and Disasters  85

écologique [ekɔlɔʒik]	ecological
l'**écologie** *f* [ekɔlɔʒi]	ecology; environmental protection
un, une **écologiste** [ekɔlɔʒist]	ecologist
s'engager [sɑ̃gaʒe]	to participate/be involved in
s'engager dans le mouvement écologiste	to be involved in the ecology movement
l'**engagement** *m* [ɛ̃gaʒmɑ̃]	commitment
agir [aʒiʀ]	to act
agir avec conviction	to act with conviction
une **action** [aksjɔ̃]	action
la **nature** [natyʀ]	nature
l'**environnement** *m* [ɑ̃viʀɔnmɑ̃]	environment
protéger l'environnement	to protect the environment
la **protection de l'environnement**	environmental protection

un **site** [sit]	site, location
préserver [pʀezɛʀve]	to preserve
préserver les sites naturels	to preserve natural monuments
sauvage [sovaʒ]	wild
désert, **déserte** [dezɛʀ, ɛt]	deserted, unpopulated
la **biosphère** [bjɔsfɛʀ]	biosphere

l'**air** *m* [ɛʀ]	air
l'**air pur/pollué**	clean/polluted air
l'**eau** *f*; les **eaux** *fpl* [o]	water
l'**eau potable**	potable water
Eau non potable!	Non-potable water!
propre [pʀɔpʀ]	clean *(See Information Box p. 44)*
polluer [pɔlɥe]	to pollute
Les produits chimiques polluent les rivières.	Chemical products pollute the rivers.
polluant, **polluante** [pɔlɥɑ̃, ɑ̃t]	polluting (adj)
un **polluant**	contaminant, pollutant
non-polluant, **non-polluante** [nɔ̃pɔlɥɑ̃, ɑ̃t]	non-polluting, environmentally-friendly
dégager un gaz polluant/non-polluant	to release a polluting/non-polluting gas
la **pollution** [pɔlysjɔ̃]	pollution
un **pic de pollution**	spike in pollution
un **pollueur**, une **pollueuse** [pɔlyœʀ, øz]	polluter

la **nappe phréatique** [napfʀeatik]	water table
une **station d'épuration** [stasjɔ̃depyʀasjɔ̃]	water purification plant
les **égoûts** *mpl* [egu]	wastewater/sewer system
les **eaux usées** *fpl* [oyze]	sewage

dangereux, **dangereuse** [dɑ̃ʒʀø, øz]	dangerous
un **danger** [dɑ̃ʒe]	danger
Attention, **danger de mort!**	Warning: Mortal Danger!
menacer [mənase]	to threaten
une **menace** [mənas]	threat
La pollution des eaux représente une menace sérieuse.	Water pollution is a serious threat.
détruire [detʀɥiʀ]	to destroy
la **destruction** [destʀyksjɔ̃]	destruction
l'**écosystème** *m* [ekosistɛm]	ecosystem
la **disparition** [dispaʀisjɔ̃]	disappearance, extinction
contaminé, **contaminée** [kɔ̃tamine]	polluted/contaminated
la **contamination** [kɔ̃taminasjɔ̃]	pollution/contamination

émettre [emɛtʀ]	to emit
l'**émission** *f* [emisjɔ̃]	emission
l'émission d'oxyde/de dioxyde de soufre/de gaz carbonique	oxide/sulfur dioxide/carbon dioxide emission
les **particules fines** *fpl* [paʀtikylfin]	fine particulates
un **produit toxique** [pʀɔdɥitɔksik]	toxic substance
nocif, **nocive** [nɔsif, iv]	harmful, toxic
la **nuisance** [nɥizɑ̃s]	(environmental) stress
se dégrader [s(ə)degʀade]	to degrade, damage
la **dégradation** [degʀadasjɔ̃]	damage, degradation
la **dégradation de l'environnement**	environmental damage
se détériorer [s(ə)deteʀjɔʀe]	to deteriorate
la **détérioration** [deteʀjɔʀasjɔ̃]	deterioration
les **dégâts** *mpl* [dgga]	damage
causer des dégâts importants	to cause major damage
la **marée noire** [maʀenwaʀ]	oil spill

les **gaz d'échappement** *mpl* [gazdeʃapmɑ̃]	exhaust fumes
le **gaz carbonique** [gɑzkaʀbɔnik]	carbon dioxide
le **smog** [smɔg]	smog
les **pluies acides** *fpl* [plɥiasid]	acid rain
la **mort des forêts** [mɔʀdefɔʀɛ]	forest dieback

déboiser [debwaze]	to deforest
le **déboisement** [debwazmɑ̃]	deforestation
aménager [amenaʒe]	to develop
l'**aménagement** *m* [amenaʒmɑ̃]	development
l'**aménagement du territoire**	land-use planning
l'**assainissement** *m* [asɛnismɑ̃]	draining, cleanup
reboiser [ʀ(ə)bwaze]	to reforest
le **reboisement** [ʀ(ə)bwazmɑ̃]	reforestation
renaturer [ʀ(ə)natyʀe]	to restore
un **CFC** (**chlorofluorocarbone**) [seɛfse]	CFC
une **bombe aérosol** [bɔ̃baeʀɔsɔl]	aerosol can
la **couche d'ozone** [kuʃdozon/dɔzɔn]	ozone layer
le **trou dans la couche d'ozone**	hole in the ozone layer
l'**effet de serre** *m* [efɛd(ə)sɛʀ]	greenhouse effect
le **réchauffement de l'atmosphère** [ʀeʃofmɑ̃d(ə)latmɔsfɛʀ]	atmospheric, global warming
le **changement du climat** [ʃɑ̃ʒmɑ̃dyklima]	climate change
le **changement climatique** [ʃɑ̃ʒmɑ̃klimatik]	climate change
les **métaux lourds** *mpl* [metoluʀ]	heavy metals
un sol contaminé par des métaux lourds	soil contaminated with heavy metals
un **détergent** *m* [detɛʀʒɑ̃]	detergent
l'**engrais** *m* [ɑ̃gʀɛ]	fertilizer
un **insecticide** [ɛ̃sɛktisid]	insecticide
un **pesticide** [pɛstisid]	pesticide
les **nitrates** *mpl* [nitʀat]	nitrates
bruyant, **bruyante** [bʀyjɑ̃, ɑ̃t]	loud, noisy
Le moteur de la moto est trop bruyant.	The motorcycle's engine is too loud.
le **bruit** [bʀɥi]	noise
calme [kalm]	quiet, calm (adj)
le **calme**	quiet, calm (n)
silencieux, **silencieuse** [silɑ̃sjø, øz]	silent
le **silence** [silɑ̃s]	silence
biologique [bjɔlɔʒik]	biological
l'**agriculture biologique**	organic farming
bio [bjo]	organic
les **aliments bio**	organic foods
les **hormones** *fpl* [ɔʀmɔn]	hormones
la **viande aux hormones**	hormone-treated meat

l'**élevage en batterie** [el(ə)vaʒɑ̃batʀi]	battery/cage farming
les **OGM** *mpl* **(organismes génétiquement modifiés)** [oʒeɛm]	GMOs (genetically modified organisms)
un **écolabel** [ekɔlabɛl]	eco-label
le **développement durable** [devlɔpmɑ̃dyʀabl]	sustainable development
la **durabilité** [dyʀabilite]	sustainability

les **ordures** *fpl* [ɔʀdyʀ]	trash, waste, garbage
les **ordures ménagères**	household waste
trier [tʀije]	to sort
le **tri** [tʀi]	sorting
le **tri des ordures**	trash sorting
la **poubelle** [pubɛl]	trash can, wastebasket
le **ramassage** [ʀamasaʒ]	pickup, collection
effectuer le ramassage des vieux papiers	to pick up scrap paper
la **décharge** [deʃaʀʒ]	landfill, dump
porter ses ordures à la décharge publique/municipale	to bring the trash to the public/municipal landfill

les **déchets** *mpl* [deʃɛ]	refuse, waste, junk, trash
éliminer les déchets	to dispose of the trash
une **usine de traitement des déchets**	waste treatment plant
les **déchets résiduels**	residual waste
les déchets spéciaux	hazardous waste
une **déchetterie** [deʃɛtʀi]	refuse processing center
les **détritus** *mpl* [detʀitys]	trash
la **collecte sélective** (**des déchets**) [kɔlɛktselɛktiv(dedeʃɛ)]	separate collection (of trash)
les **objets encombrants** *mpl* [ɔbʒɛɑ̃kʀɔ̃bɑ̃]	bulky trash
un **conteneur à verre/papier** (**usagé**) [kɔ̃tənœʀavɛʀ/papje(ɥzaʒe)]	(used) glass/paper container
récupérer [ʀekypeʀe]	to salvage
la **récupération** [ʀekypeʀasjɔ̃]	salvage (n)
le **compostage** [kɔ̃pɔstaʒ]	composting
l'**élimination** *f* [eliminasjɔ̃]	elimination
l'**incinération** *f* [ɛ̃sineʀasjɔ̃]	incineration
une **usine d'incinération des déchets**	trash incineration plant

une **bouteille consignée** [butɛjkɔ̃siɲe]	returnable bottle
une **bouteille non consignée** [betɛjnɔ̃kɔ̃siɲe]	non-returnable bottle
une **bouteille en** (**matière**) **plastique** [butɛjɑ̃(matjɛʀ)plastik]	plastic bottle
le **verre usagé** [vɛʀyzaʒe]	used glass
biodégradable [bjodegʀadabl]	biodegradable
un produit biodégradable	biodegradable product
recycler [ʀ(ə)sikle]	to recycle
du **papier recyclé**	recycled paper
recyclable [ʀ(ə)siklabl]	recyclable
un emballage recyclable	recyclable packaging
le **recyclage** [ʀ(ə)siklaʒ]	recycling (n)

une **centrale nucléaire** [sɑ̃tʀalnykleɛʀ]	nuclear power plant
un **réacteur** [ʀeaktœʀ]	reactor
radioactif, **radioactive** [ʀadjoaktif, iv]	radioactive
un nuage radioactif	radioactive cloud
la **radioactivité** [ʀadjoaktivite]	radioactivity
mesurer la radioactivité	to measure the radioactivity

l'**uranium** *m* [yʀanjɔm]	uranium
la **radiation** [ʀadjasjɔ̃]	radiation
être exposé à des radiations	to be exposed to radiation
l'**irradiation** *f* [iʀadjasjɔ̃]	irradiation
retraiter [ʀ(ə)tʀɛte]	to reprocess/recycle
Cette usine retraite des déchets radioactifs.	This plant reprocesses radioactive waste.
le **retraitement** [ʀ(ə)tʀɛtmɑ̃]	reprocessing
une **usine de retraitement**	reprocessing plant
le **stockage** [stɔkaʒ]	storage
le stockage définitif	permanent/final disposal

l'**énergie** *f* [enɛʀʒi]	energy
une **source d'énergie**	energy source
l'**énergie fossile**	fossil fuel
l'**énergie nucléaire**	nuclear power
l'**énergie solaire/éolienne**	solar/wind energy
l'**énergie géothermique**	geothermal energy
les **énergies douces/renouvelables**	alternate/renewable energy sources
La recherche se penche sur les énergies renouvelables.	Research deals with renewable energy sources.
électrique [elɛktʀik]	electric
le **courant électrique**	electrical current
l'**électricité** *f* [elɛktʀisite]	electricity

une **centrale hydroélectrique** [sɑ̃tʀlidʀoelɛkʀik]	hydroelectric power plant
le **charbon** [ʃaʀbɔ̃]	coal, carbon
le **gaz** [gaz]	gas
le **gaz naturel**	natural gas
le **pétrole** [petʀɔl]	petroleum

les **ressources naturelles** *fpl* [ʀ(ə)suʀsnatyʀɛl]	natural resources
gaspiller [gaspije]	to waste
Fais attention à ne pas gaspiller l'eau.	Be careful not to waste water.
le **gaspillage** [gaspijaʒ]	waste (n)
l'**écotaxe** *f* [ekotaks]	eco-tax
le **principe pollueur-payeur** [pʀɛ̃sippɔlɥœʀpɛyœʀ]	polluter-pays principle
un **capteur solaire** [kaptœʀsɔlɛʀ]	solar collector/panel
une **éolienne** [eɔljɛn]	wind turbine
la **bioénergie** [bjoenɛʀʒi]	biomass energy
la **biomasse** [bjomas]	biomass
le **biocarburant** [bjokaʀbyʀɑ̃]	biofuel

un **accident** [aksidɑ̃]	accident
catastrophique [katastʀɔfik]	catastrophic
une **catastrophe** [katastʀɔf]	catastrophe, disaster
une **catastrophe naturelle**	natural disaster
une **cata** *fam* [kata]	catastrophe
brûler [bʀyle]	to burn
un **incendie** [ɛ̃sɑ̃di]	fire (n)
un **incendie de forêt**	forest fire
le **feu** [fø]	fire (n)
prendre feu	to catch on fire, ignite
la **fumée** [fyme]	smoke (n)
Il n'y a pas de fumée sans feu. *prov*	Where there's smoke there's fire.
exploser [ɛksploze]	to explode
une **explosion** [ɛksplozjɔ̃]	explosion
inonder [inɔ̃de]	to overflow/inundate/flood
une **inondation** [inɔ̃dasjɔ̃]	overflow/flood (n)

désastreux, **désastreuse** [dezastʀø, øz]	disastrous
un **désastre** [dezastʀ]	disaster
imprévu, **imprévue** [ɛ̃pʀevy]	unforeseen, unexpected
imprévisible [ɛ̃pʀevizibl]	unforeseeable
avoir des répercussions imprévisibles sur la santé	to have unanticipated health repercussions
prévisible [pʀevizibl]	foreseeable
un **cataclysme** [kataklism]	cataclysm
une **tornade** [tɔʀnad]	tornado
un **ouragan** [uʀagɑ̃]	hurricane
une **avalanche** [avalɑ̃ʃ]	avalanche
Risque d'avalanches!	Avalanche Danger!
un **tremblement de terre** [tʀɑ̃bləmɑ̃d(ə)tɛʀ]	earthquake
un **tsunami** [tsunami]	tsunami
un **glissement de terrain** [glismɑ̃d(ə)tɛʀɛ̃]	landslide
une **éruption** (**volcanique**) [eʀypsjɔ̃(vɔlkanik)]	(volcanic) eruption
Le volcan est **entré en éruption**.	The volcano has begun to erupt.
une **coulée de lave** [kuled(ə)lav]	lava flow
la **sécheresse** [sɛʃ(ə)ʀɛs]	drought
une région **touchée par la sécheresse**	area affected by drought
sinistré, **sinistrée** [sinistʀe]	afflicted
déclarer une région zone sinistrée	to declare a disaster area
un **sinistre** [sinistʀ]	disaster, calamity

18.8 City, Country, Buildings, and Infrastructure  86

une **ville** [vil]	city
la **ville de** Toulouse	the city of Toulouse
une **ville de province**	country/provincial town
la **vieille ville**	old city
une **ville satellite**	commuter town
une **ville nouvelle**	new town
habiter [abite]	to live
habiter (**dans**) **une ville**	to live in a city
Ses parents **habitent** (**à**) **Lille**.	His/Her parents live in Lille.
un **habitant**, une **habitante** [abitɑ̃, ɑ̃t]	inhabitant
une **capitale** [kapital]	capital (n)
un **citadin**, une **citadine** [sitadɛ̃, in]	urbanite, city dweller

un **village** [vilaʒ]	village
un **villageois**, une **villageoise** [vilaʒwa, waz]	villager
la **campagne** [kɑ̃paɲ]	country(side)
aller* s'installer à la campagne	to move to the country
un **campagnard**, une **campagnarde** [kɑ̃paɲaʀ, aʀd]	rural inhabitant

s'urbaniser [syʀbanize]	to become urbanized
Cette région s'est urbanisée rapidement.	This region has quickly become urbanized.
urbain, **urbaine** [yʀbɛ̃, ɛn]	urban
les **transports urbains**	urban transportation
l'**urbanisation** *f* [yʀbanizasjɔ̃]	urbanization
l'**urbanisme** *m* [yʀbanism]	city planning
se dépeupler [s(ə)depœple]	to become depopulated
l'**exode rural/urbain** *m* [ɛgzɔdʀyʀal/yʀbɛ̃]	rural/urban flight
les **ruraux** *mpl* [ʀyʀo]	rural residents
une **métropole** [metʀɔpɔl]	metropolis
une **agglomération** [aglɔmeʀasjɔ̃]	population center, agglomeration
L'agglomération lyonnaise comprend Lyon et sa banlieue.	The Lyon population center includes the city of Lyon and its suburbs.
une **cité** [site]	city
une **cité-dortoir**	bedroom community
un **hameau**; des **hameaux** *pl* ['amo]	hamlet, small town

central, **centrale** [sɑ̃tʀal]	central
habiter un quartier central	to live in a central neighborhood
le **centre** [sɑ̃tʀ]	center (n)
le **centre-ville**	city center, downtown
les **environs** *mpl* [ɑ̃viʀɔ̃]	surroundings, environs
la **banlieue** [bɑ̃ljø]	suburb
dans la **proche banlieue** d'une ville	in close proximity to a city
un **quartier** [kaʀtje]	neighborhood
un **quartier chic/populaire**	stylish/unpretentious neighborhood
un **quartier ouvrier/industriel**	working-class/industrial neighborhood

l'**espace** *m* [ɛspas]	space
un **terrain** [tɛʀɛ̃]	property, site, parcel
un **terrain à bâtir**	building site
s'étendre sur [setɑ̃dʀ]	to cover/extend over
La zone industrielle s'étend sur 3 kilomètres.	The industrial zone extends over three kilometers.

la **périphérie** [peʀifeʀi]	outskirts, city limits
un **quartier résidentiel** [kaʀtjeʀezidɑ̃sjɛl]	residential area
un **faubourg** [fobuʀ]	suburb
un **projet** [pʀɔʒɛ]	project (n)
un projet de modernisation	modernization project, plan
transformer [tʀɑ̃sfɔʀme]	to transform, revamp
une **transformation** [tʀɑ̃sfɔʀmasjɔ̃]	transformation, revamping
démolir [demɔliʀ]	to demolish
construire [kɔ̃stʀɥiʀ]	to build, construct
faire construire une maison	to have a house built
une **construction** [kɔ̃stʀyksjɔ̃]	structure, building
reconstruire [ʀ(ə)kɔ̃stʀɥiʀ]	to reconstruct
un **promoteur immobilier** [pʀɔmɔtœʀimɔbilje]	real estate developer
un **chantier** [ʃɑ̃tje]	worksite
Tout le quartier **est en chantier**.	The entire neighborhood is a construction site.
restaurer [ʀɛstɔʀe]	to restore
la **restauration** [ʀɛstɔʀasjɔ̃]	restoration
rénover [ʀenɔve]	to renovate
rénover un bâtiment vétuste	to renovate a dilapidated building
la **rénovation** [ʀenɔvasjɔ̃]	renovation
s'améliorer [sameljɔʀe]	to improve
une **amélioration** [ameljɔʀasjɔ̃]	improvement
se dégrader [s(ə)degʀade]	to become dilapidated, rundown
la **dégradation** [degʀadasjɔ̃]	deterioration, damage
un **bâtiment** [bɑtimɑ̃]	building (n)
un bâtiment ancien	old building
une **maison** [mɛzɔ̃]	house
une maison neuve	new house
une **villa** [vila]	villa
un **pavillon** [pavijɔ̃]	pavilion, club house
un **immeuble** [imœbl]	(apartment) building
une **tour** [tuʀ]	tower *(See Information Box p. 201)*
un/une **HLM** (une **habitation à loyer modéré**) [aʃɛlɛm]	subsidized, low-income housing

un **édifice** [edifis]	building (n)
une **résidence secondaire** [Rezidɑ̃ss(ə)gɔ̃dɛR]	second/vacation home
une **maison de campagne** [mɛzɔ̃dkɑ̃paɲ]	country home
un **pâté de maisons** [pɑtedmɛzɔ̃]	block of houses
faire le tour du pâté de maisons	to walk around the block
un **grand ensemble** [gRɑ̃tɑ̃sɑ̃bl]	housing development
un **taudis** [todi]	slum, hovel
délabré, **délabrée** [delabRe]	dilapidated
une maison complètement délabrée	totally dilapidated house

une **rue** [Ry]	street *(See Information Box p. 17)*
jouer dans la rue	to play in the street
une **rue commerçante**	commercial street
une rue animée	lively street
un **chemin** [ʃ(ə)mɛ̃]	road
une **voie** [vwa]	road, street
une **avenue** [av(ə)ny]	avenue
un **boulevard** [bulvaR]	boulevard
une **chaussée** [ʃose]	pavement, road surface
Attention, chaussée déformée!	Caution: Uneven Road!
un **trottoir** [tRɔtwaR]	sidewalk
un **carrefour** [kaRfuR]	intersection, crossroad
un **parking** [paRkiŋ]	parking lot
un **parking souterrain**	underground garage, parking

une **piste cyclable** [pist(ə)siklabl]	bike path
une **voie sans issue** [vwasɑ̃zisy]	dead-end (road)
une **voie piétonne** [vwapjetɔn]	walkway
une **zone piétonne** [zɔnpjetɔn]	pedestrian area
une **zone industrielle** (**ZI**) [zɔnɛ̃dystRiɛl(zɛdi)]	industrial area, zone

une **place** [plas]	square
une **cour** [kuR]	courtyard *(See Information Box p. 164)*
Mon appartement **donne sur la cour de** l'immeuble.	My apartment looks out over the building's courtyard.
un **pont** [pɔ̃]	bridge
un **pont suspendu**	suspension bridge

un **parc** [paRk]	park
le parc du château de Chantilly	Chantilly Chateau park
un **jardin public** [ʒaRdɛ̃pyblik]	public garden
un **square** [skwaR]	square

une **route** [ʀut]	road, route *(See Information Box p. 17)*
sur la route de Dijon	on the road to Dijon
Route barrée.	Road closed.
une (**route**) **nationale** (**RN**)	national route
une **autoroute** [ɔtɔ/otoʀut]	major highway
un **garage** [gaʀaʒ]	garage
une **station-service**; des **station-service(s)** *pl* [stasjɔ̃sɛʀvis]	gas, service station

un **échangeur** [eʃɑ̃ʒœʀ]	interchange
un (**boulevard**) **périphérique** [(bulvaʀ)peʀifeʀik]	beltway, highway loop *(around a city)*
le **périph** *fam* [peʀif]	beltway, highway loop
une **rocade** [ʀɔkad]	bypass (n)
desservir [desɛʀviʀ]	to serve, lead to
La rocade dessert la zone industrielle.	The bypass serves the industrial area.

un **magasin** [magazɛ̃]	shop, store (n)
un **grand magasin**	department store
un **supermarché** [sypɛʀmaʀʃe]	supermarket
un **hypermarché** [ipɛʀmaʀʃe]	superstore
une **grande surface** [gʀɑ̃dsyʀfas]	supermarket, hypermarket
un **centre commercial** [sɑ̃tʀ(ə)kɔmɛʀsjal]	shopping center
une **galerie marchande** [galʀimaʀʃɑ̃d]	mall
un **marché** [maʀʃe]	market
un **marché couvert**	market hall
les **halles** *fpl* ['al]	market halls

un **hôpital** [ɔpital]	hospital
un **C.H.U.** (**centre hospitalier universitaire**) [seaʃy]	university hospital
une **clinique** [klinik]	clinic
une clinique privée	private clinic
une **maison de retraite** [mɛzɔ̃dʀətʀɛt]	retirement home
un **cimetière** [simtjɛʀ]	cemetery

une **mairie** [mɛʀi]	town hall
un **hôtel de ville** [ɔ/otɛldəvil]	city hall *(in a larger center)*
la **poste** [pɔst]	post office
une **gare** [gaʀ]	railroad station
une **gare routière**	bus station
un **musée** [myze]	museum
visiter un musée	to visit a museum
un **théâtre** [teɑtʀ]	theater
un **centre culturel** [sɑ̃tʀ(ə)kyltyʀɛl]	cultural center
une **prison** [pʀizɔ̃]	prison
un **terrain de sport** [teʀɛ̃d(ə)spɔʀ]	athletic field
un **stade** [stad]	stadium
une **piscine** [pisin]	swimming pool
une **piscine couverte**	indoor swimming pool
un **gymnase** [ʒimnɑz]	gymnasium
une **salle de sport** [sald(ə)spɔʀ]	gymnasium, sports center
une **crèche** [kʀɛʃ]	daycare center
laisser son enfant à la crèche	to put one's child in daycare
un **jardin d'enfants** [ʒaʀdɛ̃dɑ̃fɑ̃]	kindergarten, preschool
une **école** [ekɔl]	school
un **collège** [kɔlɛʒ]	secondary school, (junior) high school
un **lycée** [lise]	secondary school, high school
une **université** [ynivɛʀsite]	university
un **monument (historique)** [mɔnymɑ̃(istɔʀik)]	(historic) monument
un **château**; des **châteaux** *pl* [ʃɑto]	castle
des **ruines** *fpl* [ʀɥin]	ruins
un château **en ruines**	castle ruins
une **église** [egliz]	church
une **cathédrale** [katedʀal]	cathedral
un **port** [pɔʀ]	port
un **port maritime/fluvial**	ocean/river port
un **port de plaisance**	marina
un **quai** [kɛ]	dock

False Friends

French Word	Actual Meaning	False Friend	Correct French Word
le carton	**cardboard**	carton	*la boîte*
l'essence	**gasoline**	essence	*l'essence, le substance*
le gel	**frost**	gel	*le colloïde*
le littoral	**coastline**	literal	*littéral*
un magasin	**store**	magazine	*une revue, un magazine*
la plantation	**planting (n)**	(cotton) plantation	*la cotonnerie*
sinistré	**devastated**	sinister	*mauvais, sinistre*

My Vocabulary

19

Time and Space

19.1 Days of the Week and Dates

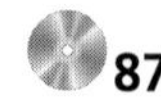 87

une **semaine** [s(ə)mɛn]	week
hebdomadaire [ɛbdɔmadɛʀ]	weekly
le **week-end**; les **week-ends** *pl* [wikɛnd]	weekend
quinze jours [kɛ̃zʒuʀ]	two weeks
une **quinzaine** (**de jours**) [kɛ̃zɛn (d(ə)ʒuʀ)]	about two weeks

INFO

The preposition *in* with time

When *in* refers to a *time period* in which an event happens, then *en* is used with a *noun group*.

But if *in* refers to a *future point in time*, then *dans* is used with a *noun group*.

Examples:

Elle a écrit ce livre en quinze jours.	*She wrote this book in (within) two weeks.*
Dans quinze jours, on sera en vacances.	*In two weeks we will be on vacation.*
Valérie viendra dans un mois.	*Valérie is coming in a month.*

les **jours de la semaine** *mpl* [ʒuʀd(ə)las(ə)mɛn]	days of the week
lundi [lœ̃di]	Monday
mardi [maʀdi]	Tuesday
mercredi [mɛʀkʀədi]	Wednesday
jeudi [ʒødi]	Thursday
vendredi [vɑ̃dʀədi]	Friday
samedi [samdi]	Saturday
dimanche [dimɑ̃ʃ]	Sunday

INFO

(Le) dimanche

Days of the week with no article designate a day of the *current, past, or coming* week:

dimanche prochain	*next Sunday*
dimanche dernier	*last Sunday*
Luc vient/viendra dimanche.	*Luc is coming on Sunday.*

The days of the week take *the definite article* when something happens *regularly*.

Le dimanche, je fais la grasse matinée.	*On Sundays I sleep in.*

le **jour** [ʒuʀ]	day
Le jour se lève.	Day is breaking.
la **journée** [ʒuʀne]	day *(duration)*
On n'a rien fait de **toute la journée**.	We have done nothing all day long.
quotidien, **quotidienne** [kɔtidjɛ̃, jɛn]	daily
un **quotidien**	daily newspaper
la **date** [dat]	date (n)
un **ami de longue date**	longtime friend

INFO

Asking and answering about the day of the week/date

Quel jour sommes-nous aujourd'hui?	*What day is it today?*
C'est quel jour aujourd'hui?	*What day is it today?*
(Aujourd'hui,) Nous sommes vendredi.	*Today is Friday.*
On est mercredi.	*It is Wednesday.*
C'est jeudi.	*It is Thursday.*
Nous sommes le combien?	*What is today's date?*
On est le combien aujourd'hui?	*What is today's date?*
Nous sommes le 1er avril/le 13 mai.	*Today is April first/May thirteenth.*
On est le 6 (mai).	*Today is the sixth (of May).*
Aujourd'hui, c'est le 13 (juin).	*Today is the thirteenth (of June).*

aujourd'hui [oʒuʀdɥi]	today
demain [d(ə)mɛ̃]	tomorrow
après-demain	day after tomorrow
À partir de demain, je me mets au régime.	I am going on a diet starting tomorrow.
hier [jɛʀ]	yesterday
avant-hier	day before yesterday
Je m'en souviens **comme si c'était hier**.	I remember it as if it were yesterday.

le **lendemain** [lɑ̃dmɛ̃]	the following day, day after
Il est reparti le lendemain de son arrivée.	He left the day after he arrived.
le **surlendemain**	two days later
la **veille** [vɛj]	the day before
la **veille au soir**	the evening before
l'**avant-veille**	two evenings before
en huit [ɑ̃ɥit]	in a week
Je serai de retour **lundi en huit**.	I will be back a week from Monday.
d'ici le/la... [disilə/la]	from now until...
Nous ne la verrons pas **d'ici la semaine prochaine**.	We won't see her until next week.

19.2 Telling Time  88

le **temps** [tɑ̃]	time
Le temps passe vite.	Time flies.
l'**heure** *f* [œʀ]	hour, time *(See Information Box p. 405)*
demander l'heure à qn	to ask s.o. for the time
un **quart d'heure**	quarter of an hour
une **demi-/demie heure**	half-hour
la **minute** [minyt]	minute
J'en ai pour une minute.	I need just a minute.
la **seconde** [s(ə)gɔ̃d]	second (n)

l'**heure d'été** *f* [œʀdete]	daylight saving time
mettre sa montre à l'heure d'été	to set one's watch to daylight saving time
l'**heure d'hiver** *f* [œʀdivɛʀ]	standard time
Demain, on passe à l'heure d'hiver, il faut retarder le réveil d'une heure.	Tomorrow standard time begins; we must set the alarm clock back an hour.
pendant des heures [pɑ̃dɑ̃dezœʀ]	for hours

... **pile** [pil]	...sharp
précis, **précise** [pʀesi, iz]	precisely...
Le cours commence **à 8 heures pile/précises**.	Class starts at eight o'clock sharp.
vers [vɛʀ]	around
Nous arriverons **vers 6 heures du soir**.	We will arrive around six o'clock in the evening.
presque [pʀɛsk]	almost, nearly

INFO

Asking for and saying the time

Quelle heure est-il?/ Il est quelle heure?	*What time is it?*
Vous avez l'heure?	*Do you have the time?*
À quelle heure...?	*At what time…?*
À quelle heure y a-t-il un train por Bordeaux?	*At what time is there a train for Bordeaux?*
Il est... ...9 heures (du matin/du soir). ...9 h 05 (neuf heures cinq). ...9 h 15 (neuf heures et quart). ...9 h 30 (neuf heures et demie). ...9 h 45 (neuf heures moins le quart). ...9 h 55 (neuf heures moins cinq).	*It is…* *… nine o'clock (in the morning/evening).* *… five past nine.* *… quarter past nine.* *… nine-thirty.* *…quarter to ten.* *…five to ten.*

INFO

Le matin, ce matin, le lendemain

ce matin/ce soir etc.	*this morning/evening*
le matin/le soir etc.	*in the morning/evening*
demain matin/soir	*tomorrow morning/evening (relative to the present time)*
le lendemain matin/soir	*the following morning/evening (relative to a point in time other than the present)*

le **matin** [matɛ̃]	morning, in the morning
de bon matin	early in the morning
la **matinée** [matine]	morning *(duration)*
dans la matinée	during the morning
faire la grasse matinée *loc*	to sleep in
de bonne heure [d(ə)bɔnœʀ]	early
Mon grand-père se couche toujours de bonne heure.	My grandfather always goes to bed early.

(le) **midi** [midi]	noon, midday
Elle déjeune ici tous les midis.	She dines here every day at noon.
l'**après-midi** *m/f* [apʀɛmidi]	(in the) afternoon
en fin d'après-midi	in late afternoon
le **soir** [swaʀ]	evening
la **soirée** [swaʀe]	evening *(duration)*
la **nuit** [nɥi]	night
La nuit tombe tôt en cette saison.	Night comes early at this time of year.
minuit [minɥi]	midnight
Nous sommes rentrés **à minuit et demi**.	We got back at half-past midnight.
Il fait jour [ilfɛʒuʀ]	It is day.
Il fait nuit [ilfɛnɥi]	It is night.
Il fait noir [ilfɛnwaʀ]	It is dark (out).

de jour [dəʒuʀ]	during the day
de nuit [dənɥi]	during the night
Ils voyagent toujours de nuit.	They always travel at night.
l'**aube** *f* [ob]	dawn, sunrise
se lever avant l'aube	to get up before dawn
le **crépuscule** [kʀepyskyl]	dusk
le **lever de/du soleil** [ləved(ə)/dysɔlɛj]	sunrise
Les oiseaux chantent dès le lever du soleil.	The birds sing as soon as the sun comes up.
le **coucher de/du soleil** [kuʃed(ə)/dysɔlɛj]	sunset

une **montre** [mɔ̃tʀ]	(wrist) watch
regarder l'heure à sa montre	to check the time/look at one's watch
avancer sa montre d'une heure	to set one's watch ahead one hour
Ma montre avance de cinq minutes.	My watch is five minutes fast.
en avance [ɑ̃navɑ̃s]	early
Tu es en avance.	You are early.
retarder [ʀ(ə)taʀde]	to be slow, to be held up
en retard [ɑ̃ʀ(ə)taʀd]	late
arriver en retard	to arrive late
à l'heure [alœʀ]	on time
Le train est toujours à l'heure.	The train is always on time.
ponctuel, **ponctuelle** [pɔ̃ktɥɛl]	punctual, on time

un **réveil** [ʀevɛj]	alarm clock
une **pendule** [pɑ̃dyl]	grandfather clock
remettre les pendules à l'heure *loc*	to make things clear
une **horloge** [ɔʀlɔʒ]	clock
régler [ʀegle]	to set

19.3 Months and Seasons  89

mensuel, **mensuelle** [mɑ̃sɥɛl]	monthly
une **revue mensuelle**	monthly magazine
le **mois** [mwa]	month
Le mois de mai a 31 jours.	The month of May has 31 days.
trois fois par mois	three times a month
janvier [ʒɑ̃vje]	January
février [fevʀije]	February
mars [maʀs]	March
avril [avʀil]	April
mai [mɛ]	May
juin [ʒɥɛ̃]	June
juillet [ʒɥijɛ]	July
Nous partons en vacances **en/au mois de juillet**.	We are going on vacation in July.
août [u(t)]	August
septembre [sɛptɑ̃bʀ]	September
octobre [ɔktɔbʀ]	October
novembre [nɔvɑ̃bʀ]	November
décembre [desɑ̃bʀ]	December
début… [deby]	at the beginning of…
Début/Au début du mois de janvier, je vais aller à Paris.	At the beginning of January, I am going to go to Paris.
fin… [fɛ̃]	at the end of…
Il viendra **fin janvier.**	He will come at the end of January.
à la fin du mois de janvier	at the end of January

le **calendrier** [kalɑ̃dʀije]	calendar
un **trimestre** [tʀimɛstʀ]	trimester
L'année scolaire française est divisée en trimestres.	The French school year is divided into trimesters.
un **semestre** [semɛstʀ]	semester
bimensuel, **bimensuelle** [bimɑ̃sɥɛl]	twice monthly, biweekly
un **magazine bimensuel**	biweekly magazine
une **année bissextile** [anebisɛkstil]	leap year

annuel, **annuelle** [anɥɛl]	annual, yearly
faire son **rapport annuel** sur qc	to make one's yearly report on s.th.
un **an** [ɑ̃]	year
par an	per year
une **année** [ane]	year
Bonne année!	Happy New Year!
l'**année scolaire**	school year

une **saison** [sɛzɔ̃]	season
Il fait beau pour la saison.	The weather is nice for the season.
le **printemps** [pʀɛ̃tɑ̃]	spring
au printemps	in the spring
l'**été** *m* [ete]	summer
en été	in the summer
l'**automne** *m* [o/ɔtɔn]	autumn, fall
en automne	in the fall
l'**hiver** *m* [ivɛʀ]	winter
en hiver	in the winter
pendant tout l'hiver	for the entire winter

printanier, **printanière** [pʀɛ̃tanje, jɛʀ]	spring (adj)
une journée printanière	spring day
estival, **estivale** [ɛstival]	summer (adj)
le Festival estival de Paris	Paris Summer Festival
automnal, **automnale** [o/ɔtɔnal]	fall (adj)
hivernal, **hivernale** [ivɛʀnal]	winter (adj)
saisonnier, **saisonnière** [sɛzɔnje, ɛʀ]	seasonal

19.4 More Time Expressions  90

le **temps** [tɑ̃]	time
avoir le temps de faire qc	to have time to do s.th.
passer du/son temps à faire qc	to spend one's time doing s.th.
gagner du temps	to save, gain time
perdre son temps à faire qc	to waste time doing s.th.
Il est temps de faire qc.	It is time to do s.th.
Je trouve le temps long.	I am bored. Time is dragging.
Le temps m'a paru court.	Time flew by.
durer [dyʀe]	to last
la **durée** [dyʀe]	duration
un **moment** [mɔmɑ̃]	moment
attendre le bon moment	to wait for the right moment
Ce n'est pas le moment.	This is not the right time/moment.
longtemps [lɔ̃tɑ̃]	for a long time
Je n'en ai pas pour longtemps.	This won't take me long.
un **siècle** [sjɛkl]	century

un **instant** [ɛ̃stɑ̃]	instant, moment
Il est arrivé **à l'instant où** j'allais partir.	He arrived at the moment I was going to leave.
une **époque** [epɔk]	epoch, time
à l'époque	at the time
une **période** [peʀjɔd]	period, time

passé, **passée** [pase]	past, last
se souvenir du temps passé	to remember past times
le **passé** [pase]	past (n)
autrefois [otʀəfwa]	formerly, earlier
ancien, **ancienne** [ɑ̃sjɛ̃, jɛn]	former *(See Information Box p. 44)*
récent, **récente** [ʀesɑ̃, ɑ̃t]	recent
récemment	recently
dernier, **dernière** [dɛʀnje, jɛʀ]	last
samedi dernier	last Saturday
le **dernier samedi** du mois	the last Saturday of the month

l'autre jour [lot(ʀə)ʒuʀ]	the other day
L'autre jour, j'ai rencontré Michel.	I bumped into Michel the other day.
de mon temps [d(ə)mɔ̃tɑ̃]	in my day
De mon temps, il n'y avait pas de cartes de crédit.	In my day there were no credit cards.
jadis [ʒadis]	formerly
Jadis, on s'éclairait à la bougie.	Formerly candles were used for illumination.
auparavant [opaʀavɑ̃]	previously, beforehand
Il est allé chez elle, mais auparavant, il lui a téléphoné.	He went to her house, but she phoned him beforehand.

présent, **présente** [pʀezɑ̃, ɑ̃t]	present (adj)
le **présent** [pʀezɑ̃]	present (n)
maintenant [mɛ̃t(ə)nɑ̃]	now
en ce moment [ɑ̃s(ə)mɔmɑ̃]	currently, at this time

pour le moment [puʀl(ə)mɔmɑ̃]	for the moment
Je suis sans emploi, pour le moment.	I am unemployed for the moment.
à présent [apʀezɑ̃]	at present, now, currently
Jusqu'à présent, tout s'est bien passé.	Up until now, everything has gone well.
actuellement [aktyɛlmɑ̃]	presently, right now
Actuellement, les fraises sont très bon marché.	Strawberries are very cheap right now.
contemporain, **contemporaine** [kɔ̃tɑ̃pɔʀɛ̃, ɛn]	contemporary
la musique contemporaine	contemporary music

l'**avenir** *m* [av(ə)niʀ]	future (n)
faire des **projets d'avenir**	to make plans for the future
futur, **future** [fytyʀ]	future (adj)
Je vous présente mon futur mari.	This is my future husband.
le **futur** [fytyʀ]	future (n)
prochain, **prochaine** [pʀɔʃɛ̃, ɛn]	next
la **semaine prochaine**	next week
La **prochaine fois**, fais attention.	Pay attention next time.
bientôt [bjɛ̃to]	soon
ensuite [ɑ̃sɥit]	then, next

à l'avenir [alav(ə)niʀ]	in the future
À l'avenir, il écoutera les conseils de ses amis.	In the future he will listen to his friends' advice.
éternel, **éternelle** [etɛʀnɛl]	eternal
croire à la **vie éternelle**	to believe in eternal life
l'**éternité** *f* [etɛʀnite]	eternity
Ça a duré une éternité.	That lasted an eternity.

l'**origine** *f* [ɔʀiʒin]	origin
commencer [kɔmɑ̃se]	to begin *(See Information Box p. 455)*
J'ai **commencé à** apprendre l'espagnol.	I have begun to learn Spanish.
Il a **commencé par** crier, puis il s'est calmé.	At first he yelled, then he calmed down.
le **commencement** [kɔmɑ̃smɑ̃]	beginning (n)
recommencer [ʀ(ə)kɔmɑ̃se]	to begin again
aller faire qc [alefɛʀ]	to be going to do s.th.
Je vais sortir tout à l'heure.	I am going to leave momentarily.
se mettre à faire qc [s(ə)mɛtʀafɛʀ]	to begin doing s.th.
Il faut que je me mette à préparer les affaires.	I must begin to get things ready.
venir de faire qc [v(ə)niʀd(ə)fɛʀ]	to have just done s.th.
Je viens d'arriver.	I have just arrived.
être en train de faire qc [ɛtʀɑ̃tʀɛ̃d(ə)fɛʀ]	to be in the process of doing s.th.
Ne me dérange pas, je suis en train de lire.	Don't bother me; I am reading.
au milieu de [omiljødə]	in the middle of
au milieu de la nuit	in the middle of the night
au bout de [obudə]	at the end of
Au bout d'un quart d'heure, j'en ai eu assez.	I'd had enough after fifteen minutes.

finir [finiʀ]	to end, finish, stop
Elle a **fini de** manger.	She finished eating.
Ils ont **fini par** nous donner raison.	They ended up admitting that we were right.
la **fin** [fɛ̃]	end (n)
terminer [tɛʀmine]	to end

---

cesser (**de faire**) **qc** [sese]	to stop (doing) s.th.
Il a cessé de pleuvoir.	It has stopped raining.
aboutir à [abutiʀ]	to amount to
S'il continue comme ça, il n'aboutira à rien.	If he continues like that, he won't amount to anything.

---

avant (**de**) [avɑ̃]	before
Passe me voir avant 6 heures.	Come see me before six o'clock.
Réfléchis avant de parler.	Think before you speak.
il y a [ilja]	ago
On a déménagé il y a 5 ans.	We moved five years ago.
d'abord [dabɔʀ]	at first
depuis [depɥi]	since (then)
Je ne l'ai pas vu depuis son retour.	I have not seen him since he got back.
à partir de [apaʀtiʀdə]	starting with
Je serai en vacances à partir du 1er août.	I will be on vacation starting August 1.
pendant [pɑ̃dɑ̃]	during
Ne me dérange pas pendant ma sieste.	Don't disturb me during my nap.
entre [ɑ̃tʀ]	between
Je prends mes vacances entre le 25 juin et le 10 juillet.	I am taking my vacation between June 25 and July 10.
jusqu'à [ʒyska]	until
Je serai à la maison jusqu'à 8 heures.	I will be at home until eight o'clock.
après [apʀɛ]	after
Tu peux m'appeler après 9 heures.	You can call me after 9 o'clock.
Et qu'est-ce que tu feras après?	And what will you do after that?
avant que + *subj* [avɑ̃kə]	before
On va rentrer avant qu'il pleuve.	We are going home before it rains.
depuis que [dəpɥikə]	since
Je ne l'ai pas vu depuis qu'il est revenu.	I have not seen him since he came back.
pendant que [pɑ̃dɑ̃kə]	while, during
Ma mère garde mon bébé pendant que je travaille.	My mother takes care of my baby while I work.

après que [apʀɛkə]	after
Il a fait la vaisselle après que les invités étaient partis.	He did the dishes after the guests left.
dès [dɛ]	as early as
dès l'aube	as early as dawn
dès que [dɛkə]	as soon as
Je t'aiderai dès que je pourrai.	I will help you as soon as I can.
au cours de [okuʀdə]	in the course of
On se verra au cours du mois de septembre.	We will see each other during the month of September.
entre-temps [ɑ̃tʀətɑ̃]	in the meantime
J'arrive dans 5 minutes. Entre-temps, sers-toi quelque chose à boire.	I will be there in five minutes. In the meantime, help yourself to something to drink.
tant que [tɑ̃kə]	as long as
Tant qu'il sera là, elle n'aura pas la paix.	As long as he is there, she will have no peace.
en l'espace de [ɑ̃lɛspasdə]	within/in the space of
En l'espace de 20 minutes, la tempête a tout détruit.	The storm destroyed everything within twenty minutes.
Quand? [kɑ̃]	When?
tout de suite [tutsɥit]	right away, immediately
Je l'ai reconnu tout de suite.	I recognized him right away.
tout à l'heure [tutalœʀ]	soon, momentarily
par la suite [paʀlasɥit]	then, subsequently
à ce moment-là [as(ə)mɔmɑ̃la]	at that time, moment
C'est à ce moment-là que je l'ai vu.	It was at that moment that I saw him.
sur le coup [syʀl(ə)ku]	immediately; at first
Sur le coup, je n'ai pas compris ce qui se passait.	At first I didn't understand what was going on.
Il a été **tué sur le coup**.	He was killed instantly.
immédiat, immédiate [imedja, jat]	immediate
immédiatement	immediately
ne… jamais [nəʒamɛ]	never
Je n'ai jamais dit ça.	I never said that.
Jamais le jardin n'a été aussi beau.	The garden has never been so beautiful.
rarement [ʀaʀmɑ̃]	rarely
de temps en temps [d(ə)tɑ̃zɑ̃tɑ̃]	from time to time, occasionally

la **fois** [fwa]	time *(See Information Box p. 98)*
C'est la deuxième fois que ma voiture tombe en panne.	This is the second time my car has broken down.
quelquefois [kɛlkəfwa]	sometimes
Je les rencontre quelquefois au cinéma.	Sometimes I meet them at the movies.
parfois [paʀfwa]	sometimes
régulièrement [ʀegyljɛʀmɑ̃]	regularly
Ils rendent régulièrement visite à leur tante.	They regularly visit their aunt.
souvent [suvɑ̃]	often
toujours [tuʒuʀ]	always
tout le temps [tul(ə)tɑ̃]	the whole time, continually
Il est tout le temps dans la lune. *loc*	He is continually daydreaming.

---

en même temps [ɑ̃mɛmtɑ̃]	at the same time
Ils sont partis en même temps que moi.	They left the same time I did.
à la fois [alafwa]	at the same time, at once
Tu ne peux pas faire deux choses à la fois.	You cannot do two things at the same time.
tout à coup [tutaku]	suddenly
Tout à coup, elle s'est mise à pleurer.	Suddenly she burst out crying.
peu à peu [pøapø]	little by little
Sa santé s'améliore peu à peu.	Her health is getting better little by little.
soudain [sudɛ̃]	suddenly
J'étais en train de dormir quand, soudain, j'ai entendu un cri.	I was sleeping when I suddenly heard a shout.

---

simultané, **simultanée** [simyltane]	simultaneous
deux actions simultanées	two simultaneous actions
simultanément	simultaneously
de suite [d(ə)sɥit]	in a row
Elle a eu deux accidents de suite.	She had two accidents in a row.

---

tôt [to]	early
déjà [deʒa]	already
Quoi? Il est déjà minuit?	What? It's midnight already?
tard [taʀ]	late
Tôt ou tard, tu admettras que j'ai raison.	Sooner or later you will admit that I am right.

au plus tôt [oplyto] — at the earliest, no sooner than
au plus tard [oplytaʀ] — at the latest, no later than
Je serai là, au plus tard à 4 heures. — I will be there no later than four o'clock.

d'avance [davɑ̃s] — in advance
Je peux te dire d'avance que ça ne marchera pas. — I can tell you in advance that that won't work.
un **délai** [delɛ] — period of time
Je demande un **délai de réflexion**. — I am asking for time to think about it.

prolonger [pʀɔlɔ̃ʒe] — to prolong, lengthen
Ils voudraient prolonger leur séjour d'une semaine. — They would like to prolong their stay for one week.

19.5 Spatial Relationships  91

l'**espace** *m* [ɛspas] — space
le temps et l'espace — time and space
dans [dɑ̃] — in
Je n'ai plus rien dans mon porte-monnaie. — I have nothing left in my wallet.
dedans [d(ə)dɑ̃] — inside
Ce sac est lourd. Qu'est-ce qu'il y a dedans? — This bag is heavy. What's inside it?
à l'intérieur (de) [alɛ̃teʀjœʀ] — inside (of)
Il est à l'intérieur de la maison. — He is inside the house.
dehors [dəɔʀ] — outside, outdoors
Allez jouer dehors. — Go play outdoors.
à l'extérieur (de) [alɛksteʀjœʀ] — outside (of)

hors de qc [ɔʀdə] — outside, out of s.th.
Il a couru hors de la pièce. — He ran out of the room.
en dehors (de) [ɑ̃dəɔʀ] — outside, beyond
La maison est en dehors du village. — The house is outside the village.

avant [avɑ̃] — before
Il faut tourner à gauche avant la mairie. — You have to turn left before the town hall.

après [apʀɛ] — after, beyond
L'accident s'est produit 5 kilomètres après Tours. — The accident happened five kilometers beyond Tours.
devant [d(ə)vɑ̃] — before, in front of
Devant la maison, il y a deux grands arbres. — In front of the house there are two large trees.
derrière [dɛʀjɛʀ] — behind
Il se cache derrière le mur. — He is hiding behind the wall.

sur [syʀ]	on
Le livre est posé sur la table.	The book is on the table.
sous [su]	under
dessus [d(ə)sy]	on top
un gâteau avec des cerises dessus	a cake with cherries on top
au-dessus de	above, over
L'avion vole au-dessus des nuages.	The plane flies above the clouds.
dessous [dəsu]	underneath, below
au-dessous de	underneath, below

le **bas** [ba]	bottom, lower part (n)
dans le tiroir **du bas**	in the lower drawer
le **haut** ['o]	upper part, top (n)
sur l'étagère **du haut**	on the top shelf
l'**arrière** *m* [aʀjɛʀ]	rear (part), back (n)
à l'arrière de	in the rear of
Je n'aime pas être assis à l'arrière du bus.	I don't like to sit at the back of the bus.
l'**avant** *m* [avɑ̃]	front (n)
à l'avant de	in the front of
le **fond** [fɔ̃]	bottom, background (n)
le **coin** [kwɛ̃]	corner (n)
au coin de la rue	at the street corner
le **côté** [kote]	side (n)
Le carré a 4 côtés égaux.	A square has four equal sides.
le **bout** [bu]	end (n)
au bout de	at the end of
Elle nous attend au bout du quai.	She is waiting for us at the end of the platform.
le **bord** [bɔʀ]	edge (n)
supérieur, **supérieure** [sypeʀjœʀ]	upper (adj)
la **lèvre supérieure**	upper lip
inférieur, **inférieure** [ɛ̃feʀjœʀ]	lower (adj)

à l'extrémité de [alɛkstʀemite]	at the end of
en bas (**de**) [ɑ̃ba]	at the bottom of
en haut (**de**) [ɑ̃'o]	at the top of
en haut d'une côte	at the top of a hill
en avant (**de**) [ɑ̃navɑ̃]	at the front (of)
Il marche en avant du groupe.	He marches at the front of the group.
en arrière (**de**) [ɑ̃naʀjɛʀ]	at the back (of); behind
au premier plan [opʀəmjeplɑ̃]	in the foreground
Au premier plan du tableau, on voit un cheval.	In the foreground of the painting there is a horse.
au second plan [os(ə)gɔ̃plɑ̃]	in the background
à la hauteur de [ala'otœʀ]	at the level of

de côté [d(ə)kote]	at the side
faire un **pas de côté**	to step to the side
à côté (**de**) [akote]	beside
Assieds-toi **à côté de moi**.	Sit down next to me.
de face [dəfas]	in front
en face (**de**) [ɑ̃fas]	facing
la **droite** [dʀwat]	right (n)
tenir sa droite	to stay/drive to the right
la **gauche** [goʃ]	left (n)
Sur votre gauche, vous pouvez voir la tour Eiffel.	On your left you can see the Eiffel Tower.
de près [d(ə)pʀɛ]	up close
de loin [d(ə)lwɛ̃]	from afar, far away
Je l'ai reconnue de loin.	I recognized him from far away.

le long de [ləlɔ̃]	along
Des roses poussent le long du mur.	Roses grow along the wall.
côte à côte [kotakot]	side by side
Ils sont assis côte à côte.	They are seated side by side.
vis-à-vis (**de**) [vizavi]	across (from)
Sa chambre est vis-à-vis de la mienne.	Her room is across from mine.
le **milieu** [miljø]	middle (n)
au milieu de	in the middle of
Il y a un arbre au milieu du jardin.	There is a tree in the middle of the garden.

19.6 Length, Width, Distance  92

la **dimension** [dimɑ̃sjɔ̃]	dimension
prendre les dimensions de qc	to take the dimensions of s.th.
long, **longue** [lɔ̃, lɔ̃g]	long
La table est **longue de** 2 mètres.	The table is 2 meters long.
avoir 10 mètres **de long**	to be 10 meters long
la **longueur** [lɔ̃gœʀ]	length
court, **courte** [kuʀ, kuʀt]	short
Elle a **les cheveux courts**.	She has short hair.
large [laʀʒ]	wide, broad
Un terrain de **100 mètres de long sur 30** (**mètres**) **de large**.	A plot 100 meters long by 30 meters wide.
la **largeur** [laʀʒœʀ]	width, breadth
étroit, **étroite** [etʀwa, wat]	narrow
haut, **haute** ['o, 'ot]	high
La maison est **haute de** 13 mètres.	The house is 13 meters high.
La tour a 50 mètres **de haut**.	The tower is 50 meters high.

la **hauteur** ['otœʀ]	height
dans le sens de la hauteur/largeur	heightwise/breadthwise, lengthwise
bas, **basse** [ba, bas]	low
un plafond bas	low ceiling
profond, **profonde** [pʀɔfɔ̃, ɔ̃d]	deep
la **profondeur** [pʀɔfɔ̃dœʀ]	depth
le **tour** [tuʀ]	breadth, circumference *(See Information Box p. 201)*
autour de [otuʀ]	around
être entouré, **entourée de** [ɑ̃tuʀe]	to be surrounded by
un jardin entouré d'une clôture	a yard surrounded by a fence
le **périmètre** [peʀimɛtʀ]	perimeter
la **circonférence** [siʀkɔ̃feʀɑ̃s]	circumference
limité, **limitée** [limite]	bordered
la **limite** [limit]	border (n)
délimité, **délimitée** [delimite]	delimited
une propriété délimitée par un mur	property delimited by a wall
près (**de**) [pʀɛ]	near
Il y a un arrêt de bus près de l'école.	There is a bus stop near the school.
proche (**de**) [pʀɔʃ]	near
C'est la station de métro **la plus proche**.	That is the nearest metro station.
les **environs** *mpl* [ɑ̃viʀɔ̃]	vicinity
dans les environs de Mulhouse	in the vicinity of Mulhouse
loin (**de**) [lwɛ̃]	far (from)
être loin du but	to be far from the goal
On voit les bateaux passer **au loin**.	We see the ships going by in the distance.
éloigné, **éloignée** [elwaɲe]	far away, distant
lointain, **lointaine** [lwɛ̃tɛ̃, ɛn]	far away, distant
Je rêve souvent de pays lointains.	I often dream of distant countries.
à… **m/km d'ici** [amɛtʀ/kilɔmɛtʀdisi]	... m/km (away) from here
La prochaine station-service est à 400 m d'ici.	The nearest gas station is 400 meters from here.
jusqu'à [ʒyska]	until, as far as, up to
aller à pied jusqu'à la poste	to walk as far as the post office
entre [ɑ̃tʀ]	between
Il y a 1 000 km entre Dunkerque et Nice.	It is 1000 km from Dunkirk to Nice.

distant, **distante de** [distɑ̃, ɑ̃tdə]	distant, apart
Les deux villes sont distantes de 5 km.	The two cities are five kilometers apart.
la **distance** [distɑ̃s]	distance
Le feu rouge se trouve à une distance de 150 mètres.	The traffic light is 150 meters away.
d'ici à... [disia]	from here to...
Il y a 3 km d'ici à la maison la plus proche.	It is three kilometers from here to the nearest house.

19.7 Location and Direction 

l'**endroit** *m* [ɑ̃dʀwa]	place (n)
par endroits	in places
le **lieu** [ljø]	place (n)
le **lieu de naissance**	place of birth
un **lieu public**	public place
le **point** [pwɛ̃]	point (n)
le **point de départ**	point of departure
local, **locale** [lɔkal]	local (adj)
les traditions locales	local traditions

la **place** [plas]	place (n)
ranger quelque chose à sa place	to put something in its place
situé, **située** [sitɥe]	located
Cette maison est située en plein centre.	This house is located right in the center.
la **situation** [sitɥasjɔ̃]	location/position
la situation géographique	geographic location
la **position** [pɔzisjɔ̃]	location/position

où [u]	where
Où est mon sac?	Where is my bag?
ici [isi]	here
là [la]	there
là-bas [laba]	over there
Tu vois ce château là-bas?	See that castle over there?
là-haut [la'o]	up there
là-dessus [lad(ə)sy]	on it
Monte là-dessus, tu verras mieux.	Climb up on it; you will see better.
là-dedans [lad(ə)dɑ̃]	inside
Allume la lumière, il fait noir là-dedans.	Turn on the light; it is dark inside.
là-dessous [lad(ə)su]	underneath

par terre [parteʀ]	on the floor/ground
à [a]	in
à Montpellier/au Portugal	in Montpellier/in Portugal
en [ɑ̃]	in
en Angleterre	in England
chez [ʃe]	at s.o.'s house
Je l'ai invité chez moi.	I invited him to my house.

---

partout [paʀtu]	everywhere
nulle part [nylpaʀ]	nowhere
Je l'ai cherché partout, mais je ne l'ai vu nulle part.	I have looked everywhere, but I have not seen it anywhere.
quelque part [kɛlkəpaʀ]	somewhere, someplace
Je ne sais pas qui c'est, mais je l'ai déjà vu quelque part.	I don't know who that is, but I have seen him someplace.
autre part [ot(ʀə)paʀ]	elsewhere
ailleurs [ajœʀ]	elsewhere, someplace else
Si tu ne te plais pas ici, va ailleurs.	If you don't like it here go someplace else.

---

la **direction** [diʀɛksjɔ̃]	direction
la **bonne/mauvaise direction**	right/wrong direction
en direction de	toward, in the direction of
vers [vɛʀ]	toward
se diriger vers [s(ə)diʀiʒe]	to go/head toward
Le bateau se dirige vers le port.	The ship is heading for the harbor.
le **sens** [sɑ̃s]	direction
dans le **sens des aiguilles d'une montre**	clockwise
l'**orientation** *f* [ɔʀjɑ̃tasjɔ̃]	orientation, direction
avoir le sens de l'orientation	to have a good sense of direction
s'orienter vers qc [sɔʀjɑ̃te]	to go in the direction of s.th.
tout droit [tudʀwa]	straight ahead
Continue tout droit jusqu'à la gare.	Continue straight ahead until you reach the train station.
droit, **droite** [dʀwa, at]	straight
une avenue **toute droite**	a perfectly straight avenue
horizontal, **horizontalel** [ɔʀizɔ̃tal]	horizontal
vertical, **verticale** [vɛʀtikal]	vertical
à droite de [adʀwatdə]	to the right of
à gauche de [agoʃdə]	to the left of
On met le couteau à droite de l'assiette et la fourchette à gauche.	The knife is placed to the right of the plate, and the fork to the left.

en avant [ɑ̃navɑ̃]	forward
En avant, marche!	Forward march!
en arrière [ɑ̃naʀjɛʀ]	rearward, backward
faire un pas en arrière	to take a step back(ward)
opposé, opposée [ɔpoze]	opposite, facing
repartir* dans la direction opposée	to go back in the opposite direction
en sens inverse [ɑ̃sɑ̃sɛ̃vɛʀs]	in the opposite direction
Elle est partie en sens inverse.	She went in the wrong direction.
parallèle à [paʀalɛl]	parallel to
La rue de la Gare est parallèle à la rue Balzac.	The rue de la Gare is parallel to rue Balzac.
perpendiculaire à [pɛʀpɑ̃dikylɛʀ]	perpendicular to
de haut en bas [də'o(t)ɑ̃ba]	from top to bottom
de long en large [dəlɔ̃ɑ̃laʀʒ]	back and forth/up and down
marcher de long en large	to walk back and forth
à travers [atʀavɛʀ]	across, through
voyager à travers la France	to travel through France
le **nord** (**N**) [nɔʀ (ɛn)]	north (N)
Lille est situé **dans le Nord** de la France.	Lille is located in the north of France.
au nord (**de**)	north of
au nord de la Loire	north of the Loire
le **sud** (**S**) [syd (ɛs)]	south (S)
au sud (**de**)	south of
l'**est** (**E**) *m* [ɛst (ø)]	east (E)
à l'est (**de**)	east of
l'**ouest** (**O**) *m* [wɛst (o)]	west (W)
à l'ouest (**de**)	west of

My Vocabulary

20

Colors and Shapes

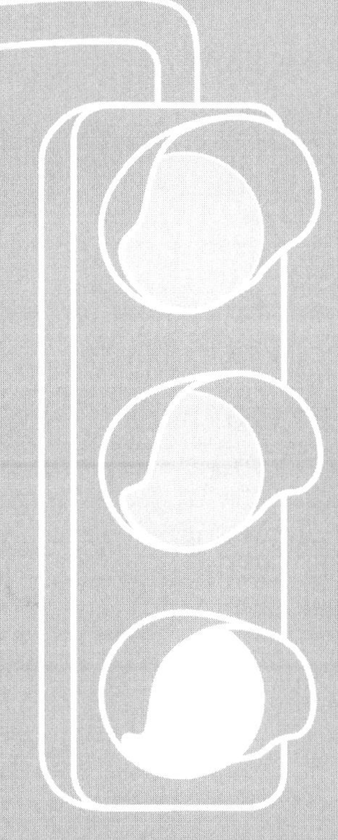

20.1 Colors  94

colorier [kɔlɔʀje]	to color
un **album à colorier**	coloring book
coloré, **colorée** [kɔlɔʀe]	colored
du **verre coloré**	colored glass
une **couleur** [kulœʀ]	color (n)
riche en couleurs	colorful
décoloré, **décolorée** [dekɔlɔʀe]	faded
incolore [ɛ̃kɔlɔʀ]	colorless
un liquide incolore	colorless liquid
un **ton** [tɔ̃]	shade/hue
une **nuance** [nɥɑ̃s]	color shade
uni, **unie** [yni]	solid color
un tissu uni	fabric in a solid color
multicolore [myltikɔlɔʀ]	multicolored
un papillon multicolore	multicolored butterfly

INFO

All about color

la couleur	*color*
la télé(vision) en couleurs	*color television*
un homme/une femme de couleur	*man/woman of color*
la peinture	*painting/paint*
un pot de peinture	*can of paint*
Il fait de la peinture.	*He paints.*

teindre [tɛ̃dʀ]	to dye
Elle s'est **fait teindre en** roux.	She has had her hair dyed red.
la **teinte** [tɛ̃t]	coloring (n)
déteindre [detɛ̃dʀ]	to fade
Sa chemise a déteint au lavage.	His shirt faded in the wash.

blanc, **blanche** [blɑ̃, blɑ̃ʃ]	white
Tu commences à avoir des **cheveux blancs**.	You are starting to get white hair.
noir, **noire** [nwaʀ]	black
gris, **grise** [gʀi, gʀiz]	gray

bleu, **bleue** [blø]	blue
jaune [ʒon]	yellow
rouge [ʀuʒ]	red
vert, **verte** [vɛʀ, vɛʀt]	green
violet, **violette** [vjɔlɛ, ɛt]	purple
Il porte une cravate violette.	He is wearing a purple tie.
rose [ʀoz]	pink

mauve [mov]	mauve
beige [bɛʒ]	beige

orange [ɔʀɑ̃ʒ]	orange
des chaussettes orange	orange socks
marron [maʀɔ̃]	brown
des chaussures marron	brown shoes
azur [azyʀ]	azure
ocre [ɔkʀ]	ocher
lilas [lila]	lilac, lavender

bleu marine [blømaʀin]	navy blue
Elle est belle, ta chemise bleu marine.	Your navy blue shirt is really pretty.
bleu ciel [bløsjɛl]	sky blue
bleu turquoise [bløtyʀkwaz]	turquoise
La mer est bleu turquoise.	The sea is turquoise blue.
rouge sang [ʀuʒsɑ̃]	blood red
vert foncé [vɛʀfɔ̃se]	dark green
une jupe vert foncé	dark green skirt
vert pomme [vɛʀpɔm]	apple green
gris clair [gʀiklɛʀ]	light gray
une cravate gris clair	light gray tie

INFO

Colors

Adjectives of color are normally *variable*:

Elle a acheté deux jupes vertes.	*She bought two green skirts.*

However, they are *invariable* when they are *nouns used as adjectives*, or when they are *composite adjectives*. Examples:

Elle a les yeux marron.	*She has brown eyes.*
Elle m'a offert trois chemises bleu clair.	*She gave me three light blue shirts as a gift.*

blond, **blonde** [blɔ̃, blɔ̃d]	blonde
brun, **brune** [bʀɛ̃, bʀyn]	brown; brunette
une **bière blonde/brune**	light/dark beer
roux, **rousse** [ʀu, ʀus]	red-haired
Elle a **les cheveux roux**.	She has red hair.
châtain [ʃatɛ̃]	light brown, chestnut
Elle est châtain.	She is a brunette/has brown hair.
Elle a les cheveux **châtain foncé**.	She has dark brown hair.
doré, **dorée** [dɔʀe]	golden
argenté, **argentée** [aʀʒɑ̃te]	silvery
clair, **claire** [klɛʀ]	light
Il a **les yeux clairs**.	He has light eyes.
foncé, **foncée** [fɔ̃se]	dark
pâle [pɑl]	pale
Elle a **le teint pâle**.	She has a pale complexion.
vif, **vive** [vif, viv]	lively, bright
une robe **rouge vif**	bright red dress
criard, **criarde** [kʀijaʀ, jaʀd]	loud, gaudy
une nappe **aux couleurs criardes**	gaudy tablecloth
sombre [sɔ̃bʀ]	dark
brillant, **brillante** [bʀijɑ̃, ɑ̃t]	shiny, bright
mat, **mate** [mat]	matte, dull

20.2 Shapes  95

former [fɔʀme]	to shape, form
Les enfants forment un cercle autour du sapin.	The children form a circle around the Christmas tree.
la **forme** [fɔʀm]	shape (n)
une boîte **en forme de** cœur	heart-shaped box
(**se**) **déformer** [(sə)defɔʀme]	to deform, distort, warp
La chaleur déforme le plastique.	Heat deforms plastic.
Le plastique se déforme sous l'effet de la chaleur.	Plastic distorts under the effect of heat.
uniforme [ynifɔʀm]	uniform, of one color
une **figure** [figyʀ]	figure (n)
une figure géométrique	geometrical figure
une **silhouette** [silwɛt]	silhouette (n)

le **point** [pwɛ̃]	point, dot (n)
un **trait** [tʀɛ]	line, stroke
tirer un trait à la règle	to draw a line with a ruler
une **ligne** [liɲ]	line (n)
une (**ligne**) **droite**	straight line

rond, **ronde** [ʀɔ̃, ʀɔ̃d]	round
La terre est ronde.	The Earth is round.
un **cercle** [sɛʀkl]	circle
un **demi-cercle**	semicircle

une **courbe** [kuʀb]	curve
un **arc** [aʀk]	arc
tracer un arc de cercle	to draw an arc
ovale [ɔval]	oval
sphérique [sfeʀik]	spherical
une **sphère** [sfɛʀ]	sphere
un **hémisphère** [emisfɛʀ]	hemisphere
Nous vivons dans l'**hémisphère Nord**.	We live in the Northern Hemisphere.
cylindrique [silɛ̃dʀik]	cylindrical
un **cylindre** [silɛ̃dʀ]	cylinder

le **bord** [bɔʀ]	edge
le bord de la table	edge of the table
un **coin** [kwɛ̃]	corner
pointu, **pointue** [pwɛ̃ty]	pointed, pointy
Attention, le couteau est pointu.	Careful, the knife has a sharp point.
une **pointe** [pwɛ̃t]	point (n)
régulier, **régulière** [ʀegylje, jɛʀ]	regular
irrégulier, **irrégulière** [iʀegylje, jɛʀ]	irregular, uneven
une surface irrégulière	uneven surface

un **angle** [ɑ̃gl]	angle
un **angle droit**	right angle
un **angle aigu/obtus**	acute/obtuse angle
triangulaire [tʀijɑ̃gylɛʀ]	triangular
un **triangle** [tʀijɑ̃gl]	triangle
rectangulaire [ʀɛktɑ̃gylɛʀ]	rectangular
un **rectangle** [ʀɛktɑ̃gl]	rectangle
carré, **carrée** [kaʀe]	square (adj)
un **carré** [kaʀe]	square (n)
une **croix** [kʀwa]	cross (n)
marquer qc d'une croix	to mark s.th. with an X
cubique [kybik]	cubical, square
la **racine cubique** d'un nombre	square root of a number
un **cube** [kyb]	cube (n)
une **pyramide** [piʀamid]	pyramid

My Vocabulary

21
Quantities, Measurements, Numbers

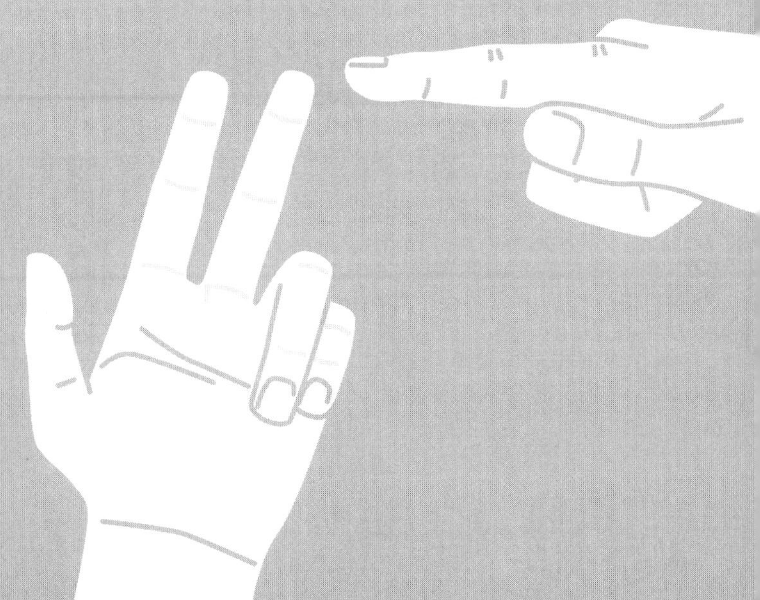

21.1 Expressions of Quantity  96

Combien? [kɔ̃bjɛ̃] — How much?/How many?
Combien coûte ce parfum? — How much does this perfume cost?
Combien de frères as-tu? — How many brothers do you have?

la **quantité** [kɑ̃tite] — quantity

nombreux, **nombreuse** [nɔ̃bʀø, øz] — many, numerous
L'accident a fait de nombreuses victimes. — The accident produced many victims.

le **nombre** [nɔ̃bʀ] — number (n)

plusieurs [plyzjœʀ] — several
Il y a plusieurs mois que je ne l'ai pas vu. — I have not seen him for several months.

quelques [kɛlkə] — some, a few
On en reparlera dans quelques années. — We will talk about it again in a few years.

quelques-uns, **quelques-unes** [kɛlkəzœ̃, zyn] — some
Je ne les connais pas tous, mais j'en ai déjà rencontré quelques-uns. — I don't know them all, but I have already met some of them.

---

ne... rien [nəʀjɛ̃] — nothing
Je n'en sais rien. — I know nothing about it.
Rien ne va plus. — No more bets!

ne... rien du tout [nəʀjɛ̃dytu] — nothing at all
Je n'y comprends rien du tout. — I don't understand anything at all.

ne... pas (**de**) [nəpa] — not, none
Je ne vois pas de solution. — I don't see any solution.

ne... pas du tout [nəpadytu] — not at all
Elle n'a pas d'argent du tout. — She has no money at all.

ne... pas un seul, **ne... pas une seule** [nəpa(z)œ̃/ynsœl] — none, not a single...
Ils ne parlent pas un seul mot d'allemand. — They don't speak a single word of German.

ne... aucun, **aucune** [nəokœ̃/kyn] — no, not a single...
Tu n'as aucune raison de te mettre en colère. — You have absolutely no reason to become angry.

aucun, **aucune (de)... ne** [okœ̃/ynnə] — none, neither
Aucun de ces deux tableaux ne me plaît. — I don't like either of these two paintings.

ne… **plus** (**de**) [nəply]	no more (of)
Je n'ai plus de monnaie.	I have no more change.
ne… **plus du tout** [nəplydytu]	absolutely no more
On n'a plus du tout de pain.	We are completely out of bread.

---

peu (**de**) [pø]	little *(See Information Box p. 448)*
Il a peu de chances de réussir.	He has little chance of succeeding.
Tu peux me prêter un peu d'argent?	Can you lend me a little money?
un (tout) petit peu (de)	a tiny bit (of)
très peu (de)	very little (of)
ne… **pas grand-chose** [nəpagʀɑ̃ʃoz]	not much
Je n'y connais pas grand-chose.	I don't know much about it.
presque pas (**de**) [pʀɛskəpas]	almost no
Cette année il n'y a presque pas eu de neige.	This year there has been almost no snow.

---

beaucoup (**de**) [boku]	lots (of)
pas mal (**de**) *fam* [pamal]	quite a few, bit (of)
Il y avait pas mal de gens à la manifestation.	There were quite a few people at the demonstration.
bien du, de la, de l'; des [bjɛ̃]	lots of, much
Je vous souhaite bien du plaisir.	I wish you lots of enjoyment.
plein (**de**) *fam* [plɛ̃]	awful lot
un tas (**de**) *fam* [ɛ̃ta]	bunch of
J'ai un tas de problèmes en ce moment.	I have a bunch of problems right now.
énormément (**de**) [enɔʀmemɑ̃]	huge amount (of)
Elle a énormément de courage.	She has a huge amount of courage.
tant (**de**) [tɑ̃]	so much
Ne bois pas tant (d'alcool).	Don't drink so much alcohol.
trop (**de**) [tʀo]	too much (of)
un **groupe** [gʀup]	group
un petit groupe de curieux	small group of curious people
une **foule** [ful]	crowd (n)
Il y avait une foule immense devant le stade.	There was a huge crowd in front of the stadium.

---

une **masse** (**de**) [mas]	mass, quantity (of)
en masse	en masse
davantage [davɑ̃taʒ]	more
Veux-tu davantage de dessert?	Do you want some more dessert?

en trop [ɑ̃tʀo]	too much, in excess
On lui a rendu ce qu'il avait payé en trop.	He was refunded the extra that he had paid.
la **majeure partie** [maʒœʀpaʀti]	majority (n)
tout au plus [tutoplys]	at the (very) most
Nous resterons là-bas 8 jours tout au plus.	We will stay there a week at the very most.

un **verre** (**de**) [vɛʀ]	glass (of)
se servir un verre de jus d'orange	to help oneself to a glass of orange juice
une **bouteille** (**de**) [butɛj]	bottle (of)
une **boîte** (**de**) [bwat]	can/box (of)
un **paquet** (**de**) [pakɛ]	package (of)
un paquet de biscuits	package of cookies

une **part** [paʀ]	part, portion (n)
Ne t'inquiète pas, tu auras ta part du gâteau.	Don't worry, you will get your portion of the cake.
une **partie** [paʀti]	part (n)
Une partie du public a sifflé la pièce.	Part of the audience booed the play.
la **plupart du, de la; des** [plypaʀ]	most of
La plupart du temps, il travaille.	Most of the time he works.
La plupart des spectateurs sont partis avant la fin du film.	Most of the audience left before the end of the film.
la **moitié** [mwatje]	half
le **reste** [ʀɛst]	rest, remainder
doubler [duble]	to double
En trois ans, il a doublé sa fortune.	He doubled his fortune in three years.
le **double** [dubl]	double (n)
la **majorité** [maʒɔʀite]	majority (n)
le **maximum** [maksimɔm]	maximum (n)
Je peux dépenser 100 euros **au maximum**.	I can spend a maximum of 100 euros.
le **minimum** [minimɔm]	minimum (n)
Il fait vraiment le minimum d'efforts.	He really puts out the minimum effort.
au minimum	at least/the minimum

comparer qn/qc à qn/qc [kɔ̃paʀe]	to compare s.o./s.th. to s.o./s.th.
plus (**de/que**) [plys]	more (of/than)
autant (**de/que**) [otɑ̃]	as much (as)
moins (**de/que**) [mwɛ̃]	less (of/than)

INFO

More or less

Que is used in comparisons after *plus/moins*; *de* is used with expressions of quantity. Examples:

Tu gagnes plus d'argent que moi.	*You earn more money than I do.*
Il gagne plus de 4 000 euros.	*He earned more than 4000 euros.*
Elle mange moins que moi.	*She eats less than I do.*
Ça vaut moins de 10 euros.	*That is worth less than 10 euros.*

tout, toute; tous *mpl*, **toutes** *fpl* [tu, tut, tus, tut]	all, every
C'est un événement dont **tout le monde** parle.	This is an event that everybody is talking about.
Tous leurs enfants vivent à l'étranger.	All their children live abroad.
Toutes mes filles sont mariées.	All my daughters are married.
le **tout** [tu]	whole (n)
l'**ensemble** *m* [ɑ̃sɑ̃bl]	whole (n)
chaque [ʃak]	each, every
Chaque jour, il quitte la maison à 7 heures.	Every day he leaves the house at seven o'clock.
chacun, **chacune** [ʃakœ̃, yn]	each (one), everyone
Il y en a assez pour chacun.	There is enough for everyone.

considérable [kɔ̃sideʀabl]	considerable
élevé, **élevée** [el(ə)ve]	high, elevated
Le prix de cette voiture est très élevé.	The price of this car is very high.
limité, **limitée** [limite]	limited
Je ne dispose que d'une somme limitée.	I have only a limited amount.
restreint, **restreinte** [ʀɛstʀɛ̃, ɛ̃t]	restricted, limited
Ses moyens sont restreints.	His means are limited.

21.2 Numbers and Numerals  97

INFO

Cardinal numbers

0	zéro [zeʀo]	40	quarante [kaʀɑ̃t]
1	un, une [œ̃, yn]	41	quarante et un, une [kaʀɑ̃teœ̃, yn]
2	duex [dø]	50	cinquante [sɛ̃kɑ̃t]
3	trois [tʀwa]	60	soixante [swasɑ̃t]
4	quarte [katʀ]	61	soixante et un, une
5	cinq [sɛ̃k]	62	soixante-deux
6	six [sis]	69	soixante-neuf
7	sept [sɛt]	70	soixante-dix
8	huit ['ɥit]	71	soixante et onze
9	neuf [nœf]	72	soixante et douze
10	dix [dis]	79	soixante-dix-neuf
11	onze ['ɔ̃z]	80	quatre-vingts [katʀəvɛ̃]
12	douze [duz]	81	quatre-vingt-un [katʀəvɛ̃œ̃, yn]
13	treize [tʀɛz]	82	quatre-vingt-deux [katʀəvɛ̃dø]
14	quatorze [katɔʀz]	89	quatre-vingt-neuf
15	quinze [kɛ̃z]	90	quatre-vingt-dix
16	seize [sɛz]	91	quatre-vingt-onze
17	dix-sept [dissɛt]	92	quatre-vingt-douze
18	dix-huit [dizɥit]	99	quatre-vingt-dix-neuf
19	dix-neuf [diznœf]	100	cent [sɑ̃]
20	vingt [vɛ̃]	101	cent un, une [sɑ̃œ̃, yn]
21	vingt et un, une [vɛ̃teœ̃, yn]	110	cent dix
22	vingt-deux [vɛ̃tdø]	200	deux cents
30	trente [tʀɑ̃t]	1 000	mille [mil]
31	trente en un, une [tʀɑ̃teœ̃, yn]	1 001	mille un, une
32	trente-deux [tʀɑ̃tdø]	2 000	deux mille
		1 000 000	un million [ɛ̃miljɔ̃]
		1 000 000 000	un milliard [ɛ̃miljar]

Cardinal numbers are used to *specify dates* and with the *names of rulers*—with the exception of the number 1. Examples: le deux/trois mai (May second/third); Napoléon III (trois), Louis XIV (quatorze).
But notice le 1er (premier) avril; Napoléon 1er (premier).

After the 1990 *Rectifications de l'orthographe* [French spelling adjustments] the *individual elements of compound numbers* can be connected with hyphens: 1284 = mille-deux-cent-quatre-vingt-quatre.

INFO

Ordinal numbers

1er	le premier	[pʀɛmje]
1ère	la première	[pʀɛmjeʀ]
2[e]	le, la deuxième	[døzjɛm]
2[e]	le second, la seconde	[s(ə)gɔ̃, ɔ̃d]
20[e]	le, la vingtième	[vɛ̃tjɛm]
21[e]	le, la vingt et unième	[vɛ̃teynjɛm]
22[e]	le, la vingt-deuxième	[vɛ̃tdøzjɛm]
71[e]	le, la soixante et onzième	[swasɑ̃teɔ̃zjɛm]
100[e]	le, la centième	[sɑ̃tjɛm]
1000[e]	le, la millième	[miljɛm]

une **dizaine** (**de**) [dizɛn] — ten, about ten
une **douzaine** (**de**) [duzɛn] — a dozen
  une douzaine d'œufs — a dozen eggs
une **quinzaine** (**de**) [kɛ̃zɛn] — about fifteen
  une quinzaine de jours — about two weeks
une **vingtaine** (**de**) [vɛ̃tɛn] — about twenty
une **centaine** (**de**) [sɑ̃tɛn] — about a hundred
  il y a une centaine d'années — about a hundred years ago
un **millier** (**de**) [milje] — about a thousand

---

un **demi** [d(ə)mi] — half
  une **demi-/demie heure** — half-hour
  une **heure et demie** — an hour and a half
un **tiers** [tjɛʀ] — a third
un **quart** [kaʀ] — quarter
  un **quart d'heure** — quarter-hour
un **cinquième** [sɛ̃kjɛm] — fifth
un **centième** [sɑ̃tjɛm] — hundredth
deux cinquièmes [døsɛ̃kjɛm] — two-fifths
un **pour cent** [puʀsɑ̃] — one percent
  Plus de 10 % des Français aimeraient que leur fille épouse un Allemand. — More than ten percent of French people would like their daughter to marry a German.

---

le **double** [dubl]	double (n)
Ça coûte le double de ce que je voulais dépenser.	That costs double what I wanted to spend.
le **triple** [tʀipl]	triple
… **fois** [fwa]	…times
Ça coûte trois fois rien. *loc*	That is dirt cheap.
un **chiffre** [ʃifʀ]	digit, number
un **nombre** [nɔ̃bʀ]	number (n)
un **nombre entier**	whole number
un **nombre premier**	prime number
un **nombre** (**im**)**pair**	uneven number
un **nombre cardinal**	cardinal number
un **nombre ordinal**	ordinal number
un **numéro** [nymeʀo]	number (n)
l'**ordre** *m* [ɔʀdʀ]	order (n)
par ordre croissant/décroissant	in increasing/decreasing order
une **unité** [ynite]	unit
compter [kɔ̃te]	to count
compter sur ses doigts	to count on one's fingers
calculer [kalkyle]	to calculate
le **calcul** [kalkyl]	arithmetic, computation, calculus
le **calcul mental**	mental calculation
une **erreur de calcul**	math error
se tromper dans ses calculs	to calculate incorrectly
la **somme** [sɔm]	sum (n)
la **différence** [difeʀɑ̃s]	difference (n)
plus [plys]	more
moins [mwɛ̃]	less
le **total** [tɔtal]	total (n)
Au total, ça fait 75 euros.	In total, that is 75 euros.
le **résultat** [ʀezylta]	product, result
correspondre à qc [kɔʀɛspɔ̃dʀa]	to correspond to s.th.
Ça correspond à peu près à mes calculs.	That corresponds closely to my calculations.

une **opération** [ɔpeʀasjɔ̃]	calculation, arithmetic procedure
additionner [adisjɔne]	to add
une **addition** [adisjɔ̃]	addition
soustraire [sustʀɛʀ]	to subtract
une **soustraction** [sustʀaksjɔ̃]	subtraction
multiplier [myltiplije]	to multiply
multiplier par trois	to multiply by three
une **multiplication** [myltiplikasjɔ̃]	multiplication
diviser [divize]	to divide
diviser par deux	to divide by two
une **division** [divizjɔ̃]	division
recompter [ʀ(ə)kɔ̃te]	to recount
J'ai recompté trois fois pour être sûr.	I counted three times to be sure.
la **virgule** [viʀgyl]	(decimal) point
deux virgule cinq	two point five (2.5)

égal, **égale** [egal]	equal
deux quantités égales	two equal quantities
l'**égalité** *f* [egalite]	equality
supérieur, **supérieure** [sypeʀjœʀ]	greater/higher than
La température est **supérieure à la normale**.	The temperature is higher than normal.
inférieur, **inférieure** [ɛ̃feʀjœʀ]	lower, less, smaller

exact, **exacte** [ɛgza(kt), ɛgzakt]	exact, precise
Avez-vous l'heure exacte?	Do you have the precise time?
précis, **précise** [pʀesi, iz]	precise, exact
Je serai là à 15 heures précises.	I will be there at exactly 3:00 P.M.
environ [ɑ̃viʀɔ̃]	around
Il a environ 35 ans.	He is around 35 years old.
à peu près [apøpʀɛ]	nearly
(**c'est**) **juste** [ʒyst]	(that is) correct, right
(**c'est**) **faux** [fo]	(that is) false, wrong, incorrect
Le résultat est juste/faux.	The result is correct/false.

21.3 Measurements and Weights  98

mesurer [məzyʀe]	to measure
mesurer une pièce	to measure a room
la **mesure** [m(ə)zyʀ]	measurement
une **unité de mesure**	unit of measurement
la **taille** [taj]	size, height
petit, **petite** [p(ə)ti, it]	small
minuscule [minyskyl]	tiny
grand, **grande** [gʀɑ̃, gʀɑ̃d]	large
immense [imɑ̃s]	huge, immense
gros, **grosse** [gʀo, gʀos]	fat
énorme [enɔʀm]	enormous
Elle a fait une énorme bêtise.	She committed a monumental blunder.

la **dimension** [dimɑ̃sjɔ̃]	dimension, size
long, **longue** [lɔ̃, lɔ̃g]	long
la **longueur** [lɔ̃gœʀ]	length
court, **courte** [kuʀ, kuʀt]	short
large [laʀʒ]	wide, broad
la **largeur** [laʀʒœʀ]	width, breadth
dans le sens de la largeur	lengthwise
haut, **haute** ['o, 'ot]	high
La tour Eiffel est **haute de** 320 mètres.	The Eiffel Tower is 320 meters high.
la **hauteur** ['otœʀ]	height
bas, **basse** [bɑ, bɑs]	low
profond, **profonde** [pʀɔfɔ̃, ɔ̃d]	deep
la **profondeur** [pʀɔfɔ̃dœʀ]	depth
un **millimètre** [milimɛtʀ]	millimeter
un **centimètre** [sɑ̃timɛtʀ]	centimeter
un **mètre** [mɛtʀ]	meter
un **kilomètre** [kilɔmɛtʀ]	kilometer
un **kilomètre de long**	a kilometer long
un **kilomètre à l'heure** (**km/h**)	one kilometer per hour

l'**échelle** *f* [eʃɛl]	scale
à l'échelle (**de**) 1/100 000[e]	on a scale of 1 to 100,000
la **graduation** [gʀadɥasjɔ̃]	scale

peser [pəze]	to weigh
Pierre pèse 70 kilos.	Pierre weighs 70 kilos.
le **poids** [pwa]	weight
la **balance** [balɑ̃s]	scale
La balance indique 80 kilos.	The scale indicates 80 kilos.
la **masse** [mas]	mass
lourd, **lourde** [luʀ, luʀd]	heavy

léger, **légère** [leʒe, ʒɛʀ]	light
net, **nette** [nɛt]	net
le **poids net**	net weight
brut, **brute** [bʀyt]	gross
le **bénéfice brut**	gross profit
un **gramme** (**de**) [gʀam]	gram
un **kilo**(**gramme**) (**de**) [kilo, kilɔgʀam]	kilogram
un kilo de pommes de terre	a kilo of potatoes
une **tonne** [tɔn]	(metric) ton

INFO

Let's shed some light on "light"

léger, légère	*light (in weight; antonym: heavy—lourd, lourde)* *minor (antonym: serious—grave)*
des bagages légers/lourds	*light/heavy baggage*
une blessure légère/grave	*minor/serious injury*
facile	*light, easy, simple (antonym: hard—difficile)*
un devoir facile/difficile	*light/hard assignment*
C'est facile/difficile à dire.	*That is easy/hard to say.*

une livre (**de**) [livʀ]	pound (of)
une **demi-livre** de beurre	half a pound of butter
un **quintal** [kɛ̃tal]	quintal, hundredweight

la **surface** [syʀfas]	surface, area
carré, **carrée** [kaʀe]	square (adj)
une pièce de 15 **mètres carrés** (m^2)	a room of 15 square meters

la **superficie** [sypɛʀfisi]	surface, area
un **are** [aʀ]	are (100 square meters)
un **hectare** [ɛktaʀ]	hectare
un terrain de 3 hectares	three-hectare plot of land

le **volume** [vɔlym]	volume
contenir [kɔ̃t(ə)niʀ]	to contain
Cette bouteille contient un litre.	This bottle contains a liter.
le **contenu** [kɔ̃t(ə)ny]	contents (n)
un **litre** [litʀ]	liter
un litre de lait	liter of milk
cube [kyb]	cubic
un **mètre cube** (m^3)	cubic meter

My Vocabulary

22

General Terms

22.1 Classifying  99

classer [klase]	to order, arrange
Tu devrais classer les photos dans un album.	You should arrange the photos in an album.
le **classement** [klasmɑ̃]	arrangement; organization
ordonner [ɔʀdɔne]	to order; to put into order
un **ordre** [ɔʀdʀ]	order, sequence (n)
classer des objets **par ordre de** taille	to organize items in order of size
une **catégorie** [kategɔʀi]	category
une **suite** (**de**) [sɥit]	sequence, succession (of)
une **série** (**de**) [seʀi]	series (of)
Cette **série de timbres** n'est pas complète.	This series of stamps is not complete.

la **classification** [klasifikasjɔ̃]	classification
procéder à la classification de qc	to classify s.th.
la **disposition** [dispozisjɔ̃]	arrangement, disposition

une **sorte** (**de**) [sɔʀt]	type (of)
une **espèce** (**de**) [ɛspɛs]	type (of)
Nous habitons une espèce de château.	We live in a type of castle.
correspondre à qc [kɔʀɛspɔ̃dʀ]	to correspond to s.th.

un **signe** [siɲ]	sign (n)
un **signe particulier**	a special sign
spécial, **spéciale** [spesjal]	special
général, **générale** [ʒeneʀal]	general
Elle manque de **culture générale**.	She is lacking in general education.
principal, **principale** [pʀɛ̃sipal]	main, principal
la **rue principale**	main road
un **détail**; des **détails** *pl* [detaj]	detail (n)
constituer [kɔ̃stitɥe]	to constitute, make up
Les différents éléments constituent un ensemble.	The various elements make up a whole.
former [fɔʀme]	to form

une **qualité** [kalite]	quality
Je préfère la qualité à la quantité.	I prefer quality to quantity.
préféré, **préférée** [prefeʀe]	preferred, favorite
St. Exupéry est mon auteur préféré.	St. Exupéry is my favorite author.
important, **importante** [ɛ̃pɔʀtɑ̃, ɑ̃t]	important

l'**importance** *f* [ɛ̃pɔrtɑ̃s]	significance, importance
une affaire **de la plus haute importance**	a matter of the greatest importance
négligeable [negliʒabl]	negligible
C'est un détail négligeable.	This is a negligible detail.

premièrement [pʀəmjɛʀmɑ̃]	first (of all)
deuxièmement [døzjɛmmɑ̃]	secondly
Premièrement, je n'ai pas envie d'y aller, et deuxièmement, je n'ai pas le temps.	In the first place, I don't feel like going there, and secondly, I don't have the time.
d'abord [dabɔʀ]	at first
ensuite [ɑ̃sɥit]	then, after that
puis [pɥi]	then, next
Ils ont d'abord eu une fille, puis deux garçons.	First they had a daughter, then two boys.
finalement [finalmɑ̃]	finally
enfin [ɑ̃fɛ̃]	finally
Il a enfin trouvé un logement.	He finally found an apartment.

en premier lieu [ɑ̃pʀəmjeljø]	in the first place
En premier lieu, je tiens à remercier M. Bernard pour son aide efficace.	In the first place I would like to thank Mr. Bernard for his efficient help.
occuper la première place [ɔkypelapʀəmjɛʀplas]	to occupy first place
être en tête de [ɛtʀɑ̃tɛt]	to be at the top of
Il est en tête du Top 50.	He is at the top of the charts.
passer* au second plan [paseos(ə)gɔ̃plɑ̃]	to take a back seat
en dernier lieu [ɑ̃dɛʀnjeljø]	in the end, final analysis

22.2 Degree, Comparison, Relationships

100

fort, **forte** [fɔʀ, fɔʀt]	strong, large
une forte majorité	strong majority
faible [fɛbl]	weak, small
un faible pourcentage	small percentage
à peu près [apøpʀɛ]	around, about
moyen, **moyenne** [mwajɛ̃, jɛn]	average, medium
Vichy est une ville moyenne.	Vichy is a medium-sized city.
en moyenne	on average
largement [laʀʒəmɑ̃]	(by) far and away

énorme [enɔʀm]	enormous, huge
Il a gagné une somme énorme au loto.	He won a huge sum in the lottery.
Il a gagné **énormément** d'argent.	He won an enormous amount of money.
fantastique [fɑ̃tastik]	fantastic
hyper/méga/giga *fam* [ipɛʀ/mega/ʒiga]	super-, ultra-
J'ai trouvé ce film hyper nul.	I found this film really lousy.
C'était une soirée méga cool.	It was a super-cool evening.
terrible [tɛʀibl]	terrible
J'ai été témoin d'un terrible accident.	I was witness to a terrible accident.
extrême [ɛkstʀɛm]	extreme
Ils vivent dans une extrême pauvreté.	They live in extreme poverty.
Il fait **extrêmement** froid.	It is extremely cold.
comparer qn/qc à qn/qc [kɔ̃paʀe]	to compare s.o./s.th. to s.o./s.th.
On le compare souvent à son père.	He is often compared to his father.
la **comparaison** [kɔ̃paʀɛzɔ̃]	comparison
le **rapport** [ʀapɔʀ]	relationship, connection
établir des rapports avec qn	to establish relations with s.o
Le succès du chanteur est **sans rapport avec** son talent.	The singer's success has no connection to his talent.
Le prix de ce vêtement n'est pas **en rapport avec** sa qualité.	The price of this article of clothing has nothing to do with its quality.
par rapport à	with respect, in comparison to
la **relation** [ʀ(ə)lasjɔ̃]	relationship
une **relation de cause à effet**	cause-and-effect relationship
le **point commun** [pwɛ̃kɔmɛ̃]	common ground
comparé, **comparée à** [kɔ̃paʀe]	compared to
comparable à [kɔ̃paʀabl]	comparable to
similaire [similɛʀ]	similar
Ils ont fait des expériences similaires.	They have had similar experiences.
égal, **égale** [egal]	equal, same
diviser qc en deux parts égales	to divide s.th. into two equal parts
pareil, **pareille** [paʀɛj]	similar, equal
Je n'ai jamais dit une **chose pareille**.	I never said such a thing.
semblable [sɑ̃blabl]	similar
ressembler à [ʀ(ə)sɑ̃ble]	to resemble, be similar to

ressemblant, **ressemblante** [R(ə)sɑ̃blɑ̃, ɑ̃t]	similar
la **ressemblance** [R(ə)sɑ̃blɑ̃s]	resemblance, similarity

la **parenté** [paRɑ̃te]	(family) relationship
l'**analogie** *f* [analɔʒi]	analogy
procéder **par analogie**	to proceed by analogy

comme [kɔm]	like
Il est bête comme ses pieds. *loc, fam*	He is dumb as a rock.
aussi... **que** [osikə]	as...as
Je cours aussi vite que toi.	I run as fast as you.
autant/tant... **que** [otɑ̃kə]	as...as
Il n'est pas aussi (si) gros que Daniel, parce qu'il ne mange pas autant (tant) que lui.	He is not as fat as Daniel because he doesn't eat as much as he (Daniel) does.
plus... **que** [plykə]	more...than
Elle est plus douée que son frère.	She is more talented than her brother.
moins... **que** [mwɛ̃kə]	less... than

de plus en plus [d(ə)plyzɑ̃ply]	more and more
Elle est de plus en plus gentille.	She keeps getting nicer and nicer.
de moins en moins [d(ə)mwɛ̃zɑ̃mwɛ̃]	less and less
Nous nous voyons de moins en moins.	We keep seeing less and less of each other.
de mieux en mieux [d(ə)mjøzɑ̃mjø]	better and better
de pire en pire [d(ə)piRɑ̃piR]	worse and worse

le **contraire** [kɔ̃tRɛR]	opposite, contrary (n)
au contraire de	in contrast to
contrairement à [kɔ̃tRɛRmɑ̃]	contrary to
Contrairement à ce qu'ils ont annoncé à la météo, il fait beau.	In contrast to what they said on the weather forecast, it is nice out.
différent, **différente de** [difeRɑ̃, ɑ̃t]	different from
Ses idées sont différentes des miennes.	His ideas are different from mine.
la **différence** [difeRɑ̃s]	difference
à la différence de	unlike, in contrast to
s'opposer à [sɔpoze]	to be opposed to
être opposé, **opposée à qc** [ɔpoze]	to be opposed to s.th.
Ils sont opposés à cette décision.	They are opposed to this decision.
à l'opposé de [alɔpoze]	in opposition/contrast to
À l'opposé de mon père, ma mère aime bien ma nouvelle coiffure.	In contrast to my father, my mother likes my new hairstyle.
l'**opposition** *f* [ɔpozisjɔ̃]	opposition

se distinguer de [s(ə)distɛ̃ge]	to be distinguished from
Il se distingue de ses frères par sa taille.	He is distinguished from his brothers by his height.
la **distinction** [distɛ̃ksjɔ̃]	distinction
contraster avec [kɔ̃tʀaste]	to contrast with
Sa voix douce contraste avec son physique de brute.	His/Her gentle voice contrasts with his/her coarse exterior.
le **contraste** [kɔ̃tʀast]	contrast (n)
différer de [difeʀe]	to differ from
être en contradiction avec [ɛtʀɑ̃kɔ̃tʀadiksjɔ̃]	to be in contradiction to
à l'inverse de [alɛ̃vɛʀs]	in contrast to
inversement [ɛ̃vɛʀsəmɑ̃]	conversely
et vice versa [evisvɛʀsa]	and vice versa
Elle aime son mari et vice versa.	She loves her husband and vice versa.
en revanche [ɑ̃ʀ(ə)vɑ̃ʃ]	on the other hand
Je n'aime pas Lyon, en revanche Marseille me plaît beaucoup.	I don't like Lyon; on the other hand, I like Marseille a lot.

le **contexte** [kɔ̃tɛkst]	context
sortir qc de son contexte	to take s.th. out of context
être lié, **liée à/avec** [lje]	to be connected to s.th.; to be friendly with s.o.
Sa façon de voir les choses est liée à son enfance malheureuse.	His way of viewing things is connected to his unhappy childhood.
Nous sommes très liés avec les Dupont.	We are very close friends with the Duponts.
le **lien** [ljɛ̃]	connection
faire partie de [fɛʀpaʀti]	to be part of, belong to
dépendre de [depɑ̃dʀ]	to depend on
Tout dépend de sa décision.	Everything depends on his/her decision.
la **dépendance** [depɑ̃dɑ̃s]	dependency

22.3 Characteristics  101

léger, **légère** [leʒe, ɛʀ]	light *(See Information Box p. 437)*
avoir **le sommeil léger**	to be a light sleeper
lourd, **lourde** [luʀ, luʀd]	heavy *(See Information Box p. 437)*
Cette valise est trop lourde.	This suitcase is too heavy.
plein, **pleine** [plɛ̃, ɛn]	full
Le verre est **à moitié plein**.	The glass is half-full.
complet, **complète** [kɔ̃plɛ, ɛt]	full
vide [vid]	empty
dur, **dure** [dyʀ]	hard
doux, **douce** [du, dus]	soft, sweet
mou, mol, molle [mu, mɔl]	soft
épais, **épaisse** [epɛ, ɛs]	thick
un brouillard épais	thick fog
mince [mɛ̃s]	thin
étroit, **étroite** [etʀwa, wat]	narrow, tight
une rue étroite	narrow street

froid, **froide** [fʀwa, fʀwad]	cold
Bois ton thé avant qu'il (ne) soit trop froid.	Drink your tea before it gets too cold.
tiède [tjɛd]	lukewarm
Il n'a pas inventé l'eau tiède. *loc*	He's not the sharpest knife in the drawer.
chaud, **chaude** [ʃo, ʃod]	hot

visible [vizibl]	visible
invisible [ɛ̃vizibl]	invisible
«L'essentiel est invisible pour les yeux.» *(St. Exupéry)*	"The essential is invisible to the eyes."
lisible [lizibl]	legible
illisible [ilizibl]	illegible

clair, **claire** [klɛʀ]	clear (adj)
tirer au clair	to clarify, clear up
obscur, **obscure** [ɔpskyʀ]	dark
une nuit obscure	dark night
coloré, **colorée** [kɔlɔʀe]	colored
incolore [ɛ̃kɔlɔʀ]	colorless
transparent, **transparente** [tʀɑ̃spaʀɑ̃, ɑ̃t]	transparent
opaque [ɔpak]	opaque

vieux, vieil, vieille [vjø, vjɛj]	old
un vieux pull; un vieil anorak; une vieille chemise	an old sweater; an old parka; an old shirt
ancien, **ancienne** [ɑ̃sjɛ̃, jɛn]	old, antique, former *(See Information Box p. 44)*
un monument ancien	ancient monument
neuf, **neuve** [nœf, nœv]	new
nouveau, nouvel, nouvelle; nouveaux, nouvelles *pl* [nuvo, nuvɛl]	new; other *(See Information Box p. 111)*
un nouveau film; un nouvel opéra; une nouvelle pièce	new film; new opera; new play
actuel, actuelle [aktɥɛl]	current
moderne [mɔdɛʀn]	modern

bon, **bonne** [bɔ̃, bɔn]	good
meilleur, **meilleure** [mɛjœʀ]	better
excellent, **excellente** [ɛkselɑ̃, ɑ̃t]	excellent
médiocre [medjɔkʀ]	mediocre
mauvais, **mauvaise** [movɛ, ɛz]	bad
être de mauvaise humeur	to be in a bad mood
normal, **normale** [nɔʀmal]	normal
anormal, **anormale** [anɔʀmal]	abnormal
ordinaire [ɔʀdinɛʀ]	ordinary, regular, usual, simple
du **vin ordinaire**	ordinary table wine
rare [ʀaʀ]	rare
étrange [etʀɑ̃ʒ]	strange, peculiar
bizarre [bizaʀ]	strange, bizarre
Elle m'a regardé **d'un air bizarre**.	She looked at me strangely.
ridicule [ʀidikyl]	ridiculous
se rendre ridicule	to make a fool of oneself

facile [fasil]	easy
C'est plus facile à dire qu'à faire.	Easier said than done.
difficile [difisil]	difficult *(See Information Box p. 437)*
une langue difficile à apprendre	a difficult language to learn
nécessaire [nesesɛʀ]	necessary
utile [ytil]	useful
inutile [inytil]	useless
essentiel, **essentielle** [esɑ̃sjɛl]	essential
aller* droit à l'essentiel	to cut right to the chase

efficace [efikas]	efficient
un remède efficace contre le mal de tête	effective/efficient remedy for headaches
inefficace [inefikas]	ineffective, inefficient
indispensable [ɛ̃dispɑ̃sabl]	indispensable
Ta présence est **indispensable à** mon bonheur.	Your presence is indispensable to my happiness.

exact, **exacte** [egza(kt), egzakt]	exact
Ma montre **indique l'heure exacte**.	My watch indicates the exact time.
inexact, **inexacte** [inegza(kt), inegzakt]	imprecise, inexact
précis, **précise** [pʀesi, iz]	precise
imprécis, **imprécise** [ɛ̃pʀesi, iz]	imprecise
vrai, **vraie** [vʀɛ]	true
Ce n'est pas vrai.	That is not true.
faux, **fausse** [fo, fos]	false, wrong
L'adresse qu'on m'a donnée est fausse.	The address I was given is wrong.
vague [vag]	vague
Je n'ai qu'une vague idée sur la question.	I have only a vague idea about the issue.
direct, **directe** [diʀɛkt]	direct
indirect, **indirecte** [ɛ̃diʀɛkt]	indirect

rapide [ʀapid]	fast, quick, speedy
vif, **vive** [vif, viv]	lively
avoir une intelligence vive	to have a quick mind
lent, **lente** [lɑ̃, lɑ̃t]	slow
Roulez lentement!	Drive slowly!

INFO

Fast

Vite (fast) is an *adverb*. As an *adjective*, the word *rapide* must be used instead.

Elle court vite/rapidement.	*She runs fast.*
But: Ils sont rapides.	*They are fast.*

cher, **chère** [ʃɛʀ]	expensive *(See Information Box p. 118)*
bon marché [bɔ̃maʀʃe]	cheap, inexpensive
Les pommes de terre sont **meilleur marché** que les asperges.	The potatoes are cheaper than the asparagus.

INFO

Good, better, best

Note the irregular comparative forms of the following adjectives and adverbs:

bon, bonne *(good)*	meilleur, meilleure	le meilleur, la meilleure
mauvais, mauvaise *(bad)*	pire	le, la pire
bien *(well)*	mieux	le mieux
peu *(little)*	moins	le moins
beaucoup *(much)*	plus	le plus

22.4 Type and Manner  102

la **manière** (**de**) [manjɛʀ] — manner (of)
  de manière que/à — so that, in such a way that
  De quelle manière? — In what way?
la **façon** (**de**) [fasɔ̃] — manner (of)
  de façon que à — so that, in such a way that
  De quelle façon? — In what way?
  de toute façon — in any case

INFO

De manière que, etc.

After the conjunctions *de façon que*, *de manière que*, *de sorte que*, the indicative is used in the subordinate clause when a factual outcome is meant. But the *subjunctive* is used when a view or an intention is meant:

Il pleut de façon/manière/sorte qu'on ne peut pas sortir.	*It is raining so hard that we cannot go outdoors.*
Exprime-toi de façon/manière/sorte qu'on te comprenne.	*Express yourself so people can understand you.*
Viens de bonne heure de sorte qu'on puisse regarder le match à la télé.	*Come early so we can watch the game on TV.*
Il est venu de bonne heure de sorte qu'on a pu regarder le match à la télé.	*He came early so we could watch the game on the TV.*

An *indicative construction* is preferred when the same subject is used in the main and subordinate clauses:

Il parle lentement de manière à être compris.	*He speaks slowly to be understood.*
Crie fort de façon à être entendu/de façon qu'on t'entende.	*Yell loudly so someone will hear you.*

une **sorte** (**de**) [sɔʀt]	type (of)
de sorte que	so that, in such a way that
le **mode** [mɔd]	means *(See Information Box p. 111)*
le **mode d'emploi**	instructions for use, directions

le **moyen** [mwajɛ̃]	means (n)
trouver le moyen de faire qc	to find a way, the means to do s.th.
Comment? [kɔmɑ̃]	What?
Comment ça va?	How goes it?
ainsi [ɛ̃si]	thus(ly)
Si tu t'y prends ainsi, tu n'y arriveras jamais.	If that's the way you go about it, you will never succeed.
aussi [osi]	also
même [mɛm]	even
J'ai même eu le temps de laver la voiture.	I even had time to wash the car.
très [tʀɛ]	very
Elle est très adroite.	She is very clever.

bien *adv* [bjɛ̃]	well
Les plantes poussent bien avec cette pluie.	The plants will grow well with this rain.
vraiment [vʀɛmɑ̃]	really
Est-ce que tu as vraiment dit ça?	Did you really say that?
seulement [sœlmɑ̃]	only
autrement [otʀəmɑ̃]	otherwise
Je ne pouvais pas faire autrement.	I could not do otherwise.

en général [ɑ̃ʒeneʀal]	in general, generally
En général, nous prenons nos vacances en été.	We generally take our vacation in the summer.
généralement [ʒeneʀalmɑ̃]	generally, usually
d'habitude [dabityd]	usually, habitually
Comme d'habitude.	As usual.
normalement [nɔʀmalmɑ̃]	normally
surtout [syʀtu]	especially
Surtout, ne faites pas ça!	Especially, don't do that!

vraisemblablement [vʀɛsɑ̃blabləmɑ̃] — probably
  Nous serons vraisemblablement absents jusqu'au 15. — We probably will be gone until the fifteenth.
au fond [ofɔ̃] — deep down, essentially
  Au fond, elle n'est pas si méchante. — Deep down, she is not so nasty.
en principe [ɑ̃pʀɛ̃sip] — in principle
en particulier [ɑ̃paʀtikylje] — in particular
particulièrement [paʀtikyljɛʀmɑ̃] — particularly
exclusivement [ɛksklyzivmɑ̃] — exclusively, only
  Elle se nourrit exclusivement de produits bio. — She eats only organic foods.

devoir [dəvwaʀ] — to have to, must
  Il doit avoir environ 40 ans. — He must be around forty.
il faut que + *subj* [ilfokə] — it is necessary (to)
  Il faut que tu ailles voir ce film. — You have to go see this film.
vouloir [vulwaʀ] — to wish, to want
pouvoir [puvwaʀ] — to be able

INFO

To be able, can

pouvoir Vous faites trop de bruit, je ne peux pas dormir.	*to be able (under certain conditions)* *You are making too much noise; I cannot sleep.*
savoir Il ne sait ni lire ni écrire.	*to know how, be able (through learning)* *He cannot read nor write*

22.5 Cause, Effect, Goal, Purpose  103

causer [koze] — to cause
  Sa santé nous cause des soucis. — His health is a source of worry to us.
la **cause** [koz] — cause, reason (n)
  à cause de — because of
  C'est à cause de toi qu'on a raté le train. — We missed the train because of you.
grâce à [gʀasa] — thanks to
  C'est grâce à vous que j'ai eu cet emploi. — I got this job thanks to you.
la **raison** (**pour laquelle**) [ʀɛzɔ̃] — the reason (why, for which)
  Je ne connais pas la raison pour laquelle elle n'est pas venue. — I don't know the reason why she didn't come.
  Pour quelle raison? — Why? For what reason?

le **motif** [mɔtif]	reason, cause, motive
Pourquoi? [puʀkwa]	Why?

le **mobile** [mɔbil]	motive
le mobile du crime	motive for the crime
le **hasard** ['azaʀ]	chance
par hasard	by chance, randomly

parce que [paʀs(ə)kə]	because
puisque [pɥiskə]	since
On est parti sans elle puisqu'elle n'arrivait pas.	We left without her since she wasn't coming.
comme [kɔm]	since
Comme il était déjà tard, il est allé se coucher.	Since it was already late, he went to bed.
car [kaʀ]	for, because
c'est pour cela/ça que [sɛpuʀs(ə)la/sakə]	that's why
c'est pourquoi [sɛpuʀkwa]	that's why
Elle travaille beaucoup, c'est pourquoi elle est fatiguée.	She works a lot; that's why she is tired.
alors [alɔʀ]	thus, so
donc [dɔ̃k]	so, therefore
«Je pense, donc je suis.» (*Descartes*)	"I think, therefore I am."
pour [puʀ]	for, in order to
Elle travaille dur pour nourrir sa famille.	She works hard in order to feed her family.
pour que + *subj* [puʀkə]	so that
Je fais tout pour qu'il soit content.	I do everything so that he will be happy.

afin que + *subj* [afɛ̃kə]	so that
Il a parlé lentement afin que nous comprenions tout.	He spoke slowly so that we would understand everything.
afin de + *inf* [afɛ̃də]	in order to
Prenez un taxi afin d'arriver à l'heure.	Take a taxi in order to arrive on time.

le **but** [byt]	goal (n)
poursuivre un but	to pursue a goal
avoir pour but	to have as a goal
dans le but de	with a view to/for the purpose of
atteindre [atɛ̃dʀ]	to reach
atteindre son but	to reach one's goal
l'**objectif** *m* [ɔbʒɛktif]	goal, objective
se fixer un objectif	to set a goal for oneself

la **fin** [fɛ̃]	end, purpose
La fin justifie les moyens. *loc*	The end justifies the means.
aboutir à [abutiʀ]	to lead to
Les négociations ont abouti à un résultat satisfaisant.	The negotiations led to a satisfactory result.
l'**intention** *f* [ɛ̃tɑ̃sjɔ̃]	intention
avoir l'intention de faire qc	to have the intention of doing s.th.

l'**effet** *m* [efɛ]	effect
Ce médicament ne **produit aucun effet sur** lui.	This medication has no effect on him.
en effet	in fact
le **résultat** [ʀezylta]	result (n)
entraîner [ɑ̃tʀɛne]	to entail, result in, bring about

la **conséquence** [kɔ̃sekɑ̃s]	consequence, result
avoir pour conséquence	to have as a result
tirer les conséquences	to learn one's lesson
par conséquent [paʀkɔ̃sekɑ̃]	consequently; as a result
Tu as désobéi, par conséquent tu seras puni.	You disobeyed; consequently you will be punished.
résulter de [ʀezylte]	to result (n)
Il ne peut rien résulter de bon de cette dispute.	Nothing good can come from this dispute.
il en résulte que	the result is

22.6 Condition and Change  104

être [ɛtʀ]	to be
l'**état** *m* [eta]	condition, state
en bon/mauvais état	in good/bad condition
être situé, située [sitɥe]	to be located
La maison est située près de la rivière.	The house is located near the river.
une **situation** [sitɥasjɔ̃]	situation
se trouver [s(ə)tʀuve]	to be located
L'hôtel se trouve à 200 mètres de la gare.	The hotel is located 200 meters from the train station.
exister [ɛgziste]	to exist
Est-ce que le Père Noël existe vraiment, papa?	Does Santa Claus really exist, Dad?
l'**existence** *f* [ɛgzistɑ̃s]	existence

mettre [mɛtʀ]	to put, place
Elle met des fleurs dans un vase.	She puts some flowers into a vase.
poser [poze]	to place, lay, put
poser les assiettes sur la table	to put the plates on the table
enlever [ɑ̃l(ə)ve]	to take away
placer [plase]	to place
placer un bon mot dans la conversation	to interject a witty remark into the conversation
déplacer [deplase]	to move to a different place; place
remplacer [ʀɑ̃plase]	to replace
remplacer un carreau cassé	to replace a broken window pane
installer [ɛ̃stale]	to install, set up
Elle installe son fauteuil face à la télé.	She set up her armchair in front of the television.
éloigner qc de [elwaɲe]	to distance s.th. from
approcher qc de [apʀɔʃe]	to move s.th. closer to
Approche la chaise de la table.	Move the chair closer to the table.
rapprocher qc de [ʀapʀɔʃe]	to move s.th. closer to
porter [pɔʀte]	to carry *(See Information Box p. 151)*
une valise **lourde à porter**	a suitcase difficult to carry
apporter qc [apɔʀte]	to bring s.th.
Apporte-moi une bière, s'il te plaît.	Bring me a beer, please.
rapporter qc [ʀapɔʀte]	to bring s.th. back, return
rapporter un livre à la bibliothèque	to return a book to the library
emporter qc [ɑ̃pɔʀte]	to take s.th.
Si tu vas en Norvège, n'oublie pas d'emporter des vêtements chauds.	If you go to Norway, don't forget to take warm clothing.
remporter qc [ʀɑ̃pɔʀte]	to take something again *(See Information Box p. 151)*
conduire qn à [kɔ̃dɥiʀ]	to drive s.o. to
Tu pourrais me conduire à la gare?	Could you drive me to the train station?
mener qn à [m(ə)ne]	to take s.o. to
mener un enfant à l'école	to take a child to school

amener qn [am(ə)ne] — to bring along
J'ai amené mon bébé, j'espère que ça ne vous dérange pas. — I have brought my baby; I hope that doesn't bother you.

ramener qn [ʀamne] — to bring s.o. back

emmener qn [ɑ̃m(ə)ne] — to take s.o. along
Je suis en voiture. Veux-tu que je t'emmène? — I am in the car. Do you want me to take you?

---

lever [l(ə)ve] — to lift, raise
lever le doigt — to raise a finger

soulever [sul(ə)ve] — to lift (up)
Je ne peux pas soulever ce sac, il est trop lourd. — I cannot lift this bag; it is too heavy.

appuyer sur qc [apɥije] — to push on s.th.
Pour mettre la machine en marche, appuie sur ce bouton. — To start the machine, push this button.

---

enfermer [ɑ̃fɛʀme] — to lock up

cacher [kaʃe] — to hide

ranger [ʀɑ̃ʒe] — to put away, tidy up

déranger [deʀɑ̃ʒe] — to disorganize, jumble up

---

tirer [tiʀe] — to pull, draw
un raisonnement **tiré par les cheveux** — strained reasoning

pousser [puse] — to push

repousser [ʀ(ə)puse] — to reject, repudiate
Elle n'a pas d'amis, tout le monde la repousse. — She has no friends; everyone rejects her.

tourner [tuʀne] — to turn

(se) **retourner** [ʀ(ə)tuʀne] — to turn around
J'ai passé la nuit à **me retourner dans mon lit**. — I spent the night tossing and turning in bed.

---

lancer [lɑ̃se] — to throw
À toi de **lancer les dés**. — Your turn to roll the dice.

jeter [ʒ(ə)te] — to throw (away)
jeter qc à la poubelle — to throw s.th. into the wastebasket

lâcher [lɑʃe] — to let go, release

ramasser [ʀamase] — to gather together, pick up
Ramasse ce papier, s'il te plaît. — Pick up this paper, please.

---

commencer qc [kɔmɑ̃se] — to begin/start s.th. *(See Information Box p. 455)*

finir qc [finiʀ] — to finish s.th. *(See Information Box p. 455)*

continuer à/de [kɔ̃tinɥe] — to continue (to)
Nous continuons à/de travailler. — We continue to work.

abandonner [abɑ̃dɔne] — to abandon, give up
Il a abandonné ses études. — He gave up his studies.

terminer [tɛʀmine] — to end, finish
Termine tes carottes, si tu veux du dessert. — Finish your carrots if you want dessert.

INFO

Commencer – finir

commencer à/de faire qc Qui commence à lire?	*to begin to do s.th.* *Who will start reading?*
commencer par faire qc Elle a commencé par préparer la salade.	*to do s.th. first* *First she made the salad.*
finir de faire qc Il n'a pas encore fini de manger.	*to finish doing s.th.* *He has not yet finished eating.*
finir par faire qc Elle a fini par s'endormir.	*to get around to doing s.th.* *She finally fell asleep.*

---

effectuer [efɛktye] — to complete, make
effectuer un achat — to make a purchase

achever [aʃ(ə)ve] — to finish, complete
Nous avons enfin achevé de payer la maison. — At last we have finished paying for the house.

interrompre [ɛ̃teʀɔ̃pʀ] — to interrupt
Ne m'interromps pas quand je parle. — Don't interrupt me when I am speaking.

une **interruption** [ɛ̃teʀypsjɔ̃] — interruption

---

la **position** [pɔzisjɔ̃] — position

rester [ʀɛste] — to remain

immobile [im(m)ɔbil] — immobile, still

l'**immobilité** *f* [imɔbilite] — immobility

---

changer [ʃɑ̃ʒe] — to change
Il a beaucoup changé depuis l'année dernière. — He has changed a lot since last year.
Elle a **changé de** coiffure. — She has changed her hairstyle.

un **changement** [ʃɑ̃ʒmɑ̃] — change (n)

inchangé, **inchangée** [ɛ̃ʃɑ̃ʒe] — unchanged
Je l'ai trouvée inchangée, toujours aussi jeune. — I found her unchanged, just as young as ever.

évoluer [evɔlɥe]	to evolve, change
Les relations parents-enfants ont beaucoup évolué.	Parent-child relations have changed a lot.
une **évolution** [evɔlysjɔ̃]	change, evolution
se développer [(s(ə)dev(ə)lɔpe]	to develop
un **développement** [dev(ə)lɔpmɑ̃]	development
un **progrès** [pʀɔgʀɛ]	progress
les **circonstances** *fpl* [siʀkɔ̃stɑ̃s]	circumstances
modifier [mɔdifje]	to modify
modifier une loi	to amend a law
une **modification** [mɔdifikasjɔ̃]	modification
faciliter [fasilite]	to facilitate, make easier
Son équipement ultra-moderne lui facilite le travail.	His ultra-modern equipment makes his job easier.
une **alternative** [altɛʀnativ]	alternative (n)
varier [vaʀje]	to vary
Le docteur m'a conseillé de varier mon alimentation.	The doctor advised me to vary my diet.
la **variation** [vaʀjasjɔ̃]	variation
ajouter (**qc à qc**) [aʒute]	to add (s.th. to s.th.)
supprimer [sypʀime]	to eliminate
Si tu veux maigrir, il faut supprimer le chocolat.	If you want to lose weight, you have to eliminate chocolate.
remplir [ʀɑ̃pliʀ]	to fill (out)
remplir un formulaire	to fill out a form
vider [vide]	to empty
Il a **vidé** son verre **d'un trait**.	He emptied his glass in one gulp.
boucher [buʃe]	to plug, stop, close, cork
boucher un trou	to plug a hole
déboucher [debuʃe]	to open, uncork
déboucher une bouteille	to open a bottle
couvrir [kuvʀiʀ]	to cover
recouvrir [ʀ(ə)kuvʀiʀ]	to cover
envelopper [ɑ̃v(ə)lɔpe]	to wrap
plier [plije]	to fold
casser [kase]	to break
arracher [aʀaʃe]	to pull up/out
abîmer [abime]	to damage

briser [bRize]	to break
Le verre s'est brisé en tombant par terre.	The glass broke when it fell to the floor.
déchirer [deʃiRe]	to tear up
rompre [Rɔ̃pR]	to break (up)
Elle a rompu avec Jean.	She broke up with Jean.
renverser [Rɑ̃vɛRse]	to knock over, spill
Elle a renversé un verre de vin sur le tapis.	She spilled a glass of wine on the carpet.
secouer [s(ə)kwe]	to shake
secouer la nappe	to shake out the tablecloth

devenir* [dəv(ə)niR/d(ə)vənir]	to become
Elle veut devenir architecte plus tard.	Later on she wants to become an architect.
transformer [tRɑ̃sfɔRme]	to transform
une **transformation** [tRɑ̃sfɔRmasjɔ̃]	transformation
augmenter [ɔgmɑ̃te]	to increase, augment
Le prix de l'essence a encore augmenté.	The price of gas has increased again.
une **augmentation** [ɔgmɑ̃tasjɔ̃]	increase (n)
diminuer [diminɥe]	to decrease, go down
Le bruit diminue d'intensité.	The noise is decreasing in intensity.
une **diminution** [diminysjɔ̃]	decrease (n)
monter* [mɔ̃te]	to go up, rise *(See Information Box p. 40)*
baisser [bese]	to go down, decrease, deteriorate
Sa vue a beaucoup baissé.	His eyesight has deteriorated a lot.

s'améliorer [sameljɔRe]	to improve
s'aggraver [sagRave]	to get worse
Son état de santé s'est encore aggravé.	His health has gotten even worse.

My Vocabulary

23

Verbal Communication

23.1 Conversing, Informing, Questioning, Answering

 105

parler [paʀle]	to speak
Il parle français avec ses enfants.	He speaks French with his children.
Je lui parlerai de tes problèmes.	I will speak to him/her about your problems.
la **parole** [paʀɔl]	word
adresser la parole à qn	to address/speak to s.o.
prendre la parole	to speak
s'exprimer [sɛkspʀime]	to express oneself
une **expression** [ɛkspʀesjɔ̃]	expression
une **expression familière**	familiar/colloquial expression
une **conversation** [kɔ̃vɛʀsasjɔ̃]	conversation
détourner la conversation	to divert the conversation
discuter de qc [diskyte]	to discuss s.th.
Je ne peux discuter de rien avec mes parents.	I can't discuss anything with my parents.
une **discussion** [diskysjɔ̃]	discussion
bavarder [bavaʀde]	to chat, converse
bavard, **bavarde** [bavaʀ, aʀd]	talkative
s'entretenir avec [sɑ̃tʀət(ə)niʀ]	to converse with
un **entretien** [ɑ̃tʀətjɛ̃]	conversation
avoir un entretien avec qn au sujet de qc	to have a discussion with s.o. about s.th.
un **interlocuteur**, une **interlocutrice** [ɛ̃tɛʀlɔkytœʀ, tʀis]	interlocutor, conversation partner
un **échange de vues** [eʃɑ̃ʒdəvy]	exchange of views
dire qc à qn [diʀ]	to say s.th. to s.o.
raconter qc à qn [ʀakɔ̃te]	to tell s.th. to s.o.
un **mot** [mo]	word
une **phrase** [fʀaz]	sentence
un **discours** [diskuʀ]	address, talk, speech
un **dialogue** [djalɔg]	dialog
prononcer [pʀɔnɔ̃se]	to pronounce
On ne prononce pas le *t* à la fin de *mot*.	The *t* at the end of *mot* is not pronounced.
prononcer un discours	to give a speech, address
proclamer [pʀɔklame]	to proclaim
chuchoter [ʃyʃɔte]	to whisper
Elle lui a chuchoté quelque chose à l'oreille.	She whispered something in his ear.

appeler [ap(ə)le]	to call
un **appel** [apɛl]	call (n)
Le Président a lancé un appel à la population.	The President put out a call to the people.
la **voix** [vwa]	voice
à haute voix/à voix haute	aloud/loud and clear
à voix basse	softly
Parle à voix basse, le bébé dort.	Speak softly, the baby is sleeping.
se taire [s(ə)tɛʀ]	to be quiet
Tais-toi, je voudrais écouter les informations.	Be quiet; I want to listen to the news.

remarquer [ʀ(ə)maʀke]	to notice
faire remarquer qc à qn	to suggest s.th. to s.o.
Je te fais remarquer que tu t'es encore trompé.	I suggest to you that you are wrong again.
une **remarque** [ʀ(ə)maʀk]	remark, comment (n)
faire une remarque	to make a remark
à propos de [apʀɔpo]	concerning, with reference to

répéter [ʀepete]	to repeat
redire [ʀ(ə)diʀ]	to repeat, say again
Je le lui ai dit et redit, mais il ne me croit toujours pas.	I repeated it to him, but he still does not believe me.
insister sur qc [ɛ̃siste]	to insist on s.th.
rappeler qc à qn [ʀap(ə)le]	to remind s.o. of s.th. *(See Information Box p. 72)*
rappeler à qn de faire qc [ʀap(ə)le]	to remind s.o. to do s.th.
ajouter [aʒute]	to add
Je dois ajouter que j'ai toujours été content de son travail.	I must add that I have always been happy with his work.

déclarer [deklaʀe]	to declare
déclarer qc sur l'honneur	to declare s.th. on one's honor
une **déclaration** [deklaʀasjɔ̃]	declaration, statement
affirmer [afiʀme]	to affirm, assert
J'affirme que je n'ai jamais vu cet homme.	I affirm that I have never seen this man.
Il affirme avoir tout payé.	He asserts that he has paid everything.
une **affirmation** [afiʀmasjɔ̃]	assertion, claim
nier [nje]	to deny
Elle nie m'avoir vu.	She denies having seen me.

présenter (**ses idées**) [prezɑ̃te]	to present (one's ideas)
défendre (**ses opinions**) [defɑ̃dʀ]	to defend (one's opinions)
influencer [ɛ̃flyɑ̃se]	to influence
L'avocat cherche à influencer le jury.	The lawyer seeks to influence the jury.
persuader qn de qc [pɛʀsɥade]	to persuade s.o. of s.th.
Tu n'as pas réussi à nous persuader de tes bonnes intentions.	You have not succeeded in persuading us of your good intentions.
assurer [asyʀe]	to assure
Je vous assure que je n'y suis pour rien.	I assure you that I can do nothing about it.
convaincre [kɔ̃vɛ̃kʀ]	to convince
convaincant, **convaincante** [kɔ̃vɛ̃kɑ̃, ɑ̃t]	convincing
une **conviction** [kɔ̃viksjɔ̃]	conviction
Il a parlé avec conviction.	He spoke with conviction.
démontrer [demɔ̃tʀe]	to demonstrate, show
Je peux vous démontrer que j'ai raison.	I can show you that I am right.
une **démonstration** [demɔ̃stʀasjɔ̃]	demonstration
faire la démonstration de qc	to demonstrate s.th.
prétendre [pʀetɑ̃dʀ]	to pretend
Il prétend que sa famille est très riche.	He pretends that his family is very rich.
Elle prétend bien connaître le Président de la République.	She pretends to know the President of the Republic well.
exagérer [ɛgzaʒeʀe]	to exaggerate
une **exagération** [ɛgzaʒeʀasjɔ̃]	exaggeration
se vanter de qc [s(ə)vɑ̃te]	to boast, brag about s.th.
Il se vante de pouvoir soulever 100 kilos.	He brags about being able to lift 100 kilos.
vantard [vɑ̃taʀ, aʀd], **vantarde**	boastful
un **vantard**, une **vantarde**	boastful person
un **prétexte** [pʀetɛkst]	pretext
sous prétexte de	under the pretext of
promettre [pʀɔmɛtʀ]	to promise
Je te promets qu'on ira à la piscine.	I promise you that we will go to the pool.
Je lui ai promis de revenir l'année prochaine.	I made a promise to him/her to return next year.
une **promesse** [pʀɔmɛs]	promise (n)
tenir ses promesses	to keep one's promises

informer qn de qc [ɛ̃fɔʀme]	to inform s.o. of s.th.
Je vous informerai de ma décision, le moment venu.	I will inform you of my decision at the right moment.
une **information** [ɛ̃fɔʀmasjɔ̃]	(piece of) information
renseigner qn (**sur qc**) [ʀɑ̃seɲe]	to inform s.o. (about s.th.)
Il nous a renseignés sur les horaires des trains.	He informed us about the train schedules.
se renseigner (**sur**)	to find out (about)
un **renseignement** [ʀɑ̃sɛɲmɑ̃]	(piece of) information
donner des renseignements à qn	to give s.o. information
expliquer [ɛksplike]	to explain
une **explication** [ɛksplikasjɔ̃]	explanation

avertir [avɛʀtiʀ]	to warn, inform
Je l'ai averti qu'il allait avoir des ennuis.	I warned him that he would have some problems.
un **avertissement** [avɛʀtismɑ̃]	warning (n)
donner un avertissement à qn	to give s.o. a warning

préciser [pʀesize]	to specify, clarify
décrire [dekʀiʀ]	to describe
Je lui ai décrit le chemin avec précision.	I described the route to him precisely.
une **description** [dɛskʀipsjɔ̃]	description

demander qc à qn [d(ə)mɑ̃de]	to ask s.th. of s.o. *(See Information Box p. 74)*
une **question** [kɛstjɔ̃]	question (n)
poser une question	to ask a question
répondre à [ʀepɔ̃dʀ]	to answer, respond to
Il m'a répondu sèchement.	He answered me abruptly.
Elle n'a pas répondu à ma question.	She did not answer my question.
une **réponse** [ʀepɔ̃s]	answer, response
donner une réponse à qn	to give s.o. an answer

signaler qc à qn [siɲale]	to indicate/point out s.th. to s.o.
Je te signale que tu as pris la mauvaise route.	I am pointing out that you have taken the wrong road.
indiquer [ɛ̃dike]	to indicate, show
Pourriez-vous m'indiquer le chemin de la poste?	Could you show me the way to the post office?
évoquer [evɔke]	to mention
Il n'évoque jamais les années qu'il a passées à l'étranger.	He never mentions the years he spent abroad.
interroger [ɛ̃teʀɔʒe]	to ask, interrogate
La police l'a interrogé pendant trois heures.	The police interrogated him for three hours.
une **interrogation** [ɛ̃teʀɔgasjɔ̃]	questioning, interrogation
un **interrogatoire** [ɛ̃teʀɔgatwaʀ]	interrogation, question
subir un interrogatoire	to undergo interrogation
soumettre qn à un interrogatoire	to interrogate s.o.

23.2 Excuses, Regrets, Consolation  106

pardonner qc à qn/à qn d'avoir fait qc [paʀdɔne]	to forgive s.o. for having done s.th.
Elle ne lui a jamais pardonné de l'avoir quittée.	She never forgave him for leaving her.
demander pardon à qn [d(ə)mɑ̃depaʀdɔ̃]	to ask s.o.'s forgiveness
Pardon! [paʀdɔ̃]	Excuse me! Sorry!
s'excuser [sɛkskyze]	to excuse oneself
Je me suis excusé auprès d'elle.	I asked her to pardon me.
Excuse(z)-moi!	Excuse me!
une **excuse** [ɛkskyz]	apology
Tu m'en veux? [tymɑ̃vø]	Are you angry with me?
C'est (de) **ma faute.** [sɛ(d(ə))mafot]	It's my fault.
regretter [ʀ(ə)gʀete]	to regret
Je regrette d'avoir été méchant avec toi.	I am sorry I was nasty with you.
Tous mes regrets. [tumeʀ(ə)gʀɛ]	I am truly sorry.
(**Je suis**) **Désolé**, **Désolée!** [dezɔle]	(I am) Sorry.

avoir honte [avwaʀ'ɔ̃t]	to be ashamed
J'ai honte de m'être comporté si bêtement.	I am ashamed to have behaved so stupidly.
être gêné, gênée [ʒɛne]	to be embarrassed
Il est tellement grossier que **j'en suis gêné pour lui**.	He is so vulgar that I am embarrassed for him.

(C'est) Dommage! [dɔmaʒ]	That's a shame!
Tu ne peux pas venir samedi? Dommage!	You can't come on Saturday? That's a shame!
Tant pis! [tɑ̃pi]	Too bad!
Je regrette, il ne reste plus de gâteau pour toi. – Tant pis!	Sorry; there is no cake left for you. Too bad!
Tant pis pour lui, il n'avait qu'à faire attention!	Too bad for him; all he had to do was pay attention!
Tant mieux! [tɑ̃mjø]	So much the better!
malheureusement [maløʀøzmɑ̃]	unfortunately
Hélas! [elas]	Alas!
Nous espérions qu'il guérirait, mais hélas, il est mort.	We were hoping that he would get better but, alas, he died.

consoler qn [kɔ̃sɔle]	to console s.o.
Mon pauvre, Ma pauvre. [mɔ̃, mapovʀ]	You poor person.
Tu es resté à l'hôpital tout l'été? Mon pauvre.	Did you stay in the hospital the whole summer? You poor thing.
rassurer qn [ʀasyʀe]	to reassure s.o.
Tes parents sont inquiets? Téléphone-leur pour les rassurer.	Are your parents worried? Call them to reassure them.
Ne t'en fais pas. [n(ə)tɑ̃fɛpa]	Don't worry about it.
Ne t'en fais pas pour moi, ça ira très bien.	Don't worry about me; I'll be fine.
Il n'y a pas de mal. [ilnjapadmal]	It doesn't matter.
Ça ne fait rien. [san(ə)fɛʀjɛ̃]	It doesn't matter./It's okay.
Ce n'est pas grave. [s(ə)nɛpagʀav]	It doesn't matter./No big deal.
Ce n'est rien. [s(ə)nɛʀjɛ̃]	It's nothing.
Ça va passer. [savapase]	It's not serious.
Ça peut arriver à tout le monde. [sapøaʀiveatulmɔ̃d]	That can happen to anybody.

23.3 Permission, Prohibition, Suggestion, Advice

 107

permettre qc à qn/à qn de faire qc [pɛʀmɛtʀ]	to allow s.o. to do s.th.
Je lui ai permis d'aller au cinéma.	I allowed him to go to the movie.
la **permission** [pɛʀmisjɔ̃]	permission
demander la permission de faire qc	to ask permission to do s.th.
donner à qn la permission de faire qc	to give s.o. permission to do s.th.
autoriser qc/qn à faire qc [ɔtɔʀize]	to permit s.o. to do s.th.
l'**autorisation** *f* [ɔtɔʀizasjɔ̃]	permission
accorder à qn l'autorisation de faire qc	to give s.o. permission to do s.th.
s'il te/vous plaît [siltə/vuplɛ]	please

prier qn de faire qc [pʀije]	to ask/beg s.o. to do s.th.
Je vous prie de vous taire et de m'écouter.	I beg you to be quiet and listen to me.
donner un ordre [dɔneɛ̃nɔʀdʀ]	to give an order
donner à qn l'ordre de faire qc	to give s.o. an order to do s.th.
ordonner à qn de faire qc [ɔʀdɔne]	to order s.o. to do s.th.
obliger qn à faire qc [ɔbliʒe]	to force s.o. to do s.th.
forcer qn à faire qc [fɔʀse]	to force s.o. to do s.th.
Tu ne peux pas la forcer à aimer Frédéric.	You cannot force her to love Frédéric.

empêcher qn de faire qc [ɑ̃pɛʃe]	to prevent s.o. from doing s.th.
interdire qc à qn/à qn de faire qc [ɛ̃tɛʀdiʀ]	to forbid s.o. to do s.th.
Elle a interdit à ses enfants de regarder des films d'horreur.	She forbade her children to watch horror movies.
une **interdiction** [ɛ̃tɛʀdiksjɔ̃]	prohibition
Interdiction de fumer.	No smoking.
défendre qc à qn/à qn de faire qc [defɑ̃dʀ]	to forbid s.o. from doing s.th.
Je te défends de me parler sur ce ton.	I forbid you to speak to me in that tone of voice.
défense de… [defɑ̃s]	No…
Défense d'entrer.	No entry.

proposer (à **qn**) **de faire qc** [pRɔpoze]	to suggest (to s.o.) to do s.th.
Je lui ai proposé d'aller au théâtre.	I suggested to him to go to the theater.
une **proposition** [pRɔpozisjɔ̃]	suggestion, proposition
rejeter une proposition	to reject a proposition
conseiller qc à qn/à qn de faire qc [kɔ̃sɛje]	to advise s.th. to s.o./s.o. to do s.th.
Le docteur m'a conseillé un séjour à la montagne.	The doctor advised me to spend some time in the mountains.
Je vous conseille de passer par Nancy.	I advise you to go by way of Nancy.
un **conseil** [kɔ̃sɛj]	advice
il n'y a qu'à faire qc *fam* [ilnijaka]	All you have to do is…
recommander qc à qn/à qn de faire qc [R(ə)kɔmɑ̃de]	to recommend s.th. to s.o./that s.o. do s.th.
Je lui ai recommandé de réserver une chambre d'hôtel.	I recommended that he reserve a hotel room.
une **recommandation** [R(ə)kɔmɑ̃dasjɔ̃]	recommendation
déconseiller à qn de faire qc [dekɔ̃sɛje]	to advise against doing s.th.
Je te déconseille de prendre la route le 1er août.	I advise against leaving on August first.
il suffit de faire qc [ilsyfi]	you only have to…
J'attends votre réponse, il suffit de me passer un coup de fil.	I await your answer; all you have to do is give me a call.
il faut/faudrait que + *subj* [ilfo/fodRɛkə]	you must/should…
Il faudrait que vous vous reposiez.	You should rest.
il vaut/vaudrait mieux que + *subj* [ilvo/vodRɛmjøkə]	it is/would be better that…
Il vaut mieux que nous partions tout de suite.	It is better that we leave right away.

23.4 Pain, Anger, Aggression  108

avoir mal (à) [avwaRmal]	to have pain (in)
J'ai **mal à la tête.**	I have a headache.
Ça fait mal.	That hurts.
Je me suis fait mal.	I hurt myself.
Aïe! [aj]	Ow! Ouch!
se plaindre de qn/qc [s(ə)plɛ̃dR]	to complain of s.o./s.th.
Ma fille se plaint de maux de ventre.	My daughter complains of stomachaches.
une **plainte** [plɛ̃t]	complaint
Ça brûle. [sabRyl]	It burns.
Ça pique. [sapik]	It burns/itches/tingles.
en avoir assez [ɑ̃navwaRase]	to have enough of s.th.
J'en ai assez de l'attendre.	I have had enough of waiting for him/her.
Ça suffit! [sasyfi]	That's enough!
Arrête! [aRɛt]	Stop!
C'est scandaleux! [sɛskɑ̃dalø]	That's scandalous!
C'est un scandale! [sɛ(t)ɛ̃skɑ̃dal]	That's a scandal!
C'est inadmissible! [sɛ(t)inadmisibl]	That is unacceptable!
en avoir marre *fam* [ɑ̃navwaRmaR]	to be fed up
J'en ai marre.	I'm fed up.
en avoir ras le bol *fam* [ɑ̃navwaRRalbɔl]	to be fed up with s.th.
Tu me casses les pieds. *fam* [tym(ə)kaslepje]	You really bug me.
Tu es vache. *fam* [tyɛvaʃ]	You are vile.
Tu es vache avec lui, quand-même.	You really treat him vilely.
Zut! *fam* [zyt]	Drat!
Zut, alors! Je ne trouve plus mon portefeuille.	Nuts! I can't find my wallet.
Mince! *fam* [mɛ̃s]	Darn!
Mince, alors!	What a bummer!
Merde! *pop* [mɛRd]	Shit!
Quel...! Quelle... ! [kɛl]	What a...!
Quel idiot, celui-là!	What an idiot he is!

jurer [ʒyʀe]	to swear
un **juron** [ʒyʀɔ̃]	swear, oath
injurier [ɛ̃ʒyʀje]	to abuse
Il l'a injuriée devant tout le monde.	He abused her in front of everyone.
une **injure** [ɛ̃ʒyʀ]	insult (n)
grossier, **grossière** [gʀosje, jɛʀ]	gross, coarse
C'est un gamin grossier et mal élevé.	That is a coarse boy with a bad upbringing.
un **gros mot** [gʀomo]	swear word
Je me demande où mon fils a appris tous ces gros mots.	I wonder where my son learned all these swear words.
insulter [ɛ̃sylte]	to insult
Tu ne vas pas te laisser insulter par ce sale type, non?	You are not going to let yourself be insulted by that creep, are you?
une **insulte** [ɛ̃sylt]	insult (n)
Menteur! Menteuse! [mɑ̃tœʀ, øz]	Liar!
Espèce de...**!** [ɛspɛsdə]	You...!
Espèce d'idiot!	You idiot!
imbécile [ɛ̃besil]	imbecilic (n)
un, une **imbécile**	imbecile
con, **conne** *pop* [kɔ̃, kɔn]	stupid
un **con**, une **conne**	stupid person, idiot
une **connerie** *pop* [kɔnʀi]	bullshit, nonsense
Arrête de dire des conneries.	Cut the bullshit.
un **abruti**, une **abrutie** *fam* [abʀyti]	jerk (n)
Regarde cet abruti qui double dans le virage.	Look at that jerk passing on a curve.
débile *fam* [debil]	idiotic
Tu es débile, ou quoi?	Are you an idiot or what?
un, une **débile**	idiot
Salaud! Salope! *fam* [salo, salɔp]	Bastard! SOB!
Salopard! *fam* [salɔpaʀ]	Sleazebag!

énerver qn [enɛʀve]	to irritate s.o.
Arrête de chanter cette chanson stupide, tu m'énerves.	Stop singing that stupid song; you are irritating me.
embêter qn [ɑ̃bɛte]	to annoy s.o.

se disputer [s(ə)dispyte]	to argue
Mes enfants n'arrêtent pas de se disputer.	My children argue constantly.
une **dispute** [dispyt]	argument
crier [kʀije]	to yell
crier après qn	to yell at s.o.
un **cri** [kʀi]	yell (n)
pousser un cri de douleur	to cry out in pain

gronder [gRɔ̃de]	to scold
Il a peur de se faire gronder par ses parents.	He is afraid to get a scolding from his parents.
gueuler *fam* [gœle]	to yell at
engueuler qn *fam* [ɑ̃gœle]	to yell at s.o.
Pierre et Juliette ont passé la soirée à s'engueuler.	Pierre and Juliette spent the evening yelling at each another.
une **engueulade** *fam* [ɑ̃gœlad]	bawling out
contredire qn [kɔ̃tRədiR]	to contradict s.o.
Chaque fois qu'il ouvre la bouche, vous le contredisez.	Every time he opens his mouth you contradict him.
une **contradiction** [kɔ̃tRadiksjɔ̃]	contradiction
avoir l'esprit de contradiction	to be contrary, confrontational
un **malentendu** [malɑ̃tɑ̃dy]	misunderstanding (n)
provoquer [pRɔvɔke]	to provoke
Tu dis ça pour me provoquer, ou quoi?	Are you saying that to provoke me or what?
une **provocation** [pRɔvɔkasjɔ̃]	provocation
interrompre [ɛ̃teRɔ̃pR]	to interrupt
Il m'a interrompu au beau milieu de ma phrase.	He interrupted me in mid-sentence.
couper la parole à qn [kupelapaRɔl]	to cut s.o. off
Je voudrais vous expliquer mon point de vue sans que vous me coupiez la parole.	I would like to explain my point of view to you without your cutting me off.

menacer [mənase]	to threaten
une **menace** [mənas]	threat (n)
mettre ses menaces à exécution	to carry out one's threats
agressif, **agressive** [agResif, iv]	aggressive
l'**agressivité** *f* [agResivite]	aggressiveness
attaquer [atake]	to attack
une **attaque** [atak]	attack (n)
une **attaque verbale**	verbal attack

La ferme! *fam* [lafɛRm]	Shut up!
La ferme! Tu as assez dit de bêtises comme ça.	Shut up! You have already talked enough crap.
Ta gueule! *fam* [tagœl]	Shut up!
Toi, ta gueule! On (ne) t'a rien demandé.	You shut up! Nobody asked for your input.
Fiche le camp! *fam* [fiʃləkɑ̃]	Get out!
Fous le camp! *fam* [ful(ə)kɑ̃]	Get out!
Dégage! *fam* [degaʒ]	Get out!
Fiche-moi la paix! *fam* [fiʃmwalapɛ]	Leave me alone!
Fous-moi la paix! *fam* [fumwalapɛ]	Leave me alone!

C'est ridicule. [sɛRidikyl]	That's ridiculous.
C'est du vol! [sɛdyvɔl]	That's highway robbery!
C'est une honte! [sɛ(t)ynə'ɔ̃t]	That's a shame!
C'est insupportable. [sɛ(t)ɛ̃sypɔRtabl]	That is unacceptable.
C'est dégoûtant! [sɛdegutɑ̃]	That's disgusting!
C'est dégueulasse! *pop* [sɛdegœlas]	That's revolting!
Arrête de roter, c'est dégueulasse!	Stop belching; it's disgusting.
C'est le comble! [sɛl(ə)kɔ̃bl]	That takes all!
Quelle horreur! [kɛlɔRœR]	How horrible!

23.5 Agreeing, Confirming, Qualifying, Refusing

 109

accepter [aksɛpte]	to accept
J'accepte tes excuses.	I accept your apology.
Il a accepté de m'aider.	He has agreed to help me.
Oui. ['wi]	Yes.
Bien sûr! [bjɛ̃syR]	Of course! Naturally!
Entendu. [ɑ̃tɑ̃dy]	Agreed.
Entendu, je passerai te chercher à 8 heures.	Agreed, I will come and get you at eight o'clock.
Bien entendu.	Sure thing!
D'accord. [dakɔR]	Agreed./Okay.
donner son accord [dɔnesɔ̃nakɔR]	to give one's agreement

approuver [apRuve]	to approve
J'approuve entièrement la décision de Claire.	I approve entirely of Claire's decision.
une **approbation** [apRɔbasjɔ̃]	approval
effectivement [efɛktivmɑ̃]	indeed, in fact
C'est effectivement la meilleure solution.	In fact that is the best solution.
à tout prix [atupRi]	at any cost
Viens vite, il faut que je te parle à tout prix.	Come quickly, I absolutely must speak with you.

Naturellement. [natyRɛlmɑ̃]	Naturally.
Absolument. [absɔlymɑ̃]	Absolutely.
Vous êtes d'accord avec elle? – Absolument.	Do you agree with her? – Absolutely.
Parfaitement. [paRfɛtmɑ̃]	Perfectly.
Exactement. [ɛgzaktəmɑ̃]	Exactly.

à coup sûr [akusyʀ]	for sure, surely
Si on va à cette fête, on va s'ennuyer à coup sûr.	If we go to this party we surely will be bored.
précisément [pʀesizemɑ̃]	precisely, exactly
Mais c'est précisément ce que j'essaie de dire depuis une heure.	But that is precisely what I have been trying to say for an hour.
sans faute [sɑ̃fot]	without fail
Alors, à jeudi, sans faute!	So, see you Thursday, without fail.
Volontiers. [vɔlɔ̃tje]	Gladly.
Vous buvez quelque chose? – Volontiers, j'ai très soif.	Something to drink? – Gladly, I am very thirsty
Pourquoi pas? [puʀkwapa]	Why not?
Si tu veux. [sityvø]	If you wish.
Bof! [bɔf]	Bah!
Il était comment, ce film? – Bof! Pas très bon, je suis déçu.	How was that movie? – Bah! Not great; I am disappointed.
Peut-être. [pøtɛtʀ]	Maybe.
On verra. [ɔ̃vɛʀa]	We shall see.
éventuellement [evɑ̃tɥɛlmɑ̃]	possibly
le cas échéant [ləkazeʃeɑ̃]	if necessary, in a pinch
Le cas échéant, on pourrait s'arrêter à Orléans pour dîner.	We could stop in Orléans for dinner in a pinch.
à la rigueur [alaʀigœʀ]	if necessary
Ce n'est pas idéal, mais ça peut aller à la rigueur.	It's not ideal, but it can work in a pinch.
sous (toute) réserve [su(tut)ʀezɛʀv]	subject to, provided
faute de mieux [fotdəmjø]	for lack of anything better, as a second-best
Faute de mieux, allons au musée, ça nous fera passer le temps.	For lack of anything better, let's go to the museum; that will pass some time.
sans plus [sɑ̃plys]	that's all, nothing more
Ils ont été polis, sans plus.	They were polite, but that's all.

être contre [ɛt(ʀə)kɔ̃tʀ]	to be against, opposed
Cette idée est mauvaise. Je suis absolument contre.	That idea is bad. I am absolutely opposed to it.
s'opposer à qc [sɔpoze]	to be opposed to s.th.
Il s'est opposé à ma candidature.	He is opposed to my candidature.
Non. [nɔ̃]	No.
Pas du tout. [padytu]	Not at all.
Pas question. [pakɛstjɔ̃]	Out of the question.
Pas question que je te prête ma voiture.	Loaning you my car is out of the question.
Rien à faire. [ʀjɛ̃nafɛʀ]	There's nothing to be done.
Jamais de la vie. [ʒamɛ̃dlavi]	No way./Never./Not on your life.
Ça (ne) **va pas, non?** *fam* [sa(n)vapanɔ̃]	That won't do!
Mais qu'est-ce que vous faites dans mon jardin? Ça (ne) va pas, non?	What are you doing in my yard? What's your problem?
Et puis quoi, encore? [epɥikwaɑ̃kɔʀ]	What else? (a pint of blood?)
Tu voudrais que nous te donnions 1 000 euros? Et puis quoi, encore?	So you would like us to give you 1000 euros? What else?
refuser qc à qn/de faire qc [ʀ(ə)fyze]	to refuse s.th. to s.o./to do s.th.
Je refuse d'écouter ces bêtises.	I refuse to listen to this nonsense.
un **refus** [ʀ(ə)fy]	refusal
à aucun prix [aokɛ̃pʀi]	under no circumstances, not for anything
Je ne lui en parlerai à aucun prix.	I will not speak to him about it under any circumstances.
bien *adv* [bjɛ̃]	well *(See Information Box p. 448)*
Bien, puisque c'est comme ça, je m'en vais.	Okay, since that's the way it is, I'm leaving.
sûrement [syʀmɑ̃]	certainly, surely
certainement [sɛʀtɛnmɑ̃]	certainly
évidemment [evidamɑ̃]	obviously, evidently
J'ai attendu, mais évidemment, il n'est pas venu.	I waited, but obviously he didn't come.
sans doute [sɑ̃dut]	definitely, no doubt
tout à fait [tutafɛ]	completely, entirely
complètement [kɔ̃plɛtmɑ̃]	completely
Il a complètement raté son examen.	He failed his test completely.
en tout cas [ɑ̃tuka]	in any case

INFO

Beyond all doubt

sans doute	*probably*
Elle a sans doute raison.	*She is probably right.*
Elle prendra sans doute le train de 15 heures.	*She will probably take the 3 o'clock train.*
sans aucun doute	*undoubtedly, certainly*
Tu es sûr que c'était Jean? – Sans aucun doute.	*Are you sure that was Jean? – Without a doubt.*

---

totalement [tɔtalmɑ̃]	completely
décidément [desidemɑ̃]	honestly, totally, certainly
Toi, décidément, on ne te changera jamais!	Honestly, you'll never change!
en somme [ɑ̃sɔm]	in short
pur et simple [pyʀesɛ̃pl]	clearly, pure and simple
C'est une escroquerie pure et simple.	That's a scam, pure and simple.
nettement [nɛtmɑ̃]	clearly
Elle est nettement plus âgée que lui.	She is clearly older than him.

---

par exemple (**p. ex.**) [paʀɛgzɑ̃pl]	for example (e.g.)
en effet [ɑ̃nefɛ]	in fact
Il ne pourra pas venir dimanche. En effet, il est gravement malade.	He can't come on Sunday. In fact, he is seriously ill.
Vous avez vu ce match? – Je l'ai vu, en effet.	Did you see that game? – In fact I did see it.
vraiment [vʀɛmɑ̃]	really
en fait [ɑ̃fɛt]	in fact
En fait, c'est tout simple, une fois qu'on a compris.	In fact it is quite simple once you grasp it.
C'est un fait que... [sɛ(t)ɛ̃fɛkə]	It is a fact that...

---

ainsi [ɛ̃si]	thus, that way
Venez tôt, ainsi vous pourrez déjeuner avec nous.	Come early; that way you can have lunch with us.
de toute manière [dətutmanjɛʀ]	in any case
De toute manière, quoique tu fasses, elle sera vexée.	In any case, she will be offended no matter what you do.
de toute façon [dətutfasɔ̃]	in any case, no matter what, anyway

d'ailleurs [dajœʀ]	after all; incidentally
Tu n'as qu'à le lui demander toi-même; d'ailleurs il sera là demain.	You merely have to ask him yourself; after all he will be there tomorrow.
après tout [apʀɛtu]	after all
Tu pourrais lui écrire; après tout, c'est ta mère.	You could write her; after all she is your mother.
finalement [finalmɑ̃]	finally
enfin [ɑ̃fɛ̃]	after all, finally, in the end
Ce n'est pas très agréable, mais enfin, on s'y habitue.	It's not very pleasant, but after all we'll get used to it.
en réalité [ɑ̃ʀealite]	in reality
autrement dit [otʀəmɑ̃di]	in other words
Elle ne me regarde plus, elle me parle à peine… autrement dit, elle ne m'aime plus.	She doesn't look at me any more, she scarcely speaks to me… in other words, she does not love me any more.
bref [bʀɛf]	in short; concise, brief
Et en plus, on nous a volé notre voiture. Bref, des vacances affreuses.	And what's more, our car was stolen. In short, a terrible vacation.

au fond [ofɔ̃]	essentially, basically
Au fond, cette idée n'est pas si bête.	That idea is essentially not so bad.
tout compte fait [tukɔ̃tfɛ]	all in all
en fin de compte [ɑ̃fɛ̃dkɔ̃t]	eventually, in the long run
pour ainsi dire [puʀɛ̃sidiʀ]	so to speak, virtually
Il n'a pour ainsi dire rien mangé.	He has eaten virtually nothing.
étant donné que [etɑ̃dɔnekə]	given (the fact) that
Étant donné qu'ils ne s'entendaient plus, il valait mieux qu'ils se séparent.	Given the fact that they didn't get along anymore, it was better for them to separate.

seulement [sœlmɑ̃]	only
uniquement [ynikmɑ̃]	solely, only, just
Elle est venue de Londres uniquement pour te voir.	She has come from London just to see you.
simplement [sɛ̃pləmɑ̃]	simply
Je voudrais simplement dire que je ne suis pas d'accord.	I simply would like to say that I do not agree.

au moins [omwɛ̃]	at least
du moins [dymwɛ̃]	at least
Du moins, c'est mon avis.	At least, that is my opinion.
plus ou moins [plyzumwɛ̃]	more or less

quand même [kɑ̃mɛm]	still, just the same
tout de même [tudmɛm]	however
Tu aurais tout de même pu te raser.	You could have, however, shaved.
plutôt [plyto]	rather, instead
Cette jupe ne te va pas, prends plutôt l'autre.	That skirt does not look good on you; get the other one instead.

malgré tout [malgʀetu]	in spite of, despite everything
Nous nous voyons rarement, mais nous sommes malgré tout restés bons amis.	We rarely see each other, but we have remained good friends despite everything.
d'autant plus que... [dotɑ̃ply(s)kə]	especially given that...
Il lui faudrait un appartement plus grand, d'autant plus qu'elle attend un bébé.	She should have a larger apartment, especially since she is expecting a baby.
d'un côté... **de l'autre** [dœ̃kotedəlotʀ]	on the one hand... on the other
D'un côté, ça m'embête de passer Noël chez ma belle-mère, mais de l'autre, ça lui fera tellement plaisir.	On the one hand, it's a drag to spend Christmas at my mother-in-law's, but on the other, it will make her very happy.
d'une part... **d'autre part** [dynpaʀdotʀəpaʀ]	on the one hand...on the other

également [egalmɑ̃]	also, equally
J'aime la musique classique, mais également le reggae.	I like classical music, but also reggae.
habituellement [abitɥɛlmɑ̃]	customarily, usually
Habituellement, nous faisons une promenade après le déjeuner.	Usually we take a walk after lunch.
d'ordinaire [dɔʀdinɛʀ]	normally, customarily
obligatoirement [ɔbligatwaʀmɑ̃]	necessarily, perforce
forcément [fɔʀsemɑ̃]	necessarily, of course
Tu connais Paul? – Forcément, c'est mon oncle.	Do you know Paul? – Of course, he's my uncle.

23.6 Praise, Thanks, Reproach  110

féliciter qn de/pour qc [felisite]	to congratulate s.o. on/for s.th.
Je vous félicite de votre courage.	I congratulate you on your courage.
Félicitations! [felisitasjɔ̃]	Congratulations!
un **compliment** [kɔ̃plimɑ̃]	compliment (n)
Tout le monde lui **fait des compliments sur** sa nouvelle coiffure.	Everyone compliments her on her new hairstyle.
louer qn pour qc [lwe]	to praise s.o. for s.th.
une **louange** [lwɑ̃ʒ]	praise (n)
chanter les louanges de qn/qc	to sing the praises of s.o./s.th.
être reconnaissant, **reconnaissante (à qn de qc)** [ʀ(ə)kɔnɛsɑ̃, ɑ̃t]	to be grateful, thankful (to s.o. for s.th.)
Elle n'a rien dit, et je lui en suis très reconnaissant.	She said nothing, and I am grateful to her for it.
la **reconnaissance** [ʀ(ə)kɔnɛsɑ̃s]	gratitude, thankfulness
manifester sa reconnaissance envers qn	to show one's gratitude to s.o.
remercier qn de qc [ʀ(ə)mɛʀsje]	to thank s.o. for s.th.
Je vous remercie de m'avoir aidé.	I thank you for helping me.
Merci. [mɛʀsi]	Thank you.
le **remerciement** [ʀ(ə)mɛʀsimɑ̃]	thanks (n)
Bravo! [bʀavo]	Bravo!
Bien! [bjɛ̃]	Good!
Super! [sypɛʀ]	Super!
Génial! [ʒenjal]	Great!
Ça y est! [sajɛ]	That's it!
Voilà! [vwala]	There (you go)!
Voilà! Tu as presque fini.	There! You are almost done.
Pas mal. [pamal]	Not bad.
Pas terrible. [pateʀibl]	Not such a big deal./Not great.
Nul./Nulle. [nyl]	Atrocious.
Ne lis pas ce livre, il est absolument nul.	Don't read this book; it is absolutely atrocious.

critiquer [kʀitike]	to criticize
dire du bien/du mal de qn/qc [diʀdybjɛ̃/dymal]	to speak well/poorly of s.o./s.th.
On m'a dit beaucoup de bien de ce restaurant.	I have heard a lot of good things about this restaurant.
donner raison/tort à qn [dɔneʀɛzɔ̃/tɔʀ]	to admit that s.o. is right/wrong

reprocher qc à qn/à qn d'avoir fait qc [ʀ(ə)pʀɔʃe]	to reproach s.o. for s.th./for having done s.th.
Je lui reproche de ne pas m'avoir dit la vérité.	I reproach him for not telling me the truth.
un **reproche** [ʀ(ə)pʀɔʃ]	reproach (n)
faire des reproches à qn sur qc	to reproach s.o. for s.th.
condamner [kɔ̃dane]	to condemn

blâmer qn de/pour qc [blame]	to blame s.o. for s.th.
un **blâme** [blam]	blame (n)

23.7 Opinion and Assessment  111

une **opinion** [ɔpinjɔ̃]	opinion
partager l'opinion de qn (sur qc)	to share s.o.'s opinion (on s.th.)
un **avis** [avi]	view, opinion
donner son avis	to give one's opinion
être du même avis que	to be of the same opinion as
être d'(un) avis contraire/opposé	to be of an opposite opinion
À mon/ton/son... avis	In my/your/his... opinion...
être en accord avec qn [ɛtʀɑ̃nakɔʀ]	to be in agreement with s.o.
être favorable à [favɔʀabl]	to be favorable toward
Le directeur a été favorable à mon projet.	The director is favorable to my project.

protester contre qc [pʀɔtɛste]	to protest against s.th.
contester qc [kɔ̃tɛste]	to protest against, challenge s.th.
Le joueur a contesté la décision de l'arbitre.	The player challenged the referee's decision.
s'élever contre qc [sel(ə)ve]	to turn against s.th.
être en désaccord avec qn [ɛtʀɑ̃dezakɔʀ]	to be in disagreement with s.o.

Ça m'est égal. [samɛ(t)egal]	It's all the same to me. Who cares?
Et après? [eapʀɛ] Et après? Qu'est-ce que ça peut te faire?	So what? So what? What's that got to do with you?
Et alors? [ealɔʀ]	So what? Who cares?
Ça ne vaut rien. [san(ə)voʀjɛ̃]	That is worth nothing.
Je m'en moque. [ʒ(ə)mɑ̃mɔk]	I don't care.
Je m'en fiche. *fam* [ʒ(ə)mɑ̃fiʃ]	I don't give a damn.
Je m'en fous. *fam* [ʒ(ə)mɑ̃fu] Elle peut penser ce qu'elle veut, je m'en fous.	I don't give a damn. She can think whatever she wants; I don't give a damn.
Ça ne me/te/le... regarde pas. [san(ə)məʀ(ə)gaʀdpa] Je peux sortir avec qui je veux, ça ne vous regarde pas.	That's none of my/your/his/her...business. I can go out with anybody I want; it's none of your business.
considérer que [kɔ̃sideʀe] Je considère que c'est stupide. Je **le considère comme** un jeune homme plein de talent.	to consider that I consider that it's stupid. I consider him a talented young man.
juger que [ʒyʒe] Fais-le, si tu juges que c'est nécessaire.	to believe, think (that) Do it if you think that it's necessary.
être sûr, **sûre (de qc/que)** [syʀ] Je suis sûr de le connaître. J'étais pourtant sûr que tu le connaissais.	to be sure (of s.th./that) I am sure I know him. I was sure that you knew him.
être certain, **certaine (de qc/que)** [sɛʀtɛ̃, ɛn] Je suis **sûre et certaine** de l'avoir vu dimanche.	to be sure, certain (of s.th./that) I am absolutely sure I saw him on Sunday.

apprécier [apʀesje]	to appreciate, evaluate, assess
une **appréciation** [apʀesjasjɔ̃]	assessment, evaluation
porter une appréciation sur	to make an assessment of
un **jugement** [ʒyʒmɑ̃]	verdict, judgment
un **préjugé** [pʀeʒyʒe]	prejudice
lutter contre **les préjugés racistes**	to fight racial prejudice
selon [s(ə)lɔ̃]	according to, in the opinion of
Selon moi, cette théorie est absurde.	In my view, this theory is absurd.
d'après [dapʀɛ]	according to
D'après mes parents, je devrais travailler plus.	According to my parents, I should work more.
ressentir qc comme… [ʀ(ə)sɑ̃tiʀ]	to take/interpret s.th. as…
Je ressens sa réflexion comme un affront.	I take his remark as an insult.

une **conclusion** [kɔ̃klyzjɔ̃]	conclusion
en conclusion	in conclusion
positif, **positiv** [pozitif, iv]	positive
négatif, **négative** [negatif, iv]	negative

relatif, **relative** [ʀ(ə)latif, iv]	relative
dépendre de [depɑ̃dʀ]	to depend on
Je ne peux rien te promettre, ça dépendra du temps qu'il fera.	I can't promise you anything; it will depend on the weather.
évident, **évidente** [evidɑ̃, ɑ̃t]	clear, obvious, evident
Il est évident que j'ai raison.	It is obvious that I am right.
clair, **claire** [klɛʀ]	clear
confus, **confuse** [kɔ̃fy, yz]	confused, muddled

il est courant que + *subj* [ilɛkuʀɑ̃]	it is usual, common that
Il est courant qu'il fasse mauvais en cette saison.	It is usual for the weather to be bad in this season.
il est (**im**)**possible que** + *subj* [ilɛ(ɛ̃)pɔsibl]	it is (im)possible that
Il est possible qu'il pleuve demain.	It's possible that it will rain tomorrow.
il est probable que [ilɛpʀɔbabl]	it is probable that
Il est probable qu'il viendra.	He probably will come.
il est improbable que + *subj* [ilɛ(t) ɛ̃pʀɔbabl]	it is improbable that

juste [ʒyst]	correct, true
faux, **fausse** [fo, fos]	false
correct, **correcte** [kɔʀɛkt]	correct
exact, **exacte** [egza(kt), egzakt]	exact, correct, accurate
Il est exact que nous nous connaissons depuis longtemps.	It is true that we have known each other for a long time.

important, **importante** [ɛ̃pɔʀtɑ̃, ɑ̃t]	important
l'**importance** *f* [ɛ̃pɔʀtɑ̃s]	importance, magnitude
de toute première importance	of the greatest importance
principal, **principale** [pʀɛ̃sipal]	main
Tu n'es pas blessé, c'est le principal.	You are not injured, that's the main thing.
secondaire [s(ə)gɔ̃dɛʀ]	secondary
C'est une question tout à fait secondaire.	That is a totally secondary consideration.

bien *adv* [bjɛ̃]	well *(See Information Box p. 448)*
Qu'est-ce que tu chantes bien!	How well you sing!
mieux [mjø]	better
Tu aurais pu mieux faire.	You could have done better.
bon, **bonne** [bɔ̃, bɔn]	good
meilleur, **meilleure** [mɛjœʀ]	better
C'est le meilleur pianiste que je connaisse.	He is the best pianist I know.
parfait, **parfaite** [paʀfɛ, ɛt]	perfect
Comme ça, c'est parfait.	It's perfect like that.
idéal, **idéale** [ideal]	ideal
Il fait un temps idéal pour un pique-nique.	The weather is ideal for a picnic.
formidable [fɔʀmidabl]	wonderful
préférer [pʀefeʀe]	to prefer
préférable [pʀefeʀabl]	preferable
Il aurait été préférable que tu te taises.	It would have been preferable for you to say nothing.

capital, **capitale** [kapital]	significant, important
un événement capital	significant event
primordial, **primordiale** [pʀimɔʀdjal]	essential, decisive
jouer un rôle primordial	to play an essential role
la **perfection** [pɛʀfɛksjɔ̃]	perfection
Yann joue du violon **à la perfection**.	Yann plays violin to perfection.
l'**imperfection** *f* [ɛ̃pɛʀfɛksjɔ̃]	imperfection
exceptionnel, **exceptionnelle** [ɛksɛpsjɔnɛl]	exceptional
Elle est d'une adresse exceptionnelle.	She has exceptional skill.
remarquable [ʀ(ə)maʀkabl]	remarkable
unique [ynik]	unique
Nous avons assisté à un spectacle absolument unique.	We attended an absolutely unique show.
convenable [kɔ̃vnabl]	appropriate

mal [mal]	badly
Tu ne trouves pas qu'ils ont mal joué?	Don't you think that they played badly?
mauvais, **mauvaise** [mo/ɔvɛ, ɛz]	bad
pire [piʀ]	worse
de pire en pire	worse and worse
grave [gʀav]	serious
Hervé est malade? **Rien de grave**, j'espère.	Hervé is ill? Nothing serious, I hope.
terrible [teʀibl]	terrible

(in)**suffisant**, (in)**suffisante** [(ɛ̃)syfizɑ̃, ɑ̃t]	(in)sufficient, (in)adequate
catastrophique [katastʀɔfik]	catastrophic
la **catastrophe**/la **cata** *fam* [kata(stʀɔf)]	catastrophe
En ce moment, au bureau, c'est la cata(strophe); presque tout le monde est malade.	It's a disaster in the office right now; almost everybody is sick.

un **avantage** [avɑ̃taʒ]	advantage
un avantage inestimable	invaluable advantage
agréable [agʀeabl]	agreeable, pleasant
pratique [pʀatik]	practical
Pour aller au bureau, je prends le bus, c'est plus pratique.	I take the bus to go to the office; it's more practical.
il semble que [ilsɑ̃bl]	it seems that
Il semble que le temps devient/devienne meilleur.	It seems that the weather is getting better.
il me semble que [i(l)m(ə)sɑ̃bl]	it seems to me that
Il me semble que Lucas a encore grossi.	It seems to me that Lucas has put on more weight.
avoir l'impression que *f* [avwaʀlɛ̃pʀesjɔ̃]	to have the impression that
avoir le sentiment que [avwaʀl(ə)sɑ̃timɑ̃]	to have the feeling that
trouver que [tʀuve]	to find that
Tu ne trouves pas que Pascal a mauvaise mine?	Don't you find that Pascal doesn't look good?
trouver qn/qc + *adj* [tʀuve]	to find s.o./s.th.
Je trouve les nouveaux voisins très gentils.	I find the new neighbors very nice.
personnellement [pɛʀsɔnɛlmɑ̃]	personally
Moi, personnellement, je lui aurais dit ce que j'en pense.	Personally, I would have told him what I think of it.
de mon côté [d(ə)mɔ̃kote]	for my part
De mon côté, je pense que Valérie a pris la bonne décision.	For my part, I think that Valérie made the right decision.
pour ma part [puʀmapaʀ]	for my part
Moi, pour ma part, je préfère la mer à la montagne.	For my part, I prefer the ocean to the mountains.
franchement [fʀɑ̃ʃmɑ̃]	frankly, really
Là, franchement, tu exagères!	Really, you are exaggerating!
heureusement (**que**) [øʀøzmɑ̃]	fortunately
Heureusement qu'on a retrouvé les clés.	Fortunately we found the keys.
malheureusement [maløʀøzmɑ̃]	unfortunately
Malheureusement, il n'est jamais là quand on a besoin de lui.	Unfortunately he is never there when you need him.

beau, bel, belle; beaux, belles *pl* [bo, bɛl]	beautiful
Quel bel oiseau!	What a beautiful bird!
magnifique [maɲifik]	wonderful
splendide [splɑ̃did]	splendid, awesome
Tu as vu ce but? Splendide!	Did you see that goal? Awesome!
laid, laide [lɛ, lɛd]	ugly
le **goût** [gu]	taste (n)
avoir bon/mauvais goût	to have good/bad taste
J'ai trouvé sa réflexion **de très mauvais goût**.	I found his remark to be in very bad taste.
charmant, charmante [ʃaʀmɑ̃, ɑ̃t]	charming
le **charme** [ʃaʀm]	charm (n)
Elle n'est pas belle, mais elle a du charme.	She is not beautiful, but she has charm.
mignon, mignonne [miɲɔ̃, ɔn]	cute, pretty, sweet
aimable [ɛmabl]	friendly, likeable, kind
Merci beaucoup, vous êtes trop aimable.	Thank you, you are too kind.
adorable [adɔʀabl]	adorable
Tu ferais ça pour moi? Tu es vraiment adorable.	You would do that for me? You are really adorable.
impressionnant, impressionnante [ɛ̃pʀesjɔnɑ̃, ɑ̃t]	impressive
intéressant, intéressante [ɛ̃teʀɛsɑ̃, ɑ̃t]	interesting
amusant, amusante [amyzɑ̃, ɑ̃t]	amusing, witty
original, originale [ɔʀiʒinal]	original, peculiar, unique
avoir des idées originales	to have some peculiar ideas
banal, banale [banal]	common, banal, trivial
Ce n'est pas banal, ce qui t'est arrivé.	What happened to you is no trifling matter.
médiocre [medjɔkʀ]	mediocre
fatigant, fatigante [fatigɑ̃, ɑ̃t]	tiring, strenuous
ennuyeux, ennuyeuse [ɑ̃nɥijø, jøz]	boring
bête [bɛt]	stupid
Ce n'est pas bête, ce que tu dis.	What you are saying isn't stupid.
désagréable [dezagʀeabl]	unpleasant, disagreeable
pénible [penibl]	painful, unbearable
Ce que tu peux être pénible, par moments!	You can be so unbearable sometimes!
détestable [detɛstabl]	horrible, hideous, hateful

moche *fam* [mɔʃ]	hideous, ugly as sin
hideux, **hideuse** ['idø, øz]	hideous, atrocious, horrendous
affreux, **affreuse** [afʀø, øz]	frightful
horrible [ɔʀibl]	horrible
épouvantable [epuvɑ̃tabl]	frightful, horrible
Les acteurs étaient bons, mais j'ai trouvé la mise en scène épouvantable.	The actors were good, but I found the production horrible.

simple [sɛ̃pl]	simple
élémentaire [elemɑ̃tɛʀ]	elementary, basic
facile [fasil]	easy *(See Information Box p. 437)*
difficile [difisil]	difficult, hard
dur, **dure** [dyʀ]	difficult, hard
Tu n'y arriveras pas, c'est trop dur.	You won't be able to do it; it's too hard.

étonner qn [etɔne]	to astonish s.o.
Ça m'étonnerait qu'il soit à l'heure.	I would be astonished if he were on time.
s'étonner [setɔne]	to be surprised
Je m'étonne toujours de l'intelligence de mon chien.	I am always surprised at my dog's intelligence.
étonnant, **étonnante** [etɔnɑ̃, ɑ̃t]	astonishing, amazing
l'**étonnement** *m* [etɔnmɑ̃]	astonishment, amazement
surprenant, **surprenante** [syʀpʀənɑ̃, ɑ̃t]	surprising (adj)
être surpris, **surprise** [syʀpʀi, iz]	to be surprised
Nous sommes surprises que tu n'aies pas encore compris.	We are surprised that you haven't yet understood.
la **surprise** [syʀpʀiz]	surprise (n)
Elle n'a pas pu cacher sa surprise quand elle l'a vu.	She could not conceal her surprise when she saw him.

émerveillé, **émerveillée** [emɛʀveje]	delighted
l'**émerveillement** *m* [emɛʀvejmɑ̃]	astonishment, amazement, delight
Le spectacle a **plongé** les spectateurs **dans l'émerveillement**.	The play plunged the audience into amazement.
stupéfait, **stupéfaite** [stypefɛ, ɛt]	shocked, stunned
Je suis stupéfait de voir comme ta fille a grandi.	I am stunned to see how your daughter has grown.
la **stupéfaction** [stypefaksjɔ̃]	astonishment
Je n'en crois pas mes yeux! [ʒ(ə)nɑ̃kʀwapamezjø]	I can't believe my eyes!
Je n'en crois pas mes oreilles! [ʒ(ə)nɑ̃kʀwapamezɔʀɛj]	I can't believe my ears!

bizarre [bizaʀ]	bizarre, strange, disconcerting
Je **trouve bizarre** qu'elle n'ait pas téléphoné.	I find it strange that she has not phoned.
étrange [etʀɑ̃ʒ]	strange
incroyable [ɛ̃kʀwajabl]	unbelievable, incredible
Incroyable, mais vrai, Véronique s'est mariée!	Incredible but true, Véronique got married.
un, une **drôle de**… [dʀol]	a strange… *(See Information Box p. 44)*
une **drôle d'histoire**	strange/peculiar story
une **histoire drôle**	funny story

curieux, **curieuse** [kyʀjø, jøz]	funny, peculiar
frappant, **frapante** [fʀapɑ̃, ɑ̃t]	striking
Qu'est-ce que tu ressembles à ton frère, c'est frappant.	How you resemble your brother; it's striking.
inexplicable [inɛksplikabl]	inexplicable
mystérieux, **mystérieuse** [misteʀjø, jøz]	mysterious
invraisemblable [ɛ̃vʀɛsɑ̃blabl]	improbable, unbelievable
inouï, **inouïe** [inwi]	unheard of, unbelievable, unprecedented
Mais c'est inouï, ce que tu dis là.	What you are saying is unheard of.

Hein? ['ɛ̃]	Huh?
Quoi? [kwa]	What?
Quoi? C'est ta sœur? Mais vous ne vous ressemblez pas!	What? That is your sister? But you don't look alike!
Comment? [kɔmɑ̃]	What?
Ah, bon? [abɔ̃]	Oh, really?
Ah, bon, c'était pour rire? Tu m'as fait peur.	Oh, really? That was a joke? You frightened me.
Tiens, tiens! [tjɛ̃tjɛ̃]	Look! Come on!
Tiens, tiens! C'est à cette heure-ci qu'on rentre?	Come on! You come home at this hour?
Eh bien! ['e/'ɛbjɛ̃]	Well!
Dis/Dites donc! [di/ditdɔ̃k]	Say!
Dis-donc! Qu'est-ce que tu as grandi!	Say! How you have grown!
Oh là là! [olala]	Oh boy!
Oh là là! Quand ma mère va voir ça, elle va être en colère.	Oh boy! When my mother sees that she will be angry.
Sans blague! [sɑ̃blag]	No kidding!
Elle a eu des jumeaux? Sans blague!	She had twins? No kidding!
Voyons! [vwajɔ̃]	Let's see!
Pas possible! [papɔsibl]	Impossible!
Ça alors! [saalɔʀ]	Indeed!/You don't say!

23.8 Commands and Wishes  112

encourager qn à faire qc [ɑ̃kuʀaʒe]	to encourage s.o. to do s.th.
Nous l'avons encouragé à continuer.	We encouraged him to continue.
un **encouragement** [ɑ̃kuʀaʒmɑ̃]	encouragement
Attention! [atɑ̃sjɔ̃]	Careful! Attention! Beware!
Allez, allez! [aleale]	Go, go!
Allez, allez! Dépêchez-vous un peu.	Go, go! Get a move on!
Vas-y! [vazi]	Go for it!
Vas-y, saute, ce n'est pas haut!	Go for it, jump, it's not high!
Halte! ['alt]	Stop!
Stop! [stɔp]	Stop!
Tais-toi! [tɛtwa]	Be quiet!
Silence! [silɑ̃s]	Silence!
Chut! [ʃyt]	Shh!
Va-t'en! [vatɑ̃]	Go away!
Laisse-moi tranquille! [lɛsmwatʀɑ̃kil]	Leave me alone!
Au secours! [os(ə)kuʀ]	Help!
À l'aide! [alɛd]	Help!
Au voleur! [ovɔlœʀ]	Stop thief!
souhaiter qc à qn [swɛte]	to wish s.th. to s.o.
Je vous souhaite une bonne nuit.	I wish you a good night.
un **souhait** [swɛ]	wish (n)
un **vœu** [vø]	wish (n)
Je vous adresse tous mes vœux de bonheur.	I send all my best wishes.
Mes meilleurs vœux (**pour la nouvelle année**).	My best wishes (for the New Year).
À tes/vos souhaits! [ate/voswɛ]	(God) Bless you!
Atchoum! – À tes souhaits!	Achoo! – Bless you!

Félicitations! [felisitasjɔ̃]	Congratulations!
Toutes nos félicitations aux jeunes mariés!	Our congratulations to the newlyweds!
Bonne fête! [bɔnfɛt]	Happy Name Day!/ Happy Birthday!
Bon anniversaire! [bɔnanivɛʀsɛʀ]	Happy Birthday!
Bonne année! [bɔnane]	Happy New Year!
Bonne année, bonne santé!	Good luck and health in the New Year!
Joyeux Noël! [ʒwajønɔɛl]	Merry Christmas!
Joyeuses Pâques! [ʒwajøzpak]	Happy Easter!
Bonne chance! [bɔnʃɑ̃s]	Good luck!
Bon appétit. [bɔnapeti]	Enjoy the meal.
Bonne journée. [bɔnʒuʀne]	Have a good day.
Bonne nuit! [bɔnnɥi]	Good night!
Bonnes vacances. [bɔnvakɑ̃s]	Have a good vacation.
Bon voyage. [bɔ̃vwajaʒ]	Have a good trip.
Bonne route. [bɔnʀut]	Have a good drive.

23.9 Phraseology in Letters

INFO

Letters preserve friendship

Le destinataire:	*Monsieur (M.), Madame (Mme.), Mademoiselle (Melle)* + nom	recipient/addressee
Le lieu et la date:	*Toulouse, le 1er avril 2009; Lyon, le 2 avril 2009*	place and date
Le debut dans une lettre officielle, on met une virgule après l'appel:	*Madame, Monsieur,* *Mademoiselle,* *Mesdames, Messieurs,* *Mademoiselles,* *Monsieur le Directeur,* *Madame la Directrice,*	Greeting in a formal letter; a comma is used after the greeting
Le début dans une lettre à des personnes qu'on connaît (un peu):	voir plus haut ou: *Chère Madame,* *Cher Monsieur,* ... (on écrit rarement le nom de famille) *Cher Philippe,* *Chére Florence,* *Bien chers tous, (1hr Lieben)*	Greeting in a letter to an acquaintance
Le premier mot de la lettre prend une majuscule.	*Chére Florence* *C'est avec beaucoup de...*	The first word in the letter is capitalized.
Formules de fin dans une lettre officielle:	*Je vous prie de croire, Monsieur, à l'expression de mes salutations distinguées.* *Je vous prie d'agréer/de recevoir, Messieurs, l'expression de mes...* *Dans l'attente de votre réponse, je vous prie de croire, Mademoiselle, à l'expression de mes salutations les meilleures.*	Closing in a formal letter: Respectfully yours, Best regards, Sincerely, I look forward to hearing from you.
Formules de fin dans une lettre à des amis:	*Amitiés* *(Bien) Amicalement* *Meilleures salutations* *Bien à toi/vous*	Closing in a letter to friends: Warmest greetings, Yours truly,
Formules de fin dans une lettre à de très bons amis:	*Salut* *Affectueusement* *Grosses bises*	Closing in a letter to very good friends: Bye for now, With love, Big hugs and kisses,

INFO

Business letters

Dans des lettres commerciales, on intercale:	*N/réf.:...(Notre référence)* *V/réf.:...(Votre référence)* *Objet:*	The following are added to business letters: Reference number: Re/Concerning:
Quelques formules utiles:		Some useful set phrases:
	J'ai bien reçu votre lettre du + date	I have received your letter dated…
	Je vous remercie de...	I thank you for…
	En réponse à votre lettre	In response to your letter…
	Je voudrais savoir si...	I would like to know if…
	En référence à votre/ma lettre...	With reference to your/my letter…
	Je vous prie de bien vouloir...	I request that you…
	Nous vous serions reconnaissants de...	We would be grateful if you…
	À la suite de votre courrier du + date	In answer to your letter of (date)…
	Je vous adresse ci-joint...	Enclosed you will find…
	Je suis heureux d'apprendre...	I am pleased to learn…
	Veuillez répondre par retour du courrier.	Please respond without delay.
	...assitôt que possible	… as quickly as possible
	Transmettez mes amitiés à...	Please convey my greetings…
La signature se trouve à droite, en bas.		The signature is below at the right.

False Friends

French Word	Actual Meaning	False Friend	Correct French Word
éventuellement	**possibly**	eventually	*en fin de comte*

24

Language Structures

24.1 Qualifiers and Pronouns  113

le, la, l'; les *pl* [lə, la, le]	the
le client, l'air; la cliente, l'eau; les clients, les clientes	the customer, the air; the (female) customer, the water; the customers, the (female) customers
du, de la, de l'; des *pl* [dy, d(ə)la, de]	some (*often not translated*)
du pain, de l'air; de la farine, de l'eau; des bonbons, des fraises	(some) bread, air; flour, water; candies, strawberries
au, à la, à l'; aux *pl* [o, ala, o]	to
je vais au marché, à l'arrêt de bus, à la banque, à l'école, aux États-Unis	I am going to the market, to the bus stop, to the bank, to school, to the United States
un, une; des *pl* [œ̃, yn, de]	a, an
un client, une cliente; des clients, des clientes	a customer, a (female) customer; customers, (female) customers

mon, ma; mes *pl* [mɔ̃, ma, me]	my
ton, ta; tes *pl* [tɔ̃, ta, te]	your
son, sa; ses *pl* [sɔ̃, sa, se]	his/her
C'est son porte-monnaie.	This is his/her wallet.
C'est sa montre.	This is his/her watch.
Ce sont ses parents.	These are his/her parents.
notre; nos *pl* [nɔtʀ, no]	our
votre; vos *pl* [vɔtʀ, vo]	your
leur; leurs *pl* [lœʀ]	their

ce, cet, cette; ces *pl* [sə, sɛt; se]	this; these
ce livre, cet appartement; cette chaise, cette orange	this book, this apartment; this chair, this orange
ces livres; ces chaises	these books; these chairs
ce livre-ci	this book
cette photo-là	that photo

tout le (l'), toute la (l') [tul(ə), tutla]	all the.../the entire...
Tout le monde est venu.	Everyone came.
Toute la famille est là.	The entire family is there.
tous les, toutes les [tule, tutle]	all
tous les garçons, toutes les filles	all the boys, all the girls
Tous mes amis sont en vacances.	All my friends are on vacation.
Toutes ces fleurs viennent de mon jardin.	All these flowers come from my garden.
tout, tous, toutes [tu, tus, tut]	all; everything
Tout s'est bien passé.	Everything went well.
Ils sont tous partis.	They have all left.
Les photos? Il nous les a toutes montrées.	The photos? He showed them all to us.

chaque [ʃak]	each, every
Chaque invité a eu un petit cadeau.	Every guest received a little gift.
chacun, **chacune** [ʃakœ̃, yn]	each
Chacun a pu donner son avis.	Each was able to give his opinion.
ne... **aucun**, **ne... aucune** [nəokœ̃, okyn]	no/none/not one
Il n'a eu aucune réaction.	He showed no reaction.
aucun...**ne**, **aucune... ne** [okœ̃nə, okyn]	no/none
Aucune (carte postale) ne m'a plu.	No postcard was to my liking.
certains, **certaines** [sɛʀtɛ̃, ɛn]	certain, some
Certaines personnes ne sont jamais contentes.	Some people are never happy.
différents, **différentes** [difeʀɑ̃, ɑ̃t]	different, various
des fromages de différentes régions de France	cheeses from different regions in France
divers, **diverses** [divɛʀ, ɛʀs]	various, different
On en a parlé à diverses personnes.	We spoke of various people.
plusieurs [plyzjœʀ]	several
On a arrêté plusieurs suspects.	Several suspects were arrested.
quelques [kɛlkə]	some, a few
Il a quelques kilos en trop.	He is a few kilos too heavy.
quelqu'un [kɛlkœ̃]	someone
Quelqu'un a téléphoné?	Did someone call?
quelques-uns, **quelques-unes** [kɛlkəzœ̃, kɛlkəzyn]	some, a few
Tu as lu tous les livres de Jules Verne? – Non, seulement quelques-uns.	Have you read all of Jules Verne's books? – No, only a few.
ne... **personne** [nəpɛʀsɔn]	no one/nobody
On n'a rencontré personne.	We met no one.
personne... **ne** [pɛʀsɔnnə]	nobody/no one
Personne n'a appelé.	Nobody called.
pas un seul, **pas une seule** [pa(z)œ̃/ynsœl]	not a single
Pas un (seul) magasin n'était ouvert.	Not a single store was open.
quelque chose [kɛlkəʃoz]	something
ne... **rien** [nəʀjɛ̃]	nothing
Je n'ai rien vu.	I saw nothing.
rien... **ne** [ʀjɛ̃nə]	no more
Rien ne va plus.	No more bets.

un, une **autre**; **d'autres** *pl* [otʀ]	another; other
Montrez-moi un autre/d'autres modèle(s).	Show me another/some other models.
le, la **même**; les **mêmes** *pl* [mɛm]	the same
Nous sommes du même avis.	We are of the same opinion.
un **tel, une telle; de tels, de telles** *pl* [tɛl]	such a(n)
Il ne faut pas rater une telle occasion.	An opportunity such as this is not to be missed.

---

je (j') [ʒə]	I
me (m') [mə]	me
Il m'a regardé.	He looked at me.
Il m'a donné un conseil.	He gave me some advice.
moi [mwa]	me
Sans moi.	Without me.

---

tu [ty]	you
te (t') [tə]	(to, for) you
Tu t'appelles comment?	What is your name?
Je te dois encore 20 euros.	I still owe you 20 euros.
toi [twa]	you
C'est pour toi.	It's for you.

---

il [il]	he, it
le (l') [lə]	him, it
Je le vois souvent.	I see him frequently.
elle [ɛl]	she, it
Elle est très sympathique.	She is very nice.
C'est Monique qui vient d'arriver? – Oui, c'est elle.	Is it Monique who just arrived? – Yes, it is she.
la (l') [la]	her, it
Si tu la vois, dis-lui de m'appeler.	If you see her, tell her to call me.
lui [lɥi]	(to) him/her
Je lui ai dit de venir.	I told him/her to come.
se (s') [s(ə)]	oneself, himself, herself, themselves
Elle s'est regardée dans la glace.	She looked at herself in the mirror.
soi [swa]	oneself
Chacun pour soi et Dieu pour tous. *loc*	Every man for himself and God for all.
on [ɔ̃]	one; we
On s'est bien amusé(e)(s).	We had a good time.
Ici, on parle espagnol.	Spanish is spoken here.

nous [nu] Nous avons faim. Écris-nous de temps en temps.	we, us We are hungry. Write us from time to time.
vous [vu] Elle vous a reconnus? Servez-vous une bière.	you Did she recognize you? Help yourself to a beer.
ils, **elles** [il, ɛl] **les** [le] Je les ai invité(e)s. **leur** [lœʀ] Je leur ai apporté des fleurs. **eux, elles** [ø, ɛl] Nous pensons souvent à eux/elles. **se (s')** [s(ə)] Ils se sont vus la semaine dernière. Ils se sont téléphoné hier soir.	they them I invited them. (to, for) them I brought them some flowers. them We often think of them. themselves They saw each other last week. They spoke by phone last night.
en [ɑ̃] Il en a parlé. Il y a assez de pommes? – Oui, nous en avons pris trois kilos. **y** [i] Je m'y intéresse beaucoup.	some, about it/them He spoke about it. Are there enough apples? – Yes, we bought three kilos (of them). there; it I am greatly interested in it.
ceci [səsi] **cela**, **ça** [s(ə)la, sa] Donne-moi cela/ça.	this that Give me that.
qui [ki] C'est une femme qui sait ce qu'elle veut. **que (qu')** [kə] C'est une vedette que j'admire. **quoi** [kwa] Il ne savait plus quoi dire. Par quoi est-ce qu'on commence? **ce qui** [s(ə)ki] Je ne sais pas ce qui est arrivé. **ce que (ce qu')** [s(ə)kə] Dis-moi ce que tu en penses.	who, which, that That is a woman who knows what she wants. which, that, whom That is a star whom I admire. what He didn't know what to say. Where shall we begin? what, that which I don't know what happened. what, that which Tell me what you think about it.

dont [dõ]	whose, of which, of whom
un film dont on parle beaucoup	a film about which people speak a lot
où [u]	where; in which
une région où j'ai passé trois ans	a region in which I spent three years
lequel (duquel, auquel) [ləkɛl]	which (of which, about which)
un événement auquel nous pensons tous	an event about which we are all thinking
laquelle (de laquelle, à laquelle) [lakɛl]	which, that
C'est une situation dans laquelle je ne voudrais pas être.	That's a situation that I would not want to be in.
lesquels (desquels, auxquels) [lekɛl]	which
lesquelles (desquelles, auxquelles) [lekɛl]	which
celui(-ci/-là), celle(-ci/-là) [səlɥi(si/la), sɛl(si/la)]	this one (here), that one (there)
Si tu n'as pas d'anorak, mets celui de Julien.	If you don't have a parka, put on Julien's.
ceux(-ci/-là), celles(-ci/-là) [sø(si/la), sɛl(si/la)]	these (here), those (there)
Ceux-ci sont trop petits, prends ceux-là.	These are too small; take those.
le mien, la mienne; les miens, les miennes *pl* [mjɛ̃, mjɛn]	mine
le tien, la tienne; les tiens, les tiennes *pl* [tjɛ̃, tjɛn]	yours
Ce pull-là, c'est le mien ou le tien?	Is that sweater mine or yours?
le sien, la sienne; les siens, les siennes *pl* [sjɛ̃, sjɛn]	his, hers, theirs
le, la **nôtre; les nôtres** *pl* [notʀ]	ours
le, la **vôtre; les vôtres** *pl* [votʀ]	yours
le, la **leur; les leurs** *pl* [lœʀ]	theirs

24.2 Question Words  114

est-ce que [ɛskə]	*formal introduction to a question*
Qui? [ki]	Who?
Qui est là?	Who is there?
De qui est ce tableau?	Who is this a picture of?
À qui est cette clé?	Whose key is this?

Que? [kə]	What?
Que veux-tu?	What do you want?
Quoi? [kwa]	What?
De quoi parlez-vous?	What are you talking about?
À quoi pensez-vous?	What are you thinking about?
Qui est-ce qui? [kiɛski]	Who?
Qui est-ce qui vient avec moi?	Who is coming with me?
Qui est-ce que? [kiɛskə]	Whom?
Qui est-ce qu'elle a appelé?	Whom did she call?
Qu'est-ce qui? [kɛski]	What?
Qu'est-ce qui est arrivé?	What happened?
Qu'est-ce que? [kɛskə]	What?
Qu'est-ce que c'est?	What is that?

Lequel? (Duquel? Auquel?) [ləkɛl]	Which one?
J'adore cet acteur. – Lequel?	I love that actor. – Which one?
Laquelle? (De laquelle? À laquelle?) [lakɛl]	Which one?
Nous pensons toujours à cette chanson. – À laquelle?	We still think about that song. – Which one?
Lesquels? (Desquels? Auxquels?) [lekɛl]	Which ones?
J'ai reçu une lettre de mes amis. – Desquels?	I received a letter from my friends. – Which ones?
Lesquelles? (Desquelles? Auxquelles?) [lekɛl]	Which ones?
Donne-moi les photos. – Lesquelles?	Give me the photos. – Which ones?

Quel? Quelle ? [kɛl]	What?
Quel âge avez-vous?/Vous avez quel âge?	What is your age?
Quels? Quelles? Quel(le)s? [kɛl]	What?
Par quelles villes êtes-vous passés?	What cities did you go through?

Où? [u]	Where?
Où habitez-vous?/Vous habitez où?	Where do you live?
D'où? [du]	(From) where?
D'où vient ce bruit?	Where is that noise coming from?
Quand? [kɑ̃]	When?
Quand est-ce qu'on mange?	When do we eat?
Comment? [kɔmɑ̃]	How?
Comment vas-tu?	How are you?
Combien? [kɔ̃bjɛ̃]	How much?
Combien ça coûte?/Ça coûte combien?	How much is that?

Pourquoi? [puʀkwa]	Why?
Pourquoi est-ce que tu ne m'aimes plus?	Why do you no longer love me?

24.3 Conjunctions  115

et [e]	and
ou (**bien**) [u(bjɛ̃)]	or (else)
Dépêche-toi, ou (bien) je pars sans toi.	Hurry up or (else) I will leave without you.
ou... **ou** [uu]	either...or
Ou tu te décides enfin ou on part sans toi.	Either you make up your mind or we will leave without you.
d'un côté... **de l'autre** [dœ̃koted(ə)lotʀ]	on the one hand... on the other
D'un côté, je l'aime bien, de l'autre, elle m'énerve.	On the one hand I like her a lot, and on the other, she annoys me.
d'une part... **d'autre part** [dynpaʀdotʀ(ə)paʀ]	on the one hand... on the other
sinon [sinɔ̃]	otherwise
Va au lit maintenant, sinon tu n'arriveras pas à te lever demain.	Go to bed now, otherwise you won't be able to get up tomorrow.
autrement [otʀəmɑ̃]	otherwise
mais [mɛ]	but
par contre [paʀkɔ̃tʀ]	on the other hand, conversely
Il est complètement idiot. Sa sœur, par contre, est très intelligente.	He is a complete idiot. His sister, on the other hand, is very intelligent.
pourtant [puʀtɑ̃]	however
Il ne me croit pas, je dis pourtant la vérité.	He doesn't believe me; however, I am telling the truth.
quand même [kɑ̃mɛm]	still, just the same
Elle est malade mais elle ira quand même à cette réunion.	She is sick, but she will still go to this meeting.
en revanche [ɑ̃ʀ(ə)vɑ̃ʃ]	on the other hand
Il est insupportable. Sa femme, en revanche, est charmante.	He is unbearable. His wife, on the other hand, is charming.
cependant [s(ə)pɑ̃dɑ̃]	however

d'abord [dabɔʀ]	at first
puis [pɥi]	then
ensuite [ɑ̃sɥit]	then, next
enfin [ɑ̃fɛ̃]	finally, at last
J'ai enfin trouvé du travail.	At last I have found work.
car [kaʀ]	for
c'est pourquoi [sɛpuʀkwa]	that's why
donc [dɔ̃k]	therefore, so
Entrez donc.	So come on in.
Je n'ai pas vu ce film; je ne peux donc pas en parler.	I have not seen this movie, so I cannot talk about it.
ainsi [ɛ̃si]	thus, that way
Passe par la rue Voltaire, ainsi tu arriveras plus vite.	Take rue Voltaire; that way you will get there quicker.
or [ɔʀ]	but
Il rêvait d'une belle voiture; or il était pauvre.	He was dreaming about a nice car, but he was poor.
par conséquent [paʀkɔ̃sekɑ̃]	as a result, thus
Il a raté son train, par conséquent il a dû prendre un taxi.	He missed his train; as a result he had to take a taxi.
voilà pourquoi [vwalapuʀkwa]	that's why
quand [kɑ̃]	when
Quand il était petit, il voulait devenir pompier.	When he was small, he wanted to grow up to be a fireman.
Je ne sais pas quand il viendra.	I don't know when he will come.
Quand tu le verras, dis-lui bonjour de ma part.	When you see him, say hello for me.
pendant que [pɑ̃dɑ̃kə]	while
Pendant qu'il dort, il ne fait pas de bêtises.	He doesn't get into any mischief while he is sleeping.
depuis que [dəpɥikə]	(ever) since
Depuis qu'il a déménagé, il n'a pas donné de ses nouvelles.	Nobody has heard from him since he moved.
avant que [avɑ̃kə]	before
Tu devrais téléphoner avant qu'il (ne) soit trop tard.	You should call before it is too late.
après que [apʀɛkə]	after
jusqu'à ce que [ʒyskas(ə)kə]	until
Reste ici jusqu'à ce que je revienne.	Stay here until I come back.

au moment où [omɔmɑ̃u]	at the instant when
dès que [dɛkə]	as soon
Je t'aiderai dès que j'aurai fini mon travail.	I will help you as soon as I finish my work.
tant que [tɑ̃kə]	as long as
Tant que tu resteras avec moi, je serai heureux.	I will be happy as long as you stay with me.
comme [kɔm]	since, because
Comme je n'avais pas de farine, je n'ai pas pu faire de tarte.	Since I didn't have any flour I couldn't bake a pie.
parce que [paʀs(ə)kə]	because
puisque [pɥiskə]	since
Ce n'est pas la peine de l'inviter puisqu'elle ne viendra pas.	No need to invite her since she will not come.
que [kə]	that; as
J'espère que tu vas bien.	I hope that you are well.
Il a le même âge que moi.	He is the same age as me.
pour que [puʀkə]	so that
Je le lui ai bien expliqué pour qu'il comprenne.	I explained it to him well so that he would understand.
de sorte que [dəsɔʀt(ə)kə]	so that, in such a way that
afin que [afɛ̃kə]	so that
On lui a prêté de l'argent afin qu'elle puisse payer son loyer.	We loaned her money so that she could pay her rent.
de manière que [d(ə)manjɛʀkə]	so that, in such a way that
de façon que [d(ə)fasɔ̃kə]	so that, in such a way that
tandis que [tɑ̃dikə]	whereas, while
J'aime bien voyager tandis que ma femme préfère rester à la maison.	I really like to travel, whereas my wife prefers to stay home.
alors que [alɔʀkə]	whereas, although, even though
Il n'est pas venu alors qu'il l'avait promis.	He didn't come even though he had promised.
quoique + *subj* [kwakə]	although, albeit
bien que + *subj* [bjɛ̃kə]	although, even though
Quoiqu'/Bien qu'il fasse froid, il se promène en tee-shirt.	Even though the weather is cold he walks around in a T-shirt.
sans que + *subj* [sɑ̃kə]	without
Ils sont partis sans que je l'aie remarqué.	They left without my noticing.

malgré que + *subj* [malgʀekə] Il a une belle situation malgré qu'il ait quitté l'école à 16 ans.	in spite of, although He has a good job in spite of having quit school at the age of sixteen.
si [si] **même si** [mɛmsi] Même si (l')on me proposait beaucoup d'argent, je ne sauterais pas en parachute. **à condition que** [akɔ̃disjɔ̃kə] Nous pouvons vous accompagner, à condition qu'on y aille tout de suite.	if even if I would not sky dive even if somebody offered me a lot of money. provided that We can go with you provided that we leave right away.
d'autant plus que [dotɑ̃ply(s)kə] Je voudrais déménager, d'autant plus que je travaille loin d'ici. **pourvu que** + *subj* [puʀvykə] Il viendra demain, pourvu que cela vous convienne.	especially, particularly, all the more so because I would like to move, especially because I work far from here. provided that He will come tomorrow, provide that's agreeable to you.

24.4 Helping Verbs  116

avoir [avwaʀ] **être** [ɛtʀ] **aller faire qc** [ale] Tu vas écrire à Paul? **venir de faire qc** [v(ə)niʀ] On vient de faire des courses. **être en train de faire qc** [ɛtʀɑ̃tʀɛ̃]	to have to be to be going to do s.th. Are you going to write Paul? to have just done s.th. We have just been shopping. to be in the process of doing s.th.
devoir faire qc [devwaʀ] **vouloir faire qc** [vulwaʀ] **pouvoir faire qc** [puvwaʀ] Peux-tu traduire ce texte aujourd'hui? – Non, je n'ai pas le temps. **savoir faire qc** [savwaʀ] Tu sais nager maintenant? – Non, toujours pas!	to have to do s.th. to want to do s.th. *(See Information Box p. 450)* to be able to do s.th. *(See Information Box p. 450)* Can you translate this text today? – No, I don't have the time. to know how/be able to do s.th. Can you swim now? – No, not yet!

faire faire qc [fɛʀ]	to have s.th. done
Il a fait réparer sa voiture.	He is having his car repaired
laisser faire qc [lese]	to allow s.th. to be done
Il laisse son fils conduire sa voiture.	He lets his son drive his car.
sembler faire qc [sɑ̃ble]	to appear to do s.th.
Tu sembles avoir des problèmes.	You appear to have problems.
paraître faire qc [paʀɛtʀ]	to appear to do s.th
Elle paraît être d'accord.	She appears to be in agreement.
avoir qc à faire [avwaʀ]	to have s.th. to do
Laisse-moi tranquille, j'ai un travail à finir.	Leave me alone, I have a job to finish.
passer pour [pasepuʀ]	to pass for
Il passe pour un bon cuisinier.	He passes for a good cook.

24.5 Negations  117

ne... **pas** (**du tout**) [nəpa(dytu)] — not (at all)
Je ne connais pas (du tout) l'Afrique. — I don't know Africa (at all).

ne... **pas encore** [nəpa(z)ɑ̃kɔʀ] — not yet
On n'a pas encore dîné. — We have not yet had dinner.

ne... **pas un seul, ne... pas une seule** [nəpa(z)œ̃/ynsœl] — not a single...
Il n'a pas bu une seule goutte d'alcool. — He has not drunk a single drop of alcohol.

ne... **plus** (**du tout**) [nəply(dytu)] — no longer (at all)

ne... **jamais** [nəʒamɛ] — never
Nous ne sommes jamais allés en Belgique. — We have never been to Belgium.

ne... **personne** [nəpɛʀsɔn] — nobody
Ils ne connaissent personne, ici. — They know nobody here.

personne... **ne** [pɛʀsɔnnə] — nobody
Personne ne me comprend. — Nobody understands me.

ne... **rien** [nəʀjɛ̃] — nothing
On n'a rien vu. — We saw nothing.

rien... **ne** [ʀjɛ̃nə] — nothing
Rien n'est plus beau que les vacances. — Nothing is better than vacation.

ne... **rien du tout** [nəʀjɛ̃dytu] — nothing at all
Je n'y comprends rien du tout. — I understand nothing at all about it.

ne… aucun, ne… aucune [nəokœ̃/okyn]	no
Tu n'as aucune raison d'être fâché.	You have no reason to be angry.
aucun… ne, aucune… ne [okœ̃/okynnə]	no, none
Aucun de ces films ne m'a plu.	None of these movies were to my liking.
ne… ni… ni [nənini]	neither…nor
Elle n'aime ni la bière ni le vin.	She likes neither beer nor wine.
ne… que [nəkə]	only
Il n'y a que deux solutions.	There are only two solutions.
ne… guère *litt* [nəgɛʀ]	scarcely, hardly
ne… nulle part [nənylpaʀ]	nowhere
Tu n'iras nulle part sans mon autorisation.	You go nowhere without my permission.

24.6 Adverbs and Adverbial Expressions  118

bien [bjɛ̃]	well; very *(See Information Box p. 448)*
Tu vas bien?	Are you well?
mieux [mjø]	better
Il joue très bien du piano, mais encore mieux du violon.	He plays the piano very well, but the violin even better.
Elle joue **de mieux en mieux**.	She plays better and better.
Tu n'en veux pas? **Tant mieux**, il y en aura plus pour nous.	Don't you want any? So much the better, all the more for us.
mal [mal]	badly
Tant pis! [tɑ̃pi]	Too bad! Tough!
Il ne vient pas? Tant pis!	He's not coming? Tough!
Tant pis pour toi!	Serves you right!/Too bad for you!
ici [isi]	here
Vous êtes d'ici?	Are you from here?
là [la]	there
là-bas [laba]	over there
Qui est cet homme là-bas?	Who is that man over there?
partout [paʀtu]	everywhere, all over
Nous avons voyagé un peu partout dans le monde.	We have traveled all over the world.

ailleurs [ajœʀ]	elsewhere
Si tu n'es pas bien ici, tu n'as qu'à aller ailleurs.	If you don't like it here, you can go elsewhere.

---

hier [jɛʀ]	yesterday
aujourd'hui [ojuʀdɥi]	today
demain [d(ə)mɛ̃]	tomorrow

---

déjà [deʒa]	already
Il est déjà trois heures.	It is already three o'clock.
bientôt [bjɛ̃to]	soon
À bientôt.	See you soon.
parfois [paʀfwa]	sometimes
souvent [suvɑ̃]	often, frequently
Je lis parfois un livre, mais **le plus souvent**, je regarde la télévision.	I sometimes read a book, but more often I watch television.
toujours [tuʒuʀ]	always
encore [ɑ̃kɔʀ]	still
Ils sont encore là?	Are they still there?
tôt [to]	soon
tard [taʀ]	late
Tôt ou tard, tu t'apercevras que nous avons raison.	Sooner or later you will see that we are right.
avant [avɑ̃]	before, previously
Avant, j'allais souvent au cinéma.	Before, I frequently would go to the movies.
maintenant [mɛ̃t(ə)nɑ̃]	now
après [apʀɛ]	after
soudain [sudɛ̃]	suddenly
longtemps [lɔ̃tɑ̃]	long (time)
Je n'en ai pas pour longtemps.	It won't take me long.
vite [vit]	quickly *(See Information Box p. 447)*
Viens vite!	Come quickly!

---

très [tʀɛ]	very
Cet enfant est très poli.	This child is very polite.
assez (**de**) [ase]	enough
J'ai assez mangé.	I have eaten enough.
Tu as dit assez de bêtises pour aujourd'hui.	You have said enough nonsense for today.
beaucoup (**de**) [boku]	much, lots (of)
Merci beaucoup.	Thank you very much.
tant (de) [tɑ̃]	so much, many (of)
Je n'ai jamais vu tant d'argent à la fois.	I have never seen so much money at one time.
Ils se sont tant aimés.	They loved each other so much.

tellement (de) [tɛlmɑ̃]	so much (of)
Il a tellement changé que je ne l'ai pas reconnu.	He had changed so much that I didn't recognize him.
plus (de) [plys]	more (of)
trop (de) [tʀo]	too much, many (of)
Il a mangé trop de chocolat.	He ate too much chocolate.
C'est vraiment trop bête.	That is really too dumb.

peu (de) [pø]	little
Le soir, on mange très peu.	In the evening we eat very little.
moins (de) [mwɛ̃]	less (than)
C'est moins loin qu'on (ne) pensait.	It is not as far as we thought.

aussi [osi]	also, so, as
Je ne savais pas que tu étais aussi bête.	I did not know you were so dumb.
plutôt [plyto]	rather
Dans l'ensemble, ils sont plutôt sympathiques.	All in all, they are rather nice.
presque [pʀɛsk]	almost, nearly
surtout [syʀtu]	especially
peut-être [pøtɛtʀ]	perhaps, maybe
Il est peut-être fatigué, mais il est surtout paresseux.	Perhaps he is tired, but he is mostly lazy.
sans doute [sɑ̃dut]	probably *(See Information Box p. 474)*
Vous avez sans doute raison.	You are probably right.
même [mɛm]	even
Bien sûr qu'elle est venue, elle est même arrivée en avance.	Of course she came; she even arrived early.
c'est-à-dire [sɛtadiʀ]	that is, in other words
par exemple (p. ex.) [paʀɛgzɑ̃pl]	for example (e.g.)

volontiers [vɔlɔ̃tje]	willingly, gladly
Vous en voulez encore? – Volontiers.	Would you like some more? – Gladly.
exprès [ɛkspʀɛ]	on purpose
Excusez-moi, je ne l'ai pas fait exprès.	Excuse me, I didn't do it on purpose.
à peine [apɛn]	scarcely, hardly, barely
Elle est à peine plus grande que toi.	She is scarcely taller than you.
en vain [ɑ̃vɛ̃]	in vain
On a essayé en vain de le joindre au téléphone.	We tried in vain to reach him by phone.

24.7 Prepositions  119

à [a] — to, in, at, on.
- Il est parti à 6 heures. — He left at six o'clock.
- Il va à Toulouse. — He is going to Toulouse.
- Elle est repartie **à pied**. — She left on foot.

de [də] — from
- Nous serons absents de lundi à jeudi. — We will be absent from Monday through Thursday.
- Il vient de Quimper. — He comes from Quimper.
- Je meurs de faim. — I am dying of hunger.

en [ɑ̃] — in, within
- On a fait la route en 4 heures. — We made the trip in four hours.
- Nous habitons en Provence. — We live in Provence.

dans [dɑ̃] — in
- Il fait froid dans cette maison. — It's cold in this house.
- On va venir dans 2 heures. — We will come in two hours.

---

depuis [dəpɥi] — since, for
- Il pleut depuis deux semaines. — I has been raining for two weeks.

il y a [ilija] — ago
- Il y a un quart d'heure qu'elle est partie. — She left fifteen minutes ago.

pendant [pɑ̃dɑ̃] — during
- Le magasin est fermé pendant tout le mois d'août. — The store is closed during the entire month of August.

jusque [ʒysk(ə)] — until, up to, as far as
- Je vous ai attendus jusqu'à 6 heures. — I waited for you until six o'clock.
- Il est allé jusqu'en Inde. — He went as far as India.

vers [vɛʀ] — toward, around
- On arrivera vers midi. — We will arrive around noon.
- Toutes ces voitures se dirigent vers Reims. — All these cars are headed toward Reims.

au bout de [obudə] — after
- Au bout de 2 heures, on était tous fatigués. — After two hours we all were tired.
- Au bout de 20 kilomètres, il est tombé en panne. — After 20 kilometers his car broke down.

---

au cours de [okuʀdə]	in the course of
Au cours des dernières années, le chômage a augmenté.	In (the course of) recent years, unemployment has increased.
dès [dɛ]	as soon as
Nous nous sommes levés dès l'aube.	We got up as soon as dawn broke.
avant [avɑ̃]	before
Ils sont arrivés avant nous.	They arrived before we did.
On s'est arrêté un peu avant Nancy.	We stopped a little before Nancy.
après [apʀɛ]	after
Après 20 heures, tous les magasins sont fermés.	After 8:00 P.M. all the stores are closed.
Tournez à gauche après l'hôpital.	Turn left after the hospital.
devant [d(ə)vɑ̃]	before, in front of
Je vous attends devant le cinéma.	I will wait for you in front of the movie theater.
derrière [dɛʀjɛʀ]	behind
C'est la maison derrière l'église.	It's the house behind the church.
par [paʀ]	through
Ils sont passés par Poitiers.	They went through Poitiers.
sur [syʀ]	on
sous [su]	under
au-dessus (**de**) [od(ə)sy]	above
Nous habitons au-dessus des Martin.	We live above the Martins.
au-dessous (**de**) [od(ə)su]	below
En Bretagne, la température descend rarement au-dessous de zéro.	In Brittany the temperature rarely goes below zero.
à côté de [akotedə]	beside, next to
à droite de [adʀwatdə]	to the right of
à gauche de [agoʃdə]	to the left of
Asseyez-vous à droite/à gauche du président.	Sit to the right/left of the president.
au milieu de [omiljødə]	in the middle of
autour de [otuʀdə]	around
Il y a un jardin **tout autour de** la maison.	There is a yard all around the house.
à travers [atʀavɛʀ]	through
La route passe à travers la forêt.	The road goes through the forest.

entre [ɑ̃tʀ]	between
Sur cette photo, je suis entre Julie et Pierre.	In this photo I am between Julie and Pierre.
parmi [paʀmi]	among
On a trouvé cette lettre parmi de(s) vieux papiers.	This letter was found among some old papers.
chez [ʃe]	at the house of
Il habite toujours chez ses parents.	He still lives with his parents.
près de [pʀɛdə]	near, close to
un village près de Montpellier	a village close to Montpellier
loin de [lwɛ̃də]	far (away) from
Ce n'est pas loin de la mer.	It is not far from the ocean.
avec [avɛk]	with
sans [sɑ̃]	without
Je prends mon café avec du lait mais sans sucre.	I take my coffee with milk but without sugar.
pour [puʀ]	for
contre [kɔ̃tʀ]	against
la **lutte contre la drogue**	the war against drugs
envers [ɑ̃vɛʀ]	toward
J'ai été injuste envers vous.	I have been unfair toward you.
malgré [malgʀe]	in spite of, despite
Malgré la chaleur, il va faire du jogging.	In spite of the heat, he is going jogging.
sauf [sof]	except (for)
Tout le monde était d'accord sauf Jacques.	Everyone was in agreement except for Jacques.
à cause de [akozdə]	because of
On ne voit rien à cause du brouillard.	We can't see anything because of the fog.
grâce à [gʀasa]	thanks to
Le film est très réussi grâce aux excellents acteurs.	The movie was a success thanks to the excellent actors.

au lieu de [oljødə] Viens m'aider au lieu de me critiquer.	instead of Come help me instead of criticizing me.
au sujet de [osyʒɛdə] On ne sait rien de précis au sujet de cet accident.	concerning, about We don't know anything certain about this accident.
à l'aide de [alɛddə] Il est monté sur le toit à l'aide d'une échelle.	with the help of He got up onto the roof with the help of a ladder.
d'après [dapʀɛ] D'après la radio, les ouvriers sont toujours en grève.	according According to the radio, the workers are still on strike.
selon [s(ə)lɔ̃] Selon la météo, il fera beau demain.	according to According to the weather forecast, tomorrow will be nice.
quant à [kɑ̃ta] Quant à Dominique, il n'a toujours rien compris.	as for, with respect to As for Dominique, he still doesn't understand anything.
excepté [ɛksɛpte] Tout le monde est venu excepté Luc.	except for Everybody came except for Luc.

24.8 Language Terminology 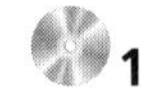 120

la **lettre** [lɛtʀ] *A* est la première lettre de l'alphabet.	letter *A* is the first letter of the alphabet.
le **son** [sɔ̃]	sound
la **voyelle** [vwajɛl] une **voyelle nasale**	vowel nasal vowel
la **consonne** [kɔ̃sɔn] une **consonne sonore**	consonant voiced consonant
la **liaison** [ljɛzɔ̃] Faites la liaison entre ces deux mots.	link, liaison Link these two words.
la **syllabe** [silab]	syllable

INFO

Language and style levels

la langue	*language*
la langue parlée	*spoken language*
la langue écrite	*written language*
la langue courante *Exemple:* Quand il a bu, il raconte n'importe quoi.	*normal speech* *Example: When he has been drinking, he talks nonsense.*
la langue familière *fam*	*familiar speech*
la langue populaire *pop* *Exemple:* Quand il est rond, il déconne à plein tube.	*colloquial/ordinary language* *Example: When he's smashed, he's really full of it.*
la langue littéraire/soutenue *litt* *Exemple:* L'excès de boisson rend ses propos confus.	*elevated, literary language* *Example: An excess of libations tends to muddle his speech.*
la langue des jeunes La langue des jeunes contient beaucoup d'expressions familières.	*teen slang* *Teen slang contains lots of colloquial expressions.*

le **point** [pwɛ̃]	period
les **deux points**	colon
le **point d'exclamation**	exclamation point
le **point d'interrogation**	question mark
la **virgule** [viʀgyl]	comma
le **point-virgule**	semi-colon
l'**accent** *m* [aksɑ̃]	accent
l'**accent aigu** *(é)*	accent aigu
l'**accent grave** *(è)*	accent grave
l'**accent circonflexe** *(ê)*	accent circonflexe
la **cédille** *(ç)* [sedij]	cedilla
le **tiret** [tiʀɛ]	dash
le **trait d'union** [tʀɛdynjɔ̃]	hyphen
la **parenthèse** [paʀɑ̃tɛz]	parenthesis
ouvrir/fermer une parenthèse	to open/close parentheses
les **guillemets** *mpl* [gijmɛ]	quotation marks
entre guillemets	in quotation marks

le **mot** [mo]	word
le **nom** [nɔ̃]	noun
le **substantif** [sypstɑ̃tif]	(concrete) noun
le **genre** [ʒɑ̃ʀ]	gender
masculin, masculine [maskylɛ̃, in]	masculine
féminin, féminine [feminɛ̃, in]	feminine
le **nombre** [nɔ̃bʀ]	number
s'accorder en genre et en nombre	to agree in gender and number
le **singulier** [sɛ̃gylje]	singular
le **pluriel** [plyʀjɛl]	plural

le **sujet** [syʒɛ]	subject
le **complément** [kɔ̃plemɑ̃]	complement
le **complément d'objet** (l'objet)	object
le **complément d'objet direct** (le COD)	direct object
le **complément d'objet indirect** (le COI)	indirect object

l'**article** *m* [aʀtikl]	article
l'**article défini**	definite article
l'**article indéfini**	indefinite article
l'**article partitif** (le partitif)	partitive article, partitive

le **déterminant** [detɛʀminɑ̃]	qualifier
le **déterminant démonstratif**	demonstrative adjective
le **déterminant possessif**	possessive adjective
le **déterminant interrogatif**	interrogative adjective
le **déterminant indéfini**	indefinite adjective

l'**adjectif** *m* [adʒɛktif]	adjective
accorder qc avec qc [akɔʀde]	to make s.th. agree with s.th.
Accordez le verbe avec le sujet.	Make the verb agree with the subject.
l'**accord** *m* [akɔʀ]	agreement
Faites l'accord de l'adjectif **avec** le nom.	Make the adjective agree with the noun.
l'**adverbe** *m* [advɛʀb]	adverb
les **adverbes de lieu/temps**	adverbs of place/time
les **adverbes de manière**	adverbs of manner
la **place** [plas]	place
Le sens d'un adjectif peut changer selon la place qu'il occupe.	The meaning of an adjective can change depending on the place it occupies.
les **degrés** (**de signification**) *mpl* [dəgʀe]	degrees (of comparison), comparative forms

le **positif** [pozitif]	basic form
le **comparatif** [kɔ̃paʀatif]	comparative
le **superlatif** [sypɛʀlatif]	superlative

---

le **numéral** [nymeʀal]	numeral
le **nombre** [nɔ̃bʀ]	number
un **nombre pair/impair**	even/odd number
un **nombre cardinal**	cardinal number
un **nombre ordinal**	ordinal number
la **fraction** [fʀaksjɔ̃]	fraction

---

le **pronom** [pʀɔnɔ̃]	pronoun
le **pronom personnel**	personal pronoun
le **pronom personnel conjoint/disjoint**	conjunctive/disjunctive personal pronoun
le **pronom adverbial**	adverbial pronoun
le **pronom réfléchi**	reflexive pronoun
le **pronom relatif**	relative pronoun
le **pronom sujet/objet**	subject/object pronoun
le **pronom démonstratif**	demonstrative pronoun
le **pronom possessif**	possessive pronoun
le **pronom indéfini**	indefinite pronoun
le **pronom interrogatif**	interrogative pronoun

---

le **verbe** [vɛʀb]	verb
un **verbe (in)transitif**	(in)transitive verb
un **verbe pronominal**	reflexive verb
la **forme** [fɔʀm]	form
la **forme simple/composée**	simple/composite form
conjuguer [kɔ̃ʒyge]	to conjugate
Conjuguez le verbe *aller* au futur simple.	Conjugate the verb *aller* in the simple future.
la **conjugaison** [kɔ̃ʒygɛzɔ̃]	conjugation
la conjugaison (ir)régulière	(ir)regular conjugation
le **radical** [ʀadikal]	root
la **terminaison** [tɛʀminɛzɔ̃]	ending
la **négation** [negasjɔ̃]	negation

---

le **mode** [mɔd]	mood
l'**infinitif** *m* [ɛ̃finitif]	infinitive
l'**indicatif** *m* [ɛ̃dikatif]	indicative
le **subjonctif** [sybʒɔ̃ktif]	subjunctive
l'**impératif** *m* [ɛ̃peʀatif]	imperative

---

le **temps** [tɑ̃]	tense
le **présent** [pʀezɑ̃]	present
Mettez le verbe au présent.	Put the verb into the present (tense).

le **passé** [pase]	past
l'**imparfait** *m* [ɛ̃paʀfɛ]	imperfect
le **passé simple** [pasesɛ̃pl]	passé simple
le **passé composé** [pasekɔ̃poze]	past perfect/passé compose
le **plus-que-parfait** [plyskəpaʀfɛ]	pluperfect
le **passé antérieur** [paseɑ̃teʀjœʀ]	past anterior
le **futur simple** [fytyʀsɛ̃pl]	simple future
le **futur composé** [fytyʀkɔ̃poze]	composite future
le **futur antérieur** [fytyʀɑ̃teʀjœʀ]	future perfect
le **conditionnel présent** [kɔ̃disjɔnɛlpʀezɑ̃]	conditional present
le **conditionnel passé** [kɔ̃disjɔnɛlpase]	past conditional
le **participe présent** [paʀtisippʀezɑ̃]	present participle
le **participe passé** [paʀtisippase]	past participle
la **voix active**/l'**actif** *m* [vwaaktiv/aktif]	active voice
la **voix passive**/le **passif** [vwapasiv/pasif]	passive voice

---

la **phrase** [fʀaz]	sentence
la **phrase/proposition déclarative**	declarative sentence/clause
la **phrase/proposition interrogative**	interrogative sentence/clause
la **phrase/proposition exclamative**	exclamatory sentence/clause
la **phrase/proposition impérative**	imperative sentence/clause
la **phrase/proposition principale**	main sentence/clause
la **phrase/proposition subordonnée**	subordinate sentence/clause
le **style** (in)**direct** [stil(ɛ̃)diʀɛkt]	(in)direct discourse
le **discours** (in)**direct** [diskuʀ(ɛ̃)diʀɛkt]	(in)direct discourse
la **concordance des temps** [kɔ̃kɔʀdɑ̃sdetɑ̃]	sequence of tenses
respecter la concordance des temps	to respect the sequence of tenses
la **mise en relief** [mizɑ̃ʀəljɛf]	emphasis

---

l'**interrogation** *f* [ɛ̃teʀɔgasjɔ̃]	question
l'**interrogation par intonation**	intonation question
l'**interrogation par inversion**	inversion question
le **mot interrogatif** [moɛ̃teʀɔgatif]	interrogative word

---

la **préposition** [pʀepozisjɔ̃]	preposition
la **conjonction** [kɔ̃ʒɔ̃ksjɔ̃]	conjunction

A

B

C

D

E

F

M

N

P

Q

R

S

T

W

X

Y

Z

My Vocabulary

Overview of Information Boxes

Index of False Friends

Track List of the MP3

Track	Title	
1	1.1	Personal Data
2	1.2	Nationality, Language, Country
3	2.1	Body Parts, Organs
4	2.2	Sexuality and Reproduction
5	2.3	Birth, Life, Death
6	2.4	Senses and Physical Reactions
7	2.5	Movements and Activities
8	2.6	Appearance
9	2.7	Cosmetics and Grooming
10	3.1	Health and Illness
11	3.2	Medical Care
12	3.3	Drugs, Tobacco, Alcohol
13	4.1	Feelings
14	4.2	Thoughts, Imagination, Desires
15	4.3	Character, Behavior
16	4.4	Activities and Skills
17	5.1	Eating and Drinking
18	5.2	Cooking, Baking, and Meals
19	5.3	Articles of Clothing
20	5.4	Jewelry and Accessories
21	5.5	Shopping
22	6.1	Construction, Houses, Buildings, and Occupants
23	6.2	Home and Furnishings
24	6.3	Household and Housework
25	7.1	People, Family
26	7.2	Greetings and Goodbyes
27	7.3	Young People
28	7.4	Social Groups, Living Conditions, Behavior
29	7.5	Relationships and Connections
30	7.6	Possession and Ownership
31	8.1	Education
32	8.2	Teaching, School
33	8.3	University, Science, and Research
34	9.1	Tools and Production
35	9.2	Office, Office Items
36	9.3	Professional Training and Professions
37	9.4	Work and Working Conditions

Track	Title	
38	10.1	Pastimes, Hobbies, and Games
39	10.2	Sports
40	10.3	Theater, Movies, and Film
41	10.4	Celebrations
42	11.1	Travel and Travel Preparations
43	11.2	Lodging
44	11.3	Gastronomy
45	11.4	Sightseeing
46	12.1	Graphic Arts
47	12.2	Music and Musical Performances
48	12.3	Literature
49	12.4	Prose, Nonfiction
50	12.5	Poetry
51	12.6	Drama
52	12.7	Working with Texts
53	13.1	History
54	13.2	Religion
55	13.3	Philosophy
56	14.1	Constitution, National Institutions
57	14.2	Public Administration
58	14.3	Parties, Political Systems
59	14.4	Laws, Justice, Crime
60	14.5	Organizations, Unions
61	14.6	Domestic Politics
62	14.7	International Relations, Globalization, Europe
63	14.8	Peace, War, Military
64	15.1	Agriculture, Fishing, and Mining
65	15.2	Industry and Trades
66	15.3	Business
67	15.4	Technology
68	15.5	Commerce and Service Industries
69	15.6	Money, Banking
70	15.7	Insurance
71	16.1	Telecommunications
72	16.2	Mail
73	16.3	Television, Radio
74	16.4	Image and Sound Recordings
75	16.5	Print and Books
76	16.6	Multimedia, Computers, Internet
77	17.1	Private Transportation
78	17.2	Public Transportation

Track	Title	
79	18.1	Universe, Earth
80	18.2	Geography
81	18.3	Climate, Weather
82	18.4	Matter, Substances
83	18.5	Plants and Garden
84	18.6	Animals, Animal Husbandry
85	18.7	Ecology, Environmental Protection, and Disasters
86	18.8	City, Country, Buildings, and Infrastructure
87	19.1	Days of the Week and Dates
88	19.2	Telling Time
89	19.3	Months and Seasons
90	19.4	More Time Expressions
91	19.5	Spatial Relationships
92	19.6	Length, Width, Distance
93	19.7	Location and Direction
94	20.1	Colors
95	20.2	Shapes
96	21.1	Expression of Quantity
97	21.2	Numbers and Numerals
98	21.3	Measurements and Weights
99	22.1	Classifying
100	22.2	Degree, Comparison, Relationships
101	22.3	Characteristics
102	22.4	Type and Manner
103	22.5	Cause, Effect, Goal, Purpose
104	22.6	Condition and Change
105	23.1	Conversing, Informing, Questioning, Answering
106	23.2	Excuses, Regrets, Consolation
107	23.3	Permission, Prohibition, Suggestion, Advice
108	23.4	Pain, Anger, Aggression
109	23.5	Agreeing, Confirming, Qualifying, Refusing
110	23.6	Praise, Thanks, Reproach
111	23.7	Opinion and Assessment
112	23.8	Commands and Wishes
113	24.1	Qualifiers and Pronouns
114	24.2	Question Words
115	24.3	Conjunctions
116	24.4	Helping Verbs
117	24.5	Negations
118	24.6	Adverbs and Adverbial Expressions
119	24.7	Prepositions
120	24.8	Language Terminology

Total running time: 15 hours and 30 minutes

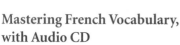

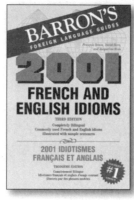

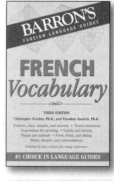